Beyond Form Criticism

Sources for Biblical and Theological Study

General Editor:
David W. Baker
Ashland Theological Seminary

1. *The Flowering of Old Testament Theology: A Reader in Twentieth-Century Old Testament Theology, 1930–1990*
   edited by Ben C. Ollenburger, Elmer A. Martens, and Gerhard F. Hasel

2. *Beyond Form Criticism: Essays in Old Testament Literary Criticism*
   edited by Paul R. House

3. *A Song of Power and the Power of Song: Essays on the Book of Deuteronomy*
   edited by Duane L. Christensen

Beyond Form Criticism

Essays in Old Testament Literary Criticism

edited by
Paul R. House

Eisenbrauns
Winona Lake, Indiana
1992

Library of Congress Cataloging-in-Publication Data

Beyond form criticism : essays in Old Testament literary criticism / edited by Paul
R. House.
    p.   cm.—(Sources for biblical and theological study. Old Testament ; 2)
    Includes bibliographical references and indexes.
    ISBN 0-931464-65-X
    1. Bible. O.T.—Criticism, interpretation, etc. 2. Bible as literature.
I. House, Paul R., 1958– . II. Series.
BS1171.2.B.49   1992
221.6′.6—dc20   92-29701

for
John D. W. Watts

CONTENTS

Series Preface. xi

Editors' Preface. xiii

Abbreviations. xv

Introduction

Paul R. House 3
    The Rise and Current Status of Literary Criticism of the
    Old Testament

Scripture and Literary Criticism

Introduction 24
David J. A. Clines 25
    Story and Poem: The Old Testament as Literature and
    as Scripture
Krister Stendahl. 39
    The Bible as a Classic and the Bible as Holy Scripture

Rhetorical Analysis

Introduction 48
James Muilenburg. 49
    Form Criticism and Beyond
J. Kenneth Kuntz. 70
    Psalm 18: A Rhetorical-Critical Analysis

Structuralist Analysis

Introduction 100
Richard Jacobson 101
    The Structuralists and the Bible

Jean Calloud 118
    A Few Comments on Structural Semiotics: A Brief Review
    of a Method and Some Explanation of Procedures
Daniel Patte and Judson F. Parker. 143
    A Structural Exegesis of Genesis 2 and 3

Formalism and Narrative

Introduction 164
    Methodology
Robert Alter. 166
    A Literary Approach to the Bible

    Structure
Shimon Bar-Efrat. 186
    Some Observations on the Analysis of Structure in
    Biblical Narrative

    Plot
Barbara Green 206
    The Plot of the Biblical Story of Ruth

    Characterization
Adele Berlin. 219
    Characterization in Biblical Narrative: David's Wives

    Narration
Meir Sternberg 234
    The Bible's Art of Persuasion: Ideology, Rhetoric,
    and Poetics in Saul's Fall

    Genre
J. Cheryl Exum and J. Williams Whedbee 272
    Isaac, Samson, and Saul: Reflections on the Comic and Tragic
    Visions

Analysis of Hebrew Poetry

Introduction 310
Adele Berlin. 311
    The Grammatical Aspect of Biblical Parallelism
J. Cheryl Exum 349
    Of Broken Pots, Fluttering Birds, and Visions in the Night:
    Extended Simile and Poetic Technique in Isaiah

Reader-Response Analysis

Introduction 374
Robert M. Fowler....................................... 376
    Who Is "The Reader" in Reader Response Criticism?
Willem S. Vorster...................................... 395
    Readings, Readers, and the Succession Narrative:
    An Essay on Reception

The Future of Old Testament Literary Criticism

Introduction 410
    Narrative
David M. Gunn 412
    New Directions in the Study of Biblical Hebrew Narrative

    Poetry
Mona West.. 423
    Looking for the Poem: Reflections on the Current and Future
    Status of the Study of Biblical Hebrew Poetry

Index of Authorities...................................... 433

Index of Scripture References.............................. 438

SERIES PREFACE

Old Testament scholarship is well served by several recent works which detail, to a greater or lesser extent, the progress made in the study of the Old Testament. Some survey the range of interpretation over long stretches of time, while others concern themselves with a smaller chronological or geographical segment of the field. There are also brief *entrés* into the various subdisciplines of Old Testament study included in the standard introductions as well as in several useful series. All of these provide secondary syntheses of various aspects of Old Testament research. All refer to, and base their discussions upon, various seminal works by Old Testament scholars which have proven pivotal in the development and flourishing of the various aspects of the discipline.

The main avenue into the various areas of Old Testament inquiry, especially for the beginner, has been until now mainly through the filter of these interpreters. Even on a pedagogical level, however, it is beneficial for a student to be able to interact with foundational works firsthand. This contact will not only provide insight into the content of an area, but hopefully will also lead to the sharpening of critical abilities through interaction with various viewpoints. This series seeks to address this need by including not only key, ground-breaking works, but also significant responses to these. This allows the student to appreciate the process of scholarly development through interaction.

The series is also directed toward scholars. In a period of burgeoning knowledge and significant publication in many places and languages around the world, this series will endeavor to make easily accessible significant, but at times hard to find, contributions. Each volume will contain essays, articles, extracts, and the like, presenting in a manageable scope the growth and development of one of a number of different aspects of Old Testament studies. Most volumes will contain previously published material, with synthetic essays by the editor(s) of the individual volume. Some volumes, however, are expected to contain significant, previously unpublished works. To facilitate access to students and scholars, all entries will appear in English and will be newly typeset. If students are excited by the study of Scripture and scholars are encouraged in amicable dialogue, this series would have fulfilled its purpose.

DAVID W. BAKER, *series editor*
Ashland Theological Seminary

EDITOR'S PREFACE

The time is particularly ripe for an introduction to the major methods and figures in Old Testament literary criticism. Several factors point to this conclusion. First, the field's relative youth has led to some misconceptions about its nature. Definitions need to be set where none have existed. For instance, because there have been so many kinds of literary studies, some readers may wonder what literary analysis seeks to accomplish. Related to this initial concern is a second reason a survey may be helpful. Many readers identify literary criticism with a single methodology. To them, literary analysis *is* structuralism, or rhetorical study, formalism, etc. Thus, a survey of the discipline must define its aims and demonstrate its complexity. The literary critic possesses definite goals, plus a number of methodological options.

Third, a survey will help beginning students learn about this expanding movement. Many texts on other methods are available, but few exist that are devoted to a literary study of the Old Testament. Studying the early trends in the field will help students judge the advisability of using the method themselves. Theological students must also read literary critical approaches to stay in touch with major currents in Old Testament studies.

Fourth, some standards need to be set. Much poor work has appeared in which writers have not exhibited a sound knowledge of generally acceptable literary criticism. But, more happily, it is appropriate to celebrate the major accomplishments of the discipline's early years. Affirming strong studies should encourage similar excellence. Literary analysis has stimulated discussion in many areas, generated excitement among scholars, and offered new ways of studying the Bible for a wide variety of readers.

This volume may not achieve these goals. No doubt some will disagree with the choice of authors and articles. Various items had to be sacrificed due to space limitations. Yet the works chosen exhibit why literary criticism has grown from a "passing fad" to a, hopefully, lasting part of old Testament research.

The format of this collection seeks to address two very basic areas. Biblical studies both introduce and implement critical methodologies.

Scholars choose approaches and then use them to explain texts. Therefore at least two articles appear for each literary approach in the sections below. One article has been chosen to help the reader define an individual type of literary analysis. Subsequent articles then use the methodology to explain an Old Testament text. In this way both an approach's theoretical and practical value can be judged.

Other aims also helped structure this volume. A historical concern is shown by at least partially ordering the sections to reflect the sequence in which the methodologies or issues gained prominence. The studies chosen also reflect the fact that Hebrew prose and poetry, the Old Testament's two major genres, have both been analyzed extensively. Finally, this volume attempts to anticipate literary criticism's future. Readers need to sense what may or may not be ahead for the discipline, even though absolute certainty cannot be achieved.

Hopefully this selection will reflect accurately the opinions of the authors of the articles. Sometimes segments from a scholar's body of work may misrepresent the person's overall viewpoint. No doubt several of the writers may have stronger articles on other subjects, but those pieces do not fit the collection's scheme. Only time will tell which of these authors and writings remain significant. For now, they represent what is best in this exciting and growing discipline.

PAUL R. HOUSE
Taylor University

Publisher's Note
Foreign terms are translated for the assistance of English readers. All articles originally published in English are edited only minimally to achieve consistency in such matters as form of reference. Matters of substance, including grammar and punctuation, remain as in the original publication.

ABBREVIATIONS

General

AV	Authorized Version
ET	English translation
JPS	Jewish Publication Society Bible
LXX	Septuagint
MT	Masoretic Text
NEB	New English Bible
NJPSV	New Jewish Publication Society Version
NT	New Testament
OT	Old Testament
RSV	Revised Standard Version
Targ.	Targum
Vg./Vulg.	Vulgate

Books and Periodicals

AB	Anchor Bible
AcOr	*Acta Orientalia*
ALUOS	*Annual of the Leeds University Oriental Society*
AnBib	Analecta Biblica
ANET	J. B. Pritchard (ed.), *Ancient Near Eastern Texts Relating to the Old Testament*
BEvT	Beiträge zur evangelischen Theologie
BH	*Biblia Hebraica*
BHS	*Biblia Hebraica Stuttgartensia*
Bib	*Biblica*
BibOr	Biblica et Orientalia
BJRL	*Bulletin of the John Rylands Library*
BKAT	Biblischer Kommetar: Altes Testament
BTB	*Biblical Theology Bulletin*
BWANT	Beiträge zur Wissenschaft vom Alten and Neuen Testament

BZ	*Biblische Zeitschrift*
BZAW	Beiheft zur Zeitschrift für die Alttestamentliche Wissenschaft
CBQ	*Catholic Biblical Quarterly*
EBib	Etudes Bibliques
GKC	*Gesenius' Hebrew Grammar*, ed. E. Kautzsch, trans. A. E. Cowley
HAT	Handbuch zum Alten Testament
HKAT	Handkommetar zum Alten Testament
HSM	Harvard Semitic Monographs
HVS	M. O'Connor, *Hebrew Verse Structure*
HTR	*Harvard Theological Review*
HUCA	*Hebrew Union College Annual*
IB	*Interpreter's Bible*
Int/Interp	*Interpretation*
JAAR	*Journal of the American Academy of Religion*
JBL	*Journal of Biblical Literature*
JJS	*Journal of Jewish Studies*
JNES	*Journal of Near Eastern Studies*
JQR	*Jewish Quarterly Review*
JR	*Journal of Religion*
JSOT	*Journal of the Study of the Old Testament*
KAT	Kommentar zum Alten Testament
KHAT	Kurzer Hand-Commentar zum Alten Testament
NCB	New Century Bible
OTS	*Oudtestamentische Studiën*
RGG	*Religionen in Geschichte und Gegenwart*
RSR	*Recherches de Science Religieuse*
SBLDS	Society of Biblical Literature Dissertation Series
SBT	Studies in Biblical Theology
UF	*Ugarit-Forschungen*
VT/VetT	*Vetus Testamentum*
VTS(up)	Supplements to Vetus Testamentum
WMANT	Wissenschaftliche Monographien zum Alten und Neuen Testament
ZAW	*Zeitschrift für die Alttestamentliche Wissenschaft*

Introduction

The Rise and Current Status of Literary Criticism of the Old Testament

PAUL R. HOUSE

Many external factors led to the rise of literary criticism in biblical studies. Philosophy had stressed linguistic issues for several years (Gross 1970: 13). New views of historiography replaced older means of analyzing the past (Breisach 1983). Some literary scholars, perhaps most notably Northrop Frye (1967) and Robert Alter (1975, 1976, etc.), wrote serious studies of the Bible. Though these trends cannot be explained here in detail, they must be mentioned in passing. Biblical scholarship does not operate in a vacuum. As in the past, the discipline responded to the larger academic world.

Besides the influence of interdisciplinary trends, literary criticism arose at least in part because of impasses in older ways of explaining Scripture. Many thinkers concluded that historical criticism, the standard means of biblical analysis, had almost run its course (Clines 1978: 7–15). Old issues could either be reworked or new paths could be charted. Too, numerous scholars began to recognize that some of the established approaches divide and atomize texts. These methodologies obscure the unity of large and small texts alike. Efforts to date, categorize, and scrutinize even short passages had produced reorganized texts not all could appreciate. An overemphasis on historical detail cost readers a proper understanding of plot, theme, and character. Pre-textual matters subsumed textual issues. The achievements of historical criticism were appreciated, but new ways to illuminate the Bible were desired.

3

From several directions, then, literary criticism became a force in Old Testament analysis. Its emergence allowed biblical studies to interact with other disciplines, and at the same time gave interpreters new avenues into exegesis. For convenience, this essay divides the first twenty years of Old Testament literary criticism into three historical segments, each with one dominant literary methodology. Though this ordering is imperfect, it does reflect definite high points in the growth of the discipline. Some overlap of important approaches occurs, yet how critics have examined the Bible has evolved over time.

The first period includes 1969–1974. In 1969 James Muilenburg's seminal work "Form Criticism and Beyond" appeared, and in 1974 the influential journal *Semeia* was founded. Muilenburg argued that rhetorical criticism could advance Old Testament study. Many authors followed Muilenburg's suggestion and produced careful rhetorical analyses of Old Testament texts. These detailed linguistic treatments paved the way for other literary approaches, such as structuralism. Partly because of its affinity with form criticism, rhetorical analysis gained respect among Old Testament scholars. Still, certain commentators wondered if this new emphasis on the text itself would minimize historical methods.

By 1974 enough rhetorical-critical articles had been published to make the discipline more-or-less acceptable in scholarly circles. Then literary criticism turned in another direction. Perhaps due to its influence in other fields, structuralism now dominated many discussions of biblical passages. The writings of Lévi-Strauss, Barthes, and Ricoeur were particularly significant for structuralist biblical critics. This trend continued until 1981, when another method gained popularity. Structuralism was significant enough that *Interpretation* and *Semeia* devoted whole issues to it. Also, *Semeia* published a steady number of structuralist pieces during 1974–1981, and the method still retains faithful practitioners.

In England literary studies were advanced during 1974–1981 by the founding of the *Journal for the Study of the Old Testament* in 1976. Though it produced many important articles and reviews between 1976 and 1980, the journal's influence grew most after that time period. With *Semeia* in the United States and *Journal for the Study of the Old Testament* in Britain, literary criticism now had strong voices on both sides of the Atlantic. With rhetorical analysis and structuralism, it also had two methodologies that were accepted by many other, more traditional, journals.

From 1981 to 1989 literary criticisms blossomed into a major force in Old Testament studies. Debate raged over whether it deserved a place in the family of critical approaches. There remain opponents to the method, but even those critics *normally* accept its validity. More than any other work, Robert Alter's *The Art of Biblical Narrative* (1981) advanced Old Testament literary criticism during the 1980s. Alter primarily followed American formalism, which focuses on examining the main elements of plot, structure, character, and themes in narratives. This approach made literary criticism more accessible to students and teachers unaccustomed to the discipline. Unlike structuralism, the use of formalism requires no extensive specialized vocabulary or philosophical background.

With *Semeia* and *Journal for the Study of the Old Testament* in place, Alter's book helped fuel the growing discipline. Writers continued to produce structuralist and rhetorical-critical analyses, but more authors penned material from a broadly formalist viewpoint. The significant literary critic Northrop Frye added an ambitious volume based on an archetypal look at the whole Bible. New studies of both Hebrew narrative and poetry appeared regularly in such standard periodicals as the *Journal of Biblical Literature*, which had published Muilenburg's article in 1969. Literary criticism had "arrived."

Alongside formalism, more as a partner than a rival, reader-response criticism developed. Perhaps this approach will have greater long-term effect than formalism. Indeed, later I may wish I had set it apart as a fourth pillar of these early years. Right now, however, it has yet to gather the same following as the others. Still, it takes issues raised by the whole of literary criticism and pushes them to important limits. David Gunn's 1987 piece reprinted in this volume states this point very well.

Seeds of a Discipline: 1969–1974

Literary approaches to the Bible existed long before 1969. Indeed, O. B. Hardison notes that

> when the ancient tradition was assimilated by the Christian authors, comparisons were drawn between Latin and Hebrew authors. Jerome was fond of such comparisons. "David," he remarked, "is our Simonides, our Pindar, our Horace," and it is to Jerome that Latin tradition owes its conception of Job as a tragedy, Pentateuch as a heroic poem, and Ecclesiastes as elegy. Bede . . . takes the same approach (Preminger, Hardison, and Kerrane 1974: 11).

Martin Luther understood the value of literary expertise in biblical exegesis. David Clines quotes Luther as arguing that

certainly it is my desire that there shall be as many poets and rhetoricians as possible, because I see that by these studies, as by no other
means, people are wonderfully fitted for the grasping of sacred truth
and for handling it skillfully and happily (1980: 115).

Luther also believed that interpreters of Scripture should possess historical and hermeneutical skills as well, but this quotation points out a
gap in most people's view of Luther's exegetical method. The great reformer acknowledged the need to grasp the Bible's literary components.

Richard G. Moulton's 1899 work, *The Literary Study of the Bible*, assigned genres to Old Testament material, broke books into component
parts (acts, scenes, etc.), and generally explored the basic aspects of
biblical literature. Like many current scholars, Moulton was more com-
fortable with narrative than poetry. He found it especially difficult to
categorize prophecy (1899: 363–89). Certain aspects of Moulton's work
remain solid. Almost no biblical critics followed his lead, however, so
literary analysis of Scripture did not develop at this time.

Of course, several authors have sought to treat the Bible "as literature." They have argued for the value of reading Scripture, especially
the Old Testament, as an example of great world literature. To them,
the Bible deserves a place among the best literary art. This position is
fine to a certain point. Yet to explain the Old Testament's narrative and
poetic techniques, while retaining respect for all types of biblical analysis, is a quite different matter. The Bible-as-literature proponents seem
to say, "The Bible is one thing, but we will treat it as another." On the
other hand, Old Testament literary critics contend that the Hebrew
Scriptures *are* literature, and that therefore literary analyses possess inherent validity. Other methods are not discarded. But literary criticism
is not some sort of outsider. It does not have to prove its potential merit.

When Muilenburg delivered his 1968 Society of Biblical Literature
address, subsequently published as "Form Criticism and Beyond"
(1969), Old Testament studies needed some new horizons. A full century of source criticism had passed. Form criticism had been practiced
for seven decades, and redaction criticism had been prevalent for over
a generation. Old methods are not automatically bad methods. Nor do
new methods, just because they are new, deserve preference over
older, sounder approaches. Still, even when good methods are applied
to the same material over a long period of time a certain regularity,
even staleness, can creep into a discipline. Apparently the time had
come for a new way of reading the Old Testament.

Another factor in the rise of literary criticism was the occurrence of
certain impasses in traditional approaches. For instance, source critics
had subdivided the four standard Pentateuchal sources into a number of

splinter groups (Rendtorff 1986: 157–64). Redactional-compositional studies of the prophetic books had produced such diverse results within single prophecies that little if any sense of unity remained (Muilenburg 1969: 6). Jeremiah, because of its complexity, seemed a particularly hopeless case. Writers believed they knew more than ever about the Old Testament's composition, yet not all considered these results an advance in understanding and application. Further, debate continued to rage over the authorship, dating, and theology of the accepted redactional layers. Progress had been made, but where to go next was a distinct problem.

Muilenburg recognized some of these difficulties in his article. He noted the significance of source criticism and form criticism for Old Testament studies, and observed that perhaps form criticism had "outrun its course" (1969: 4). He says that even within kindred literary types, such as Deuteronomy 32 and Micah 6:1–8, "the stylistic and rhetorical differences outweigh the similarities" (1969: 5). Thus, Muilenburg believed some new means of analyzing texts was needed. This method must be consistent enough to illuminate every literary type in Scripture, yet it must also reveal the individual qualities of single texts.

To meet this need, Muilenburg turned to "stylistics or aesthetic criticism." As he explains, this discipline was already contributing to biblical studies, with Luis Alonso Schökel's *Estudios de Poética Hebraea* (1963) serving as a prime example of the method's value (1969: 7). Fundamental issues were at the heart of Muilenburg's decision:

> For the more deeply one penetrates the formulations as they have been transmitted to us, the more sensitive he is to the rôles which words and motifs play in a composition; the more he concentrates on the ways in which thought has been woven into linguistic patterns, the better able he is to think the thoughts of the biblical writer after him (1969: 7).

Simply put, language and style may reveal as much about an author's intentions as that author's historical situation. How may this philosophical principle be applied to texts?

> And this leads me to formulate a canon which should be obvious to us all: a responsible and proper articulation of the words in their linguistic patterns and in their precise formulations will reveal to us the texture and fabric of the writer's thought, not only what it is that he thinks, but as he thinks it (1969: 7).

Intention and meaning will emerge as a thorough examination of linguistic patterns and artistic texture takes place. Muilenburg summarizes:

> What I am interested in, above all, is in understanding the nature of Hebrew literary composition, in exhibiting the structural patterns that

are employed for the fashioning of a literary unit, whether in poetry
or in prose, and in discerning the many and various devices by which
the predications are formulated and ordered into a unified whole.
Such an enterprise I should describe as rhetoric and the methodology
as rhetorical criticism (1969: 8).

Obviously, "rhetorical criticism" shifts the interpreter's attention
from historical, precompositional matters to the text itself. This paradigm shift places the Old Testament in a whole new light. Now each
text has individual value, since each biblical writer possessed distinct
powers of artistic expression. Interpretation now lies in the text, rather
than in what lies behind the text. Passages must no longer serve simply
as avenues back into history.

Rhetorical criticism employs a logical exegetical procedure. First,
the exegete divides a passage into units. Then, Muilenburg adds, the
rhetorical critic must note how the single unit moves, "shifts or breaks
in the development in the writer's thought" (1969: 10). Poetic devices
and word play are particularly helpful in this stage of the process.
Next, how the writer's thought progresses from one unit to the next
must be charted (1969: 13). Finally, the data should be assembled to
explain the author's basic intention or intentions for the piece.

Muilenburg's ideas work best, though not exclusively, on poetic
texts. These principles *can* apply to narrative, but are really formulated
for Hebrew poetry. Since rhetorical analysis grows out of form criticism, this tendency is hardly surprising. Muilenburg states that he does
not want to eliminate form criticism (1969: 18), but various writers began to implement these ideas and go "beyond form criticism." No
doubt other scholars had concepts like Muilenburg's, yet it was his article that paved the way for rhetorical studies of the Old Testament.

Two authors can serve as examples of how this methodology
gained prominence. J. Cheryl Exum's "A Literary and Structural
Analysis of the Song of Songs" (1973) exhibits many of the principles
Muilenburg espouses. Exum divides the book into poems, sections,
and strophes. She explains how passages work internally and how they
relate to subsequent sections. Important words are analyzed to show
their significance in the text. Even the article's title reveals a shift away
from straightforward historical and form criticism. Exum's rhetorical
analysis ends with a hope for more works of this type

> We have seen that we have in the Song a complex and highly sophisti-
> cated love poem. The limited scope of our investigation gives us indi-
> cations that the artistry in the Song is even more intricate than we have

been able to suggest here. Much more investigation of the poet's style needs to be done. In addition, it remains for further study to relate the intricate workings of the poet's style to the problems of the over-all interpretation and exegesis of the Song. We hope that our analysis has provided some ground work for the undertaking of this task (1973: 79).

In short, Exum not only demonstrates the method's value on a demanding text, but also claims the approach has long-term worth.

Lawrence Boadt exhibits a similar methodology in "Isaiah 41:8–13: Notes on Poetic Structure and Style" (1973). Though he does not venture as far from form criticism as Exum, Boadt represents other writers who shifted slowly to rhetorical analysis. Boadt leans heavily on the work of Westermann (e.g., 1966) and Muilenburg. His goal is to move past source criticism to a means of examining and illuminating poetry rather than historical background:

> The aim is rather to illustrate the technique of Second Isaiah whereby a carefully structured accumulation of repetitive and rhythmic elements is skillfully used to create an emphatic and euphonious result, a result that reveals the special genius of Second Isaiah in which sense units coincide with a determined sound pattern (1973: 22).

So Boadt, like Muilenburg and Exum, views literary artistry as an important component in biblical passages.

Much of Boadt's exegesis parallels Exum's conclusions. He examines the meter, parallelism, and word play of the chosen poem. Boadt divides the surrounding sections into stanzas. Also, his analysis focuses on how Scripture means by what it says. Finally, the fact that Exum's piece appeared in *Zeitschrift für die Alttestamentliche Wissenschaft* and Boadt's in *Catholic Biblical Quarterly* meant that rhetorical criticism had attained a measure of academic respectability by 1973. More space has been used to introduce this methodology than will be used to describe others, but without the emergence of rhetorical criticism all types of literary analysis would have waited much longer for prominence.

In many ways 1974 was a watershed year for literary criticism. Bridges were built between old and new ways of analyzing Old Testament literature. Rhetorical criticism by no means disappeared, yet structuralism began to move to the forefront of scholarly discussion. Perhaps most importantly, *Semeia* was founded as an experimental journal dedicated to exploring new means of interpreting Scripture.

Most of the individuals involved in founding *Semeia* were New Testament scholars who were especially interested in Gospels and parables research. Much of the impetus for the journal came from Robert Funk,

Dan Otto Via, James M. Robinson, and Norman Perrin (Wilder 1974: 1–2). In his explanation of the journal's purpose in the initial issue, Amos Wilder states that hopefully *Semeia* "would serve as a vehicle for innovative work in progress and for communication among workers in all aspects of language running from literary criticism to linguistics" (1974: 2). Like Muilenburg, Wilder claims that an emphasis on new methods should pose no threat to older disciplines (1974: 3). Rather, the journal would seek to strengthen an already vibrant area of study:

> Our newer approaches to language and text are not therefore discontinuous with the tradition. At the various levels of vocabulary, grammar, syntax and discourse we seek to take advantage of new sophistications. These investigations have to do with such matters as the dynamics of human speech and communication, language modes and patterns, the apperception of hearer or reader, the social-cultural nexus of all language-phenomena, and the relation of language to referent and to reality (1974: 4).

Such an ambitious program would obviously allow the periodical to chart a number of interesting directions.

By its third issue, *Semeia* was exploring Old Testament narrative. Writers for *Semeia 3* included David Gunn, Burke Long, and Robert Polzin. Later issues of the journal also examined Old Testament subjects, so the publication's founding soon advanced beyond New Testament concerns. Literary critics now had their own vehicle of expression in the United States. This vehicle was published by Scholars Press, which tied it closely to the Society of Biblical Literature. Therefore, literary analysis now had a more established status than in the past.

Even in its first article, *Semeia* speaks of the importance of structuralism. Wilder concludes that

> mankind is always the prisoner of its language and its long accumulation of mental habit. Theological tradition is thus subverted and we need the more direct kind of thrust beneath the incubus of sedimentation, whether of language or categories, that is afforded by structuralism (1974: 10).

Thus, Wilder hoped that structuralism could provide an objective means of looking at biblical linguistics. Whether through an initial "structure" (1974: 12), or a subsequent "deep structure" (1974: 13), the goal was to discover without prior prejudice how the Bible speaks. While *Semeia*'s appearance proved that rhetorical criticism had paved the way for a respect for literary analysis, Wilder's comments show that a new methodology was gaining momentum. How that method advanced will be a main subject of the next section of this survey.

Roots for a Discipline: 1974–1981

Besides the emergence of *Semeia,* another publishing event acknowledged the growth of literary criticism and highlighted structuralism.
The April 1974 issue of *Interpretation* featured structuralism as its topic.
As usual in these early years, the editors felt the need to justify this selection. Their main reason was that

> first in France, then in Germany, and more recently in North Amer-
> ica, structuralism is attracting the investigative energies of biblical
> scholars and beginning to take shape in a new "frontal system" of
> freshening breezes. Whether the front will form and move, it is too
> early to say (Mays 1974: 132).

Though structuralism was growing as a means of exegetical exploration, the editors note, "the matter stands at present very much in the
exploratory stage where definition is being clarified through practice"
(Mays 1974: 132).

Those chosen to write for this volume demonstrated well how
structuralism can explicate biblical texts. Richard Jacobson charted
the discipline's major proponents, explained its basic characteristics,
and gave some brief examples of how the method works on Scripture
(1974: 146–64). Robert Polzin examined Job's framework from a structural viewpoint (1974: 182–200). He basically uncovered the book's
primary structural level, and left deeper matters for future studies
(1974: 200). Despite the issue's explanatory format, however, certain
difficulties surfaced that still hamper a usage of structuralism by a
broad spectrum of interpreters.

Jacobson's article reveals a primary problem for those utilizing
structuralism. Interpreters must accumulate a specialized vocabulary
and philosophical orientation to use the discipline. Jacobson lists various terms that must be mastered. First, one must recognize that each
word is a "sign," and that "the sign is the relation arising from the two
parts, one of which, the signifier, is a sound-image, the other of which,
the signified, is a mental image or concept" (1974: 147). Each word,
then, indicates more than meets the eye.

Three more sets of terms deserve mention. A reader must discern
the difference between "language/speaking (*langue/parole*), diachrony/
synchrony, metaphor/metonymy" (1974: 147). The first of these pairs
distinguishes between commonly stored "word-images," and how each
individual uses those images in a society. As for the second pair of opposites, Jacobson states that

diachrony/synchrony is the distinction between a study oriented toward change or development over time, and the language state at any one time. Traditional philology and etymology are of course diachronic studies. The study of the sign at any given time, or of the relations among signs in a given language-state, is synchronic (1974: 147).

Finally, "metaphor" speaks of similar words, while "metonymy" indicates how an author orders these words (see 1974: 148). All these factors must be weighed in a structuralist reading. In short, what, why, and how an author speaks is analyzed.

All these concepts constitute a first layer, or structure, of meaning. Next, the exegete must uncover a work's "deep structure," or second level of understanding. To reach this level, interpreters must realize that "deep structures express themselves as codes" (Robertson 1976: 549). Corina Galland defines "code" as the means "to decipher the message or the collection of rules which permits a text to produce meaning and to be communicable" (1979: 184). How does one break this "code"? First, a reader should examine all the syntactical material Jacobson mentions (Galland 1979: 184). Then, the exegete explores the semantic aspects of a narrative (Galland 1979: 186). The ways in which characters relate to one another, the plot unfolds, and the narrator tells the story must be charted and graphed. These artistic elements are all interrelated, thus revealing the narrative's complexity. For clarity, structuralists often draw grids and diagrams to present the results of their analysis.

Psychology enters structuralist interpretation next. If the deep structures of a text can be unlocked, then the basis of a writer's or society's thought processes can also emerge. David Robertson observes that the structuralist's ultimate goal is to explain the psychology of language in society: "By decoding human activities one can not only discover the reality behind the appearances of everyday life, but can also, potentially, map the structure of the mind" (1976: 549). Obviously, if successful, the method could uncover the intent of biblical writers. Even if an author does not claim this much for a structuralist analysis, the inner workings of a biblical story may be discussed in a new and effective way.

For those who learned its terminology, accepted its philosophy, and embraced its complexity, structuralism opened new doors of understanding. Throughout the 1970s and into the next decade writers published structuralist examinations of the Old Testament (see *Semeia* 18 [1980]). Some of the authors, like Robert Polzin, were scholars of religion. Still others, were teachers of literature or philosophers. For example, *Semeia* 4 chose "Paul Ricoeur on Biblical Hermeneutics" as its theme. Many commentators believed that structuralism was overly technical and subtle, and hoped for a more accessible literary theory.

Whatever one's feelings about structuralism, all would agree that the method continued the emphasis on the value of texts for interpretation that rhetorical criticism had begun. More people than ever focused on meaning garnered through literary analysis. Thus, Jacobson summarizes the continuing influence of structuralism when he writes that

> one thing is clear about the work of structuralists on the Bible and radically distinguishes it from previous scholarship: The focus of attention shifts from questions of document, composition, and *kerygma* to those of "reading" (*lecture*), text, and signification (1974: 157).

During the same time period, another method was taking root— formalism. This approach, like structuralism and rhetorical criticism, was not new to literary scholarship in general, but it was new to biblical studies. In fact, this method is perhaps the most widely used approach in university literature classes.

As when speaking of rhetorical criticism and structuralism, one must be cautious when discussing formalism. Various types of formalism exist. Different "schools" of the discipline developed, for instance, in Russia and the United States. So one could define the method in a number of ways. What is clear, however, is that formalism is quite different in nature than rhetorical, structuralist, or reader-response analysis. It embraces several literary topics and seeks to explain individual aspects of poetic and narrative works.

Formalistic analysis studies a text's components to uncover its meaning. Texts are seen as valuable in and of themselves. Therefore formalism does not stress a story's historical background, authorship, or psychology in any detail. Instead, a text is analyzed to interpret its themes, motifs, and messages (what it says), and to uncover its plot, characterization, setting, and imagery (how it says). Formalism holds that a text must be understood from within rather than without.

Robert Alter describes common formalistic analysis in his plea for "A Literary Approach to the Bible":

> By serious literary analysis I mean the manifold varieties of minutely discriminating attention to the artful use of language, to the shifting play of ideas, conventions, tone, sound, imagery, narrative viewpoint, compositional units, and much else; the kind of disciplined attention, in other words, which through a whole spectrum of critical approaches has illuminated, for example, the poetry of Dante, the plays of Shakespeare, the novels of Tolstoy (1975: 70).

Here Alter simply claims that the methods of "secular" literary criticism, the most prominent of which was formalism, can unlock new doors of meaning in the study of Scripture. Alter followed this 1975 piece with articles on "Biblical Narrative" (1976) and "Character in the

Bible" (1978). Certainly these discussions helped create a climate for literary analysis of the Old Testament in the 1970s, but Alter was to be more significant in the 1980s, as will be noted later. At this point it is sufficient to realize that a standard, accessible literary method was about to challenge structuralism.

While Alter's initial comments were read by a mostly nonreligious-studies audience, a trio of scholars in England were establishing a voice for Old Testament literary analysis. David Clines, Philip Davies, and David Gunn, all of whom taught at the University of Sheffield, launched *Journal for the Study of the Old Testament* in 1976. They listed several reasons in the first issue for starting the periodical, including the "backlog of papers that have been accepted by the usual journals," the price of current journals, and the lack of periodicals that accepted works in progress (1976: 2). Left unsaid was that the editors were moving toward literary analysis themselves, and hoped to encourage others in the same direction. Along with the journal, a supplement series was begun as well (1976: 3).

Clines and Gunn had already published articles that went beyond an interest in oral literature to analysis of written narrative. An example of this change is Gunn's "Narrative Patterns and Oral Tradition in Judges and Samuel" (1974). He then contributed a study of narrative, "David and the Gift of the Kingdom," to *Semeia* 3 (1975). This article shifted almost entirely to literary means of interpretation. Clines authored the first volume of the *Journal for the Study of the Old Testament* supplement series. Entitled *I, He, We, and They: A Literary Approach to Isaiah 53*, this 1976 effort linked older methods with a commitment to literary criticism. Again, like other writers trained in historical-critical methods, Clines and Gunn were making a gradual transition, and formalistic-type methods were what they utilized.

Gunn and Clines soon completed their move from historical to literary criticism. Clines attempted to highlight the unity of the Pentateuch in his 1978 monograph, *The Theme of the Pentateuch* (vol. 10). Here he combats two tendencies that he feels have hindered Pentateuch research: *atomism* and *geneticism* (1978: 7). The former problem is that scholars have broken the Pentateuch into an excessive number of sources, while the latter is that scholars have overemphasized "the origins and development of the extant Biblical text" (1978: 9). Clines argues for a literary approach that will focus on the unity of texts. This methodological concern leads Clines to admit, "on one level, then, this is an essay about the Pentateuch; on another, it is a programme for work in Biblical studies. It is both about matter and about method" (1978: 15). Thus, Clines does not hide his attempt to do scholarship that would point out the value of literary analysis.

Two books in the *Journal for the Study of the Old Testament* supplement series demonstrated Gunn's preference for a text-oriented approach to the Old Testament. First, he published *The Story of King David: Genre and Interpretation* (vol. 6), in which he discussed the David narrative as "story." By stressing the narrative details of Samuel, Gunn advanced the notion that solely literary analyses are legitimate for exegesis. When he published *The Fate of King Saul* in 1980 (vol. 14), he showed that literary analysis can indeed raise serious theological issues. The method was versatile enough to illuminate text, theme, and theology.

Other significant thinkers wrote in *Journal for the Study of the Old Testament* and its supplement series, but Gunn and Clines, because of their primary role in these ventures, have been used as representatives of a growing movement. By the end of the 1980s, then, *Journal for the Study of the Old Testament* had joined *Semeia* as a vehicle for Old Testament literary criticism. Authors now had new options when traditional journals rejected literary projects. Structuralism and formalism vied for prominence in the field, with the former having many academic adherents and the latter gaining widespread usage and acceptance. Now literary criticism had roots on two continents and in major intellectual circles. The question was whether or not the movement had the impetus to move forward.

Flowering of the Discipline: 1981–1989

Literary criticism still awaited some means of further definition and expansion. That mechanism was provided in 1981 with the appearance of Robert Alter's *The Art of Biblical Narrative*. Some of the book's chapters were reworked articles already published in *Commentary* and other journals, while some of the material was new. Alter's combination of clear writing, interpretative insight, and critical expertise gave the monograph a wide audience. For the first time many biblical and literary critics noticed the growing methodology. Having authored works on Fielding, the picaresque novel, and Stendhal, among other subjects, his literary skills were readily accepted. Since he knew Hebrew and modern Hebrew literature, Alter's ability to read Old Testament narrative was unquestioned. Not all of his conclusions were embraced by other commentators, but his work showed that one can glean insight through literary analysis and treat the material as Scripture at the same time.

Alter later followed his work on narrative with *The Art of Biblical Poetry* (1985). This second volume was excellent as well, though it did not gain the notoriety of its predecessor. What were Alter's main contributions to Old Testament literary criticism to that point? First, he showed a wider audience the value of the method. Second, he helped shift the field's interest from structuralism to a more formalistic analysis. His approach made sense to many who could never learn all the intricacies of structuralism. Third, Alter explained that biblical narrative has many unique traits. Thus, biblical literary critics must develop unique theories as to how an Old Testament narrative works. In short, Alter produced what is very hard to create—a scholarly book that gains a measure of popular success. The influence of this monograph for the growth of literary methods for biblical interpretation can hardly be overestimated.

The next year another, perhaps more prominent, literary critic published a work on the Bible. This event gave literary methods even more credibility and momentum. Northrop Frye's *The Great Code: The Bible and Literature* (1982) traced major themes and archetypes through the whole Bible. An expert in romanticism, Frye had written previously on biblical topics in *Anatomy of Criticism* (1957). This sweeping look at literary history noted the Bible's place in English-speaking literary life. Here Frye examined the Bible's generic character, basic thematic material, and vastly influential passages (e.g., Genesis 3).

The Great Code advances the notion of the Bible's unity, a topic once scorned by biblical analysts, in a variety of ways. Frye first cites a historical reason for reading Scripture as a unified construction, which is "that 'the Bible' has traditionally been read as a unity, and has influenced Western imagination as a unity" (1982: xiii). Next, he notes a practical reason for reading Scripture as a unity: "Those who do succeed in reading the Bible from beginning to end will discover that at least it has a beginning and an end, and some traces of a total structure" (1982: xiii). Finally, he adds an interpretative reason. Frye believes the Bible deserves both historical and literary exploration. Any literary analysis, he concludes, must include a consecutive, unified reading of the text.

> A genuine higher criticism, I should think, would observe that [the] account of creation stands at the beginning of Genesis, despite its late date, because it belongs at the beginning of Genesis. That would lead to an integrated study of the Book of Genesis, and eventually of the whole Bible, as it now stands, concerning itself with the question of why the Bible as we know it emerged in that particular form (1982: xvii).

In short, "the end product needs to be examined in its own right" (1982: xvii).

Frye reads the whole biblical text with vigor. He surveys the nature of language, myth, and metaphor to give a background as to how societies think and express themselves. Chapters on typology explain how symbols gather power as they are used and reused. Frye even shows how each section of the English Bible flows into the next (1982: 105–38). No doubt the book's greatest contribution to Old Testament literary criticism is its insistence that the Bible is a book, and as a book has meaning as a whole that cannot be grasped if an interpreter ignores this point.

Problems arise when one attempts to apply Frye's methods to the Old Testament. His choice of the English Bible's order for Scripture may not yield the best results. Also, like structuralism, Frye's archetypal approach becomes overly psychological and individualistic at times. Few commentators can do what Frye can do with his methods. Still, Frye helped encourage a literary approach to Scripture by his emphasis on biblical unity. Like Alter, Frye gave the general notion of literary analysis of the Old Testament academic legitimacy and popular appeal.

Because of all these various currents in Old Testament criticism, several insightful writers sought to examine the nature not only of biblical narrative, but of biblical poetry as well. Adele Berlin contributed to both discussions. She aided formalistic analysis of texts in *Poetics and Interpretation of Biblical Narrative* through her comments on characterization and point of view (1983: 23–82). Berlin particularly showed the peril of neglecting characterization when examining biblical artistry. In these and other ways Berlin supplemented and, at times, corrected Alter's observations.

Meir Sternberg shifted the discussion of biblical narrative a bit. While acknowledging the value of terms like *fiction* and *literary*, Sternberg seeks biblical categories in *The Poetics of Biblical Narrative: Ideological Literature and the Drama of Reading* (1985). More specifically, he argues that the Old Testament fuses both what moderns call history and fiction to make ideological points. Historical and literary critics alike must pay attention to the text's historical and artistic components. Therefore, he declares:

> Herein lies one of the Bible's unique rules: under the aegis of ideology, convention transmutes even invention into the stuff of history, or rather obliterates the line dividing fact from fancy in communication. So every word is God's word. The product is neither fiction nor historicized fiction nor fictionalized history, but historiography pure and uncompromising (1985: 34–35).

Few could doubt that such observations will help stimulate debate about what biblical narrative is and does. Such discussions are now underway, and will doubtlessly continue for some time.

Poetic studies stand at a similar crossroads of opinion. Traditional viewpoints have been challenged and clarified. Of course poetic analysis received a boost from rhetorical analysis, although form criticism and similar techniques had offered interpretations of poetry for many years. For two centuries Robert Lowth's opinion (1753) that Hebrew poetry is based on parallel thought and line sequences had been the starting place for theoretical discussions. Hebrew poetry exhibits either synonymous, antithetical, or synthetic parallelism in this view.

James Kugel attacked this traditional position in *The Idea of Biblical Poetry* (1981). His thesis is that Hebrew poetry is a series of statements that second, then move beyond, original comments. In this way, Kugel fights the notion that Old Testament poetic lines merely restate, or state the opposite of, one another. For Kugel, Lowth's ideas are too restrictive because they are too broad. Hebrew poetry serves a number of functions, and cannot be limited to a few set purposes:

> What is the essence of biblical parallelism? . . . Sharpness, sequences of actions and cause-effect sequences, differentiation, differences in the *other* words in "fixed pair" parallelism, B's going beyond A in repetitive parallelism, the nonsynonymity of numerical and "self-contradictory" parallelism, the "B-clause *kol*"—each is, in its way, an argument against fixing on the similarity of A and B as central. This is not to say that paralleling is not important. . . . But focusing on it is just somewhat beside the point (1981: 51).

Later in the book Kugel finds great similarities between Hebrew prose and poetry, so many, in fact, that he questions whether some texts commonly called poetic are poetry at all.

Despite certain agreements with Kugel, other writers believed that his assessment of poetry left it without a real identity. Adele Berlin had already pointed out various kinds of morphological and syntactical parallelism in her 1979 article "Grammatical Aspects of Biblical Parallelism." Kugel was not alone in rejecting an overly rigid approach to poetry. Further, Robert Alter cautions in *The Art of Biblical Poetry* (1985: 4) that Kugel virtually eliminates Hebrew poetry as a literary category. Alter claims that Hebrew poetry exists, and that it differs from prose in that a succeeding line "heightens," "focuses," and "pushes" actions and themes forward through linguistic means. Thus poetry can even create narrative as it moves "from line to story" (see Alter 1985: 27–61). So Alter and Berlin object more to Kugel's alleged diminishing of poetry than his refinements of parallelism. As was noted earlier, this debate will surely go on, with a host of other commentators continuing to contribute to the discussion.

With all these advancements in the status of literary criticism, a number of new books and articles on related topics have appeared.

Since much of the early efforts had to be theory oriented, few commentaries and introductions had appeared by 1985. But even this gap is beginning to be filled. Several examples of both genres now exist, but only a few can be mentioned.

Peter Miscall's *1 Samuel: A Literary Reading* (1986) examines a whole Old Testament book from a literary perspective. Miscall believes that 1 Samuel is part of a larger book, Genesis–Kings, yet acts as a major piece of that book (1986: viii). The various intricacies of the text's narrative, already explored by Gunn and others, are developed in detail. Plot and character receive serious treatment. In these and other ways Miscall pays homage to the creative skill of 1 Samuel's author, and does so with a basically formalistic format. Robert Polzin makes a similar contribution using a more structuralist approach in *Moses and the Deuteronomist* (1980) and *Samuel and the Deuteronomist* (1989).

Though great strides have been made in narrative and lyric studies, more work needs to be done on prophecy. John Watts regards Isaiah as unified drama in his two-volume commentary (1985, 1987). My own *Zephaniah: A Prophetic Drama* (1988) attempts to demonstrate that prophecy can be dramatic, and thus convey a discernible plot. Such works are simply starting points, however, and have in no way exhausted the subject. How prophetic scenes and speeches create plot, in particular, deserves more analysis.

In a way, *The Literary Guide to the Bible* (1987), edited by Robert Alter and Frank Kermode, signaled an end to literary criticism's search for acceptance. Published by Harvard University Press, this volume employs many significant Old Testament literary critics in an attempt to introduce Hebrew Scripture. Most of the narrative sections are well crafted, but the prophetic books' commentators may yet need to go "beyond form criticism." In another way, this volume points out the need for literary analysis to move ahead to new and better understandings. Narrative theory and interpretation need to sharpen their definitions and comments. Poetic and prophetic studies may still be in their infancy. Only continued research can bridge these gaps. Still, commentaries and introductions have begun to surface.

Perhaps in time reader-response criticism will overshadow all the methodologies mentioned above. This approach emphasizes the reader's reception of Scripture as the main goal of the Old Testament. Such a switch completes a pendulum swing from pre-textual to post-textual matters. For now, however, reader-response analysis awaits its turn, along with methods like a feminist-oriented approach, as the major means of reading Old Testament texts. Formalistic types of analysis, fueled by Alter and others, continue their lead role in the field.

Conclusion

At present (1989), literary criticism of the Old Testament stands on fairly firm ground. Certainly many scholars, journals, and publishing houses remain skeptical of its worth. But *Semeia, Journal for the Study of the Old Testament,* Indiana University Press, and other presses and periodicals are enthusiastic about literary methods. Work groups within the Society of Biblical Literature, which have been much more influential than I have had space to indicate, continue to provide a place for new ideas to develop and a forum for debating old issues. Rhetorical criticism, structuralism, and reader-response analysis are fairly well known and well received. Various kinds of formalism are practiced on a wide scale. A hard-won respectability may have been achieved.

Other writers in this volume will chart the discipline's future. This article cannot do so, and has merely sought to describe a few of the movement's highest points in its first twenty years. Another writer might choose different, or better, books and authors. Even with these disclaimers, no one can legitimately deny the achievements of literary criticism of the Old Testament. At worst it has attempted to provide new insight and to apply fresh approaches to Scripture. At best, it has succeeded in breaking an impasse in Old Testament studies and in forging a new way of reading the Hebrew Bible based on its literary unity and its poetic and narrative genius.

Bibliography of Works Cited

Alonso Schöckel, Luis
    1963   *Estudios de Poética Hebraea.* Barcelona: Juan Flors.
Alter, Robert
    1975   "A Literary Approach to the Bible." *Commentary* 60/6:70–77.
    1976   "Biblical Narrative." *Commentary* 61/5:61–67.
    1978   "Character in the Bible." *Commentary* 66/4:58–65.
    1981   *The Art of Biblical Narrative.* New York: Basic Books.
    1985   *The Art of Biblical Poetry.* New York: Basic Books.
Alter, Robert, and Frank Kermode (editors)
    1987   *The Literary Guide to the Bible.* Cambridge: Belknap Press of Harvard University Press.
Berlin, Adele
    1979   "Grammatical Aspects of Biblical Parallelism." *Hebrew Union College Annual* 50:17–43.
    1983   *Poetics and Interpretation of Biblical Narrative.* Bible and Literature Series 9. Sheffield: Almond.

Boadt, Lawrence
1973   "Isaiah 41:8–13: Notes on Poetic Structure and Style." *Catholic Biblical Quarterly* 35:20–34.

Breisach, Ernst
1983   *Historiography: Ancient, Medieval, and Modern.* Chicago: University of Chicago Press.

Clines, David J. A.
1976   *I, He, We, and They: A Literary Approach to Isaiah 53.* Journal for the Study of the Old Testament Supplement 1. Sheffield: JSOT.
1978   *The Theme of the Pentateuch.* Journal for the Study of the Old Testament Supplement 10. Sheffield: JSOT.
1980   "Story and Poem: The Old Testament as Literature and as Scripture." *Interpretation* 34:115–27.

Exum, J. Cheryl
1973   "A Literary and Structural Analysis of the Song of Songs." *Zeitschrift fur die Alttestamentliche Wissenschaft* 85:47–79.

Frye, Northrop
1957   *Anatomy of Criticism: Four Essays.* Princeton: Princeton University Press.
1982   *The Great Code: The Bible and Literature.* New York: Harcourt Brace Jovanovich.

Galland, Corina
1979   "A Structural Reading Defined." Pp. 183–87 in *Structuralism and Biblical Hermeneutics: A Collection of Essays.* Edited by Alfred M. Johnson Jr. Pittsburgh Theological Monograph Series 22. Pittsburgh: Pickwick.

Gross, Barry R.
1970   *Analytic Philosophy: An Historical Introduction.* New York: Pegasus.

Gunn, David M.
1974   "Narrative Patterns and Oral Tradition in Judges and Samuel." *Vetus Testamentum* 24:286–317.
1975   "David and the Gift of the Kingdom (2 Sam 2–4, 9–20, 1 Kgs 1–2)." *Semeia* 3:14–45.
1978   *The Story of King David: Genre and Interpretation.* Journal for the Study of the Old Testament Supplement 6. Sheffield: JSOT.
1980   *The Fate of King Saul: An Interpretation of a Biblical Story.* Journal for the Study of the Old Testament Supplement 14. Sheffield: JSOT.

House, Paul R.
1988   *Zephaniah: A Prophetic Drama.* Bible and Literature Series 16/Journal for the Study of the Old Testament Supplement 69. Sheffield: Almond.

Jacobson, Richard
1974   "The Structuralists and the Bible." *Interpretation* 28:146–64.

Kugel, James L.
1981   *The Idea of Biblical Poetry: Parallelism and Its History.* New Haven: Yale University Press.

Lowth, Robert.
1753   *Lectures on the Sacred Poetry of the Hebrews.* Reprinted 1829. Translated by G. Gregory. Boston: Crocker & Brewster/New York: Leavitt.

[Mays, James Luther]
    1974   "Editorial." *Interpretation* 28:131–32.
Miscall, Peter D.
    1986   *1 Samuel: A Literary Reading.* Indiana Studies in Biblical Literature.
              Bloomington: Indiana University Press.
Moulton, Richard G.
    1899   *The Literary Study of the Bible: An Account of the Leading Forms of Litera-
              ture Represented in the Sacred Writings.* Revised edition. Boston:
              Heath.
Muilenburg, James
    1969   "Form Criticism and Beyond." *Journal of Biblical Literature* 88:1–18.
Polzin, Robert
    1974   "The Framework of the Book of Job." *Interpretation* 28:182–200.
    1980   *Moses and the Deutoronomist: A Literary Study of the Deuteronomic His-
              tory, Part One: Deuteronomy, Joshua, Judges.* New York: Seabury.
    1989   *Samuel and the Deutoronomist: A Literary Study of the Deuteronomic His-
              tory, part two: I Samuel.* New York: Harper & Row.
Preminger, Alex S., O. B. Hardison, Jr., and Kevin Kerrane
    1974   *Classical and Medieval Literary Criticism: Translations and Interpreta-
              tions.* New York: Ungar.
Rendtorff, Rolf.
    1986   *The Old Testament: An Introduction.* Translated by John Bowden.
              Philadelphia: Fortress.
Robertson, David.
    1976   "Literature, The Bible as." Pp. 547–51 in *The Interpreter's Dictionary
              of the Bible: Supplementary Volume.* Edited by Keith Crim. Nashville:
              Abingdon.
Sternberg, Meir
    1985   *The Poetics of Biblical Narrative: Ideological Literature and the Drama of
              Reading.* Bloomington: Indiana University Press.
Watts, John D. W.
    1985   *Isaiah 1–33.* Word Biblical Commentary 24. Waco: Word.
    1987   *Isaiah 34–66.* Word Biblical Commentary 25. Waco: Word.
Westermann, Claus
    1966   *Das Buch Jesaja: Kapitel 40–66.* Das Alte Testament Deutsch 19. Göt-
              tingen: Vandenhoeck & Ruprecht.
Wilder, Amos N.
    1974   "*Semeia,* An Experimental Journal for Biblical Criticism: An Intro-
              duction." *Semeia* 1:1–16.

Scripture and Literary Criticism

Introduction

As the introduction has indicated, literary criticism has employed several methodologies during the past twenty years. Because these approaches were new to biblical studies, their validity was challenged. By the time David J. A. Clines (1980) and Krister Stendahl (1984) published the articles reprinted in this chapter, however, literary analysis was accepted, or at least tolerated, by most of the scholarly community. Clines and Stendahl reflect how this legitimization was achieved.

Clines demonstrates that examining the literary aspects of the Old Testament in no way diminishes its status as holy Scripture. Indeed, even the great reformer Martin Luther felt individuals trained in literary studies could illuminate biblical interpretation (see the epigraph to Clines's article, p. 25). This realization that literary criticism enhances the value of Scripture relieves the need to reject the discipline on the basis that it is detrimental to faith development and serious scholarly inquiry.

Stendahl steers a middle course in his article, which was his Society of Biblical Literature presidential address. Rather than arguing for or against literary or historical criticism, Stendahl claims both methods are possible approaches for interpretation. Whereas Clines urges acceptance of literary analysis, Stendahl asks that it receive a fair hearing.

Since these articles appeared, literary analysis has gained more adherents. Discussions about its legitimacy occur less frequently. Still, it is important to realize that this acceptance emerged gradually. Few disciplines achieve immediate acceptance, and Old Testament literary criticism is no exception to this rule.

Story and Poem:
The Old Testament as Literature and as Scripture

DAVID J. A. CLINES

[[115]] I am persuaded that without knowledge of literature pure theology cannot at all endure, just as heretofore, when letters have declined and lain prostrate, theology too has wretchedly fallen and lain prostrate; nay, I see that there has never been a great revelation of the Word of God unless He has first prepared the way by the rise and prosperity of languages and letters, as though they were John the Baptists. . . . Certainly it is my desire that there shall be as many poets and rhetoricians as possible, because I see that by these studies, as by no other means, people are wonderfully fitted for the grasping of sacred truth and for handling it skillfully and happily. . . . Therefore I beg of you that at my request (if that has any weight) you will urge your young people to be diligent in the study of poetry and rhetoric.[1]

Luther's encouragement seems to have little effect on biblical studies since his time. With some important exceptions,[2] Old Testament studies in particular have been obsessed with philological and historical questions. And where biblical "poetry and rhetoric" have been attended to, the focus has [[116]] very often been upon the devices or mechanics

Reprinted with permission from *Interpretation* 34 (1980) 115–27.

1. Preserved Smith and Charles M. Jacobs (eds.), *Luther's Correspondence* (United Lutheran Publication House, Philadelphia, 1918) II, 176f.

2. E.g. Johann Gottfried Herder, *Vom Geist der ebräische Poesie* (Stuttgart, 1782–83), trans. by James Marsh as *The Spirit of Hebrew Poetry* (Edward Smith, Burlington, 1833), 2 vols. From the nineteenth and early twentieth century we could mention George Gilfillan, *The*

of biblical literature[3] rather than upon broader issues of the literary character of the Bible or, most importantly, what it signifies that the Bible (scripture) exists as literature.

The decade of the seventies has seen changes, though not always great advances. Two years ago in *Interpretation* John Dominic Crossan gave a useful sketch of the trends of that decade in literary approaches to biblical texts: structuralism, the genre parable, narrative syntax, the genres tragedy and comedy.[4] He omitted mention of the work of James Muilenburg, of which his well-known SBL Presidential address of 1968 was only a sample; his call for a movement "beyond form criticism"[5] generated a proliferation of studies, some sensitive and some mechanistic, under the banner of "rhetorical criticism."[6] More influential, however, in the English-speaking world at least, has been the heady development of schools of religious studies in secular universities; the Bible has been taught in these schools not for the reasons that have accorded it prominence in the seminaries and divinity schools. It has not even always been taught by professional biblical scholars, but by professors of English for the sake of acquainting their students with what is arguably the greatest and certainly the most influential literary work of world civilization.[7]

Those who have been quick to applaud this movement as a restoration of the Bible to its rightful place in education had perhaps better restrain themselves for the time being; for it is by no means determined

---

Bards of the Bible (Hamilton, Adams, and Co., London, 1850); and Richard G. Moulton, *The Literary Study of the Bible* (D.C. Heath, Boston, 1899[2]); J. H. Gardiner, *The Bible as English Literature* (T. Fisher Unwin, London, 1906).

3. So, e.g., Eduard König, *Stilistik, Rhetorik, Poetik in Bezug auf die biblische Literatur* (Weicher, Leipzig, 1900).

4. "Waking the Bible. Biblical Hermeneutic and Literary Imagination," *Interp.* 32:269–85 (1978).

5. James Muilenburg, "Form Criticism and Beyond," *JBL* 88:1–18 (1969).

6. See Jared J. Jackson and Martin Kessler (eds.), *Rhetorical Criticism. Essays in Honor of James Muilenburg* (Pittsburgh Theological Monograph Series, 1; Pickwick Press, Pittsburgh, 1974). For two excellent surveys of the field, see Martin Kessler, "A Methodological Setting for Rhetorical Criticism," *Semitics* 4:22–36 (1974); and Isaac M. Kikawada, "Some Proposals for the Definition of Rhetorical Criticism," *Semitics* 5:67–91 (1977). Cf. also David Greenwood, "Rhetorical Criticism and Formgeschichte: Some Methodological Considerations," *JBL* 89:418–26 (1970); Roy F. Melugin, "Muilenburg, Form Criticism, and Theological Exegesis," in Martin J. Buss (ed.), *Encounter with the Text. Form and History in the Hebrew Bible* (Semeia Supplements, 8; Fortress Press, Philadelphia and Scholars Press, Missoula, 1979) 91–100.

7. Perhaps the finest in the collection of *Literary Interpretations of Biblical Narratives*, ed. by Kenneth R. R. Gros Louis, with James S. Ackerman, and Thayer S. Warshaw (Abingdon, Nashville, 1974), was the essay by one such literary critic, D. F. Rauber, originally published as "Literary Values in the Book of Ruth," *JBL* 89:27–37 (1970).

in advance that when the Bible is studied in the context of comparative literature it must emerge at the apogee of humanistic or even religious texts.[8] But much more serious than the possibility that the Bible will not retain or regain a position of lordship over its rivals, peers, or congeners when considered as literature is the sociological problem now becoming [[117]] apparent. That is, that there is a danger that particular contexts of reading and studying the Bible will tend to dictate particular ways in which the Bible is approached. In the church and the seminary the Bible will be heard as scripture; in the University and the world it will be heard, when it is heard, as literature. It would be painful if at this moment, when theologians and literary critics have so much to learn from one another, such a distinction should become institutionalized.

It would be doubly distressing if such should come about since the distinction between the Bible as literature and the Bible as scripture is largely artificial. Indeed, it is my contention here that the church can properly hear its Bible as Scripture only when it reads it as literature. Even the "authority" of the Bible as Scripture is experienced in no different way from that in which the "authority" of any great literary work is felt. Ontologically there may be a world of difference between the Bible and the Shakespearean or Dostoyevskian canons, but the way in which they impose themselves upon their readers, impel them to reexamine their values, and win for themselves lodgement in those recesses of the mind where behavior is determined, is one and the same.[9]

If one cannot, or should not, read the Bible as Scripture except as literature—and the proposition has yet to be defended—may one read the Bible as literature and not as Scripture at all? Yes, and this is why the distinction between "as literature" and "as scripture" is not wholly artificial. But whenever the values of the Bible are assented to, whenever indeed they are seriously engaged with and not dismissed as, for example, primitive or anti-humanistic, the line of demarcation between "literature" and "scripture" becomes somewhat blurred. Nevertheless, my primary concern here is to explore, not the way biblical literature may function as Scripture, but the way Scripture must be allowed to function as literature.[10]

8. See e.g. David Robertson, *The Old Testament and the Literary Critic* (Fortress Press, Philadelphia, 1977).

9. In rooting the authority of the Bible in its "function," I am more sanguine about the value of that concept than is James Barr, *The Bible in the Modern World* (SCM, London, 1973).

10. See Barr, *op. cit.*, pp. 53–74; *idem*, "Reading the Bible as Literature," *BJRL* 56:10–33 (1973–74). As far as Brevard S. Childs's *Introduction to the Old Testament as Scripture* (SCM, London, 1979) is concerned, I should comment that while for him the Old Testament *is* Scripture, whether it is recognized as such or not, I am not engaging with that position; I am arguing that whether or not the Old Testament is Scripture, it *is* literature.

The literature of the Old Testament is essentially story or poem. Whether we take the historical books, wisdom, prophecy, or psalmody, it is only some geneological lists, land allocations, prose sermons, and laws (all of them set within a narrative framework) that escape the net of these two literary forms.[11] The two genres are not, of course, mutually exclusive. It so happens, however, that examples [[118]] of blends of story and poem (narrative poetry, ballads, epics) are rare, if not nonexistent, in Old Testament literature. Even the Song of Deborah (Judges 5), the nearest approach the Old Testament makes to ballad, is set in the framework of a hymn and so functions as a song of praise to Yahweh rather than as a narrative poem.[12] Further, it must be acknowledged that each of these principal genres, story and poem, is by no means homogeneous. But the fact that the Old Testament consists very largely of two types of imaginative literature and only to a minor degree of straightforward "referential" or "non-literary" literature, makes one think. It means that so long as we regard the Old Testament as essentially conveying information about theological truth or historical truth we make a serious category mistake. No matter how reliable its information on such matters is, to imagine that we can move with any kind of speed or assurance from the face value of the Old Testament text to such information is to deceive ourselves.[13] The *Dogmatic Constitution on Divine Revelation* of Vatican II accords on this point with Luther's concern for the activity of "poets and rhetoricians" in handling the biblical texts:

> Those who search out the intention of the sacred writers must... have regard for "literary forms." For truth is proposed and expressed in a variety of ways, depending on whether a text is history of one kind or another, or whether its form is that of prophecy, poetry, or some other type of speech.... For the correct understanding of what the sacred writer wanted to assert, due attention must be paid to the customary and characteristic styles of perceiving, speaking, and narrating which prevailed at the time of the sacred writer.[14]

Overarching the multiplicity of literary forms (*Gattungen*) discovered within the Old Testament literature are these two catch-all forms

11. Cf. Barr, "Story and History in Biblical Theology," *JR* 56:1–17 (1977), (5): "The long narrative corpus of the Old Testament seems to me, as a body of literature, to merit the title of story rather than of history."

12. Joseph Blenkinsopp, "Ballad Style and Psalm Style in the Song of Deborah," *Bib* 42:61–76 (1961).

13. Cf. Barr, *Bible in the Modern World*, p. 142; David F. Kelsey, *The Uses of Scripture in Recent Theology* (SCM, London, 1975).

14. *Dogmatic Constitution on Divine Revelation*, III.12 (=W. M. Abbott, S. J. [ed.], *The Documents of Vatican II* [The American Press, New York, 1966] 120).

of story and poem. To manifestations of each of these and to some comments on their significance I now turn.

Story

To observe the effect of taking the Old Testament narrative primarily as *story*, we shall have to consider a few selected examples.

In the case of the Book of *Jonah*, we note first that we are relieved of the need to decide whether, or to what extent, the narrative recounts events that actually happened. Most readers of this article will find no need to be relieved of that ⟦119⟧ decision, since they have already decided that Jonah was not swallowed by a "great fish" (though they may not be certain whether the Jonah of the story was an historical personage or whether Nineveh ever repented). But very many readers of the Book of Jonah itself, I suppose, do not doubt that it tells of what in fact happened, and have not seen any need to make a decision about its historicity. If we come to the story as *story*, both kinds of readers can enjoy the story, value the story, and engage in potentially fruitful discussion with each other about the meaning(s) of the story. It is not necessary to disbelieve, or to believe, in the story's historicity in order to understand it. The question of historicity does not have to be swept under the carpet, but neither does it have to be the *pièce de resistance*.

Next, if the book is viewed as story, we can sit looser to the idea that we should search for *the* message or point or kerygma of the book. When it is regarded primarily as Scripture, we are perhaps more likely to ask what it has to say, teach, affirm, assert, deny. When it is regarded primarily as literature, we are more inclined to say, I think: The simplicity of this book is only superficial; what it has to says is not likely to be simple. The history of recent scholarship confirms this presumption.[15] For the conventional view has been that the book is "a tract against particularistic intolerance and arrogance."[16] By some the implication of such polemic has been thought to be a call to mission to the heathen. Some have seen its purpose as a demonstration of the possibility of repentance. Other have found in it a statement about true and false prophecy, about the relation between conditional and unconditional prophecy, or about the problem of the non-fulfillment of prophecy against the nations. Yet again, the message of the book may

15. See Childs, *Introduction*, pp. 419ff., 425; Ronald E. Clements, "The Purpose of the Book of Jonah," VTS 28:16–28 (1975).

16. Georg Fohrer, *Introduction to the Old Testament* (Eng. Tr., SPCK, London, 1970) 443, referring to Artur Weiser, *An Introduction to the Old Testament* (Eng. Tr., Darton, Longman, and Todd, London, 1961) 250.

be regarded as essentially a statement about God, whether in a positive vein, that he is willing to override his prophetic word for the sake of the nations' salvation; or in a more negative vein, that God's capacity for change of mind can destroy the credibility of his prophets and be in any case ultimately ineffectual in converting the heathen. Even the old allegorical interpretation in which Jonah represents the people of Israel swallowed up in exile by the world powers is still advocated.

Most of these interpretations of the thrust of the Book of Jonah have so much for them and against them in the book, that we can seriously question whether the search for *a* message is not, in this case at least, incompatible with the "literary" view of the book. May not Jonah have nothing in particular to "teach" but be an imaginative story (traditional or not) in which various serious concerns of the author are lightly and teasingly sketched? The delicate echoing ironies of the book [[120]] and the tantalizing note on which it ends would tempt us to believe so. This story, a literary critic might say, is a field not so much for conflicting arguments but for interpenetrating visions.[17]

If we turn now to the *David* story, we can see, not how the quest for a single theological message or "kerygma" can disintegrate when the dimensions of the text as literature are explored, but how a ruling historical-critical consensus about the purpose of the work, which lacks any significant theological spin-off, can be overcome by a literary approach that liberates the work to function theologically and humanistically. The story of David as king (2 Samuel 9–20; 1 Kings 1–2) has long been recognized as a unity in virtue of the "succession" motif: The thread that binds the story together is the suspenseful question, Who is to succeed David? In other words, the work has been seen as political propaganda for Solomon's place on the Davidic throne.[18]

Against this view is the rather obvious fact that the succession motif is not strongly enough marked to function as the integrating theme. It will not account for the focus of the story on *David*, the man, the king, and the father. One relatively straightforward reconceptualization of the material is to envisage a distinction between 2 Samuel 2–5 where David is "under the blessing" and 2 Samuel 9–24 where he is "under the curse," the pivotal point being the knot of David's misdeeds in the Bathsheba

17. The formulation is Northrop Frye's (cited by Martin Kessler, SBL Proceedings, 1972, II, 525).

18. Leonhard Rost, *Die Überlieferung von der Thronnachfolge Davids* (BWANT III/6; Kohlhammer, Stuttgart, 1926) (=*Das kleine Credo und andere Studien zum Alten Testament* [Quelle und Meyer, Heidelberg, 1965] 119–253); R. N. Whybray, *The Succession Narrative* (SBT II/9; SCM, London, 1968).

episode (2 Samuel 11).[19] Since David is evidently not always under the curse through chapters 9–24, a more subtle and more persuasive approach to the story is one that explores various levels in the characterization of David and in his relationships with other persons in the story.[20] There is a tension between David as king and David as man (husband, father), a tension that defeats David at times; for example, when his son Absalom, who ought to belong to the private family sphere, moves over into the political sphere and becomes David's enemy militarily. At another level the story of David can be read in terms of the paradigm of "giving" and "grasping," both in his private and public life. When David is content to be given to (2 Samuel 2–5) or to give (2 Samuel 15–18) he is at his finest. Grasping, as portrayed quintessentially in the seizure of Bathsheba, is always destructive; it boils over into the sorry story of the family [[121]] and the state with the rape of Tamar, the killing of Amnon, and the rebellion of Absalom following in rapid succession.

In this narrative there is

> no simple *Tendenz* or moralizing but rather a picture of the rich variety of life that is comic or ironic in its contrasting perspectives and conflicting norms. Not that the author is amoral or immoral; but his judgment is tempered by his sense of the intricacy and ambivalence of the situations that confront his characters—a sense, also, that is not without significance for his treatment of Providence in the story.[21]

Those who would read the David story as Scripture will not neglect, indeed, the narrative's indications of the rather mysterious but also rather infrequent incursions of Yahweh into the tale; but they will sap the life out of the story if they search primarily for religious or moral truths or lessons. They will hear it best as the "things . . . written aforetime . . . for our learning" (Rom 15:4) if they engage with the story in its irony and ambiguity and find themselves witnesses of a story about a man's strengths and weaknesses.

Yet even where Yahweh is wholly absent from an Old Testament story, as in the case of *Esther*, the story is not precluded from having any theological "pay-off." For it has been precisely through a literary study of this tale that a most satisfying account of the book's religious

---

19. R. A. Carlson, *David, The Chosen King. A Traditio-Historical Approach to the Second Book of Samuel* (Almqvist & Wiksell, Stockholm, 1964).

20. David M. Gunn, "David and the Gift of the Kingdom," *Semeia* 3:14–45 (1975); *idem, The Story of King David: Genre and Interpretation* (JSOT Supplement Series, 6; JSOT Press, Sheffield, 1978).

21. *Ibid.*, 111.

significance has been given.[22] Mordecai's words in 4:13–14, "If you keep silence at such a time as this, relief and deliverance will arise for the Jews from another quarter," are to be recognized as the structural center of the book, artistically considered. From this perspective, rather than by decoding the term "another quarter" as a cipher for "God," we can discern the storyteller's belief in a "hidden causality" that lies beneath the events of history. Like the Joseph story, the Esther tale evinces no visible activity of God; unlike the Joseph story, the Esther tale does not even allow at the end that all that has happened has in reality been God's doing (as Gen 45:5; 7–8; 50:20). In Esther, no theologoumenon breaks the spell of the story; but the fact that Esther is in a position of power "as such a time as this" and that, even if she will not speak out on behalf of her people, "help" from some quarter or other can be confidently expected bespeaks an assurance that history is neither random nor directed exclusively by human forces. The whole story speaks, though always obliquely, of a hidden presence of Yahweh in the world. The storyteller "mirrors the nature of history in his method of narration,"[23] and as an artist makes Yahweh conspicuous by his absence.

[122] There is another unexpressed theologoumenon that is mouthed rather than spoken by the tale: "the preservation of the Jewish people is in itself a religious obligation of the first magnitude."[24] Nothing in the book says so, but the institution of Purim as the perpetual sequel to the story and the presence of the story within both Jewish and Christian Scripture testify to a consummate art in storytelling that broadcasts its fundamental world-views by saying nothing, apparently, about them.

A further benefit to be gained from approaching the Old Testament as literature appears when we consider the *Pentateuch*. A truly literary approach will hardly hesitate to regard the Pentateuch as a unitary work, largely because it has been Torah to Jews and the "fivefold volume" to Christians for many centuries. Moreover, it is chronologically sequential and, with the exception of Genesis, which could no more be separated from what follows than could Exodus be separated from what precedes, its beginning, middle, and end correspond with the life story of a single dominant individual. A wise literary critic cannot afford to ignore the vast investment of scholarly effort in analysis of

---

22. See Sandra Beth Berg, *The Book of Esther: Motifs, Themes and Structure* (SBL Dissertation Series, 44; Scholars Press, Missoula, 1979).

23. *Ibid.*, 178.

24. Robert Gordis, *Megillat Esther* (The Rabbinical Assembly, New York, 1972) 13; cf. Childs, *Introduction*, 606: "The strongest canonical warrant . . . for the religious significance of the Jewish people in an ethnic sense."

the pre-history of the Pentateuchal text, but in the end he has to take his stand with the text that won out, and not with JEDP or whatever.

Two important consequences result.[25] First, a single unifying theme in the Pentateuch may be sought (though perhaps not necessarily found). I would locate it in the triple promise (formulated variously in Genesis) of descendants, land, and relationship with God—and in the (partial) fulfillment of those promises. Secondly, the point at which the Pentateuch concludes is a powerful determinant of the meaning of the Pentateuch as a whole: Israel's canon within its canon speaks not of the realization of the divine promises, except in part and proleptically, but of the simple existence and continuing reaffirmation of the promises. Israel is left by this literary work with the future, which can be an occasion for hope or despair, for trust in the God of the promise or doubt in his capability.

When this Scripture is read as story, no unambiguous kerygma asserts itself; but the hearers expand their experience of what life under a promise can be like and ask themselves serious questions about how long they can go on living in expectation, with hope deferred, and with their heart sick.

These stories are, according to one influential analysis, "world-establishing" myths.[26] But they need not be comforting assurances just for that reason; they ⟦123⟧ can be every bit as much "world-subverting" as the highly acclaimed "parable" form. If Georg Büchner rightly depicted literature as a *Möglichkeit des Daseins*, "a rehearsal of the possibilities of being in the world . . . not a confirmation of what one is but a proposal to be something different,"[27] all these stories are potentially subversive and have the capacity to function as a literature critical of any world-view brought to it by the preunderstanding of its readers.

Poem

A first example may be taken from *Psalms* 42–43, where a single *dominating image* seems to offer the best insight into the poem.[28] In the first strophe the image is that of water as life; in the second, of water as death. In the first strophe, water is life for the thirsty hart in the desert; the psalmist's anxious desire for God is the instinctual drive of the desperate

---

25. See Clines, *The Theme of the Pentateuch* (JSOT Supplement Series, 10; JSOT Press, Sheffield, 1978).

26. Cf. John Dominic Crossan, *The Dark Interval* (Argus, Niles, 1975) 57–62.

27. Cited by J. P. Stern, *The Times' Higher Education Supplement*, June 4, 1976, 11.

28. See Luis Alonso Schökel, "The Poetic Structure of Psalm 42–43," *JSOT* 1:14–11 (1976) (first published as "Estructura Poetica del Salmo 42–43," in *Wort, Lied und Gottesspruch. Festschrift für Joseph Ziegler* [Echter Verlag, Würzburg, 1972]).

animal for self-preservation; it is a search for the one who is his water, his life. In the second strophe, however, the psalmist knows himself to be overwhelmed by hostile water which, like the water he craves, also comes from God: "Your torrents and your breakers have engulfed me" (42:7). In seeking water, he finds it; but it is not the life-giving water that he finds. Does this not mean that "God, who was to have been the life of the psalmist, has become his death; he has become an elemental force, oceanic, irresistible"?[29] The poem is projecting the tension in the mind of the psalmist between his contrary experiences of God: God is at once his joy and fate.[30] This tension expresses itself also in the dialogue within the psalmist himself: "Why are you cast down, O my soul . . . Hope in God; for I shall again praise him" (42:5, 11; 43:5). Here is polarity of the psalmist's experience: "At one level of consciousness nostalgia and dismay predominate; at a deeper level confidence and hope emerge and grow."[31]

What does this poem teach us about God? That God may be experienced negatively as well as positively? Certainly. That God *is* both comforting and hostile? Possibly. But does this poem exist in order to teach? Does it not exist in order to be sung—or chanted or read? Will not the polarity in the psalmist's experience of God—to speak only of this aspect of the poem—be felt and heard differently by its hearers in their differing circumstances? Of course, as we all know; a psalm that makes one person weep can rejoice another. When the psalm ⟦124⟧ works in this variegated manner, it is functioning as literature. To acknowledge it as Scripture in addition is to say no more than that the community of faith welcomes, and is sustained by, the possibilities that it opens up.

Next, the *Song of Songs* may be chosen as an illustration of the role of a sustained *cluster of metaphor* in Old Testament poetry. Country (with its flocks, vineyards, sun, flowers, hills, fields and villages) and court (with its king, chambers, curtains, maidens, jewels, couches, perfumes, banquets, streets and squares) function as a brilliant but transparent metaphoric system for the disjunction of the lovers that is always striving towards union. The imagery is everywhere sensuous, with fragrances, breezes, natural beauty, delights of food and wine; and the emotional language is highly pitched, with ravishment of heart, lovesickness, desperate longing, exultation, and its images of animal energy and grace (gazelle, stag, goats, raven, doves, fawns).

---

29. *Ibid.*, 7.
30. The phrase is from Solomon ibn Gabirol.
31. Alonso Schökel, *op cit.*, 8.

Again, the imagery of enclosed gardens, walls, doors, or absence and presence, of losing and finding, pervades the poem with the tension of sexual desire, frustration, and fulfillment. It is not the explicit reference to breasts and kissing that creates the erotic quality of this poem, but the consistent play of metaphor. The language is rarely direct and explicit (hence the difficulties in reconstructing a drama from the poem, or even in some places of assigning speeches); rather it is "subtle and seductive, leaving many things unspoken but nonetheless present."[32] The poem does not allow love to evaporate into a philosophical abstraction, for it persistently makes physical attraction and excitement of feeling the chief ingredient in romantic love; but on the other hand, its emphatic sexuality is not expressed in physical terms and it makes no appeal to the voyeuristic instinct.[33]

The metaphoric systems pervading the poem exist, in the first place, to be savored and appreciated. "The beginning of literary criticism lies in the recognition [that] . . . the work of art . . . exists not to be used but to be understood and enjoyed."[34] It does not exist in order to "teach" or "affirm" the value of sexual love. It does not even "celebrate" it in any self-conscious way. It is true that the Song has been appropriated for Scripture, but that only means that its horizon of reference has been broadened so that it can function as teaching (wisdom) if need be. Certainly it may be *used* in protest against distorting and limiting views of human sexuality. But when it is no longer time for protest or battle or the restoring of balances, the Song comes into its own again not as some "useful" artifact but as an invitation to delight in the mysterious reality of joyful physical love.

For a third example of Old Testament poetry, we may consider *Hosea* 2 and [[125]] the function of *structure* in poetry.[35] Though not a narrative poem in any usual sense of that term, this poem of Yahweh and his wife is structured in two shapes (at least). It first appears in linear or sequential shape, that is, as a plotted poem. We can make out seven acts in its plot, one earlier act being presupposed by the poem. What is going on in the poem, we may say, is this:

32. Roland E. Murphy, "Interpreting the Song of Songs," *BTB* 9:99–105 (1979) 104.

33. Cf. Leland Ryken, *The Literature of the Bible* (Zondervan, Grand Rapids, 1974) 217–30.

34. Helen Gardner, *The Business of Criticism* (OUP, Oxford, 1959) 15.

35. Cf. David J. A. Clines, "Hosea 2: Structure and Interpretation," in *Studia Biblica 1978. I. Papers on Old Testament and Related Themes. Sixth International Congress on Biblical Studies*, ed. E. A. Livingstone (JSOT Supplement Series, 11; JSOT Press, Sheffield, 1979) 83–103.

0. Yahweh and Israel have related harmoniously to each other as husband and wife [this is presupposed as the past state of affairs].
1. Israel has begun to love the Baalim, but that cannot be combined with love for Yahweh. So although Yahweh still wishes to be husband to Israel, Israel has blocked that relationship ("she is no wife to me" [v. 2a]).
2. The result is that Yahweh abandons his normal marital relationship with Israel, so that there is a blockage on his side as well as hers ("I am not her husband," viz. "I can be no husband to her" [v. 2a]).
3. The next move in the plot is not a response, but an initiative, by Yahweh: he sets up a blockage (thorn hedge, wall) between Israel and the Baalim (v. 6), which denies her access to them but does not remove her longing for them (5b, 7a).
4. In the next step, Israel contemplates a return to Yahweh (v. 7b), but she finds that that route also is blocked because she does not "know" Yahweh and his gifts (v. 8).
5. The result is stalemate. The three *personae* at the corners of the triangle remain, but Israel's lines of communication both to Yahweh and to the Baalim stay blocked; she is trapped.
6. The only way out of stalemate is for Yahweh to remove the blockage between himself and Israel; this he does in removing Israel from the sphere of the Baalim's influence by taking her into the desert (v. 14).
7. Finally, the reciprocal relationship between Yahweh and Israel that existed before the poem began is restored: Yahweh speaks and Israel answers (vs. 14–15). The Baalim are remembered only to be forgotten (v. 17)!

The poem plainly lends itself to being read in this linear fashion. But it also contains another structure which permits a different reading. This second structure emerges from the function of the triple *lākēn* ("therefore") in the poem:

Appeal to Israel to abandon her harlotry (vs. 2–5).

[Because she has played the harlot]
1. *Therefore* (*lākēn*) I will bar her way (v. 6a) ⟦126⟧
   (viz. I will end her harlotry) (vs. 6–7)
   But she does not acknowledge me as giver (v. 8a).

[Because she does not acknowledge me as giver]
2. *Therefore* (*lākēn*) I will take back my gifts (v. 9a)
   (viz. I will end her enjoyment of them) (vs. 9–13)

But me she has forgotten (v. 13b).

[Because she has forgotten me]
3. *Therefore* (*lākēn*) I will persuade her . . . woo her (v. 16)
   (viz. I will cause her to remember me and [by implication] to abandon her harlotry) (vs. 16–17).

Each "therefore" (*lākēn*) strophe is grounded upon a misdeed of Israel's mentioned at the end of the previous strophe. So there is a sequential air to the poem. Yet each of Israel's misdeeds have taken place at the same time: to have played the harlot with the Baalim, to have failed to acknowledge Yahweh as her benefactor, to have forgotten Yahweh, are all the same sin. So the poem can be read not as a *sequence* of actions that Yahweh proposes to take in response to a sequence of misdeeds, but as a *set of options* he opens himself up to, a range of possibilities that he passes in review. The mood of the poem is, on this reading, one of divine bafflement, of God's struggling with himself (cf. 6:14; 11:8).[36] Does he dismiss the first two options in favor of the third, or does he take a yet further alternative of forging a wholeness out of all three available options? His options arise from deep feeling (both resentment of Israel and a craving for her companionship), and any decision that attempts to ignore something that is real to him will reduce (will it not?) the wholeness of his being.[37]

The poem does not allow us to choose definitively between these various readings. It permits itself to be read horizontally as well as vertically, that is, as presenting impulses that exist simultaneously within Yahweh as well as a sequence of actions he plans to carry out. It permits itself to be read as the coming to a decision out of a conflict of competing feelings, or as one total response to the reality of Israel's infidelity. We may lean to one reading or another, but we will be good readers of this intense and finely wrought piece of scriptural literature if we can be alert to all reasonable readings of it.

Story and poem are alike enough to allow a common set of reflections on their significance in Old Testament literature.

1. Story and poem are oblique modes of communication. Neither Genesis nor [[127]] the Song of Songs sets out to tell us what to do or to convey a "message" to us. Indeed, it would be excessively doctrinaire to assert that a literary work has no meaning beyond itself ("A poem should

36. Cf. Hans Walter Wolff, *Hosea* (Eng. Tr., Hermeneia; Fortress Press, Philadelphia, 1974) 119.
37. See J. Gerald Janzen, "Metaphor and Reality in Hosea 11," *SBL 1976 Seminar Papers*, ed. George McRae (Scholars Press, Missoula, 1976) 413–45.

not mean, but be"),[38] but almost equally doctrinaire to claim to nail down *the* "kerygma" of a literary work. A literary approach to the Old Testament lowers our expectations for clear messages and general truths or for proof texts to equip arsenals for theological warfare. But it heightens our sensitivities to being moved, amused, elated, angered, persuaded. And when the literature provokes in us the kinds of reaction it has the capacity to create—what more could one ask of a *scripture?*

2. Old Testament story and poem reach us as texts. Texts are monuments; they signal the presence of what is dead but "survives" and can be awakened.[39] We cannot hear these stories and poems as their first hearers heard them, recreating the world of the teller of tales or wishing ourselves back into the audience of an Amos. But the texts themselves still exist, endlessly replicated. They are given to springing to life and taking even casual readers by surprise. *We* do not make the leap into the past, *we* do not have to devise some scheme for bridging the gap between the "then" of the text and the "now" of the hearer. Any literature worth the name jumps the time-gap of its own accord. For this reason, the church is entitled to regard its scripture as "lively oracles."

3. What is happening in imaginative literature such as story and poem is the creation of worlds alternative to our own present reality. Though they bear a resemblance to our everyday world, we are aware that things are done differently there, values we recognize are differently esteemed, and our own personal security may be troubled as we realize that our way is not the only way for humans to be. If we are fascinated into acknowledging the alternative world as part, at least, of what we want to have as our own real world, two horizons merge: that of our prior world and that of the alternative world. In religious language, this is called "hearing" Scripture. If the Old Testament as literature wins this kind of assent from us, has it not become our Scripture?

38. Archibald MacLeish, "Ars Poetica," in *Streets in the Moon* (Houghton Mifflin, Boston, 1926).

39. Cf. Walter J. Ong, "*Maranatha*: Death and Life in the Text of the Book," *JAAR* 45:419–49 (1977).

The Bible as a Classic and the Bible as Holy Scripture*

KRISTER STENDAHL

⟦3⟧ Thirty years ago there was hardly any attention to an alternative like the Bible as a classic and the Bible as Holy Scripture. Then the proper discussion was about the Bible as history and the Bible as Holy Scripture. And the battle was about *geschichtlich und historisch*, historic and historical, about historicity and myth, the historical Jesus and the kerygmatic Christ, history of salvation and just plain history.

Now there has been a shift from history to story: the Bible as story, theology as story.[1] For both philosophical and literary reasons the focus on language and on forms of literary criticism demand the center stage. The odd idea of a "language event" strikes me as a hybrid in the transition from the one perspective to the other.

Reprinted with permission from *Journal of Biblical Literature* 103 (1984) 3–10.

*The Presidential Address delivered 18 December 1983 at the annual meeting of the Society of Biblical Literature held at the Loews Anatole Hotel, Dallas, TX.

1. This shift has many facets. There is the literary dimension as found in Northrop Frye, *The Great Code: The Bible and Literature* (New York/London: Harcourt, Brace, Jovanovich, 1982). There is the movement represented by the Society of Biblical Literature journal *Semeia* (1974–), edited by J. Dominic Crossan and foreshadowed by the pioneering work of Amos N. Wilder (see *Semeia* 12–13, 1978). The depth of the philosophical and theological shifts are perhaps best expressed in David Tracy, *The Analogical Imagination: Christian Theology and the Culture of Pluralism* (New York: Crossroad, 1981). Tracy significantly uses as one of his main categories "The Classic." For a theological critique see the review by Peter Manchester, *Cross Currents* 31 (1981/82) 480–84. See also Patrick A. Kiefert, "Mind Reader and Maestro: Models for Understanding Biblical Interpreters," *Word and World* 1 (1980/81) 153–68; and in the same issue (entitled "The Bible as Scripture") Karlfried Froehlich, "Biblical Hermeneutics on the Move," 140–52.

It is tempting to speculate about deeper cultural forces at work in
this shift. Could it be that preoccupation with history comes natural
when one is part of a culture which feels happy and hopeful about the
historical process? Hegel's pan-historic philosophy belongs, after all,
to the ascendancy of western imperialism—it was even said that other
parts of the world were lifted "into history" when conquered, colo-
nized, or converted by the West. Now the western world is not so sure
or so optimistic about where history—that is, "our" history—is going.
So the glamour, the glory, the Shekinah has moved away from history.

[4] There is a striking analogy to such a move from history to
story and wisdom. I think of the major move of rabbinic Judaism after
the fall of Jerusalem and the Bar Kokhba catastrophe. Rabbinic Judaism—a child of the very tradition which is often credited with having
given "the idea of history" to the world—cut loose from the frantic attempts at finding meaning in and through history. At Jamnia and
through the Mishnah the center of religious existence was placed in
Halakah, i.e., in the lifestyle and wisdom of Torah. To be sure, the historical consciousness remained strong in Judaism, but not any more as
the center of attention. It becomes exactly "story," Haggadah, with far
less binding authority. To be sure, the Mishnah and the Talmud are
not the sum total of Judaism. There are the prayers and the memories,
but the center, the equivalent to what Christians came to call theology,
is in Torah as Halakah. Those Jewish writings that struggled with
meaning in and through history, writings like 4 Ezra and 2 Baruch,
have survived through Christian transmission.[2] They were not part of
the living tradition of Judaism. It was the Christians, new on the block,
who inherited and renewed the historical mode. To them history was
not mute, for now "in these last days God has spoken to us by a Son"
(Heb 1:2). With continuity and with fulfillment, history worked well—
or what turned out to be a very long time—a time which now may
come to an end in western theology.

Whatever the value and truth of such rather wild speculations, the
shift in contemporary biblical and theological work from history to
story is obvious and well substantiated by a perusal of the program for
the annual meeting of our Society of Biblical Literature and of our sister, the American Academy of Religion.

Thus it has become natural to think in the pattern of the Bible as a
classic and the Bible as Holy Scripture. The shift is appealing for a very

---

2. See now Jacob Neusner, *Ancient Israel After Catastrophe: The Religious World View of the
Mishnah* (Charlottesville, VA: University Press of Virginia, 1983). Note also Neusner's observation about the revelatory style of 4 Ezra and Baruch in contrast to the Mishnah (p. 26).

simple additional reason. It expresses so much better the way in which the Bible actually exists within our western culture, and sometimes even beyond its confines: as a classic with often undefined distinctions on a sliding scale of holiness and respect.

By "classic" I mean any work that is considered worth attention beyond its time, and sometimes also beyond its space—although I doubt there is any truly global classic—across all cultures. It would be western myopia to claim such recognition for Homer or for Shakespeare, or even for the Bible. For it is its recognition that makes a classic a classic, not its inner qualities. Hence I try to avoid the more romantic terminology in which modern studies abound, such as "excess of meaning" or "the [5] power of disclosure." Such terminology tends to obscure the societal dimension of a classic. It is common recognition by a wide constituency of a society that makes a certain work into a classic. No inner quality suffices unless widely so recognized.

Thus I limit myself to western culture and its classics. There is the Bible, Dante, Milton, Cervantes' Don Quixote, and Shaw's Pygmalion—becoming even more of a classic by dropping the Greek name for the English title, "My Fair Lady." And there are the classics of philosophy and science: Plato, Aristotle, Kant's Critiques, and Darwin's Species. There are classics of law and classics of medicine. There is even Kierkegaard, who wrote a novel with the title *Fear and Trembling*—he did call it a novel.

Furthermore, as the West broadens its perspective there are ways in which the Quran and the Gita become classics in our eyes. We read the holy texts of other communities as classics, mostly without consciousness of their being "only" classics. Readers find that such classics speak to them, often in undefined ways.

So there are many types of classics, and they come in many shapes and forms, in various styles and genres. And awareness of the genre is part of their being a classic for the reader. To speak of the Bible as a classic is therefore not the same as speaking of it as a literary classic. The issue is rather how to assess what kind of a classic we are dealing with. Scholars are of course free to pronounce it—or its various parts—a literary classic, or a classic of language, or a classic of history, or a classic of philosophy, or whatever. But as a living classic in western culture the perceptions of common discourse on a more democratic basis are decisive. And it is my contention that such perceptions include an irreducible awareness of the Bible as Holy Writ in church and/or synagogue.

What then about Holy Scripture? That designation is not innocent of culture and theology. It is our language. After all, Quran means "recitation," not "scripture," and the Hebrew Bible knows not only the *kĕtîb* but also the *qĕrê*—Jesus presumably never used the *kĕtîb* Yahweh.

It is as Holy Scripture, Holy Writ, that the Bible has become a classic in the West. Personally, I prefer the plural form, Holy Scriptures. I do so not primarily in recognition of the fascinating and often elusive ways in which the Hebrew Bible is common to Jews and Christians—the same text word for word, and yet so different when it becomes the Old Testament of the Christian Bible. I speak rather of "Holy Scriptures," plural, in order to highlight the diversity of style and genre within the scriptures. In various ways such diversity becomes important for those to whom the scriptures function as the bearer of revelation.[3] When the [[6]] Bible functions as a classic in culture, such distinctions play no significant role, but for theological and philosophical reflection it is crucial. In the scriptures we have the oracles, the laws, the prophets, the dreams, the interpreters of dreams, the wisdom, the history, the stories, the psalms, the letters, and so on. To be sure, it is a whole library. Bible means, after all, "the little books."

Nevertheless, what makes the Bible the Bible is the canon. Here is where the Bible as a classic and as Holy Scripture meet: the canonical books, bound together by those complex historical acts of recognition in the communities of faith which we can trace as the history of canonization. For it is as Bible that the biblical material has become a classic of the western world, and whatever part of the Bible is in focus—be it Job or Leviticus, the Christmas story or the Sermon on the Mount—it functions as a classic by being part of the Bible. It is perceived and received as a classic by being part of the Bible.

The Bible as a classic exists in western culture with an often undefined but never absent recognition of its being the Holy Scriptures of the church and/or the synagogue. I have my doubts that it—or substantial parts of it, at least—would have ever become a classic were it not for its status as Holy Scripture. Perhaps not even Job, the literary favorite; certainly not Leviticus, except as a legal classic. And Arthur Darby Nock used to say that the Gospel of John did not become beautiful as literature until 1611, when the King James Version gave it a beauty far beyond what the Greeks perceived.[4]

---

3. See Paul Ricoeur's Dudleian Lecture at Harvard Divinity School, "Toward a Hermeneutic of the Idea of Revelation," *HTR* 70 (1977) 1–37. Here Ricoeur differentiates Prophetic Discourse, Narrative Discourse, Prescriptive Discourse, Wisdom Discourse. The first constitutes to him the "basic axis of inquiry" concerning revelation. Indeed, this is the discourse which declares itself to be "pronounced in the name of [God]," 3. Cf. the Book of Revelation—the only NT book which claims such authority.

4. For a penetrating understanding of the glories of the King James Version see J. L. Lowes, "The Noblest Monument of English Prose," *Essays in Appreciation* (1936) 3–31.

It is as Holy Scripture that the Bible is a classic in our culture. Therefore there is something artificial in the idea of "the Bible as literature." Or rather, it can be artificial and contrary to the perception of both most believers and most unbelievers, as artificial as "the Bible as history" or "the Bible as a textbook in geology or biology" or—the Bible as anything but Bible.

Most readers know, in often undefined ways, that the Bible is Holy Scripture, and it is a classic exactly as that special kind of classic. I wonder if some of our attempts at literary analysis—be it structuralism or not so new "new criticism"—are not, when all is said and done, a form of apologetics, sophisticated to a degree which obfuscates the apologetic intention even to its practitioners.

I do not consider apologetics to be a sin, provided that the apologetic intention is conscious and not obscured by having it masquerade as ⟦7⟧ something else or offered as an alternative to a traditional apologetic of theological and doctrinal special pleadings. About such apologetics Northrop Frye says: "Such systems of faith, however impressive and useful still, can hardly be definitive for us now, because they are so heavily conditioned by the phases of language ascendant in their time, whether metonymic or descriptive." Then he continues:

> A reconsideration of the Bible can take place only along with, and as part of, a reconsideration of language, and of all structures, including the literary ones, that language produces. One would hope that in this context the aim of such a reconsideration would be a more tentative one, directed not to a terminus of belief but to the open community of vision, and to the charity that is the informing principle of a still greater community than faith (*The Great Code*, p. 227).

It seems rather obvious to me that Frye's program of reconsideration in all its humble tentativeness is an apologetic attempt with its own theology, appealing to charity over against the outdated "systems of faith," and addressing "a still greater community than faith." In short, here is an attempt at cutting loose from the moorings of Holy Writ. It is an attempt at allowing the text to speak as literature freed from the very claims which made the Bible a classic in the first place.

That can be done, and with great effect, not least in the hands of masters of exposition like the Auerbachs and the Fryes of literary criticism. In Frye's case the very fact that the Bible is already in itself a continuum of interpretation and reinterpretation, then becomes a glorified manifestation of a "capacity of self-re-creation," and that "to an extent to which I can think of no parallel elsewhere" (p. 225).

Such an approach yields significant insights and opens the senses that have been numbed by overly familiar ways of reading, greedily hunting proof texts for cherished doctrines. Titles like *Mimesis* and *The Great Code* help our mental liberation.

Or to shift to Ricoeur's proposal of a "non-heteronomous dependence of conscious reflection on external testimonies," a literary approach allows new space for the imagination. He suggests that we "too often and too quickly think of a will that submits and not enough of an imagination that opens itself . . . For what are the poem of the Exodus and the poem of the resurrection addressed to if not our imagination rather than our obedience?" Thus there is the non-heteronomous possibility of encountering revelation "no longer as an unacceptable pretension, but a nonviolent appeal."[5]

Frye and Ricoeur both address the imagination, but while Frye looks away apologetically from the revelatory dimension of Scripture, Ricoeur [[8]] defines a way in which revelation can be revelation in a "nonviolent" manner. But Ricoeur is driven toward a dichotomy between imagination and will or obedience. Yet in speaking of an appeal, be it nonviolent, it seems that the issue for him is not will versus imagination, but rather *how* the scriptures affect the readers, in their full persons, imagination as well as will and action.

This attention to revelation, will, obedience, and action is important for our discussion, and it would seem that any culture-apologetics that circumvents those dimensions of scripture misjudges the ways in which the Bible is actually perceived as a classic by the common reader in western culture. For such readers do recognize the Bible as a classic just in its belonging to the genre of Holy Scripture. Thereby there is a recognition of the normative nature of the Bible. That is an irreducible component in the kind of classic that the Bible is. In this it is different from Shakespeare or from the way one now reads Homer.[6]

How one relates to that normativeness is a very different question. The spectrum here is wide indeed, both within and outside the communities of faith, all the way from rejection of that claim to the most minute literal obedience. But that does not change the fact that the normative claim is recognized as intrinsic to the Bible.

It may be worth noting that the more recent preoccupation with "story" tends to obscure exactly the normative dimension. Following

5. *HTR* 70 (1977) 37.

6. There was, of course, a time when Homer served as a "sacred" text which became the object for religious and philosophical interpretation. The Stoics are famous for this approach, and such commentaries on Homer came to serve as prototypes for both Jewish and Christian commentators on the Bible in the Hellenistic and Graeco-Roman world. See Rudolf Pfeiffer, *History of Classical Scholarship: From the Beginnings to the End of the Hellenistic Age* (Oxford: Clarendon, 1968) 237ff.

upon the history-kerygma preoccupation—via the "language event"—
we come to story. It should be remembered, however, that even much
of biblical story was preserved and shaped by the halakic needs of the
communities of faith, rather than by the kerygmatic urge of communication. What was told or remembered was shaped by the need for guidance in the life of the communities; hence the normative nature of the
texts as they are given to us.

It is this element of the normative which makes the Bible into a peculiar kind of classic. This is of course true in an intensive sense within
the Christian community (and what a sliding scale of intensity there is).
But I find it important to remember that the normative character is
present also in the minds of most people who read the Bible "only as a
classic."

When biblical scholarship has become greatly enriched by learning
methods of literary criticism, it seems that this sense of the "normative
expectation" has been lost or overlooked, for the literary models have
〚9〛 been non-normative genres. To ask poets (or artists) what they actually meant or intended with a piece of art is often an insult, and they
are apt to answer: "It is for you to answer what it means to you." That is
fair enough. The more meanings the merrier.

The normative nature of the Bible requires, however, a serious attention to original intentions of texts. The intention of the original
sayings, or stories, or commandments can hardly be irrelevant, as they
might well be in other genres of literature. Let me give only one example, the "lex talionis" (Exod 21:22–25; Lev 24:20): " . . . eye for eye,
tooth for tooth, hand for hand . . . ," words that must strike most contemporary readers as ferocious. Self-serving Christians even quote it as
an example of that spirit of vengeance which is supposed to characterize Judaism as compared with Christianity, the religion of love and forgiveness.[7] But attention to "what it meant," to the intention of the
legislation, to descriptive historical exegesis, all make it abundantly
clear that the point made was the quantum jump from "a *life* for a
tooth." Thus it was a critique of vengeance, not a sanction for vengeance. Such examples could be multiplied seventy times seven—and
more.

All of this leads me to the conclusion that it is exactly the Bible as a
classic *and* as Holy Scripture which requires the services of the descriptive biblical scholars and their simple reminder "that from the beginning

---

7. On the Jewish interpretation of the *lex talionis*, see W. Gunther Plaut, et al., *The
Torah: A Modern Commentary* (New York: Union of American Hebrew Congregations,
1981) 568, 571–75; and Jakob J. Petuchowski, *Wie unsere Meister die Schrift erklären*
(Freiburg: Herder, 1982) 58–64.

it was not so," as Jesus said. That is as true about the commandments as it is about the theological constructs or the human self-understandings of the Bible.

Actually, the more intensive the expectation of normative guidance and the more exacting the claims for the holiness of the Scriptures, the more obvious should be the need for full attention to what it meant in the time of its conception and what the intention of the authors might have been.[8] But also where the Bible is enjoyed in a far more relaxed mood as a classic, people do like to find its support or sanction for their thoughts and actions. The low intensity of the normativeness often makes such use of Scripture less careful. Many even think they give honor to God and Christianity by such use of the Bible. Not least in such [[10]] situations, the call to historical honesty by access to what it meant is necessary and salutary, lest vague biblical authority become self-serving, trivializing or even harmful.

In conclusion: we are a Society of Biblical Literature. The word "biblical" includes both the Bible as a classic and the Bible as Holy Scripture, and I have tried to argue that in both respects the normative dimension is an irreducible part of biblical literature. Hence our responsibilities include the task of giving the readers of our time free and clear access to the original intentions which constitute the baseline of any interpretation. This task is both one of critique and of making available those options which got lost in the process. For true criticism is also the starting point for new possibilities, hidden by the glories and by the shame of a long history under the sway of the Bible.

---

8. Since I have placed so much emphasis on the Bible as canon, it is important to stress this point. Contemporary stress on the Bible in its canonical wholeness is often coupled with disregard for the intention of the various strata and theologies within the Bible. I would argue rather that exactly the normative quality of scripture necessitates the attention to original intentions; see my discussion with Brevard Childs in the introductory essay in my forthcoming book *Meanings* (Philadelphia: Fortress, 1984) and also the essay on "One Canon is Enough" in that volume.

Rhetorical Analysis

Introduction

Rhetorical analysis helped establish literary criticism in at least three ways. First, its most influential initial proponent, James Muilenburg, was a well-known form critic. His call for rhetorical criticism was therefore more readily accepted than a similar urging by a novice Old Testament critic. Second, its ties with form criticism helped ease several scholars' transition from historical background issues to the text itself. A huge hermeneutical leap was not necessary. Third, its emphasis on linguistic detail encouraged further text-oriented studies of the Old Testament.

Muilenburg (1969) and Kuntz (1983) represent opposite ends of the development of rhetorical criticism. Muilenburg helps define the method. He urges the utilization of "stylistics or aesthetic criticism" that analyze "words in their linguistic patterns" in a way that uncovers the "texture and fabric of the writer's thought" (p. 56). Fourteen years later, J. Kenneth Kuntz's article demonstrates how well rhetorical analysis fulfills Muilenburg's goals. Kuntz's careful analysis of Psalm 18 shows how a text's overall meaning can be explained through close attention to its smaller literary units. His article also reflects rhetorical criticism's continuing impact on biblical studies.

Form Criticism and Beyond*

JAMES MUILENBURG

[1] The impact of form criticism upon biblical studies has been profound, comparable only to the subsequent influence of historical criticism as it was classically formulated by Julius Wellhausen about a century ago. Its pioneer and spiritual progenitor was Hermann Gunkel, for many years professor of Old Testament at the University of Halle. The magnitude of his contribution to biblical scholarship is to be explained in part by the fact that historical criticism had come to an impasse, chiefly because of the excesses of source analysis; in part, too, by Gunkel's extraordinary literary insight and sensitivity, and, not least of all, by the influence which diverse academic disciplines exerted upon him.[1] At an early age he had read Johann Gottfried Herder's work, *Vom Geist der ebräischen Poesie* (1782–83), with ever-growing excitement, and it kindled within him an appreciation not only of the quality of the ancient Oriental mentality, so characteristic of Herder's work, but also and more particularly of the manifold and varying ways in which it came to expression throughout the sacred records of the Old and New Testaments. Then there were his great contemporaries: Eduard Meyer and Leopold von Ranke, the historians; Heinrich Zimmern, the Assyriologist; Adolf Erman, the Egyptologist; and perhaps most important of all Eduard Norden, whose *Antike Kunstprosa* (1898) and *Agnostos Theos* (1913) anticipated Gunkel's own work in its recognition of the categories of style and their application to the NT records.

Reprinted with permission from *Journal of Biblical Literature* 88 (1969) 1–18.

*The Presidential Address delivered at the annual meeting of the Society of Biblical Literature on December 18, 1968, at the University of California, Berkeley, California.

1. W. Baumgartner, "Zum 100. Geburtstag von Hermann Gunkel," *Supplements to VetT*, 1962, 1–18.

Mention must also be made of his intimate friend and associate, Hugo
Gressmann, who in his detailed studies of the Mosaic traditions pursued much the same methods as Gunkel,[2] and, more significantly, produced two monumental volumes on *Altorientalische Text und Bilder*
(1909[1], 1927[2]), surpassed today only by the companion volumes of
James B. Pritchard (1950; 1954). Gunkel possessed for his time an extraordinary knowledge of the other literatures of the ancient Near
East, and availed himself of their forms and types, their modes of discourse, and their rhetorical features in his delineation and elucidation
of the biblical ⟦2⟧ texts. What is more—and this is a matter of some
consequence—he had profound psychological insight, influenced to a
considerable degree by W. Wundt's *Völkerpsychologie*, which stood him
in good stead as he sought to portray the cast and temper of the minds
of the biblical narrators and poets, but also of the ordinary Israelite to
whom their words were addressed. It is not too much to say that
Gunkel has never been excelled in his ability to portray the spirit
which animated the biblical writers, and he did not hesitate either in
his lectures or in his seminars to draw upon the events of contemporary history or the experiences of the common man to explicate the interior meaning of a pericope.

(+)   One need not labor the benefits and merits of form-critical methodology. It is well to be reminded, however, not only of its distinctive
features, but also of the many important contributions in monograph,
commentary, and theology, in order that we may the better assess its
rôle in contemporary biblical research. Professor Albright, writing in
1940, remarked that "the student of the ancient Near East finds that the
methods of Norden and Gunkel are not only applicable, but are the
only ones that can be applied."[3] The first and most obvious achieve-
∽ ment of *Gattungsforschung* is that it supplied a much-needed corrective
to literary and historical criticism. In the light of recent developments,
it is important to recall that Gunkel never repudiated this method, as
his commentary on the Book of Genesis demonstrates, but rather
averred that it was insufficient for answering the most pressing and natural queries of the reader. It was unable, for one thing, to compose a literary history of Israel because the data requisite for such a task were
either wanting or, at best, meager. Again, it isolated Israel too sharply
from its ethnic and cultural environment as it was reflected in the literary monuments of the peoples of the Near East. Further, the delineation of Israel's faith which emerged from the regnant historico-

2. *Mose und seine Zeit* (1913).
3. *From the Stone Age to Christianity*, 44.

critical methodology was too simply construed and too unilinearly conceived. Not least of all, its exegesis and hermeneutics failed to penetrate deeply into the relevant texts. The second advantage of the form-critical methodology was that it addressed itself to the question of the literary genre represented by a pericope. In his programmatic essay on the literature of Israel in the second volume of Paul Hinneberg's *Die Kultur der Gegenwart* Gunkel provided an admirable sketch of the numerous literary types represented in the OT, and many of the contributions to the first and second editions of *Die Religion in die Geschichte und Gegenwart* bore the stamp and impress of his critical methodology. It is here where his influence has been greatest and most salutary because the student must know what kind of literature it is that he is reading, to what literary category it belongs, and what its characteristic features are. The third merit of the method is its concern to discover [[3]] the function that the literary genre was designed to serve in the life of the community or of the individual, to learn how it was employed and on what occasions, and to implement it, so far as possible, into its precise social or cultural milieu. Of special importance, especially in the light of later developments in OT scholarship, was its stress upon the oral provenance of the original genres in Israel, and beyond Israel, among the other peoples of the Near East. Finally, related to our foregoing discussion, is the comparison of the literary types with other exemplars within the OT and then, significantly, with representatives of the same type in the cognate literatures. Such an enterprise in comparison releases the Scriptures from the bondage to parochialism.

The reflections of form-critical methodology are to be discerned all along the horizons of OT studies since the turn of the century, although it must be added that it has also been consistently ignored by substantial segments of OT scholarship. Thus R. H. Pfeiffer in his *magnum opus* on the *Introduction to the Old Testament* (1941) scarcely gives it a passing nod, in sharp contrast to the introductions of Otto Eissfeldt (1934[1]; Engl. transl. 1965), George Fohrer (1965; Engl. transl. 1968), Aage Bentzen (1948), and Artur Weiser (1948; Engl. transl. 1961), all of whom devote a large part of their works to the subject. In many commentaries, too, the literary types and forms are seldom mentioned. On the other hand, there have been many commentaries, such as those in the *Biblischer Kommentar* series, where they are discussed at some length. Equally significant is the important rôle that form criticism has played in hermeneutics. In theology, too, it has influenced not only the form and structure of the exposition, but also the understanding of the nature of biblical theology, as in the work of Gerhard von Rad, which is based upon form-critical presuppositions. Many works have been devoted to detailed studies of the particular literary genres, such as Israelite law,[4] the lament and dirge,[5] historical narrative,[6] the various types of Hebrew prophecy,[7] and wisdom.[8] In quite a different fashion, the method is [[4]] reflected in recent studies of the covenant formulations,[9] the covenantal lawsuits,[10] and the covenant curses.[11]

Now, having attempted to do justice to the substantial gains made by the study of literary types, I should like to point to what seem to me to be some of its inadequacies, its occasional exaggerations, and especially its tendency to be too exclusive in its application of the method. In these reservations I do not stand alone, for signs are not wanting, both here and abroad, of discontent with the prevailing state of affairs, of a sense that the method has outrun its course. Thus its most thoroughgoing exponent, H. G. Reventlow, in a recent study of Psalm 8, comments: "One gets the impression that a definite method, precisely because it has demonstrated itself to be so uncommonly fruitful, has arrived at its limits."[12] It would be unfortunate if this were taken to mean that we have done with form criticism or that we should forfeit its manifest contributions to an understanding of the Scriptures. To be sure there are clamant voices being raised today against the methodol-

---

4. G. von Rad, *Deuteronomium-Studien* (1948; Engl. transl. 1953); A. Alt, *Die Ursprünge des israelitischen Rechts* in *Kleine Schriften zur Geschichte des Volkes Israel*, I (1959) 278–332; Engl. transl. in *Essays on Old Testament History and Religion* (1966) 79–132; Karlheinz Rabast, *Das apodiktische Recht im Deuteronomium und im Heiligkeitsgesetz* (1949).

5. Hedwig Jahnow, *Das hebräische Leichenlied im Rahmen der Völkerdichtung*, BZAW, 36 (1923).

6. R. A. Carlson, *David, the Chosen King* (1964).

7. J. Lindblom, *Die literarische Gattung der prophetischen Literatur* (1924); and *Prophecy in Ancient Israel* (1962); C. Westermann, *Grundformen prophetischer Rede* (1960), Engl. transl., *Basic Forms of Prophetic Speech* (1967).

8. W. Baumgartner, *Israelitische und altorientalische Weisheit* (1933); J. Fichtner, "Die altorientalische Weisheit in ihrer israelitisch-jüdischen Ausprägung," BZAW, 62 (1933); J. Hempel, *Die althebräische Literatur und ihr hellenistisch-jüdisches Nachleben* (1930).

9. V. Kurošec, *Hethitische Staatsverträge* in *Leipziger rechtswissenschaftliche Studien* (1931); G. E. Mendenhall, *Law and Covenant in Israel and the Ancient Near East* (1955); K. Baltzer, *Das Bundesformular. Wissenschaftliche Monographien zum alten Testament* (1960); Dennis J. McCarthy, *Treaty and Covenant, Analecta Biblica*, 21 (1963).

10. H. B. Huffmon, "The Covenant Lawsuit in the Prophets," *JBL*, 78 (1959) 285–95; G. E. Wright, "The Lawsuit of God: A Form-Critical Study of Deuteronomy 32," in *Israel's Prophetic Heritage* (1962) 26–67; Julien Harvey, S.J., "Le 'Ribpattern,' requisitoire prophetique sur le rupture de l'alliance," *Biblica*, 45 (1962) 172–96.

11. Delbert R. Hillers, "Treaty Curses and the Old Testament Prophets," in *Biblica et Orientalia*, 16 (1964); H. J. Franken, "The Vassal-Treaties of Esarhaddon and the Dating of Deuteronomy," *Oudtestamentische Studiën*, 14 (1965) 122–54.

12. H. G. Reventlow, "Der Psalm 8" in *Poetica: Zeitschrift für Sprach- und Literatur-Wissenschaft*, 1, 1967, 304–32.

ogy, and we are told that it is founded on an illusion, that it is too much influenced by classical and Germanic philology and therefore alien to the Semitic literary consciousness, and that it must be regarded as an aberration in the history of biblical scholarship.[13] If we are faced with such a stark either-or, my allegiance is completely on the side of the form critics, among whom, in any case, I should wish to be counted. Such criticisms as I now propose to make do not imply a rejection so much as an appeal to venture beyond the confines of form criticism into an inquiry into other literary features which are all too frequently ignored today. The first of these is the one that is most frequently launched against the method. The basic contention of Gunkel is that the ancient men of Israel, like their Near Eastern neighbors, were influenced in their speech and their literary compositions by convention and custom. We therefore encounter in a particular genre or *Gattung* the same structural forms, the same terminology and style, and the same *Sitz im Leben*. ⟦5⟧ Surely this cannot be gainsaid. But there has been a proclivity among scholars in recent years to lay such stress upon the typical and representative that the individual, personal, and unique features of the particular pericope are all but lost to view. It is true, as Klaus Koch says in his book, *Was ist Formgeschichte?* (1964), that the criticism has force more for the prophetic books than for the laws and wisdom utterances; and I should add for the hymns and laments of the Psalter too, as a study of *Die Einleitung in die Psalmen* by Gunkel-Begrich will plainly show, although the formulations exhibit diversity and versatility here too. Let me attempt to illustrate my point. In the first major section of the Book of Jeremiah (2:1–4:4*) we have an impressive sequence of literary units of essentially the same *Gattung*, i.e., the *rib* or lawsuit or legal proceeding, and the *Sitz im Leben* is the court of law. Yet the literary formulation of these pericopes shows great variety, and very few of them are in any way a complete reproduction of the lawsuit as it was actually carried on at the gate of the city.[14] What we have here, for the most part, are excerpts or extracts, each complete in itself, to be sure, but refashioned into the conventional structures of metrical verse and animated by profuse images. Only the first (2:1–13) and final pericopes (3:1–4:4*) are preserved with any degree of completeness. But what is more, precisely because the forms and styles are so diverse and are composed with such consummate skill, it is clear that we are dealing with imitations of a *Gattung*. Even when we compare

---

13. Meir Weiss, "Wege der neuen Dichtungswissenschaft in ihrer Anwendung auf die Psalmenforschung," *Biblica*, 42 (1961) 255–302.

14. Ludwig Köhler, "Justice in the Gate," in *Hebrew Man* (1956) 148–75.

such well-known exemplars of the type as Deuteronomy 32 and Micah 6:1–8, the stylistic and rhetorical differences outweigh the similarities. The conventional elements of the lawsuit genre are certainly present, and their recognition is basic to an understanding of the passage; but this is only the beginning of the story. To state our criticism in another way, form criticism by its very nature is bound to generalize because it is concerned with what is common to all the representatives of a genre, and therefore applies an external measure to the individual pericopes.[15] It does not focus sufficient attention upon what is unique and unrepeatable, upon the particularity of the formulation. Moreover, form and content are inextricably related. They form an integral whole. The two are one. Exclusive attention to the *Gattung* may actually obscure the thought and intention of the writer or speaker. The passage must be read and heard precisely as it is spoken. It is the creative synthesis of the particular formulation of the pericope with the content that makes it the distinctive composition that it is.

Another objection that has often been made of the criticism of literary types is its aversion to biographical or psychological interpretations and its resistance to historical commentary. This is to be explained [6] only in part as a natural, even inevitable, consequence of its disregard of literary criticism. One has only to recall the rather extreme stress upon the nature of the prophetic experience of former times. The question is whether the specific text or passage gives any warrant for such ventures. There are cases, to be sure, as with Jeremiah and Ezekiel, where it is difficult to see how one can cavalierly omit psychological commentary of some kind. The call of Jeremiah, for example, is something more than the recitation of a conventional and inherited liturgy within the precincts of the temple,[16] and the so-called confessions of the prophet are more than the repetition and reproduction of fixed stereotypes, despite all the parallels that one may adduce from the OT and the Near Eastern texts for such a position. Perhaps more serious is the skepticism of all attempts to read a pericope in its historical context. The truth is that in a vast number of instances we are indeed left completely in the dark as to the occasion in which the words were spoken, and it is reasonable to assume that it was not of primary interest to the compilers of the traditions. This is notably the case with numerous passages in the prophetic writings. In Jeremiah, for example, more often than not, we are simply left to conjecture. Nevertheless, we have every reason to assume that there were situations which elicited particular

---

15. H. G. Reventlow, *op. cit.*, 304.
16. H. G. Reventlow, *Liturgie und prophetisches Ich bei Jeremia* (1963) 24–77.

utterances, and we are sufficiently informed about the history of the times to make conjecture perfectly legitimate. The prophets do not speak *in abstracto*, but concretely. Their formulations may reflect a cultic provenance as on the occasion of celebration of a national festival, although one must be on his guard against exaggeration here, especially against subsuming too many texts under the rubric of the covenant renewal festival, as in the case of Artur Weiser in his commentaries on Jeremiah and the Book of Psalms, or of the festival of the New Year, as in the case of Sigmund Mowinckel in his *Psalmenstudien.*

The foregoing observations have been designed to call attention to the perils involved in a too exclusive employment of form-critical methods, to warn against extremes in their application, and particularly to stress that there are other features in the literary compositions which lie beyond the province of the *Gattungsforscher.* It is important to emphasize that many scholars have used the method with great skill, sound judgment and proper restraint, and, what is more, have taken account of literary features other than those revealed by the *Gattung,* such as H. W. Wolff's commentary on Hosea in the *Biblischer Kommentar* series. Further, we should recognize that there are numerous texts where the literary genre appears in pure form, and here the exclusive application of form-critical techniques has its justification, although one must be quick to add that even here there are differences in formulation. But there are many other passages where the literary genres are being ⟦7⟧ imitated, not only among the prophets, but among the historians and lawgivers. Witness, for example, the radical transformation of the early Elohistic laws by the deuteronomists, or, perhaps equally impressively, the appropriation by the prophets of the curse formulae, not only within the OT, but also in the vassal treaties of the Near Eastern peoples.[17] Let me repeat: in numerous contexts old literary types and forms are imitated, and, precisely because they are imitated, they are employed with considerable fluidity, versatility, and, if one may venture the term, artistry. The upshot of this circumstance is that the circumspect scholar will not fail to supplement his form-critical analysis with a careful inspection of the literary unit in its precise and unique formulation. He will not be completely bound by the traditional elements and motifs of the literary genre; his task will not be completed until he has taken full account of the features which lie beyond the spectrum of the genre. If the exemplars of the *Gattung* were all identical in their formulations, the OT would be quite a different corpus from what it actually is.

17. See n. 11.

It is often said that the Hebrew writers were not motivated by distinctively literary considerations, that aesthetics lay beyond the domain of their interests, and that a preoccupation with what has come to be described as stylistics only turns the exegete along bypaths unrelated to his central task. It may well be true that aesthetic concerns were never primary with them and that the conception of *belles lettres,* current in ancient Hellas, was alien to the men of Israel. But surely this must not be taken to mean that the OT does not offer us literature of a very high quality. For the more deeply one penetrates the formulations as they have been transmitted to us, the more sensitive he is to the rôles which words and motifs play in a composition; the more he concentrates on the ways in which thought has been woven into linguistic patterns, the better able he is to think the thoughts of the biblical writer after him. And this leads me to formulate a canon which should be obvious to us all: a responsible and proper articulation of the words in their linguistic patterns and in their precise formulations will reveal to us the texture and fabric of the writer's thought, not only what it is that he thinks, but as he thinks it.

The field of stylistics or aesthetic criticism is flourishing today, and the literature that has gathered about it is impressive. Perhaps its foremost representative is Alonzo Schökel, whose work, *Estudios de Poetica Hebraea* (1963), offers us not only an ample bibliography of the important works in the field, but also a detailed discussion of the stylistic phenomenology of the literature of the OT. In this respect it is a better work than Ed. König's *Stilistik, Rhetorik und Poetik* (1900), an encyclopedic compendium of linguistic and rhetorical phenomena, which nevertheless has the merit of providing many illuminating parallels [[8]] drawn from classical literature and of availing itself of the many stylistic studies from the earliest times and throughout the nineteenth century. It would be an error, therefore, to regard the modern school in isolation from the history of OT scholarship because from the time of Jerome and before and continuing on with the rabbis and until modern times there have been those who have occupied themselves with matters of style. One thinks of Bishop Lowth's influential work, *De sacra poesi Hebraeorum praelectiones academicae* (1753), and of Herder's work on Hebrew poetry (1772–83), but also of the many metrical studies, most notably Ed. Sievers' *Metrische Studien* (I, 1901; II, 1904–05; III, 1907).[18] Noteworthy, too, are the contributions of Heinrich Ewald, Karl Budde, and Bernhard Duhm, and more recently and above all of Umberto Cassuto. W. F. Albright has devoted himself to subjects which are to all intents and pur-

18. For literature on the subject see Otto Eissfeldt, *The Old Testament: An Introduction* (1967) 57.

poses stylistic, as *inter alia* his studies on the Song of Deborah and his most recent work on *Yahweh and the Gods of Canaan* (1968). His students too have occupied themselves with stylistic matters, notably Frank M. Cross and D. N. Freedman in their doctoral dissertation on *Studies in Yahwistic Poetry* (1950) and in their studies of biblical poems.[19] Among the many others who have applied stylistic criteria to their examination of OT passages are Gerlis Gerleman in his study on the Song of Deborah,[20] L. Krinetski in his work on the Song of Songs,[21] Edwin Good in his analysis of the composition of the Book of Hosea,[22] R. A. Carlson in his scrutiny of the historical narratives of 2 Samuel in *David, the Chosen King* (1964), and William L. Holladay in his studies on Jeremiah.[23] The aspect of all these works which seems to me most fruitful and rewarding I should prefer to designate by a term other than stylistics. What I am interested in, above all, is in understanding the nature of Hebrew literary composition, in exhibiting the structural patterns that are employed for the fashioning of a literary unit, whether in poetry or in prose, and in discerning the many and various devices by which the predications are formulated and ordered into a unified whole. Such an enterprise I should describe as rhetoric and the methodology as rhetorical criticism.

The first concern of the rhetorical critic, it goes without saying, is to [[9]] define the limits or scope of the literary unit, to recognize precisely where and how it begins and where and how it ends. He will be quick to observe the formal rhetorical devices that are employed, but more important, the substance or content of these most strategic loci. An examination of the commentaries will reveal that there is great disagreement on this matter, and, what is more, more often than not, no defence is offered for the isolation of the pericope. It has even been averred that it does not really matter. On the contrary, it seems to me to be of considerable consequence, not only for an understanding of how the *Gattung* is being fashioned and designed, but also and more especially for a grasp of the writer's intent and meaning. The literary unit is in any event an indissoluble whole, an artistic and creative unity, a unique formulation. The delimitation of the passage is essential if we are to learn how its major motif, usually stated at the beginning, is resolved. The

19. "A Royal Song of Thanksgiving—II Samuel 22 = Psalm 18," *JBL*, 62 (1953) 15–34; "The Song of Miriam," *JNES*, 14 (1955) 237–50; "The Blessing of Moses," *JBL*, 67 (1948) 191–210. See also Freedman's "Archaic Forms in Early Hebrew Poetry," *ZAW*, 72 (1960) 101–7.

20. "The Song of Deborah in the Light of Stylistics," *VetT*, 1 (1951) 168–80.

21. *Das Hohelied* (1964).

22. "The Composition of Hosea," *Svensk Exegetist Årsbok*, 31 (1966) 211–63.

23. "Prototype and Copies, a New Approach to the Poetry-Prose Problem in the Book of Jeremiah," *JBL*, 79 (1960), 351–67; "The Recovery of Poetic Passages of Jeremiah," *JBL*, 85 (1966) 401–35.

latter point is of special importance because no rhetorical feature is more conspicuous and frequent among the poets and narrators of ancient Israel than the proclivity to bring the successive predications to their culmination. One must admit that the problem is not always simple because within a single literary unit we may have and often do have several points of climax. But to construe each of these as a conclusion to the poem is to disregard its structure, to resolve it into fragments, and to obscure the relation of the successive strophes to each other. This mistaken procedure has been followed by many scholars, and with unfortunate consequences.

Now the objection that has been most frequently raised to our contention is that too much subjectivity is involved in determining where the accents of the composition really lie. The objection has some force, to be sure, but in matters of this sort there is no substitute for literary sensitivity. Moreover, we need constantly to be reminded that we are dealing with an ancient Semitic literature and that we have at our disposal today abundant parallel materials from the peoples of the ancient Near East for comparison. But we need not dispose of our problem so, for there are many marks of composition which indicate where the finale has been reached. To the first of these I have already alluded, the presence of climactic or ballast lines, which may indeed appear at several junctures within a pericope, but at the close have an emphasis which bears the burden of the entire unit. A second clue for determining the scope of a pericope is to discern the relation of beginning and end, where the opening words are repeated or paraphrased at the close, what is known as ring composition, or, to employ the term already used by Ed. König many years ago and frequently employed by Dahood in his commentary on the Psalter, the *inclusio*. There are scores of illustrations of this phenomenon in all parts of the OT, beginning with the opening literary unit of the Book of Genesis. An impressive illustration is the literary complex of Jer 3:1–4:4, with deletion of the generally recognized [[10]] prose insertions. While most scholars see more than one unit here, what we actually have before us is a superbly composed and beautifully ordered poem of three series of strophes of three strophes each. The major motif of turning or repentance is sounded in the opening casuistic legal formulation and is followed at once by the indictment:

> If a man sends his wife away,
>   and she goes from him,
> and becomes another man's wife,
>   will she return to him [with the corrected text]?

> Would not that land
>   be utterly polluted?
> But you have played the harlot with many lovers,
>   and would you return to me? (Jer 3:1).

The word שׁוּב [['return']] appears in diverse syntactical constructions and in diverse stylistic contexts, and always in strategic collocations.[24] The poem has of course been influenced by the lawsuit, but it also contains a confessional lament and comes to a dramatic climax in the final strophe and in the form of the covenant conditional:

> If you do return, O Israel, Yahweh's Word!
>   to me you should return (Jer 4:1a).

The whole poem is an Exhibit A of ancient Hebrew rhetoric, but it could easily be paralleled by numerous other exemplars quite as impressive.

The second major concern of the rhetorical critic is to recognize the structure of a composition and to discern the configuration of its component parts, to delineate the warp and woof out of which the literary fabric is woven, and to note the various rhetorical devices that are employed for marking, on the one hand, the sequence and movement of the pericope, and on the other, the shifts or breaks in the development of the writer's thought. It is our contention that the narrators and poets of ancient Israel and her Near Eastern neighbors were dominated not only by the formal and traditional modes of speech of the literary genres or types, but also by the techniques of narrative and poetic composition. Now the basic and most elemental of the structural features of the poetry of Israel, as of that of the other peoples of the ancient Near East, is the parallelism of its successive cola or stichoi. Our concern here is not with the different types of parallelism—synonymous, complementary, antithetic, or stairlike, etc.—but rather with the diversities of sequence of the several units within the successive cola, or within the successive and related bicola or tricola. It is precisely these diversities which give the poetry its distinctive and artistic character. It is always tantalizing to the translator that so often they cannot be reproduced into English or, for that matter, into the other Western tongues. In recent years much attention has been given to [[11]] the repetitive tricola, which is amply illustrated in

---

24. William L. Holladay, *The Root ŠÛBH in the Old Testament* (1958).

Ugaritic poetry.[25] But this repetitive style appears in numerous other types of formulation, and, what is more, is profusely illustrated in our earliest poetic precipitates:

> The kings came, they fought;
>> then fought the kings of Canaan,
> at Taanach, by the waters of Megiddo;
>> they got no spoils of silver.
> From heaven fought the stars,
>> from their courses they fought against Sisera.
> The torrent Kishon swept them away,
>> the onrushing torrent, the torrent Kishon.
> March on, my soul with might (Judg 5:19–21).

Within so small a compass we have two instances of chiasmus, the four-fold repetition of the verb נִלְחָמוּ [['they fought']], the threefold repetition of נַחַל [['torrent']], and a concluding climactic shout. There are numerous cases of anaphora, the repetition of key words or lines at the beginning of successive predications, as in the series of curses in Deut 27:15–26 or of blessings in the following chapter (Deut 28:3–6), or the prophetic oracles of woe (Isa 5:8–22), or the repeated summons to praise (Psalm 150), or the lamenting "How long" of Psalm 3. Jeremiah's vision of the return to primeval chaos is a classic instance of anaphora (Jer 4:23–26). In the oracle on the sword against Babylon as Yahweh's hammer and weapon, the line "with you I shatter in pieces" is repeated nine times (Jer 50:35–38). Examples of a different kind are Job's oaths of clearance (Job 31) and Wisdom's autobiography (Prov 8:22–31). These iterative features are much more profuse and elaborate in the ancient Near Eastern texts, but also more stereotyped.[26]

The second structural feature of Israel's poetic compositions is closely related to our foregoing observations concerning parallel structures and is particularly germane to responsible hermeneutical inquiry and exegetical exposition. The bicola or tricola appear in well-defined clusters or groups, which possess their own identity, integrity, and

25. H. L. Ginsberg, "The Rebellion and Death of Baʿlu," *Orientalia*, 5 (1936) 161–98; W. F. Albright, "The Psalm of Habakkuk," *Studies in Old Testament Prophecy*, ed. by H. H. Rowley (1950) 1–18; *idem, Yahweh and the Gods of Canaan* (1968) 4–27; J. H. Patton, *Canaanite Parallels in the Book of Psalms* (1944) 5–11.

26. S. N. Kramer, *The Sumerians* (1963) 174ff., 254, 256, 263; A. Falkenstein and W. von Soden, *Sumerische und Akkadische Hymnen und Gebete*, 59f., 67f., J. B. Pritchard, *ANET*, 385b–86a, 390, 391b–92.

structure. They are most easily recognized in those instances where they close with a refrain, as in the prophetic castigations of Amos 4:6–11 or in Isaiah's stirring poem on the divine fury (9:7–20, 5:25–30) or the personal lament of Psalms 42–43 or the song of trust of Psalm 46 in its original form, or, most impressively in the liturgy of thanksgiving of Psalm 107. They ⟦12⟧ are readily identified, too, in the alphabetic acrostics of Psalms 9–10, 25, and 119 and in the first three chapters of Lamentations. But, as we shall have occasion to observe, there are many other ways to define their limits. In the literatures of the other peoples of the ancient Near East the same structural phenomena are present.[27] But how shall we name such clusters? The most common designation is the *strophe*, but some scholars have raised objections to it because they aver that it is drawn from the models of Greek lyrical verse and that they cannot apply to Semitic poetic forms. It is true that in an earlier period of rhetorical study scholars were too much dominated by Greek prototypes and sought to relate the strophes to each other in a fashion for which there was little warrant in the biblical text. If we must confine our understanding to the Greek conception of a strophe, then it is better not to employ it, and to use the word *stanza* instead. The second objection to the term is that a strophe is to be understood as a metrical unit, i.e., by a consistent metrical scheme. There is also some force in this objection. Many poems do indeed have metrical uniformity, but often this is not the case. Indeed, I should contend that the Hebrew poet frequently avoids metrical consistency. It is precisely the break in the meter that gives the colon or bicolon its designed stress and importance. But we can say with some confidence that strophes have prevailingly consistent meters. My chief defense for employing the word *strophe* is that it has become acclimated to current terminology, not only by biblical scholars, but also by those whose province is Near Eastern literature. By a strophe we mean a series of bicola or tricola with a beginning and ending, possessing unity of thought and structure. The prosody group must coincide with the sense. But there is still another observation to be made which is of the first importance for our understanding of Hebrew poetry. While very many poems have the same number of lines in each strophe, it is by no means necessary that they be of the same length, although in the majority of cases they are indeed so. Where we have variety in the number of lines in successive strophes, a pattern is usually discernible. In any event, the time has not yet passed when scholars resort to the precarious practice of emendation in order to produce regularity. Just as we have outlived the practice of deleting

27. See A. Falkenstein and W. von Soden, *op. cit.*, for full discussion, especially pp. 37ff.

words *metri causa* for the sake of consistency, so it is to be hoped that we refuse to produce strophic uniformity by excision of lines unless there is textual support for the alteration.

Perhaps there is no enterprise more revealing for our understanding of the nature of biblical rhetoric than an intensive scrutiny of the composition of the strophes, the manifold technical devices employed for [[13]] their construction, and the stylistic phenomena which give them their unity. Such a study is obviously beyond the province of our present investigation. We may call attention, however, to a number of features which occur with such frequency and in such widely diverse contexts that they may be said to characterize Hebrew and to a considerable extent ancient Near Eastern modes of literary composition. We have already mentioned the refrains which appear at the close of the strophes. There are not a few examples of where they open in the same fashion. Thus the succession of oracles against the nations in Amos 1:3–2:16 are all wrought in essentially the same mold, and the stylistically related sequence of oracles in Ezek 25:3–17 follows precisely the same pattern. Psalm 29 is, of course, a familiar example with its iteration of קוֹל יהוה [['the voice of the LORD']] in five of the seven strophes. In the opening poem of Second Isaiah (40:1–11) the poem comes to a climax in the cry, קִרְאוּ אֵלֶיהָ [['declare to her']]. This now serves as a key to the structure of the lines that follow: קוֹל קוֹרֵא [['a voice rings out']] (3a), קוֹל אֹמֵר קְרָא (6a) [['a voice rings out: "Proclaim!"']], and הָרִימִי בַכֹּחַ קוֹלֵךְ (9b) [['raise your voice with power']]. The poem which follows is a superb specimen of Hebrew literary craft and exhibits the same sense of form by the repetition of key words at the beginning of each strophe, and the succession of interrogatives couched in almost identical fashion reach their climax in the awesome וּרְאוּ מִי־בָרָא אֵלֶּה [['and see: Who created these?']], which is answered in the final strophe by the words to which all the lines have been pointing:

> Yahweh is an everlasting God,
> Creator of the ends of the earth (40:28b).

Perhaps the most convincing argument for the existence of strophes in Hebrew poetry as in the poetry of the other ancient Near Eastern peoples is the presence within a composition of turning points or breaks or shifts, whether of the speaker or the one addressed or of motif and theme. While this feature is common to a number of literary genres, they are especially striking in the personal and communal laments. Psalm 22, which fairly teems with illuminating rhetorical features, will illustrate. We cite the opening lines of each strophe:

My God, my God, why hast thou abandoned me? (1–2)
But Thou art holy (3–5)
But I am a worm and no man (6–8)
Yet thou art he who took me from my mother's womb (9–11)
I am poured out like water (14–15)
Yea, dogs are round about me (16–18)
But thou, O Yahweh, be not far off (19–21)
I will tell of thy name to my brethren (22–24)
From thee comes my praise in the great congregation (25–28)
Yea to him shall all the proud of the earth bow down (29–31)
(emended text. See B. H. *ad loc.*).

Particles play a major rôle in all Hebrew poetry and reveal the rhetorical cast of Semitic literary mentality in a striking way. Chief [[14]] among them is the deictic and emphatic particle כִּי, which performs a vast variety of functions and is susceptible of many different renderings, above all, perhaps, the function of motivation where it is understood causally.[28] It is not surprising, therefore, that it should appear in strategic collocations, such as the beginnings and endings of the strophes. For the former we may cite Isaiah 34:

> For Yahweh is enraged against all the nations (32:2a)
> For my sword has drunk its fill in the heavens (34:5a)
> For Yahweh has a sacrifice in Bozrah (34:6c)
> For Yahweh has a day of vengeance (34:8a).

The particle appears frequently in the hymns of the Psalter immediately following the invocation to praise, as in Psalm 95:

> For Yahweh is a great God,
>   and a great King above all gods (95:3),

or later in the same hymn:

> For he is our God,
>   and we are the people of his pasture (95:7).

The motivations also conclude a strophe or poem:

> For Yahweh knows the way of the righteous,
>   but the way of the wicked shall perish (Ps 1:6);

28. James Muilenburg, "The Linguistic and Rhetorical Usages of the Particle in the Old Testament," *HUCA*, 32 (1961) 135–60.

or, as frequently in Jeremiah:

> For I bring evil from the north,
>   and great destruction (Jer. 4:6b);

> For the fierce anger of Yahweh
>   has not turned away from us (Jer 4:8b);

> For their transgressions are many,
>   their apostasies great (Jer 5:6c).

Significantly, in the closing poem of Second Isaiah's eschatological "drama" (Isaiah 55) the particle is employed with extraordinary force, both at the opening and closing bicola of the strophes, and goes far to explain the impact that the poem has upon the reader. As the poems open with the threefold use of the particle in the opening strophe, so they close with a fivefold repetition of the word.

‏‎A second particle, frequently associated with כִּי is הִנֵּה or הֵן, the word which calls for our attention. Characteristically it appears in striking contexts, either by introducing a poem or strophe or by bringing it to its culmination. Thus the third and climatic strophe of the long and well-structured poem of Isa 40:12–31 begins dramatically after the long series of interrogatives:

> Behold (הֵן), the nations are like a drop from a bucket,
>   and are accounted as dust on the scales;
> Behold, he takes up the isles like fine dust (40:15).

[[15]] The poem which follows is composed of three series of three strophes each, and the climax falls in each case upon the third strophe. The "behold" always appears in crucial or climactic contexts. The judgment of the nations appears at the close of two strophes:

> Behold, you are nothing,
>   and your work is nought;
>   and abomination is he who chooses you (Isa 41:24);

> Behold, they are all a delusion
>   their works are nothing;
>   their molten images are empty winds (Isa 41:29).

It is at this point that the Servant of Yahweh is now introduced:

> Behold my servant, whom I uphold,
>   my chosen, in whom I delight;

I have put my spirit upon him,
    he will bring forth justice to the nations (42:1).

The last of the so-called Servant poems begins in the same way:

Behold, my servant yet shall prosper,
    he shall be exalted and lifted up,
    and shall be very high (Isa 52:13).

The particle may appear in series, as in Isa 65:13–14:

Therefore thus says Yahweh God:
"Behold, my servants shall eat,
    but you shall be hungry;
behold, my servants shall drink,
    but you shall be thirsty;
behold, my servants shall rejoice,
    but you shall be put to shame;
behold, my servants shall sing for gladness of heart,
    but you shall cry out for pain of heart,
    and shall wail for anguish of spirit."

Frequently it brings the strophe or poem to a climax:

Behold your God!
Behold, the Lord Yahweh comes with might,
    and his arm rules for him;
behold, his reward is with him,
    and his recompense before him (Isa 40:9–10).

The particle appears in many other modes and guises in the OT, as, for example, in introducing oracles of judgment where הִנְנִי is followed by the active participle.[29]

    There are other particles which would reward our study, among which we may mention לָכֵן [['therefore']], which characteristically introduces the threat or verdict in the oracles of judgment, or לָמָּה [['why?']], with which the laments so frequently open, or וְעַתָּה [['and now']], so central to the covenant formulations, but perpetuated in the prophets and singers of Israel.

---

29. Paul Humbert, *Opuscules d'un Hebraïsant* (1958) 54–59.

⟍   ⟦16⟧ Numerous other stylistic features delineate the form and structure of the strophes. Most frequent are the vocatives addressed to God in the invocations. Take the opening cola of the successive strophes in Psalm 7:

> O Yahweh, my God, in thee do I take refuge 7:1a (Heb. 2a);
> O Yahweh, my God, if I have done this 7:3a (Heb. 4a);
> Arise, O Yahweh, in thy anger 7:6a (Heb. 7a).

Or the inclusio of Psalm 8:

> O Yahweh, my Lord,
>   how spacious is thy name in all the earth (8:1, 9 [Heb. 2, 10]);

or the entrance liturgy:

> O Yahweh, who shall sojourn in thy tent?
> Who shall dwell on thy holy hill? (15:1).[30]

⟍   Rhetorical questions of different kinds and in different literary types appear in strategic collocations. As we should expect, they are quite characteristic in the legal encounters:

> What wrong was it then that your fathers found in me
>   that they went far from me? (Jer 2:5);
>
> Why do you bring a suit against me? (Jer 2:29).[31]

⁻The questions often provide the climatic line of the strophe:

> How long must I see the standard,
>   and hear the sound of the trumpet? (Jer 4:21),

⁓ or in the moving outcry of the prophet:

> Is there no balm in Gilead?
>   Is there no physician there?
> Why then has the health of the daughter, my people, not
> been restored? (Jer 8:22).

30. Cf. also Pss 3:1 (Heb. 2), 6:1 (Heb. 2), 22:1 (Heb. 2), 25:1, 26:1, 28:1, 31:1 (Heb. 2), 43:1, 51:1 (Heb. 2).

31. Cf. also Pss 2:1, 10:1, 15:1, 35:17, 49:5 (Heb. 6), 52:1 (Heb. 2), 58:1 (Heb. 2), 60:9 (Heb. 11), 62:3 (Heb. 4); Jer 5:7a; also Isa 10:11, 14:32, 42:1–4; Jer 5:21d, 9:9.

Especially striking is the threefold repetition of a keyword within a single strophe. This phenomenon is so frequent and the words are so strategically placed that it cannot be said to be fortuitous. We have observed it in connection with our study of the particles. We select an example almost at random, though it is lost in translation:

קוּמִי אוֹרִי כִּי בָא אוֹרֵךְ וּכְבוֹד יְהוָה עָלַיִךְ זָרָח:
כִּי־הִנֵּה הַחֹשֶׁךְ יְכַסֶּה־אֶרֶץ וַעֲרָפֶל לְאֻמִּים
וְעָלַיִךְ יִזְרַח יְהוָה וּכְבוֹדוֹ עָלַיִךְ יֵרָאֶה:
(Isa 60:1–3) וְהָלְכוּ גוֹיִם לְאוֹרֵךְ וּמְלָכִים לְנֹגַהּ זַרְחֵךְ:

⟦Arise, shine, for your light has dawned;
    The Presence of the LORD has shone upon you!
Behold! Darkness shall cover the earth,
    And thick clouds the peoples;
But upon you the LORD will shine,
    And His Presence be seen over you.
And nations shall walk by your light,
    Kings, by your shining radiance.   (NJPSV)⟧

⟦17⟧ Amos' oracle on the Day of Yahweh is another good example (Amos 5:18–20). If we may accept the present masoretic text of Isa 55:1, it is not without significance that the prophet's final poem opens with the urgent invitations, which is all the more impressive because of its assonance:

Ho, every one who thirsts,
    come (לְכוּ) to the waters;
and he who has no money
    come (לְכוּ) buy and eat!
Come (לְכוּ), buy wine and milk
    without money and without price (Isa 55:1).[32]

Repetition serves many and diverse functions in the literary compositions of ancient Israel, whether in the construction of parallel cola or parallel bicola, or in the structure of the strophes, or in the fashioning and ordering of the complete literary units. The repeated words or lines do not appear haphazardly or fortuitously, but rather in rhetorically significant collocations. This phenomenon is to be explained perhaps in

---

32. Cf. Judg 5:19–21; Pss 25:1–3, 34:1–3 (Heb. 2–4), 7–10 (Heb. 8–11), 121:7–8, 139:11–12 (Heb. 12–13), 145:1–3; Isa 55:6–9; Jer 5:15c–17.

many instances by the originally spoken provenance of the passage, or by its employment in cultic celebrations, or, indeed, by the speaking mentality of the ancient Israelite. It served as an effective mnemonic device. It is the key word which may often guide us in our isolation of a literary unit, which gives to it its unity and focus, which helps us to articulate the structure of the composition, and to discern the pattern or texture into which the words are woven. It is noteworthy that repetitions are most abundant in crucial contexts. Perhaps the most familiar of these is the call of Abram (Gen 12:1–3) which opens the Yahwist patriarchal narratives. As Ephraim Speiser has seen, it is a well-constructed poem of three diminutive strophes of three lines each. But what is notable here is the fivefold repetition of the word *bless* in differing syntactical forms, which underscores the power of the blessing that is to attend not only Abram, but all the nations of the earth. It is not surprising, therefore, that the motif should recur again and again and always in decisive places. An example of another kind is the much controverted verse at the beginning of the book of Hosea:

לֵךְ קַח־לְךָ אֵשֶׁת זְנוּנִים   וְיַלְדֵי זְנוּנִים
כִּי־זָנֹה תִזְנֶה הָאָרֶץ   מֵאַחֲרֵי יהוה   (1:2)

⟦Go, get yourself a wife of whoredom
  and children of whoredom;
for the land will whore away
  from following the LORD.   (NJPSV marg.)⟧

In the following chapter the motif of the new covenant reaches its climax in another repetitive text:

> And I will betroth you to me for ever; I will betroth you to me in righteousness and in justice, in steadfast love, and in compassion. I will betroth you to me in faithfulness; and you shall know that I am Yahweh (Hos 2:19–20 [Heb 21–22]).

⟦18⟧ The structure of the first chapter of Ezekiel is determined by the recurring motif of the *demuth* at the beginning of each of its major divisions, and in the finale reaches its climax by the dramatic threefold repetition:

> And above the firmament over their heads was the likeness of a throne, in appearance like sapphire; and seated above the likeness of a throne was a likeness as it were in human form (Ezek 1:26).

Persistent and painstaking attention to the modes of Hebrew literary composition will reveal that the pericopes exhibit linguistic patterns, word formations ordered or arranged in particular ways, verbal sequences which move in fixed structures from beginning to end. It is clear that they have been skillfully wrought in many different ways, often with consummate skill and artistry. It is also apparent that they have been influenced by conventional rhetorical practices. This inevitably poses a question for which I have no answer. From whom did the poets and prophets of Israel acquire their styles and literary habits? Surely they cannot be explained by spontaneity. They must have been learned and mastered from some source, but what this source was is a perplexing problem. Are we to look to the schools of wisdom for an explanation? It is difficult to say. But there is another question into which we have not gone. How are we to explain the numerous and extraordinary literary affinities of the *Gattungen* or genres and other stylistic formulations of Israel's literature with the literatures of the other peoples of the Near East? Were the prophets and poets familiar with these records? If not, how are we to explain them? If so, in what ways?

But there are other latitudes which we have not undertaken to explore. T. S. Eliot once described a poem as a raid on the inarticulate. In the Scriptures we have a literary deposit of those who were confronted by the ultimate questions of life and human destiny, of God and man, of the past out of which the historical people has come and of the future into which it is moving, a speech which seeks to be commensurate with man's ultimate concerns, a raid on the ultimate, if you will.

Finally, it has not been our intent to offer an alternative to form criticism or a substitute for it, but rather to call attention to an approach of eminent lineage which may supplement our form-critical studies. For after all has been said and done about the forms and types of biblical speech, there still remains the task of discerning the actuality of the particular text, and it is with this, we aver, that we must reckon, as best we can, for it is this concreteness which marks the material with which we are dealing. In a word, then, we affirm the necessity of form criticism, but we also lay claim to the legitimacy of what we have called rhetorical criticism. Form criticism and beyond.

Psalm 18: A Rhetorical-Critical Analysis

J. KENNETH KUNTZ

[[3]] This essay seeks to demonstrate that a rhetorical-critical analysis of Psalm 18 is of significant help in our attempt to understand the message of its author and to appreciate his talents as a Hebrew poet of high rank. In what follows no diligent comparison between Psalm 18 and its parallel recension in 2 Samuel 22 will be attempted since that has been definitively accomplished by Cross and Freedman.[1] Of course, those textual variants which relate most directly to the literary craft of the poet will require some attention. In my own translation I have often benefited from Cross and Freedman's renderings as well as from those provided by Stuart.[2] Also with these scholars I accept the tenth century B.C. as the *terminus a quo* of the poem and would entertain the notion that at its inception the one to whom the psalm referred was David. Indeed, one might think of Psalm 18 as the product of a gifted poet at work within the Davidic court.

While Gunkel's classification of the entire composition as a *Dankpsalm des Einzelnen* is not unfounded,[3] Psalm 18 is more accurately identified as a royal song of thanksgiving. The one who voices the thanksgiving for divine help on the battlefield and to whom the psalm persistently refers is the king. Moreover, a rhetorical-critical investigation

Reprinted with permission from *Journal for the Study of the Old Testament* 26 (1983) 3–31.

1. F. M. Cross, Jr., and D. N. Freedman, "A Royal Song of Thanksgiving: II Samuel 22 = Psalm 18," *JBL* 72 (1953) 15–34; more recently published in *Studies in Ancient Yahwistic Poetry* (SBLDS 21; Missoula: Scholars Press, 1975) 125–58.

2. Douglas K. Stuart, *Studies in Early Hebrew Meter* (HSM 13; Missoula: Scholars Press, 1976) 171–86.

3. Hermann Gunkel, *Die Psalmen* (HKAT; Göttingen: Vandenhoeck & Ruprecht, 1926) 62.

of this extensive composition is in no position to minimize the sound judgment established on form-critical grounds that this royal personage stands within the Israelite cult that is witness to the present narration of Yahweh's saving deed and to individual thankful response. Here is the thanksgiving of a king who speaks throughout. Mainly it is a testimony about the deity cast in the third person which emphasizes the deliverance and eminence he has conferred on his king.

⟦4⟧ Our rhetorical inquiry will confine itself to attempting answers to the following five questions:

1. What can be posited concerning the strophic structure of Psalm 18 and asserted about the scope, interest, and movement of its strophes?
2. Granting that the portrayal of the theophany of Yahweh in vv. 8–16 constitutes one of the high points of this composition, how do its majestic style and graphic vocabulary impart something of the reality and splendor of divine presence that operated on the king's behalf?
3. Over against Schmidt's judgment that two psalm prayers of thanksgiving are discernible in Psalm 18, one (vv. 2–31) spoken by an individual, and the other (vv. 32–51) voiced by the monarch,[4] can a case based on rhetorical considerations be made for claiming that the entire composition manifests a certain unity? In particular, what literary elements within vv. 32–51 facilitate the integration of 'Part II' (the celebration of victory over the enemy) with 'Part I' (vv. 2–31, the celebration of enemy dispersion)?
4. How is the poet's total portrayal of the deity appreciably enriched by use of diverse divine names and epithets? Similarly, what rhetorical achievement is attained by the psalmist's use of varied terminologies in the depiction of the king's enemies?
5. Given the fact that Psalm 18 tells the story of the king's rescue from an oppressive—even life-threatening—situation and his ensuing triumph over his foes, what manifestly spatial imagery does the writer employ within the heightened discourse of his poetry, and what overall impact is thereby made on the reader?

In anticipation of all five questions, and most notably the first, I submit the following translation which, by virtue of its layout and headings, signals the strophic delineation that will soon be defended.

---

4. Hans Schmidt, *Die Psalmen* (HAT: Tübingen: J. C. B. Mohr, 1934) 27.

1 To the choirmaster. To the servant of Yahweh, to David, who
spoke the words of this song to Yahweh on the day when Yahweh
delivered him from the hand of all his enemies, and from the
hand of Saul. 2 He said

I. *Introductory hymnic praise* (vv. 2–4)

I exalt[a] you, O Yahweh, my strength.
3 Yahweh is my rock, and my fortress, and my deliverer,
    my God, my rock, in whom I take refuge,
    my shield, and the horn of my salvation, my stronghold. ⟦5⟧
4 I call on Yahweh who is worthy to be praised,
    and from my enemies I am saved.

II. *The desperate peril of the king* (vv. 5–7)

5 The waves[b] of death encompassed me,
    the floods of Belial assailed me;
6 The cords of Sheol entangled me,
    the snares of death confronted me,
7 In my distress I called, 'Yahweh!'
    to my God I cried for help;
From his temple he heard my voice,
    and my cry for help[c] came into his ears.

III. *Theophanic intervention emphasizing initial unfolding* (vv. 8–11)

8 Then the earth did shake and quake,
    the foundations of the hills trembled,
    they were shaken, for he was wroth.
9 Smoke arose from his nostrils,
    and fire from his mouth devoured;
    coals flamed forth from him.
10 Then he bowed the heavens and descended;
    darkness was under his feet.
11 He rode upon a cherub, and flew,
    he swooped down upon the wings of the wind.

---

    [a] Reading *ʾarōmimkā* for *ʾerḥomekā*, an emendation to be discussed in our analysis of Strophe I,
    [b] With 2 Samuel 22 reading *mišberê* for *heblê* which itself is present in the next bicolon and seems to have been introduced here into the text from that point.
    [c] Deleting *lepānāw* as an explanatory gloss or alternative reading (lacking in 2 Samuel) thereby rescuing a manifestly overburdened colon.

IV. *Theophanic intervention emphasizing divine hiddenness* (vv. 12–13)

12 He set darkness[d] round about him,
   his pavilion was the rain cloud.[e]
13 Thick clouds were before him [*or*, Before him his clouds
      passed by],[f]
   hail and coals of fire.

V. *Theophanic intervention emphasizing its efficacy* (vv. 14–16)

14 Yahweh also thundered from the heavens,
   and the Most High uttered his voice;[g]
15 And he sent forth arrows,[h] and scattered them;
   he flashed[i] lightenings, and discomfited them.
16 The channels of the sea[j] then appeared,
   and the earth's foundations were laid bare,
   At thy menacing rebuke, O Yahweh,
   at the blast of the breath of thy nostrils. [[6]]

VI. *The accomplishment of divine deliverance* (vv. 17–20)

17 He sent from on high, he took me;
   he drew me out of many waters.
18 He delivered me from my enemies though strong,[k]
   from my foes though mightier than I.
19 They confronted me in the day of my calamity;
   but Yahweh became a support for me.
20 He brought me forth into a roomy place;
   he delivered me, for he delighted in me.

---

[d] Deleting *sitrô*, which, owing to its absence in 2 Samuel, is likely an alternative reading for *ḥōšek* which stands just prior to it.

[e] With 2 Samuel reading *ḥašrat* for *ḥōšek*, undoubtedly influenced by previous mention of *ḥōšek* in this verse.

[f] Following Cross and Freedman (*op. cit.*, p. 25) that in ʿābê *š*ḥāqîm minnōgah and negô ʿābāw ʿābᵉrû we have a dual reading which is signaled by a dittography involving the final *Mem* in *š*ḥāqîm and the initial *Mem* in *minnōgah* that immediately follows.

[g] Following 2 Samuel and the LXX version of Ps. 18, the third colon is deleted as a dittography from v. 13.

[h] With 2 Samuel and LXX reading *ḥiṣṣîm* for *ḥiṣṣāw* to secure the plural congenial with the colon that immediately follows.

[i] With 2 Samuel reading *bārāq* for *rāb* (cf. Ps 144:6).

[j] With 2 Samuel reading *yām* for *mayim*; the initial *Mem* undoubtedly originated as an enclitic *Mem* terminating the preceding word of the construct chain.

[k] With LXX and Syriac reading plural *mē*ʾōyᵉbay for MT singular, thereby coordinating with mention of 'foes' in v. 18b and of 'enemies' in v. 4b; also inserting *kî* with the parallel colon and emending ʿōz to ʿazzû in the light of the plural ʾāmᵉṣû to follow.

VII. *Declaration of the king's righteousness* (vv. 21–25)

21 Yahweh rewarded me according to my righteousness,
    according to the cleanness of my hands he requited me.
22 For I have kept the ways of Yahweh,
    and have not turned wickedly from my God.
23 For all his ordinances are before me,
    and his statutes I have not put aside from me.
24 I was blameless before him,
    and I was on my guard against iniquity.
25 And Yahweh requited me according to my righteousness,
    according to the cleanness of my hands in his sight.

VIII. *Declaration of Yahweh's faithful dealings* (vv. 26–31)

26 With the loyal you show yourself loyal;
    with the blameless you show yourself blameless.
27 With the pure you show yourself pure;
    but with the crooked you show yourself perverse.
28 For a humble people you deliver,
    but haughty eyes you abase.
29 For you are[l] my lamp, O Yahweh,
    my God brightens my darkness.
30 For with your help I storm over a bank,[m]
    and with the help of my God I jump over a wall.
31 God's way is perfect;
    the word of Yahweh is fire-tested;
    he is a shield to all who take refuge in him.

IX. *The king divinely prepared for battle* (vv. 32–37)

32 For who is God, apart from Yahweh?
    and who is a rock, except our God?
33 The God who girds me with strength,
    and makes my way safe.
34 Who makes my feet like those of hinds,
    and upon the heights[n] he sets me secure. ⟦7⟧

---

[l] With 2 Samuel deleting *tāʾîr*; presumably this variant verb was added to provide a verbal equivalent with *yaggîah* employed in the colon which immediately follows.

[m] Reading *gādēr* (wall of fieldstones) for *gᵉdûd* in attempting to make sense of a more difficult verse.

[n] With 2 Samuel and LXX omitting the suffix and reading *bāmôt* for *bāmōtay*.

35 Who trains my hands for war,
   and my arms in bending the bronze bow.
36 You give me your saving shield,
   and your right hand upholds me,
   and your answering[o] makes me great.
37 You have lengthened my strides beneath me,
   and my ankles do not falter.

X. *The king invincible in battle* (vv. 38–43)

38 I pursue my enemies and overtake them;
   and turn not back till I make an end of them.
39 I smite them down, so that they cannot rise;
   they fall beneath my feet.
40 And you gird me with strength for war;
   you bring down my adversaries beneath me.
41 You give me the neck of my enemies,
   and those who hate me I exterminate.
42 They cry for help, but there is none to save,
   unto[p] Yahweh, but he answers them not.
43 I pulverize them as the dust before the wind;
   like the mire of the streets I crush[q] them.

XI. *The king's conquest of the nations* (vv. 44–46)

44 You deliver me from the strife of the people,
   you set me at the head of the nations;
   a people I had not known serve me.
45 Upon hearing,[r] they obey me,
   foreigners cringe before me.
46 Foreigners cower,
   and stagger forth from their bulwarks.

XII. *Concluding praise of Yahweh* (vv. 47–49)

47 Yahweh lives! and blessed be my Rock,
   and exalted be the God of my salvation.

[o] Reading *ʿ*^{a}*nôt*^{e}*kā* for *ʿanwat*^{e}*kā*.

[p] With 2 Samuel reading *ʾel* for *ʿal*.

[q] With 2 Samuel reading *ʾ*^{a}*diqqēm* for *ʾ*^{a}*riqem* since this corresponds well with the parallel verb in the preceding colon and acknowledges the common confusion of the Hebrew consonants *Rēsh* and *Dāleth*.

[r] With 2 Samuel reading *lišmôaʿ* for *l*^{e}*šēmaʿ*.

48 The God who gives me vengeance,
    and makes people subject to me;
49 Who delivers me from my enemies;
    truly above my adversaries you exalt me;
    from the violent man you deliver me.

Liturgical postlude (vv. 50–51)

50 Therefore I will proclaim you, O Yahweh, among the nations,
    and to your name I will sing praise. [[8]]
51 Who increases the triumphs of his king,
    and shows favor to his anointed,
    to David and his posterity for ever. [[9]]

Strophic Structure

Our first enquiry challenges us to ascertain the strophic structure of
the royal psalm and to perceive the scope, interest, and movement of
its several strophes. How are the major poetic units to be identified?
What fundamental pattern did the psalmist confer upon these poetic
lines as he gave them birth? While full confidence is not attainable, I
would suggest that Psalm 18 consists of a dozen strophes and a concluding two-verse liturgical postlude. The briefest strophe (vv. 12–13)
contains but two bicola while the two longest strophes (vv. 26–31 and
32–37) each hosts five bicola and one tricolon.

   Strophe I (vv. 2–4) functions as introductory hymnic praise. Its
rapid accumulation of epithets for Yahweh aptly extols him as the un-
breakable support of the king. The colon attested in v. 2, *ʾerḥomᵉkā
YHWH ḥizqî*, and to be rendered, 'I love you, O Yahweh, my strength,' is
unique as an introductory component in biblical hymnody. Not only is
the verb a Qal hapax, but the root *rḥm*, being reserved to designate the
deepest fathomed divine compassion, is never elsewhere attested as an
expression of man's love toward the deity. In the light of Ps 30:2;
145:1; and Isa 25:1, many commentators posit that the original form of
the first word in v. 2 is *ʾᵃrōmimkā* and read, 'I exalt you, O Yahweh.'
This is the heartfelt word of praise with which the psalm is begun, the
chain of epithets introduced, and the recounting of the theophany undoubtedly anticipated. As such it need not be dismissed as a liturgical
addition.[5] Since rhetorical critics should obviously exercise caution in
pressing for what is wholly unique in a given composition, this emendation, though a vote for typicality, commends itself. Clearly, the pil-

---

5. As does E. J. Kissane, *The Book of Psalms* (Dublin: Browne & Noland, 1954) 78.

ing up of divine appellatives is imposing. The deity is the psalmist's 'strength', 'rock' (*sela*^{c} and *ṣûr* both appear), 'fortress', 'deliverer', 'shield', 'horn of salvation', and 'stronghold'. The appellative 'my deliverer' (*mᵉpalṭî*) might be deleted in v. 3a either in an attempt to shorten the colon[6] or in recognition that it is the only appellative that is not a metaphor. Such textual surgery, however, is not all that compelling. Even if some of the epithets in v. 2 should be subsequent additions, we have no solid basis for establishing a definitive list.[7] Suffice it to say that the poet appears to have moved in a deliberate and artful manner as he incorporated several divine appellatives of high antiquity that were available to him. He thereby fashioned a rhetorically strong introductory element capable of serving the entire lengthy poem that would ensue. Equally impressive [[10]] is the use of the Tetragammaton in each verse of this introductory strophe. Yahweh is the effective agent of the king's signal deliverance and the one 'who is worthy to be praised' (v. 4).

Strophes II (vv. 5–7) and VI (vv. 17–20) frame the theophany. The former conveys in rich metaphorical detail, and with a noticeable alternation of perfect and imperfect tenses, the anguished situation of the king which provoked him to entreat the deity to intervene. Hymnic form now yields to narrative. The peril of death is effectively described by means of a chiastic construction consisting of four plural construct chains and four plural verbs with first-person singular suffixes. In vv. 5a and 6b the cola are *introduced* by the verb, while in vv. 5b and 6a they are *terminated* by the verb. This poignant portrayal of the monarch's plight is followed by the tetracolon of v. 7 with its reference to the king's cry for help which is divinely heard and responded to in the theophanic act itself. The divine names used in Strophe II, *Yₕwₕ* and *ᵓᵉlōhîm*, intentionally balance those of Strophe I where *Yₕwₕ* and *ᵓēl* are employed. Then in v. 7cd the voice of the entreater (*qôlî*) is represented as heard by the one entreated (*bᵉᵓoznāw*). The poet's talent for subjecting this colorful strophe to the service of one key thought should not be underestimated. As a self-contained sense unit, Strophe II declares that the environmental odds confronting the king were so overwhelming that only by his turning to the deity could he dare hope for deliverance.

Strophes III (vv. 8–11), IV (vv. 12–13), and V (vv. 14–16) are devoted to an elaborate depiction of Yahweh's theophanic intervention. A

---

6. The concern of H.-J. Kraus, *Psalmen*² (BKAT; Neukirchen-Vluyn: Neukirchener Verlag, 1961) 138, who identifies this appellative as an inner-textual variant.

7. In agreement with A. A. Anderson, *The Book of Psalms* (NCB; Grand Rapids: Eerdmans, 1972) I, 155.

substantial body of expressive cola readily evokes the attention of the
listener or reader. To be sure, it is not altogether clear that vv. 8–16
can be divided into three separate strophes. Perhaps they should be
taken as one elaborate strophe. At best, *yāšet* heading v. 12 and *way-
yar͑ēm* at the outset of v. 14 are subtle indications that new strophes are
unfolding. The many cola spanning vv. 8–16 offer sustained third-
person description which effectively contrasts with Strophe II (vv. 5–7),
set in the first person, and Strophe VI (vv. 17–20), where third-person
statement continues but where first-person suffixes are attached to six
of its ten verbs.[8] Moreover, Jeremias notes that vv. 9–15, which describe in ever new colors and images Yahweh's coming, are artistically
enclosed by vv. 8 and 16, which denote highly disruptive terrestrial reaction to divine manifestation.[9] In the absence of clear rhetorical clues
for new strophes, it can nonetheless be said that in vv. 12–13 the hiddenness of Yahweh is especially emphasized. Yet does [[11]] Yahweh's
elusive presence there affirmed adequately distinguish these verses
from others in the theophany? A firm answer is not readily evident. In
our quest for strophic identity, it might be asked whether anything is
to be made of the fact that within the theophany *per se*, only in vv. 14–
16 is the deity explicitly named. 'Yahweh' is mentioned in v. 14a and
that is balanced by reference to 'the Most High' (*͑elyôn*) in v. 14b. Then
in v. 16c we meet the vocative, 'O Yahweh.' Yet if this is meant to distinguish vv. 14–16 from that which immediately precedes, the actual
nouns and verbs here employed press us into admitting that this is at
most a nuanced separation that ought not be overemphasized. The
efficacy of Yahweh's self-manifestation, however, is artfully imparted in
vv. 14–16 and a perceptible climax is reached.

We shall bring this particular inquiry to a close by submitting that
even if many interpreters of this composition should persist in accepting vv. 8–16 as a single strophe, vv. 8–11, 12–13, and 14–16 still merit
recognition as its logical thought sequences. Since the presence of two
tricola and eight bicola within a single strophe seems excessive, the
strophic delineation of Yahweh's self-manifestation here advanced at
least constitutes a reasonable proposal.

In Strophe VI (vv. 17–20) the purpose of Yahweh's presence is set
forth as effectively accomplished. The deity is presented in v. 17b as
having reached down and drawn (*mšh*) the monarch out of 'many waters' (*mayim rabbîm*) which vividly symbolize the historical enemies who

---

8. It is surely not fortuitous that none of the verbs within vv. 8–16 possesses an inseparable suffix.

9. Jörg Jeremias, *Theophanie: Die Geschichte einer alttestamentlichen Gattung* (WMANT;
Neukirchen-Vluyn: Neukirchener Verlag, 1965) 36.

had overpowered him. In the day of the king's calamity (v. 19a), when adversity had almost fully overwhelmed him, Yahweh, who is the subject of all but two verbs in this strophe, took pleasure in the king (v. 20b) and acted for his welfare. A coherence is achieved in this strophe through the varied use of suffixed prepositions in strategic collocations, and through a six-fold use of the third-person singular imperfect verb with first-person suffix, which on all but one occasion (v. 19a) denote the deity's salvific way with the king. Two instances each of the third-person singular imperfect with suffix are present in vv. 17 and 20 which envelop the strophe, and one instance each occurs in vv. 18 and 19. At the end of the bicola in vv. 18, 19, and 20, the prepositions *mimmennî*, *lî*, and *bî* respectively appear and undoubtedly reflect the poet's conscious design. The last-mentioned, which is utilized in the final colon (*kî ḥāpēṣ bî*), helps the strophe to come to rest on an emphatic note: 'for he [Yahweh] delighted in me.' Here the poet succinctly provides the very reason why the deity intervened—he was pleased with his royal servant.[10]

[[12]] Strophe VII (vv. 21–25) proclaims the king's righteous relation with the deity. As an instance of ring composition, strikingly similar initial and concluding bicola readily define the scope of this strophe. Cross and Freedman hold that v. 25 is out of place in its present context and that its verbal links with v. 21 suggest that it is a doublet.[11] A close reading of the Hebrew, however, reveals that the wording is not all that similar. Though repetition of entire cola, with requisite allowance for artistic variation, is not a pronounced feature in Psalm 18, it may well be warranted here as the poet's means for affirming the efficacious nature of Yahweh's theophany: *deliverance of the righteous king was forthcoming.* As one who is well aware of the covenant relation binding him meaningfully with his Lord, the monarch announces that his hands are clean (v. 21b) and that he has respected Yahweh's ways (v. 22a), ordinances (v. 23a), and statutes (v. 23b). The nouns *derek*, *mišpāṭ*, and *ḥuqqâ* confer a welcome note of specificity on vv. 22–23 which affects a contrast with the sweeping statement of v. 24a, 'I was blameless (*tāmîm*) before him.' As a meaningful sense unit, this strophe is committed to the assumption that as Yahweh's servant, the king's righteousness is firmly anchored in his unwavering commitment to Yahweh and his covenant. Accordingly, royal self-exultation is in no wise permitted.

10. To be sure, the deictic particle *kî* has its own service to render in making the reason for divine intervention all the more explicit.

11. Cross and Freedman, *op. cit.*, 28.

A declaration of Yahweh's faithful dealings appropriately follows in Strophe VIII (vv. 26–31) which concludes the first half of the psalm. With the conspicuous use of the preposition ʿim at the head of all four cola, vv. 26–27 have been aptly judged by Cross and Freedman to be an ancient gnomic quatrain characterized by 'sing-song rhythm and anthropopathic conceptions' which the poet appropriated.[12] Undoubtedly he was attracted by its assonance and alliteration. The strophe is rounded out by means of three emphatic bicola (vv. 28–30) all headed with the deictic particle kî and a tricolon (v. 31) containing two divine names (ʾēl and Yʜwʜ) and the crucial epithet 'shield' (māgēn) already offered in v. 3 and to be mentioned once more in v. 36. The second-person discourse of the gnomic quatrain in vv. 26–27 is maintained throughout most of the strophe, though in v. 30b the poet switches to the first person and v. 31 is entirely cast in the third person. Such shifts are smoothly executed. Certainly v. 30b balances nicely over against v. 30a, and v. 31 in its third-person speech presumably instructs other faithful members within the Israelite community and in so doing performs in a manner typical of thanksgiving compositions in the Hebrew Bible. The metonymy [13] located roughly midway in this strophe ('but haughty eyes you abase,' v. 28b) readily advertises the composer's capacity to fashion intensely poetic discourse. Moreover, in the rich tricolon of v. 31 he ushers the first half of this elaborate psalm to a strong finish. Notwithstanding its resemblance to Deut 32:4, the colon in v. 31a ('God's way is perfect') is superbly suited to the psalm at this juncture. Its adjective tāmîm replicates a key term used of deity in v. 26b, near the start of the strophe, though a somewhat different English translation is here invited. The celebration of the benefits of covenantal fellowship and fidelity successfully links all of the elements of this strophe into a meaningful sense unit.

Clearly, the exact strophic arrangement of the second half of the psalm is difficult to determine and what is here presented is admittedly provisional. There is extensive disagreement in the commentaries, though major breaks are often noticed at the end of vv. 43 and 46. Strophe IX (vv. 32–37) opens in a determined manner with its emphatic kî particle and two rhetorical questions each introduced by the interrogative 'who' (mî). As an artfully employed stylistic device, both rhetorical questions glorify Yahweh by underscoring his incomparability. He alone is fully capable of ensuring the king's victory over against his enemies. Moreover, the poet may have v. 31 still well in mind, for once more we discover that multiple divine names (ʾelôah, Yʜwʜ, and

12. *Ibid.*, 21; Stuart, *op. cit.*, 185, concurs.

$^{\supset e}l\bar{o}h\hat{\imath}m$ all appear) as well as a significant divine appellative—'rock'
($\hat{sur}$). Thus the second half of this poem begins to unfold smoothly
from that junction where the first half came to rest. An intentional
symmetry obtains in the third-person language of vv. 33–35. These bicola are so formulated that in each instance the first member features
a Piel participle denoting some favor that the deity bestows on the
king. Then the second member attests either an imperfect or perfect
verb which further extends the poetic assertion of its predecessor. Also
the word about divine support is more generally stated in v. 33 than is
the case in vv. 34–35 where attention is called to the king's feet, hands,
and arms which are divinely enabled. In vv. 36–37, which are framed
in the second person, the more general statement about divine support (v. 36) precedes the specific concern about the king's sure footing
amid the battle (v. 37).[13] In this strophe, the expression of God's personal concern in equipping his chosen servant for battle borders on
the extravagant. From first to last, the deity is the subject of the many
verbs employed in this strophe and the king is their object. Though
the poet portrays the girding and training of his royal [[14]] servant in
some detail, he is successful in creating a strophe which throughout
maintains its focus on Yahweh.

If these verses and those in Strophes X and XI resume the narrative about divinely answered need, most verbs invite past-tense translations.[14] Yet Eaton cogently claims that 'the verses could be taken more
generally, expressing the capacity for triumph which Yahweh has now
bestowed on his king, to be translated with present and future
tenses'[15] and several translations have pressed in this direction.[16]
While I favor a dominantly present-tense rendering, that does not require the selling of one's soul to radical views about the possibilities of
sacral kingship in biblical Israel. Since the choice of verb tense does
not play all that determinative a role in shaping the rhetorical craft of
Psalm 18, we need not say more on the matter in this context.

13. While a break has sometimes been identified after v. 35, the mere shift of persons alone is insufficient to justify this. There are no words or grammatical constructions
in v. 36 which would signal a new strophe, and the logic of the thought begun in v. 32
continues through v. 37.

14. As undertaken, for example, by Gunkel, *op. cit.*, 16–62; Kraus, *op. cit.*, 137–38;
Mitchell Dahood, *Psalms I* (AB: Garden City, N.Y.: Doubleday, 1966) 103–104.

15. J. H. Eaton, *Kingship and the Psalms* (SBT, II/32; Naperville: Alec R. Allenson,
1976) 114.

16. For example, A. R. Johnson, *Sacral Kingship in Ancient Israel* (Cardiff: University
of Wales Press, 1955) 112–114; Cross and Freedman, *op. cit.*, 30–34; Stuart, *op. cit.*, 181–
82; and the NEB.

The shift to the first person in v. 38 coupled with a new thought unit signal the beginning of a new strophe (vv. 38–43). The king who has been readied for battle by Yahweh now pursues his enemies and is victorious. Though first-, second-, and third-person cola are present, first-person statement dominates. It appears in six of the twelve cola and is particularly evident at the extremities of the strophe. The king's success in eradicating all enmity and opposition is sketched in admittedly harsh language. The scene is a busy one and may well reach its climax in the concluding bicolon of the strophe (v. 43) where the king says of his enemies, 'I pulverize them (*ʾešḥāqēm*) as dust before the wind; like the mire of the streets I crush them (*ʾadiqqēm*).' In its totality, however, Strophe X conveys a tone of awe, moving under a firm recognition that such regal success depends on Yahweh's substantial undergirding. Three cola cast in second-person discourse and located midway in the strophe (vv. 40–41a) are quite explicit on the matter.

Closely related to the theme of Strophe X is Strophe XI (vv. 44–46) in which the king's conquest of the nations is announced. Opening with an imperfect form of *plṭ* ('to deliver'), a root which plays a vital role elsewhere in the psalm (vv. 3 and 49), the strophe first utilizes second-person speech in v. 44ab to acknowledge what Yahweh has done for the king. Then in v. 44c, with its shift to the third person, it moves immediately to mention the king's universal dominance over peoples and nations as the deity's vicegerent. So impressive is the king's fame that the cowering enemy surrenders without the necessity of physical combat. Here a degree of intensification is rhetorically realized through the poet's artful use of repetition.

[15] Strophe XII (vv. 47–49), which offers concluding words of praise, opens emphatically with the joyous and ancient cultic formula, *ḥay YHWH* ('Yahweh lives'). In its first three cola the deity is mentioned by three different names (*YHWH*, *ʾelōhîm*, and *ʾēl*) as well as by the appellative 'rock' (*ṣûrî*) most recently met in the first bicolon of the second half of the psalm (v. 32b) and previously attested in the introductory hymnic praise (v. 3b). An intense personal feeling is deftly communicated by the attachment of the first-person singular suffix to four nouns (vv. 47ab, 49ab), three verbs (v. 49abc), and two prepositions (v. 48ab). Accordingly, the poet successfully recaptures the hymnic mood which had been struck at the outset of the poem in Strophe I. We are led full circle.

The muting of such personal expression in vv. 50–51, along with the formal presence of the particle *ʿal-kēn* ('therefore'), induce our identifying the last two verses of the psalm as a liturgical postlude. While our strophic investigation stands in rather minimal agreement with that advanced by Kraft, his designation of vv. 50–51 as a liturgical postlude and interest in contrasting their mood with that projected in vv. 47–49 are well founded.[17] With its proclivity for a formal yet forthright mode of discourse, this postlude is dedicated to declaring that the king's testimony resounds for all the nations of the world to hear. It is a testimony which confidently proclaims Yahweh as one who is, and ever will remain, unwavering in his fidelity (*ḥesed*, v. 51b) to his covenant with David and his descendants.

The Theophany and Its Rhetoric

Our second rhetorical inquiry, concerning the poet's rich portrayal of the theophany of Yahweh in vv. 8–16, returns us to Strophes III, IV, and V. In what manner do the majestic style and graphic vocabulary of its eight bicola and two tricola impart something of the reality and splendor of God's intervening presence that made possible the king's deliverance?[18]

At the outset it should be noted that with the exception of v. 16cd, the poet has cast his lines in third-person language and made deliberate use of a quite diverse terminology. A minimal repetition of nouns and verbs alike suggests to us that an indirect, if not intentionally allusive, element is operative within the theophanic description. Apart from the twofold use of the root *gᶜš* in v. 8, each of the other twenty-one verbs in these strophes appears only once. Of the [[16]] thirty-one different nouns employed, approximately one in six is repeated and then but once.[19] Neither are certain particles, prepositions, or other word elements duplicated as emphatic descriptive components. If the significance of those few words which are repeated should not be overlooked, it is clear that nothing momentous is here achieved by this commonly employed rhetorical device.

17. C. F. Kraft, *The Strophic Structure of Hebrew Poetry as Illustrated in the First Book of the Psalter* (Chicago: University of Chicago Libraries, 1938) 63.

18. For another analysis of the theophany in Psalm 18 which addresses several issues that do not particularly concern us in the present study (e.g., the capacity of Psalm 18 to reflect the ongoing tradition about the theophany of Yahweh on Mount Sinai), see J. K. Kuntz, *The Self-Revelation of God* (Philadelphia: Westminster, 1967) 173–89.

19. Thus we discover *ûmôsᵉdê* in v. 8 and *môsᵉdôt* in v. 16; *bᵉʾappô* in v. 9 and *ʾappekā* in v. 16; *ʾēš* in both vv. 9 and 13; *geḥālîm* in v. 9 and *wᵉgaḥᵃlê* in v. 13; and *šāmayim* in v. 10 and *baššāmayim* in v. 14. In what may be alternative readings in v. 13 we meet both *ʿābê šᵉḥāqîm* and *ʿābāyw* which allude to the same phenomena. While *rûaḥ* appears in both vv. 11 and 16, in the former instance it can only mean 'wind', and in the latter 'breath'. In sum, the repetition of nouns is minimal.

Nevertheless, the descriptive components in these strophes seem to be well ordered and the careful reader can detect specific indications of movement. To be sure, there is throughout a proclivity for imprecision. A sharply focused image is not projected. One metaphor is piled upon another in such manner that a note of splendor, rather than coherence, is secured. Of necessity, Yahweh's earthly visitation is narrated by means of indirect modes of speaking. Yet what is wanting in straightforward statement is compensated in the august impact of Yahweh's theophanic intervention which is achieved through forceful poetic formulation. That impact mainly derives from the aggregation of carefully aligned descriptive elements whose arrangement invites our inspection.

Theophanic engagement is first denoted through the tricolon of v. 8 with its mention of the reverberations of the earth. Thus Yahweh's imminent visitation is announced. The short Hebrew rhyme produced by the introductory *wattig͑aš wattir͑aš*, as retained in our translation, 'did shake and quake',[20] presents itself as the premeditated expression for recording the movement of the earth that is evoked at the outset of Yahweh's appearance. This image is then buttressed by the two remaining cola of v. 8. There a new verb root, *rgz*, is introduced and the first-mentioned verb, *g͑š*, reappears. The culminating effect of the terrestrial agitation in the tricolon cannot escape the notice of even a casual reader. Moreover, in v. 8c the cause of the upheaval is directly attributed to Yahweh's wrath (*kî ḥārâ lô*) which had been awakened by the turn of events (whatever they might have been) against his royal servant.[21] In the tricolon that immediately follows (v. 9), the description begins, and at some length will continue, to focus on the unfolding self-manifestation of Yahweh himself. No concrete image of the deity is offered, but outright mention is made of the smoke, fire, and coals that are emitted by him. These nouns further signal his advent. In v. 9 the awful manifestation of divine wrath is represented by admittedly bold figures of speech. Yet in this depiction of Yahweh's angry approach, the poet does not presume to expose the divine form itself. [[17]] While he enumerates several parts of Yahweh's body—his nos-

---

20. Cross and Freedman, *op. cit.*, 23, use the term 'rhyme mechanism' to identify this phrase; they also rightly detect its presence in vv. 26–27.

21. Admittedly, some scholars have dismissed v. 8c as a gloss. Cross and Freedman, *op. cit.*, 23, regard the duplication of the verb *g͑š* as suspect, and Kraus, *op. cit.*, 138, calls this colon intrusive and points to its 'erklärenden und belehrenden Charackter.' Certainty on the matter is not possible. We have retained v. 8c, however, since the presence of tricola is not unusual in this psalm and the element of divine anger is elsewhere mentioned in this portrayal of Yahweh's theophany.

trils (v. 9a), mouth (v. 9b), and feet (v. 10b)—he stops short of fabricating a concrete image of the deity.

Then in a pair of bicola (vv. 10–11) which concludes this first of three strophes devoted to the theophany, Yahweh's arrival from the high heavens is depicted in a way that calls attention to a whole series of imperfect verbs—Yahweh 'bowed' (*wayyēṭ*), 'descended' (*wayyērad*), 'rode' (*wayyirkab*), 'flew' (*wayyāᶜōp*), and 'swooped down' (*wayyēdeʾ*). The poet assuredly favors *spatial* imagery in his attempt to portray Yahweh's descent. Cross and Freedman aptly remark on the use of the root *nṭh* (*nṭy*) in v. 10a that the proper meaning is 'to spread out, to spread apart, to spread open'.[22] Thus the poet imagines the heavens to be curtains which Yahweh pushes aside as he begins his journey toward the earth. Moreover, as the *terminus technicus* of Yahweh's theophanic descent, the verb *wayyērad* rigorously affirms the actuality of divine approach. Even so, his concealment is at once assured, for the poet declares that 'darkness was under his feet' (v. 10b). The one who is enthroned high in the heavens condescends to the urgent invocation of the king, but he is enveloped by a protective cloud covering which is perceived as sheer darkness. As the *Deus revelatus*, Yahweh remains the *Deus absconditus*. The figures used by the poet for describing Yahweh's advent are more suggestive than explicit, and this imprecision, though it may well be a hallmark of masterful poetry, cannot help but prove frustrating for any contemporary interpretation of this composition. For example, v. 11 establishes a synonymous parallelism between 'cherub' and 'the wings of the wind' upon which Yahweh is said to have 'swooped down.' The portrayal, which may involve the personification of the storm-cloud, is rather mystifying. At least it is curious that the cloud itself is nowhere specified in Psalm 18 as the divine vehicle, for elsewhere in biblical theophanies it is so understood.[23] Again we note that the psalmist is more determined to highlight the grandeur and dynamic of intervening theophanic presence than he is to furnish a sharply coherent sequence of thought.

The next brief strophe (vv. 12–13) speaks even more intently about divine hiddenness by placing several nouns in prominent position. The poet alludes to the darkness (*ḥōšek*) that Yahweh sets about himself, the pavilion of rain cloud (*sukātô*) that protects him, and the cloud bank (*ḥašrat mayim* and *ᶜabê šᵉḥāqîm*) that stages itself before him. The 'coals of fire' referred to at the close of v. 13 [[18]] surely must refer to the lightning that is emitted through the rain cloud. Here is a unique

---

22. Cross and Freedman, *op. cit.*, 24; similarly, Dahood, *op. cit.*, 107.
23. So Exod 16:10; 40:34–38; Num 17:7; and implicitly in Exod 19:9; 24:16.

expression standing for the flash of lightning which in its brightness resembles burning coals.

With its introductory mention of the deity thundering in the heavens, a new strophe (vv. 14–16) brings the theophanic description to a finish by referring to the telling impact of Yahweh's self-manifestation on the king's adversaries and, no less, on creation itself. Theophanic intervention is presented in this strophe as being remarkably efficacious. The author's capacity to highlight the august divine voice in the opening bicolon of the strophe (v. 14), and to render it with a vivid Canaanite flavor,[24] is noteworthy. Also his mastery at poetic design is evident in the descriptive bicolon that follows. The same word sequence appears in both verse members—the verb with its unexpressed pronoun subject, the object of the verb, and the effect of the action ('And he sent forth arrows, and scattered them; / he flashed lightnings, and discomfited them'). Amid the tumult attending his self-revelation, Yahweh causes the thunderbolt to hurl forth. Moreover, in the light of what is affirmed in vv. 4 and 18, we accept the twofold mention of 'them' in v. 15 as a reference to the king's opponents, and not merely an allusion to lightning.[25] Having established that the enemies of the monarch have, amid earthly battle, been confounded by divine intervention, the strophe concludes with mention of the effects of the theophany on the created order as the awful expression of divine wrath. As Strophe V begins to retard in v. 16ab, an effective *inclusio* is indulged. The thought returns to that which was of main concern in v. 8, namely the drastic effect of Yahweh's advent on all terrestrial creation. As the earth is said to have responded with its agitations at the outset of Yahweh's coming (v. 8), its very bases are now splendidly revealed and the ireful aspect of Yahweh's theophanic intervention is deftly set forth.

In their totality, vv. 8–16 constitute a grandiose description that imparts in a most convincing manner the stupendous might of Israel's covenant God. Indeed, the poet may have made use of ancient material that was available, but he worked it most creatively into an impressive whole. Throughout, Yahweh's omnipotence, presence, and hiddenness

24. As previously noted by Cross and Freedman, *op. cit.*, 25.

25. It cannot be denied that in this composition, the enemies, from whose power the king is rescued by virtue of Yahweh's immediate intervention, stand in a direct connection with the theophany itself. For a rather recently expressed opposing view on the meaning of the pronominal suffix on *waypîṣēm* in v. 15a, see Othmar Keel, *The Symbolism of the Biblical World* (New York: Seabury, 1978) 215, who states, 'In order to portray the zigzag path of the lightning, the psalmist has Yahweh scatter his arrow-shots.' In the light of this colon's larger context, however, this interpretation is not particularly viable.

are depicted in compelling terms. His coming evokes violent rumblings of nature. While they signal his presence, the bank of clouds and mantle of darkness that envelop the deity effectively conceal him from human gaze. All of the natural elements are gathered here as powerful figures of speech which are [19] regarded by the poet as his most suitable vehicle for representing the awesome and real advent of the deity for the purpose of securing the king's deliverance.

Vibrant with archaic imagery which is not always easily, much less confidently, perceived by the biblical interpreter, vv. 8–16 collectively convey an accomplished portrait of Yahweh's coming which confers an unmistakable note of excellence on the total psalm.

Psalm 18 as an Integrated Whole

The next question to be addressed can be put very simply—may Psalm 18 be understood along rhetorical-critical lines as an integrated whole? As has already been noted, in 1934 Schmidt held that Psalm 18 hosts two distinct compositions, the first terminating with v. 31 and the second commencing with v. 32.[26] Two decades later Cross and Freedman wrote, 'It remains a question as to whether the psalm is an amalgamation of two or more independent odes, or a single poem sharply divided into separate parts.'[27] A close reading of the psalm does suggest that its second half, with its enthusiastic praise of Yahweh for being a sturdy support in battle, applies more specifically to an Israelite monarch than does the first. While there is nothing stated in vv. 2–31 which would be especially ill-suited on the lips of a warrior king who is intent on expressing thanksgiving to Yahweh within the worshipping congregation, that observation is at best a second-rate claim that Psalm 18 is in fact an integrated whole. To be sure, those who regard the psalm's total narrative as a depiction of a past event or a series of past events may contend that the dispersion of the king's enemies is affirmed in the first portion of the psalm (v. 15), but only in the second (vv. 38–46) is the victory over them presented as an established fact. Moreover, those who hold that past, present, and even future royal triumphs are all being grasped by the mind of the poet can maintain that only in its entirety can the psalm register so sweeping a sentiment.

---

26. See note 4.

27. Cross and Freedman, *op. cit.*, 21. More recently Frank Crüsemann, *Studien zur Formgeschichte von Hymnus und Danklied in Israel* (Neukirchen-Vluyn: Neukirchener Verlag, 1969), has questioned the unity of the psalm. Only with some concession does he write, 'Aber auch, wer an der Einheit festhält oder unentschieden bleibt, muss von zwei formal und inhaltlich ganz verschiedenen Hälften sprechen' (p. 254).

As rhetorical critics, we shall argue for the unity of Psalm 18 by making three specific observations. First, the old gnomic quatrain (vv. 26–27), to which reference has already been made, may claim a more strategic position within the total composition than we first imagined. It answers the question, 'Why does the deity come to the aid of the psalmist and to all who humbly seek him for refuge?' Here a lesson is being taught to the attending congregation which directs [[20]] them both backward and forward. It directs them *backward* to vv. 5–25 which collectively affirm that Yahweh does mightily intervene in order to deliver those who are loyal to him. Likewise it directs them *forward* not only to vv. 28–31 which conclude with the statement that Yahweh 'is a shield to all who take refuge in him,' but beyond to vv. 32–46 where God's chosen servant is superbly equipped to win the battle and to taste the fruits of victory. In our estimation, this gnomic quatrain, located at the psalm's midpoint, fulfills a crucial pivotal function in effectively uniting the poem in its several parts.

Second, Psalm 18 achieves some degree of integration by the manner in which divine names and appellatives are employed. Five different names are used for deity—*YHWH* (16x), *ʾelōhîm* (6x), *ʾēl* (4x), and *ʾelyôn* and *ʾelôah* each once. In the first half consisting of thirty verses, the Tetragrammaton appears a dozen times and in four cases it is employed in the vocative (vv. 2, 7, 16, 29). In the second half consisting of twenty verses, it appears four times, and once in the vocative (v. 50). With a rather similar distribution, the name *ʾelōhîm* is attested four times in the first half and twice in the second, and aside from its use in v. 47, it persistently contains a first-person suffix. Likewise, *ʾēl* is seen in both halves—not only in vv. 3 and 31, but also in vv. 33 and 48. Moreover, with the exception of v. 3, it is rendered with the definite article. This distribution of divine names also exerts a unifying force on the entire psalm. Absent only in Strophes III, IV, and XI, which span a total of merely nine verses, these names definitely contribute to the composition's overall richness of expression, and their basic uniformity of application throughout the psalm should not be overlooked.

With regard to the appellatives, one thrice-attested divine title, 'rock' (*ṣûr*), appears in both halves of Psalm 18. With first-person singular suffix, it is intentionally used near the extremities of the poem, in v. 3b within the introductory hymnic praise and in v. 47a within the concluding praise. Also *ṣûr* without suffix is met in v. 32b within the second of two crucial rhetorical questions which are carefully framed by the poet as the suitable introduction to the second half of the psalm. In passing it might be noted that the noun 'shield' (*māgēn*), which is unmistakably a divine appellative in v. 3, is something less

than an appellative in v. 31, and functions in a quite different manner
in v. 36 within the second half of the poem ('You give me your saving
shield, / and your right hand upholds me'). Of the various epithets
which might have been used, in selecting *ṣûr* as [[21]] a *Leitwort* for his
composition, the poet has seemingly chosen the best one available for
this royal thanksgiving and appropriated it in such a manner as to facilitate an artful integration of the entire psalm.

Our third rhetorical observation in defense of the unity of Psalm
18 concerns the poet's employment of still other nouns as well as verbs
within both halves. Though the specific use of some words militates
against our selecting them as evidence tending toward unity,[28] at least
several require a mention. This assuredly includes the poet's use of two
nouns, 'enemies' (*ʾōyēb* in vv. 4, 18, 38, 41, and 49) and 'haters' (*śōnēʾ*
in vv. 18 and 41, and both with first-person suffix).[29] Moreover, we
dare not ignore the significant presence of five verbs. One denotes crying for help (*šwʿ* in vv. 7 and 42), three relate to salvation (*yšʿ* in vv. 4,
28, and 42; *nṣl* in vv. 18 and 49; and *plṭ* in vv. 3, 44, 49), and one refers
to exaltation (*rwm* in vv. 2, as emended, 28, 47, and 49). A recognition
of their use speaks a further persuasive word in behalf of the psalm's
oneness and the capacity of its two halves to function in a mutually reinforcing manner.

In summary, we believe on rhetorical-critical grounds that Psalm
18 can, and should, be comprehended as an integrated whole, that
there is no compelling reason to posit the existence of two distinct poetic compositions. Admittedly, the break between vv. 31 and 32 is considerable and it will remain useful for scholars to refer to the two
halves of the psalm in their exegetical discussions. Even so, the psalm
as primarily the product of one talented Israelite poet summons us to
interact with it as a single composition having an integrity of its own.
In short, this is how we perceive the text intends to be understood.

Rhetorical Mention of the King's God and Enemies

A fourth rhetorical-critical inquiry turns on the poet's portrayal of
both the deity who is the subject of the psalm's praise and thanksgiving

28. For example, the noun *derek* ('way') is attested in both halves, but in the first half
(vv. 22 and 31) refers to Yahweh and in the second to the king (v. 33). As such, it has
nothing to say either for or against the psalm's unity. The noun *yad* ('hand') is used of
the king in both halves (in vv. 21 and 25, as well as in v. 35), but is too common a noun
to be of help here. The same thing might be said of the verb root *ntn* ('to give') which is
found in v. 14 and in vv. 33, 36, 41, and 48, and always has the deity as its subject.

29. Rendered in v. 18 as 'my foes'.

and the enemies who so overwhelmed the king that amid his distress he was compelled to call out, 'Yahweh!' Our concern, however, will limit itself to specific names, appellatives, and terminologies which the poet employs in his attempt to depict the king's God and foes. Though we shall not wish to repeat what has already been asserted about the psalmist's use of divine names in this composition, we should take note of the poet's reference to the deity as $^{c}ely\hat{o}n$ in [[22]] v. 14 ('Yahweh also thundered from the heavens, / and the Most High uttered his voice'). There the king confesses that salvation has dawned, yet he recognizes the mystery and distance of the one who does not divest himself of his otherness when he comes in theophanic intervention. Moreover, given the covenant relation which binds the king with his God, the dominant use of the Tetragrammaton over all other divine names is most fitting.

The poem is manifestly rich in divine titles though few are mentioned more than once.[30] Collectively they are intended to denote in an obviously picturesque manner the king's perception of his God. Accordingly, the deity is claimed by the kind in v. 2 to be 'my strength' ($hizq\hat{i}$), and in v. 3 he is designated as 'my rock' ($sal^{c}\hat{i}$ and $\hat{sur}\hat{i}$ are both to be so translated), 'my fortress' ($m^{e}\hat{sud}\bar{a}t\hat{i}$), 'my deliverer' ($m^{e}pa\underline{l}t\hat{i}$), 'my shield' ($m\bar{a}ginn\hat{i}$), 'the horn of my salvation' ($qeren\ yi\check{s}^{c}\hat{i}$), and 'my stronghold' ($mi\acute{s}gabb\hat{i}$). Moreover, in 2 Sam 22:3c, in the colon which finds no counterpart in Psalm 18, the predicates 'my refuge' ($m^{e}n\hat{u}s\hat{i}$) and 'my savior' ($m\bar{o}\check{s}\hat{i}^{c}\hat{i}$) are met. Then in v. 29 the king speaks of the deity as 'my lamp' ($n\bar{e}r\hat{i}$). Two of these divine appellatives reappear in subsequent cola. In v. 31 Yahweh is presented as 'a shield' ($m\bar{a}g\bar{e}n$) for those seeking refuge, in v. 32 he is called 'a rock' ($\hat{sur}$), and in v. 47 'my rock' ($\hat{sur}\hat{i}$).

In v. 3 the breathlessly articulated cluster of qualifying nouns, including participles, all applying to the deity is singularly impressive. Without exception, these predicates within the hymnic introit celebrate Yahweh as the deliverer and helper *par excellence* of the oppressed. So sweeping is the protection that God extends to his royal servant within the mountainous Judean countryside that the king cannot help but experience strong feelings of safety and trust. If the central idea of v. 3 is best captured in the epithet 'my deliverer' ($m^{e}pa\underline{l}t\hat{i}$),[31] it is admittedly less vivid than the predicate 'the horn of my salvation' ($qeren\ yi\check{s}^{c}\hat{i}$) which boldly celebrates Yahweh as one whose strength is irresistible, not unlike that of wild oxen with their horns. In v. 3 the poet has artfully employed traditional and stereotypical lan-

---

30. For a helpful listing with succinct analysis, see D. N. Freedman, "Divine Names and Titles in Early Hebrew Poetry," in Freedman, *Pottery, Poetry, and Prophecy: Studies in Early Hebrew Poetry* (Winona Lake, Ind.: Eisenbrauns, 1980) 97–99.

31. So Kraus, *op. cit.*, 142.

guage so as to emphasize that Yahweh, and he alone, provides needful asylum in times of grave danger. Undoubtedly, the one divine appellative which is the most suggestive metaphorically is that of the rock whose deliberate recurrence in the psalm is striking. Gottwald observes that among nature's inanimate objects, only the rock is attested in the Hebrew Bible as a divine epithet with any [[23]] frequency: 'What is implied in calling Yahweh "rock," "crag," or "stone" is reference to his role as the sure support and protector of his people—as a rock provides the foundation and material for solid building, shade from the scorching summer sun, and a hiding place for the guerrilla fighter.'[32] That epithet above all others lavishly extols the deity in his determination to support the king.

One other divine title merits our notice—'my lamp' (*nērî*, v. 29). This image is unmistakably useful to the poet in his desire to highlight the ongoing personal relation that ensues between monarch and deity. Appearing roughly midway in Strophe VIII with its resolute declaration of Yahweh's faithful dealings, this epithet finds itself parallel with two divine names, 'Yahweh' in v. 29a and 'my God' (*ʾelōhay*) in v. 29b. The king's confession of his own dependency on the deity as lamp is well intimated by the suffixed noun, 'my darkness' (*ḥōškî*), which stands as the final word of the bicolon. He knows Yahweh to be the source of light that effectively penetrates into the recesses of his endangered existence and renews in him a sense of well-being. Finally, several well placed participles, not mentioned in the two preceding paragraphs, serve the poet in his desire to identify the God who is here celebrated. These include *hamʾazzerēnî* in v. 33a, *magdil* in v. 51a, and *ʿōśeh ḥesed* in v. 51b, which respectively designate Yahweh as the one 'who girds me [with strength],' 'who increases [the triumphs of his king],' and 'who shows favor [to his anointed].' All three active participles testify to the deity's personal concern for his royal servant that makes deliverance from danger and military triumph possible. Finally, the poet's inclusion of the passive participle *mehullāl* in his introductory hymnic strophe (v. 4a) aptly presents the deity as the one 'who is worthy to be praised'; and obviously a plethora of poetic lines to follow spells out the reasons why. In summary, a wide range of terminology, much of which consists of vivid poetic figures, is used by the author in his portrayal of the covenant deity whom he is intent upon celebrating.

The king's enemies are likewise depicted in this composition through varied terminology—five in all, though one finds no verse about them swarming with predicates which is the equal of v. 3 in its

---

32. N. K. Gottwald, *The Tribes of Yahweh* (Maryknoll, N.Y.: Orbis Books, 1979) 684.

portrait of God. In five instances the noun 'enemy' (*ʾōyēb*) is used to designate the king's opposition and in every instance a first-person singular
pronominal suffix is attached (vv. 4b, 18a, 38a, 41a, and 49a). No other
term denoting the hostility is employed so frequently. [[24]] Twice the
poet refers to those who hate the king (vv. 18b and 41b) and again
the same suffix is met. In our translation, however, we have rendered
the root *śnʾ* as 'my foes' in v. 18b and as 'those who hate me' in v. 41b.
The opposition is designated in vv. 40b and 49b as 'my adversaries'
(*qāmay*, the Qal active participle with pronominal suffix from the root
qwm, 'to rise up'). In adjacent cola (vv. 45b and 46a) the noun construct
bᵉnê nēkār ('foreigners') is encountered. As those who 'cringe,' 'cower,'
and 'stagger forth,' they present no threat on the battlefield. Even so,
these submissive persons are surely no friends of the king and should at
least be associated with those hostile forces which would, whenever possible, stand counter to him. In v. 49c the poet rather curiously refers to
'the violent man' (*ʾîš ḥāmās*) from whom he is divinely delivered. Its
function in the tricolon where it exists parallel with 'my enemies'
(v. 49a) and 'my adversaries' (v. 49b) induces our interpreting it as a collective noun. Finally, in many cola the king's enemies are mentioned in
a less explicit way through object pronouns which are attached to the
verb (vv. 15ab, 38ab, 39a, 42b, and 43ab).[33] Somewhat less frequently
the enemies are the implied subjects of imperfect verbs which sketch
the behavior of the king's opposition (vv. 19a, 39ab, 42a, 45a and 46b).

By limiting ourselves to the poet's use of specific terminologies for
the king's enemies, it may be observed that one third of the mention
occurs in two strongly hymnic strophes (I and XII) which envelop the
psalm (vv. 4b, 49abc), one third occurs in Strophe X with its focus on
the invincibility of the king in battle (vv. 38a, 40b, 41ab), with the remaining third falling equally in Strophe VI portraying the king's deliverance in the context of Yahweh's theophanic intervention (vv. 18ab)
and in Strophe XI where the king's universal rule is affirmed (vv. 45b,
46a). It is tempting to attribute this rather persistent reference to the
enemy in the hymnic strophes and in Strophe X, with its sketch of the
battle scene, to the poet's conscious rhetorical design.

In Strophe X where the portrayal of the enemy is more lavishly
wrought than anywhere else in the poem, Yahweh is credited with or-
chestrating the decisive defeat. The deity's direct involvement is denoted by the active verbs employed in vv. 40ab and 41a. Moreover, with
consummate literary skills the poet reports in v. 42 Yahweh's unwilling-

---

33. Ordinarily this involves the imperfect form of the verb, though we meet in v. 38b
an infinitive construct with suffix (*kallôtām*) and in v. 42b a suffixed verb form (*ʿānām*).

ness to respond to the enemy's plea for help. There the use of contrast as a compelling rhetorical device is twice evident. First, in v. 7b the king's cry for help was effective; Yahweh heard and moved [[25]] into action. In v. 42a the same verb root ($\check{s}w^c$) is used of the enemies but their appeal falls on divine ears that are now deaf. Moreover, in v. 36c it is Yahweh's answering that ensures the king's success in battle. By contrast, in v. 42b it is his *failure* to answer (the root ^cnh is needed in both instances) that pulls the enemy down to defeat. Also, another rhetorical device is manifested in v. 42, namely, the use of synonymous sequential parallelism, revealing the poet's desire to confer a welcome freshness on his discourse by deliberately breaking up stereotypical expressions. This verse has as its *continuous* segment, 'they cry for help unto Yahweh,' whereas its parallel segment incorporates the two phrases, 'but there is none to save' and 'but he answers them not.' Accordingly, the initial word in the first colon, $y^e\check{s}aww^{e^c}\hat{u}$ ('they cry for help') is furthered and completed by the initial element in the second, $^{\supset}el$ *YHWH* ('unto Yahweh').[34] Finally, we should not fail to acknowledge the poet's talent in v. 49 where three different terms—'my enemies,' 'my adversaries,' and 'the violent man'—appear in a synonymous relation, as do two verbs of deliverance ($m^epall^e\c{t}i$ and $ta\d{s}\d{s}\hat{\imath}l\bar{e}n\hat{\imath}$ which respectively open and close the verse). Such a poetic intensification late in the psalm ably succeeds both in enlivening all previous mentionings of the king's enemies and in reaffirming that it is Yahweh, and he alone, who makes the king's hoped-for deliverance and victory a reality.[35] In sum, a rich vocabulary, careful balancing and structuring, and a keen imagination have all served the poet well in his quest to portray royal deliverance and triumph which necessarily involve the king's interaction with both his God and his enemies.

Spatial Imagery in Psalm 18

The remaining question which requires an answer in our rhetorical analysis concerns the manifestly spatial imagery which the poet

34. As pointed out by P. D. Miller, Jr., "Synonymous-Sequential Parallelism in the Psalms," *Biblica* 61 (1980), 256, who uses Ps 18:42 as one of several illustrations of this phenomenon.

35. Robert Alter, *The Art of Biblical Narrative* (New York: Basic Books, 1981), 97, reminds us that in biblical poetry synonymous parallelism by its very nature is more approximate than exact. Not only is 'every restatement . . . a new statement,' but 'the conscious or intuitive art of poetic parallelism was to advance the poetic argument in seeming to repeat it—intensifying, specifying, complementing, qualifying, contrasting, expanding the semantic material of each initial hemistich in its apparent repetition.' Especially with respect to v. 49 this observation is germane.

employs as he narrates the story of the king's successful deliverance
from an oppressive—even life-threatening—situation[36] and his ensuing triumph over his enemies. In our discussion of the function of
vv. 10–11 within the theophany, we already had occasion to observe
that spatial imagery plays a crucial role in the poet's description of
Yahweh's earthward descent. Moreover, in a prior colon (v. 7c) the
psalmist states that 'from his temple' (*mēhêkālô*), and in the light of
Canaanite associations, undoubtedly his *heavenly* dwelling or palace,
Yahweh hears the king's supplicating voice. In a [[26]] subsequent colon (v. 14a) Yahweh thunders 'from the heavens' (*baššāmayim*) as the
omnipotent Most High God (*ᶜelyôn*). That thundering exerts an immediate impact on the earth below. So extensive are the terrestrial con-
vulsions in response to Yahweh's theophanic intervention (v. 8ab) that
'the channels of the sea' (*ᵓᵃpîqê yām*) and 'the earth's foundations'
(*môsᵉdôt tēbēl*) are exposed. Clearly, spatial imagery presents itself as an
essential ingredient within the total theophanic description.

The poet's fascination with the spatial, however, is not confined to
this portion of the psalm. It is already evident at the outset of Strophe
II where the king's anguished condition is set forth in highly expressive figures of speech. As one who is being victimized by 'the waves of
death' (*misbᵉrê māwet*) and 'the floods of Belial' (*naḥᵃlê bᵉliyyaᶜal*, v. 5),
the king finds his own world under heavy siege. Here the historical
foes of the king (v. 4b) are closely linked with the forces of chaos which
would defy creation itself. Though more than one interpretation is
possible, we find helpful Dahood's observation that Belial is the 'Swal-
lower' whose name derives from the root *blᶜ* ('to swallow') and that 'the
engorging capacity of the nether world' prominent in Canaanite my-
thology is here reflected.[37] The king's struggle with powerful national
opponents is portrayed as a struggle with Death itself, 'the adversary
par excellence,'[38] and by virtue of the poetic imagery here employed, a
spatial aspect is strongly hinted. As the king pursues his tenuous
course, his world is threatened by the breakers of the cosmic sea. The
presumptuous powers of chaos, which have been held in check by the
Creator, now proceed to defy all constraints and overtake the king. In
a spatial sense, the king is portrayed as one who is plunged into the
deep, engulfed and even swallowed by waves and billows as he is thrust
downward to Sheol, the very kingdom of death. Then references in v. 6
to 'the cords of Sheol' (*ḥeblê šᵉᵓôl*) and 'the snares of death' (*môqᵉšê*

36. Well symbolized by the presence of the noun *ṣār* in the opening element of v. 7,
'in my *distress* I called upon Yahweh.'

37. Dahood, *op. cit.*, 105.

38. *Ibid.*

māwet) to a lesser degree emphasize the spatial, for the mysterious nether world is pictured here as a huntsman who moves about the landscape setting traps and snares for his prey. In sum, the poetic narrative about the rude encroachment of death into the king's world is expressed in unmistakably spatial terms.

Similarly, the poet relies on spatial imagery in his depiction of the king's deliverance and military triumph. In some measure this is true of the psalm's references to the king's scaling a wall (v. 30), running with lengthening strides (v. 37), and causing his enemies to fall [[27]] beneath his feet (v. 39). The spatial rhetoric, however, is more fully realized at three other junctions in the poem, namely, vv. 17ab, 20a, and 34b. The first and second, contained in Strophe VI, relate to the king's deliverance; the third, found in Strophe IX, is associated with his military triumph. All three references focus on what Yahweh does for his royal servant.

In v. 17 the portrayal of the king's rescue from death involves a reversal of the action depicted in v. 5—'He sent from on high, he took me; / he drew me out of many waters.' Again we meet a merger of cosmic and historical realities. The rapid pace of three imperfect verbs contributes to the overall rhetorical effect. The deity who has descended in theophanic intervention now rescues the king from the insurgent waters of the nether world (*mayim rabbîm*), indeed, from the realm of chaos itself. The verb *mšh* ('to draw out') is met elsewhere in the Hebrew Bible only twice—in the parallel text of 2 Sam 22:17 and in Exod 2:10, where the infant Moses is saved on the water and given a name meaning 'drawn from the water.' Thus, it is tempting to infer that, as the poet constructed the bicolon in Ps 18:17, he may well have had in mind this earlier deliverance of one who would become one of Yahweh's notable servants. In any event, the portrait of Yahweh's reaching down and lifting his chosen one out of the waters of chaos is presented in unmistakably graphic terms. Here is a bold affirmation in behalf of the God whose sovereignty embraces creation and history alike. And in this poetic statement of his condescension in order to address dire human need, an act which involves the deity's intrusion into the arena where the awesome battle between creation and chaos must be waged, the spatial element is prominent.

The description of this saving deed is continued in v. 20a with its own spatial figure, 'He brought me forth into a roomy place (*lammerḥāb*).' Apart from its use here and in the parallel Samuel text, the noun *merḥāb* appears but four times in the OT. In Hos 4:16 it denotes the 'broad pasture' which the lamb inhabits, and in Hab 1:6 'the breadth of the earth' over which the Chaldean army will confidently tread.

More significant for our own interpretation is the metaphorical presence of this noun in Ps 31:9 and 118:5. In the former text, an individual lament, the suppliant anticipates that Yahweh will graciously set his
feet 'in a broad place' (*bammerḥāb*) rather than deliver him into the
hand of the enemy (*ʾôyēb*). In the latter text, a thanksgiving for deliverance in battle, the psalmist states ⟦28⟧ within his narrative that when
he called to Yahweh out of his distress (*mēṣār*), the deity 'answered me
in a broad place' (*bammerḥāb*)—the RSV offers the admittedly smoother
translation, 'the Lord answered me and set me free.' Here a striking
contrast is secured through the studied use of two picturesque Hebrew
nouns. *Mēṣār* denotes a narrow place which hems in the one who is
afflicted, whereas *merḥāb* points to a broad expanse occupied by one
who has been rescued from adversity and allowed to roam freely. This
same contrast, surely to be understood as a deliberately employed rhetorical device, is present in Psalm 18, for the image of the king's being
delivered to a liberating 'broad place' (*merḥāb*) is set over against his
former narrow condition of distress (*ṣar*, v. 7).[39]

Finally, v. 34b, with its first-person statement, 'and upon the
heights (*bāmôt*) he sets me secure (*yaʿamîdēnî*),' perceives Yahweh's support of the king spatially; and its Hiphil verb, 'to cause to stand/set secure,' is no less vivid than that offered in v. 20 ('to cause to go out/
bring forth'). This colon nicely balances that contained in v. 34a where
in an expressive simile the king's feet are compared with those of swift-
moving hinds. The entire bicolon reflects the realities of ancient warfare where victory comes only to the warrior who conducts himself in a
rapid, yet sure-footed, manner as he takes possession of coveted mountain strongholds. That critical military prowess, which is understood by
the poet as divinely given, involves the king's confident spatial movement across the Judean landscape. To summarize, among the poet's
many rhetorical talents reflected in this magnificent composition is his
masterful use of spatial imagery as a most helpful means for emphasizing both the king's hazardous situation and Yahweh's effective intervention in his servant's behalf which enables royal deliverance and
military triumph to occur.

The poet of Psalm 18 appears to have been quite well qualified in
his literary craft. In this achieved work of poetry, which admittedly has
its full share of textual perplexities, he has excelled in presenting human need and divine deliverance in equally graphic terms. Through

---

39. Dahood's suggestion, *op. cit.*, 111, that *merḥāb* functions in v. 20 as a poetic name
for the nether world because the realm of the dead is often perceived by the ancient as
being vast, belongs more to the category of possibility than probability.

his richly developed introductory and concluding hymnic lines of praise, detailed portrayal of Yahweh's theophanic intervention, expressive depiction of the king in battle, and soaring verse which persistently places the spotlight on what the deity has wrought in the king's behalf, our poet has demonstrated a high level of rhetorical skill.

Structuralist Analysis

Introduction

Structuralism furthered literary criticism's academic credibility by linking it with secular literary analysis and philosophy, where structuralism was already popular. For instance, biblical scholars used the theories of Paul Ricoeur and Roland Barthes to analyze Scripture. Thus, Old Testament literary criticism was infused with new ideas from sources outside biblical studies.

Because it mixes linguistics, philosophy, and psychology, structuralism is a hard methodology to master. Despite its difficulties, however, several biblical scholars used the approach, especially between 1974 and 1981. The articles in this section reflect both the difficulty and usefulness of structuralism. Once its principles have been grasped, the method can illuminate texts in a number of ways.

Richard Jacobson's 1974 essay introduces structuralism to those unfamiliar with its intricacies. Major ideas and proponents are outlined. Without this basic information no one can implement structuralist techniques. Jean Calloud's 1979 article explains the terms and procedures Jacobson mentions, but in more detail. Even with this more in-depth discussion, structuralism is not easily grasped, yet Calloud clarifies the method very efficiently.

Once Jacobson's and Calloud's comments have been absorbed, readers can better understand Daniel Patte and Judson F. Parker's 1980 analysis of Genesis 2–3. Most major tenets of structuralism appear in this study. The text's superstructure, linguistic units, and deep structures are analyzed. Graphs of the passage's important linkages are included, which reveals a number of details not readily uncovered by other types of analysis. Thus, structuralism informs interpreters who accept its philosophy, learn its terminology, and embrace its complexity.

The Structuralists and the Bible

RICHARD JACOBSON

⟦146⟧ The French critic Tzvetan Todorov has noted that a "science does not speak of its object, but speaks itself with the help of its object." I expect this is no less true of God-centered than of man-centered studies. One wishes to know about nature, but studies physics or chemistry; one wishes to study the nature of divinity, and learns theology or comparative religion. In large measure, structuralism, which is not quite a science but an array of methods, is very much in the process of "speaking itself"; and it is in its own elaboration that most of its energies are invested. The extent and the way in which this is so will, I hope, become clear in the exposition which follows.

A definition is in order. "Structuralism" is the application of principles derived from certain movements within linguistics to other areas of discourse. These other areas may be transphrastic, that is units of speech greater than the sentence, such as narrative; or they may be the social discourse of ritual, kinship rules, law.[1] Structuralism is seen by its ⟦147⟧ literary practitioners as part of the more global enterprise of semiology or semiotics, conceived by the classic exponent of structural linguistics, Ferdinand de Saussure, as the general science of signifying systems, of which linguistics would be a part.[2]

Reprinted with permission from *Interpretation* 28 (1974) 146–64.

1. See Jean Piaget, *Structuralism* (New York, Harper & Row, Publishers, 1971), for an account of "structuralism" in such diverse disciplines as mathematics, physics, biology, as well as linguistics and psychology.

2. *Course in General Linguistics* (Fr. ed., 1915; ET New York, McGraw-Hill, 1966) 16. The series *Approaches to Semiology*, published by Mouton, has some thirty-odd volumes dealing with narrative, costume, psychiatry, information theory.

By way of introduction to structuralist practice on the Bible, it would be well to briefly summarize the major elements of structuralist analysis. The first key principle is the arbitrary nature of the sign. There is no necessary relation of similarity between its two parts-in-relation, the signifier and the signified. The bond between the two elements is none other than the social convention according to which, for speakers of English, the sounds /tri/ conjure up the mental image of a tree. The sign is the relation arising from the two parts, one of which, the signifier, is a sound-image, the other of which, the signified, is a mental image or concept.

Many of the remaining principles are conveniently arranged in dichotomies. These are language/speaking (*langue/parole*), diachrony/synchrony, metaphor/metonymy.

Language is everything which is social about speech. "If we could embrace the sum of word-images stored in the minds of all individuals, we could identify the social bond that constitutes language (*la langue*)."[3] *Parole*, speaking, is all that is individual in the particular utterance. By analogy with chess, *langue* is the set of rules, *parole* each move. Recent developments in cognate fields allow for some approximate equivalents. Thus code/message in computer work, and competence/performance in transformational linguistics describe more or less the same dichotomy.

Diachrony/synchrony is the distinction between a study oriented toward change or development over time, and the language state at any one time. Traditional philology and etymology are of course diachronic studies. The study of the sign at any given time, or of the relations among signs in a given language-state, is synchronic.

Any utterance is constructed along the principles of selection and combination (metaphor/metonymy). For each position in the phrase, there exists a class of potential substitutes united by a principle of [[148]] *similarity*, while the words so chosen are united in a linear unit governed by *contiguity*. The class of potential words is a *paradigm*, "present" in a sense, *in absentia*. The utterance as realized along the linear chain is a *syntagm*. The paradigm is united by *metaphor*, the syntagm by *metonymy*.[4]

Linguists since Saussure have added two important concepts to his; these are metalanguage and the principle of the double articulation of language.

Broadly speaking, metalanguage is any statement of a second-order language whose signified or signifier is a sign of the first order system.

3. Saussure, *op. cit.*, 13.

4. One indication of the widespread applicability of these terms may be seen in Frazer's twofold classification of magic as "contagious" and "sympathetic." Cf. Freud in the Third Essay of *Totem and Taboo*.

Thus if I say "'moron' means imbecile," my statement is meta-linguistic in that a sign (moron) becomes the concept (signified) of the second-order system. If I see the formula $e=Mc^2$ on the cover of a physics text-book, the formula, itself a sign, is also the signifier of a second-order meaning, "physics" or "science." A second-order statement may be a proposition or other complex sign—for example an advertisement bearing a photograph of a well-dressed person driving one or another car may carry a second-order meaning such as "Driving a Cadillac is the prosperous thing to do."

The "double articulation" of language has been most clearly stated by the linguist André Martinet.[5] Human speech is composed of two distinct levels of articulation, first into *significant units* ("monemes," or words) and these significant units into purely *differential* units (pho-nemes, or sounds). Phonemes have no meaning in themselves: their purpose is only to be different from one another, while meaning arises from their combination into words. But there is a related question concerning articulation which must be dealt with in any structural analysis: How is the syntagm to be divided up for the purposes of analysis, and how, indeed, is the syntagm to be separated from the larger and ultimately infinite text of all speech? There are, in effect, two parallel undifferentiated entities, one of concepts of ideas (the signified), the other of sounds (signifiers). By relating one group of sounds to an idea, a certain area is delimited, which gains its value pre-cisely from its ⟦149⟧ contrast to every other such "articulation." Barthes explains this concept by an example: There exists in nature the spectrum of light, which is a continuum—there is nothing in na-ture to define the point where yellow merges into green. Language, through the connection of signifiers with concepts, accomplishes this articulation into discontinuous units.[6]

It was by way of the Russian formalist studies into the inter-relations between language and poetic process that the possible exten-sion of means of linguistic analysis to other kinds of discourse was first suggested. Filipp Federovic Fortunatov, one of the founders of the Moscow linguistic school, seems to be the first to have articulated the view that language is not "a means for the expression of ready-made ideas" necessarily, but primarily "an implement for thinking."[7] "In a

5. "Structure and Language," in Jacques Ehrmann, ed., *Structuralism* (Garden City, Doubleday & Co., 1970).

6. Roland Barthes, *Elements of Semiology* (Boston, Beacon Press, 1970) 56f., 64f.

7. Cited in Roman Jakobson, *Selected Writings*, Vol. II (The Hague, Mouton, 1971) v, vi, 527–38.

certain respect, the phenomena of language themselves appertain to the phenomena of thought."

With the migration to the West of Russian formalists following the Russian revolution, social scientists began to appreciate the range of formalist and structuralist approaches. In particular the French anthropologist Marcel Mauss, in his *Essai sur le don*,[8] first suggested that the rules governing the structure and exchange of messages within society might be applied to other key items of exchange, such as women and goods. It was presumably from his acquaintance first with the work of Mauss, and then with the Russian linguist Roman Jakobson, that Claude Lévi-Strauss came to apply structuralist methods to the analysis of kinship system and later so fruitfully to myth.

Virtually all the structuralist analysis of the Bible harks back to Lévi-Strauss' classic essay, "The Structural Study of Myth."[9] An account of this essay should give a particularly clear view of the application of the principles of structuralist analysis introduced above.

Lévi-Strauss notes "the astounding similarity between myths collected in widely differing regions," despite the fact that the restrictions of everyday reality are relaxed in myth. This bears comparison with languages, which use much the same restricted body of phonemes yet differ ⟦150⟧ vastly among themselves. Just as meaning arises in language from the combination of arbitrary phonemes, so it seems likely that meaning in myth ought to arise not from the intrinsic meaning of the actions, but from their combinations.

But special procedures are called for, since myth is not merely language: it is something different which begins with language. The first approximation as to this difference may be seen in the special relations between *langue* and *parole* in myth. *Langue* belongs to reversible time; its nature is synchronic, while *parole* is necessarily bound to nonreversible time. Myth belongs to both aspects at once: It unites synchrony and diachrony in that it is told in past time, and yet is felt to have a real effect on the present.

Now myth is composed of *actions*, with a determined similarity to one another: "Myth is the part of language where the formula *traduttore, tradittore* reaches its lowest truth value." The minimal units of articulation in myth, analogous to phonemes in speech, will be simple actions and relations. The minimum significant units, analogous to words, will be "bundles of such relations." The "bundles" amount to paradigms, of which the individual relations are related to one another by a principle of similarity.

---

8. An ET is *The Gift*, trans. by I. Cunnison (Glencoe, Ill., Free Press, 1954).

9. Chap. xi of *Structural Anthropology* (Garden City, Doubleday & Co., 1967).

It was inevitable that Lévi-Strauss' methods of analyzing myth should be applied to the Old Testament. The first such work was carried out by the English anthropologist Edmund Leach, whose essay in two versions, "Lévi-Strauss in the Garden of Eden,"[10] and "Genesis as Myth,"[11] is an attempt to provide a structuralist analysis of the early chapters to Genesis. Leach goes so far as to relate this analysis, quite validly, to communications theory, singling out the elements of *redundancy* and *binary opposition*. Redundancy arises from the fact that "all important stories recur in several versions." Binarism, which is "intrinsic to the process of human thought," is the discrimination of opposing categories which are mutually exclusive. The most important such oppositions in human experience are life/death, male/female, and perhaps for myth, human/divine. The value of redundancy is the correction [[151]] of errors introduced through "noise," that is, those elements of a message which are accidental to meaning. Meaningful relations are distinguished from noise by their presence in a pattern observable through all the variants of the narrative.

The major problem for myths of origin is a "childish intellectual puzzle": there are those women of our kind with whom one must not have sexual relations (due to the incest taboo) and those of the other kind who are allowed. "If our first parents were persons of two kinds, what was that other kind? But if they were both of our kind, then their relations must have been incestuous and we are all born in sin." This to Leach is the central contradiction to be resolved in the Garden of Eden story, and of similar myths in other cultures.

Leach provides an elaborate diagram intended to summarize the binary distinctions and mediations of the Creation myth, which following the principle of redundancy, appears in three permutations (the two Creation stories and the Cain-Abel sequence). Genesis 1 divides into two three-day periods, the first characterized by the creation of the static or "dead" world, the second the creation of the moving, sexual, "live" world. Just as the static triad of grass, cereals, and fruit-trees is created on the third day, the triad of domestic and wild animals and creeping things appear on the sixth, "but only the grass is allocated to the animals. Everything else, including the meat of the animals, is for Man's use." Finally, man and woman are created simultaneously and commanded to be fruitful and multiply, "but the problems of Life versus Death, and Incest versus Procreation are not faced at all."

10. "Lévi-Strauss in the Garden of Eden," in *Transactions of the NY Academy of Science*, Ser. II, 23, No. 4 (Feb. 1961) 386–96. Also in E. N. Hayes and T. Hayes, *Lévi-Strauss: The Anthropologist as Hero* (Cambridge, M.I.T., 1970).

11. *Genesis as Myth and Other Essays* (London, Jonathan Cape, 1969).

The Garden of Eden story then takes up the very problems left at the end of the first account. The creation of Eve is analogous to that of the creeping things in that both are anomalous, the creeping things to the other animals and Eve to the man/animal opposition. The serpent, a creeping thing, is mediator between man and woman. When the first pair eat the forbidden fruit, death and the capacity for procreation enter the world together.

The Cain and Abel story repeats the earlier oppositions: Abel, the herdsman, represents the living world; and Cain, the gardener, represents the static. Cain's fratricide is a reprise of Adam's incest, which Leach believes to be demonstrated by the similarity between God's questioning and cursing of Cain and the questioning and cursing of Adam, Eve, and [[152]] the Serpent (It has "the same form and sequence"). Since the latter part of 3:16 is repeated exactly (so Leach) in 4:7, "Cain's sin was not only fratricide but also incestuous homosexuality." Just as Adam must eliminate a sister in order to acquire a wife, so Cain must eliminate a brother.

Leach's work demands scrutiny both in terms of what it says and what it fails to say. I do not wish to call into question his application of structuralist principles, with the priority of synchronic analysis, but to point up some problems.

The whole question on text is a complicated one. Granted that for Leach's purpose a single text is taken as authoritative (in this instance the "English Authorized Version," i.e. the King James Bible of 1611), Leach still fails to do it justice. His claim that meat is given to man in 1:29, for example, is a misreading. The AV says, "Behold, I have given you every herb bearing seed, which is upon the face of all the earth, and every tree, in the which *is* the fruit of a tree yielding seed; to you it shall be for meat." The phrase "for meat" translates *l^coklah*, which can only mean "for food" in contemporary English. But even the AV, in its own idiom, clearly means that both men and animals are to be restricted to a *vegetarian* diet. This is no small error, since questions of diet are central in a number of Genesis myths (if not in the myths of many nations) and naturally call for comparison with the meat diet first expressly permitted in the Noah sequence.

Leach introduces further problematic interpretations of the plain (or corrupt) meaning of the words in the text. God's questioning of Adam and Cain are very dubiously compared. The second of these is very difficult to decipher. Oesterley and Robinson point out that "Readers of *Genesis* in Hebrew will know that this is somewhat in the nature of a paraphrase of an ungrammatical and untranslateable passage."[12]

---

12. W. O. E. Oesterley and T. H. Robinson, *Hebrew Religion, Its Origin and Development*, (London, S.P.C.K., 1937) 116.

Whatever the original meaning of 4:7, an interpretation of homosexual incest between the brothers based upon it seems weak indeed. It is of course possible to reverse the order of the argument and argue for such a meaning based on a structural pattern present throughout Genesis. Such an argument has merit, but Leach does not make it.

This point does however raise the whole question of text and translation [[153]] in structuralist work. These seem to be separate though related issues. An examination of Hebrew myth cannot rest upon any particular translation. Sole reliance on the AV or the Revised Version can lead to valid discussion only of the point of view of King James' translation commission or the scholarship of Oxbridge dons of the last century. The critic, whoever he is and whatever his stance, needs a clean text.

And here a further difficulty arises, for we may well be at a loss to locate the Hebrew myth at all. In the welter of primary documents and conjectured sub-documents, whatever was in fact primary and mythic may well be obscured. By itself the documentary hypothesis need not invalidate a structuralist approach, which *seeks* repetitions, parallelisms, inversions—all possible variants of a myth in order to establish the correlations and oppositions through which the structure may be read. But awareness of the two factors of multiple documents and sacredness of text leads to suspicion of the authenticity of any given text or reading.

This is because the myths before us are both *sacred* and *text*. The various mythological materials collected in the field by anthropologists (notably, of course, by Lévi-Strauss in his four volumes of *Mythologiques*)[13] must be properly distinguished from literary material. In effect, each report from a native informant *is* the myth. But a biblical myth is so much less the thing itself by virtue of its paradoxical fixity and fluidity. Once a myth is written down, it must cease to be the product of the unconscious generative force (question, contradiction, paradox, whatever) and becomes instead the report of that force acting upon given materials at one moment—though it enters the (written) culture as the myth itself. The assumption behind a Lévi-Straussian analysis must be that the audience of the myth is aware, if "unconsciously," of the permutations and transformations of the myth because they have heard some and will yet hear others. The individual narrative element (*parole*) has the living redundancy which at whatever level of articulation is the speaking sense of the story. Once it becomes a fixed and written part of the culture, the myth (now transformed into sacred

13. The four volumes of *Mythologiques* are *Le cru et le cuit* (Paris, Plan, 1964; ET—*The Raw and the Cooked*, New York, Harper & Row, Publishers, 1969); *Du miel aux cendres* (1966; ET—*From Honey to Ashes*, trans. by John and Doreen Weightmann, Harper & Row, Publishers, 1973); *L'origine des manieres de table* (1968), *L'homme nu* (1971).

history) must inevitably sacrifice much of that structure which becomes evident in the [[154]] variations of repeated telling. In effect, the competency of the culture to state the myth (*langue*) and the performance (*parole*) become identified—and the generative power and meaning of the myth must together become moribund.

And fluidity of a sort arises from the sacred character of the text as well. Despite the Deuteronomic injunction (4:2), alterations have occurred for a variety of reasons, such as the scribal errors of haplography, dittography, or a scribal practice of *lectio difficilior*.

But more significant than the alteration of written material in the hands of scribes and revisers is the work of redaction, which may transform the material either through conscious or unconscious means. A myth, by virtue of its presence in a written text, may enter into dialectical relations of a sort with other material whose contiguity to it in scroll or codex is strictly contingent. It may also, of course, have been affected by a dialectical process with other nonpreserved texts from its own culture area. The work of the redactor may advance this process by his attempt to harmonize originally disparate works reflecting aetiological tales, true history, pristine myth. He may wish to propagandize for religious doctrine, he may suppress material which is apparently contradictory on the syntagmatic plane, or he may unite conflicting material by means of new additions or suppression of old, all in the interests of one or another aesthetic end. In any case his work could well, like that of a careless archaeologist, obscure or destroy what it most wishes to preserve. His intrusion of conscious material may serve to destroy the unconscious logic and coherence of which he is most likely unaware.

Considerations similar to these were raised in a fascinating colloquy between Paul Ricoeur and others, and Lévi-Strauss which appeared in the November 1963 issue of the French journal *Ésprit*. Here Ricoeur and Lévi-Strauss show some agreement in doubting the applicability of a structuralist analysis to the Bible. For Ricoeur, following von Rad, the significant content of the Hexateuch is the "declaration of the great deeds of the Lord." "The method of comprehension applicable to this network of events consists in restoring the *intellectual working-out*, the result of this historical faith set out in a confessional framework." Consequently, in the Old Testament "we are faced with an historical interpretation of the historical . . . the tradition corrects itself by additions, and it is these additions which themselves constitute a theological dialectic." [[155]] Lévi-Strauss, citing the early work of Leach, largely agrees, "because of scruples which join with those of M. Ricoeur. First because the Old Testament, which certainly does make use of mythic materials, takes them up with a view to a different end from their original one . . . the myths have then been subjected, as M. Ricoeur well says, to an intellectual operation." Further, symbols, whose meaning is only "by position," can only be understood "by reference to the ethnographic context" which "is almost entirely lacking."

Leach discusses these matters briefly in "The Legitimacy of Solomon." His disagreement with Lévi-Strauss is based on the contradictory nature of Lévi-Strauss' doubts; he has no qualms, for one thing, about applying structuralist principles to South American Indians, "peoples of whom our ethnographic evidence is sketchy to say the least."

But even in the comparative lack of other ethnographic data, the successive reinterpretations of the same material amount to an ethnographic datum *par excellence.* The difference is that the informants are oriented diachronically, across time rather than across space. But beyond all this, the goals of a structuralist/semiological analysis need not be the same as those of an anthropologist at work on traditional society.

For better or worse, structuralist work on the Bible starts with a text conceived as a synchronous whole. In this fact we have a definite parting of the ways with other and more traditional modes of biblical interpretation. The object of study differs: it is now to be biblical text as it entered the culture of the West. While such analysis might conceivably yield information about the prehistory of the text, such information is necessarily secondary to the kind of information provided by the text as a given whole. The object of study then changes from the textual and cultural processes, which gave to the text, to the structure of the text as it enters the cultural life of the West. It may well have been the hope and intention of biblical scholars of the past century to reveal the secrets of the text by exposing the history behind it. While such textual study has been elaborate and refined, the text still preserves a good many secrets. While I am not certain how many further secrets will be exposed by structuralist methods, I think the very conditions of the obscurity of certain texts will be explained.

For the question arises precisely where to locate the structures which a structuralist analysis brings to light. Taking the linguistic definition ⟦156⟧ of structures (one of many similar definitions), "a whole formed of mutually dependent elements, such that each depends on the others and can only be what it is by its relationship with them,"[14] what can we say about the *source* of that structure in our biblical text, particularly in light of the heterogeneous sources of that text?

14. Émile Benveniste, *Problems in General Linguistics,* trans. by M. E. Meek (Coral Gables, University of Miami Press, 1971) 82.

Is the structure present in the first composition, or first writing: Is it a product of the mind of the first author, or of his culture? If so, can we guarantee that the narrative structure of Genesis 1 will be similar to that of Genesis 2 or Genesis 4? Will the structure of Mark be that of Matthew or of Luke? Or is it something present in the mind of the reader—not then a rule of composition, but a rule of reading? Or does it have yet some third kind of existence?

For Lévi-Strauss, the source of this structure seems to have changed. Early in his work on myth he seems to believe in the objective presence of structure governing the elaboration of discourse: it is present in the writing, and open to decipherment in the reading.[15] But later in his work Lévi-Strauss posits an *esprit* which, according to Leach, "appears as part of an extremely involved interchange relationship in which it is the casual (sic: causal?) force producing myths of which its own structure is a precipitate."[16] I do not feel at the same loss which Leach claims to feel in understanding this term, but I do recognize a reasonable doubt as to its existence except at the highest reaches of abstraction, in which case it is clearly an *a posteriori* construct, the "mind" posited behind the total cultural product. The *esprit* of a culture may be identified with the set of implied rules which govern its discourse in all possible modes. It does seem a bit contradictory that so materially based an approach as structuralism should generate so ideal a concept. But taken as the potential formalized model of the organization of discourse, it is worth seeking—and where better to seek such a spirit than in the very interplay of successive interpretations of "the great deeds of the Lord" provided the modern world by the Bible?

Finally, we need not unduly bother about the "intellectual distortion" introduced by successive interpreters of the same mythic material. Each naive telling of the myth is equally a "distortion" because of the contingencies ⟦157⟧ of individual variation—each telling will be skewed in terms of the situation which calls it forth. Even the attempt at editing need not necessarily interfere with the operation of structural rules, if they are indeed the expression of the *esprit* of a culture. The editor or reviser is aware of the *content* of what he wishes to change in the text; he is as unconscious as the first teller of the pristine myth of the structure of his story. We ought to find the structure repeated no less in the intrusion than in the original. All we need are the analytical tools.

15. *Structural Anthropology*, 272.
16. *Genesis as Myth and Other Essays*, 25.

As noted early in this essay, structuralist methodology is still very much in the process of "speaking itself," and that rather self-consciously. One has the impression that there is a greater fascination among structuralists and semioticians with the development of the theory than with practical applications. This theoretical self-centeredness may be due to an aspiration inherited from Lévi-Strauss, the aspiration of ultimately describing the structure of mind through an account of symbolic processes. If this is so, then the goal of analysis is as much to reflect upon the development of theoretical as practical results. In any event, there has developed a kind of canonical form of structuralist exposé, somewhat along the lines of Lévi-Strauss' Oedipus essay: the methodical and theoretical considerations are first laid out, a morphological discussion follows, and the morphology leads to a semantic statement.

One thing is clear about the work of structuralists on the Bible and radically distinguishes it from previous scholarship: The focus of attention shifts from questions of document, composition, and *kerygma* to those of "reading" (*lecture*), text, and signification. These will be the issues of method and theory which we will see discussed by such structuralist researchers as Roland Barthes, Claude Chabrol, and Louis Marin. A glance at the footnotes will show that many of these essays appear together in a number of journals. As Chabrol points out, "plurality is a necessity for [semiotic analysis] and its reading of texts is always 'with several voices.'" The idea is to bring together a body of work by different scholars on similar texts and then advance the constitution of the theory by the observation of separate analyses based upon similar principles.

The French critic Roland Barthes occupies a position of considerable prominence in French intellectual life as the main force behind the journal *Tel Quel,* and as the author of works of cultural criticism and [[158]] literary theory. His contributions to the analysis of the Bible are presented as applications of his work on theory of narrative. What is most interesting about his two essays on the Bible is the considerable distance between the claims he makes for his standpoint and the practice he carries out. This is perhaps truer of the later work, "La lutte avec l'ange,"[17] a "textual" analysis of Gen 32:23–32, which appears in a work intended to present for comparison the work of two "structuralists" and two exegetes.

Barthes introduces a refinement on the traditional structuralist analysis, introducing an approach he calls "textual" but which has little

---

17. *Analyse structurale et exégèse biblique,* ed. F. Bovon (Neuchâtel, Delachaux et Niestlé, 1971).

to do with traditional textual approaches. Text is defined for Barthes as "a production of significance and not at all as a philological object."[18] The text takes part in an "open network, which is the very infinitude of language." The goal of such study is not to determine where the text comes from or how it is made, but "how it undoes itself, breaks open, disseminates: according to what coded paths it *goes on its way.*"[19]

In one sense Barthes seems to be calling for most extreme arbitrariness of interpretation, and on the other hand to be suggesting no more than the inevitable consequence of a synchronic approach. Leaving aside the colorful language with which he characterizes his method, he invites us to determine what relations the text establishes, what its rules of organization may be, how it *allows* for meaning—all of these part of the common aspiration of the structuralist school. Presumably an examination of a given text as one utterance (*parole*) governed by a code (*langue*) will lead to reflection upon the nature of those rules and consequently to the goals of structuralist analysis: formalized, exhaustive, and simple statements of the nonconscious determination of the text.

Barthes' major contribution is his pointing up of the range of ambiguity and paradox in the "struggle with the angel" story. First of all, the story of the passage over the Jabbok may be taken two ways: Jacob either crosses the ford or he does not. "If Jacob remains alone *before* having crossed the Jabbok, we are drawn toward a 'folkloristic' reading," ⟦159⟧ the resting of the hero before he can cross an obstacle. If Jacob remains alone *after* having crossed over, the "passage is without structural finality, but on the other hand acquires a religious finality." Jacob is then marked by solitude. The location of the struggle is ambiguous in an equivalent way: "Passage over the Jordan would be more comprehensible than passage over the Jabbok; we find ourselves, in sum, before the passage of a neutral place." While the exegete must reach a conclusion about the intention of the text, the "textual" analyst will "relish this sort of *friction* between two ways of understanding."

In his earlier work on Acts, Barthes had suggested that "the proper narrative analyst must have a sort of imagination of the *counter-text*, an imagination of the aberration of the text, of what is scandalous in a narrative sense."[20] In connection with the struggle at the ford, Barthes carries out an imagination of such a countertext: He invites us to consider a nonparadoxical battle. If A fights B, and must win at whatever cost, he

18. "Texte, qui doit être entendu comme production de signifiance et pas du tout comme object philologique," "Lutte," 28.

19. "Comment il se défait, explose, dissémine: selon quelles avenues codées it *s'en va,*" *ibid.*

20. "L'analyse structurale due récit: à propos d'Actes x–xi," *RSR* 58:17–37 (1970).

may deal a low blow. In the logic of the narrative this should bring about A's victory. "The mark of which the blow is structurally the object cannot be reconciled with its ineffectiveness"—that is, it must work. But, paradoxically, the low blow fails, the adversary is not victorious; he is subject to an unannounced rule; he must depart at dawn. In two senses, then, the struggle marks one of the combatants: He is physically marked (he limps afterward), and he is also marked as the bearer of an illogical disequilibrium. This disequilibrium may be related to the disequilibrium of Jacob vis-à-vis Esau. The generational equilibrium of brothers is conventionally upset by the preference given the elder. But in the case of the sons of Isaac, it is the younger who upsets the arrangement by carrying off the ancestral blessing. In the struggle at the passage, "the conflict with Esau is *displaced* (every symbol is a *displacement*)." Barthes might have carried the pattern further and developed an extra-textual correlation with other instances of such fraternal disequilibrium: Isaac/Ishamel, Ephraim/Manasseh, Zerah/Perez, Joseph/his brothers.

Barthes applies a second formal pattern to this brief narrative, the actantial model of A. J. Greimas.[21] Greimas posits six formal classes of "actants"—three pairs of narrative positions or statuses which the characters [[160]] in a narrative may occupy. These are subject/object (the one who must carry out a task or quest and the goal of his action), destinator/destinee (the one who sets the task for the subject and the one for whose benefit the destinator sets the task), and adversary/helper. Note that in this scheme the parts are distributed as follows:

Subject: Jacob	*Destinator:* God	*Adversary:* God
Object: passage	*Destinee:* Jacob	*Helper:* Jacob

There is no particular ambiguity in Jacob's having the actantial status of subject and destinee, nor even in his being his own helper. But it is extremely odd that the destinator and adversary should be the same person. Barthes sees only one kind of story which properly uses this paradoxical scheme: blackmail. He might well have added a class of stories in which the destinator *wants* the hero to succeed in the task he sets him but makes the task more difficult in order better to point up the hero's virtue.

The programmatic statements in "problèmes de la sémiologie narrative des récits bibliques,"[22] show Claude Chabrol's adherence to much the same views as Barthes'. But Chabrol's reflections on the central problems raised at various points in this essay offer some progress

---

21. *Sémantique structurale* (Paris, Larousse, 1966) 172–91.
22. *Langages* 22:3–12 (juin, 1971).

toward a resolution, less in answering doubts than in creating a more fully coherent program. The reading (*lecture*) of a text amounts to the constitution of a new object, composed of text and reader and not identical with either one. "To read is always to destroy (*perdre*) the text and the meaning, and this definitively. In place of this destroyed text and meaning, there is constituted a 'subject wishing to know' whose quest is not an object but a desire . . . which creates this particular relation of interlocution from which the reading is taken up . . . a creation interior to the text which articulates the connection which establishes a 'textual' narrator and reader."

Meaning (*sens*) had been to Barthes, "any type of correlation, intertextual or extratextual, that is to say, any trait of a narrative which refers to another element of the narrative or to another locus of the culture necessary to read the narrative."[23] To Chabrol, meaning "is not [[161]] *behind* the text; it is the system of rules which permits the engenderment of the differential interplay of oppositions which governs my reading the length of an 'infinite' text of which the text I read is only a contingent and limited—which is to say historical—actualization." There is no "hidden signified," but rather the hidden signifier, which is a "network of correlations." Instead of the notion of a "final signified" of the biblical text, there is the statement of the order which produces the infinite set of cross-references between signifiers and signifieds within and beyond the portion of text to be analyzed.

Chabrol's essay, "Analyse du 'texte' de la Passion,"[24] does make a major contribution to understanding the *meaning* of the biblical text, even while remaining true to the program of demonstrating the *functioning* of the text. The essay posits an "operational model" of the text, taking the three Gospel accounts of the passion as three variants of a single "meta-text." Chabrol then sets out to establish "the semantic universe which underlies the text" by comparing the three Synoptic accounts, among themselves and with the Peter and Cornelius episode in Acts. The object of the Cornelius episode is "beyond the reduction of the geographic distance, the abolition of 'distance' between Judaism and Otherness." Observe the stories of healing of the Centurion's servant and the daughter of the Canaanite woman, along with the Peter/Cornelius episode.

1. Jesus goes toward the foreign province//but does not enter it.
2. Jesus goes toward the foreign house//but does not enter it.

23. Barthes, "Actes," 21.
24. *Langages* 22:75–96.

3. The pagan woman leaves her territory//and enters Galilee.
4. The Centurion leaves his house//and goes toward Jesus.
5. Peter goes toward the foreign province//and enters it.
6. Peter goes toward the foreign house//and enters it.
7. The Centurion does not leave his province//he remains in the foreign country.
8. His representatives go alone to Judea to bring Peter back.

In the case of Peter, a certain negation of the separation between the worlds of "identity" and "otherness" takes place. This is related to the various indications in the New Testament that Jesus and his followers committed *minor* infractions of the ritual prescriptions, such as eating without washing of hands, eating with sinners, not fasting. The text ⟦162⟧ thus sets up both a homology, Identity : Purity : : Otherness : Impurity, and the beginning of the mediation of the opposition. Jesus carries out a "non-distantiation" by approaching the foreign territory and by healing (at a distance) the daughter of the Canaanite. He does not affirm the opposite pole of "distantiation," proximization, but he does in some way deny the distance. Each of these semantic distinctions, purity/impurity, distance/proximity, is mediated, placing Jesus in a "neutral" position neither proximate nor distant, neither ritually pure nor impure, and ultimately in the position of "communal indifferentiation." A new turn is created, as expressed in Peter's declaration, "Of a truth God is no respecter of persons. But in every nation he that feareth him . . . is accepted," and this new term must be something like "universalism," however different from the "hierarchical" universalism of Old Testament eschatology.

I must confess I feel myself at a loss before the work of Louis Marin, the most subtle, rich, and complex of the structuralists/semioticians who have published on the Bible. I very much hope his work finds an adequate translator soon. The best I can offer is a brief summary and paraphrase of a small part of his already quite large body of analytical work.[25]

Much of Marin's work is concerned with questions of communication as represented within the text. He has concerned himself with parable and other forms of narrative in which questions of the embedding of one narrative within another appear, with questions of communications in

25. Marin's works on the Bible include, "Essai d'analyse structurale d'Actes 10, 1–11, 18," *RSR* 58 (janv.–mars 1970); "Essai d'analyse structurale d'um récit-parabole: Matthieu 13/1–23," *Etudes Theologiques et Réligieuses* 46 (1971); two essays in *Langages* 22; *Semiotique de la Passion* (Paris, Biblioteque de Sciences Réligieuses, 1972); "Du corps au texte," *Esprit* (avril 1973); *Le récit évangelique* (Paris, BSR, 1973), with Claude Chabrol.

the larger sense not only of messages but of spirit in terms of hospitality, with the relations between locutionary forces in language, and between silence and speech. At the same time his methodological observations are the most extended and the most clear.

Since the text is defined "not in the irreversible temporality of *a* meaning (direction and signification) but like a network of tangled relations, with reversible orientation,"[26] it demands a *lecteur attentif*, particularly since the biblical text makes efforts to define its own reading (by means [[163]] of the metalinguistic fragments Marin examines). "By '*lecteur attentif*' I mean one who refuses the naivete of the simple route of reading the thread of the text, one who interrogates the text, which is to say rereads it, and in this rereading, works it out—makes it work—who consequently accepts the task of listening to the relations and the multiple echoes which guide him to the depths where, it seems, what he had read the first time is dismembered and rebuilt without ever being resolved." "Still, the reading is a construction of the object, and as such, is at the same time regressive and progressive— constitutive."[27] A text "*provokes* correlations between elements and totality, (and) this provocation, at the level of each text, unveils its rules of reading." But at the same time the text's *infinitization*, its relentless intertextuality, defines the principle of incertitude of reading. "As much as reading (*lecture*) adds signified by an articulation of the signifier of the text different from that which the text lays claim to, by just so much the text harbors signified at another point on its surface. Incertitude means the impossibility of stopping this movement between signified and signifier, a movement which *is* the reading, and whose exemplary form the text gives us in the parable."

In his essay on "The Women at the Tomb,"[28] Marin offers a structural analysis based on the Greimas "actantial model." The overall model for the Passion may be diagrammed as follows:

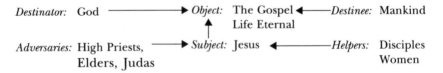

What is significant is that the recognition of Jesus as risen is only effective when performed by the community. All the recognitions by individuals

---

26. "Récit-parabole: Matthieu 13/1–23," 40.
27. "En guise de conclusion," *Langages* 22:120.
28. "Les femmes au tombeau," *Langages* 22:39–50.

fail or are incomplete. When the women come to the tomb, their actantial "object," the focus of their desire, is the body of the crucified Jesus. But in place of the object they seek they find the Angel, the bearer of the message "Jesus is risen." The women *intend* to look after a dead body; their relation with the hero is individual and passive. This double relation is opposed to (1) the recognition that the hero is indeed alive and [164] (2) the recognition of the hero in the community of disciples. "This double opposition is a modulation of the two great profound semic categories: life/death, individual/society."

At the tomb, they find the annulment of their desire and its satisfaction in one. It is the verification of the earlier prophetic utterance of Jesus: "He is not here, for he is risen, as he said." "The prophetic word, recalled and verified in the form of a quotation by the angel, makes disappear the body of the crucified." When the angel tells the women, "Tell his disciples that he is risen from the dead: and behold, he goeth before you into Galilee: there shall you see him," his statement is both *factum* and *dictum*. Just as the fact of the absent body becomes something said ("I tell you I shall rise"), this second statement, by the speech-act of the angel, becomes fact ("You shall see him").

Thus there is, within a narrative centered on an occurrence, a discourse which speaks of a *thing*, there appears another discourse "centered upon itself and its texture . . . upon its own communication, its own transmission. It is that exceptional moment in the narrative where things, the referent, the body, are effaced and absent, and where, in their place, there appear words, messages—in brief, where words become things."

A Few Comments on Structural Semiotics:

Brief Review of a Method and Some Explanations of Procedures*

JEAN CALLOUD

What It Is All About

[[51]] We all know how to read texts. All that is necessary is that a text be written in (or translated into) [[52]] a language we know, and not be too far removed from the "genres" of texts with which we are familiar. To read means to understand or "perceive the meaning." Texts are nothing more than outward and visible signs of what we call meaning. They belong to the order of language (and therefore of signs), and their function is to enable us to move from the level of sense (hearing,

Reprinted with permission from *Semeia* 15 (1979)

*Translated from an unpublished paper, "Quelques mots sur la sémiotique structurale: présentation sommaire d'une méthode et explications des procédures," by John C. Kirby, Faculty of Religious Studies, McGill University. This paper was not originally produced with publication in mind but rather as a brief statement to assist some relative beginners in the method. The editor asked for permission to translate and publish it for two reasons. It presents a brief outline of the Greimasian method as used at CADIR [[Centre pour l'Analyse du Discours Religieux in Lyon]] on biblical and other religious texts (for fuller discussion, see the "Rudiments" in each issue of *Sémiotique et Bible*). Then too, the article may provide a useful introduction to the following article on Jonah [[not reproduced in this volume]], an attempt to apply some elements of this approach to an OT text. [[No bibliography was published with this article.]]

sight) to the conceptual level. Like two sides of a sheet of paper, a text is made up of two inseparable parts: "signifiers" chosen from the vocabulary of a given language and a structured universe of "signifieds," or, to use another pair of words, a combination of "expression" and "content" offered together to one and the same perception-comprehension. Linguistic competence (knowledge of a language) and semiotic competence (knowledge of the rules which govern the different mechanisms of meaning), both being skills which can be improved, make it possible to compose and to use texts. The majority of readers are satisfied at this point and see no reason to pursue the matter further.

If, however, we have only an empirical perception of the meaning of a text obtained by reading it or by hearing it read, can we claim to have a complete knowledge of that text, a knowledge which can be rigorously checked? We may have a certain "experience" of it, but do we have a genuine "knowledge"? The natural sciences have shown us how wide the gap is between a perceived phenomenon and its scientific representation. In the framework of a more-or-less precise theory of universal gravitation, the apparent rotation of the sun around the earth is shown to be the very reverse of what actually happens. Light and color have become wave lengths. Material reality is described in terms of molecules, atoms, and particles. All these new creations, born of scientific discourse, obey the laws of measurement, of mathematics. The truth intrinsic in this elaborate system of models, of systems, of laws, is seen in the fact that they work, that successful experiments can be carried out when they are used. The reverse [[53]] is also true: the phenomena are obedient to the laws which they have suggested to the human mind.

What is true of the order of nature is also true at the human level. As for the meaning, or signification, which we continually create and which constitutes us, is it not subject to the same approach if we wish to arrive at understanding? Must we not analyze a text, break it down into its constituent elements, and then put it together again starting from these same elements, which have been clearly defined with a view to a precise handling of a text? The objective of semiotics is to enable us to speak of meaning other than in terms of empirical perception or of interpretative procedures. It proposes a way of arriving at a formal description of that which we call meaning, which is immanent in the text and therefore not directly perceptible. The text (written or oral) remains the "real" to be known. The reading of it remains the place where the signifying phenomena are perceived. To the text we must always return, in the text we must set up our laboratory, and by the text we must judge the models we have devised in order to discover how its meaning functions. But, as far as semiotics is concerned, it is useless to expect that we will discover meaning by passively observing the surface of the text, by picking out editorial idiosyncracies, or by trying to capture the message directly, be it actually or allegedly new. The *form*, or knowable aspect of the signifying phenomenon, must be drawn out by starting from the text and then applying it to the text, but this must be done by using a theory and a method neither of which is to be found in the words, phrases, or paragraphs of the text, but only in the mind of the analyst. The text must be confronted by a kind of "double," constructed out of a theoretical language which conforms to the rules of the method and which is suitable for coherently questioning the different aspects of the text with precision and discrimination. For analysis is an activity, a well-ordered though admittedly difficult method of tackling a text and of stretching out before it the net of a formal elaboration. [[54]] The text will either validate the method by showing that it worked with that particular text, or it will question it by drawing attention, not to the meaning inherent in the text but to another method better suited to bringing out that meaning. In the semiotic approach to a text, attentive and careful reading is the visible side of a hidden mental activity which concerns itself primarily with the coded message that the method with its different permutations and combinations has unearthed. The analyst speaks at the same time two languages: the language of the text, the "natural language," which he must neither forget nor subvert, and the "metalanguage" through which he puts into code the information received from his reading; with the laws and constraints of this metalanguage he must be completely familiar. When agreement is produced between the two readings, approximately if not completely, the formal "image" of the text constitutes the knowable side of it or the description of the signifying phenomenon. When the nature of the language of description (metalanguage) is taken into consideration, it is clear that relationships will show up here rather than correlated terms and systematic coherence rather than stylistic agreement or harmony of ideas. The order and the strict control of meaning, the principle of which does not appear on the surface of the text, are thus brought to light. This is a significant gain with regard to the knowledge of the text and an indispensable aid to the never-ending task of analyzing it.

The Theory of Signification:
Two Principles of Semiotics

The purpose of analysis is to bring to light the *form* of the signification. It uses for this purpose a *formalized* language, i.e., one reduced to the elements strictly necessary to make the form clear without the intrusion of nonformal elements, which unremittingly "sponge" on the text and prevent us from seeing its structure. The [[55]] analyst must be the master of this metalanguage and have used it enough for it to be a help and not a hindrance to him. He cannot do this without at first knowing something of the *form* proper to the meaning that at least one semiotic theory presents. Better still, he must be able to anticipate in broad outline, if not exactly, what he is looking for or, to put it another way, what essential characteristics every descriptive mechanism must present and to what conditions it is subject.

First Principle

The elementary structure of meaning is composed of differences and opposites. There is no signification except on the basis of differences. The universe of meaning as compared with the physical universe is a discontinuous one made up of discrete elements differing enough from each other, even arbitrarily, to make confusion impossible. Recognition of the signifying phenomena lies in locating the pertinent differences which make them what they are and in evaluating them more closely.

The semiotic form will be seen in the form of pairs of semantic "characteristics" or "values" which are opposite to each other. These are called "semes" (s).

$$s^1 \qquad \text{vs.} \qquad s^2$$
$$\text{(high)} \qquad\qquad \text{(low)}$$

The relationship between s^1 and s^2 is one of opposites and contraries. The two values are in a relation of double implication from the point of view of their definition. They are contrary to each other on a given axis, e.g. the vertical, an axis defined by its relationship with its contrary, the horizontal. They are also incompatible from the point of view of their realization in discourse (the selection of one entails the exclusion of the other).

Different characteristics belonging to different axes can be combined to form complexes of meaning called "sememes." From the basic elements and the play of selection-combination appropriate to each semantic [[56]] universe, we can constitute what is sometimes called the "signified" of words. This meaning cannot be considered as something fixed and final, closely and definitively tied to a particular "signifier." The signifying material thus formed is obtained from the network of the expression (lexemes) which helps us to have access to the manifestation. It is the relative autonomy of the expression and of the content and the instability of the structured formations of the content that make the difficult analysis of the semantic universe necessary. We have direct access only to the differences in the signifier (the expression), and we must therefore establish the differences in the signified (the content) which organize discourse. It is sometimes said that in order to assure the coherence of the content both in itself and in its connections with the expression, every text, by means of a mechanism differentially adapted, uses a "code" (an ordered system of differences, e.g. red or green, high or low, in its "traffic lights" corresponding to the values it wishes to make known, e.g. permitted or forbidden) to produce a "message." This is a good way of describing how things are. We must remember, however, that we are dealing with a highly complex problem when we attempt to analyze a discourse in natural language. We must, on the one hand, organize the movement from the expression to the content (in the technical sense of these words) and, on the other, do the same thing within the semantic material itself in order to describe the different levels of articulation and the different superimposed layers of structure.

Second Principle

The movement from the expression (the signifier) to the content (the signified) which constitutes the essential problem of all systems of signs must be seen, not as a word-for-word correspondence (the red always and everywhere meaning "forbidden" and the green "permitted") but as the play of equivalences between systems of relationships. We are looking for correlations between terms, not for meanings to be given to individual [[57]] terms. In the set of fractions $\frac{1}{2} = \frac{2}{4} = \frac{12}{24} = \frac{48}{96} = \frac{144}{288} \ldots$, their equality is defined by the relationship of each set of numbers not by the numbers separately. The semiotic model will always have the shape of a relationship between several terms, either in

the simple form s^1 vs. s^2, or in the complex form $\frac{s^1}{s^2} = \frac{s^3}{s^4} = \frac{s^4}{s^6} = \ldots$ or

in the form of a square (more about this later):

Analysis begins only when, for the surface effects (word contrasts, of situation, differences, vague oppositions, gaps, nuances, etc.), we can substitute a precise model of differential relationships which take into account, at a deep level, the variations recorded in the text that has been read. Since we must, in this descriptive operation, maintain the relationship "expression/content," the totality of the differences which make up the model will reproduce this organization. Every system of relationships can claim to be considered as a content with respect to an expression and as an expression with respect to a content. Either of these may be seen more easily than the other or before the other; if it is, then it belongs to the "expression" side of the relationship. Thus, step by step, in the course of our analysis, we set out the "code" or system of relationships which assure us an entry into and progress in the world of meaning of a text.

Strangely enough, and only experience will convince us of this, it is the simplest, the most elementary, and therefore the least debatable set of correlations which are the most fundamental. On it the whole game of meaning depends. It also stands out the most clearly and occurs most often on the surface of the text, although the least easy to mark off. It almost belongs to the expression [[58]] and is tied to it very closely, though it is undeniably part of the content. It is not easy for us to see a code, however, because we habitually look for the message. It is only by becoming more sensitive to these elementary systems of differential relationships that we learn to distinguish "analysis" from "interpretation."

The application of this second principle also avoids the confusion between "analysis" and "abstraction," or the search for general ideas. Analysis uses a method for discerning semantic values which forces us to break with the figurative level of the text. In no case must it start with a search for general ideas which are sometimes thought to be the best summary of a text or of its content. Analysis gives us valid results when it discerns, in the apparent disorder of the surface of the text, some of the indicators of the elementary categories which ensure the cohesion of the text and its functioning in terms of meaning. These elementary categories are themselves inserted into the text wherever necessary, not to convey a message but to indicate the road that must be followed in exploring "the country of meaning." They are not to be found at the level of great thoughts but in the most concrete, often the most commonplace, material in the text. There is thus opened up, as a source of continual pleasure, the land of meaning where language and its productions recover their playful character—playful in a multiple sense of that word, for if the reader catches himself playing with words and allows himself to get into the game, he will also find that he is part of it.

The Two Aspects of Analysis

Not all the signifiers which give us the differences can be found at the same time. In order to speak about meaning in the strictest possible terms, we must ascertain levels of relevance, particular points of view. We can thus ensure the homogeneity of semiotic discourse. Two levels of analysis have been the object of extensive [[59]] research: the "narrative" level and the "discursive" level. The former deals with a very important element in narrative (though it is found in all the genres of literature) and can be found in a variety of "languages" (films, comic strips, etc.). The latter deals with the element which is characteristic of the way in which language is used in a given "language." In literary semiotic analysis we must be continually aware of both levels. Every text is a discourse, something produced in a given language. Every text "relates," even if it does not "narrate." Some texts, naturally, show this more clearly than others.

The Narrative Component

This is brought out by means of a narrative model, the basis of which is the difference (very general and reductionist—but useful in analysis) between *state* and *transformation* (corresponding to the difference between *being* and *doing*), or between "statements of fact" and "statements of transformation." Its purpose is to reduce the narrative to short general statements. We thus get a simple definition of a narrative: a sequence of states and of transformations.

What is a state? By state we mean a relationship between two terms, defined in the method as S (subject) and O (object). We know nothing about either of these in themselves but only about the relationship which binds them together. This is a relationship of *junction* (S → O) and it may be either *disjunction* ∨ or *conjunction* ∧. Since it can be reversed, it obeys the principle of differences. Two statements about state are therefore possible: S ∨ O and S ∧ O.

We need to get into the habit of describing situations found in texts in terms of the relationship S ∧ ∨ O. This is easy when S and O are represented by clear-cut "figures" of "someone who possesses or is dispossessed," or of "something which can be possessed, lost or found." The verb "have" or similar verbs are normally used to describe this relation in natural language. It is [[60]] not so easy when the semiotic "object" does not stand out clearly and is represented in a very subtle way or not at all. This may also be true when the subject pole itself is uncertain in the visible distribution of roles (actantial). The verb "to be" is then used (or a similar verb or no verb at all). Thus we need to become sensitive to variations, inversions or other modifications of states.

What is a transformation? State is defined in a way which does not include the power of reversing itself. In our method, we must therefore define the operation which ensures this power of reversal. This is called "transformation," or "performance," and is represented by the following formula:

$$A(S) \quad \rightarrow \quad [(S \vee O) \quad \rightarrow \quad (S \wedge O)]$$
$$\text{or} \quad [(S \wedge O) \quad \rightarrow \quad (S \vee O)]$$

where by the action (A) of a subject (S), state 1 (S ∨ O) is transformed into state 2 (S ∧ O). This is the formula for all performance.

We see therefore that the distinction between the statement of a state (*énoncé d'état*), and the statement of an action (*énoncé du Faire*), entails a distinction between the subject of a state and the subject of an action. They can be represented by one personage (reflexive operation) or by several personages (transitive operation).

With these two types of statements and the symbols which represent them, we are in possession of the metalanguage which we need to talk about the narrative component of all texts. With it we can begin to encode the language of a text into its metalanguage for it allows us to substitute for a series of descriptive phrases, actions, movements, confrontations, agreements, or eliminations, a series of simple and well-defined operations. The advantage of this extremely restricted vocabulary (S, O, ∧, ∨, A, etc.) is found in its exactitude and its formal character; it is a good method to permit the *form* (narrative) to emerge. Its disadvantage lies in its reductionist nature; it takes into account only very general [[61]] differences and therefore does not bring out the uniqueness of any given text. We shall see how this defect is partly corrected by further steps in narrative analysis in what follows.

The Narrative Programs.   As we proceed to rewrite a text in this metalanguage in order to bring out its narrative form, we see that it is composed of sequences of operations and of states. By putting a text into a series of sequences we get, in our model, the order of the statements in the narrative, what is sometimes called the syntagmatic dimension of the text. We then discover that certain actions succeed each other in complete conformity and in a coherent order. They work together to achieve a common goal. This set of coherent, similar operations is called the "narrative program" (NP). It includes all the operations necessary to transform an initial state, after many partial operations, into a final state.

We also note that this first series is duplicated in another series of actions which attempt to do the very opposite of the first narrative program by cancelling out the transformation which occurred in it and by substituting objects. This is called the anti-narrative program ($\overline{\text{NP}}$). We cannot escape from this duplication of the narrative model for the simple reason that the situation at the beginning of the narrative is the result of an adverse intervention, the "lack," being the result of a "misdeed." This duplication is of great importance for the following reasons.

(a) Narrative program and anti-narrative program explain the often polemic nature of narrative and indeed of the majority of texts. We can therefore record simultaneously the actions and the situations which are opposed to each other at the same time that they succeed each other. Often the polemic character of the text is either not apparent at all or is very muted. It is therefore necessary to make explicit what is implicit in the text as it stands: the potential narrative program which is the opposite of the one found in the text. Apart from this [[62]] twofold division at the level of the model, how is it possible to bring out the differential nature of the meaning in discourse? If this difference is made clear in the form of precise categories which indicate the lexemes or the statements, it must also resonate in the narrative component of the story and be translatable into syntagms. The values assumed in the narrative program are definable only in terms of opposition to anti-values assumed by the anti-narrative program even if either of them is hidden by the selective word game being played in the text.

(b) This systematic duplication of the narrative program sets in motion and presupposes, at this point in the analysis, the discovery of values and anti-values. Starting from them we will be able to formalize the discursive level. The duplication organizes the narrative model with a view to its articulation in the discursive model.

(c) The duplication draws attention to the importance and the difficulty of effectively identifying objects. It is in order to discover the latter that the two narrative programs are often necessary. A narrative may have two different endings, even with the same characters. This is a sign of two potential narratives, one incompatible with the other, and therefore of two narrative programs. When a text does not show any clearly contrasted characters, one of which will confront and inevitably eliminate the other, it is a good idea to raise questions about the two kinds of possible endings by the attribution of opposing objects.

The Narrative Algorithm.   Whether the text reveals one or two narrative programs (or more in certain cases), it sets up a trajectory (*parcour*) more or less, made up of opposing positions which must lead from the initial situation to the final situation. This is sometimes called the "narrative algorithm." The trajectory which explores to the fullest the potentialities of the narrative structure is one with four [[63]] phases or stages: manipulation, competence, performance, recognition. Such a trajectory is found, for example, in fairy tales or in detailed narratives or events or adventures.

Phase 1. Manipulation. This is a matter of having something done to somebody (*Faire-Faire*), of communicating to him the volition or the obligation to do something (*Vouloir-Faire* and *Devoir-Faire*). These are usually called modalities or modal objects. A subject to whom something is to be done (sometimes called the sender) is brought on stage, together with the subject of an action. The latter is then the subject of a state, separated from and then linked up to the modal object. It is potential before having the volition or the obligation and actual afterwards.

Phase 2. Competence. This is a question of qualifying somebody to do something (*Etre du Faire*). The subject of the action, still in the position of subject of a state, must receive the power to act (*Pouvoir-Faire*) or the knowledge of how to act (*Savoir-Faire*) which are necessary for him to act. It becomes an actualized or qualified subject.

Phase 3. Performance. By this is meant the working of the transformation which turns the initial state into the final state (*Faire-Etre*). Here one of the narrative programs dominates the other and the object is attained. The modalities previously acquired are seen only insofar as they are utilized. The subject is brought to fulfillment.

Phase 4. Sanction. By this is meant the recognition of the subjects as they really are (*l'Etre de l'Etre*). The subjects of the narrative program which have been actualized are seen to be the "heroes," and those of the unrealized narrative program to be the "villains." Here the truth (*véridiction*) about the subject is revealed by the communication of knowledge (*Savoir sur l'Etre*). Previously it could remain hidden or be distorted by pretence or by lying. By the "truth-operation," the subject ⟦64⟧ is then recognized. This is the end of the trajectory of the narrative.

Two observations can be made here. (1) In each of the four phases (or subprograms), we find the typical succession of states and transformations. We therefore do not need to create a new formula in order to describe each subprogram. The formula of performance is enough. The difference between the phases is represented by a change in the attributed object. Manipulation and competence bring into play a *modal object* (volition/obligation or power/cognition). Performance is centered on a *value object* (the nature of this will vary with the type of narrative). Sanction is centered on a *cognition object*. (2) Cognition appears twice. Competence can include cognition; here it is cognition of how to act. Sanction is also constituted by cognition, but this is cognition of being (of subjects).

It must also be added that, before the transmission of volition or obligation, an initial cognition is brought forward which leads to volition or obligation to act. This is therefore knowledge of the existence of possible values or of the possible object. The subject normally passes from potentiality to actuality by accepting the cognition which he previously lacked. The subject of the manipulation is therefore often a subject to whom cognition is communicated (subject of a persuading action [*Faire Persuasif*]). We see then how important the *cognitive* area is in narrativity and also the operations of the transformations which can take place there, with all the possible complications.

The presentation of the narrative algorithm just given replaces that which was current when semiotics was directly dependent upon the analysis of folktales. The following correspondences can be noted: manipulation (contract), competence (qualifying test), performance (principal test), and sanction (glorifying test).

How do we carry out a narrative analysis? With our knowledge of the formal construction which the method [[65]] and its possible variants gives us, all that we need to do is to let a text, attentively read, and the model of narrativity react on each other. If we are fortunate, we shall obtain some knowledge of the text by juxtaposing an object to be known and a form known. The difficulty arises from the fact that the text cannot be compared with the model we hold beside it until we have submitted it to a preliminary treatment which replaces the lexemes by units which have been analyzed enough to uncover their semiotic nature. For in order to establish a narrative program we need to know what a state or a transformation, subject or object, conjunction or disjunction, are. We must evaluate the different objects and their relationship before dividing the narrative, often linear on the surface, into two narrative programs. This initial operation sometimes appears risky and unnecessary since it looks like abandoning the surface of the text. But we should not shy away from this first step for two reasons: mistakes always lead to an impasse in the analysis and we cannot evade the verification process. The "take-off" from the surface of the text does not go in the direction of an interpretation, which could bring doubtful options into play and prevent us from hearing the message of the text correctly. It goes rather in search of the elements of the "code," the knowledge of which is, in any case, prior to our getting into the game of meaning. Nobody can avoid this and risk is not appropriate for an analyst! As has been said earlier, this type of analysis, far from being concerned with general ideas which could be substituted for a careful examination of the text, wishes to draw our attention to the unobtrusive appearance of the system of signals necessary to meaning. This method appears to allow a great deal of freedom but in fact demands a rigorous fidelity to the form which the content takes with regard to what is fairly obvious and not in need of "interpretation."

The Discursive Component

⟦66⟧ Narrative Analysis can grasp only one formal aspect of signification, the one which corresponds to the syntagmatic dimension and sets in motion the mechanism which enables us to "relate." We know that this narrative component never exists in isolation and forms part of all texts (even narratives) in tune with the component proper to the linguistic material which gives it its means of manifestation. In a very large number of texts, the second (discursive) component is clearly the dominant one. It is therefore necessary to establish a second stage, or level of relevance, in order that the differences which produce meaning, the form of the content, may be grasped from other points of view with new and further means of definition. To take into consideration this new series of constraints (which are a new face given to the form of the content), a new metalanguage is needed; it must, as in the analysis of the narrative component, give priority to the system of relationships, and therefore make use of a model in which we will insert the units of the text in order to show their correlations and bring out their value in the system.

We find ourselves, in effect, in a paradoxical situation: reading gives us an understanding of the words which seem to have in themselves, independently of each other, a definite meaning assigned to them in the language system. We know, however, that the content (or the signified) of the text is not the addition of the fixed meanings given to each of the words but a semantic material, arranged according to its own characteristic structure and hidden to a greater or lesser degree by a network of signifiers. We therefore have to look for this characteristic structure and discover the indicators of it which are nearest to the surface of the signification, searching in the strata of the content most closely bound up with the expression, in the sort of twilight zone between the signifier and the signified where the relationship between ⟦67⟧ the code of values deduced from the former and the values of the latter can be most easily agreed upon. It is here that the relational model must be applied and the basic units which are easiest to organize brought to the surface; these in turn are able to organize the semantic material. While taking the text at its word, we are as far as possible from a study of vocabulary! The treatment to which the lexemes are submitted is not a lexical treatment nor a simple account of the usages of words, but an insertion into a system, a relational model where the words lose their autonomy in order to signify by means of difference the value they have in that particular text. This value cannot be deduced a priori from what the word appears to mean in the lexicon of the language.

The rooting of the discursive analysis in this textual stratum, abstracted, so to speak, from the distinction signifier/signified guarantees its applicability to the text. In simpler terms, it could be said that the text shows, more or less clearly, in its lexical and figurative composition the code which articulates the semantic material. It is enough for us, difficult though it is, to hear between the words the proclamation of this code. For that reason we must remain open to expressions of the code and stop trying to find the message. Our work is made easier when we know the relational model to which the semantic values are submitted and some of the more common relationships between figures and values. This double necessity calls for the use of the semiotic square to which we must now turn. What is the semiotic square? What is the relationship between what is read in the text and what is inscribed in the semiotic square? In conclusion, it will be enough to remember how this discursive component is connected with the narrative component.

The Semiotic Square. The situation here is different from the one we met in narrative analysis: we have only a relational model. We do not know the terms which are suitable to use there. ⟦68⟧ We have not yet defined a precise, limited vocabulary, starting from which we could set up the text in code. We will have to invent this vocabulary in order to name the units which we retain as characteristic of the discursive level and of its organization. Verification will be made when they are inscribed in the basic relational model and by the operational character (generative) of the completed model. Semiotic square is the name given to the model used to bring out the three principal relationships to which all the signifiers must be submitted so that they can give us a demonstrable semantic universe.

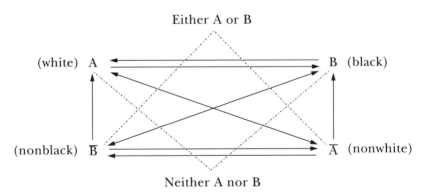

A, B, A̅, B̅ denote the places which the signifying units of all levels can occupy and also the places reserved for the basic organizational units of signification and indicators of the classification of the figures.

Between A and A̅ there is a relationship of *contradiction*. A̅ is the negation of A. We must choose between them. No third option is possible. This is the law of the alternative: of *two* things, *one*.

Between A and B there is a relationship of *contrariety*. B is the contrary of A. B is incompatible with A in the actualized signification. But B can only be thought of as the contrary of A and vice versa. There is between them a relationship of double implication. This verifies what we have said about the relational definition of configurations (*figures*) of content. Contraries have ⟦69⟧ this peculiarity that they never present themselves in terms of alternatives. Their incompatibility always offers us a third position, neither A nor B. The law of contraries is therefore: of *three* things, *one*.

Between A̅ and B̅ there is a relationship of *subcontrariety*, so that A̅ and B̅ may be in a position of exclusion or of conjunction. They also allow for a third position, either A or B (complex position as opposed to the neutral position, neither A nor B). The law of subcontraries is then: of *three* things, *two*.

Between A̅ and B or B̅ and A there is a relationship of *narrative implication*. The position of the negative term (A̅ or B̅), by negating one of its contraries, makes possible the affirmation of the other. The negative and therefore indeterminate terms are the points par excellence where we may pass from one type of content to its opposite.

N.B. The relationship between the contraries is sometimes called the *axis* or *semantic axis*, since we can bring out the value by listing a characteristic common to two opposing categories: the axis of color, for example, for the opposition black vs. white. The relationship between two contradictories is called a *schema*. *Deixis* is the name given to the unit made up of a contrary and an identical subcontrary: A + B̅ and B + A̅.

It will probably be useful to add to this general description further precise information about the use of this model. Four points merit attention.

(a) *Contradictories and Contraries*. From the semantic point of view, there is no difference of meaning between A and A̅ or B and B̅. Only the presence or absence of the negative differentiates them. We can always form A̅ and B̅ by starting from A and B: all we need to do is negate them. By doing this we alter the meaning but we do not alter the mechanism through which the meaning is given. On the other hand, the difference between A and B is one of meaning: the two words take on value only because they ⟦70⟧ are contrary the one to the other. To put one forward as a unit of meaning is, implicitly at least, to postulate the other. We can never, as with the contradictories AA̅ and BB̅ deduce one from the other or produce one by starting from the other. We must put them together as terms in a relationship productive of meaning. The analysis of the semantic component has for its goal the establishment, for every text, of the relevant opposition (or the group of oppositions), and then to take note of, or take out of the text, at a fairly elementary level, the pair of contraries which create and regulate the signification. The contraries are not given as such in nature. They are the effect of discourse and of the application of language to reality. We can see the truth of this when we realize that we distinguish only what we name and that the complexities of vocabulary always precede the classification of objects in reality. To see better is always the result of speaking more precisely. Hence the introduction of a new vocabulary, e.g. that of semiotics, is not simply a matter of words and memory but of a different view and a new understanding. Words seldom enter into the language one by one, but rather two by two, even if the second arrives a little later than the first, or if the new word is in reality the second one in a pair. In any case, strict contrariety is not a lexical phenomenon which would always and inevitably be seen in the words per se; it is established only within a discursive semantic structure, at the level of highly organized values, of classificatory indicators. The rest is a matter of after-effects, of echoes more or less muffled. We shall return to this later when dealing with the relationship of "figurative" and "thematic." All we need to know now is that words keep, like the memory of their different usages, vestiges of the oppositions that they have represented and that they most often represent. That is why we sometimes consider as established contraries, universal and unchangeable, pairs of oppositions which are only statistically more frequent [[71]] than others: black vs. white, day vs. night, heaven vs. earth. These customary pairs are only indicative of language in general. Every text can either reorganize its contents differently or select other lexemes to cover the same meaningful whole.

(b) *Usefulness of the Semiotic Square.* We must not put too high a value on this model nor hold it in such high regard that it invades all our analysis. Our anxiety about constituting a good (or even a beautiful) square should not hinder us from carrying out our first observations and putting the contents in elementary order. But we need to recognize its character as a working model whose aim it is to establish and check microsystems which have been devised to describe a text. As a formal model, already tested, it is ready to receive the signifying units, the relational character of which we wish to bring out, since by themselves they have little meaning. It helps to reconstitute the network of correlations that are hidden or distorted in ordinary language, and therefore gives a good sampling of the order or the system in which the units of the text begin to take on meaning. For this reason we can use it fairly early in the course of our analysis as a way of discovering the network of signifiers. It functions then as a model for classifying the figures and so allows us to isolate their relevant aspects. This first use of it is only a preliminary step; it must be developed further in order to include the elementary units which structure the text, that is, the *code* proper to the particular text which is being analyzed. Each of the elementary units is integrated into its proper place in the code. In this connection, it must be pointed out that the semiotic square in its final form is never a summary of the message of the text, but rather a pre-condition of that message or a key to it. Even if the writing down of the different figures which are representative of the text give us the appearance of a summary of its substance, we must remember that what it actually gives us is only the 〚72〛 *form* of it. It is precisely for this reason that the semiotic square, even if it is considered to be the end of the analysis, gives us only the turning point in our journey. It calls us to return to the surface of the text of which it is the root and of which it gives us a new "re-cognition." It thus shows us its true function: a way of knowing a text as an empirical object.

(c) *Semiotic Square and Narrative Model.* In order to play its proper role, the semiotic square must fulfill one necessary condition: it must be linked up with the narrative model. Questions are often raised about the continuity between the narrative and discursive phases of analysis. People sometimes have the impression that there is an insurmountable dichotomy between them: how can the results of narrative analysis serve as an entry into discursive analysis? How can we give to the whole course of the analysis its unity and coherence? We know, of course, that all our procedures lie within the confines of the semantic field since it is an analysis of the "signified," or "content," and that from a certain point of view narrative analysis and discursive analysis have the same goal. But there is often some difficulty in seeing any connection between them. That connection is one of secret complicity rather than one of open points of contact. This must be understood if we are right from the start to direct the narrative algorithm into the form that will be useful to us.

Both models, the narrative model (the algorithm) and the discursive model (the semiotic square) have two sides and can therefore represent the duplication which is absolutely essential to the basic structure of signification. In the narrative model it is in the form of two contrary narrative programs (narrative program and anti-narrative program) that we find the structure of opposites which underlies the syntagmatic unfolding of the text. In the discursive model it is in the duality of the *deixis* (the contrary vertical spaces) that we expect to find the 〚73〛 structure of the semantic content and its classificatory indicators (classemes). We can therefore establish, without too much difficulty, a correspondence between the two narrative programs and the two deixies. The opposing

values, controlled by each of the two narrative programs (one actualized, the other potential), appear in the relationship of contrariety on
the semiotic square. The incompatibility of the contraries corresponds
to the incompatibility found in the two narrative programs.

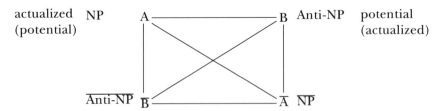

The square differs from the narrative model in that it represents directly not the series of operations under the form of an algorithm but the
static mechanism (achronic) of relationships. It therefore corresponds
best to the paradigmatic dimension of the discourse. However, and this is
highly advantageous, certain arrows on the semiotic square which designate relationships are also able to be interpreted in terms of operations.
This is the case for the relationship of contradiction which corresponds
to the operation of a negation: we move from A to A̅ by negating A. This
is also true for the relationship of narrative implication which corresponds to the assertion. Thus from A to A̅ and to B, and from B to B̅ and
to A, sets up a trajectory in which four terms can be successively placed.
As these operations, logical in nature, can be represented in a text by
figurative operators, words, narrative figures (confrontation, domination,
cancellation, elimination, attribution), it is possible to effect a movement
between the text and its double representation, syntagmatic and paradigmatic. Here is the square of the ⟦74⟧ trajectory.

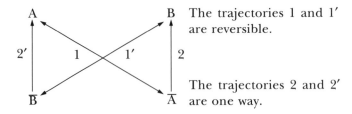

The trajectories 1 and 1′ are reversible.

The trajectories 2 and 2′ are one way.

Attention is drawn to the form the trajectories take in this diagram.
We cannot go directly from A to B nor from A̅ to B̅. The relationship of
contrariety and of subcontrariety cannot be interpreted in terms of logical or narrative operation. A close look at narratives justifies this decision. On the other hand, we can move only in one direction on the

vertical arrow, from bottom to top, never from top to bottom. The square, when substituted for the simple binary relationship A vs. B, gives us the important advantage of allowing us to make a correct representation of the movement from one value to a contrary value, i.e., from a narrative program to an anti-narrative program. The analysis of a number of texts quickly shows us the advantage of this model. The shifting of the attribution of value-objects always includes the invalidation of a contrary situation, the elimination or neutralization of opposing forces.

(d) *Some Examples.* By way of illustrating the way in which the square functions, we present here the way in which it makes use of the modalities.

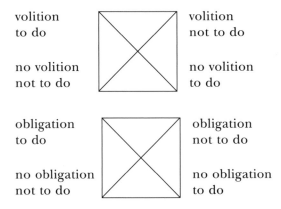

volition
to do

volition
not to do

no volition
not to do

no volition
to do

obligation
to do

obligation
not to do

no obligation
not to do

no obligation
to do

Each square draws attention to four different possibilities of the subject and thus allows us to locate the narrative positions more precisely.

〚75〛 In superimposing the squares of several modalities, we obtain more complex definitions of the same subjects. If we take into consideration the fact that modal positions can vary for each modality, we can see that the possibilities are multiplied and our ability to make more precise observations about the text increased. We can find a subject defined where the modalities of volition, obligation and power are in opposition.

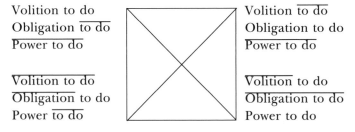

Volition to do
Obligation $\overline{\text{to do}}$
$\overline{\text{Power to do}}$

Volition $\overline{\text{to do}}$
Obligation to do
$\overline{\text{Power to do}}$

$\overline{\text{Volition to do}}$
$\overline{\text{Obligation}}$ to do
Power $\overline{\text{to do}}$

$\overline{\text{Volition}}$ to do
$\overline{\text{Obligation to do}}$
Power to do

Figurative and Thematic. The difficulties of analysis and of constructing semiotic squares are caused by the distance which separates the surface of the text (its linguistic manifestation) and the level of its semantic articulation. The textual surface, the only empirical reality, is the place where all the levels, which we separate out for analytic purposes, meet: expression and content, narrative component and discursive component. It is seen as a sequence of words (lexemes), paragraphs, chapters, etc., and reveals nothing but a stylistic distribution of contents, not directly representing the order and the signifying system properly speaking. It is the place where the "effects of meaning," the "effects of style," and the "effects of presentation" are seen. What we have are complex units which contain within them aspects that must be dealt with separately. A simple breakdown of these units in order to point up certain words or parts of words would not give us material which per se could be inserted into a semiotic square. That would be just a breaking down into its components, not an analysis, for it would not succeed in getting at the relevant aspects of the text, the constraints which [[76]] make that particular text what it is. Analysis must, first of all, make a distinction between expression and content and then move inside the content at a deeper level than that of sign. Semiotics differs fundamentally in its operation from the method by which we pass from text to language, the results of which are a grammar and lexicon. In semiotics we move from a text to a system of correspondences which organize the many movements from one level of text to another. If "meaning" "circulates" through a text, we need to show the direction it takes and the laws by which it circulates. These laws are not general laws (they do not exist prior to the text), nor are they clearly revealed in discourse. They are inscribed in filigree, as it were, between the words clearly enough for a sound reading to be possible but discreetly enough not to distract the attention of the reader. They are like the source of light which illuminates a sign without needing to be looked at directly itself.

Since each text must establish its own laws, language preserves traces of them either in the form of memory of past texts or of potentialities of future ones. In no way can a language explicitly foresee or imperiously dictate these constraints of the discursive code. But as texts are not outside language and its use, we have to imagine a sort of compromise between what it is possible to do with words, sentences, sequences of sentences, and what it is necessary to organize on a semantic-logical model in the form of a structured semantic universe. Everything will then be a matter of words (signs) and of significant autonomous relationships in their order. The game of language (spoken or written), reverberates like an echo in a semantic space which is not directly perceptible, producing there its effects of organization, regularity, selection, neutralization, etc., which constitute meaning. It is these effects which presuppose the differential nature of the minimal units in a semantic space. The conclusion of all this may be more simply expressed as follows: [[77]] to arrive at the relevant level of semantic values where the order and the form become clearly demonstrable in the models, we have to start from a level which is less ordered and nonformal but more immediately perceptible. Order and form, postulated at a deep level, must then find their reflection in the surface of the text. Every text points to its code at the same time as it expresses its message. All language has this twofold ability: to point to the code and to express the message. In order to practice semiotic analysis, it is not enough to know the formal models in a general kind of way. We need to read (or to hear) these surface images of the code.

(a) *The Two-Tiered Stage.* We may define a text as a place where the same signifying action unfolds in two modes: a *figurative* mode, a direct manifestation, and a *thematic* mode, a secondary one. The first stage is the *reading*, the second that of the semantic-logical operations where *analysis* is attempted. To understand how meaning functions, it is the thematic level which is important and which controls the figurative level. The latter can only be represented in ordinary language, the former only in metalanguage. The technique of analysis consists in replacing the language of the surface by a thematic representation. The word *thematic*, defined from a semiotic point of view, must not be confused with what is usually called "theme" or "thematic" in the sense of literary motif, i.e., subjects dealt with or dominant ideas, all of which belong to a certain way of understanding the message of texts. *Thematic* here refers to the level of values and the level of the code, as contrasted with *figurative* which refers to the representation of these things in ordinary language. The semantic values are translated into "figures," and the "figures" can be interpreted in semantic values. This relationship is analogous to the relationship between words and their meanings, between "lexemes" and "sememes," between potential and actualized meaning. Many results flow from this. [[78]]

(b) *Discursive Configurations and Thematic Roles.* The values which constitute the semantic network underlying a text are fewer in number than the "figures" which represent them in the text. It may even be said that they are limited in number and that a technical vocabulary will one day replace them. Theoretically, there is nothing to prevent a particular semantic value from being represented in a text by an unlimited number of figures. Verticality, for example, can be represented by a tree, a cliff, a slope, a fall, standing upright, etc. Although certain figures are more suitable than others to represent certain things, it is always possible to reduce them by synecdoche or metonymy. This characteristic of the way in which texts function semantically shows that the precise value of a figure is not fixed for all time. It depends on the reason for which it is used.

This distinction between figurative and thematic is related to the connection between language and discourse. By having in store, as potential sources of meaning, all lexemes which can be employed, language is a vast reservoir of figures always within reach. These figures are organized in more or less homogenized groupings, gathering the terms which are normally used together or are capable of being so used, e.g. everything connected with the sea: navigation, dangers, materials, professions connected with the sea, geography, symbols of the ocean and so on. These groupings in the language are vestiges of previous texts and sketches of future ones. They represent a system of particular constraints: horse races are not run on the ocean nor boat races on a field of snow! If this kind of thing is said, it is said by means of a complementary system of relationships: irony, metaphor, fantasy or the like. These groupings of figures anterior to the discourse itself are called *discursive configurations*. They always contain more elements than can be used in any given discourse. The selection of a part of a configuration (a figurative track or trajectory, *parcours figuratif*) is indicative of [[79]] the value that is being represented. Depending on the words we borrow from the configuration of words connected with the sun, we will infer the value /heat/, /light/, /star/ or /destruction/, all of which belong to the thematic level. These values or semantic headings which bring that particular configuration into the discourse may indicate persons, things, places or actions. To assign one of these values to a particular person defines him as an *actor* who is given a thematic role. It is precisely the meeting, in the *actor*, of the *thematic* role and the *actantial role* (arising out of the narrative structure) which qualifies the actor to enter into the discourse and to "figure" or appear there in both narrative and discursive aspects of it.

(c) *The Classification of the Figures in Discourse.* The reduction of the figures, many in number and uncertain in value, to one precise semantic value is called classification. It is accomplished in the discourse and is the condition for its intelligibility. Analysis ought to make this quite clear. When the semantic values are correctly established, they are arranged into pairs of opposites which can then be arranged in squares. The squares can then serve as a basis for establishing the groups or classes into which the figures can be put. The semantic values have a classificatory value which extends more or less through the whole of any given discourse. Some of them can mark the difference between two or three figures only, some operate on them all. It is these latter which determine the *isotopie* (or homogeneous level of meaning) of the discourse. They are quite repetitive or redundant. They are called *classemes*, i.e., classificatory semes. These are the essential terms in a semiotic square.

(d) *Return to the Semiotic Square.* The establishment of the classificatory semes, as a result of our observation of the discursive configurations and the figurative trajectories, allows us to make the semiotic squares and use them to classify the figures. In order to [[80]] remain coherent, the semiotic square must first record the classemes. Sometimes, however, it happens that when we are doing our first analysis our attention is drawn to a resemblance between certain figures and an initial classification can give us a provisional square. There is nothing to stop us from doing this.

As for the classificatory semes which provide the basis of the code, we do not need to think of them as abstract ideas but as distinctive markings, always discoverable on the surface of the text, sometimes indicated, as has been said above, by odd impressions of emphasis or by details which do not have much to do with the expression of the message. We will find them only by paying close attention to the text. This is just a matter of practice.

Note on the Typology of the Discourse

We have just noted that a discourse always links up a figurative level with a thematic level, and that analysis endeavors to bring to light a system of semantic features which can be classified. This means that, thanks to a metalanguage (language of definition and description), it is possible to speak of that which the discourse itself does not speak directly, and which turns out to be its starting point. If it is possible to enclose a descriptive (semiotic) discourse within a figurative discourse, it is because a word can be extended by means of language used as metalanguage to the nonfigurative dimension of discourse. This possibility is exploited in certain discourses which are constituted more directly at the thematic level and aim at designating their semantic values and their articulation with a minimal use of figures. They thus bring together analysis and quasi-semiotic description. We can indeed establish a scale of figurativity on which discourse could be classified, from the story (maximal figurativity) and semiotic discourse (minimal figurativity).

⟦81⟧ This has repercussions on our ideas of natural language and of metalanguage. Indeed, the distinction between them is artificial. Although metalanguage has for its function to point to that which has no name in any language (the units of the signified), it can never be defined without using natural language. It is always with words (even if they are neologisms) that we designate semes and classemes. Even if we are to designate them by pure symbols or by numbers, we could never escape completely from the semanticizing of the indices. Is it possible to speak in a nonsignifying way about meaning?

Thus language is enriched by new signs in proportion as points of view on reality increase and methods of analysis vary. It is language itself which possesses the means of talking about itself and which creates its own metalinguistic mechanism. This is already seen in the dictionary where the movement from the word to the definition shows us the application of language to itself.

Note on Veridiction

Attention must be drawn to this particularly important effect in discourse. It is bound up with the communication of knowledge and can be defined as one of its qualifications (or modalities). It can be true, false, secret, deceptive (misleading, illusory). These positions can be represented on the semiotic square in this way:

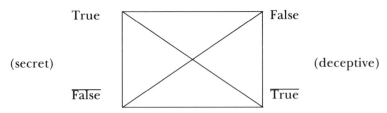

We can see that veridiction is a subsystem of the discursive mechanism of meaning.

Knowledge plays an important role in discourse. When discussing the narrative algorithm, we mentioned the two phases which are normally put in the cognitive space: manipulation (which includes an attribution of knowledge ⟦82⟧ of an object before the attribution of volition or of obligation) and sanction (the attribution of knowledge on the being of a subject). To this can be added the phase of competence which sometimes brings into play a modality of knowing how to do instead of the modality of being able to do. In these three cases, the relationship of knowledge to the system of veridiction controls the position of the personages in their exchanges and their mutual relationships. All limitation on the knowledge of the truth that they have about each other has an effect on their qualifications and therefore on their performance. Depending on whether or not appearance corresponds to reality, their exchanges are normal or abnormal. Veridiction is therefore linked with appearance and reality as the following model shows.

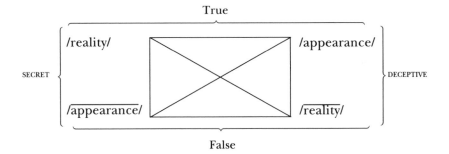

We may use this more basic definition of the figures of veridiction:

true	= /reality/ + /appearance/
false	= /r̄ēālīty/ + /āppēārance/
secret	= /reality/ + /āppēārance/
deceptive	= /r̄ēālīty/ + /appearance/

But the problem of veridiction (saying what is true) is posed at another level, that of the communication of the discourse itself between the speaker and the hearer. It is a bit of knowledge which moves on this axis and it must be specified as true (or possibly false, secret or deceptive). The problem of the veracity of the discourse ⟦83⟧ is not usually raised at the beginning of an analysis and it will not be dealt with here. But we need to be put on our guard about it and gradually get used to recognizing the procedures associated with the mechanism of signification in order to construct the overall effect of truth. The procedures for this vary: putting a narrator in the text who is truthful and sure of what he knows, affirmation of truth, actions which point to it, the speaker implicitly giving evidence in its favor, truth which is self-evident.

All that remains to be determined is the conditions necessary and sufficient to link the implicit action of persuading on the part of the speaker to the interpretative (believing) act on the part of the hearer and to pose the total effect of truth so that no further questions need be asked. Semiotics is making progress in this direction now.

Conclusion

What has been written above is not a complete resume of all one needs to know to speak of structural analysis. It is rather a reflection on methods, goals, and practice. Semiotics is not so much concerned with knowledge as it is with know-how.

A Structural Exegesis of Genesis 2 and 3

Daniel Patte
and Judson F. Parker

The Specific Goal of Our Exegesis

⟦55⟧ Our exegesis follows a well defined method based upon a theoretical model of a part of the structural network operating in narrative texts (presented in Patte and Patte 1978a, 1978b). Its ultimate goal is to elucidate the system of deep values, or semantic universe, presupposed by the text in its present form. These deep values (or symbolic values, or again convictions as "self-evident truths") are elements of the vision of life and of the world held as self-evident or ⟦56⟧ revealed by the author or redactor (whether collective or individual). They constitute the semantic framework within which the author thinks, speaks, acts, (and thus they must be contrasted to the symbolic system that the author dominates, transforms, and creates, at least to a certain extent). These deep values constitute the "meaning horizon" of the text. As such they are NOT the central values (or themes) manifested by the text's symbolism. They are peripheral although foundational. They are not that upon which the text is focused, although they are what focuses the text, its *visée*. The deep values of the semantic universe should not, therefore, be confused either with the codes (studied by Boomershine) which are cultural systems used in a text, or with the semantic categories (studied by Jobling) which are semantic/symbolic themes.

These deep values are also termed symbolic values because they are manifested by certain symbolic dimensions of the text—namely by

Reprinted with permission from *Semeia* 18 (1980) 55–75.

the connotations of textual elements, by metaphorical relations, in brief, by the text's "symbolic system" (a technical term which does NOT intend to designate all the symbolic dimensions of a text). Both the system of deep values and the symbolic system are organized paradigmatically in such a way as to constitute a series of inter-related isotopies (we define isotopy as a coherent set of deep values). The quasi-logical relations of the semantic square are the fundamental principles governing their paradigmatic organization.

Our research has demonstrated that there is, in any narrative, a *correspondence* between the organization of the symbolic system and the narrative organization, despite the fact that these are governed by quite different principles (the former is paradigmatic, the latter syntagmatic). By virtue of this correspondence, the study of the narrative organization (usually an easier task) provides criteria for the establishment of the symbolic system of the text and for the study of the system of deep values. In fact, each step of the analysis can be verified by each of the others.

Our exegesis, because of its very goal, is exclusively focused upon *certain* aspects of the text: Those which manifest the system of deep values. Thus, we account for certain features, and certain features only, of the syntagmatic and paradigmatic organization of the text's *signification systems*. We do NOT account for the textual manifestations related to the participation of the text in a *communication process*. In our view (cf. also Greimas and Courtés 1979: 157–160) these later features, through which the text has a rhetorical and aesthetic effect, include (a) the action sequences (studied by Culley), the narrative trajectories, and the unification of the syntagmatic organization in terms of characters, times and places; (b) the paradigmatic organization in terms [[57]] of (semantic) themes expressed in symbolic figures; and (c) the correlation of these syntagmatic and paradigmatic figures by means of rhetorical devices (studied by Boomershine) and enunciative manifestations such as direct and third person discourses (studied by White). According to our method, all these features are better studied after the completion of the analysis which is aimed at elucidating the text's semantic universe through a study of its symbolic system, which is, in turn, based upon a study of the narrative organization; yet we do not deny that they can be studied on their own.

Relevant Aspects of the Narrative Organization of Genesis 2 and 3

Our theoretical and methodological research has shown that the syntagmatic organization into "narrative levels" and "systems of pertinent transformations" corresponds to the paradigmatic organization of the "symbolic system" and "semantic universe." In the narrow confines of this article, we cannot present either the method or the analytical process aimed at establishing the narrative levels of the systems of pertinent transformations of Genesis 2 and 3. (For the complete presentation of the method and an example, see Patte and Patte 1978a: chapters 2–3.) A few remarks and the presentation of the results of the analysis will have to suffice here.

Establishment of the Narrative Levels

When one studies the narrative development, one can note, among other phenomena, places where this development is carried forward on the *sole basis* of an interpretation (by a character) of the value of another part of the narrative. This is to be contrasted with the usual unfolding of the narrative development through the transmission of somatic or cognitive Objects (whether or not this process involves an interpretation). This phenomenon is significant because it signals a shift from one narrative level to another. Such a narrative shift corresponds to a shift from an isotopy to another. Thus, by identifying these interpretive prolongations of the narrative development one can break down the text into narrative units—the narrative levels—which correspond to units of the semantic universe.

In the text under consideration we have identified two narrative levels:

Primary level: Gen 2:4–15 and 3:22–24
Secondary level: Gen 2:16–3:21

⟦58⟧ After the narrative development recounting the first creative acts and its "parallel" narrative about the rivers (primary level), Yahweh Elohim gives a command to the man (2:16) which presupposes a specific interpretation by Yahweh of the value of the first creative acts, and therefore introduces a secondary level. These values attributed respectively to the man and the garden (and its various components) demand that the two be in a specific relationship expressed in the command. In 2:18 we find a second interpretation by Yahweh of the same situation focused this time on the loneliness of man. The serpent's interpretation presupposes another and conflicting interpretation of the relationship between man and garden. The narrative unfolds on the basis of these three interpretations, and this without changing level up through 3:21. (The status of 3:20–21 as belonging to the secondary level becomes clear only at the next stage of the analysis.)

With 3:22 an interpretation of what happened at the secondary level is presupposed: Yahweh Elohim's statement draws the consequences

TABLE I *System of Pertinent Transformations of Level I*

3:23b Adam (cultivation → Adamah)	: 2:5d	Adam (cultivation ↛ Adamah)
3:24b Cherubim (guarding → tree of life)	: 3:33d	Adam (hand of Adam → tree of life)
2:10b river(s) (moistness → garden)	: 2:6b	²ed (moistness → Adamah)
2:9a Y.E. (springing up → edible trees)	: 2:5b	Eretz (springing up ↛ herbs)
2:7d Y.E. (breath of life → Adam)	: 3:22g	Adam (eternal life → Adam)
2:4b Y.E. (state of creation → Eretz)	: 2:5c	Y.E. (not rain → Eretz)

from what happened. This narrative shift indicates either a return to the primary level or a passage to a tertiary level. The next stage of the analysis shows that the former option is the correct one.

Establishment of the Systems of Pertinent Transformation

Each narrative level is a self-contained narrative unit insofar as it is the narrative space in which a series of polemical programs are overcome or neutralized by a corresponding series of principal programs. A number of programs are therefore opposed by pairs in that they manifest opposite "functions" (Propp's and Lévi-Strauss' term) or "transformations" (Greimas' term). Since a transformation can be defined in terms of the actantial model as the relation between the Object and the Receiver (O → R), there is opposition between two transformations when they belong to opposite narrative axis (principal and polemical) and when they have either contradictory Objects, or contradictory Receivers, or again contradictory functions (represented by ↛).

The analysis proceeds in several steps: (a) a representation of each program according to the model, Subject (Object → Receiver), using appropriate abbreviations (their choice is somewhat arbitrary, the essential is that they be used consistently through the analysis); (b) listing of these programs according to the axis to which they belong (either principal or polemical); (c) the identification of the pertinent oppositions (i.e., those opposed by pairs); (d) the organization of the systems of pertinent transformation according to the order of the narrative development (which is not necessarily the textual order) on ⟦59⟧ the axis which commands the narrative development. We give below the results of this analytical process (space requirements prohibit its description).

System of Pertinent Transformations of the Primary Level. This system is represented in Table 1.

In this table one will note that the identification of some of these pairs of pertinent transformations has required that we evaluate the se-

TABLE II   *System of Pertinent Transformations of Level II*

3:16e	her *ish* (domination → woman)	: 3:17b	Adam (listening → woman)
3:16b	Y.E. (labor pain → woman)	: 3:6e	woman (pleasing fruit → woman)

b) *Transformations of the woman parallel*

3:15a	Y.E. (emnity for the serpent → woman)	: 3:13d	serpent (fascination for the serpent → woman)
3:14c	Y.E. (greater curse than every beast → serpent)	: 3:1b	Y.E. (greater craft than every beast → serpent)

a) *Transformations of the serpent parallel*

3:21	Y.E. (skin garments → *ish* and woman)	: 3:7e	*ish* and woman (leaf aprons → *ish* and woman)
3:19e	Adam (dust → Adam)	: 3:4b	tree in middle of garden (not death → man and woman)
3:18a and 3:19a	Adam (bread in sweat and thorns → Adam)	: 3:6h	*ish* (fruit of tree in middle of garden → *ish*)
2:25b	Adam and woman (not shame → Adam and woman)	: 3:7b, c	*ish* and woman (cognition of nakedness → *ish* and woman)
3:3e	tree in middle of garden (death → man and woman)	: 3:5c and 7a	fruit of tree in middle of (open eyes → man and woman)
2:17a	Adam (not fruit of tree → Adam)	: 3:6g	woman (fruit of tree → her *ish*)
3:3b	Elohim (command about eating (= 2:16a) and death → man and woman)	: 3:1d	Elohim (command about eating of any tree → man and woman)
2:22d	Y.E. (woman → man)	: 2:20b	Y.E. (not matching helper → man)

2:10b	river(s) (moistness → garden)	: 2:6b	*'ed* (moistness → Adamah)

mantic relations of certain symbolic manifestations (e.g., the judgment that "edible trees" and "herbs of the field" are two representations of the same category "edible plants"). Note also that "garden" and "adamah" are shown to be representations of two opposed categories because of the oppositions of the principal and polemical programs concerning watering (same verb in 2:10b and 2:6b). This table is to be read from bottom to top. ⟦Y.E. indicates the deity, Yahweh Elohim.⟧

System of Pertinent Transformations of the Secondary Level: 2:16–3:21. We represent the system of pertinent transformations of the secondary level in Table II. Two remarks are necessary. First, this system of transformations is articulated upon the system of level I through the opposition of 2:10b *vs.* 2:6b (the last pertinent transformation of the story about the first creating acts). Second, this system becomes threefold towards its end: in the part corresponding to the threefold curse. Only a three-dimensional graph could allow us to represent the parallelism of the transformations related to the story of the man (3:19a, 3:18a *vs.* 3:6h and 3:19e *vs.* 3:4b) and those related to the stories of the serpent (respectively 3:14c *vs.* 3:1b and 3:15a *vs.* 3:13d) and of the woman (respectively 3:16b *vs.* 3:6e and 3:16e *vs.* 3:17b) which we write at the top of Table II. These three parallel sets of transformations do not correspond to each other narratively (their respective transformations are different) but they occupy the same place in the system of pertinent transformations since each of them prolongs [[60]] the narrative development beyond the opposition 2:25b *vs.* 3:7b, c. The last transformation (3:21b *vs.* 3:7e) prolongs both the man's and the woman's story and not the serpent's story.

[[61]] Thus, the system of pertinent transformations of level II splits into three parallel narratives, two of which recombine, as in the sketch Table IIb.

The Symbolic System and the Semantic Universe

[[62]] The identification of the systems of pertinent transformations of both narrative levels gives us an entry into the symbolic and semantic organization of the text. A symbolic and semantic field (what Lévi-Strauss would term a "state") is associated with each pertinent transformation (what Lévi-Strauss called a "function"). By using Greimas' actantial categories, we can say that this symbolic and semantic field is manifested symbolically by the Subject and its various qualifications, i.e., the investments of the actantial positions of Helper, Opponent and Sender. Thus our first task is to go back to the text and make a list of the qualifications of each Subject at the specific stage of the narrative development where the corresponding pertinent transformation is found. This list should include whatever, *according to the text*, the Subject uses or has when performing the program: will (*vouloir*), i.e., what motivates the Subject; cognition (*savoir*), i.e., what knowledge the Subject has; and power (*pouvoir*), i.e., what enables the Subject. Note that the Helpers include eventually the proper time and location, and often the possession of the Object which will be communicated. It is important at this point to include in this list only what is expressed in the text.

Among the numerous semantic connotations (or *semantic features*) that each bundle of qualifications has, the text selects a few pertinent semantic features by including them in transformations which are contradictory in one of the ways mentioned above [[p. 146]]. That the pertinent transformations in the text in turn disclose the pertinent se-

TABLE IIb

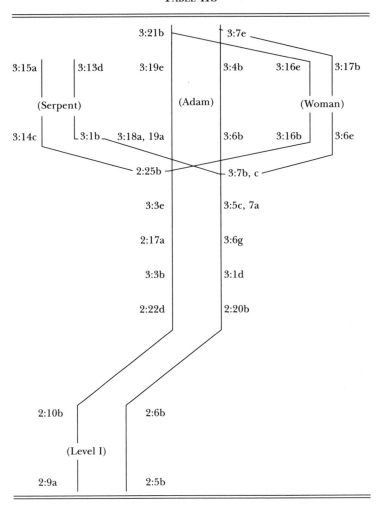

mantic features of the text we regard as a major contribution of this method, and some further remarks are perhaps in order.

Following a suggestion by Greimas, it has been shown (in Patte and Patte 1978a: chapter 2) that to a *narrative opposition* (an opposition of narrative transformations) corresponds a *semantic opposition* (an opposition of semantic features manifested symbolically by the qualifications) *of contradiction* (the "diagonal" of a semiotic square, such as A and non-A). For several theoretical reasons based on this principle, it appears that the bundles of qualifications associated with the transformations are in the proper position as terms of semiotic squares when they are organized as the system of pertinent transformations, although with an important difference: the polemical axis must be slid upwards so that the opposition corresponding to a narrative opposition be a contradictory opposition. (Once more, it is not the place to justify or to present this theory.) Thus, by studying the relations of contrariety, contradiction and implication among the bundles of qualifications, one can identify the semantic features which have been selected by the text ⟦63⟧ for each bundle of qualifications so that the symbolic system of the text might be coherent. In this way, the system of deep values presupposed by the text can be disclosed.

When studying this mass of symbols, one needs to use the "cultural dictionary" (i.e., the mass of knowledge elucidated by historical research devoted to the text's cultural milieu) in order to be aware of the potential connotations of these qualifications. Obviously, as New Testament scholars we do not pretend to have the necessary background in Old Testament research to perform fully such an analysis. Despite this limitation we hope to be able to identify the main categories presupposed by our text.

A full description of this twofold process would be too long in the limited space of the present essay. We simply provide tables showing the symbolic system of each level, that is, the network of relations among the bundles of qualifications corresponding to the pertinent transformations (the qualifications are suggested as concisely as possible). Without discussing the numerous relations which have to be considered so as to identify the pertinent semantic features, we shall merely present a second set of tables showing the semantic features which account for the three types of relations in the semiotic squares. The phrases we use in order to express these semantic features form a metalanguage which is, at best, an approximation. In fact, it is an attempt to express in a referential way, i.e., as ideas, what belongs to the connotative realm. On this basis we will draw some conclusions as to what characterizes the semantic universe presupposed by Genesis 2 and 3. ⟦64⟧

Level I

The symbolic system of level I ⟦is expressed in table III⟧.

The symbolic system forms a series of interrelated semiotic squares (four complete squares and two half squares). The only semantic features which appeared to be pertinent (that is to account for all the re-

TABLE III *The Symbolic System of Level I*

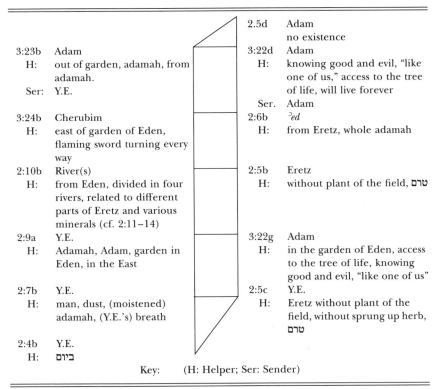

			2.5d	Adam
				no existence
3:23b	Adam		3:22d	Adam
H:	out of garden, adamah, from		H:	knowing good and evil, "like
	adamah.			one of us," access to the tree
Ser:	Y.E.			of life, will live forever
			Ser.	Adam
3:24b	Cherubim		2:6b	ʾed
H:	east of garden of Eden,		H:	from Eretz, whole adamah
	flaming sword turning every			
	way			
2:10b	River(s)		2:5b	Eretz
H:	from Eden, divided in four		H:	without plant of the field, טרם
	rivers, related to different			
	parts of Eretz and various			
	minerals (cf. 2:11–14)			
2:9a	Y.E.		3:22g	Adam
H:	Adamah, Adam, garden in		H:	in the garden of Eden, access
	Eden, in the East			to the tree of life, knowing
				good and evil, "like one of us"
2:7b	Y.E.		2:5c	Y.E.
H:	man, dust, (moistened)		H:	Eretz without plant of the
	adamah, (Y.E.'s) breath			field, without sprung up herb,
				טרם
2:4b	Y.E.			
H:	ביום			

Key: (H: Helper; Ser: Sender)

lations which exist among the bundles of qualifications) can be
represented in table IV. [[65]]

On the basis of this analysis it appears that the set of deep values
(the isotopy) which undergirds both the narrative development and
the themes and figures of this part of the text is a series of presuppositions (self-evident truths) related to the /power to create/ (we use "/ /"
to make clear that our formulation of the semantic features is approximate: other terms could certainly be used to express them). In this
phrase "power" must be read as a technical term designating a modality, i.e., a value which modifies the value of an action; "to create" must
be read in the broad sense of "causing to be."

[[66]] By the phrase "power to create" we attempt to express the
overarching value which is manifested in a more specific way by each of
the symbolic/semantic fields of the positive axis. In 2:7b, Y.E. manifests

TABLE IV   *The System of Values of Level I*

		2:5d	Adam no existence
3:23b	Adam existence in own realm, power to make Adamah fertile	3:22d	Adam in divine realm, power to disrupt order of cosmos
3:24b	Cherubim power to order the cosmos	2:6b	ᵓed no power to make Adamah fertile, no power to give order
2:10b	river(s) power to give order to Eretz from Eden = from the divine going out of Eden	2:5b	Eretz does not belong to the divine realm, without specified origin, no power to produce vegetable life
2:9a	Y.E. power to produce vegetable life for others, will produce vegetable life	3:22g	Adam not going out of Eden for oneself, power to appropriate life
2:7b	Y.E. power to give human life, will go give oneself	2:5c	Y.E. no will to produce vegetable life, no will to give oneself, no will to create Eretz and heavens
2:4b	Y.E. will to create Eretz and heavens		

a /power to give human life/; in 2:9a, Y.E. manifests a /power to produce vegetal life/; in 2:10b the river(s) manifest(s) a /power to give order to Eretz/; 3:24b the cherubim manifest a /power to give order to the cosmos/; 3:23b Adam manifests a /power to make adamah fertile/. Each of these values is further defined by their relations of contrariety and of contradiction with the negative values and by the relations of implication which exist among them.

Thus, the two semantic features of /power to give human life/ are further defined: giving human life involves /giving of oneself/; the power to do so is before all a manifestation of the /will/ to do so rather than the manifestation of an ability (force). This appears when one notes that the /power to give human life/ (2:7b) is contradictory with Adam's /power to appropriate life for oneself/ (3:22g). Appropriating for oneself is /not giving/, or more specifically /not giving of oneself/, a feature that the text selects among the potential connotations of the symbol "(Y.E.) breathed into his nostrils the breath of life." This observation already suggests that the power to give human life is associated with the /will to give of oneself/ (giving of oneself is a matter of the "will" and not merely of a "power"). It is through this latter feature that this value appears to be in contrary relation with the qualifications of Y.E. in 2:5c: the absence of creation does not result from a lack of power, nor from an opposed power (nothing in this part of the text can be construed as having such connotations). The only limiting qualification is the temporal notation, טרם, a time "before" the (proper) day, i.e., a time which is not appropriate, a time when Y.E. has /no will to create/, /no will to give of oneself/, by contrast with "the (appropriate) day" when Y.E. has the /will to create/ (2:4b).

The /power to produce vegetal life/ (2:9a) which involves the /will/ to do so (as contradictory to 2:5c) is further characterized as being /for others/. This feature which sets 2:9a as contrary to 3:22g (/for oneself/) is symbolically manifested by the description of the vegetal life as "pleasant to the sight and good to eat" which makes it clear that it is not created by Y.E. for his own sake but *for others.*

Considering the relation of implications between 2:7b and 2:9a, it appears that the /power to give human life/ involves the conjunction of the /divine/ (Y.E. self) and /adamah/, thus human life is by nature both /divine/ and /earthy/ while the /power to produce vegetal life/ merely involves the use of /adamah/, /for others/, this second feature implying (i.e., manifesting in another way) the /divine/. By contrast the Eretz by itself which symbolizes something without the divine in either [[67]] of its forms (this lack being symbolically represented as lack of rain) is sterile (2:5c and also 2:5b). Similarly, "in the garden of Eden" which qualifies the negative power of Adam in 3:22g (the /power to appropriate life for oneself/) must be read as symbolizing a /power exclusively based on the divine/. We shall see below that the connotation /divine/ or /divine realm/ appears as a pertinent feature of the "garden of Eden" (and of "Eden") throughout our text.

The river(s) (2:10b) manifest(s) a /power to give order to Eretz/: its function is not only to water the garden but also to divide Eretz into various regions (cf. 2:10–14, note the repeated designation "Eretz"). By contradiction with Adam's power (3:22g) this ordering power is defined as going out of Eden (as well as out of the garden): it has a divine origin (from Eden) but is "outgoing." Through its contrary relation with 2:10b, the powerlessness of Eretz (2:5b) is simultaneously defined once more as /not from the divine/, /not belonging to the divine realm/ or more specifically /without specified origin/.

The contradictory relation of river(s) (2:10b) and *ʾed* (2:6b) shows that the latter symbolizes (among other things to be discussed below) a /lack of power to give order/. The connotations /undivided watery mass/ and thus /chaotic waters/ are therefore without any doubt pertinent. *ʾed* has here connotations similar to the corresponding Accadian term: "flood water" and not "mist" (cf. R.S.V.).

Since the cherubim (3:24b) manifest the values /power to give order to the cosmos/ (i.e., power to separate the human realm from the divine realm) which is derived from the fact that they /belong to the divine realm/ (a connotation which is shown to be pertinent because of the contradictory opposition to Eretz, 2:5b), the cherubim and *ʾed* are in opposition of contrariety as /divine power/ *vs.* /chaotic power/. Yet this chaotic power is not defined as an active (evil) power but rather as a twofold absence of power: as a /lack of power to give order to Eretz/ (cf. the relation to 2:10b) and as a /lack of power to make Adamah fertile/ by contrast to Adam's /power to make Adamah fertile/ (3:23b)—our way of formulating the power to cultivate Adamah.

Adam's /power to make Adamah fertile/ (3:23b) is defined as associated with the fact that /man is in his own realm/ (no longer in the garden but with Adamah) by contrast with its contrary /man in the divine realm/ (in the garden) the situation of Adam in 3:22d. Both through the relation of contradiction with the "non-existent" Adam (2:5d) and the relation of implication with the cherubim (3:24b), Adam's power is further defined as /having existence/ as a result of Y.E.'s creative act, and thus being the conjunction of a divine element and of Adamah. As such he is in relation with the divine realm but does not belong to it. In fact for man to be in the divine realm is to be a [[68]] /power disrupting the order of the cosmos/ (by disrupting the distinction between the human realm and the divine realm, by being "like gods") (3:22d).

These values, the main characteristics of which we briefly described (many details being left out for the sake of space), appear to be what form the semantic framework in which the text of the first narrative level unfolds its symbolism.

Level II

[[The symbolic system of level II is expressed in Table V; the system of values of level II is expressed in Table VI. Both tables should be read from bottom to top.]] [[71]] The set of values (isotopy) which gives unity and coherence to the symbolic system of the secondary level (cf. Table VI) endorses as proper *a relational view of human existence* and denounces as wrong various monolithic views of human existence. As

TABLE V   *The Symbolic System of Level II*

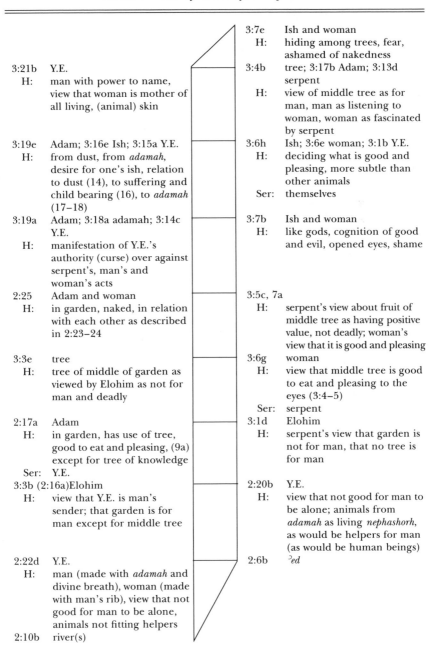

3:7e   Ish and woman
H: hiding among trees, fear,
        ashamed of nakedness

3:21b   Y.E.
H: man with power to name,
        view that woman is mother of
        all living, (animal) skin

3:4b   tree; 3:17b Adam; 3:13d
        serpent
H: view of middle tree as for
        man, man as listening to
        woman, woman as fascinated
        by serpent

3:19e   Adam; 3:16e Ish; 3:15a Y.E.
H: from dust, from *adamah*,
        desire for one's ish, relation
        to dust (14), to suffering and
        child bearing (16), to *adamah*
        (17–18)

3:6h   Ish; 3:6e woman; 3:1b Y.E.
H: deciding what is good and
        pleasing, more subtle than
        other animals
Ser: themselves

3:19a   Adam; 3:18a adamah; 3:14c
        Y.E.
H: manifestation of Y.E.'s
        authority (curse) over against
        serpent's, man's and
        woman's acts

3:7b   Ish and woman
H: like gods, cognition of good
        and evil, opened eyes, shame

2:25   Adam and woman
H: in garden, naked, in relation
        with each other as described
        in 2:23–24

3:5c, 7a
H: serpent's view about fruit of
        middle tree as having positive
        value, not deadly; woman's
        view that it is good and pleasing

3:3e   tree
H: tree of middle of garden as
        viewed by Elohim as not for
        man and deadly

3:6g   woman
H: view that middle tree is good
        to eat and pleasing to the
        eyes (3:4–5)
Ser: serpent

2:17a   Adam
H: in garden, has use of tree,
        good to eat and pleasing, (9a)
        except for tree of knowledge
Ser: Y.E.

3:1d   Elohim
H: serpent's view that garden is
        not for man, that no tree is
        for man

3:3b   (2:16a)Elohim
H: view that Y.E. is man's
        sender; that garden is for
        man except for middle tree

2:20b   Y.E.
H: view that not good for man to
        be alone; animals from
        adamah as living *nephashorh*,
        as would be helpers for man
        (as would be human beings)

2:22d   Y.E.
H: man (made with *adamah* and
        divine breath), woman (made
        with man's rib), view that not
        good for man to be alone,
        animals not fitting helpers

2:6b   ⁾ed

2:10b   river(s)

TABLE VI   *The System of Values of Level II*

		3:7e — Ish and woman belonging to the vegetal world, hiding for fear, rejecting sexuality as shameful
3:21b — Y.E. sexuality as the source of life, belonging to the animal world		3:4b — tree/3:17b Adam/3:13d serpent like gods, transcending one's nature
3:19e — Adam/3:16e Ish/3:15a Y.E. each dominated according to own nature, dominated by that from which one originates, not like gods		3:6h — Ish/3:6e woman/3:1b Y.E. having excessive freedom of choice, transcending one's origin
3:19a — Adam/3:18a Adamah/3:16b Y.E./3:14c Y.E. no choice regarding nature, Y.E. has authority to establish nature		3:7b, c — Ish and woman acting as gods, not according to human nature, separation by shame
2:25b — Adam and woman man's full union with woman, man's separation from parents, according to human nature, choice of an order for the world of living creatures		3:7a =3:5c — fruit man has a choice of an order for the cosmic and/or world, good and pleasing
3:3e — tree man does not belong together with center of garden, center produces death for man		3:6g — woman like gods, totally identified with the divine, integrally part of the garden
2:17a — Adam not integrally part of the garden but related to it, earthly but not totally		3:1d — Elohim man and woman do not at all belong to the garden, totally unrelated to the divine
3:3b =2:16a — Elohim man and woman belong together with the garden (with the divine), man and woman not integral with the divine		2:20b — Y.E. man and woman related exclusively to *Adamah*, man is totally earthly living *Nephesh*, man made with *Adamah* alone
2:22d — Y.E. woman made with rib of man, man made with Adamah and divine breath, relational power		2:6b — *ᵓed* undifferentiated power with total claim, monolithic, chaotic power, no power to order Eretz
2:10b — river power to order Eretz, diffentiated power from Eden		

such this isotopy develops one of the characteristics of the isotopy of the first level. The "power" (or "lack of power") has often as its predicate "ordering," i.e., /setting in specific relations certain elements/.

These two isotopies are articulated upon one another through the pair of bundles of qualifications 2:10b river(s) *vs.* 2:6b *ʾed*. In the context of our discussion of the first level we have seen that this contradictory opposition can be represented in summary from as /differentiated, and from Eden, power to order Eretz/ *vs.* /undifferentiated, and from Eretz, chaotic power, i.e., lack of power to order Eretz/. In addition to features emphasizing in a specific way /power/ (the overarching values of the first isotopy), this pair also involves specific features expressing the importance of proper relationships within the creation (the characteristic of the second isotopy).

The river has the power to order Eretz because it is "from Eden" and "*divided*" (into four "heads"), while *ʾed* lack such a power because it is "from Eretz" and an "undifferentiated mass."

The following contradictory opposition (2:22d *vs.* 2:20b) associates the semantic features /divided/ or /relational/ and /undifferentiated/ or /monolithic/ to views of human nature. Note first that if the animals and birds are not fitting helpers for Adam (2:20b) it is because each is a /totally earthly living nephesh/, i.e., /made with adamah alone/, a value contradictory to the value manifested by the woman (part of the bundle of qualifications of Y.E. in 2:22d) who is /made with the rib of man/ and thus shares with Adam his twofold nature as /made with adamah *and* the divine breath/. This first observation, which by itself would be quite tenuous, is confirmed by the other relations in which 2:20b and 2:22d are involved. The woman's twofold nature (conjunction of the /divine/ and the /earthly/) is associated with a similar semantic feature manifested by the nature of Y.E.'s power in 2:22d: a power that Y.E. shares with man (who, through his naming, participates in the creation of the animals and of woman), that is, a /relational power/ (a power exerted in relation with others) which is contrary to the /monolithic chaotic power/ of the flood, an /undifferentiated power with total claim/ (covering the *whole* adamah, 2:6). Thus 2:22d serves as a first hinge between the two isotopies by linking the relational nature of human existence with the relational nature of Y.E.'s power. This link being established, the new isotopy can unfold its own network of values.

⟦72⟧ First we find that human beings are characterized as being related to the divine but not as an integral part of it. In 3:3b (2:16a) the pertinent qualification of Elohim (Y.E.) is his view of man (and woman) presupposed and expressed in his command. Man has his place in the garden; he can eat of every tree, yet he is not an integral part of it, he should not eat from the "tree of the knowledge of good and evil" (2:17a) that is, from the "tree in the middle of the garden" (3:3b). The positive injunction manifests that man and woman /belong together with the garden (with the divine)/, while the negative injunction denying them access to the center emphasizes that they are not an integral part of it. This positive relation to the divine which is the main emphasis of 3:3b (2:16a) is contrary to the /exclusive relation to adamah/ of the animals (non-human beings) found in 2:20b.

2:17a manifests semantic features similar to those of 3:3b (2:16a) but with the opposite emphasis: the view of /*man not integrally part of the garden* (*as earthly*) *although he is related to it*/. Such an emphasis sets 2:17a in contradictory relation to 2:20b: man as /earthly although not totally/ vs. /totally earthly/ animal. To be earthly is not to be man (2:17a) as well as not to be a woman (2:22d).

On the negative axis we find two new expressions of the monolithic view of human existence as contradictory to 3:3b (2:16a) and 2:17a respectively: the view according to which human beings do /not at all belong to the garden/ (they cannot eat of any tree) found in 3:1d manifests that they are /totally unrelated to the divine/; the view according to which human beings are /integrally part of the garden/ (they can eat of any tree) found in 3:6g manifests that they are /totally identified with the divine/, they are "like gods." In 3:3e (2:17b) the "deadly" conjunction of the tree in the middle of the garden with the human beings manifests quite emphatically that such a total identification with the divine is a wrong view of human nature: /human beings do not belong with the center of the garden/. The "day" they would pretend to appropriate the divine for themselves they would be /annihilated/, /dead/ instead of "like gods," although this does not mean that they do not belong together with other parts of the garden (contradictory relation with 3:1d).

As the isotopy unfolds what is implied by this twofold and relational view of human nature appears. The proper human existence involves separation from (i.e., non-identification with) any one element from which one originates: one's parents as well as the divine. This is manifested by the relation of implication between 3:3e (2:17b) and 2:25b (a bundle of qualifications which includes the textual elements found in 2:23–24). The /separation from the center of the garden/ and thus /from the divine/ (3:3e) is correlated with /man's separation from his ⟦73⟧ parents/ (in which "separation" must be understood as "non-identification" according to the relations previously considered). This separation is the necessary condition for the realization of the proper interrelation between man and woman (and possibly, more generally,

between human beings?). Indeed, the same relation of implication correlates /separation from center of garden/ and /from one's parents/
with /man's full union with woman/ the normal (shameless) relation
which is /fulfillment of the human nature/, by contrast with /not being
according to human nature/, i.e., /like gods/ (cf. the contradictory relation with both 3:6g and 3:7b, c).

The twofold human nature and the correlated non-identification
with any one element from which one originates establish a "space" in
which human beings have freedom of /choice/ (for lack of a better
term). Yet this space is strictly delimited. This first appears when considering the contrary relation between 2:25b and 3:5c, 7a. In 2:19–23
(part of the bundle of qualifications of 2:25b), man's role as choosing a
name for each living nephesh and further as choosing among them a
fitting helper has been strongly emphasized (to the point that this
choice is a limitation to Y.E.'s power, cf. 2:22d). Thus the /choice to select a helper among the living creatures/ or more generally the /choice
of an order for the world of the living creatures/ is marked as a positive
value. By contrast the "fruit" (which opens the eyes, 3:5c, 7a) is qualified as having been recognized as "good for food and pleasing to the
eyes" by the woman who in this way has chosen among the trees, i.e.,
among the elements of the garden, what is "good and pleasing" over
and beyond the order established by Y.E. (cf. 2:9). This involves the
/choice of an order for the cosmic (and/or vegetal) world/ which is
marked as a negative value and is contrary to the freedom of /choice of
an order for the world of living creatures/ (a positive value) and also
contradictory with the values manifested by Y.E.'s curses (3:14c, 3:16,
3:18a, and 3:19a). These curses manifest with utmost emphasis that any
living creature including man and woman has /no choice regarding
one's nature/ even if it is "not pleasing." Serpents have to go on their
own belly but they eat dust (thus they have food); women have to
suffer, and they bear children; men have to suffer hard work because
of the hostile nature of *adamah* and they have food from it. In other
words, /man's freedom to choose an order establishing the relation of
each living creature to himself/ (2:25) is correlated with (and limited
by) /Y.E.'s authority to establish the nature of each/ (3:14c, 3:16, 3:18a
and 19a). It is illegitimate for /human beings to choose their relationship to the world/, that is, /to establish their own natures/ (3:5c, 7a).
Thus the negative value /to be like gods rather than according to their
own nature/ is progressively defined. The pertinence of these values
(which could certainly be better formulated) is confirmed by the negative ⟦74⟧ bundle of qualifications found in 3:1b, 3:6h, and 3:6e where
we find once more the man and the woman choosing their relation to

the world and, in addition, the serpent qualified as ערום, a term usually translated by "shrewd," "subtle," "crafty," which must be understood as /having an excessive freedom of choice/.

The freedom of choice, which characterizes the existence of human beings (and the serpent) is strictly limited by their nature which involves that they are dominated. Indeed, each is /dominated according to one's nature/ as expressed in 3:15a (for the serpent), in 3:16e (for the woman), and 3:19e (for the man). In the two latter cases, it is more specifically /to be dominated by that from which one originates/. The woman is dominated by the man from whom she has been taken; the man is dominated by the adamah from which he has been taken. (Logically the serpent should be viewed as being dominated by the woman..."from whom it has been taken"! Could it be in the sense that it is through the quest for the woman that it was created!?) At any rate, the wrong view of human existence, being like gods (expressed in 3:4b and manifested indirectly in 3:17b and 3:13d where the woman and the serpent are "like gods" because they are accepted as Sender instead of God), is /transcending one's origin/, /transcending one's nature as living creature/. In the last resort, human beings are thus defined as /belonging to the world of living creatures/, the "animal" world: this is one of the features of 3:21b (the view of man and woman presupposed by Y.E. who gives them "*skin*-garments"). It is in this world only that they have the freedom of choice, sharing one of Y.E.'s attributes, according to their nature. By attempting to transcend their own nature they end up *not* in the divine realm (like God) but alienated from the divine (in fear, and hiding from Y.E.) and /in the vegetal world/ (cf. 3:7–8: they wear leaf aprons, they hide "in the middle *of the trees* of the garden," identifying themselves with the trees, and not "in the middle *of the garden*" which would have symbolized the identification with the divine). Human life is thus limited to the animal world, even though human beings dominate it through their freedom of choice which relates them to the divine realm. Human life is (exists as such) if, and only if, human beings maintain the proper relationship inside their own realm, the realm of living creatures. This proper relationship includes sexuality, the full, un-ashamed union of the man and the woman. It is in this relationship that the source of life is: Adam can see the woman as "the mother of all living."

Our formulation of these deep values, in a metalanguage which certainly could be improved upon, attempts to account for the semantic universe, the "meaning horizon" of our text. Let us repeat it, these ⟦75⟧ deep values are *not that upon which the text is focused*. The text which narrativizes these values is focused upon certain themes and figures which have rhetorical and aesthetic effects. These deep values are rather *what focuses the text* and its thematic and figurative dimensions. This analysis can serve as a basis for further study of the text's symbolism. Yet in and of themselves these deep values have a special interest for us in that they are held as self-evident truths: they characterize most directly the faith of the author/redactor.

Works Consulted

Boomershine, T.
  1974   *Mark the Storyteller: A Rhetorical Critical Investigation of Mark's Passion and Resurrection Narrative.* Union Theological Seminary Dissertation. Ann Arbor, Michigan. Microfilm.
Culley, R. C.
  1978   "Action Sequences in Gen 2–3." Pp. 51–60 in *SBL Seminar Papers,* vol. 1. Chico: Scholars Press.
Greimas, A. J., and J. Courtés
  1979   *Sémiotique. Dictionnaire raisonné de la théorie du langage.* Paris: Hachette.
Jobling, D.
  1977   "A Structural Analysis of Numbers 11 and 12." Pp. 171–203 in *SBL Seminar Papers.* Chico: Scholars Press.
  1978   *The Sense of Biblical Narrative: Three Structural Analyses in the Old Testament (I Samuel 13–31, Numbers 11–12, I Kings 17–18).* Journal for the Study of the Old Testament Supplement Series, 7.
Lévi-Strauss, C.
  1967   "The Structural Study of Myth" in *Structural Anthropology.* Trans. Claire Jacobson. Garden City, New York: Doubleday.
  1969   *The Raw and the Cooked.* Trans. J. and D. Weightman. New York: Harper & Row.
Patte, D., and A. Patte
  1978a   *Structural Exegesis: From Theory to Practice.* Philadelphia: Fortress Press.
  1978b   *Pour une Exégèse structurale.* Paris: Seuil.
White, H. C.
  1978   "Direct and Third Person Discourse in the Narrative of the 'Fall.'" Pp. 121–140 in *Seminar Papers: SBL,* vol. 1.

Formalism and Narrative

Introduction

Formalism popularized Old Testament literary criticism during the 1980s. Rhetorical criticism was employed by form critics and linguistic experts, and structuralism aided scholars who mastered its intricacies, but formalism made literary analysis accessible to a large number of scholars. Most literature departments in major universities have used formalism since the 1940s, so practically everyone who has studied literature has at least been exposed to the approach. Formalism also focuses on common literary topics, such as plot, characterization, themes, etc., which makes it more understandable than structuralism. Because of formalism's widespread use, this section is the longest in the collection.

Robert Alter's *The Art of Biblical Narrative* (1981) set the recent agenda for formalistic analysis of the Old Testament in at least two ways. First, Alter defined formalism as "attention to the artful use of language" that explains a literary piece's "ideas, conventions, tone, sound, imagery, narrative viewpoint, compositional units, and much else" (p. 175 below). In other words, he advocated the use of a method that had illuminated world literature for years (p. 175). Second, because Alter's book was distributed more widely than earlier works on biblical narrative, it encouraged similar studies. Alter's essay (originally published in *Commentary* in 1975) serves admirably to introduce this section on formalism because it carefully explains how formalism works.

Formalists tend to focus on the interpretation of narrative. Therefore, many studies of structure, plot, characterization, narration, and genre have appeared. Structure and plot are vital elements in narrative. Shimon Bar-Efrat (1980) and Barbara Green (1982) demonstrate that a story's superstructure and action often dictate its meaning in subtle and creative ways. Characterization is one of the most overlooked subjects in literary analysis. Adele Berlin (1982) chooses this neglected emphasis to examine some neglected Old Testament personae—David's wives. Her essay illustrates how literary analysis can illuminate forgotten

164

details in biblical texts. Narratology has grown in importance in all literary criticism during the past twenty-five years. Meir Sternberg (1983) argues that narrators are not neutral. Rather, they champion persons, causes, and ideologies. It is part of the interpretative task, then, to uncover the narrator's underlying motives. All literature takes a definite form. It contributes to a genre. J. Cheryl Exum and J. William Whedbee (1984) explore the possibility that biblical narrative reflects comic or tragic viewpoints. Though such categories are imperfect, they at least begin the discussion of whether or not biblical authors consciously created certain kinds of plots.

Each of the articles in this section is representative of the work of other scholars. Interest in biblical narrative continues to increase. Though some critics still prefer to employ structuralist techniques on narrative passages, a majority of scholars now probably prefer formalistic methods. This trend will likely continue, so the analyses of the past ten years will serve as the foundation for more advanced studies of Old Testament narrative.

A Literary Approach to the Bible

ROBERT ALTER

[[3]] What role does literary art play in the shaping of biblical narrative? A crucial one, I shall argue, finely modulated from moment to moment, determining in most cases the minute choice of words and reported details, the pace of narration, the small movements of dialogue, and a whole network of ramified interconnections in the text. Before we weigh the theoretical considerations that may explain why this should be so, and also the circumstances of intellectual history that have prevented this essential literary dimension from being sufficiently observed, it would be well to follow the sustained operation of narrative art in a biblical text.

Let me propose for analysis a supposedly interpolated story because it will give us an opportunity to observe both how it works in itself and how it interacts with the surrounding narrative material. I should like to discuss, then, the story of Tamar and Judah (Genesis 38), which is set in between the selling of Joseph by his brothers and Joseph's appearance as a slave in the household of Potiphar. This story is characterized by E. A. Speiser, in his superb Genesis volume in the Anchor Bible series, as "a completely independent unit," having "no connection with the drama of Joseph, which it interrupts at the conclusion of Act I."[1] The interpolation does, of course, as Speiser and others have recognized, build [[4]] a sense of suspense about the fate of Joseph and a feeling of time elapsed until Joseph shows up in Egypt, but Speiser's failure to see its intimate connections through motif and theme with

Reprinted with permission from *The Art of Biblical Narrative* (New York: Basic Books, 1981) 3–22.

1. *Genesis*, The Anchor Bible (New York, 1964) 299.

the Joseph story suggests the limitations of conventional biblical scholarship even at its best. I shall begin with the last five verses of Genesis 37 in order to make clear the links between frame-narrative and interpolation. My translation will at a number of points be awkwardly literal to reproduce verbal repetitions or syntactic peculiarities of the original for the purposes of analysis.

Joseph's brothers, one recalls, after selling him into slavery, dip his cherished tunic in goat's blood to show to their father.

"They had the ornamented tunic brought to their father [note the indirection of their approach to Jacob, even more marked in the Hebrew syntax], and they said: 'This [*zot*] have we found. Please recognize [*haker-na*], is it your son's tunic or not?'" (Gen 37:32). The brothers are careful to let the contrived object, "this [*zot*]," do their lying for them—it goes before them literally and syntactically—and of course they appropriately refer to Joseph as "your son," not by name nor as their brother. Jacob now has his prop, and from here on he can improvise his own part: "He recognized it [*vayakirah*], and he said: 'My son's tunic! An evil beast has devoured him, / Joseph has fallen prey'" (Gen 37:33). *Haker*, the verb for recognition (which we will be seeing more of), stated by the brothers in the imperative, immediately recurs in the perfect tense, Jacob responding at once as the puppet of his sons' manipulation.

It should be observed (I am sure the scholars have) that when Jacob goes on here to invent a disastrous explanation, left unstated by his sons, for the bloodied tunic, his speech ("An evil beast... ") switches into formal verse, a neat semantic parallelism that scans with three beats in each hemistich: *hayáh ra⁽áh ⁾akhaláthu / taróf toráf Yoséf.* Poetry is heightened speech, and the shift to formal verse suggests an element of self-dramatization in the way Jacob picks up the hint of his son's supposed death and declaims it metrically before his familial audience. If this seems fanciful, I would direct attention to how Jacob's bereavement is described in the next two verses: "Jacob tore his clothes, put sackcloth on his loins, and mourned his son many days. All his sons and daughters tried to console him but he refused to be consoled, saying, 'No, I will go down to my son in the underworld mourning,' thus did his father bewail him" (Gen 37:34–35). In two brief verses half a dozen different activities of mourning are recorded, including the refusal to be consoled and direct speech in which the father expresses the wish to mourn until he joins his son in death. (Later, ironically, he will "go down" to his son not to Sheol, the underworld, but to Egypt). One can hardly dismiss all these [[5]] gestures of mourning as standard Near Eastern practice, since the degree of specification and synonymity is far beyond the norms of the narrative itself. Thus, just a few verses earlier (Gen 37:29), when Reuben imagines Joseph is dead, his sincere sense of bereavement is expressed quite simply with "He tore his clothes"—in the Hebrew only two words and a particle.

Finally, the extravagance of Jacob's mourning is pointed up by the verse that immediately follows it and concludes the episode: "And the Midianites sold him in Egypt to Potiphar, courtier of Pharaoh, his chief steward" (Gen 37:36). Modern translations usually render the initial *vav* of this verse with something like "meanwhile," but that loses the artful ambiguity of the Bible's parataxis. In this cunningly additive syntax, on the same unbroken narrative continuum in which Jacob is mourning his supposedly devoured son, Midianites are selling the living lad: "And his father bewailed him and the Midianites sold him"— for even the sentence break would not have been evident in the ancient text. The original syntax, to be sure, does indicate some opposition and perhaps a past perfect sense of the verb by placing the subject before the verb ("and the Midianites sold him"), not the normal Hebrew order, and by switching the verb form when the Midianites are introduced. In any case, the transition from Jacob mourning to Joseph sold is more nearly seamless, less relationally marked, than modern translations make it seem.

At this point (Genesis 38), with an appropriately ambiguous formulaic time indication, *vayehi ba^{c}et hahi*, "at about that time," the narrative leaves Joseph and launches on the enigmatic story of Tamar and Judah. From the very beginning of the excursus, however, pointed connections are made with the main narrative through a whole series of explicit parallels and contrasts:

> 1. At about that time Judah parted from his brothers and camped with an Adullamite named Hirah. 2. There Judah saw the daughter of a Canaanite named Shua, married her, and lay with her. 3. She conceived and bore a son, whom they named Er. 4. She conceived again and bore a son, whom she called Onan. 5. Then she bore still another son, whom she called Shelah; he was in Chezib when she bore him. 6. Judah got a wife for Er his firstborn, and her name was Tamar. 7. Er, Judah's firstborn, displeased God, and God took his life. 8. Judah said to Onan: "Lie with your brother's wife and fulfill your duty as a brother-in-law, providing seed for your brother." 9. But Onan, knowing the seed would not be his, let it go to waste on the ground whenever he lay with his brother's wife, in order not to give seed for his brother. 10. What he did displeased God and He took his life, too. 11. Then [6] Judah said to Tamar his daughter-in-law, "Stay as a widow

in your father's house until Shelah my son grows up," for he thought,
"He, too, might die like his brothers." And Tamar went off to dwell in
her father's house.

The story begins with Judah parting from his brothers, an act conveyed with a rather odd locution, *vayered m³et*, literally, "he went down
from," and which undoubtedly has the purpose of connecting this
separation of one brother from the rest with Joseph's, transmitted with
the same verb-root (see, for example, the very beginning of the next
chapter: "Joseph was brought down [*hurad*] to Egypt"). There is thematic justification for the connection since the tale of Judah and his
offspring, like the whole Joseph story, and indeed like the entire Book
of Genesis, is about the reversal of the iron law of primogeniture,
about the election through some devious twist of destiny of a younger
son to carry on the line. There is, one might add, genealogical irony in
the insertion of this material at this point of the story, for while Joseph, next to the youngest of the sons, will eventually rule over his
brothers in his own lifetime as splendidly as he has dreamed, it is
Judah, the firstborn, who will be the progenitor of the kings of Israel,
as the end of Genesis 38 will remind us.

In any case, the preceding block of narrative had ended with a
father bemoaning what he believed to be the death of his son. Genesis
38 begins with Judah fathering three sons, one after another, recorded
in breathless pace. Here, as at other points in the episode, nothing is
allowed to detract our focused attention from the primary, problematic subject of the proper channel for the seed (since this is thought of
both figuratively and in the most concretely physical way, I have translated it literally throughout). In a triad of verbs that admits nothing adventitious, Judah sees, takes, lies with a woman; and she, responding
appropriately, conceives, bears, and—the necessary completion of the
genealogical process—gives the son a name. Then, with no narrative
indication of any events at all in the intervening time, we move ahead
an entire generation to the inexplicable death ("he displeased God")
of Er, Judah's firstborn, after his marriage to Tamar. The firstborn
very often seem to be losers in Genesis by the very condition of their
birth—the epithet "firstborn," hardly needed as identification, is asserted twice here, almost as though it explained why Er displeased
God—while an inscrutable, unpredictable principle of election other
than the "natural" one works itself out. The second son, Onan, however, makes the mistake of rebelling by *coitus interruptus* against the legal obligations of the system of primogeniture, refusing to act as his
[7] dead brother's proxy by impregnating the widow in the brother's

name, and so he, too, dies. Interestingly, after we have been exposed
to Jacob's extravagant procedures of mourning over the imagined
death of one son, Judah's reaction to the actual death in quick sequence of two sons is passed over in complete silence: he is only reported delivering pragmatic instructions having to do with the next
son in line. If this striking contrast underscores Jacob's excesses, it
surely also makes us wonder whether there is a real lack of responsive-
ness in Judah, and thus indicates how parallel acts or situations are
used to comment on each other in biblical narrative.

After the death of the second son, the narrator gives us (Gen
38:11) Judah's direct speech to Tamar as well as Judah's interior
speech explaining his motive, but no response on the part of Tamar is
recorded. This may suggest silent submission, or at least her lack of
any legal options as a childless young widow, and it certainly leaves us
wondering about what she is feeling—something which her actions
will presently elucidate. There is one small but tactically effective hint
that Judah is in the wrong: when he addresses Tamar, she is identified
as "Tamar his daughter-in-law," an otherwise superfluous designation
that reminds us of his legal obligation to provide her a husband from
among his sons.

At this point we are given another time indication to mark the next
stage of the story, in which the tempo of narration will slow down dras-
tically to attend to a crucial central action:

> 12. A long time afterward, Judah's wife, the daughter of Shua, died;
> after being consoled, he went up toward Timnah to his sheepshearers,
> together with his friend Hirah the Adullamite.

All the information in this verse is essential for what follows. Tamar has
been allowed to linger mateless "a long time," so that her own perception, reported two verses later, that she has been deliberately neglected is given an objective grounding. Judah has been widowed and
the official period of mourning has passed—that is the meaning of
"being consoled," but it is worth translating literally because it stands
in contrast to Jacob's previous refusal to be consoled—so Tamar can
plausibly infer that Judah is in a state of sexual neediness. Here begins
her bold plan:

> 13. And Tamar was told, "Your father-in-law is coming up to Timnah
> for the sheepshearing." 14. Then she took off her widow's garments,
> covered her face with a veil, wrapped herself up, and sat down at the
> entrance to Eynaim on the road to Timnah, for she saw that Shelah
> [8] was grown up and she had not been given to him as a wife. 15.

Judah saw her and took her for a harlot because she had covered her face. 16. So he turned aside to her by the road and said, "Look here, let me lie with you," for he did not realize that she was his daughter-in-law. She answered, "What will you pay me for lying with me?" 17. He replied, "I'll send you a kid from my flock." She said, "Only if you leave a pledge until you send it." 18. And he said, "What pledge should I leave you?" She replied, "Your seal and cord, and the staff you carry." He gave them to her and he lay with her and she conceived by him. 19. Then she got up, went away, took off her veil, and put on her widow's garments. 20. Judah sent the kid by his friend the Adullamite to redeem the pledge from the woman, but he could not find her. 21. He inquired of the men of the place, "Where is the cult prostitute, the one at Eynaim by the road?" and they answered, "There has been no cult prostitute here." 22. So he went back to Judah and told him, "I couldn't find her, and the men of the place even said, 'There has been no cult prostitute here.'" 23. Judah said, "Let her keep the things, or we shall become a laughingstock. I did, after all, send her this kid, but you could not find her."

Until this point Tamar had been a passive object, acted upon—or, alas, not acted upon—by Judah and his sons. The only verbs she was the subject of were the two verbs of compliance and retreat, to go off and dwell, at the end of verse 11. Now, a clear perception of injustice done her is ascribed to Tamar (verse 14), and she suddenly races into rapid, purposeful action, expressed in a detonating series of verbs: in verse 14 she quickly takes off, covers, wraps herself, sits down at the strategic location, and after the encounter, in verse 19, there is another chain of four verbs to indicate her brisk resumption of her former role and attire. (One might usefully compare this to the rapid series of verbs attached to Rebekah's activities [Gen 27:14–17] as she prepares through another kind of deception to wrest the blessing from Isaac for her son Jacob.) Judah takes the bait—his sexual appetite will not tolerate postponement though he has been content to let Tamar languish as a childless widow indefinitely—and here we are given the only extended dialogue in the story (verses 16–18). It is a wonderfully businesslike exchange, reinforced in the Hebrew by the constant quick shifts from the literally repeated "he said" (*vayomer*) to "she said" (*vatomer*). Wasting no time with preliminaries, Judah immediately tells her, "Let me lie with you" (literally, "let me come to you," or even, "let me enter you"), to which Tamar responds [[9]] like a hard-headed businesswoman, finally exacting the rather serious pledge of Judah's seal and cord and staff, which as the legal surrogate of the bearer would have been a kind of ancient Near Eastern equivalent of all a person's major credit cards.

The agreement completed, the narrative proceeds in three quick verbs (the end of verse 18)—he gave, he lay, she conceived—to Tamar's single-minded purpose, which, from her first marriage, has been to become the channel of the seed of Judah. When the Adullamite comes looking for Tamar, he asks, decorously enough, for a cult prostitute (*qedeshah*), though Judah had in fact thought he was dealing with a ordinary whore (*zonah*).[2] The local people answer quite properly that there has been no *qedeshah* in that place, an assertion which receives special emphasis through the narrative contrivance by which it is repeated verbatim in Hirah's report to Judah. Nor, we may be led to think, has there been a *zonah* in that place, but only a wronged woman taking justice into her own hands. We are now prepared for the climax of the story.

> 24. About three months later, Judah was told, "Tamar your daughter-in-law has played the harlot [*zantah*] and what is more she is with child by harlotry [*zenumim*]." And Judah said, "Take her out and let her be burned."

The naked unreflective brutality of Judah's response to the seemingly incriminating news is even stronger in the original, where the synthetic character of biblical Hebrew reduces his deadly instructions to two words: *hotzi'uha vetisaref.* As elsewhere, nothing adventitious is permitted to intervene between intention and fulfilled purpose, and so the next two words of the text go on from Judah's command almost as if there had been no time lapse, as though there were no perceptible interval between magically powerful speech and the results of speech: Judah says, *hotzi'uha*, take her out, and the next two words, in a rare present passive participle, are *vehi mutz'et*, literally, "And she is being taken out." But this is the last instant before Tamar's triumphant revelation:

> 25. As she was being taken out, she sent word to her father-in-law, "By the man to whom these belong, by him am I with child." And she added, "Please recognize [*haker-na*], to whom do these belong, this ⟦10⟧ seal and cord and staff?" 26. Judah recognized [*vayaker*] them and he said, "She is more in the right than I for I did not give her to my son Shelah." And he had no carnal knowledge of her again.

The whole inset of Genesis 38 then concludes with four verses devoted to Tamar's giving birth to twin boys, her aspiration to become the mother of male offspring realized twofold. Confirming the pattern of

---

2. In ancient Near Eastern pagan religion, there were special temple prostitutes with whom male worshippers consorted as part of a fertility cult. Their activity would not have had the base mercenary motives that impelled common prostitutes.

the whole story and of the larger cycle of tales, the twin who is about to be secondborn somehow "bursts forth" (*parotz*) first in the end, and he is Peretz, progenitor of Jesse from whom comes the house of David.

If some readers may have been skeptical about the intentionality of the analogies I have proposed between the interpolation and the frame-story, such doubts should be laid to rest by the exact recurrence at the climax of Tamar's story of the formula of recognition, *haker-na* and *vayaker*, used before with Jacob and his sons. The same verb, moreover, will play a crucial thematic role in the dénouement of the Joseph story when he confronts his brothers in Egypt, he recognizing them, they failing to recognize him. This precise recurrence of the verb in identical forms at the ends of Genesis 37 and 38 respectively is manifestly the result not of some automatic mechanism of interpolating traditional materials but of careful splicing of sources by a brilliant literary artist. The first use of the formula was for an act of deception; the second use is for an act of unmasking. Judah with Tamar after Judah with his brothers is an exemplary narrative instance of the deceiver deceived, and since he was the one who proposed selling Joseph into slavery instead of killing him (Gen 37:26–27), he can easily be thought of as the leader of the brothers in the deception practiced on their father. Now he becomes their surrogate in being subject to a bizarre but peculiarly fitting principle of retaliation, taken in by a piece of attire, as his father was, learning through his own obstreperous flesh that the divinely appointed process of election cannot be thwarted by human will or social convention. In the most artful of contrivances, the narrator shows him exposed through the symbols of his legal self given in pledge for a kid (*gedi ᶜizim*), as before Jacob had been tricked by the garment emblematic of his love for Joseph which had been dipped in the blood of a goat (*seᶜir ᶜizim*). Finally, when we return from Judah to the Joseph story (Genesis 39), we move in pointed contrast from a tale of exposure through sexual incontinence to a tale of seeming defeat and ultimate triumph through sexual continence—Joseph and Potiphar's wife.

It is instructive that the two verbal cues indicating the connection between the story of the selling of Joseph and the story of Tamar and [[11]] Judah were duly noted more than 1500 years ago in the Midrash: "The Holy One Praised be He said to Judah, 'You deceived your father with a kid. By your life, Tamar will deceive you with a kid' . . . The Holy One Praised be He said to Judah, 'You said to your father, *haker-na*. By your life, Tamar will say to you, *haker-na*' " (*Bereshit Rabba* 84:11, 12). This instance may suggest that in many cases a literary student of the Bible has more to learn from the traditional commentaries than from modern scholarship. The difference between the two is ultimately the difference between assuming that the text is an intricately interconnected unity, as the midrashic exegetes did, and assuming it is a patchwork of frequently disparate documents, as most modern scholars have supposed. With their assumption of interconnectedness, the makers of the Midrash were often as exquisitely attuned to small verbal signals of continuity and to significant lexical nuances as any "close reader" of our own age.

There are, however, two essential distinctions between the way the text is treated in the Midrash and the literary approach I am proposing. First, although the Midrashists did assume the unity of the text, they had little sense of it as a real narrative continuum, as a coherent unfolding story in which the meaning of earlier data is progressively, even systematically, revealed or enriched by the addition of subsequent data. What this means practically is that the Midrash provides exegesis of specific phrases or narrated actions but not continuous *readings* of the biblical narratives: small pieces of the text become the foundations of elaborate homiletical structures that have only an intermittent relation to the integral story told by the text.

The second respect in which the midrashic approach to the biblical narratives does not really recognize their literary integrity is the didactic insistence of midrashic interpretation. One might note that in the formulation recorded in the passage just cited from *Bereshit Rabba*, God Himself administers a moral rebuke to the twice-sinning Judah, pointing out to him the recurrence of the kid and of the verb "to recognize" that links his unjust deception of his father with his justified deception by Tamar. That thematic point of retaliation, as we have seen, is intimated in the biblical text, but without the suggestion that Judah himself is conscious of the connections. That is, in the actual literary articulation of the story, we as audience are privileged with a knowledge denied Judah, and so the link between kid and kid, recognize and recognize, is part of a pattern of dramatic irony, in which the spectator knows something the protagonist doesn't and should know. The preservation of Judah's ignorance here is important, for the final turn of his painful moral education must be withheld for the quandary in which he will find himself later when he encounters ⟦12⟧ Joseph as viceroy of Egypt without realizing his brother's identity. The Midrash, on the other hand, concentrating on the present moment in the text and on underscoring a moral point, must make things more explicit than the biblical writer intended.

Indeed, an essential aim of the innovative technique of fiction worked out by the ancient Hebrew writers was to produce a certain indeterminacy of meaning, especially in regard to motive, moral character, and psychology. (Later we shall look at this indeterminancy in detail when we consider characterization in the Bible.) Meaning, perhaps for the first time in narrative literature, was conceived as a *process*, requiring continual revision—both in the ordinary sense and in the etymological sense of seeing-again—continual suspension of judgment, weighing of multiple possibilities, brooding over gaps in the information provided. As a step in the process of meaning of the Joseph story, it is exactly right that the filial betrayal of Genesis 37 and the daughter-in-law's deception of Genesis 38 should be aligned with one another through the indirection of analogy, the parallels tersely suggested but never spelled out with a thematically unambiguous closure, as they are in the Midrash.

These notes on the story of Judah and Tamar are not, of course, by any means an exhaustive analysis of the material in question, but they may illustrate the usefulness of trying to look carefully into the literary art of a biblical text. This sort of critical discussion, I would contend, far from neglecting the Bible's religious character, focuses attention on it in a more nuanced way. The implicit theology of the Hebrew Bible dictates a complex moral and psychological realism in biblical narrative because God's purposes are always entrammeled in history, dependent on the acts of individual men and women for their continuing realization. To scrutinize biblical personages as fictional characters is to see them more sharply in the multifaceted, contradictory aspects of their human individuality, which is the biblical God's chosen medium for His experiment with Israel and history. Such scrutiny, however, as I hope I have shown, cannot be based merely on an imaginative impression of the story but must be undertaken through minute critical attention to the biblical writer's articulations of narrative form.

It is a little astonishing that at this late date literary analysis of the Bible of the sort I have tried to illustrate here in this preliminary fashion is only in its infancy. By literary analysis I mean the manifold varieties of minutely discriminating attention to the artful use of language, to the shifting play of ideas, conventions, tone, sound, imagery, syntax, narrative viewpoint, compositional units, and much else; the kind of disciplined attention, in other words, which through a whole spectrum of ⟦13⟧ critical approaches has illuminated, for example, the poetry of Dante, the plays of Shakespeare, the novels of Tolstoy. The general absence of such critical discourse on the Hebrew Bible is all the more perplexing when one recalls that the masterworks of Greek and Latin antiquity have in recent decades enjoyed an abundance of astute literary analysis, so that we have learned to perceive subtleties of lyric form in Theocritus as in Marvell, complexities of narrative strategy in Homer or Virgil or in Flaubert.

In making such a sweeping negative assertion about biblical criticism, I may be suspected of polemical distortion impelled by the animus of a modern literary person against antiquarian scholarship, but I do not think this is the case. There has been, of course, a vast amount of scholarly work on the Bible over the past hundred years or more. It would be easy to make light of the endless welter of hypotheses and counter-hypotheses generated in everything from textual criticism to issues of large historical chronology; but the fact is that, however wrong-headed or extravagantly perverse many of the scholars have been, their enterprise as a whole has enormously advanced our understanding of the Bible. Virtually all this activity has been what we might call "excavative"—either literally, with the archeologist's spade and reference to its findings, or with a variety of analytic tools intended to uncover the original meanings of biblical words, the life situations in which specific texts were used, the sundry sources from which longer texts were assembled. Although much remains debatable—necessarily so, when we are separated from the origins of the texts by three millennia—the material unearthed by scholarship has clearly dispelled many confusions and obscurities.

Let me offer one brief example. The ancient city of Ugarit at the site of Ras Shamra on the Syrian coast, first excavated in 1929, has yielded a wealth of texts in a Semitic language closely cognate to biblical Hebrew, some of them strikingly parallel in style and poetic convention to familiar biblical passages. Among other things, the Ugaritic texts report in epic detail a battle between the regnant land god, Baal, and the sea god, Yamm. Suddenly, a whole spate of dimly apprehended allusions in Psalms and Job came into focus: an antecedent epic tradition had been assimilated into the recurrent imagery of God's breaking the fury of the elemental sea or shackling a primordial sea monster. Thus, when Job cries out (Job 7:12), *ha-yam ʾani ʾim tanin*, he is not asking rhetorically whether he is the sea (*yam*), but, with a pointed sardonic allusion to the Canaanite myth, he is saying: "Am I Yamm, and I the Sea Beast, that you should set a guard over me?"

Excavative scholarship, then, demonstrably has its place as a necessary [[14]] first step to the understanding of the Bible, but until the last few years there was little evidence that much more than excavation was going on, except, of course, for the perennial speculations of the theologians built on biblical texts. A systematic survey of the state of knowledge in the field, Herbert F. Hahn's *The Old Testament in Modern*

Research,[3] delineates source analysis, anthropology, sociology, comparative religion, form criticism, archeology, and theology as the relevant major areas of professional study—but nothing at all that any literary person would recognize as literary inquiry. The uneven but sometimes valuable literary commentary occasionally provided by such scholars as Umberto Cassuto and Luis Alonso-Schökel (the former writing mainly in Hebrew, the latter in Spanish and German) was apparently deemed so peripheral to the discipline as not to be worthy of categorization.

Still more revealing as a symptom of the need for a literary perspective is Otto Eissfeldt's massive *The Old Testament: An Introduction*,[4] widely regarded as one of the most authoritative general reference works in the field. Most of Eissfeldt's considerations, of course, are purely excavative, but when the nature of the biblical materials confronts him with literary categories, his apparent authoritativeness begins to look shaky. Thus, he divides biblical narrative into myths, fairy tales, sagas, legends, anecdotes, and tales, using these problematic terms with a casualness and a seeming indifference to their treatment in other disciplines that are quite dismaying. Or again, his eight-page summary of conflicting scholarly theories on biblical prosody painfully illustrates how the scholars have read biblical poetry with roughly the intellectual apparatus appropriate to the decipherment of cuneiform inscriptions, multiplying confusion by the invention of elaborate pseudo-mathematical systems of scansion or by the wholesale importation of terms and concepts from Greek prosody. The latest trend, moreover, in describing biblical prosody is a system of syllable-counting proposed by the American scholar David Noel Freedman, which reflects the most likely conception of how lines of poetry operate and also requires a dubious hypothetical reconstruction of the "original" Hebrew vowel-system. The inadequacy of all this becomes transparent when one compares it to the wonderfully incisive analysis of biblical verse as a "semantic-syntactic-accentual" rhythm by Benjamin Hrushovski—not a Bible scholar but a leading authority in the field of poetics and comparative literature—in his synoptic article on Hebrew prosody for the 1971 edition of the *Encyclopedia Judaica*. In a few packed paragraphs, Hrushovski manages to cut through generations of confusion ⟦15⟧ and to offer a general account of biblical prosody at once plausible and elegantly simple, avoiding the far-fetched structures and the strained terminology of his predecessors.

3. New York, 1954, 1st ed.; updated to 1970 through an appended bibliographical essay by Horace D. Hummel.

4. Rev. ed., trans. P. R. Ackroyd, New York, 1965.

Until the mid-1970s, the only book-length study in English by a professional Bible scholar that made a sustained effort to use a literary perspective was Edwin M. Good's *Irony in the Old Testament*.[5] One sympathizes with Good's complaints about the general indifference of his colleagues to literary issues and with the reasonableness of his declared intention merely to make a modest start in the right direction. His book succeeds in doing that, but no more than that. (Good's most recent articles, however, reflect an admirable advance in literary sophistication over this early work.) *Irony in the Old Testament* is an engaging book, and one that offers useful local perceptions, but it has no clearly defined critical method, no way of adequately discriminating the complex distinctive forms of biblical literary art. The concept of irony becomes so elastic that it threatens to lose descriptive value, though perhaps one might argue that this is a problem almost equally perceptible in the work of many literary critics who discuss irony. Elsewhere, of course, we have had sensitive appreciations of the Bible's imaginative power by literary people like Mark Van Doren, Maurice Samuel, and Mary Ellen Chase. Good's book often seems more like such an appreciation than a rigorous literary analysis, though it has the advantage of being supported by a professional knowledge of Hebrew philology, source criticism, and ancient Near Eastern history.

Over the last few years, there has been growing interest in literary approaches among the younger generations of Bible scholars—in this country, especially those associated with the new journal, *Semeia*—but, while useful explications of particular texts have begun to appear, there have been as yet no major works of criticism, and certainly no satisfying overviews of the poetics of the Hebrew Bible. As elsewhere in the academy, the manifest influence of the vogue of Structuralism on these Bible scholars has not been a very fruitful one; and one too often encounters in their work rather simple superimpositions of one or another modern literary theory on ancient texts that in fact have their own dynamics, their own distinctive conventions and characteristic techniques. One sometimes gets the impression that scholars of this sort are trying manfully, perhaps almost too conscientiously, to make a start, but that literary analysis, after all those seminars in graduate school on Sumerian law and Ugaritic cult terms, remains for them a foreign language laboriously learned, whose accents and intonations they have not yet gotten right.

Three recent first books by Bible scholars may be partly exempted, ⟦16⟧ though only partly, from these strictures. Michael Fishbane's *Text*

---

5. Philadelphia, 1965.

and Texture[6] provides a series of sensitive close readings of a variety of biblical texts, but it does not propose any general critical method; it is often a little ponderous in its formulations and in its application of Structuralist or ethnopoetic notions; and it seems finally less concerned with poetics than with homiletics. The Dutch scholar, J. P. Fokkelman, in *Narrative Art in Genesis*,[7] a book strongly influenced by the Swiss-German *Werkinterpretation* school of literary criticism (an approximate analogue to the American New Criticism), gives us some brilliant analyses of formal patterns in the Hebrew prose and of how they function thematically; but he also shows a certain tendency to interpretive overkill in his explications, at times discovering patterns where they may not be, and assuming with a noticeable degree of strain that form must always be significantly expressive. Finally, the Israeli Bible scholar, Shimon Bar-Efrat, has attempted in *The Art of the Biblical Story* the first serious book-length introduction in any language to the distinctive poetics of biblical narrative.[8] He makes a valuable beginning, offering some splendid readings of individual scenes and nicely observing certain general principles of biblical narrative; but whether out of an uncertain sense of audience or because of his own relation to the subject, rather too much space is devoted to belaboring the obvious, especially in regard to basic matters of how literary narratives work. These recent publications, then, indicate that things may be in the early stages of changing within the field of biblical studies proper, but also that the discipline still has a considerable way to go.

The one obvious reason for the absence of scholarly literary interest in the Bible for so long is that, in contrast to Greek and Latin literature, the Bible was regarded for so many centuries by both Christians and Jews as the primary, unitary source of divinely revealed truth. This belief still makes itself profoundly felt, in both reactions against and perpetuations of it. The first several waves of modern biblical criticism, beginning in the nineteenth century, were from one point of view a sustained assault on the supposedly unitary character of the Bible, an attempt to break it up into as many pieces as possible, then to link those pieces to their original life contexts, thus rescuing for history a body of texts that religious tradition has enshrined in timelessness, beyond precise historical considerations. The momentum of this enterprise continues unabated, so that it still seems to most scholars in the field much more urgent to inquire, say, how a particular psalm might have been

6. New York, 1979.
7. Assen and Amsterdam, 1975.
8. (Hebrew) Tel Aviv, 1979.

used in a hypothetically [[17]] reconstructed temple ritual than how it
works as an achieved piece of poetry. At the same time, the potent res-
idue of the older belief in the Bible as the revelation of ultimate truth
is perceptible in the tendency of scholars to ask questions about the
biblical view of man, the biblical notion of the soul, the biblical vision
of eschatology, while for the most part neglecting phenomena like
character, motive, and narrative design as unbefitting for the study of
an essentially religious document. The fact that such a substantial proportion of academic biblical studies goes on in the theological seminaries, both here and in Europe, institutionally reinforces this double-
edged pursuit of analyzed fragments and larger views, with scarcely any
literary middle ground.

The rare exceptions to this general rule have often occurred, as in
the case of the Hrushovski article, when a literary scholar with a grasp
of biblical Hebrew has addressed himself to biblical materials, approaching them from some larger literary perspective. The one celebrated instance is the immensely suggestive first chapter of Erich
Auerbach's *Mimesis*,[9] in which the antithetical modes of representing
reality in Genesis and the Odyssey are compared at length. Auerbach
must be credited with showing more clearly than anyone before him
how the cryptic conciseness of biblical narrative is a reflection of profound art, not primitiveness, but his insight is the result of penetrating
critical intuition unsupported by any real method for dealing with the
specific characteristics of biblical literary forms. His key notion of biblical narrative as a purposefully spare text "fraught with background" is
at once resoundingly right and too sweepingly general. Distinctions
have to be made for narratives by different authors, of different periods, and written to fulfill different generic or thematic requirements.
An arresting starkness of foreground, an enormous freight of background, are beautifully illustrated in the story of the binding of Isaac
which Auerbach analyzes, but those terms would have to be seriously
modified for the psychologically complex cycle of stories about David,
for the deliberately schematic folktale frame of the Book of Job, or for
a late (in part, satirical) narrative like Esther, where in fact there is a
high degree of specification in the foreground of artifacts, costume,
court customs, and the like.

Moving beyond Auerbach toward the definition of a specific poetics of biblical narrative are four important articles by Menakhem Perry
and Meir Sternberg, two young Israeli literary scholars, which appeared in the Hebrew quarterly, *Ha-Sifrut*. The first of these, "The

9. Trans. Willard Trask, Princeton, 1953.

King through Ironic Eyes,"[10] is a brilliant verse-by-verse analysis of the story of David [[18]] and Bathsheba demonstrating—to my mind, conclusively—that an elaborate system of gaps between what is told and what must be inferred has been artfully contrived to leave us with at least two conflicting, mutually complicating interpretations of the motives and states of knowledge of the principal characters. This reading, which insists on a structural analogy between the story in 2 Samuel and Henry James's deliberate ambiguity in *The Turn of the Screw*, stirred up a hornet's nest of protest after its initial publication. The most recurrent theme of the article's critics was that the biblical story was, after all, religious, moral, and didactic in intention, and so would hardly indulge in all this fancy footwork of multiple ironies that we moderns so love. (Implicit in such a contention is a rather limiting notion of what a "religious" narrative is, or of how the insight of art might relate to a religious vision. This is a central question to which we shall return.) Perry and Sternberg responded with a rejoinder of over 50,000 words in which they convincingly argued that they had not imposed modern literary criteria on the Bible but rather had meticulously observed what were the general norms of biblical narrative itself and in what significant ways the story in question diverged from those norms.[11]

More recently, Sternberg, writing alone, has provided a shrewdly perceptive analysis of the story of the rape of Dinah, concluding his discussion with a general description of the spectrum of rhetorical devices, from explicit to (predominantly) oblique, through which biblical narrative conveys moral judgments of its characters.[12] Finally, Sternberg, in still another lengthy article, has catalogued with apt illustrative explications the repertory of repetitive devices used by the biblical writers.[13] Anyone interested in the narrative art of the Bible has much to learn from all four of these articles. The rigor and subtlety of Perry and Sternberg's readings in themselves lend support to the programmatic assertion they make at the end of their response to their critics: "The perspective of literary studies is the only relevant one to the consideration of the Bible *as literature*. Any discipline, real or imagined, runs the danger of inventing groundless hypotheses and losing touch with the literary *power* of the actual biblical story."

Having been taught so much by Perry and Sternberg, I would like to express two small reservations about this approach, one perhaps just a quibble over formulation, the other an issue of method. The notion

10. *Ha-Sifrut* 1:2 (Summer 1968) 263–92.
11. *Ha-Sifrut* 2:3 (August 1970) 608–63.
12. *Ha-Sifrut* 4:2 (April 1973) 193–231.
13. *Ha-Sifrut* 25 (October 1977) 110–50.

of "the Bible as literature," though particularly contaminated in English by ⟦19⟧ its use as a rubric for superficial college courses and for dubious publishers' packages, is needlessly concessive and condescending toward literature in any language. (It would at the very least be gratuitous to speak of "Dante as literature," given the assured literary status of Dante's great poem, though the *Divine Comedy* is more explicitly theological, or "religious," than most of the Bible.) Perry and Sternberg, answering their critics, characterize the biblical story as "a junction of purposes which generate relations of complementarily and tension." "One such purpose," they go on to say, "is the 'aesthetic' aim" to which at least one of their critics makes a gesture of concession. Rather than viewing the literary character of the Bible as one of several "purposes" or "tendencies" (*megamot* in the original), I would prefer to insist on a complete interfusion of literary art with theological, moral, or historiosophical vision, the fullest perception of the latter dependent on the fullest grasp of the former. This point has been aptly made by Joel Rosenberg, a young American scholar and poet, in an admirably intelligent general rationale for a literary perspective on the Bible published in *Response*: "The Bible's value as a religious document is intimately and inseparably related to its value as literature. This proposition requires that we develop a different understanding of what literature is, one that might—and should—give us some trouble."[14] One could add that the proposition also requires, conversely, that we develop a somewhat more troublesome understanding of what a religious document might be.

One leading emphasis of the Rosenberg essay points to what I think is a methodological deficiency in Perry and Sternberg's otherwise apt analyses. They tend to write about biblical narrative as though it were a unitary production just like a modern novel that is entirely conceived and executed by a single independent writer who supervises his original work from first draft to page proofs. They turn their backs, in other words, on what historical scholarship has taught us about the specific conditions of development of the biblical text and about its frequently composite nature. Rosenberg, by contrast, is keenly aware of historical scholarship, and he sees its findings, in a way the historical scholars themselves do not, as aspects of the distinctive artistic medium of the biblical authors. Here is his comment on the Pentateuch, the set of biblical narratives most thoroughly analyzed into antecedent sources by the scholars: "It may actually improve our understanding of the

---

14. "Meanings, Morals, and Mysteries: Literary Approaches to the Torah," *Response* 9:2 (Summer 1975) 67–94.

Torah to remember that it is *quoting* documents, that there is, in other words, a purposeful documentary *montage* that must be perceived as a unity, regardless of the [[20]] number and types of smaller units that form the building blocks of its composition. Here, the weight of literary interest falls upon the activity of the *final* redactor, whose artistry requires far more careful attention that it has hitherto been accorded." The last clause if anything understates the case, since biblical critics frequently assume, out of some dim preconception about the transmission of texts in "primitive" cultures, that the redactors were in the grip of a kind of manic tribal compulsion, driven again and again to include units of traditional material that made no connective sense, for reasons they themselves could not have explained.

There is no point, to be sure, in pretending that all the contradictions among different sources in the biblical texts can be happily harmonized by the perception of some artful design. It seems reasonable enough, however, to suggest that we may still not fully understand what would have been perceived as a real contradiction by an intelligent Hebrew writer of the early Iron Age, so that apparently conflicting versions of the same event set side by side, far from troubling their original audience, may have sometimes been perfectly justified in a kind of logic we no longer apprehend. (We shall be considering this phenomenon more closely later, in chapter 7.) In any case, the validity of Rosenberg's general claim can, I think, be demonstrated by a careful reading of countless biblical narratives. Genesis 38, which we have examined in detail, is generally ascribed by scholars to the so-called Yahwistic or *J* Document after a mingling of *J* and *E* (the Elohistic Document) in the previous episode. But even if the text is really composite in origin, I think we have seen ample evidence of how brilliantly it has been woven into a complex artistic whole.

Accustomed as we are to reading narratives in which there is a much denser specification of fictional data, we have to learn, as Perry and Sternberg have shown, to attend more finely to the complex, tersely expressive details of the biblical text. (Traditional exegesis in its own way did this, but with far-reching assumptions about the text as literal revelation which most of us no longer accept.) Biblical narrative is laconic but by no means in a uniform or mechanical fashion. Why, then, does the narrator ascribe motives to or designate states of feeling in his characters in some instances, while elsewhere he chooses to remain silent on these points? Why are some actions minimally indicated, others elaborated through synonym and detail? What accounts for the drastic shifts in the timescale of narrated events? Why is actual dialogue introduced at certain junctures, and on what principle of selectivity are specific words assigned to characters? In a text so sparing in epithets and relational designations, [[21]] why are particular identifications of characters noted by the narrator at specific points in the story? Repetition is a familiar feature of the Bible, but it is in no way an automatic device: when does literal repetition occur, and what are the significant variations in repeated verbal formulas?

Finally, to understand a narrative art so bare of embellishment and explicit commentary, one must be constantly aware of two features: the repeated use of narrative analogy, through which one part of the text provides oblique commentary on another; and the richly expressive function of syntax, which often bears the kind of weight of meaning that, say, imagery does in a novel by Virginia Woolf or analysis in a novel by George Eliot. Attention to such features leads not to a more "imaginative" reading of biblical narrative but to a more precise one; and since all these features are linked to discernible details in the Hebrew text, the literary approach is actually a good deal *less* conjectural than the historical scholarship that asks of a verse whether it contains possible Akkadian loanwords, whether it reflects Sumerian kinship practices, whether it may have been corrupted by scribal error.

In any case, the fact that the text is ancient and that its characteristic narrative procedures may differ in many respects from those of modern texts should not lead us to any condescending preconception that the text is therefore bound to be crude or simple. Tzvetan Todorov has shrewdly argued that the whole notion of "primitive narrative" is a kind of mental mirage engendered by modern parochialism, for the more closely you look at a particular ancient narrative, the more you are compelled to recognize the complexity and subtlety with which it is formally organized and with which it renders its subjects, and the more you see how it is conscious of its necessary status as artful discourse. It is only by imposing a naive and unexamined aesthetic of their own, Todorov proposes, that modern scholars are able to declare so confidently that certain parts of the ancient text could not belong with others: the supposedly primitive narrative is subjected by scholars to tacit laws like the law of stylistic unity, of noncontradiction, of nondigression, of nonrepetition, and by these dim but purportedly universal lights is found to be composite, deficient, or incoherent. (If just these four laws were applied respectively to *Ulysses*, *The Sound and the Fury*, *Tristram Shandy*, and *Jealousy*, each of those novels would have to be relegated to the dustbin of shoddily "redacted" literary scraps.) Attention to the ancient narrative's consciousness of its own operations, Todorov proposes, will reveal how irrelevant these complacently assumed criteria generally are.[15] Todorov bases his argument on examples from the *Odyssey*; but his questioning the existence of primitive [22] narrative could be equally well supported by a consideration of the Hebrew Bible.

What we need to understand better is that the religious vision of the Bible is given depth and subtlety precisely by being conveyed through the most sophisticated resources of prose fiction. In the example we have considered, Judah and Jacob-Israel are not simply eponymic counters in an etiological tale (this is the flattening effect of some historical scholarship) but are individual characters surrounded by multiple ironies, artfully etched in their imperfections as well as in their strengths. A histrionic Jacob blinded by excessive love and perhaps loving the excess; an impetuous, sometimes callous Judah, who is yet capable of candor when confronted with hard facts; a fiercely resolved, steel-nerved Tamar—all such subtly indicated achievements of fictional characterization suggest the endlessly complicated ramifications and contradictions of a principle of divine election intervening in the accepted orders of society and nature. The biblical tale, through the most rigorous economy of means, leads us again and again to ponder complexities of motive and ambiguities of character because these are essential aspects of its vision of man, created by God, enjoying or suffering all the consequences of human freedom. Different considerations would naturally have to be explored for biblical poetry. Almost the whole range of biblical narrative, however, embodies the basic perception that man must live before God, in the transforming medium of time, incessantly and perplexingly in relation with others; and a literary perspective on the operations of narrative may help us more than any other to see how this perception was translated into stories that have such a powerful, enduring hold on the imagination.

15. *The Poetics of Prose*, trans. Richard Howard (Ithaca, New York, 1977) 53–65.

Some Observations on the Analysis of Structure in Biblical Narrative

SHIMON BAR-EFRAT

⟦154⟧ In recent years an increasing number of studies has been published devoted to the investigation of the literary features of biblical narratives.[1] Whereas in the past biblical scholars paid attention primarily to

Reprinted with permission from *Vetus Testamentum* 30 (1980) 154–73.

1. Among the early advocates and practitioners of this line of investigation the following deserve to be mentioned above all: M. Buber, "Leitwortstil in der Erzählung des Pentateuchs," M. Buber and F. Rosenzweig, *Die Schrift und ihre Verdeutschung* (Berlin, 1936) 211–38; E. Auerbach, *Mimesis: Dargestellte Wirklichkeit in der abendländischen Literatur* (Bern, 1946), chap. 1: Die Narbe des Odysseus, 7–30; J. Muilenburg, "A Study in Hebrew Rhetoric: Repetition and Style," *Supp. to VT* 1 (1953) 97–111; E. Galbiati, *La struttura letteraria dell'Esodo* (Alba, 1956); L. Alonso-Schökel, "Erzählkunst im Buche der Richter," *Bib.* 42 (1961) 143–72; M. Weiss, "Einiges über die Bauformen des Erzählens in der Bibel," *VT* 13 (1963) 456–75, and "Weiteres über die Bauformen des Erzählens in der Bibel," *Bib.* 46 (1965) 181–206. Some of the more recent contributions are: L. Krinetzki, "Ein Beitrag zur Stilanalyse der Goliathperikope (1 Sam 17,1–18,5)," *Bib.* 54 (1973) 187–236; J. L. Crenshaw, "The Samson Saga: Filial Devotion or Erotic Attachment?" *ZAW* 86 (1974) 470–504; M. Fishbane, "Composition and Structure in the Jacob Cycle," *JJS* 27 (1975) 15–38; J. P. Fokkelman, *Narrative Art in Genesis: Specimens of Structural and Stylistic Analysis* (Assen-Amsterdam, 1975); R. Alter, "A Literary Approach to the Bible," *Commentary* 60 (1975) 70–77, and "Biblical Narrative," *Commentary* 61 (1976) 61–67; J. Magonet, *Form and Meaning: Studies in Literary Techniques in the Book of Jonah* (Bern-Frankfurt, 1976); J. T. Walsh, "Genesis 2:4b–3:24: A Synchronic Approach," *JBL* 96 (1977) 161–77; J. Licht, *Storytelling in the Bible* (Jerusalem, 1978). See also the publications in *Semeia* and the survey by J. D. Crossan, "Waking the Bible (Biblical Hermeneutic and Literary Imagination)," *Int.* 32 (1978) 269–85.

genetic questions, with a view to restoring the "original," "authentic" form of the narratives by peeling off additions and disposing of alterations, lately there has been evidence of a growing tendency to deal with the biblical narrative in its present shape. Needless to say, this new literary approach is not to be confused with the form-critical method, which occupies itself mainly with questions of genre, formulas and other more or less fixed forms, and with their *Sitz im Leben.*[2] The present literary method is concerned mainly with the ⟦155⟧ individual narratives. Its aim is to bring to light their artistic and rhetorical characteristics, their inner organization, their stylistic and structural features. This preoccupation with the literary rather than with the historical aspects of the biblical narrative—or to put it differently, with its synchronic rather than with its diachronic facets—is no doubt influenced by similar trends in other realms of scholarly endeavour. Structuralism has secured a position of considerable importance in the sciences as well as in the humanities, and conspicuously so in anthropology, in linguistics and in literary criticism.[3] Structuralism is itself only one manifestation of the current attempt to look at things as they are, to investigate the arrangement of the constituent parts rather than to inquire how they originated and how they developed.[4]

It appears, however, that there is some lack of clarity with regard to the method of analysing structure. When examining specimens of structural analysis of biblical narratives one sometimes senses a lack of awareness of the exact nature of the structural elements employed. In a certain number of cases the analysis evinces an indiscriminate use of heterogeneous elements, which is of course detrimental to the quality of the structural analysis and may even impair its validity. Therefore it might be useful to clarify the subject to some extent by surveying the chief varieties and constituents of narrative structure and illustrating them by reference to biblical narratives.

Structure can be defined as the network of relations among the parts of an object or a unit. This definition at once raises the question what is to be considered a unit in the area of biblical narrative. Should biblical scholars focus their attention on the smallest literary units or

---

2. Both methods are represented in the work of Gunkel; his successors, however, have applied themselves almost exclusively to form-criticism.

3. Cf. J. Culler, *Structuralist Poetics: Structuralism, Linguistics and the Study of Literature* (Ithaca, N. Y. and London, 1975); J. Piaget, *Le structuralisme* (Paris, 1968); R. Scholes, *Structuralism in Literature: An Introduction* (New Haven, 1974).

4. Already in 1925 J. L. Palache expressed the opinion with regard to the biblical narrative that its being rather than its becoming should be studied. See his *Het karakter van het Oud-Testamentische verhaal* (Amsterdam, 1925) 7–8.

should the literary work as a whole be the object of investigation? The correct reply to this question seems to be that the limits of the literary unit cannot be fixed a priori, but that they are dynamic and vary according to the kind of questions the literary critic desires to pose,[5] provided of course that the delimiting of the unit has its justification in the text.

[[156]] In the field of biblical narrative particularly it seems to be impossible to define the boundaries of the literary unit rigidly. In the Bible narratives which are more or less complete in themselves link up with one another so as to create larger literary units. In other words, narratives which on the one hand can be considered as self-contained units may be regarded on the other hand as parts of larger wholes. Those larger units in their turn become components of whole biblical books, whose books again being incorporated into comprehensive literary works. Structure can be discerned and may legitimately be studied in small sections as well as in comprehensive units—in a short segment such as Job 1:13–19 or in a complete composition such as the Book of Ruth.

In Job 1:13–19 it is shown how four messengers come to Job one after another, each one informing him of a new catastrophe that had befallen him. The fourfold structure of this passage is made prominent by means of recurrent words and phrases, e.g. "and I only have escaped alone to tell you," "this one was yet speaking when another came." Also, the first and third disasters are caused by men (Sheba and the Kasdim respectively), whereas the second and the fourth disasters are caused by nature (fire from heaven, which is to be understood as lightning, and a strong wind). The calamities are arranged in such order that they reach their climax in the fourth and last one, which is again emphasized by a recurrent word: in all four calamities "the young men" (*hann^e^{c}ārīm*) are killed, but in the first three "the young men" are Job's servants, whereas in the fourth they are his children.

The Book of Ruth also has a clear structure, though it is less manifest. In the middle of the book (chapters 2 and 3) we find the two central scenes depicting the encounters between Boaz and Ruth in the field (in the first of these scenes there appear in succession Boaz with his servant, Boaz with Ruth, and again Boaz with his servants). These two large scenes are each preceded and followed by two brief scenes showing Ruth and Naomi at their home. In the first chapter of the book of Ruth is portrayed by contrasting her with Orpah, and correspondingly in the

---

5. Cf. M. Sternberg, "What Is Exposition?" in J. Halperin (ed.), *The Theory of the Novel: New Essays* (New York, 1974) 30.

last chapter Boaz is portrayed by contrasting him with the redeemer. Subsequently in both the first and the last chapter we find the women of Bethlehem in the role of a chorus commenting on Naomi's condition, which is most unhappy in the first chapter and most happy in the last one. The book opens with information about people who died before the beginning of the main action and it ends ⟦157⟧ with a list of the generations that were born after the conclusion of the main action. Thus we obtain the following scheme of the structure of the book:

1   People who
    died before
    main action
                          Ruth ↔ Orpah
                          Women of Bethlehem
2   Naomi-Ruth
                                                Boaz-servant
                                                                Boaz-Ruth
                                                Boaz-servants
                                            Naomi-Ruth
3   Naomi-Ruth
                                                                Boaz-Ruth
                                            Naomi-Ruth
4   *Boaz ↔ redeemer*
                          Women of Bethlehem
    People who
    were born after
    main action

Elements of Structure

It is appropriate now to consider the various elements upon which structural analysis may be based. With regard to these elements four different levels should be distinguished: (1) the verbal level; (2) the level of narrative technique; (3) the level of the narrative world; (4) the level of the conceptual content.

The Verbal Level

The analysis of structure on this level is based on words and phrases. For example, the Creation account in the first chapter of Genesis has a very distinct structure, which even the most superficial reader cannot fail to notice. This structure, which divides the whole account into seven well-defined sections, is clearly marked by the recurrent phrase: "And it was evening and it was morning, the nth day." In addition we find repetition of phrases such as: "And God said, Let . . . ," "and God saw that it was good," which also contributes to the manifestation of the structure. But the structure is brought to light in this case not only by repetition, but also by ordered variation: "the *first* day," "the *second* day," "the *third* day," etc.

Another instance is furnished by the narrative of Samson and Delilah (Judg 16:4–31). Here we encounter the recurrent phrases: [[158]] "Tell me please wherein your great strength lies and wherewith you may be bound"; "then I shall be weak and be as another man"; "Philistines upon you, Samson!" The repetition of these phrases brings out the structure of the narrative: three times Delilah questions Samson about the secret of his strength; three times he gives a false reply, but the fourth time he yields to her entreaties and tells her the truth and he is consequently overpowered by the Philistines.

➤ Stylistic features such as metaphors, similes, unusual grammatical and syntactical constructions and the like also belong to the verbal level.

➤ A distinction should be made, however, between the analysis of structure on the verbal level and the analysis of texture. Texture is structure looked at through a magnifying glass. It consists of the small-scale relations among the subordinate and generally proximate parts of the narrative, whereas structure proper consists of the relatively large-scale relations among the main and possibly distant parts.[6] Structural analysis, even if it is based on words or phrases, does not usually concern itself with texture (the investigation of texture is carried out by means of stylistic analysis).

The Level of Narrative Technique

➤ The analysis of structure on this level is based on variations in narrative method, such as narrator's account as opposed to character's speech (dialogue), scenic presentation versus summary, narration as against description, explanation, comment, etc. For example, the narrative about David and Achish at Aphek (1 Samuel 29) is constructed in the following manner: first, the narrator relates that the Philistines gathered their armies together to Aphek, not far from the Israelite encampment in Jezreel, and that David and his men passed on with Achish in the rear of the lords of the Philistines. Following that, there are two rather elaborate dialogues, one between the commanders of the Philistines and Achish, and the other between Achish and David; both

6. Cf. M. C. Beardsley, *Aesthetics—Problems in the Philosophy of Criticism* (New York, 1958) 168–69, 221.

dialogues are concerned with the question of David's loyalty to the Philistines and his presence in their camp. The narrative concludes with the narrator's statement that David departed early in the morning to return to the land of the Philistines, whereas the Philistines went up to Jezreel. Thus the bulk of the narrative is made up of two dialogues of considerable length, which are framed by two short communications by the narrator. ⟦159⟧

Narrator's account	(verses 1–2)
Dialogue	(verses 3–5)
Dialogue	(verses 6–10)
Narrator's account	(verse 11)

The story of Samuel's birth (1 Sam 1:1–2:11) is composed mainly of three scenes. The first and largest scene takes place at the House of God in Shiloh and it shows Hannah before the birth of her son. The second scene takes place at Elkanah's home in Ramathaim and it shows Hannah after the birth of Samuel. The third scene takes place again at the House of God in Shiloh and it shows Hannah presenting her son at the sanctuary. These three scenes are preceded, joined and concluded by brief summaries. The first summary, by way of introduction, supplies the necessary background information about the participating characters and tells of their custom to go up to Shiloh every year. The second summary reports that Elkanah and his family returned to their home at Ramathaim, where Hannah conceived and gave birth to Samuel. The third summary relates that Hannah gave suck to her son until she weaned him and the last summary informs us that Elkanah went to his house, while Samuel remained at Shiloh.

Thus we find that the narrative is organized in the following way:

Summary	(1:1–3)
Scene	(verses 4–18)
Summary	(verses 19–20)
Scene	(verses 21–23a)
Summary	(verse 23b)
Scene	(1:24–2:10)
Summary	(verse 11)

The alternation of scenic presentation and summary account is closely related to the handling of time. As is well known the author can vary the relations between narrated and narration time freely according to his wish. In scenic presentation narrated time flows rather slowly, whereas in summary it runs quickly, relative to narration time. Thus we find in the story of David and Bathsheba (2 Samuel 11) that the opening and concluding parts of the narrative, which are concerned with Bath-sheba—David seeing her from his roof and lying with her and in the end bringing her to his house and making her his wife—are told in such a manner as to make narrated time flow very fast. On the other hand, the two sections in the middle of the narrative, which are concerned with Uriah—David's attempts to make him go down to his house and lie with his wife and the messenger's report of Uriah's death—contain a large amount of direct speech, with the [[160]] result that time passes relatively slowly. Only the factual account by the narrator of Uriah's death itself is related rather quickly. So in this case the narrative displays the following construction in terms of time-velocity:

Quick:		Bathsheba	(verses 2–5)
	Slow:	Uriah	(verses 6–15)
Quick:		Uriah	(verses 16–17)
	Slow:	Uriah	(verses 18–25)
Quick:		Bathsheba	(verses 26–27)

The molding of time in narrative pertains not only to its (relative) rate of progress, but also to its order. The author can begin his story at the beginning, in the middle or at the end; he can introduce flash-backs, anticipations, etc. In biblical narrative events are arranged as a rule in successive order and time flows in one direction only. However, in a number of cases flashbacks can be found.

For example, the narrative dealing with the armed conflict be-tween David and the Amalekites (1 Samuel 30) begins with a flashback by the narrator relating what had happened at Ziklag before David re-turned there from Aphek: "And it came to pass when David and his men came to Ziklag on the third day, the Amalekites had made a raid upon the Negeb and upon Ziklag and smitten Ziklag and burned it with fire. And had taken captive the women that were in it; small or great, they killed no one, but carried them off and went their way" (verses 1–2).

As against this reversal to the past at the beginning of the narra-tive, there is a leap into the future at the end of the narrative: "And it was so from that day forward, he made it a statute and an ordinance for Israel to this day" (verse 25).

In the narrative of David and Abigail (1 Samuel 25) several brief flashbacks are to be found, which all occur at central points and func-tion as markers of the structure. These flashbacks are clearly indicated by the use of the *qāṭal* form of the verb denoting the past perfect tense instead of the usual *wayyiqṭol* form. The narrative, which relates of Abigail's successful attempt to deter David from killing Nabal and destroying everything belonging to him, focuses first on David, then on Abigail, then on the encounter between the two. The flashbacks are all located at the points of transition.

The first section of the narrative dealing with David ends with the statement that David set out with four hundred men, all girded with swords, towards Nabal (verse 13). The second section telling of ⟦161⟧ Abigail begins with a flashback: "Now Abigail, Nabal's wife, had been told by one of the servants, 'Behold, David sent messengers from the wilderness to salute our master ... '" (verse 14). This section concludes as follows: "Now as she was riding on the ass and coming down under the cover of the mountains, behold, David and his men coming down toward her, and she met them" (verse 20). At this point—the beginning of the third section—when the meeting between the two chief characters is about to materialize, we are again carried back in time: "And David had said, 'Surely in vain have I guarded all that belongs to this one in the wilderness ... '" (verse 21).[7] At the end of the third section, just as the meeting between David and Abigail is brought to an end and she is about to return to Nabal, another flashback occurs: "And to her he had said, 'Go up in peace to your house, see I have listened to your voice and I have lifted up your countenance'" (verse 35). In view of the foregoing it hardly comes as a surprise to find flashbacks at the end of the last section and the conclusion of the narrative as a whole: "And Ahinoam had been taken by David from Jezreel, and so both of them became his wives. But Saul had given Michal his daughter, David's wife, to Palti the son of Laish, who was of Gallim" (verses 43–44).

The Level of the Narrative World

The analysis of structure on this level is based on the narrative content as created by the language and the techniques. The two chief components of narrative content are characters and events (other components are setting, clothes, arms and similar items).

Characters.   Several aspects of the characters, such as their identity, their nature and their function in the story, may serve as a basis for structural analysis of the narrative.

---

7. Cf. 1 Sam 9:14ff., where the narrator also shifts the time back to the past at the very moment when the encounter between Saul and Samuel is to take place: "So they went up to the city and as they were entering the city, behold, Samuel coming out toward them, to go up to the high place. And God had revealed to Samuel one day before the coming of Saul ... " In both instances the flashback occurs at the exact point of time when Abigail/Saul sees David/Samuel drawing near, that is when they are already very close, but before they actually meet.

With regard to structure based upon the identity of the characters it is instructive to re-examine the narrative of Samuel's birth (1 Sam 1:1–2:11) referred to above. In the first scene of that narrative Elkanah ⟦162⟧ talks to Hannah and afterwards Eli talks to Hannah, following her prayer to God. In the second and third scenes Hannah talks to Elkanah and subsequently she talks to Eli, this time preceding her prayer to God. This gives us the following scheme:

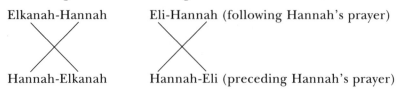

Elkanah-Hannah   Eli-Hannah (following Hannah's prayer)

Hannah-Elkanah   Hannah-Eli (preceding Hannah's prayer)

A striking illustration of structure based upon identity of characters is provided by the narrative of Amnon and Tamar (2 Samuel 13). This narrative is constructed in the manner of a chain: in each link composing the chain two characters are to be found. The narrative begins with an opening section introducing the main participating characters. Afterwards, in the first link of the story proper, Jonadab and Amnon appear, in the second link Amnon and David, in the third David and Tamar, in the fourth Tamar and Amnon, in the fifth Amnon and the servant, in the sixth the servant and Tamar and in the seventh Tamar and Absalom. Following the seventh link there is a short concluding section.

The joining together of the links is effected by means of the second character in each link, who is invariably the first character in the next link:

Jonadab-Amnon (verses 3–5)
     Amnon-David (verse 6)
         David-Tamar (verse 7)
             Tamar-Amnon (verses 8–16)
                 Amnon-servant (verse 17)
                     servant-Tamar (verse 18)
                         Tamar-Absalom (verses 19–20)

It should be observed that Amnon is found in the first two links, whereas Tamar is found in the last two. Moreover, Tamar is also found in the third link from the beginning and Amnon in the third link from the end. In the middle link, which is much larger in size than any of the other ones (9 verses), Amnon and Tamar meet and here the climax of the story is reached.

It is noteworthy too that Amnon is present in links 1 and 2, Tamar in links 3 and 4, Amnon in links 4 and 5 and Tamar again in links 6 and 7. An additional contribution to the symmetry of the structure is achieved by means of the fact that Jonadab, who is close to Amnon 〚163〛 and his ally, is mentioned in the first link, whereas Absalom, who is close to Tamar and her ally, is mentioned in the last link. However, this last symmetry no longer belongs to the aspect of the identity of the characters, but to the aspect of their function in the story.

The aspect of the function of the characters includes distinctions such as hero and opponent, assistants to either side, instigators, obstacles, pursuer and pursued, etc. The aspect of the nature of the characters comprises characteristics such as virtuous versus vicious, hospitable versus inhospitable, loyal versus disloyal, fruitful versus barren. Analysis of structure may be based on any of these matters.

Events. The events of the story in their mutual relationships make up the plot. The plot always has a structure. Contrary to real life no accidental and irrelevant facts are included and the incidents are connected with each other both temporally and causally. Often when narrative structure is referred to generally, what is meant in fact is structure of the plot.

Most narratives in the Bible have single plots, but some have complex ones. For instance, in the Book of Esther, the main plot deals with Haman's design to exterminate all the Jews in the empire and with the steps taken by Mordecai and Esther to counteract Haman's intention. But besides the main plot a secondary, independent plot can be detected. The second plot is concerned with the conspiracy of the two chamberlains, Bigthan and Teresh, who plan to murder the king. They are discovered by Mordecai, who much later is rewarded for his saving of the king's life. The secondary plot underlines and reinforces the primary one: both culminate in Mordecai's victory over Haman.

Although every plot has a structure, it is not always necessary or indeed fruitful, to describe its structure. In practice the description of plot structure often boils down simply to paraphrasing. The description of plot structure is as a rule of interest only if it serves a special purpose such as comparing various narratives or if it reveals unusual and outstanding patterns.

Plot structures are usually compared in order to establish similarity. For instance, it has been shown that a number of prophetic miracle stories have a common plot structure: A brings his problem to the attention of B, who has the power to provide miraculous help; B 〚164〛

responds by taking action on the problem; as a result of a miracle the problem is removed.[8]

A common plot structure can be found also in the three narratives in Genesis telling of a patriarch who begs his wife to pass herself off as his sister in order to save him from being killed by the ruler of a foreign country; the ruler, when the truth is revealed to him, reprimands the patriarch, but does not harm him; eventually the patriarch acquires great wealth in the foreign country.[9]

In these examples it is perhaps not too surprising to find similar structures, since the narratives under consideration are also more or less similar in subject-matter. Of course, resemblance in subject-matter does not necessarily entail resemblance in structure, but such resemblance would not come quite unexpectedly,[10] and in any case it would be much more remarkable to detect similar plot structures in narratives that differ from each other completely in respect of their subject-matter. This is the case, for example, in the narrative of Isaac's blessing (Genesis 27), the narrative of the Gibeonites (Joshua 9) and the narrative of the wise woman from Tekoah (2 Samuel 14). In spite of the great divergence in subject-matter, these narratives display a common plot structure, which can be summarized as follows: A (Jacob, the Gibeonite envoys, the Tekoite woman) is sent by B (Rebekah, the Gibeonite people, Joab) to achieve some good, greatly valued and not material (a blessing, a covenant, a remission of punishment) from C (Isaac, Joshua, David). Since it is impossible for A to attain his object in a straightforward manner, he is directed by B to have recourse to deceitful means. A disguises himself, appears before C in a false role and in the ensuing conversation gives him wrong information about himself. In this way he succeeds in gaining his end. C soon discovers the fraud, but nevertheless he cannot annul A's achievement (he only modifies it to a certain extent).

It should be emphasized at this point that in comparing narratives it is essential not to describe the plots in too abstract and general [[165]] terms, because obviously the more abstract and general the formulations, the greater the number of narratives that will fit the given plot

---

8. The stories referred to are to be found in Exod 15:22–27, 17:1–7; 1 Kgs 17:17–24 = 2 Kgs 4:18–37; 2 Kgs 2:19–22, 4:1–7, 4:38–41, 6:1–7. Cf. R. C. Culley, *Studies in the Structure of Hebrew Narrative* (Philadelphia-Missoula, 1976) 72–96.

9. Gen 12:10–20, 20:1–18, 26:1–14. Cf. R. C. Culley, *Studies*, 33–41.

10. The similarity might easily be explained as being due to the narratives being variant versions of the same story (as in the case of the narratives about the patriarch's wife) or to their belonging to the same genre (as in the case of the prophetic miracle stories).

outline. Especially problematical in this respect are those plot abstracts which state the content or development in terms of broad themes or concepts, like broken relationship–restored relationship, disobedience–obedience, unnatural behaviour–natural behaviour. Also, by means of symbolic or metaphorical interpretation and by delving into the "deep" structure (as opposed to the surface structure)[11] of the plot it is relatively easy to discover similarities among plot structures. In other words, it is meaningful to point out common plot structures only if the plots are delineated in a rather specific and detailed manner.[12]

In addition to the structure consisting of a factual outline of the plot development narratives possess what may be designated as dramatic structure. Dramatic structure involves the building up and relaxation of tension. Many biblical narratives are organized in this respect so as to exhibit the classical pyramid pattern. From a peaceful initial situation the action rises towards the climax where the decisive step determining the outcome of the conflict is taken, and from there it drops again to a more or less tranquil situation at the end. This, for instance, is the structural pattern of the narrative of Abraham's sacrifice (Genesis 22) and of the Book of Esther.

These two stories also display the device of reversal, which is a central feature in the plot structure of many biblical narratives. At the crucial point of the story of Abraham's sacrifice, at the very moment when Abraham is about to reach out his knife to slaughter his son, the action veers round to its opposite. Unexpectedly an angel of [166] God appears and prevents Abraham from carrying out his intention, making it known to him that God desires only the willingness to sacrifice his son and not the sacrifice itself. Likewise in the story of Esther a reversal in the development of the plot is effected at the crucial point, when during the second banquet the King is suddenly filled with anger at his favorite

11. I refer to analyses such as those carried out by E. Leach in his *Genesis as Myth and Other Essays* (London, 1969). Although both belong to the structuralist school there is a fundamental difference between the work of Leach and that of R. Barthes in favour of the latter. Cf. his "La lutte avec l'ange: Analyse textuelle de Genèse 32.23–33," R. Barthes et al., *Analyse structurale et exégèse biblique: Essais d'interprétation* (Neuchâtel, 1972) 27–39.

12. For instance, the following outline set down by Culley as shared by six "deception" stories or episodes seems too general (it is certainly applicable to much more than six stories or episodes): (1) an opening situation presenting the necessity for action by a person or a group; (2) a response involving a deception by that person or group; (3) the outcome of the action taken in response, reflecting an improvement on the opening situation for the person or group. The proposed outline reduces the stories to three sequences only, two of which (the first and the last) are stated in rather indefinite terms. Cf. R. C. Culley, "Structural Analysis: Is It Done with Mirrors?" *Int.* 28 (1974) 165–81, especially pp. 173–74.

Haman and gives orders to hang him on the very gallows which Haman
had prepared for Mordecai.

A most conspicuous example of reversal in the direction of the
plot development is to be found in the narrative dealing with Jacob's
return after his twenty years of service with Laban (Genesis 32–33).
The story stresses in various ways that Jacob is very much afraid at the
prospect of meeting his brother Esau, whom he had infuriated many
years earlier by cheating him out of the blessing due to him as firstborn. Now upon hearing that Esau has set out towards him with four
hundred men, Jacob is panic-stricken. He takes several measures to
decrease the impact of the impending blow and to abate Esau's anger;
he divides all his belongings and all his family into two camps, he
sends many herds one after another as presents to Esau and he offers
fervent prayer to God. On the last night before the fateful encounter
Jacob fights with a mysterious "man," who in a sense may be taken to
stand for Esau,[13] and compels him to give him his blessing. In the
morning he approaches his brother with the greatest apprehension
manifested by his bowing down to the ground seven times. Now Esau
runs to meet him, but contrary to expectations, Esau embraces and
kisses his brother. There is no longer any rancour in Esau's heart and
the brothers are reconciled.

A number of biblical narratives reveal a somewhat different plot
structure. Instead of rising to the climax and afterwards descending
quickly to the tranquil end, they ascend to the climax, descend, but
then they rise again to a second climactic point, and only afterwards
do they finally fall off to the equilibrium of the end.

The narratives of Isaac's blessing (Genesis 27) and of Job's trial
(Job 1–2, 42) provides examples of this type of pattern. The narrative
of Isaac's blessing reaches its climax when Jacob comes very close to
the suspicious Isaac and is subjected to bodily examination. A resting
point is reached when Isaac, apparently satisfied, gives Jacob his blessing. But when immediately after Jacob's departure Esau enters ⟦167⟧
his father's tent the story flares up again. A new resting point is
reached only after Jacob departs from his home and a physical distance is created between the hostile brothers.

The narrative of Job's trial reaches its first climax when he is informed, in close succession, of the four catastrophes that have befallen
him. The demonstration of Job's steadfastness and firm maintenance
of faith and integrity at the end of the first chapter could bring the

---

13. Cf. F. Rosenzweig, "Das Formgeheimnis der biblischen Erzälungen," M. Buber
and F. Rosenzweig, *Die Schrift und ihre Verdeutschung* (Berlin, 1936) 252–53.

story to an end. But the situation is stirred up again and the story reaches a new climax when Job meets with a new disaster which is even harder to bear. Again Job is unswerving in his belief and conduct, but tranquility is not reached until everything is restored to its original state and Job receives his deserved reward in the last chapter of the book.

Along with dramatic structure mention should be made of spatial and temporal structure of the plot.

The narrative of Job's trial, to which reference has just been made, provides a very clear example of spatial structure. After the introduction, telling of Job and his piety, the action takes place alternately in heaven, on earth, in heaven and on earth again. The scenes in heaven are very similar to each other, and so are the scenes on earth. In this way a very pronounced symmetry is achieved.

In numerous biblical narratives the scene of action is not confined to one single place, but it shifts from one region to another, thus creating a distinct structure. For instance, in the story of the suing for Rebekah (Genesis 24) the introductory and concluding scenes are located in and near Abraham's dwelling place in Canaan, whereas the two main scenes in the middle of the narrative are situated near and in the city of Nahor in Mesopotamia (at the well and in the house of Bethel respectively).

Canaan		(verses 1–10)
	Mesopotamia	(verses 11–31)
	Mesopotamia	(verses 32–61)
Canaan		(verses 62–67)

The temporal structure of the plot is established by means of dates and other indications of time, stating when the action took place and how long it lasted. Those indications of time are not at all uncommon in biblical narrative. They are especially abundant in the narrative of Noah and the Flood (Genesis 6–8).[14]

⟦168⟧ The dates mentioned in this narrative refer for the most part to the 600th year of Noah. The flood began on the seventeenth day of the second month (7:11) and the earth became completely dry on the twenty-seventh day of the second month one year later (8:14). That means that altogether the flood lasted 365 days, or one solar year. This period is divided in the following way. On the seventeenth day of

---

14. Cf. U. Cassuto, *A Commentary on the Book of Genesis* II (Jerusalem, 1964) 43–45; G. J. Wenham, "The Coherence of the Flood narrative," *VT* 28 (1978) 336–48, especially p. 343.

the second month the flood commenced (7:11). On the seventeenth
day of the seventh month, that is exactly five months later, the ark
rested on the mountains of Ararat (8:4). The tops of the mountains
were seen on the first day of the tenth month (8:5). On the first day of
the first month (in the 601st year), i.e. exactly three months later, the
waters had dried from the ground (8:13).

In addition to dates, periods of time are mentioned in the Flood
narrative. The flood began seven days after God had commanded
Noah to enter the ark with his family and all the animals (7:10). The
rain was upon the earth for forty days (7:12, 17). The waters prevailed
for 150 days (7:24, 8:3). Noah opened the window of the ark forty days
after the tops of the mountains had become visible (8:6). Noah waited
seven days (twice) until he sent the dove out again (8:10, 12). This gives
us the following scheme of periods of time:

7 days
     40 days
          150 days
     40 days
7 days

Another example of temporal structure can be found in the Book of
Judges, where periods of distress and warfare are separated by spells of
peace and quiet, lasting forty years each (once eighty years) (Judg 3:11,
30, 31; 8:28).[15]

The Level of Conceptual Content

On this level the analysis of structure is based on the themes of the narrative units or the ideas contained therein. Themes and ideas are closely
related. But themes are usually formulated in the form of short phrases,
ideas in the form of complete sentences. Themes define the central
issue of the narrative. They are embodied in the various narrative elements discussed before and serve as their focal point and as a unifying
and integrating principle. Ideas are the meanings and ⟦169⟧ lessons
contained in the narratives, their message or "philosophy." In the majority of cases neither themes nor ideas are stated explicitly. They are
implied in the narrative and have to be abstracted by interpretation.

A basic theme to be discerned in 1 Samuel and functioning as a cor-
nerstone of its structure is the transference of leadership—from Eli to
Samuel, from Samuel to Saul and from Saul to David. The process is carried out smoothly and harmoniously in the case of Eli; it is accompanied

15. Cf. also Judg 15:20, 16:31; 1 Sam 4:18; 1 Kgs 2:11.

by discord and conflict in the case of Samuel; and it leads to outbreaks of violence and undisguised hostility in the case of Saul. This theme is a determining factor in the overall composition of the book. The book can be divided roughly into three parts. The first quarter (chapters 1–7) deals with Eli and Samuel, the second quarter (chapters 8–15) with Samuel and Saul, while the third and fourth quarters of the book (chapters 16–31) are devoted to Saul and David. The theme mentioned is accompanied of course by other themes.

Another example can be found in the narratives of David, Bathsheba and Uriah (2 Samuel 11), Amnon and Tamar (2 Samuel 13), Absalom's rebellion (2 Samuel 15–19) and Adonijah's attempt at the throne (1 Kings 1–2). These four narratives are brought into close relationship by means of a thematic structure which is shared by all of them. Just as in the case of David sexual offence is followed by murder, so in the case of Amnon, Absalom and to a certain extent Adonijah too, sexual offense is followed by murder:

David × Bathsheba	→ killing of Uriah
Amnon × Tamar	→ killing of Amnon
Absalom × David's concubines	→ killing of Absalom
(Adonijah × Abishag)	→ killing of Adonijah[16]

A word of warning should be uttered here. Since themes or ideas are not stated overtly, but have to be extracted by means of interpretation, one should exercise a good deal of self-restraint and self-criticism before proceeding to the delineation of thematic or ideational structures. Even when dealing with phenomena that are objectively present in the narrative text a certain amount of subjectivity is involved when pointing out structures. This is due to the necessity to single out among a multitude of diverse phenomena those elements ⟦170⟧ with which a significant structure can be realized. The subjective factor increases considerably when the ingredients of the structure are themselves the product of the rather subjective process of interpretation. So in order to steer clear of undue arbitrariness themes and ideas should be borne out by the facts of the narrative as clearly and unambiguously as possible. Also, vague and general formulations should be avoided.

Patterns of Structure

Most of the examples offered above display special structural patterns characterized by symmetry. The main ones to be distinguished are the

---

16. Cf. J. Blenkinsopp, "Theme and Motif in the Succession History (2 Sam. xi 2ff.) and the Jahwist corpus," *Supp. to VT* 15 (1966) 47–57, especially pp. 47f.

parallel pattern (similar or antithetical), the ring pattern, the chiastic
pattern and the concentric pattern. These patterns are created by repetition of certain elements of the structure:

> A A'   (parallel pattern)
> A X A'   (ring pattern)
> A B B' A'   (chiastic pattern)
> A B X B' A'   (concentric pattern)

The repeated elements may belong to any of the structural levels discussed above—the verbal level, the level of narrative technique, the level
of the narrative world or the level of conceptual content. It is not to be
concluded, of course, that all biblical narratives are characterized by
neat symmetrical patterns or that the symmetry in those narratives that
do possess such patterns is always perfect. On the contrary, one should
beware of detecting symmetrical arrangements in every narrative unit,
large or small. It is easy to exaggerate this practice, as can be observed
in the work of some authors, who display an excessive tendency to discover chiastic structures. However, it cannot be denied that a number of
narrative units in the Bible do feature remarkable structural patterns. As
an additional example the structural analysis of a short narrative unit,
viz. the speech of Hushai (2 Sam 17:8–13), will be presented here.

> A   You *know your father* and his men, that they are *powerful* and
>   embittered,
> B   *Like a bear* robbed of her cubs in the field.
> C   And your father is skilled in war and he will not pass the
>   night with *the people.*
> X   Behold, even now he is hidden in one of the pits or IN ONE OF
>   THE PLACES.
> C'   And it will be when some of them will fall at the beginning,
>   whoever hears it will say: "There has been a slaughter
>   among *the people* who follow Absalom."⟦171⟧
> B'   Then even the brave man, whose hart is *like* the heart of *a
>   lion*, will utterly melt.
> A'   For all Israel *knows* that *your father* is *powerful* and brave men
>   are those who are with him.
>   Therefore I counsel—
> D   Let *all Israel* be completely *gathered* to you, from Dan to
>   Beersheba,
> E   *As the sand by the sea* for multitude; and you in person go to
>   battle.
> X'   And we shall come upon him IN ONE OF THE PLACES where he
>   is to be found,

E'   And we shall light upon him *as the dew falls on the ground*;
      and of him and all the men that are with him not even
      one will be left.

D'   And if he be *gathered* into a city, *all Israel* will carry ropes to
      that city, and we shall drag it into the brook, until not
      even a small stone is to be found there.

The structure of the speech is characterized by a marked division
into two parts. The first part (A–A') is devoted to revealing the weak
points in Ahitophel's advice (which are in fact the strong points, but
Hushai aims at presenting them as the weak ones). The second part (D–
D'), following the words "Therefore I counsel," offers an alternative
plan, which is supposedly better.

The first part is divided again into two sections. At first (ABC)
Hushai shows why Ahitophel's plan has no chance of succeeding. Afterwards (C'B'A') he explains that not only will this plan fail to achieve
the desired aim, but it will furthermore harm Absalom and bring about
his destruction. The sentence between these two sections (X) is common to both and serves as a transition, because it is connected both
with the idea that Ahitophel's plan cannot succeed and with the idea
that this plan is dangerous to Absalom himself.

The second part also is divided into two sections. In the first section
(DE) the elaborate preparations to be taken before embarking on the
pursuit of the king are set forth. The second section (ED) describes the
effects of the attack on the king. Again there is a connecting sentence
(X'), which refers to the finding of the king, marking the end of the
pursuit on the one hand and the prelude to the attack on the other.

The organization of the speech on the verbal level corresponds with
and confirms its structure on the thematic level. In A and A' the words
"know," "your father" and "powerful" recur, B and B' contain similes
which mention beasts of prey and which represent qualities 〚172〛 ("like
a bear," "like the heart of a lion") and in C and C' the word "people" is
repeated. Likewise in the second part the words "all Israel" and "gathered" occur in both D and D' and comparisons which refer to inanimate
nature and which depict quantities ("as the sand by the sea," "as the dew
falls on the ground") are to be found in E and E'. The two central sentences X and X' are contrasted with each other. In both the phrase "in
one of the places" occurs, but whereas David is "hidden" in one of the
places according to the first phrase, he is "found" in one of the places
according to the second.[17]

17. For a stylistic analysis of Hushai's speech see the writer's *The Artistic Shape of the
Biblical Narrative* (Tel Aviv, 1979) (Hebrew) 32–43.

In this example the analysis is based both on verbal and thematic elements. These reinforce each other, thus providing a firm foundation for the analysis. But structural analysis may very well be based on one type of element only and yet have a high degree of plausibility. What should be avoided, however, is the mixing of miscellaneous elements. It is definitely undesirable to base the structure analysis partly on verbal elements, partly on elements of technique and partly on characters, on events, on themes or on other varieties of narrative or conceptual content.

Functions of Structure

In conclusion a few remarks must be made about the utility of structural analysis. Since structure is an indispensable aspect of narrative it goes without saying that its investigation will provide us with a fuller and richer understanding of the narratives. In particular our sense of their literary and artistic qualities will be greatly enhanced. But structural analysis has value not only for its own sake. Structural arguments can be and in fact have been used to prove the unity of a given narrative or to determine the boundaries of a literary unit. Moreover, structure has rhetorical and expressive value: it is one of the factors governing the effect of the work on the reader and in addition it serves to express or accentuate meaning.

Stating the rhetorical implications of structure and the meanings to be elicited from it significantly complements the analysis of structure itself. The actual interpretation of structure must of course be adapted to each individual narrative.

It should be borne in mind, however, that the interpretation of structure is much more prone to subjectivity than its mere description. In order to endow the proposed interpretation with a high degree of ⟦173⟧ probability and convincing power it is recommendable to look for data in the text, apart form the structure, that confirm or support it.

Although questions of interpretation are beyond the scope of the present article the extraction of meaning from structure will be briefly illustrated. To this end use will be made of two examples that have both been mentioned before.

It was noted above that the Creation story in Gen 1:1–2:3 is characterized by a very prominent structure. The unmistakable emphasis on structure and order in this case hints at the conception that the act of creation consisted chiefly in ordering, in making distinctions, in fixing boundaries, in arranging parts and establishing relations among them with the corollary that the universe is an ordered whole. In this respect the creation account in Gen 1:1–2:3 differs remarkedly from the creation account in Gen 2:4ff. The second creation story neither displays a pronounced structure nor does it convey the idea that creation consists primarily in separating undifferentiated elements and arraying them in order.

The second example refers to the narrative of David, Bathsheba and Uriah (2 Samuel 11). It may be recalled that this narrative is made up of two sections relating to David and Bathsheba in which time elapses quickly, two sections relating to David and Uriah in which time passes rather slowly and one central section relating to Uriah in which time flows quickly. This structural arrangement based on narrative technique places great emphasis on Uriah, who is the subject of two elaborate scenes lingered upon by the narrator and of the central section of the narrative, whereas relatively little space and only minor attention is accorded to Bathsheba. The meaning to be drawn from this is that the main issue of the narrative is to be sought in David's conduct towards Uriah—his efforts to conceal the consequences of his adultery and his order to have Uriah killed in battle. David's moral baseness is brought out by his behaviour towards Uriah even more than by his conduct towards Bathsheba. The conclusion that David's acts with respect to Uriah are the primary concern of the narrative is corroborated by Nathan's rebuke (2 Sam 12:7–10). Nathan does not mention David's adultery, but he convicts him of having killed Uriah the Hittite with the sword and of having taken Uriah's wife to be his wife. Additional confirmation of this interpretation can be found in 1 Kgs 15:5, where it stated "that David did what was right in the eyes of the Lord and turned not aside from anything that he commanded him all the days of his life, save only in the matter of Uriah the Hittite."

The Plot of the Biblical Story of Ruth

Barbara Green

[[55]] There is a great deal more to be said about meaning in the biblical story of Ruth even after the elements of its plot have been discussed, but there is no doubt that an adequate understanding of exactly how those elements work is a prerequisite for further understanding. Though the story is judged to be fairly simple, as biblical narratives go, there is still no clear consensus on the plot even after a number of articles—some recent—dealing with this topic. One more attempt, standing on the shoulders of some of those predecessors, seems justified. The storyteller of this particular tale is so careful in his or her use of detail that I think it is possible to figure out the storyline satisfactorily. The method for this attempt will consist of a blend of stated assumptions, questions put to the text and careful consideration of its manifold clues.

The first step of the process is to lay down the literary assumptions behind the interpretation about to be proposed. There are eight of them, falling into three clusters.

First, the plot of the story is plausibly constructed so that there is no serious discontinuity or incompatibility between the steps. The audience must be able to understand what is happening.[1] Second, however, is the fact that a good storyteller must be sure that there is some suspense in the story both for the audience and for the characters. And third, once the climax of the story has been reached and the coup has been accomplished, the audience should be able to look back and

Reprinted with pemission from *Journal for the Study of the Old Testament* 23 (1982) 55–68.

1. D. R. G. Beattie, "Ruth III," *JSOT* 5 (1978), 39–41 who opens an article on the topic in a similar way, calls this principle coherence and intelligibility.

see by what steps and with what hints the pathway was paved. A relishing of these hints is part of the enjoyment of re-reading or re-hearing the same stories.

A fourth principle governing a narrative such as this one is that our storyteller is reliable and will not only not deceive us but will give us whatever information is essential for our understanding.[2] Balancing that, however, is a fifth assumption, [[56]] that there is an inevitable distance between ourselves and the storyteller, a distance which always exists, but which in certain situations (e.g., written text, large time gap, significant cultural differences) becomes a difficulty. In the case of the Old Testament we can never be totally or even substantially sure what important silent understandings the storyteller shared with his or her audience. A sixth factor, however, softens the fifth a bit, for in certain kinds of stories—notably love stories—a time or culture gap does not deprive us of much insight that comes simply from sharing human nature with the storyteller, characters and an audience contemporary with them.

The seventh and eighth principles are even more specific to the story of Ruth itself. I presume that it counts on a general attitude of conformity with law and custom, and in fact shows how the characters act in ways that surpass strict legal obligations. And I presume some purposeful resonance between the story of Ruth and material in both Genesis 38 and Deuteronomy 25. We are meant to interrelate the stories, though not necessarily to conclude that they are referring to exactly the same legal customs.

With these eight assumptions stated—assumptions which are themselves part of an *a priori* reasoning process but which seem justified on the basis of the skill of this particular storyteller, the interpretation process can begin. There are two main points to be made. First, in terms of content, the story's main intent is to relate the restoration of seed: food in the land, food for Naomi and Ruth, a husband for Ruth, a redeemer for Naomi and an heir (leading to a king) for the whole people. These particular things are all lacking at the outset of the story, and they are restored one by one. The field, a symbolic representation of the woman, is the locus of resolution of all these needs. The second observation to be sustained by this analysis of the plot is that the way in which the restoration is detailed fits the story's basic field-seed symbolism well. Each of the six main sections is decisive within its limits, but none is complete. Each depends on hints from previous sections to have prepared the ground or on an unfurling of

2. Beattie, ibid., 40, calls this principle self-sufficiency.

details in the next sections to give us the clarity we need—or on both techniques simultaneously. The whole story of seed restoration depends on appropriate timing and fortuitous conditions.

Ruth 4:1–12

The most suitable place to begin the search for understanding [[57]] is the scene where the climax of the story occurs. And the first question to ask is what tensions are present as it opens.[3] The secrecy of the previous scene (3:1–18) suggests that no one except the three main characters (Boaz, Ruth and Naomi) and the audience has any inkling that the story's decisive moment is about to begin. Ruth knows that Boaz has responded positively to her marriage request. Naomi has been told that and has received an additional communication as well: a gift of seed. Boaz has also stated that he will see to the question of redemption, though he is not the holder of the first option. The question we have been left with, I believe, is: How will the problem of the nearer redeemer be resolved? How will events have to be managed so that Boaz is able to perform this function as well as the others he has already undertaken? The tension for Boaz is whether he will be able to accomplish his plans fully: to get the nearer redeemer to cede to him the option for redemption and the rights and obligations connected with it.

The first four verses serve to underline the legality of the whole scene. The principals and witnesses are positioned, the details of the situation are carefully stated, the order of precedence is given. The unnamed redeemer—if surprised by the suddenness with which the situation clamors for a decision from him—seems to have no immediate trouble deciding what to do. He declares that he will accept his option, apparently envisioning no way in which he can lose. J. M. Sasson speculates, reasonably I think, on what thoughts might have run through the man's mind.[4] As long as Naomi and Ruth remain husbandless and childless and since Naomi is elderly,[5] there is little chance that the man would—having spent to redeem the land—have

3. It is impossible both to work backwards from the climax and at the same time to have already underlined the points of tension. So I choose the former procedure and will take care to substantiate farther on what I maintain here.

4. J. M. Sasson, *Ruth: A New Translation with a Philological Commentary and a Formalist-Folklorist Interpretation* (Baltimore: Johns Hopkins University Press, 1979) 115.

5. E. F. Campbell, Jr., *Ruth: A New Translation with Introduction, Notes and Commentary* (Garden City, N.Y.: Doubleday & Co. Inc., 1975) 97, 107, 110, 116, 127, points out a number of ways in which both Boaz and Naomi are portrayed as seniors.

to give it up even at a time of jubilee. By redeeming, he will act justly and gain a portion of land.

The trap of the whole story is sprung in the controversial 4:5 by the verb that is written in one way and pointed in another.[6] Boaz says, in effect: You take the land, then, as is your right as nearest redeemer. But know that *I* am going to marry Ruth—and in fact marry her precisely for the purpose of raising an heir for Mahlon, an heir who can claim Elimelek's field.[7] Boaz's words must be seen as having two characteristics. First, they reveal the care with which he has thought out his position, a position so certain that he cannot lose by revealing it. And second, his words come as a surprise to the unnamed redeemer—a surprise whose effect we see in his next words. The secrecy of [[58]] chapter 3 has guarded the marriage plans of Ruth and Boaz from all except themselves, Naomi and us: the rhetorical devices suggesting that Boaz is a contemporary of Naomi have had the same effect. On the other hand, chapters 2 and 3 have symbolically prepared us for his marriageability by describing him in terms of productivity: he is a successful sower of seed. But even we, who stand at the city gate knowing that he has already promised to marry Ruth, are surprised to learn that he is entering a marriage "to raise the name of the dead man over his inheritance" (4:5, 10), a "levirate" marriage. The surprise only works, of course, if there is no legal connecting obligation between a redeemer

6. Virtually all interpreters of the story must contend with this verse, whether they call much attention to their reasons or not. D. R. G. Beattie, "*Kethibh* and *Qere* in Ruth IV 5," *VT* 21 (1971), 490–94, sets forth the suggestion that in spite of rather consistent agreement to the contrary among scholars, the written text is to be preferred to the one pointed for reading (though his reasons are not identical with mine). The combination of letters preceding the name Ruth is also a problem in relation to the rest of the sentence. If they are to be read as "and from the hand of Ruth," then there is no direct object in the sentence. Campbell, 146, refers us to the verse below (v. 10) where a similar statement indicates that Ruth is the object acquired. He suggests that the letters *wm'*t are best read as the conjunction "and" followed by an enclitic *mem* and the direct object marker. Other commentators, G. Gerleman, *Ruth. Das Hohelied* (Neukirchen-Vluyn: Neukirchener Verlag des Erziehungsvereins, 1965) 35; P. Joüon, S.J., *Ruth: Commentaire philologique et exégétique* [Rome: Institut Biblique Pontifical, 1953) 83; A. R. S. Kennedy, *The Book of Ruth: The Hebrew Text with Grammatical Notes and Vocabulary* (London: SPCK, 1928) 55, prefer to see the letters *wm'*t as reflecting *wgm-'*t (and also), with the *ghimel* having dropped out. In either case, Ruth is the direct object, not the object of the preposition "from."

7. T. C. Vriezen, "Two Old Cruces," *OTS* 5 (1948) 87, points out the specifically voluntary nature of the marriage, noting that there is no extant law covering the sort of action Boaz is undertaking. To make my methodology slightly clearer here: some choices must be made, resting inevitably on presumptions. I prefer to base my choices on literary presumptions rather than on sociological ones and to leave the legal questions as open as they can be left, since detailed knowledge of them is so slight.

and a "levir" and if there is no marriage obligation for the redeemer or for the widow of a Jewish man. Only if a marriage between Ruth and Boaz is a bit startling, and a "levirite" marriage is even less usual, is the surprise a good one. Since there is no extant Hebrew narrative where the three customs are interrelated in a binding way, it seems preferable to assume—on the basis of good storytelling—that they need not be related rather than that they must have been. What is normally done cannot be an effective surprise.

The nearer redeemer's change of mind is made explicit in 4:6, where without giving a specific reason he simply says he cannot redeem without destroying his inheritance. And he cedes his place to Boaz, who has now achieved his plan fully. As several commentators point out, if the change of mind cannot be explained on the grounds that the man is ignorant of who his dependants are or of what his own obligations entail, or on the grounds that Boaz is trying to slip across some illegal procedure, it can only be explained by Boaz' introducing consequences which the other man had not anticipated but which clearly threaten him in some way. Those consequences would be something like the following (again, letting the story itself supply a small part of the absence of any clear legal detail): if the unnamed redeemer redeemed the field, he would be out the purchase price but could expect to keep the field, since there was apparently no prospect of any male heir who might have come between Naomi and the nearest redeemer; he had no obligation to marry Ruth when acting as redeemer, nor was she part of the acquisition.[8] Even if Ruth married, as she was free to do (as is clear from Boaz' words to her in chapter 3), and even if she had a son, there would be no threat to the field, unless the marriage were a "levirate" marriage. But if someone were to contract a "levirate" marriage, then a child so [[59]] sired could reclaim the land of his "father" from the redeemer.[9] Only when Boaz announces that he is going to marry Ruth and raise issue for Mahlon does the problem of the destruction of the nearer redeemer's estate enter plausibly.[10] One further point: if the

8. W. McKane, "Ruth and Boaz," *Transactions of the Glasgow Oriental Society* 19 (1961–62) 34, notes that there is no clear Old Testament evidence that levirate (and to this I add redemption) included inheriting the widow.

9. Sasson, *Ruth*, p. 114, comes to the same conclusion. Again, in absence of clear legal material, this is a guess that seems validated not only by the story's logic but even by terminology: "to raise the name of the dead over his inheritance" seems to link the new child to the land of its dead "father." Sasson hypothesizes (p. 139) that any time the male heir or his family were in need, he (or they) could offer the field to the redeemer, hence the threat to his estate. The solution is total relinquishment of his redemption rights—just the step Boaz has desired.

10. Ibid., 139.

nearer redeemer had any rights or obligations in regard to marriage, Boaz would have been running a risk that his clever idea would have such appeal that the nearer redeemer would act upon it himself. Once again it seems clear that Boaz is risking very little—the actual redemption of the field—and that even that facet is pretty well under the control of his plan. To those who wonder why Boaz would have undertaken such responsibilities Sasson points out that not only does Boaz love Ruth but also that the heir will be his in at least some way[11]—which we see also from the genealogy at the end of the story.

The next few verses detail the ceremony of confirmation, the gesture and words by which the unnamed redeemer cedes his option on Elimelek's field to Boaz. Verse 9 calls the elders to witness Boaz' acquisition of all that belonged to Elimelek and his sons; verses 10–11 call them to witness Boaz' resolution to marry Ruth and to raise an heir for Mahlon. The witnesses acknowledge the transaction and bless the marriage.

Before looking at the rush of concluding events which follow from this scene at the gate, there are a few more questions to be examined. One question mentioned occasionally in commentaries is how Boaz knew what Naomi wanted done with the field. Prior to that are queries such as: how could Naomi have a field? How were they so poor if they owned land? Why had not the nearer redeemer acted earlier? Why did we not know about the field before chapter 4? The question of how Boaz decided what to do is basically unanswerable and best explained as a literary device to preserve the surprise of the story and the tempo of its events as they unfold between the threshing floor and the city gate. The legal questions are not answerable from available legal evidence, though I presume that the audience contemporary with the storyteller would have been able to supply an understanding that would satisfy them. And the question of why we were not told about the field is again a literary question involving the sensitivity of both artist and interpreter. The field is a key theme throughout the story, and the reader who understands that the land is the focus of the whole story is not totally surprised when a portion of it becomes the specific device for the tale's resolution. [60]

Ruth 4:13–22

The story is not yet complete at the climax, for the actions so carefully articulated in the preceding section must be seen to bear fruit. The details are not quite so clear as might be desired, but on the assumption

11. Ibid., 140.

that they conform in general to what has been so carefully prepared for, some suggestions can be offered with confidence.

The marriage, conception and birth of a son are related in 4:13. The remaining verses indicate how the child resolves the various problems with which the story has dealt. He is first of all proof that the barrenness of Ruth and the emptiness of Naomi have ended. The blessing of 4:11–12 is accomplished, as the foreign woman builds the house of Israel once again. The second point that is clear is that the birth of the boy furthers the line which will produce the king. The reference to Perez, the genealogy and the royal nuances of the blessing[12] all support this conclusion.

The remaining two pieces of information that it seems reasonable to expect are first, that the baby is Boaz' heir and hence possibly (presumably) also in a position to be Naomi's redeemer; and second, that the child is also heir to Elimelek and Mahlon. The first point seems reasonably well confirmed by the genealogy which lists Obed as Boaz' son and by the blessing which indicates that it is Boaz' house which Obed will build, just as Perez built Judah's (not Er's). The exact relationship of the child to Naomi through Elimelek and Mahlon is less clearly implied. Boaz' words in 4:5 and 10 which were interpreted as his commitment to "levirate" marriage refer to Mahlon's name and to his heritage. There are two other references to "name": 4:11 has a parallel set of phrases, the first of which seems to refer to Boaz' ability to sire a son[13] and the second of which seems to allude to a name being called in Bethlehem—Mahlon's over his heritage, possibly. The final reference to "name" occurs in 4:14, where the women are blessing the Lord for not leaving Naomi without a redeemer, "whose name is called in Israel." I would suggest that both references are applicable (at least) to Obed and that the reference to "name" serves to link his two roles: Naomi's redeemer through Boaz and Elimelek's heir through Mahlon and Ruth. His relationship to the field—as both redeemer and heir—is an equivalent link. These end verses, then, show Ruth to have a husband and a son; Naomi to have a redeemer (Boaz), a grandson (through Mahlon), a second redeemer (Boaz' son); Mahlon's name is raised over his [[61]] inheritance, called in Bethlehem, and the heritage of the father goes to the son; Boaz has a son whose line will produce kings.

---

12. S. B. Parker, "The Marriage Blessing in Israelite and Ugaritic Literature," *JBL* 95 (1976) 23–30, argues a case for the royal overtones of the words spoken.

13. Campbell, 153, follows C. J. Labuschagne, "The Crux in Ruth 4:11," *ZAW* 79 (1967) 364–367, in maintaining that both clauses beginning with imperatives refer to Boaz' procreativity: "to bestow a name" is parallel to the phrase "to sire a child."

Ruth 3:1–18

The events of chapter 3 are crucial to the whole story and to the climax scene in particular. Having already discussed the climax affords the advantage of letting the most significant preparations for it be visible. The interpretation can go in four main blocks, responding to the following questions. First, what is Naomi's plan? What does she intend in sending Ruth to the threshing floor? Second, what exactly do Ruth's actions and words entail? Does she alter Naomi's plan? Third, what are the elements of Boaz' response? To what does he agree? And fourth, what does Naomi learn, and what might we be expected to learn, from the closing scene of the chapter?

The first set of questions is addressed by the opening verses (1–4), consisting of the words of Naomi to Ruth, words whose full meaning is not readily apparent. The "rest" of which she speaks connotes the security and benefits a woman might expect as she enters married life,[14] and more metaphorically in this story, the rest that the land is and gives (Deut 12:9; Ps 95:11). A related word was used previously in the story (1:9) and the home of the husband was where such rest was to be found. The directions regarding Ruth's personal preparation, her washing and anointing and donning her cloak, are obvious enough in their meaning on the rational level, as a young woman goes forth to meet a man, but their fuller significance must be gotten at as well. One signification of the words is to show that the period of mourning in the story is over. David performs the same sequence of actions after the death of his young son (2 Sam 12:20). The time of sorrow for Ruth (and for the people of Yahweh whom she represents) is at an end. The sequence of actions also suggests sexual readiness. The prophet Ezekiel performs these actions for his bride prior to betrothing her (Ezek 16:9). Naomi bids Ruth adorn herself as a bride. She next directs her daughter-in-law to uncover the legs of the sleeping man, who will then make known to her what she should do (3:3–4). Whatever the exact denotation of uncovering the feet or legs of a sleeping man includes, it would be difficult to argue that the connotation is not suggestive of sexual activity and that such an association is not clearly intended by the storyteller. The verb *glh* (to uncover) is frequently used in connection with nakedness, and the noun *regel* (foot) to which [[62]] *marg^elōtāw* (legs) is related is used often for both male and female genitals.[15] Taken together, the various nuances of the verses are most coherently

---

14. G. A. Cooke, *The Book of Ruth* (Cambridge: Cambridge University Press, 1913) 3. Other commentaries generally agree.

15. Campbell, 21, discusses the passages.

accounted for if Naomi is sending Ruth to Boaz to suggest marriage.[16]
The appearance of Ruth and her gesture will convey the message. A
crucial question left vague here but one which is obviously important
in view of the development in chapter 4 is whether Naomi understood
Boaz to be obliged to marry Ruth. In absence of any clear indication
that she did, it seems more consistent with the rest of the story to understand that she did not, and that her allusion to his being a kinsman
and to his having shown kindness already (3:2) is a reassurance and an
inducement for Ruth and possibly a way of juxtaposing in the mind of
the audience the fact that Boaz has some legal tie to Naomi and that
he may be a suitable husband for Ruth. Surely if Boaz were obliged to
marry Ruth it would be difficult to understand the need for the plan
Naomi unfolds.[17]

There are two aspects to Ruth's part of the scene (vv. 5–9). On the
one hand the storyteller emphasizes through dialogue and through narrative description that Ruth does as she has been told; she goes to Boaz,
embodying the suggestion of marriage. At 3:9, however, she first verbal-
izes the request she was sent to make: "Spread your garment (*kᵉnāpeka*)
over your handmaid . . . " Her words are no doubt meant to recall for us
Boaz' blessing spoken to her in 2:12, where he prays that the Lord may
shelter her fully with his wings (*kᵉnāpāw*). The particular combination of
spreading a garment (*kānāp*) or wings (*kᵉnāpim*) occurs in the context of
protection. Deuteronomy 32 describes the scene where the Lord finds
his portion Israel in a desert place and hovers over his charges and under them, spreading his wings to bear his fledgling young along. The
combination also occurs in a context that is sexual. Ezekiel 16 tells of
the Lord's finding the young Jerusalem at the age for love, spreading
his garment over her nakedness and plighting his troth with her (v. 8).
On the understanding that the institutions of marriage and redemption
are kept distinct in the story for purposes of artistry, and that marriage
imagery pervades this scene, I understand Ruth's request as relating primarily to marriage, but the very expression maintains its relation with
protection language and thus helps move us to her next request.

16. The connotations are far from making Ruth a harlot, though, since both Naomi
and Boaz have shown themselves concerned for Ruth's safety. A number of scholars prefer to distinguish a request for sexual relations from a marriage proposal. I am not sure
such a distinction can be made in this particular story. Again, though, I think we can assume on the basis of the rest of the story that the actions of the characters are not contrary to the law but virtuous beyond the demands of the law.

17. E. Robertson, "The Plot of the Book of Ruth," *BJRL* 32 (1950) 218. Once again it
is worth repeating that if someone else were obliged to marry Ruth or she him, Boaz
would not be likely—given his character in the story—to usurp another's role or to be
successful at doing so in public.

For at 3:9 Ruth not only does what she has been told, but she then takes the initiative and asks something else as well: she reminds the man that he is a redeemer. The crucial question is ⟦63⟧ what is the nature of the relationship between the two statements. Is Ruth requesting marriage *because*[18] Boaz is a redeemer, or is she requesting marriage and redemption? What is unclear—and purposefully ambiguous in fact—in Ruth's requests may be clarified by Boaz' responses, assuming that his words respond directly to hers.

Boaz' words (3:10–13) first bless Ruth for two acts of kindness, the second of which refers to her having chosen him over other men. One implication of these words seems to be that Ruth was free to marry as she pleased;[19] a second is that Boaz interpreted Ruth's request (at least part of it) as a marriage suggestion.[20] In 3:11 he states that he will do all she has asked, which in view of what has preceded and in view of what will follow in chapter 4 is surely marriage.

But in 3:12 he responds to a second topic, redemption, evidently in response to Ruth's second request in 3:9, a request for redemption. The complication Boaz refers to is the one he will resolve at the city gate. Boaz responds, then, to the two requests Ruth has made. The first he can promise to do; the second depends on one factor outside his control, but he will make sure that one of the redeemers acts. The connection of the two roles, marriage and redemption, is not obligatory; the juxtaposing of them here is a literary arrangement in this story[21] which serves to inform us of the general plan of Boaz but leaves us unclear as to exactly how his plan can serve the purposes we are coming to appreciate. We are not meant to infer the complete *dénouement* from this

---

18. Most commentators assume that the conjunctive word *ky* connecting the two statements requires its most common translation, "because." However, it needs to be noted that this is the sole possibility only if one presumes that the redeemer has the obligation to perform a "levirate" marriage—a presumption that cannot be drawn too quickly from this story and hence there should not be too quickly applied to it. Correspondence between Sasson and Beattie (both of whom agree that the redemption and "levirate" marriage responsibilities are being carefully distinguished by the storyteller) addresses the meaning of the word *ky*. Sasson argues that it is corroborative and emphatic: "The Issue of Geʾullah in Ruth," *JSOT* 5 (1978) 57; Beattie finds that explanation rather dubious and prefers to base his explanation of the verse on an understanding of Ruth's whole statement as a general request for assistance because Boaz had been kind in the past; Beattie sees here neither a specific marriage request nor a specific and technical request for redemption: "Redemption in Ruth and Related Matters: A Response to Jack M. Sasson," *JSOT* 5 (1978), 65–66. I prefer Sasson's judgment that the particle is emphatic rather than conjunctive.

19. Robertson, 218; Sasson, "Geʾullah," 55–56.

20. Beattie, "Ruth III," 45.

21. Beattie, "Response," 67.

scene, so part of the ambiguity protects the surprise climax of the story. In this scene Ruth is sent to request marriage; she asks that—and also redemption. Boaz says (if not explicitly) that he will marry her and that he will see redemption accomplished.

The last question is what Naomi learns at the end of the chapter that enables her to speak so confidently, and how she learns it. Once again the information is partially sheltered from us. Boaz pours barley into Ruth's shawl and sends it to Naomi, we are told. The shawl is spoken of in Isa 3:22 in a description of the daughters of Zion, whose finery will be replaced by the garb of exile and disgrace. It is an image of fine clothing and an image of freedom from oppression. It is a synonym for the cloak Ruth wore to the threshing floor, the same word used in Exod 12:34 to describe the garment in which the liberated Israelites carry unleavened bread dough in their journey of liberation from Egypt. The clothing is a symbol of redemption. The grain [[64]] itself is the gift of food most frequently given by Boaz in this story, as well as a suggestion that he will sire a child. Naomi undoubtedly understands the symbolism of Boaz' gift of seed in terms of marriage and quite possibly in terms of redemption of Elimelek's field. Once we see the end of the story, even the implications of seed for the two women in terms of "levirate" marriage can be seen.

Ruth 2:1–23

The first half of the story is not quite so dense as the second half and requires less explanation of the plot. The events of chapter 2 move the problems already introduced by chapter 1 towards resolution and also set up the factors on which chapter 3 depends.

The first details about the resolution of lack of food (already announced in 1:6) appear in this chapter, and the resolution has a number of aspects: custom will offer the resolution of gleaning; Boaz will give Ruth food and water, and in sufficient amount for her to share with Naomi; he will also allow her to do more than glean from his field since she will actually gather grain from the bundles. The solutions to famine range from temporary (2:14, 18) to more adequate (2:17) to more long-term (2:8–9, 15–16, 21–23). The first introduction to the man who will help resolve the lack of human seed occurs here, too, though there is not much detail of the shape of his contribution (only hints).

This chapter prepares for the threshing floor scene. Ruth and Naomi are given ample basis for their requests of Boaz. We, too, are able to be forming our ideas about him. Naomi presumably first knows him as a friend or relative of her husband and as a redeemer of herself. Ruth's first encounter with him introduces him as a man who acts with kindness and generosity. Once they pool information, each woman knows sufficient for her to act. Naomi can anticipate that Boaz might well agree to marry Ruth since he has shown special interest in her; Ruth can expect that since Boaz is a redeemer he will act in the interests of herself and Naomi. The storyteller has given us both sets of information at the beginning of the chapter. Boaz is a man of worth, which implies wealth, success, productivity, upright behavior and character.[22] He is successful as an agriculturalist, gracious to a stranger, generous to his people—in offering Elimelek's daughter-in-law food and drink, protection and a plentiful source of food. The chapter sets up the [[65]] question of whether Boaz will act decisively or not. There are hints that he will, and yet his actions are not quite what we might have expected, and his words indicate that he is leaving much of Ruth's need to be supplied by the Lord.[23] Ruth's initial plan would seem in accord with practices like those described in the law (Lev 19:9; 23:22; Deut 24:19) since she is an alien and a widow.[24] She requests an additional permission and gets at least that, if not more. The generosity of Boaz to Ruth is illustrated by hospitality (2:8–9), refreshment while she works (2:9, 14), words of consolation (2:11–12), privileges in his field (2:15–16) and a supply of food (2:17–18).

Ruth 1:6–23

The scene which composes most of chapter 1 announces the resolution of the problem of food supply (1:6, 22), leaving chapter 2 to differentiate the various aspects, as has been noted. Verses 6–22 focus also on the apparent hopelessness of the other seed deficiencies of the story: there are no prospects of husbands or children, little hint that a redeemer or "levir" will make an appearance. Naomi's words both raise and dismiss the possibility of "levirate" marriage. The other way in which this section anticipates the food resolution is Naomi's reference to the Lord as the one responsible for her empty state. The legal genre in which she makes her accusation[25] will be the medium for its redress. Most of the plot of 1:6–22 concerns the question of who will accompany

---

22. Campbell, 109–11.

23. D. F. Rauber, "Literary Values in the Bible: The Book of Ruth," *JBL* (1970) 32.

24. Some commentators wonder why Ruth needs "favor" in order to do what is apparently her right. Sufficient explanation would seem to lie in the rather persistent prophetic accusation that the poor are not being cared for as the law had envisioned.

25. Campbell, 62, argues the case for the legal overtones of her statement.

Naomi, and though it is important to the story, it is not particularly complex.

Ruth 1:1–5

The five opening verses introduce the themes of death from which the story will draw life: famine in nature leading to exile; death and barrenness leading to Naomi's being without any family except foreign daughters-in-law.

Conclusion

The plot of the story is one of several ways in which the storyteller seeks to communicate the basic meaning of the story. The careful way in which the nuptials of this alien and dispossessed woman and her beloved are arranged contributes to our readiness to see the biblical story of Ruth as more than a simple love story. It is the story of the liberation of God's people from the land of oppression and death and the re-seeding [[66]] of them and their land. It is the recounting of the nuptials of the Lord and his people.

Characterization in Biblical Narrative: David's Wives

ADELE BERLIN

[[69]] Literary approaches to the Bible have proliferated in recent years, and have been fruitful, especially in their analyses of the style and structure of biblical material. What has been somewhat lacking is broader studies of literary interest—studies concerned with characterization, point of view, etc. Toward this end I offer a literary study of several narratives in the books of Samuel and Kings, all of which concern David and the women who became his wives, with the primary focus on the characterizations of the women and an indirect view of the characterization of David.

Literary criticism of biblical material may take many forms. I will not attempt to fit mine into the mold or methodology of anyone else. In most cases the slavish application of one particular method or approach to a text produces a mechanical, lifeless criticism. Rather, the starting point should be the text. Different texts lend themselves to different types of criticism.

A word of justification of the material selected may be in order. The stories discussed here have, of course, been dealt with before. For example, an American scholar has done an admirable literary analysis of the Abigail story, and from it draws a historical conclusion.[1] An Israeli scholar, having explored literary aspects of the Bathsheba story,

Reprinted with permission from *Journal for the Study of the Old Testament* 23 (1982) 69–85.

1. Jon D. Levenson, "I Samuel 25 as Literature and History," *CBQ* 40 (1978) 11–28. See also a follow-up by J. Levenson and B. Halpern, "The Political Import of David's Marriage," *JBL* 99 (1980) 507–18.

concludes that the author intended to convey a moral lesson.[2] These scholars are using literary analysis as a means to an end. I feel, naively some will think, that literary criticism of the Bible is an end in itself. There is no need to make it yield a theological or historical discovery. That these are also to be found may, indeed, be true, but this is a different level of interpretation completely. For whatever else it is, the Bible is certainly a literary work, and as such becomes subject to literary criticism—the purpose of which is to bring into clearer focus the [[70]] subtleties of language, style, and meaning that are the fabric of the text. Moreover, the goal of this paper is not only a new clarification of individual texts, but the literary perspective that emerges from an overview of a number of related texts.

The importance of David as a national hero, and, therefore, a focal point for tales, can never be overestimated. Stories about him abound— whether as part of an official court history, traditional folktales, or the creations of literary artists. We do not know whether the body of stories that have been preserved in the Bible were meant for entertainment, propaganda, historiography, or a combination of these and perhaps other purposes.[3] For this study it does not matter; regardless of their purpose, literary criteria can be applied to them with meaningful results.[4]

2. M. Garsiel, "The Character and Aim of the Story of David and Bathsheba," *Beth Miqra* 40/2 (1972) 162–83. Cf. also M. Garsiel, "A Review of Recent Interpretations of the Story of David and Bathsheba," *Immanuel* 2 (1973) 18–20.

3. D. M. Gunn (*The Story of King David, Genre and Interpretation* [JSOT Supplement Series 6: Sheffield, 1978]) reviews the various hypotheses on the genre of the so-called Court History or Succession Narrative (2 Samuel 9–20, 1 Kings 1–2). His own conclusions are that this should be labelled a "story" whose purpose is serious entertainment. The story is an artistic work which draws on traditional structures and motifs. He also modifies the boundaries of the story, including in it most of 2 Samuel 5 and 6. He does not, however, relate the "Story of King David" to the David stories which precede it in 1 Samuel; thus the stories of David's marriages to Michal and Abigail are not part of the unit which Gunn discusses.

4. Of course, literary analysis is demanded even more if we assume, with Gunn, that the works are primarily literary. But even if one insists that they are part of a historical narrative, this does not obviate the need for literary analysis, for there are similarities between fictional and historical narrative in the Bible. E. F. Campbell, Jr., writes: "I have rather badly blurred the distinction between historical narrative and the short narrative tale. . . . The prose style is really similar. . . . In fact, I rather doubt that we can draw a clean and clear line between historical narrative and the short story genre here proposed. . . . I would even hazard the observation that there is not much difference between this genre and that of what most agree is the first great piece of Israelite historical writing—namely, the Court History of David" ("The Hebrew Short Story: A Study of Ruth," *A Light Unto My Path. Old Testament Studies in Honor of Jacob M. Myers* [Philadelphia, 1974] 93). Robert Alter expresses a similar view in "Sacred History and the Beginnings of Prose Fiction," *Poetics Today* 1 (1980) 143–62.

The stories examined below are all about David, yet, strangely enough, David is not the main character in all. What they have in common is that they all portray a relationship between David and a woman; they differ in that the characterization of each woman (and even of the same woman in different stories) is quite different. It is this difference in characterization which interests us here.

Michal and Bathsheba

Michal was the first, and in some ways the most interesting, of David's wives. Robert Alter has given a vivid description of this character and the personal tragedy surrounding her, and it need not be repeated here.[5] What I would like to add is the aspect of Michal's characterization that emerges when it is compared with Jonathan's. This comparison cries out to be made: both Michal and Jonathan are the children of Saul who show more love and loyalty to their father's competitor than to their father. The biblical author further invites the comparison by juxtaposing their stories in 1 Samuel 18–20. The results are surprising: the characteristics normally associated with males are attached to Michal, and those usually perceived as feminine are linked with Jonathan.

The first of Michal's unfeminine traits is found in the notice that she loved David and made it known. It is recorded twice (1 Sam 18:20, 28), and is the only time in the Bible that a woman seems to have chosen a husband instead of the usual pattern of a husband choosing a wife.[6] (Of course, the marriage could only take place because father Saul approved, for his own ulterior motives.) David, on his part, married Michal not for [[71]] love but because "it pleased David well to be the king's son-in-law" (18:26). His relationship to her is always colored by practical considerations. He apparently did not (or could not) object when she was married to someone else during his absence (1 Sam 25:44), and his later demand for her return was motivated by political reasons (2 Sam 3:13–15). In this last incident Michal's feelings are not recorded, but her second husband appears somewhat effeminate as he tags along after her crying until Abner commands him to go back home.

The feelings of love and tenderness that David might have been expected to have for Michal are all reserved for Jonathan. Jonathan,

---

5. "Character in the Bible," *Commentary* 66/4 (Oct., 1978) 58–65.

6. The initiative taken by Naomi and Ruth is more complex and differently motivated.

too, like his sister, made known his warm feelings for David (1 Sam
18:1; 19:1; 20:17), but in his case they were reciprocated. The parting
of the friends in the field describes how "they kissed one another and
wept upon each other until David exceeded" (20:41). At their final
parting David laments "I am distressed over you, my brother,
Jonathan; you have been very pleasing to me—more wonderful was
your love to me than the love of women" (2 Sam 1:26).

David, then, seems to have related to Michal as to a man and to
Jonathan as to a woman. It is not a question of sexual perversion here,
but a subtle suggestion that this reflects something of the essence of
these two characters. Michal is the aggressive and physical one. She
saves David by physically lowering him out of a window,[7] and arranging
the bed so as to appear that he is in it. She lies to the messengers, telling them that David is sick in bed, and then, after the ruse is discovered and Saul himself questions her, she brazenly fabricates the story
that David threatened to kill her if she did not aid in his escape (1 Sam
19:12–17). Jonathan, too, saves the life of his friend, but it is never by
physical means; it is through words (talking Saul out of killing him in
1 Sam 19:4–5), and words with a coded meaning (the episode of the
arrows in 1 Sam 20:20ff.). Jonathan's most physical action is the shoot-
ing of the arrows for the pre-arranged signal—hardly a show of
strength. The "little white lie" that he told to his father to explain
David's absence from the new moon feast (20:28–29) had actually been
concocted by David himself (20:6). Jonathan is just the messenger boy.
His words and deeds are certainly much less daring than Michal's.

The last bit of information we have about Michal is that she never
bore a child (2 Sam 6:23). Not only is this the culmination of the disappointment of her life, and a hint that the [72] husband who never
loved her now stopped having marital relations with her,[8] but, in the
light of the foregoing discussion, it suggests that Michal never filled a
female role, or at least the role that the Bible views as the primary female role. Significant, too, may be the fact that Michal, unlike many
women in biblical narrative, is never described as beautiful. Far from
being a typical woman, Michal has been cast in a most unfeminine role.

Whether one evaluates the character of Michal positively or negatively, it seems clear that she stands as a character in her own right—
an important figure in the episodes in which she is involved.

7. The lowering of a person through a window may be a motif connected with fe-
males; compare Josh 2:15 where Rahab does the same. Nevertheless, Michal's actions
throughout appear more physical and aggressive in contrast to Jonathan's.

8. Cf. Alter, "Character in the Bible," 63.

Not so Bathsheba in 2 Samuel 11–12. She enters the story as a passive object, someone seen from a rooftop.[9] Her naked beauty caught the eye of David and he made inquiries about her. The reader does not know whether she obeyed David's summons eagerly or because she could not refuse a royal command. Her announcement of her pregnancy is stated matter-of-factly in two words, *hārāh ʾānōkî*, "I'm pregnant." That leaves the problem for David, who first tries to have Uriah visit his wife in an attempt to pass off the child as legitimate. When this fails, David arranges to have Uriah killed in battle.

When next we hear of Bathsheba, David's plan has been carried out. Her reaction and the subsequent events are told as follows: "And when the wife of Uriah heard that Uriah her husband was dead, she made lamentation for her husband. And when the mourning was past, David sent and took her home to his house, and she became his wife, and bore him a son" (11:26–27a). One and a half cold, terse verses to sum up the condition of a woman who has had an adulterous affair, become pregnant, lost her husband, married her lover, the king of Israel, and borne his child! These are crucial events in the life of any woman, yet we are not told how they affected Bathsheba. The end of verse 27 is significant, too: "But the thing that David had done displeased the Lord." Now both parties were equally guilty of adultery, and both should have incurred the wrath of God, yet not a word is said of Bathsheba's guilt; only David's is mentioned.[10]

His punishment is not to be his own death (the prescribed punishment for an adulterer) but the death of his illegitimate son. While the child is sick, David is portrayed as a loving and distraught father. So extreme is his emotional state that his servants fear to inform him when the child has died. Again the [[73]] narrative is silent about Bathsheba's feelings. Was she not a loving mother, deeply grieved by the illness and death of her infant? The only hint of this is given in 12:24: "And David comforted Bathsheba his wife. . . ."

Throughout the entire story the narrator has purposely subordinated the character of Bathsheba. He has ignored her feelings and

9. Traditional commentators fault Bathsheba for not closing her curtains while bathing. Even E. M. Good (*Irony in the Old Testament* [London, 1965] 36) says: "We may hazard the guess that Bathsheba may not have been unaware of David's whereabouts." I think this is reading too much into the text. The scene is necessary for the plot; it enables David to develop a desire for Bathsheba.

10. For this reason some commentators explain that the thing that displeased the Lord was the murder of Uriah, not adultery, and thus Bathsheba is free from guilt. But the parable that Nathan tells emphasizes the taking of the wife more than the killing of the husband.

given the barest notice of her actions. The reader can feel the whole range of David's emotions: sexual desire, frustration at not being able to get Uriah to go home, indignation at the rich man in Nathan's parable, shame when the parable is explained, grief during the child's illness, and finally acceptance of his death. The only emotions ascribed to Bathsheba are mourning at the death of her husband and grief at the death of her child. The first is presented in a perfunctory manner, as if it were done out of respect for decency rather than from the need to mourn, and the second is mentioned indirectly.

All this leads us to view Bathsheba as a complete non-person. She is not even a minor character, but simply part of the plot. This is why she is not considered guilty of adultery. She is not an equal party to the adultery, but only the means whereby it was achieved. This is evident from the way she is referred to. She is introduced as "Bathsheba, the daughter of Eliam, the wife of Uriah the Hittite," doubtless a historical personage known to us from other biblical references. But she does not appear here as a historical figure. Her proper name is not used for most of the story. The few times she is mentioned she is called "the woman" (11:5) or "the wife of Uriah" (11:26; 12:9, 10, 15), a phrase which emphasizes that her status in the story is Married Woman.[11] She is called Bathsheba only in 12:24, after the sin has been expiated and David's marriage to her begins with a clean slate. Bathsheba, then, is not a full-fledged character. She cannot even be viewed as a type. For lack of a better designation I will call her an "agent." An Aristotelian term which describes the performer of an action necessary to the plot. How an agent may come to be perceived as a character is explained by Frank Kermode: "the plot has agents, and the agents have proper names . . . so that we come to think of them as characters."[12] The plot in 2 Samuel 11 calls for adultery, and adultery requires a married woman. Bathsheba fills that function. Nothing about her which does not pertain to that function is allowed to intrude into the story.[13] [[74]]

11. Alter has noted how Michal is called either David's wife or Saul's daughter, depending on which relationship the story wishes to stress. This is added evidence that we should pay more attention to epithets in the Bible.

12. *The Genesis of Secrecy. On the Interpretation of Narrative* (Cambridge, Mass., 1979) 78. This view is in some ways similar to that of the Formalists, who see all characters as *actants* rather than as *personnages*. For a fuller discussion of Aristotle's definition of character, and that of the Formalists, see Seymour Chatman, *Story and Discourse* (Ithaca, 1980), 108–11. I am not looking for a way to explain character in literary theory, but am trying to differentiate between levels of characterization.

13. The only other piece of information we have about her is that she has cleansed herself from her impurity (2 Sam 11:4). For the function of this phrase in the narrative see the Appendix.

Bathsheba and Abishag

Bathsheba's function as an agent in 2 Samuel 11–12 is in marked contrast to Bathsheba as a character in 1 Kings 1–2. Here she is a "real" person, a mother concerned with securing the throne for her son. She emerges in these episodes as one of the central characters, important in affairs of state as well as in family matters (the two are inseparable).

There is, however, also an agent in these chapters. She is not Bathsheba, but Abishag. Abishag was the fair damsel who ministered to the king "but the king knew her not." In her first appearance in the story she provides a contrast to David—her youth and beauty offset his age and feebleness. This occurs in 1 Kgs 1:4. In verse 15, when Bathsheba enters the king's chamber, we are again told that "the king was very old, and Abishag the Shunamite woman ministered unto the king." There is no need to remind the reader so soon about Abishag's ministrations. The repetition of this information must serve a different function here. It is not made for the contrast with David, but for the contrast with Bathsheba. It is Bathsheba who is now noticing the presence of Abishag as she enters the room. Bathsheba, who was once young and attractive like Abishag, is herself now aging, and has been, in a sense, replaced by Abishag, just as she comes for the purpose of replacing David with Solomon. One can feel a twinge of jealousy pass through Bathsheba as she silently notes the presence of a younger, fresher woman. Or is it perhaps sad irony that the once virile David who could not restrain his passion is now oblivious to the young woman who "lies in his bosom" to provide him with warmth?

Abishag's usefulness to the narrative does not end there. After David has died and Solomon ascended the throne, Adonijah, the elder brother and displaced heir, asks Bathsheba to present his request that Solomon permit Adonijah to marry Abishag. The dialogue that ensues goes as follows:

B: Do you come with peaceful intentions?
A: Yes, with peaceful intentions. I have something to say to you.
B: Say on.
A: You know that the kingdom was mine and everyone expected me to be king, but things have been turned around and the kingdom is my brother's, because the Lord willed it. [[75]]
Now I have one favour to ask of you; please don't refuse me.
B: Say on.
A: Speak, please, to Solomon the king, for he will not refuse you, that he should give me Abishag for a wife.
B: Very well, I will speak for you to the king.

The actions of both parties are difficult to understand. If claiming a former king's concubine is tantamount to claiming the throne, as it is often interpreted, then surely this is a rash move on the part of Adonijah, although one could understand how desperately he wanted to be king. It is even more rash on the part of Bathsheba, who has just done her utmost to insure Solomon's succession.[14] On the face of it, it seems that she is here undermining the very cause for which she worked so hard. Why did she agree to speak on behalf of Adonijah? Several suggestions could be offered, all of them speculative in the extreme. (i) Bathsheba is naive. She is convinced that Adonijah really does come with honorable intentions, and feels sorry enough for him to aid him in this (unimportant?) request. (ii) A naive Bathsheba, in light of what we already know of her, is difficult to accept. Perhaps she is really hateful, expecting Solomon to react violently. This would then be an opportunity to get her son's rival out of the picture once and for all. Prior to this, Solomon had agreed to permit Adonijah to live in peace, leaving the possibility of a future uprising against the king. Bathsheba would be glad to prevent this, and through her intervention, Adonijah loses his life.[15] (iii) In conjunction with the latter explanation, there may be an additional element involving Abishag, the object of the request. We have already noted how the narrative hints at Bathsheba's perception of her. Perhaps Bathsheba is really jealous of

14. Gunn (*The Story of King David*, 137 note 4) notes the other cases in which claiming a royal concubine has been viewed as making a claim to kingship; he also expresses doubts about the correctness of this interpretation. In the case of Bathsheba and Adonijah, he says that "such interpretation requires the implication that both Adonijah and Bathsheba are to be viewed as imbeciles." The second suggestion (below) answers this difficulty, at least on Bathsheba's part. Adonijah may have been willing to try anything, even something as dangerous as this, especially if he thought that Bathsheba would support him. That Adonijah's request is a bid for the throne is generally thought to be confirmed by Solomon's reaction. Gunn views this as an over-reaction—"any request for anything would have served to trigger Solomon's paranoia." That is, of course, possible; but if the request was indeed innocuous then the story becomes even more difficult to explain. Why did Adonijah want Abishag? (Certainly love is not an issue here.) And why would such a story be told at this juncture if it were not perceived as a threat to the kingship of Solomon? The context is: how Solomon secures the throne and destroys the opposition. The killing of the opposition must be for good reasons, either because of David's death-bed command and/or because it is truly merited—not because of a paranoid over-reaction. (I am indebted to Prof. Gunn for calling to my attention several of these points in a private communication.)

15. Both of the foregoing are reflected in *The Jerome Biblical Commentary* (Englewood Cliffs, 1968) I, 183–184. If Bathsheba is, indeed, leading Adonijah on toward catastrophe, then she is following the dying David's lead in dealing with the opposition. This is also a contrast to her actions in 1 Kings 1, which were initiated by Nathan. Here she is clearly working on her own for the benefit of her son.

her and does not want Solomon to have her. In any case, the opportunity to have Abishag at the center of a troublesome issue would not be lost on Bathsheba.

I have presented the dialogue in order to call attention to the narrative technique. The slowing down of the action, both here and when Bathsheba appears before Solomon, gives some insight into the minds of the characters. Adonijah carefully and delicately leads up to the favor he has come to ask, assuring Bathsheba that he has come to terms with the loss of the throne. Bathsheba's interjections of "Say on" suggest that she is considering at each step what it all means and where it might [[76]] lead. Some amount of ambivalence or hesitation is evident when she keeps her promise to Adonijah. The narrative records each detail of her entrance into the audience with Solomon, as if we are moving through the action in slow motion along with her. Her words to Solomon are almost identical to Adonijah's words to her, with several significant changes. "I have one *small* favor to ask of you" (v. 20); the favor has become a small favor, either in an attempt to convince Solomon that there is really no harm in it (the naive Bathsheba), or, as an ironic comment (the scheming Bathsheba). She also transforms the syntax from "let him give me Abishag" to "let Abishag be given," making Abishag the subject instead of the object, and thereby emphasizing her action and minimizing Solomon's (in support of my third explanation).

Bathsheba's part in the story ends here, but, no matter what motivated her, it is clear that she is a full-fledged character, important to the plot but with feelings and reactions developed beyond the needs of the plot. There is a different literary use of Bathsheba here from the one in 2 Samuel 11; there she was an agent, here she is a character.

Abigail

The story of Abigail (1 Samuel 25) precedes the story of David and Bathsheba chronologically, and in some ways it is a mirror image of it. First of all, Bathsheba's husband Uriah was a good man (too good) while Abigail's was a base fellow. Despite this Bathsheba apparently did (or could do) nothing to save him. Abigail, on the other hand, resorted to elaborate measures in order to save her husband. Secondly, the story of Bathsheba capitalizes on illicit sex. This is completely absent in the Abigail story. Although David was obviously attracted to Abigail, as witnessed by the speed with which he married her when she became widowed, there is no hint of any unseemly behavior between the two, although there was ample opportunity. Finally, in the Bathsheba story David commits murder because of a woman. In the Abigail story David, as he himself recognizes, has been prevented from committing murder because of a woman.[16]

There have been several fine discussions of 1 Samuel 25, and my understanding of this chapter is in many ways dependent on them.[17] However, our interest here is not the story itself, but its characters, for here we find individuals who are neither agents nor full-fledged characters. Rather they are types. Abigail [[77]] and Nabal are both exaggerated stereotypes.

Nabal, meaning "churl," is what he is named and what he is.[18] This is expressed twice: once when the character is introduced (v. 3—the point of view of the narrator), and again as part of Abigail's statement to David (v. 25—Abigail's point of view). Although his only offense is his failure to recognize David's authority (and this is quite understandable), his wife, his servants, and the reader all think poorly of him. He is pictured only as obstinate, boorish, drunk, and stunned by what his wife has done. We have no idea why he is like this, what motivated him; it is simply his nature to be so.

If Nabal is the proverbial "fool," then Abigail epitomizes the *ʾēšet ḥayil* [['capable woman']].[19] She is described as intelligent and beautiful, and portrayed as sensitive, assertive, and ready to protect her husband though he does not deserve it. In short, she is a model wife and modest woman. This is clearest, and most exaggerated, when she addresses David as lord and refers to herself as his maidservant. This might be interpreted as correct etiquette, or the politic thing to do when trying to convince David not to harm her husband, but it is out of all proportion at the end of the story when David proposes marriage. The widow of the wealthy rancher answers the young upstart by saying: "Behold, your handmaid is a servant to wash the feet of the servants of

16. Cf. P. Miscall, "Literary Unity in Old Testament Narrative," *Perspectives on Old Testament Narrative, Semeia* 15 (1979) 27–44. Concerning the relationship of 2 Samuel 11 to 1 Samuel 25 Miscall states (p. 39): "Transformations in regard to 1 Samuel 25 are . . . transparent. . . . In both stories, David gains a wife but the processes by which he gets them could not differ more radically." Miscall is not so much interested in showing the structural similarities of these two stories—which are obvious—as showing how both are related structurally to the three stories of the patriarch and his wife in a foreign land in Genesis.

17. Levenson, *CBQ* 40 (1978) 11–28; and D. M. Gunn, *The Fate of King Saul* (JSOT Supplement Series 14; Sheffield, 1980) 96–103.

18. Gunn (*The Fate of King Saul*, 155 note 9) discusses whether the name really has this meaning, and, if so, whether it could then be a real name; or whether the real meaning of Nabal has been lost. In any case, I feel that the character is a stereotype. Abigail is the same, even though her essence is not conveyed in her name.

19. So P. Kyle McCarter, Jr., *I Samuel* (Anchor Bible, Garden City, 1980) 401.

my lord!" Finally, in antithesis to Nabal, Abigail has the prescience that David will be "prince over Israel" and is therefore entitled to respect.

The plot, as well as the characters, is unrealistic. It could be reduced to: "fair maiden" Abigail is freed from the "wicked ogre" and marries "prince charming." This suggests that this is not just another episode in the biography of David, but an exemplum.[20] Chapter 25 presents more abstractly the theme found in chapters 24 and 26—David has the power to kill but declines to use it. He triumphs over his opponent without the need to kill him himself, for God sees to it. The Abigail story, no less than the Saul stories, is a strong endorsement of David's destiny to reign as the chosen favorite of God. As Abigail says: "And though a man rise up to pursue you, and seek your life, the life of my lord shall be bound up in the bond of life with the Lord your God, and the lives of your enemies shall He sling out . . . and He appointed you prince over Israel" (vv. 29–30). This is hardly relevant to the events of the Abigail story, but exactly the point that it, along with its adjacent chapters, is trying to make.[21] ⟦78⟧

Conclusions

Four women, Michal, Bathsheba, Abishag, and Abigail, have been presented here, and we have seen how differently they are characterized. Michal and Bathsheba in 1 Kings 1–2 are full-fledged characters in the modern sense. They are realistically portrayed; their emotions and motivations are either made explicit or are left to be discerned by the reader from hints provided in the narrative. We feel that we know them, understand them, and can, to a large extent, identify with them. Abigail, on the other hand, is much more of a type than an individual; she represents the perfect wife. Different from both the character and the type is what I have called the agent. Examples of agents are Bathsheba in 2 Samuel 11–12 and Abishag. Both of these women appear in the narrative as functions of the plot or as part of the setting.[22] They

20. Cf. Levenson, *CBQ* 40 (1978) 22: "In this little tale, we are close to the world of moral allegory. . . . " Gunn (*The Fate of King Saul*) traces the themes of good and evil in the story but then concludes that "retribution is not decided on moral grounds" (p. 102). It is thus not a true *moral* allegory, but could certainly be considered an exemplum or allegory.

21. Levenson (p. 23) cites the thematic links between chapter 25 and its adjacent chapters. His conclusions are close to my own on this matter.

22. On the difficulty in distinguishing characters from setting see S. Chatman, *Story and Discourse*, 138–41. It is possible to have characters that are not human, especially in fairy tales or science fiction, e.g. animals, magical objects, natural phenomenon, robots, etc. It is also possible to have humans, even individual, named humans, that are not characters.

are not important for themselves, and nothing of themselves, their feelings, etc., is revealed to the reader. The reader cannot relate to them as people. They are there for the effect that they have on the plot or its characters. They are necessary for the plot, or serve to contrast with or provoke responses from the characters.

These are the levels of characterization that have emerged from a study of a small number of stories. I would venture to put these three on a continuum: 1. the agent, about whom nothing is known except what is necessary for the plot; the agent is a function of the plot or part of the setting; 2. the type, who has a limited and stereotyped range of traits, and who represents the class of people with these traits; 3. the character, who has a broader range of traits (not all belonging to the same class of people), and about whom we know more than is necessary for the plot. There may, of course, be other levels of characterization in the Bible that await discovery. The fact that there are at least three should caution us against hasty generalizations about characterization in biblical narrative.[23]

It is interesting to note that none of the characters analyzed here is really a main character in the broad sweep of the stories in Samuel and Kings. The main concern of all of the episodes is the king and the kingship, yet David is the dominant character only in 2 Samuel 11–12. In the Michal story in 1 Samuel 19 his role is secondary to Michal's; he is not even given any words to say. The scene does not shift away from Michal after David has exited, but remains focused on Michal and the encounter with her father. The same is true of the Abigail story, in which [[79]] David is supporting actor for the leading lady. Again, most of the action takes place at Abigail's home, in the absence of David. The scene shifts to David's location only when Abigail is there. In 1 Kings 1–2 David is barely alive. To be sure, it is his extreme condition that motivates the struggle for succession, and his word that confirms the winner, but he is hardly a main character in the narrative. It is Bathsheba who emerges as the main character even though the story is really not about her.

The result in all of these cases is an indirect presentation of David, in which various aspects of his character emerge naturally, outside of the glare of direct scrutiny. These episodes are then combined, in the mind of the reader, with the episodes in which David is the main char-

---

23. A penetrating study by M. Sternberg ("The Truth *vs* All the Truth: The Rendering of Inner Life in Biblical Narrative," *Hasifrut* 29 [1979] 110–46) refutes the notion that the Bible does not present the inner life of its characters, and shows in great detail the techniques that are used to do just that. I hope to pursue another aspect of this in a future study on point of view in biblical narrative.

acter. It has already been shown how the David stories alternate between a presentation of the private man and the public figure, so that in the end family affairs and affairs of state are intermingled, each having an effect upon the other.[24] What has not been observed is that there is also an alternation in the narratives between David as main character and David as subordinate character, and that these correspond roughly to the public and private domains.[25] Furthermore, there is a correspondence between the public and private stages in David's life in terms of his responses to his wives:[26]

Michal	emotionally cold, but uses her to political advantage	the cold, calculated gaining of power
Abigail	eager but gentlemanly response	self-assurance as a popular leader
Bathsheba	lust, grasping what is not his	desire to increase his holdings, expand his empire
Abishag	impotence	loss of control of the kingship

The David stories have been woven into a masterful narrative in which all facets of the hero's complex personality are allowed to emerge. This is accomplished by highlighting him at times, and by showing him in the reflection of lesser characters at other times. This shift in focus and in clarity of presentation produces a narrative which has depth, which is credible to the reader, and which never fails to engage his interest. [[80]]

Appendix: A Note on 2 Sam 11:4:
" . . . she having been purified from her uncleanness"

Since this is the only bit of information about Bathsheba that the reader is given, and since we have stressed that nothing about Bathsheba *per se*

---

24. See K. Gros Louis, "The Difficulty of Ruling Well: King David of Israel," *Semeia* 8 (1977) 15–33; and Gunn, *The Story of King David*, 87–111.

25. In the case of 2 Samuel 11 there is a reversal. David is the main character in the private episode and absent totally from his public role as commander of the Israelite forces against Ammon.

26. This is observed, in the cases of Bathsheba and Abishag, by Gunn, *The Story of King David*, 90–93.

intrudes into the story, it is necessary to clarify the meaning of this phrase and its function in the narrative.

Some find it ironic that David should be so concerned with ritual purity when he was about to commit adultery.[27] But there is nothing in the story to suggest that David would have refrained from sexual intercourse had Bathsheba not been in a pure state.[28] Moreover, the phrase is for the benefit of the reader, not David; the whole verse, containing a series of actions, is the narrator's way of informing the audience what took place. Our phrase is a parenthetic note describing Bathsheba's condition at the time of the action, and is thus to be rendered in English by a perfect tense (i.e. it is something that happened before but about which the reader learns only now). The Hebrew text has no suggestion of cause and effect, such as is conveyed by the incorrect translation "and he lay with her, *for* she was purified. . . . "[29]

Others have found in this phrase an explanation for the bath which first attracted David's attention. It does refer back to the bath, but surely a bath was not such an unusual occurrence that it required an explanation. If it did, it would have been better to place it in v. 2, where the bath is mentioned, rather than in v. 4, which describes action subsequent to the bath.

Actually, the phrase is in precisely the right place. Its purpose was neither to explain the bath nor David's religio-sexual values. Its purpose has been discerned by A. B. Ehrlich, who explains that the verse is meant to inform the reader that Bathsheba was clearly not pregnant when she came to David, since she had just been "purified from her uncleanness." Shortly thereafter she found that she was, and that leaves no doubt that the child is David's, since her husband had been out of town during the interlude between the bath and her visit to the palace.[30]

27. Cf. the commentary of David Kimhi. It is cited on p. 270 of M. Perry and M. Sternberg, "The King through Ironic Eyes: The Narrator's Devices in the Biblical Story of David and Bathsheba and Two Excursuses in the Theory of the Narrative Text," *Hasifrut* 1 (1968–69) 263–292. This article has generated a number of responses: cf. the articles by B. Arpali, U. Simon, and the response of Perry and Sternberg in *Hasifrut* 2 (1970).

28. This brings to mind the scene in Bernard Malamud's *The Fixer* when Bok, already in bed with the daughter of his Russian benefactor, discovers that she is menstruating and is so filled with repulsion that he cannot continue his lovemaking. I cite this to emphasize that it is *not* parallel to the Bathsheba story. The plot of 2 Samuel 11 requires that David have sexual relations with Bathsheba; the plot of *The Fixer* requires that the sexual relationship not be consummated.

29. Thus the old Jewish Publication Society translation (1955). The New JPS translation (1978) and the RSV correctly omit "for." The NEB reads: "though she was still being purified after her period," thereby making David guilty of two offenses.

30. *Mikra Ki-Pheshuto* (reprinted New York, 1969) vol II, p. 210. This is also the conclusion arrived at by Perry and Sternberg.

Moreover, the phrase may also alert the reader to the fact that Bathsheba was, at this time in her cycle, most likely to become pregnant.[31] Thus there is some foreshadowing even before the pregnancy is announced (in the next verse). The phrase, then, gives the reader plot information, not character [[81]] information.

31. Cf. H. P. Smith, *Samuel* (New York, 1899) 318; H. W. Hertzberg, *I and II Samuel* (Philadelphia, 1964) 310.

The Bible's Art of Persuasion:

Ideology, Rhetoric, and Poetics in Saul's Fall

MEIR STERNBERG

I

[[45]] What goals does the biblical narrator set himself? What is it that he wants to communicate in this or that story, cycle, book? What kind of text is the Bible, and what roles does it perform in context? These are all variations on a fundamental question that students of the Bible would do well to pose loudly and sharply: the question of the narrative as a functional structure, a means to a communicative end, a transaction between the narrator and the audience on whom he wishes to produce a certain effect by way of certain strategies. Like all social discourse, in short, biblical narrative is oriented to an addressee and regulated by a purpose or a set of purposes involving him. Hence our primary business as readers is [[46]] to make purposive sense of it, so as to explain the *what's* and the *how's* in terms of the *why's* of communication.

Posing such a question in the clearest terms is a condition for reasonable and systematic inquiry, rather than a panacea or a shortcut to unanimity. The answers to it would doubtless still vary as well as agree, since the reticent narrator gives us no clue about his intentions except in and through his art of narrative. To reconstruct the principles underlying the textual givens, therefore, we must form hypotheses that will relate fact to effect; and these may well differ in interpretive focus

Reprinted with permission from *Hebrew Union College Annual* 54 (1983) 45–82.

and explanatory power. But even the differences, including those not or not immediately resolvable, would then become well-defined and intelligible and fruitful. That they are not remarkable for being so in the present state of affairs is largely due to the tendency to read biblical texts out of communicative context, with little regard for what they set out to achieve and the exigencies attaching to its achievement. Elements thus get divorced from the very terms of reference that assign to them their role and meaning: parts from wholes, means from ends, forms from functions. Nothing could be less productive and more misleading. Even the listing of so-called forms and devices and configurations—a fashionable practice, this, among aspirants to "literary criticism"—is no substitute for the proper business of reading. Since a sense of coherence entails a sense of purpose, it is not enough to trace a pattern; it must also be validated and justified in terms of communicative design. After all, the very question of whether that pattern exists in the text—whether it has any relevance and any claim to perceptibility—turns on the question of what it does in the text. Unless firmly anchored in the relations between narrator and audience, therefore, formalism degenerates into a new mode of atomism.

What, then, does the biblical narrator want to accomplish, and under what conditions does he operate? To answer this question, we must take into account the distinctive as well as the universal features of his communication. Like all speakers, from the humblest dialogist going about his daily business to the most highbrow artist in his ivory tower, the biblical storyteller is a persuader in that he wields discourse to shape response and manipulate attitude. Unlike most speakers, however, his persuasion is not only geared to an ideology but designed to vindicate and inculcate it. Even among ideological persuaders, he has a special claim to notice, due not so much to the theology preached as to the rules and rhetoric of its preaching.

Of the various challenges facing the biblical narrator as ideological persuader, the most basic and formidable derives from the tension [[47]] between two constraints. One is his commitment to the divine system of norms, absolute and demanding and in application often ruthless; the other, his awareness of the necessity and difficulty of impressing it on a human audience. The problem is always how to harmonize rhetoric and ideology: how to get man to adopt a world-picture that both transcends and threatens man; how to win the audience over to the side of God rather than of their fellow-mortals; how to accomplish the task of persuasion without dwarfing, betraying or compromising the object of persuasion. This would make the narrator the servant of two masters, were it not for the fact that one of these he serves with a view of subjecting him all the more effectively to the other. Only a fool like Rehoboam—whose fate is indeed a lesson in rhetorical as well as political control—would disregard the advice of the wise old men about apparent service as the way to real domination.

Thus suspended between heaven and earth, the narrator must perform feats of tightrope walking in order to maintain his balance and achieve his dual goal. The trickiness of that performance has few equivalents in literature, religious or secular, ancient or modern. Obviously, nothing like it constrains Homer's narrative strategy in the *Iliad*, where the gods' squabbling provides comic relief from the intensity of the human tragedy, and their petty score-keeping, a contrastive background to the hero's absolute norms. And the irreverent treatment of the gods in Homeric epic has its counterpart in the rough handling of the audience in prophetic discourse, for a Jeremiah can afford to lash out where the storyteller would entice and manipulate. In the absence of either license, the narrator must establish consensus while observing both the articles of faith and the decorums of communication.

On top of all this, as if to make things even more difficult for himself, the biblical narrator avoids the line of least resistance in presenting character, event, and the march of history.[1] Unlike the didactic [48] persuader, with whom he is so often confused, he will rarely stoop to the polarization of values and effects, with repulsive villains pitted against all-round paragons; nor to the wholesale evocation of stereotype and stock-response; nor to homiletic address and lecturing. Didacticism is ideological writing, but not vice versa, and the dividing

---

1. In this, the Bible's ideological rhetoric corresponds to its rhetoric of interpersonal relations as I described it in "Delicate Balance in the Rape of Dinah: Biblical Narrative and the Rhetoric of the Narrative Text," *Hasifrut* (1973), 193–231. That analysis concludes with a spectrum of fourteen rhetorical devices, ranging from the explicit to the covert, through which the Bible shapes our response to character and event: (1) Narratorial evaluation through a series of epithets; (2) through a single epithet; (3) through a choice of loaded words, without at all interrupting the flow of the action; (4) explicit judgment left ambiguous between narrator and characters; (5) as in (1), (2) and (3), except that the judgment is made by characters; (6) judgment through a nonverbal objective correlative: drastic action that speaks for itself; (7) charged dramatization, lingering over and thus foregrounding the plot elements designed for judgment; (8) informational redundancy; (9) direct inside-view of the characters and the play of perspectives; (10) order of presentation; (11) order of presentation involving the manipulation of conventional patterns, i.e. chronological gapping and syntactic displacement; (12) analogical linkage and confrontation: straight, contrasted, dynamic; (13) recurrence of key-words along the sequence; (14) neutral or pseudo-objective narration, where incidental details seem to gain not just equality but sometimes even priority to essentials. These control measures, we shall see, characterize doctrinal as well as interpersonal rhetoric, with the preference again given to the arts of indirection.

line is precisely where ethics and aesthetics meet to generate the *art* of persuasion.

Still, at times the Bible's task is relatively simple. Even the God of wrath, after all, does not always need much vindication. In the story of David and Bathsheba or Ahab and Naboth, for example, the king's sins are so odious that the human and the divine systems of norms converge and point the same way. But in many other instances, likewise based on a scheme of "crime and punishment," the narrator's rhetorical powers are stretched to the utmost, because the plain facts of the tale by no means suffice to ensure such harmony. Where God condemns, man may well condone.

These are accordingly the real test-cases, and the story of Saul and Amalek (1 Samuel 15) illustrates the challenge they present. Does Saul's sparing of "Agag and the best of the sheep and the oxen" justify God's tearing the kingdom from him? Hasn't Saul followed the essential instructions in destroying Amalek "from Havilah as far as Shur," and doesn't this make his one aberration forgivable, if not negligible? Isn't there a glaring disproportion between achievement and reward, sin and penalty? There are the normative questions that the reader is sure to pose. And these are indeed the very questions that the narrator prepares to meet and resolve, by way of subtle persuasive art rather than blunt ideological fiat.[2]

Nothing else can account so well for the tale's selective and combinatory procedures, notably for the manifold repetition that governs its whole sequence. This striking feature seems here not merely to incur redundancy, as usual, but to carry it far in excess of normal biblical practice. While the biblical structure of repetition requires (and often makes do with) only two members, Saul's ordeal involves all the three [49] possible types: (1) *the member of prospect* (command, prophecy, scheming), defined in terms of expectation about the narrative future: God orders Saul to smite the Amalekites; (2) *the member of action* (performance, realization, accomplishment): Saul smites Amalek; (3) *the member of report* (about prospect and/or action), defined in terms of retrospection on the past: Saul tells Samuel how he smote Amalek.[3] Even more excessive, the first type of member repeats a long-standing prospection from Deuteronomy (25:17–19) and is in turn repeated to

2. Of the kind imposed by the Chronicler, who lays down the law without going to any trouble to make it intelligible, let alone palatable: "Saul died for his unfaithfulness to the Lord, on account of the commandment of the Lord that he did not keep" (1 Chr 10:13).

3. For further discussion of these concepts and the compositional principle as a whole, see my "The Scripture of Repetition in Biblical Narrative: Strategies of Informational Redundancy," *Hasifrut* 25 (1977) 109–50.

Saul after as well as before the smiting of Amalek; and the last type re-curs again and again in Saul's apologetics. Finally, this extended series of repetitions alternates with another that centers in Samuel, once he arrives on the scene to confront the king. What might otherwise appear a hodge-podge of redundancies, however, makes perfect rhetorical sense in terms of an overall strategy that wields repetition as a battering ram against Saul and, indirectly, the possibly doubting reader.

In fact, the rhetorical strategy devised to justify the ways of God to man begins as early as the opening member of the repetition, in that it gives the divine command its shape and emphases:

> And Samuel said to Saul, It was me the Lord sent to anoint thee king over his people, over Israel; now therefore listen to the voice of the Lord. Thus says the Lord of hosts, I remember what Amalek did to Is-rael, how he waylaid him when he came up from Egypt. Now therefore go and smite Amalek and utterly destroy all that he has; and do not spare him, but kill both man and woman, both infant and suckling, both ox and sheep, both camel and ass ([1 Sam] 15:1–3).

At this point, of course, the normative crux is still hidden from the reader's eyes: not just left unannounced but, in fact, artfully cam-ouflaged, since the opening focuses attention on Amalek's rather than Saul's crime and punishment. But the narrator looks ahead and, hav-ing misled the reader about his target and intentions, prepares the real line of attack. Seemingly concerned only to highlight the odium and justify the doom of the past offender, he actually lays the ground for producing the very same effects in regard to the future offender who desecrates the workings of retribution. If Amalek's fate now appears to the reader well deserved, so will Saul's later: it is this logic that drives the hidden persuader to start by manipulating our response to future developments in [50] a variety of ways, each turning on a "prospect + prospect" mode of repetition.

First, to anticipate and offset the ruthlessness of the extermination order, the text leads up to it by a specific exposition. As regards the se-quence of discourse, it is not just that the member of prospect ante-cedes the action, as is the rule in the Bible. Within the members of prospect itself, a retrospect leads the way: the explanation comes be-fore the command, the cause before the effect, the mention of the crime ("what Amalek did to Israel" etc.) before the demand for punish-ment ("Now therefore go and smite Amalek"). Thus, the expository movement from past to future, the wording of the retrospect, even the general-particular relation between its parts—all these bring to mind the original *memento mori* in Deuteronomy:

Remember what Amalek did to thee on the way as you came out of Egypt. How he beset thee on the way and cut off at the rear all who straggled behind, when thou wert faint and weary; and he feared not God. Therefore, when the Lord thy God has given thee rest from all thy enemies round about, in the land which the Lord thy God gives thee for an inheritance to possess, thou shalt blot out the remembrance of Amalek from under heaven. Thou shalt not forget (25:17–19; cf. Exod 17:8–16, Num 14:45).

To reinforce the parallels, by way of structural as well as thematic allusion, is to reinforce the present command by investing it with historical resonance and continuity.

Second, again as with the original command from the times of the desert, the explanation is cast in terms that are national no less than religious: "I remember what Amalek did to Israel." This is not a private quarrel, then, between God and Amalek. Nor is this just an ancestral grudge, an exceptional *casus belli* within an otherwise harmonious coexistence. The speech does not explicitly indicate that, apart from the first unforgivable act of aggression, Israel also has more recent scores to settle with Amalek, from the days of the Judges. Rather, these later contexts are now implicitly activated by way of pointed intertextual allusion. Note the verbal analogy devised between Israel's coming revenge and Amalek's periodic invasions in the Gideon era: the prospective "both ox and sheep, both camel and ass" rhymes with the retrospective "they left no sustenance to Israel, neither sheep nor ox nor ass . . . and their camels were without number" (Judg 6:3–5). The tit-for-tat patterning, so dear to the biblical rhetoric of retribution,[4] not only eliminates all traces [[51]] of arbitrariness from the divine command, but also evokes a long and eventful history of one-sided aggression.

Third, the intertextual analogy also serves to explain an otherwise obscure point. Why is the command addressed to Saul rather than to one of his predecessors or successors, and why at this particular moment? The answer lies in another artfully, pinpointed link between past and present. The historical visions expressed in Deuteronomy to a landless people in the words "when the Lord thy God has given thee rest from all thy enemies round about [*misaviv*]" have now come true to the last detail: the end of the previous chapter describes Saul's victories against "all his enemies round about [*saviv*], against Moab and against the Ammonites and against Edom and against the kings of Zobah and against the Philistines." Repatriation, settlement, national

---

4. On the use of verbal echoes to imply or pinpoint causal links between action and counteraction see "Delicate Balance in the Rape of Dinah," esp. 212, 230.

security *misaviv*: all the promises in the subordinate clause having now been kept, the main clause falls due. No wonder God picks up the thread ("I remember") just where he dropped it ("Thou shalt not forget"). The time for revenge has finally come, and it is Saul's duty and privilege to settle the outstanding account.[5]

Indeed, the fourth feature of the rhetorical preparations consists in making Saul (as well as the reader) aware of his personal responsibility for closing that account. The opening reference to Saul's having been anointed "king over [God's] people, over Israel" already implies his role in dealing with "what Amalek did to Israel." And that implication is soon made explicit in the grammatical person of the imperatives, which (with the one exception I have italicized) assumes the singular form: "Go and smite . . . and *utterly destroy* . . . and do not spare . . . but kill."[6] Again, the allusion to Deuteronomy sharpens and validates the effect. While in the early prospect the second-person singular refers to the people, in the version repeated here its reference shifts to their king: God is "I," Saul "thou," and Israel "he." The shift in reference pinpoints a shift in responsibility, one that hints at the recent transformation of social structure with the rise of the monarchy and will later prove of crucial importance as soon as Saul tries to shift responsibility back to the people who delegated it to him.

Finally, as with the burden of responsibility so with its object. It is not [[52]] only that the charged language of the ban (*ḥerem*), reserved for holy war and fortified by the absolute "all," imposes the duty of total destruction. Its operational meaning is at once spelt out. Cast in blunt terms and symmetrical specifications, the decree leaves no room for misunderstanding and excuses, in regard to either enemy population or property: "both man and woman, both infant and suckling, both ox and sheep, both camel and ass."

At the stage of prospection, then, the preliminary rhetoric serves a complex of functions, apparently straightforward but in fact double-edged. It is designed (1) to base the command on the widest possible (and hence most widely acceptable) normative grounds; (2) to issue it to the most definite addressee and in the most definite terms; (3) to gain understanding and assent for its various conditions (timing, dras-

---

5. The very same structure recurs later in the book (2 Sam 7:1–3 alluding to Deut 12:10–11), so as to suggest the contrast between David and Saul as keepers of ancestral obligations. Far from needing a reminder to build a temple "when the Lord had given him rest from all his enemies round about," David takes the initiative at the earliest possible moment.

6. Even that single plural disappears in the Targum and Septuagint versions, perhaps by analogy to v. 18.

ticness, responsibility, and all); and thus (4) to maximize the reader's desire for, as well as expectations of a swift and meticulous performance on the king's part.

That performance indeed starts on an encouraging, though unexpected, note. Having summoned the people,

> Saul came to the city of Amalek, and lay in wait in the valley. And Saul said to the Kenites, Go, depart, come down from among the Amalekites, lest I put an end to thee with them; and thou showedst kindness to all the people of Israel when they came up from Egypt. And the Kenites departed from among Amalek ([1 Sam 15:]5–6).

It is precisely what looks like a divergence from the letter of the divine command that proves so encouraging, since it manifests a remarkable grasp of the spirit informing that command. God having sent him on his mission armed with a reason as well as a sword, Saul wisely infers that those who showed Israel kindness "when they came up from Egypt" must not perish with those who stabbed Israel in the back "when he came up from Egypt." If the terms of reference are the settling of historical debts, then gratitude counts no less than revenge: the execution of justice must work both ways.

At this point, then, the tale goes out of its way—even literally so, the Kenite episode being a digression from the main line of events—to give Saul credit for his energetic ("Go, depart, come down") initiative. Its very inclusion speaks for itself; the echoing reference to the time of the Exodus confirms the approval by way of analogy; and that nobody chides Saul for having thereby jeopardized the whole campaign suggests that the risk was well worth taking. But within the rhetorical strategy as a whole, the very normative insight displayed by Saul here is later to be [53] turned against him, in more than one way. It enables the narrator to avoid black-and-white portraiture (an avoidance that forms not only an aesthetic feature of his storytelling but a shrewd weapon of persuasion as well: "Who wishes to blackguard the man? Whenever he deserves praise, he gets it"). An even more boomerang-like effect produced by Saul's insight is that it serves to reimpress on the reader's mind the historical rationale of the war, this time from the positive side, and concretize the distinction between justified and unjustified divergence. And in terms of the play of expectations about the future, it looks as good as a promise that Amalek, too, will get his just deserts from the scrupulous king. Given the pointed contrast in regard to the past, the logic of analogy would seem to leave no room for any other development.

That expectation is even further reinforced by the immediate sequel, especially since the member of action starts ("And Saul smote

Amalek") by echoing the member of prospect ("go and smite Amalek").
So its frustration, just when everything seemed to be going so well, re-
doubles our surprise, disappointment, condemnation:

> Saul smote Amalek, from Havilah as far as Shur, which is east of
> Egypt. And he took Agag the king of Amalek alive, and all the people
> he utterly destroyed with the edge of the sword. And Saul and the
> people spared Agag, and the best of the sheep and of the oxen and of
> the fatlings, and the lambs, and all that was good, and would not ut-
> terly destroy them; and all the despised and rejected property, this
> they utterly destroyed ([[1 Sam 15:]]7–9).

Actional and rhetorical surprise come together. For through the sudden unfolding of Saul's misconduct, the narrator also unfolds for the
first time his own focus of interest and object of attack. Such drastic
shifts and turns are far from rare, still less accidental. As argued in my
analysis of the story of Dinah, based on a double twist, they relate to
the Bible's management of the narrative sequence and the narrator's
control of our response throughout the reading-process.[7] The Bible's
persuasive repertory thus includes the disappointment of both the
reader's expectation (in terms of the structure of probabilities) and his
preference or judgment (in terms of the structure of values). For each
mode of frustration produces surprise, a retrospective repatterning of
anterior elements, and hence a sharpening of impressions and attitudes. The effect of the newly-revealed material then derives not only
from the preparations [[54]] made by the narrator but also the unpre-
paredness of the reader, whose attention has been diverted elsewhere
till the moment judged suitable for springing the surprise that will can-
alize it into the desired grooves.

Consider the present case of sequential shift in focus. Only when
his hero falls into sin does the narrator show his hand. It is (we now
discover) Saul's crime, not Amalek's, that forms the real theme, and
his punishment that raises the moral-ideological question marks and
hence calls for justification. But this does not at all mean that the narrator has so far been wasting his time on a mere effort to mislead us
about his target and intentions. Nor is it just that lulling our suspicions
about what lies ahead serves his purposes because it lowers any possible resistance on our part to his initial manipulations and then
enables him to catch us unprepared at the transitional stage of disclosure. The point is that as soon as Saul emerges as the real center of interest and judgment, all that has gone before appears in a new light

---

7. For theoretical background see my *Expositional Modes and Temporal Ordering in Fiction* (Johns Hopkins: Baltimore and London, 1978).

and acquires new significance in relation to him. The whole normative weight of the tale's opening, seemingly designed to crush the Amalekites or any pity their fate may evoke, now recoils upon Saul.

This is evidently the case with the member of prospect, now transformed all along the line from an explicit judgment on the original offenders into an implicit judgment on the appointed avenger of their offense. But take the distinction just made between what deserves to be annihilated (Amalekites) and what spared (Kenites). Having so far served to vindicate the divine command, by emphasizing its ideological basis, it now serves to condemn the human performance, by emphasizing the mercenary basis of its distinctions, whether motivated by vanity (Agag) or greed (sheep, cattle, etc.). The contrastive effect extends even further. That divergence from the letter of God's order now opposes, and thus exposes, the violation of its very spirit. It is not simply that the holy war is desecrated by the looting, but that its whole point is rudely reversed by the principle of choice: the pride of Amalek should have been the first object of total destruction, not of selective "sparing."

Still, despite its boomerang-like effect at this point in the sequence, Saul's behavior toward the Kenites at least reflected some credit on him at the time. In contrast, his handling of the Amalekites instantly bristles with condemnation and leaves him no leg to stand on in the future. The act itself is bad enough, of course, but its impact on the reader can largely be traced to the shape given to it by verse 9. A turning-point in the action and the rhetorical strategy alike, this forms one of the most intricate pieces of persuasion in the Bible: [[55]]

> Saul and the people spared Agag, and the best of the sheep and of the oxen and of the fatlings, and the lambs, and all that was good, and would not utterly destroy them; and all the despised and rejected property, this they utterly destroyed.

Since the performance of the command is a nonlinguistic object—a member of action that the narrator could render in any number of ways—each of the choices involved in its representation assumes a special significance:

(a) Of all the verbs and verbal forms available to the rendering of the offense, the narrator chooses that root ("spare") and that number (singular, though the subject is plural) which will most directly conflict with the language of God's order: "spared" (*vayaḥmol*) in the action as against "do not spare" (*loʾ taḥmol*) in the prospection.

(b) From the semantic and perspectival standpoint, moreover, "spare" (literally, "have pity") does not merely denote an action or omission. Unlike otherwise equivalent verbs like "took" or even "failed to destroy," it gives us an *inside view* of the agent, so that the subjective motive for the omission emerges together with its objective result. The same verb becomes even more conspicuous in retrospect, since (coupled with "would not destroy them," which validates and reinforces its import) it provides the only inside view of Saul throughout the narrative. And this monopoly over the inner life ensures its crushing effect in relation to later as well as foregoing members of the structure of repetition. The king's long series of prevarications in the coming members of report—from the versions that it is the people who did the sparing to the version that it is his fear of the people that drove him into sin— will be exposed and denounced vis-à-vis the authoritative reference-point established by the narrator in the member of action.

(c) Even within the present sentence itself, the combinatory features of the verb sharpen the rhetorical effect of its selection. Thus, in his rendering of the sin the narrator not only takes preventive action by dissociating the "sparing" from the natural (and hence emotionally problematic) objects of pity, like the infant and the suckling named in the command. He goes so far as to lay an ironic trap for the reader: "spared"—whom? the weak? the helpless?—"Agag and the best of the sheep and of the oxen." (The surprise-and-irony are even finer in the original word order—literally, "And spared Saul and the people of Agag and the best" etc.—since the interposition of the grammatical subject between the predicate and the objects gives the reader more time to entertain the illusive [56] hypothesis.) So the miniature twist within the sentential sequence, like the coincident large-scale twist marking the whole tale's structure of expectations, impresses on our minds that there is no question here of any humanitarian motives whatsoever: sparing (*kh-m-l*) is nothing but an ironic euphemism for greed (*kh-m-d*).[8]

(d) Order of presentation is also put to another artful use within the verbal microcosm. Given the flexibility and ambiguity of syntactic coordination, one cannot tell whether in the course of events itself the "sparing" really followed any order (e.g. whether it was initiated by Saul or perpetrated in concert with the people). But the narrator takes advantage of the fact that in language things cannot be simultaneously communicated to arrange the subjects of the sentence in the order most unfavorable to Saul: "Saul and the people spared." An initial subject, Saul appears to be the initiator of action, since the sequence of

8. This ironic wordplay gains support from the analogous misdeed in Josh 7:21, where Achan himself admits that he "coveted" the spoils.

words gives an impression of a corresponding sequence of events. And even if placed first on hierarchical rather than chronological grounds, the king must still shoulder most of the blame.[9]

(e) As the sentence continues to unfold, one pattern of coordination gives place to another, more extended but on the face of it equally innocent. In fact, like that of the grammatical subjects, the series of objects is so ordered as to invite and deepen the reader's condemnation while pretending to supply him with factual information. Take the strongest and most perceptible points in any sequence, the beginning and the ending. Agag's appearance at the head of the list of the "spared" startles the reader and hardens his response in advance. And the closure of the list with the jarring phrase "all that was good"—referentially indeterminate (What does it indicate or include?), normatively incongruous (How can an abomination be "good"?), and perspectivally ambiguous (Who thinks in such terms? surely not the narrator?)—operates to shock the reader anew into a retrospective hardening of judgment. Moreover, the fact that both the subjects and the objects of the "sparing" fall into two groups (Saul: people, Agag: livestock) places Saul in a serial position corresponding to Agag's, and thus reinforces our sense of his personal responsibility for the survival of Amalek's very epitome.[10] "Reinforces," [[57]] because the wording of verse 8 ("And he took Agag the king of Amalek alive") has already coupled the two kings in a similar form.

(f) Finally, the selectional art of the sentence as a whole (What is said? What is not said? How such is said?) effectively dovetails with its combinatory pattern. There is not even a hint of the kind of extenuating circumstance later adduced by Saul: that the army was actuated by the desire to keep the best of the spoil for sacrifice. On the contrary, the narrative does its utmost to demolish any possible illusion about mistaken zeal, and instead to bring home to us that their motives were pure only in the sense of being purely self-regarding. For Agag, who heads the list, is hardly a prospective sacrifice. The ensuing series of objects manifests, apart from sheer length, such stylistic inelegance and such odd shifts between the general and the particular (the general term "the best of the sheep and of the oxen" followed by the

9. Again, this device is still more effective in the original. Since the Hebrew text both preposes the verb and casts it in singular form, the reader integrates predicate and kingly subject into a well-formed whole ("spared Saul") before discovering that another, coordinate subject ("and the people") lies ahead.

10. Not for nothing does Josephus claim that Saul "took prisoner the enemy king, Agag, out of admiration for his beauty and his status," while the people "spared the beasts and the cattle . . . and all the chattels and riches" (*Jewish Antiquities*, bk. VI, 7:2).

particular "the fatlings and the lambs" followed by the all-inclusive "all that was good") as to produce an impression of an orgy of looting. The progression from the human (Agag) through the animate (the live-stock) to the miscellaneous (the "good") deepens this impression by suggesting the range and variety of the plunder. And the glaring con-trast between the destroyed and the preserved, in both representa-tional form (order vs. disorder) and proportions (phrase vs. catalogue), dispels any remaining doubt about motivation. Considering the mem-ber-of-action's role in hardening our heart against the offender, it is no accident that the negative first-impression generated here about the looters is more intense and homogeneous than in any of the subse-quent stages. There, the very location of Saul and his army in Gilgal implies a possible intention to share the pickings with God. But, how-ever dubious its mitigating effect, even the geographical picture emerges only later; and when it does, the tale already has additional weapons to direct against Saul.

By the end of verse 9, then, the case for the prosecution becomes so formidable that it is hard to believe that the narrator has put it to-gether without uttering so much as a single word of overt condemna-tion. Another look at the fourteen devices ranged along our rhetorical scale (see footnote 1) will establish that the first four have not been employed at all—nor will they be in the sequel—while all the rest have variously been put to work in the space of a few verses. Rather than di-rectly operating against his target, the narrator prefers to shape and manipulate response through his favorite indirections, whose power derives [[58]] from a sophisticated art of relations. His control strategy includes selective ratios and combinatory modes of presentation, inter-textual and intratextual linkage, repetition and variation on all levels, devices of sequence and suprasequential patterns of analogy, the inter-play of grammatical design and semantic context, and the mutual rein-forcement of language and world. And no less notable than the repertory of indirections is the skill with which they are coordinated into a single persuasive whole.

Accordingly, the clash between prospect and action maneuvers the reader into concluding that Saul has seriously abused, if not betrayed, his office. But does his sin justify a punishment so final and terrible as dismissal? After all, the prophet Samuel himself protests that it does not:

> And the word of the Lord came unto Samuel, saying, I repent that I have made Saul king, for he has turned away from following me and has not performed my commandments. And Samuel was enraged and he cried to the Lord all night ([[1 Sam 15:]] 10f.).

To persuade us that the sin nevertheless does justify such rejection, to narrow and bridge and smooth over any possible gap between divine and human judgment, ideally to the point of perfect accord: this is the narrator's main task, whose trickiness shows him operating at his rhetorical best.

II

But before proceeding to trace the strategy by which the reader is manipulated into the desired judgment, we need to understand more precisely the nature of the task and the rules for its performance. By rules I mean a set of self-imposed limitations as well as self-authorized license, since the Bible does not consider that the end of serving two masters and bringing their points of view into harmony justifies all means. Thus, as a matter of artistic principle, the biblical narrator does not make things easy for himself by minimizing in advance the rhetorical problems to be overcome. Just as in the story of the rape of Dinah he does not present the Hivites as monsters, just as his historico-ideological commitment to Jacob does not preclude giving Esau a sympathetic hearing, just as none of his righteous men is perfect and few of the unrighteous wholly evil—so in our tale he avoids the line of least resistance. The narrator does not rob Saul of his impressive victory over Amalek, not even to the customary extent of adverting to some intervention [[59]] on God's part. Nor does he turn Saul into a rebel against God. Nor does he burden Saul with such a heinous crime against his fellowmen as will (like the murder of Naboth) immediately warrant the most extreme retaliation according to human as well as divine norms. It is precisely here that he rejects the ideological simplifications of didacticism and melodrama: his is the art of self-constraint, of meeting challenges, of dancing in chains. Even in ideological commitment and strait he takes risks where lesser or more single-minded persuaders would take shortcuts.

On the other hand, it is equally typical of the biblical artist that, as a matter of rhetorical principle, he should avoid both the normative evenhandedness open to uncommitted literature and the dogmatist's suicide missions of the "all or nothing" variety. Whatever the appeal of truth or balance or the *difficulté vaincue* or psychological complexity and realism, the persuader's main business is to carry his audience with him to the predetermined terminus. Where this is at stake in the Bible, no wonder that any other ideal, aesthetic or historical, should bend to the pressures of ideology. The wonder is rather that the narrative should deny them anything like full control over its choices and procedures. It usually observes such constraints only in regard to doctrinal essentials; and even then it usually so implements their dictates as to leave room for other interests and to suit with the poetics of indirection. Not that the narrator is lacking in ideological zeal, but that he abounds in the artistic energy which impels and qualifies great literature to reconcile opposites without unduly sacrificing either. His zeal itself, moreover, is pragmatic rather than dogmatic: this is a distinctive feature with enormous explanatory power, and the failure to appreciate it has led Bible studies into endless error and trouble. Being pragmatic means, as I shall soon argue, that when the exigencies of manipulating the audience do require some sacrifice, the doctrine as well as the art or the history may have to pay the price of indoctrination.

When things come to the crunch, therefore, we find the rhetoric determined indeed to produce the appropriate effect, but not by the easy, certainly not the easiest way. It is not just that the narrator prefers winning the audience over to (what often proves the undoing of the dictatorial speaker, God and his prophets included) laying down the law to them. Nor is it just that he favors the indirect approach through the mediation of a represented world, where the preacher would go in for a frontal assault, direct address and all. Some of this favorite techniques as indirect persuader cannot be accounted for in terms of mere expediency. Thus, faced with a task of persuasion that bristles with difficulty, [[60]] the biblical narrator would rather go to extra compositional trouble than simply load the dice for or against the problematic character or cause. A typical solution for him would be to distribute the difficulty over a number of episodes (as well as elaborating the devices within each) with a view to overcoming our possible resistance by degrees. This is the case with many biblical doublets, usually explained in genetic terms. Take Hagar's flight from Abraham's house before she is forcibly driven out years later, or Esau's sale of his birthright to Jacob before being cheated out of his blessing. In each variation on the principle, the narrator so extends and divides his treatment as to lead up to a crucial scene that might otherwise prove too much for the reader: the first episode softens our response to the second by getting us used to the idea of the antagonist's deprivation or, more radically, splitting it into two gradated and differently motivated acts on the protagonist's part.

Where the art of sequential distribution will not reduce the problem to manageable size by itself, it may be buttressed or replaced by some biased tampering with plot or character. Whether invidious or apologetic or laudatory, however, such tampering is akin to, but not quite identical with, the notorious loading of the dice in doctrinal writing. For one thing, it shows a moderation that stops well short of dichotomizing the world into paragons and brutes, attractive protagonists and repulsive antagonists. Esau and Saul, even Abimelech and Ahab, have their sympathetic features; while Jacob and David, or even Elijah, are certainly not idealized. For another, it tends not so much to simplify as to shift or "deflect" the terms of the normative conflict, freely switching from one set of norms to another in order to produce the desired impression. The result is a foregone conclusion, but not the means to its achievement or vindication; the fight has indeed been fixed, but often athwart rather than along ideological boundaries.

Hence many a tricky clash, where merit opposes merit, is actually resolved by the Bible in terms of the persons rather (or no less) than the causes involved. Examples would be the characterization of the Hivites as twisters in the Dinah story, or of Esau as a glutton indifferent to his primogeniture, both designed to complicate, if not to confuse, the moral issue in favor of the inevitable victor: Jacob and his line. Were the antagonist treated differently—the Hivites portrayed as scrupulously honest, Esau as self-controlled as well as loving—his cause would assume such weight as to meet the opposite cause on something like even terms, enforce a clear-cut choice between right and right or value and value, and thus endanger the protagonist's moral status. As it is, the point may have been made to some extent on the "wrong" (e.g. personal or emotional [[61]] rather than doctrinal) grounds, but it has nevertheless been made.

In general, the biblical narrator neither loads the opposed terms of a conflict (or the responses they elicit) with the total partiality of the didacticist, nor sharpens and balances them with the total impartiality open to the freethinking artist. Instead, he prefers to subject opposites to such (and so much) mixing, blunting and even twisting operations as will have the most persuasive impact on his audience. Naturally, far from serving to project what a philosopher would regard as an integrated doctrine and a moralist as a clear lesson, such shifting or deflection of terms produces normative blurs, if not discontinuities and inconsistencies. But the narrator aims at effective rather than coherent theology, at pragmatic rather than dogmatic morality. As long as he can maintain (and drive home) his general frame of reference, the details worry him far less than they seem to worry so many of his critics, as unmindful of the exigencies of communication as of the arts and licenses of storytelling. This means, in short, that to gain his rhetorical ends he is ready to pay even in ideological coin.

It is this logic of persuasion that now explains two measures taken by the narrator in the Amalek story, viewed as an ideological drama where Saul plays antagonist to God's protagonist. One measure consists in an anticipatory softening-up of our moral resistance to God's decision, by way of a precedent located at an earlier stage of the same book. The Amalek affair operates not as an isolated exception but as an intensified re-enactment of a foregoing drama of sin and punishment:

> And Samuel said to Saul, Thou hast done foolishly; thou hast not kept the commandment of the Lord thy God, which he commanded thee; for now God would have established thy kingdom over Israel forever. But now thy kingdom shall not endure (1 Sam 13:13–14).

Saul's first sin of disobedience, in the war against the Philistines, now combines with the second to give him the image of an habitual offender; and its having already cost him the hope of founding a dynasty now leaves his own position the only target for God's wrath. Thus, the narrator orders and welds the double pattern into a two-phase process of retribution, which enables him not just to proceed gradually but to "improve" the moral proportion (or moderate the disproportion) between cause and effect. On the one hand, Saul having learnt nothing from his previous aberration, the sin now looms larger; on the other hand, the dynasty having already been doomed, the punishment now looks milder.

[[62]] This gradated and cumulative progression makes rhetorical sense not only of an otherwise disturbing redundancy, predictably dismissed by scholars in genetic terms, like multiple origin. It likewise integrates other sequential features of the cycle. Note the curiously delayed introduction of Saul's sons—above all, of the heir who will play such a decisive role in the first war. That he is hardly mentioned previous to his father's clash with the prophet, while richly drawn thereafter, forms a preventive measure within the overall rhetoric of retribution. For even the dynastic doom must appear a foregone conclusion before the reader can be allowed to encounter its immediate victim: the lovable and brave and pious Jonathan, whose trust in God presents such a contrast to his father's lack of faith. Jonathan being endowed with the very moral attributes in which Saul is deficient, his premature spotlighting would compromise God's first decree—far from unworthy of succeeding, he would seem the natural choice—and thus endanger the whole tactics of gradual deposition. Whereas, the punishment having fallen on more or less anonymous heads, Jonathan's emergence after the fact minimizes the incongruity and even serves to expose Saul anew by way of opposition. It is all a matter of persuasive timing, the order of presentation being determined by ideological rather than chronological exigencies.

If this anticipatory step forms a characteristic "rhetorical softening-up," then its complement within the tale itself forms a characteristic "rhetorical deflection." The tale, that is, refrains from putting the opposition between the divine and the human norms to the supreme test. Instead, it correlates the two sets of norms, operating against Saul with a double or mixed standard, persuading on two fronts, so to speak. True, the prophet formulates the relations between sin and punishment in the stark and lucid terms of *lex talionis*, "Because thou hast rejected the word of the Lord, he has rejected thee from being king." But the narrator himself will not balance them on such a razor's edge. He could easily manage to stand a head-on collision between the will of God (as moral protagonist) and the disobedience of man (as moral antagonist): for instance, to depict Saul as a king perfect by all social as opposed to divine standards, and to risk everything on the attempt to persuade us that even such a Saul deserves to go the way of all offenders. Here as elsewhere, however, the narrator avoids this line of showdown (reserving it for Moses alone, the model leader denied entrance into the promised land for having struck instead of spoken to the rock). And its avoidance, as Mose's case indeed shows, hardly lends itself to explanation in the simplistic (if not circular) terms that such a polarity is inconceivable within his world-picture. It is for reasons of rhetoric rather than [[63]] doctrine that he chooses throughout to broaden as far as possible the basis and area of agreement between the reader and himself by exposing Saul to a two-pronged attack.

The narrator, caught between the ideological rage for coherence and the rhetorical need for consensus, thus "deflects" the moral drama that the prophet, who faces no such task of persuasion, can afford to sharpen and radicalize. The persuader is willing to settle for less than the absolute measure for measure—"rejection" for "rejection"—as long as he can maintain the principle of the rightness and supremacy of God's judgment. Hence, far from operating on purely religious grounds, right from the start he presents the war against Amalek as a national affair and later he goes out of his way to demonstrate Saul's unfitness for kingship from the social as well as the divine viewpoint. It is not that this deflection makes the job of bringing the viewpoints into harmony easy to perform, but that it entails a doctrinal compromise, certainly a complication. The difference between "almost-all or nothing" and "all or nothing" is equally vital for the understanding of the Bible's structure of norms and its art of narrative.

All this explains the variety of devices now marshalled against Saul (and in a different sense, the reader). One is the allusion to historical precedents, both without and within the Book of Samuel. Like that of

prospect, the members of action and report derive much of their rhetorical force from implicit intertextual and interepisodic relations. The
intertextual analogy-by-allusion is this time to Joshua 7, which follows
the earliest instance of total destruction, with spoils put under the ban
and all. The conquest of Jericho, we are made to recall, involved an
analogous transgression ("Achan, the son of Carmi . . . took some of
the banned things, and the anger of the Lord burned against the
people of Israel"); and, again, the points of similarity between the two
tales are specified far beyond this broad thematic correspondence.
The similarity established is also linguistic (e.g., the recurrence of the
charged term *ḥerem* [['ban', 'spoil']], or the epigrammatic turn given to
the judgment), geographical (both crimes have "Gilgal" for a setting),
and, most remarkably, situational. For the Jericho narrative likewise
dramatizes, in the same terms and even the same sequence, a normative distinction between justified and unjustified deviation from God's
command: between going beyond its letter (and again, in favor of a
benefactor of Israel, "only Rahab the harlot shall live") and going
against its spirit (like Achan).

Of the two looters, the text now invites us to conclude, Saul deserves death even more than Achan, in view of the difference in status
and enemy. And it is another impressive measure of the deliberateness
of the [[64]] whole intertextual coupling that, the allusion once perceived, not only Saul's death itself but its circumstances and concomi-
tants become predictable. For the dynamics of this analogy involve its
covert extension or propulsion from the phase of sin to that of punishment. The expectation generated as early as this stage, that Achan's
end foreshadows Saul's, comes true later in the book. Like his historical mirror-image, Saul dies a violent death, his sons fall with him, and,
what is otherwise inexplicable in terms of Jewish culture and has indeed always puzzled scholars, the corpses are set on fire (the phrase
"burnt them" of Josh 7:25 recurring in 1 Sam 31:12).[11]

Moreover, by a kind of associative chain reaction, some features of
Achan's story also bring to mind the war with the Philistines that immediately precedes the Amalek affair. In each case, God turns away
from the embattled Israel due to a "breach of contract" on the part of
some warrior—Achan's theft, Jonathan's tasting the honey—whose
identity and offense finally come to light through the drawing of lots
(Josh 7:14–21, 1 Sam 14:36–64). The associated violations thus fall

---

11. The Chronicler, who omits the Amalek episode, also omits the unusual detail of
burning from the parallel account of the exploit performed by the Jabesh-gileadites
(1 Chr 10:10–11).

into a tripartite analogy, which directs against Saul a telling *argumentum ad hominem* (or more precisely, *argumentum ex concessis*): even the precedents and premises he himself set now rise to condemn him. If Saul wanted to execute ("thou shalt surely die, Jonathan") his victorious son ("who has wrought this great deliverance in Israel") for having unwittingly broken ("Jonathan had not heard") the king's impulsive and senseless oath ("Cursed be the man who eats any food until evening"), then what penalty does he himself deserve for violating God's reasoned command?

Furthermore: the two external analogies, established as early as the member of action, combine with two internal analogies that open and round off the sequence of reports. One is the contrast between the king and the prophet, who objects to the mission God lays on him ("Samuel was enraged and he cried to the Lord all night") and yet hastens to perform it ("Samuel rose early to meet Saul in the morning"). The other is the parallel that surprisingly bridges the distance between the two kings. For the prophet's arrival on the scene leads to an ironic peripety in the fates of both. Saul falls from the heights of victory ("behold, he set up a monument for himself") to the depths of rejection; Agag has a rude awakening from the illusion of survival ("Surely the bitterness of death is past") to the reality of death by the sword ("Samuel hewed Agag in ⟦65⟧ pieces"). And the double peripety culminates in the figurative-literal relations between the "tearing" away of one's kingdom and the "hewing" of the other's body. Apart from reinforcing the dramatic irony and extending the appearance-and-reality theme, this tripartite pattern carries the most unpleasant normative implications for Saul, due to the "unnaturalness" of the two pairings: on the one hand, the disparity revealed between king and prophet, whom we would expect to stand together, and on the other hand, the parity between king and king, whom we would expect to form diametric opposites all along the line. In fact, the two royal enemies are drawn so close together, as brothers in crime and self-delusion and sudden reversal of fortune, that their analogy looks like a realization of another old promise *cum* warning: the Lord "will give their kings into thine hand and thou shalt make their name perish from under heaven. . . . And thou shalt not bring an abomination into thine house, lest thou become an accused thing [*ḥerem*] like it" (Deut 7:24–26).

But what proves most damaging to Saul's image is the final development of the repetition structure, effected between these internal analogies and occupying the whole middle of the tale (verses 13–31). Actually, we encounter here two interlinked structures of repetition— one consisting in the series of Saul's "reports" about his performance and the other in Samuel's "reports" about God's judgment. In dialogic combination, they assume the following form:

Samuel came to Saul,

and Saul said to him: "Blessed be thou to the Lord! I have performed the commandment of the Lord."

And Samuel said: "What then is this bleating of the sheep in my ears and this lowing of the oxen that I hear?"

And Saul said: "They have brought them from Amalek; for the people spared the best of the sheep and of the oxen, to sacrifice to the Lord thy God. And the rest we have utterly destroyed."

And Samuel said: "Stop, and I will tell thee what the Lord said to me this night. . . . Though thou art small in thine own eyes, art thou not the head of the tribes of Israel? The Lord anointed thee king over Israel and the Lord sent thee on a mission and said: 'Go and utterly destroy the sinners, the Amalakites, and fight against them until they are consumed.' Why [[66]] then didst thou not listen to the voice of the Lord, but didst swoop on the spoil and didst what was evil in the eyes of the Lord?"

And Saul said to Samuel: "I did listen to the voice of the Lord, and I have gone on the mission on which the Lord sent me, and I have brought Agag the king of Amalek, and I have utterly destroyed Amalek. And the people took of the spoil, sheep and oxen, the best of the things devoted to utter destruction, to sacrifice to the Lord thy God in Gilgal."

And Samuel said: "Is the Lord as pleased with burnt offerings and sacrifices as with listening to the voice of the Lord? Behold, listening is better than sacrifice, to hearken better than the fat of rams. For rebellion is the sin of divination, and stubbornness is iniquity and idolatry. Because thou hast rejected the word of the Lord, he has rejected thee from being king."

And Saul said to Samuel: "I have sinned, for I have transgressed the utterance of the Lord and thy commandments, because I feared the people and listened to their voice. Now, pray, forgive my sin and

And Samuel said to Saul: "I will not return with thee; for thou hast rejected the word of the Lord, and the Lord has rejected thee from being king over Israel."

return with me, and I shall prostrate myself before the Lord."

> And Samuel turned to go,
> and he laid hold of the skirt of his robe,
> and it tore.

> > And Samuel said to him: "The
> > Lord has torn the kingdom of Is-
> > rael away from thee this day, and
> > has given it to a neighbor of thine,
> > who is better than thou. Also, the
> > Strength of Israel will not lie and
> > will not repent, for he is not a man
> > that he should repent."

And he said: "I have sinned. Now
honor me, pray, before the elders of
my people and before Israel, ⟦67⟧
and I shall prostrate myself before
the Lord thy God."

> And Samuel returned with Saul,
> and Saul prostrated himself before the Lord.

Vertically, we have in each column a sequence of reportive variations
that gradually but inexorably moves towards a climax. Saul comes all
the way from the exulting "I have performed the commandment of the
Lord" to the about-facing "I have sinned"; and Samuel, from the mild
query about the bleating of the sheep to a brutal statement of rejection. Horizontally, we have a sequence of exchanges whose speech-
and-counterspeech logic dramatically motivates the nature, extent and
movement of the repetition and produces one of the Bible's most
elaborate dialogues.

The development and interweaving of the two structures of repetition in terms of dialogic alternation indeed yields a coherent and striking pattern. But to appreciate its goal and achievements, one needs to
understand the difficulty with which the formation of that natural-
looking pattern confronted the narrator. The difficulty derives from the
unequal status of the two series of "repetitive" speeches: the equality
they show in the text, far from a natural feature, is the result of brilliant

craftsmanship. As far as concerns the aims of the tale—indeed, of the whole book—the vital part of the dialogue centers in the speeches made by Saul, who is meant to condemn himself by his incessant shifts and turns. And this structure of repetition makes excellent sense in dramatic (psychological, situational) as well as rhetorical terms: Saul has every reason to conceal or whitewash his sin, and he retreats only step by step, version by defensive version. But what about Samuel's structure of repetition, each of whose members causally leads to a future retreat on Saul's part? How can it be likewise justified? How can it be made not only to avoid a monotonous reiteration of the same message, but to progress in terms of dramatic logic, notably including the give-and-take of dialogue?

This problem inspired a solution that turns the difficulty to rich compositional account. In the first place, the narrator leaves Samuel considerable freedom of action—certainly of speech—in that he refrains from specifying the prophet's terms of reference as envoy. In this respect, there emerges a suggestive contrast in the handling of his two missions to the king. The tenor of the first mission having been developed into a central fact, that of the second is now reduced to an informational gap. For if the Saul-centered structure of repetition opens [[68]] with a quote of God's peremptory command, the Samuel-centered structure opens with a general statement by God ("I repent that I have made Saul king") and suppresses all the rest: not only Samuel's nightlong appeal but even God's final instructions. Whatever took place between them, we are kept in the dark about it; and for all dramatic and rhetorical purposes, therefore, Samuel is burdened with no categorical message to the king. That blurring and withholding of information makes it possible for the narrator to have the best of both worlds—to present Samuel as one who (unlike Saul) adheres to the spirit of God's orders and yet adjusts his conduct to the situational requirements—since we can never tell which of the messenger's first verbal shots derives from God's original message and which comes on his own initiative. This goes to show, again, the flexibility of the Bible's principle of repetition. Underrepetition (to the point of gapping) is no less feasible and functional than overrepetition (to the point of redundancy), and the two can even perfectly well dovetail to serve an overall strategy.

Second, the informational gap that results from the blurring of the member of prospect addressed to Samuel is exploited in another way for the same end. The part disclosed to the reader complements and reinforces the effect of the part suppressed. If the suppression makes a flexible Samuel acceptable, then the disclosure gives his flexibility an active causal legitimation: it suggests that God himself has not yet irrevocably committed himself to deposing Saul. For compared with normal expressions of divine wrath and to the prophet's own violence in the sequel, what we actually find in verse 11 is cast in relatively mild language. In fact, it emphasizes past misdeed ("he has turned back from following me") and present emotion ("I repent") more than the future scenario typical of a prospect. And the sense of an *open* future gains further support from the built-in reminder that God is quite capable of changing his mind with the change of circumstance. Having started by repenting, he may well finish by repenting this repentance.

That Samuel denies this possibility—"the Strength of Israel will not lie and will not repent, for he is not a man that he should repent"—rather highlights than precludes it. It is not only that Samuel speaks in anger and towards the end of the dialogue, when Saul has already convicted himself beyond redemption; that Samuel's moral and informational viewpoint has by then long been distinguished from God's; that God often forgives (or at least, as with Ahab in 1 Kings 21, reprieves) the penitent, to the despair of the Jonahs among his prophets. In flat opposition to Samuel's absolute denial the narrator himself opens God's counteraction with "I repent" and ends it with "the Lord repented." Still, [[69]] given the differences in speaker and context, nothing could be more gratuitous than the popular appeal to an interpolator to explain the "contradiction." Except to a reader bent on imposing harmony on the perspectives that the Bible takes such care to discriminate and play off against one another, the three statements are perfectly easy to accommodate in a single tale. Even if Samuel literally meant what he says—and his own conduct suggests that he knows better—then his claim would just expose his own unreliability. To guide our expectations, we look to the lord of history and the master of narrative, rather than to any creature of theirs, however eminent; and these two speak here with one voice.

Hence the impression that, whether or not Samuel has a formal mandate to suit the judgment to the results of the confrontation, there is still room for another "repentance" on God's part. Saul still has a chance, even after the fact, and everything now depends on his response to the charges made against him. As regards the internal structure of time, the future is thus left opaque, indeterminate, contingent on moral choice; and to good effect. This effect forms a rhetorical end in itself, in that it "improves" God's image and the proportions between sin and punishment; and also a means to justify the repetitive series, in that it heightens our sense of the prophet's legitimate freedom of action.

Third, the narrator gives Samuel a good psychological reason to make use of that freedom: his sympathetic attitude to Saul, not much in evidence in their previous dealings but now established beyond doubt by the "anger" and "crying" of verse 11. The reader cannot help asking himself why for two whole rounds the prophet does not simply tell his interlocutor about his dismissal but rather asks him questions—first one pretending ignorance of what happened ("What then is the bleating of the sheep" etc.?) and then a sharper follow-up ("Why then didst thou not listen to the voice of the Lord," etc.?). The most probable explanation is that he wants to put Saul to the test, and only when convinced of his favorite's hopelessness does he pronounce sentence, with understandably escalating brutality.[12] This produces a striking correspondence between the character's psychological and the narrator's rhetorical motives for drawing out the interview: the gradated and dilatory ("repetitive") tactics employed by Samuel are also the best tactics for demonstrating to the reader that even one who starts by appealing [[70]] against God's judgment must finally come to admit its justness. The prophet's very sympathy for Saul thus becomes a weapon for condemnation at the hands of the artful persuader.

As the crucial dialogue opens, then, the structure of point of view is characterized by informational and normative tensions between the various perspectives involved. On the axis of information, the omniscient narrator and God contrast with the benighted Saul, who has no knowledge of either past commotion or impending catastrophe. In between the poles, Samuel knows at least what he has been instructed to say the night before; while the reader's view of past and future has been sufficiently blurred (gapped, ambiguated) to generate the impression of a fluid state of affairs, where events wait on the moral character of the agents and Saul once again holds his fate in his own hands at the crossroads of history.

On the axis of judgment, another perspectival division shows itself here. The narrator and God stand together, as usual, their rejection of Saul equally absolute, though the one's is silent and the other's vocal. And again, this coalition is not only poles apart from Saul's own view of his behavior, but also faces a less extreme and yet more serious opposition, likewise composed of one silent and one vocal member.

---

12. The alternative explanation—that Samuel starts with questions because he is ignorant of the facts behind God's displeasure—would make no sense. It plays havoc with the relations between God and prophet, and is flatly contradicted by the reference to "what the Lord has said to me this night." The informational gap about the member of prospect is the reader's, not the prophet's.

These are of course the reader, who still needs to be persuaded, and Samuel, torn between duty and feeling.

On the face of it, while the informational discrepancies effectively serve the tale's overall strategy, the normative variations appear self-defeating. For if the end of every rhetorical strategy is to resolve or at least to minimize ideological tensions, so as to bring the audience's viewpoint into alignment with the text's—here obviously represented by the God-narrator alliance—then the multiplication of differences in judgment would seem to go counter to that end. Above all, the prophet's midway position splits the divine front and threatens the whole rhetoric of retribution: if the Lord's own seer grieves and wavers, can the ordinary man (including the reader) be expected to do less?

However, what looks like a damaging oversight is actually a calculated risk and proves a source of strength throughout. In general, the difference between running and running away from such risks corresponds to nothing less than the difference between two orders of rhetoric, largely exemplified by biblical narrative and poetry respectively. Naive rhetoric plays the ostrich in all that concerns attitudes (norms, responses, valuations, perspectives, world-pictures) other than its own, whether by simply ignoring or dismissively caricaturing them, Jeremiah fashion. Whereas sophisticated rhetoric gives (or at least pretends to give) such [[71]] divergent attitudes not just recognition and voice but something like a fair hearing, with a multiple end in view. Aesthetically, this goes to meet the poetic demands for tension and variety and complexity, for courting danger as a challenge and a source of interest. Thematically, rather than reducing issues to opposites, this makes (at least on the personal and interpersonal level) for a polyphonic treatment, richer in opportunities for nuancing character and viewpoint. Even on the rhetorical balance sheet itself, the dangers incurred are more than compensated for by the gains: the impression of open-mindedness, even-handedness, awareness of alternatives and variations, etc., strengthens the persuader's reliability and ultimately improves his chances of bringing the audience over to his side.

In short, if the final end of persuasion consists in aligning the addressee's viewpoint with the speaker's, the tactics employed along the route to that terminal may well include ideological understatement, complication, plurality, even disharmony and conflict. Hence a whole set of features typical of biblical narrative, especially when dealing with major cruxes and figures. Consider the avoidance of preaching and black-and-white portraits; the abstention from a fully explicit moral evaluation of the dramatis personae, sometimes leading to a judgment of the act rather than the agent; the establishment of normative gradations in preference to stark polar extremes; and what immediately concerns us, the (not always illusive) distribution of "authoritative" commentary between narrator, God, and prophet.

Accordingly, though the game that the narrator plays in splitting the forces against Saul is indeed dangerous, the rendering of the prophet as a character in conflict proves one of the story's most telling devices. Rhetorically, where strict orthodoxy on Samuel's part would just stamp and distance him as a mouthpiece for God's thunder, his surprising ambivalence draws him closer to us. It reflects the reader's (actual or possible) state of mind at this point along the sequence. His mixed feelings thus turn him at once into "our man" in the represented world and will invest his final judgment, precisely because it is wrung from him, with tremendous power and authority. Just as, in dramatic terms, they motivate the prolongation of his dialogue with Saul—impelling him to inquire and check and double check before delivering the final blow.

III

All this makes sense of the dialogue that gradually unfolds and consistently interweaves the two alternating structures of repetition. In fact, its [[72]] progress has been rendered so natural and its implications so forceful that the narrator can dispense with all overt commentary. Carrying the dialogic principle to an extreme, he effaces himself more than ever. His presence manifests itself in little more than the neutral reporting verb "said" that punctuates the ping-pong movement of the dialogue. Despite the extraordinary length of the exchange, by biblical standards, he does not even provide any stage directions (as regards tone, gesture, setting) till he comes to the punch-line. Despite the seriousness of the things revealed, he makes no normative comment except through the art of relations: the internal patterning of the scenic give-and-take, its linkage with the foregoing discourse, and the intertextual analogies. Despite the agitation and the play-acting and the maneuvering of the two speakers—both deeply troubled, Samuel in conflict and increasing rage, Saul fighting for survival—no inside-view of their minds is given. Instead of exposing Saul's inner life, the narrator lets Saul expose himself. And instead of formulating the pressures that lead to the prophet's ever-sharpening attacks and the king's series of retreats, he leaves the whole task to the reader: we are invited to fill in the gaps, to reconstruct motive and psychological process, to draw the normative conclusions for ourselves. "Let them play before us," the reportorial voice seems to be saying; but like every stage manager, he always remains in control by pulling the strings from behind the scenes.

Saul, little suspecting what awaits him and perhaps genuinely un- aware of any wrongdoing ("behold, he set up a monument for himself"), greets Samuel with the elated "I have performed the com- mandment of the Lord." Still, the prophet does not come out with the crushing refutation ready to his hand—God's "he has not performed my commandments"—but prefers to counter with a question: "What then is this bleating of the sheep in my ears, and the lowing of the oxen which I hear?" Since Samuel already knows the truth, the reader has no doubt about the rhetorical nature of this question. At the same time, the very choice to open not with blunt denunciation but with ob- lique sarcasm immediately raises the possibility that Samuel is first con- cerned to test Saul's response.[13]

[[73]] Unlike the reader, however, Saul does not know that Samuel knows. He apparently thinks his visitor has come on his own initiative and, misled by the questioner's appeal to sense-data ("in my ears," "hear") rather than to supernatural knowledge imparted by God, takes at face value the newcomer's show of innocence. Hence his treatment of the question not as a piece of irony but as a genuine call for information:

> "They have brought them from Amalek; for the people spared the best of the sheep and of the oxen, to sacrifice to the Lord thy God; and the rest we have utterly destroyed."

This counter-show of innocence launches a complex play of view-points and levels of awareness, with Saul as its ironic target. While actually

13. The Septuagint, favored by some modern scholars, prefaces the dialogue with the stage direction that Samuel found Saul "offering as holocausts to the Lord the best of the spoils he had brought from Amalek." This addition (together with the corollary that the Masoretic Text has lost the passage as a result of scribal haplography) makes even less sense than usual, because it goes against both the situational logic of the tale and the struc- tural logic of biblical repetition in general. Situationally, if Samuel discovered Saul at sac- rifice, he would cast his opening question not in terms of hearing ("in my ears . . . hear") but of sight (e.g., "in my eyes . . . see"). Nor does such sacrifice cohere with Samuel's later accusation of "swooping on the spoil" or Saul's own admission of having "feared" the people: to reduce the point at issue to a difference between summary and more ceremo- nial destruction is to deprive the king's plea, not to mention God's judgment, of all color of reason. In fact, structurally speaking, we have here a typical instance of the Septuagint's misdirected rage for harmony in repetition. True to its policy of retrospectively squaring the early (v. 13) with the late (vs. 15+21), regardless of contextual and informational vari- ations, it produces here a montage of the member of "action" with that of "report" and thus identifies the narrator's objective with Saul's unreliable version. (See also n. 14 below, and "The Structure of Repetition," 111–13.) This goes to show, again, the need for con- sidering—and often deciding between—textual variants in the light of textual poetics.

invited to make a moral response—a full confession of guilt being the only gesture that might save him—Saul delivers a factual report. Having misinterpreted the present state of affairs, Saul now misrepresents the past and thus leaves himself no future. And blind to his own informational disadvantage, he seeks to take advantage of his addressee's.

Saul, in other words, now realizes that his opening account cannot stand. But, clinging to the optimistic assumption of Samuel's ignorance, he still hopes to extricate himself from trouble by means of a revised version. And this version departs from the objective truth, as established by the narrator in verses 7–9, at quite a few material points. First, it makes no reference to the heaviest sin of all—the sparing of Agag—but confines itself to explaining the facts ("sheep" and "oxen") directly indicated by the question. If Samuel does not know, why volunteer information? Even in regard to what it must and does disclose, Saul's version ("the best of the sheep and of the oxen") is strikingly selective compared with the narrator's ("the best of the sheep and of the oxen and of the fatlings, and the lambs, and all that was good"). Strikingly, because the truncation of the original catalogue—the reported whole is only the actional beginning—brings out the anxiety to play things down. Moreover, these factual omissions go together with an explanatory addition designed to [[74]] whitewash the offense by assigning to it a pious motive: "to sacrifice to the Lord thy God." Since the dialogue does take place in the sacral Gilgal, the reader must thereupon review the effect produced by the member of action: that the looting was motivated by pure self-interest. But the reviewing does not lead to a definite revision for the better, because nothing in the text now shakes the first impression of orgiastic plunder. The alleged intention shows no sign of past or coming fulfillment. The new semantic twist given to the verb "spare"—in the direction of thrift rather than greed—looks doubly forced, therefore, its irony heightened both by the factual groundlessness of the claim and the textual resonance of the language. And so does the replacement of the narrator's distinction between what the army "would not utterly destroy" and what "they utterly destroyed" by a new ingenious distinction between what was reserved for sacrifice and what relegated to destruction. When joined to the telltale failure to mention Agag, these forms of incongruity combine to establish that Saul is lying. His version introduces the element of doubt only to expel it, with another boomerang effect, and to pave the way for Samuel's dismissal of the excuse on theological as well as factual grounds.

Finally, exploiting what I would call the rhetoric of grammatical person, Saul tendentiously redistributes the credit (and correspondingly also the blame, which however barely surfaces at this stage). His tale falls into three parts, each with its grammatically distinct agent ("they," the collective "he" of the people, "we") and its morally distinct action ("brought," "spared," "destroyed"). Those parts are arranged in hierarchical rather than chronological sequence, so that the report progresses by correlating two movements: the tripartite shift in person goes with a tripartite shift in merit. First, some undefined "they" are made to bear the responsibility for the problematic act of looting, euphemized into "they have brought them from the Amalekites." The redeeming motive for the problematic act is then attributed to the people, likewise cast into the third person but differentiated (in Hebrew) by number: "for the people spared the best of the sheep and of the oxen to sacrifice to the Lord thy God." And only when he comes to the wholly unexceptionable item, the performance of the command itself, does Saul give himself a role and a share: "And the rest we have utterly destroyed." According to this ascending order of merit, then, everyone (except perhaps for the conveniently anonymous "they") has both meant well and done well, but none more so than the king.

Suppression, invention, manipulation: from the reader's vantage point of dramatic irony, this distorted account of what we know to have [[75]] happened aggravates the effect of the happenings themselves. The evasion of the truth is scandalous as it is futile; and so is the evasion of responsibility, manifested in the acrobatics of grammatical person. In this, the royal report diverges from each of the preceding members within the structure of repetition. It diverges from the initial command, dominated by the second-person singular that holds the king accountable for the performance. It also diverges from the narrator's representation, which laid most of the actual (and all the "ministerial") blame on Saul, using the identical verb and person (*vayahmol*) that Saul now reserves (*hamal*) for the people. (Hence another reason for the narrator's choice in verse 9 to couple a verb in the singular with a plural subject: just as his "spared" maximized at the time the retrospective clash with God's "do not spare," so does it now prove to have anticipated Saul's own "spared"). And it even diverges from Saul's previous and exclusively first-person version: "I have performed the commandment of the Lord." Once the monopoly (*I*) over the "performance" turns out to be double-edged, the king is at most prepared to share with his subjects (*we*) the credit for "destroying" but none of the guilt (*they, he*) of "bringing" and "sparing."

This is how the narrator activates the twofold (human-divine or religio-social) frame of normative reference, whose establishment as early as the stage of prospect and importance for his rhetorical opera-

tions I have already discussed. From now on, he will consistently bring
it to bear on his target, employing Samuel's responses in each dialogic
round both as overt aids to judgment on Saul's versions and as situational pressures that elicit from Saul some future pieces of double self-
incrimination. Of course, Samuel performs this service against his will.
His judgments are oriented to God rather than society, and his pressures meant to save Saul himself rather than damn him in the eyes of
others. But the narrator so stage-manages the play of speech and coun-
terspeech as not only to accommodate or neutralize but even to exploit
such perspectival discrepancies. He lets the two speakers express themselves in their own terms and for their own ends—as if they were free
agents and he merely an impartial recorder—while canalizing their
discourse (the illusion of autonomy included) into his strategy of
persuasion.

Thus, Samuel having been stationed at a point of observation analogous to the reader's, his response to the king's current tale is
sufficiently familiar to confirm the socially-based judgment, sufficiently
prophetlike to echo God's voice and thus forward the theological line
of attack, and yet sufficiently restrained to leave the door open. He will
not take the 〚76〛 trouble to dispute Saul's claims. By implication, he
does wave away the pronominal sophistry, not only as irrelevant and
dishonorable ("thou art the head of the tribes of Israel") but also, mentioning for the first time his official status and divine sources of information ("Stop, and I will tell thee what the Lord has said to me this
night"), as lacking in fullness ("until they are consumed," i.e., you've
forgotten Agag) and in truth ("thou didst swoop on the spoil"). But his
main concern is to re-establish the proper frame of reference for the
issue, namely, that consisting in the original decree which he himself
relayed at the very start and now repeats. In its terms, the responsibility
falls on the king alone. The second-person singular, which in the
member of prospect functioned to assign responsibility, thus becomes
in second transmission a series of blows: "The Lord anointed
thee . . . and sent thee . . . and said, Go and utterly destroy . . . and
fight. . . . Thou didst not obey . . . thou didst swoop . . . thou didst evil."
Nevertheless, having clarified the issue, the prophet is in no hurry to
close it by pronouncing sentence. Instead, he ends with another rhetorical question ("why then didst thou not obey?"), overtly an expression of bitterness and disappointment, but covertly also an invitation
to repentance that may still avert disaster.

But Saul receives none of these signals. Blind to the folly of rewrit-
ing history in the presence of God's envoy, to the implications of shirk-
ing responsibility, to the chance secretly offered him to retrieve his

fortunes, he persists in denial. A concrete measure of the enormity as well as the futility of this proceeding is the contrast it forms with three analogical instances, past, present, and future. Achan after the Jericho battle ("indeed I have sinned against the Lord God of Israel"), Jonathan ("Here I am, ready to die") in contemporary times, David in the next generation: each promptly confesses his sin once charged with it.

Even worse than the denial itself, if Saul's response now varies from that of the previous round, it is only in carrying prevarication to new lengths. The repetition with variation thus follows the pattern of causal balance that shapes the whole dialogue: Samuel having just sharpened his censure, Saul now recasts his protestations of innocence into a form that will hopefully withstand the attack. He starts by flatly denying God's general charge of disobedience ("Why didst thou not obey the voice of the Lord?"→"I have obeyed the voice of the Lord"), and then goes on to contest its details, point by point and often phrase by phrase. To the wording of the divine command, as just requoted by Samuel, he selectively opposes formulations of his own that are meant to establish the impeccability of his performance. (Hence the echoing of "the Lord sent thee on a mission and said, Go" by "I have gone on the mission on which [[77]] the Lord sent me," and of "utterly destroy the sinners, the Amalekites" by "I have utterly destroyed the Amalekites.") The taking of Agag alive, no longer omissible, gets interpolated in the middle of the denial, for reasons that the dialogic text leaves unspecified along with the rest of the inner life. Is it because Saul hopes to smuggle it in between "positive" neighbors? Because he wants to demonstrate that he did not "swoop on the spoil" in any gross material sense? Because he wishes to minimize the single aberration by contrasting it with the impressive sum-total ("I have utterly destroyed the Amalekites")? Or, strange but perhaps most probable, because of a confused idea that the seizure of Agag may somehow redound to his credit? Clearly, in the absence of any inside-view, each gap-filling hypothesis damns Saul on different grounds.

From the social viewpoint, what makes this new retrospect even more damning is that it involves still another, third distribution of positives and negatives. The pressure on Saul having increased, he counteracts it by a more drastic forging of the balance sheet. The three-point ascending scale of merit gives place to a descending order that unfolds something like an opposition between good and evil. This time Saul takes all the credit (probably including the capture of Agag) for himself: on the plus side of the balance sheet, the first person is no longer plural ("we have utterly destroyed") but uniformly singular ("I have obeyed

... I have gone ... I have brought ... I have utterly destroyed").[14]
Whereas all the blame for the looting gets squarely thrown on the
people (who "took of the spoil, sheep and oxen, the best of the things
devoted to utter destruction"), with certain variations that on the whole
tend to show them in a more negative light than before.

On the one hand, Saul indeed replaces the problematic verb
"spare," directly conflicting with the original decree, by the neutral
"take"; he still retains the extenuating motive ("to sacrifice to the Lord
thy God") and even heightens its plausibility by indicating the geographical location ("in Gilgal," i.e. they have not taken the livestock
straight home). On the other hand, the blackening far outweighs the
whitewashing. For Saul now drops the anonymous scapegoat in the form
of the third-person singular and transfers its role directly to the people
("they have brought them"→"the people took"). He injects into the people's share of the [[78]] report the charged phraseology ("spoil," "*ḥerem*")
that he took such care to avoid (e.g., by omitting "the sinners" from his
echo of Samuel's words) when glorifying his own. And far from highlighting, as he has just done in regard to himself, he does not even
glance at the creditable part of their activities, namely, the collective destruction of "all the despised and rejected property" or (in his own recent euphemism) "the rest."

Accordingly, if in his first version Saul monopolized the credit but
suppressed the blame and if in the second he turned aside the blame
but shared out the credit, now he radicalizes the opposition between
himself (who did well) and the people (who only meant well). Whether
these shifts are improvised in panic or in cold blood—the narrator, as
usual, provides no inside-view but lets the results speak for themselves—Saul's mendacity and unmanliness as well as his ungodliness
are beyond doubt. What becomes increasingly doubtful is his fitness
for kingship.

Indeed, this is precisely the conclusion that "our man" in the
drama likewise reaches from his own viewpoint. Samuel not only continues to disdain Saul's wriggling, but despairs of getting him onto the
right track. Modulating into formal discourse, he begins with a tongue-
lashing about the duty of obedience as supreme value ("Is the Lord as
pleased with burnt offerings and sacrifices as with listening to the voice

14. Predictably, the Septuagint (again with a following among modern scholars) already reads "*I* have utterly destroyed" in the previous report to Samuel. In its eagerness
to smooth away apparent inconsistencies by way of retrospective adjustment, it again
misses and skews the effect designed by the structure of repetition—this time not the disharmony between the narrator's and Saul's versions but between Saul's shifting versions
themselves.

of the Lord?" With his bitter experience in mind, he hastens to supply his own answer to the rhetorical question, "Behold, listening is better than sacrifice," etc.). And the ideological statement having paved the way for the application, the prophet ends by delivering the long-deferred sentence. Appropriately echoing the judgment pronounced by Joshua on Achan ("Why hast thou troubled us? The Lord shall trouble thee this day"), his sentence assumes a tit-for-tat form that matches crime with punishment and encapsulates the logic in the language of retribution: "Because thou hast rejected the word of the Lord, he has rejected thee from being king."[15]

IV

The three opening rounds of dialogue thus unfold a pattern of causal symmetry: as one side gets increasingly entangled and demoralized, the other gets straightforward and resolute. Given the series of Saul's "repetitive" [[79]] versions, the reader needs little other guidance to trace the erosion of self-confidence, of moral fibre, of royal dignity. The breakdown under pressure takes place before our eyes, gradual enough to compel belief, rapid enough to suggest organic weakness, thoroughgoing and many-sided enough to justify drastic counteraction. At the same time, within the chain of repetition formed by Samuel's speeches, the recurrent formal and semantic elements bring out the three-stage progression that has just reached a climax. We see him moving from a question so innocent-sounding that the addressee may (and does) interpret it as genuine, through a question whose factual antecedent underlines its rhetorical nature, to a question from which the inquirer himself draws the operative conclusion; from a colloquial tone through prophetic thundering to the solemn and measured accents of doom; from ironic criticism through formal reproof to utter rejection.

As for the dialogue's (and the whole tale's) correlated structure of repetition, it also progresses from speech to speech and from round to

15. While the epigrammatic balance is common to both instances, though, its force is significantly heightened here. The whole rhetorical strategy being devised to maximize our sense of proportionateness, the narrator does not rest content with verbally pinpointing, Joshua fashion, the relations between crime and punishment. To preclude any impression of arbitrariness, the key-term that does the pinpointing by appearing on both sides of the equation must follow from the represented developments. That is why we find it drawn from the account of the crime itself, so as to link the verb "reject" and the adjective "reject(ible)" into suggestive wordplay: "Whoever devoted the reject to God, sealed his own rejection."

round, but in a more complex manner than either of its dramatic
flanks. Here the reticent narrator does indeed (and will continue to)
benefit from all the rhetorical advantages yielded to him by the expressive prophet: from the articulation of the judgments themselves, from
their escalating sharpness, and from the weight they carry by virtue of
being wrung from a secret sympathizer. But he commits himself to
none of their rhetorical disadvantages, notably the narrowness and ab-
stractness of the ideological basis for judgment. While the prophet's ti-
rades are geared to divine law, the narrator exploits Saul's string of
responses to bring into play the social code as well. The conclusion
reached and preached is the same, and so is the timing, but not the
grounds or frames of reference. So the two perspectives meet rather
than coincide, and the prophet's voice forms only one component
within the orchestration that reflects the narrator's more inclusive
viewpoint and implements his strategy. But since the frames of reference are compatible and the judgments oriented to them increasingly
converge as the dialogue progresses, this stage also marks a climax of
normative harmony: the dovetailing of the explicit and the implicit, of
divine and human viewpoint, of the attitudes taken by the doctrinally
committed and the reluctantly aligned and the artfully persuaded.

Hence this stage is also a landmark in the relations between what I
⟦80⟧ called the informational and the normative axes of point of view.
These relations manifest a notable shift along the sequence of the dialogue. At the starting point, Saul's informationally the least privileged
of the five relevant viewpoints, since he knows nothing about the
threat hanging over his head; but he is still closer to the reader than to
Samuel, let alone to God and the narrator. Normatively, Saul's is also
the least reliable perspective, but, again, at this point it still has more
in common with the ambivalent and undecided reader than with the
polar extreme of divine wrath. As the dialogue moves forward, however, these perspectival positions change along both axes, in an equally
gradual but otherwise almost diametrically opposed fashion. Saul, who
discovers something about his plight with each round, draws closer
and closer to the reader (as well as to the other participants and ob-
servers) till their viewpoints reach the stage of virtual synchronization.
But the further Saul progresses towards the reader along the informational axis, the further does the reader (together with the prophet) retreat from him along the normative axis towards God and the narrator,
till their viewpoints reach the stage of virtual polarization. Conver-
gence in knowledge goes with divergence in judgment; as dramatic
irony decreases, emotional and moral distance increases. And the two
opposed movements are not only juxtaposed or correlated but causally

related. For what may be excusable with an agent ignorant of his own offense and its implications ("I have performed the commandment of the Lord") becomes intolerable once that agent learns the true state of affairs. Even our pity for the floundering man is hardly a proper emotion for a king to elicit. Indeed, God is right: Saul must go.

The Q.E.D. secured, it may seem that the art of persuasion has done its work and it only remains to wind up the tale. But the narrator, resolved to make doubly sure, has a final surprise in store for us. Saul has not given up hope yet:

> I have sinned, for I have transgressed the utterance of the Lord and thy words, because I feared the people and listened to their voice. Now, pray, forgive my sin and return with me and I will prostrate myself before the Lord.

This is a weapon for rhetorical overkill, launched on both normative fronts to deepen conviction and broaden consensus. If any reader has a lingering doubt about the justice of Saul's rejection, the newly fabricated account will banish it for good. Saul indeed starts by confessing his sin, at long last. But he immediately relapses and, blind to the implications of his argument, throws the blame on others. He thus disqualifies himself on all possible grounds. In social terms, the blatancy of his lie ("I feared [[81]] the people") exceeds all previous limits; and even if this were the whole truth, what better proof would one need of his unfitness for kingship? And in religious terms, he in effect admits that he fears the people more than he fears God. He also chooses the unhappiest (from the hidden persuader's side, the happiest) phrase to express the results of his fear: "I listened to their voice." This loaded verb, whose sense extends from hearing to obedience, resonates more than any other throughout the structure of repetition: as a command ("Now therefore *listen* to the voice of the Lord"); as a call to battle ("Saul *summoned* the people"); as a sarcastic show of innocence ("What then is this bleating . . . which I *hear?*"); as a direct accusation ("Why then didst thou not *listen to* the voice of the Lord?"); as a self-justifying denial ("I *did listen* to the voice of the Lord"); and as a doctrinal priority ("Is the Lord as pleased with burnt offerings and sacrifice as with *listening* to the voice of the Lord?"). So its new appearance, in the context of *vox populi*, galvanizes in retrospect a whole chain of meaning: it infringes the command, confirms the accusation, denies the denial, reverses the scale of priorities. And that the voice of the army has been falsely invoked only makes things worse, if possible, while sparing the persuader the awkwardness of enforcing an ideological choice between *vox populi* and *vox dei*.

It is in this state of double betrayal—where he allegedly betrayed God for fear of the people and actually betrays the people for fear of God—that Saul still expects a happy ending. But that blindness only provokes increasingly trenchant responses, so trenchant indeed as to arouse the suspicion that Samuel finds relief for his personal feelings in the cruelty of his prophetic diatribes. First comes an answer that sharpens the foregoing, religiously-oriented version by hinting at Saul's disgraceful treatment of his subjects ("the Lord has rejected thee from being king *over Israel*") and crowns the verbal rebuff with the drastic act of refusing to appear with the king in public ("I will not return with thee"). Then comes the symbolic interpretation given to the tearing of the coat as a visual figuration of history, barbed by the reference to the unkinging as an accomplished fact ("The Lord *has* torn the kingdom of Israel from thee"), the disclosure that a successor has already been chosen ("and given it to a neighbor of thine, who is better than thou"), and the emphasis on the finality of the sentence ("the Strength of Israel will not lie and will not repent, for he is not a man that he should repent").

Only this terrible crescendo of rejection manages to bring it home to Saul that what is done cannot be undone. He now completely inverts his first version ("I have performed"→"I have sinned") and resigns himself to the loss of God's favor ("I will prostrate myself before the Lord" modulates ⟦82⟧ into "I will prostrate myself before the Lord thy God"). All he wishes is to save his face by turning the worship of God in the prophet's company into a public show of solidarity ("before the elders of my people and before Israel"). In typical disregard for the dynamics of repetition, this natural finale has been twisted into incongruity and explained away as the second of the tale's "two conclusions: (1) vv 24–29, in which Saul confesses his sin, asks Samuel to return to Gilgal with him to worship, and is sharply refused; and (2) vv 30–31, in which Saul confesses his sin, asks Samuel to return to Gilgal with him to worship, and is obliged."[16] In fact, the two units form structural rather than genetic variants. For the confessions are not identical but discrepant, not alternative but successive and gradated, moving from qualified to plain avowal of guilt. Rhetorically, of course, Saul must finally confess in proper form, too late to escape punishment but just in time to seal its vindication. Yet it also makes good psychological sense that he should thus confess, if not from his heart, then at least with a view to moving the prophet.

16. P. Kyle McCarter, Jr., *I Samuel* (The Anchor Bible: New York, 1980) 268.

Samuel, his mixed feelings easily imaginable and soon to find a catharsis of sorts in the dismemberment of Agag, Saul's formal antagonist and veiled analogue, indeed yields to that new appeal—as if to illustrate his recent generalization that man may repent. But no later than the next chapter will he be burdened with a mission destined to undermine Saul's social prestige as well. Still mourning for one king, Samuel is dispatched to anoint another, whose conduct toward God and people, in adversity as well as in prosperity, will exhibit the sharpest contrast to his predecessor's. This is the king who, having committed his first offense and listened to the prophet's denunciation, at once responds by the simple words "I have sinned" that only a series of rounds can wring from Saul. This is also the king who, having committed his second (and last) sin and brought God's wrath down on the people, has only one request to make: "Behold, I have sinned and I have done wickedly; but these sheep, what have they done? Let thine hand, pray, be against me and my father's house" (2 Sam 24:17). While one of the persuader's eyes focuses on the individual episode unfolding in the narrative present, the second looks ahead to the future and the development of the book as a whole. With David, as with Saul, the two normative frames of reference inextricably fuse together. But the difference that emerges from their joint application motivates the different fates of the two leaders and is supposed to explain the course of history.

Isaac, Samson, and Saul:

Reflections on the Comic and Tragic Visions[1]

J. Cheryl Exum
and
J. William Whedbee

Holy Books never laugh, to whatever nations they belong.

Baudelaire

I

[[5]] Within the more standard approaches of biblical criticism, the categories of comedy and tragedy have played a peripheral role. At first glance such a state of affairs should not be surprising: after all, the terms are Greek in origin, usually Aristotelian in their literary critical application, and hence seemingly remote from the central and characteristic genres of biblical literature. Yet in the long history of the

Reprinted with permission from *Semeia* 32 (1984) 5–40.

1. An earlier version of this paper was presented at the 1982 Annual Meeting of the Catholic Biblical Association. Dr. Exum's research for this study was supported by a grant from the National Endowment of the Humanities, administered by the American Schools of Oriental Research, and by a grant from the Penrose Fund of the American Philosophical Society.

Bible's place in the Western tradition, comedy and tragedy have had a powerful involvement with the Bible—an involvement often subtle, sometimes strained, at times fascinating. Interpretation has swung from one extreme to the other; comedy, in particular, has had a checkered past: from early on some interpreters opposed any significant link between comedy and the Bible, whereas Dante immortalized the Christian biblical vision in the ⟦6⟧ grand Medieval poem he named the *Commedia.* More recently Northrop Frye has made the Dantesque view a central aspect of his own approach to the Bible:

> From the point of view of Christianity . . . tragedy is an episode in that larger scheme of redemption and resurrection to which Dante gave the name of *commedia.* This conception of *commedia* enters drama with the miracle-play cycles, where such tragedies as the Fall and the Crucifixion are episodes of a dramatic scheme in which the divine comedy has the last word. The sense of tragedy as a prelude to comedy is hardly separable from anything explicitly Christian (1964: 455).

What is striking is that biblical scholarship has paid so little attention to the implications of Frye's claims. Thus the potential of comedy and tragedy as illuminating perspectives for explicating biblical texts has never been carefully and systematically explored, at least to our knowledge. To be sure, biblical scholarship has not totally ignored the usefulness of comic and tragic models: here we would point to H. Gunkel's trenchant remarks on comic episodes in Genesis (see below) and single out for special praise E. M. Good's *Irony in the Old Testament,* a volume that offers pioneering, provocative interpretations of comic and tragic irony in the Hebrew Bible. Apart from Good's book, we find articles on Job and Saul as tragic figures (see below) or on tragic dimensions of the crucifixion. But comedy in particular as an interpretive category appears infrequently in the standard biblical commentaries and journals, though as we have noted, outside biblical scholarship comedy holds a higher, more honored place. Even when tragedy or comedy enters the picture in biblical criticism, its particular form is usually unclear and ill-defined. In recent years biblical scholars have begun to look more seriously at the possibilities, but the exceptions are rare that seek to lay a solid groundwork in literary criticism before building an interpretive edifice.

In this article we wish to make some amends for the desultory application of comedy and tragedy to the Hebrew Bible, with the necessary qualification that we keenly recognize the limited, tentative scope of our treatment. We hope our reflections will be suggestive as to what could and should be done, but we offer them in all diffidence before the enormity of the task.

As an epigraph for our presentation we have cited Baudelaire's assertion, "Holy Books never laugh . . . "—an assertion we have chosen ironically as a backdrop against which to offer a contradictory thesis: the holy book we call the Bible revels in a profound laughter, a divine and human laughter that is endemic to the whole narrative of creation, fall [[7]] and salvation, and finally a laughter that results in a wondrous, all-encompassing comic vision. Moreover, we wish to argue that the passion and depth of this comic vision derives precisely from its recognition of the place and power of tragedy, of that vision of the dark, jagged side of human existence which knows of unredeemed death and unmitigated disaster, and which holds in unresolvable tension the facts of human culpability and hostile transcendence (Ricoeur: 220; see below). But the tragedy is episodic in the overarching structure of the Bible and ephemeral in its ultimate effects; though nonetheless excruciating in its reality. The comic vision can embrace the tragic side of existence without eliminating or negating it. Tragedy cannot be felt in its full force apart from comedy, nor can comedy be understood and fully appreciated apart from tragedy. So it is in general—and so it is, we suggest, in the concrete forms of biblical literature.

If N. Frye is correct that the book of Job is "the epitome of the narrative of the Bible" (1982: 193), and if he and others are correct that Job is best construed as a comedy, then the book of Job with its subtle subordination of the tragic vision to the more dominant view of comedy tellingly illustrates our thesis (see Whedbee). We do not wish, however, to argue again the thesis of the comedy of Job; we want rather to move to the narratives about Israel's patriarchs, judges, and kings to explore the centrality of comedy and the paradoxical, powerful interplay between the tragic and comic visions in the Hebrew Bible—visions that ultimately are reincorporated and refocussed in the Christian Bible.

Before turning to Genesis, Judges, and 1 and 2 Samuel, we need to consider briefly the nature of the comic and tragic visions. We do not wish to offer a definition as such or a reductive formula where voluminous critical discussion is available; rather we want to draw out certain recurrent dimensions of comedy and tragedy—dimensions which reflect established lines of literary criticism and which appear in major comic and tragic works. Here we are acutely sensitive to the risk of imposing later and perhaps alien schemas on the Bible. Obviously the persuasiveness of any interpretation of biblical literature in terms of comic and tragic visions depends on the degree to which one can argue for a form of comedy or tragedy that is intrinsic to the biblical texts within their native Hebraic and Near Eastern setting. We would hasten to add, however, that a larger comparative context embracing the relationship between the Bible and its ongoing role in Western culture is also a germane factor: going back and forth between the Bible and its literary and dramatic "afterlife" may open up the possibility for new insights into both the original biblical texts and later works which have been influenced by the Bible.

[[8]] We wish to focus on the comic and tragic visions from three major perspectives: (1) plot; (2) thematic and stylistic patterns; (3) characterization of heroes. First, the plot lines of comedy and tragedy follow similar trajectories, but then conventionally break apart at the decisive endpoint. Thus both comedy and tragedy usually begin with a view of a harmonious, integrated society, a situation that is challenged or tested in some way as the action unfolds; but comedy typically swings upward at the end and shows the hero happily reintegrated within her or his rightful society, whereas tragedy typically ends with a fallen hero and a vision of disintegration, alienation, and death. To use N. Frye's apt image, comedy follows a U-shaped plot line, whereas tragedy has an inverted U-shaped movement. Tragedy may grant its protagonist a moment of glory, but then descends into darkness and stays there, whatever the glimmerings of a new day. Comedy, on the other hand, ultimately ascends from any momentary darkness and concludes with celebration, joy, and new life. In a word, tragedy ends in catastrophe, whereas comedy ends in carnival. Using this pattern of parallel but ultimately diverging plot lines, D. Robertson has offered a stimulating comparative treatment of Exodus 1–15 as a comedy over against Euripides' tragedy, *The Bacchae.*

Second, comedy and tragedy have characteristic thematic and stylistic habits which set them apart, yet here too one should not think of polar opposites. Comedy typically delights in various forms of verbal artifice such as word plays, parody, exaggerated repetitiousness, burlesque, hyperbole and understatement. Comedy exploits incongruity, stressing specifically the ludicrous and ridiculous. Though comedy cannot be reduced to a simplistic equation with the humorous and laughable, comedy nevertheless seeks habitually to elicit laughter— even though the laughter sometimes might be pained and embarrassed, not joyous and celebrative. Thus the laughter may be at someone's expense when comedy takes the form of satire in order to deflate the pretentious. Comedy indeed celebrates the rhythm of life with its times of play and joyous renewal, but frequently comedy must first resort to ridicule and bring down the boastful who block the free movement of life. Comedy takes up its arms against the forces that stifle life and laughter; and though its barbed arrows can sting fiercely, they usually do not kill. If satire fails to move on to the genuinely restorative and celebrative, then it becomes a real question whether it still remains in the domain of comedy (cf. Frye, 1966: 233–39).

When we turn to tragedy, we find that its thematic movement, so intimately interwoven with its plotline, characteristically oscillates between the fatedness of the hero's fall and the fierceness of the hero's [[9]] assertion of transcendence. The issue of the hero's so-called flaw is subordinate to the inexorable movement toward catastrophe and the increasing isolation of the hero in a cosmos that appears inhospitable and capricious. At the heart of tragedy is always "a vision of extremity"—to borrow M. Krieger's telling phrase. Any tempering of this extremity beclouds the clarity of the tragic vision (see G. Steiner: xiiff.). Such a sombre thematic configuration typically demands an elevated, even exalted style: "The rhetoric of tragedy requires the noblest diction that the greatest poets can produce" (Frye, 1966: 210). To be sure, the presence of common rhetorical strategies such as irony, parody, and repetition in central tragic works reveals the stylistic crossovers between comedy and tragedy. Thus any distinction between so-called "low" and "high" styles must be precisely delineated in the context of particular texts and their discrete literary traditions.

Third, the characterization of comic and tragic heroes differs, though again it is often a matter of degree and relative emphasis. As Frye reminds us, "comedy tends to deal with characters in a social group, whereas tragedy is more concentrated on a single individual" (1966: 207). The tragic hero's glory and burden is that he or she is isolated, an individual who stands somehow apart from or above humanity, yet is still one of us. Social stratification often plays a pivotal role in this process of differentiation and isolation; hence in antiquity and in fact until recently the tragic hero was customarily a king, prince, or warrior, and rarely a person of low rank. (A. Miller's *Death of a Salesman* illustrates how twentieth century attempts at tragedy are far removed from the dominant tradition.)

On the other side, the characteristic figures of comedy—rogues, tricksters, buffoons, fools, clowns—incarnate the human, all too human, sometimes in fact assuming sub-human or animal form. When seemingly great or noble personages appear, they are usually satirized and subjected to ridicule, thus undercutting their pretentiousness and reducing them to the common lot of humanity. Even when comedy isolates a figure for some sort of special attention, the ultimate goal is still reintegration into the social group to which he or she properly belongs.

II

We have indulged enough in generalities and must now attempt to give life to these dry bones of critical commonplaces about comedy and tragedy. Analysis of concrete texts must come into play in order to test the illuminating power of such categories. We begin with Genesis, which in many respects may be more appropriately called "the epitome of the narrative of the Bible" than the book of Job. Against the backdrop ⟦10⟧ of the exile from Eden and the wandering of the children of Adam and Eve—a backdrop which Milton justly treated as tragic in *Paradise Lost*—we have the narratives about Israel's fathers and mothers. If the comic vision animates the whole Bible, then surely we should expect to find its seeds in the patriarchal and matriarchal traditions. Although all three major patriarchs provide appealing subjects for analysis from the perspective of comedy, we have space here to consider only Isaac, often overlooked because he appears so bland and uninteresting, a figure overshadowed by his father Abraham, on the one side, and his son Jacob, on the other. Yet perhaps his shadowy presence in the biblical tradition makes him all the more inviting as a test case for our exploration.

Isaac at first glance appears the least likely candidate for the role of comic figure, whereas Abraham and Jacob have occasionally been portrayed in a comic light. Jacob, for instance, can be viewed as a rogue or trickster who by dint of his guile and wit makes his way successfully in the world (cf. Good and Williams). Isaac, however, has usually been represented as a tragic figure, especially in light of the story of Abraham's near sacrifice of young Isaac. Elie Wiesel, for example, illustrates the more common approach in "Isaac: A Survivor's Story," where he calls Isaac "the most tragic of our ancestors" (97). We wish, however, to argue an alternative position: whatever the fate of Isaac in the many "after-lives" of his tale, he is better represented in the biblical narratives as one of the *most comical* of Israel's ancestors. The evocation of various forms of laughter in the name "Isaac" precisely finds its most congenial home in a narrative best defined as comedy, a narrative which embodies all the ingredients that have conventionally made up the comic vision.

To capture the full panorama of Isaac's story we must go back before his birth and look at those engrossing accounts of the promise of his birth. Yhwh reiterates the promise of numerous progeny to the aging father-to-be in Genesis 17, narrowing the promise to focus on the single son in the closing speech to Abraham, who responds with skeptical laughter. Yhwh then repeats the promise in Genesis 18, where it meets with Sarah's amused but incredulous laughter.

However we evaluate the traditio-historical and theological interpretations of the aged couple's laughter in response to promises about a new baby, their laughter at bottom is most easily taken as an all too human reaction to an incongruous situation filled with amusing, even absurd ingredients. Despite all the sombre trappings of a theophanic revelation, Abraham's laughter and his skeptical questions are not surprising—at least from his intense human awareness as to how things customarily work in the world: "Shall a child be born to a man who is a [[11]] hundred years old? Shall Sarah, who is ninety years old, bear a child?" (Gen 17:17); nor is his petition in behalf of his "other" son unreasonable: "O that Ishmael might live in your sight!" (Gen 17:18). Yhwh simply brushes aside Abraham's concerns, reiterates Sarah's maternal role, and then adds a significant new element—the name of the promised child: "No, but Sarah your wife shall bear you a son, and you shall call his name Isaac" (יצחק, "he laughs," Gen 17:19). Yhwh does not allow the sound of laughter to die in Abraham's throat, but rather seizes upon the verb יצחק and declares that it will be the name of the coming heir. In so doing Yhwh permanently embeds laughter into the line of Israel's ancestors: Isaac will bear in his very being the image of laughter.

After this first outburst of incredulous laughter and the ensuing dialogue between the skeptical Abraham and the insistent Yhwh, we will hear again and again the echoes of laughter around this promised child. Thus the following narrative about Sarah's equally incredulous laughter with her even more earthy reaction stands as a perfect complement to the preceding story about Abraham: it is a case of like husband, like wife. The narrative is one of the master strokes of Genesis, which must be read in its entirety to appreciate fully its artistry (see Gen 18:9–15). The seemingly preposterous promise of a new baby, the eavesdropping Sarah who is discovered, the divine visitor who feels insulted, the tête-à-tête between Yhwh and Sarah who attempts to cover up her laughter by lying to her guest(s)—all these elements add up to something equivalent to Hebrew farce. That the dialogue breaks off without any clear resolution heightens the suspense and leaves the reader hanging in the balances—not to mention the aging couple.

Before Abraham and Sarah have their long awaited son, the major story line is complicated twice more. First, the rather dreary story of the destruction of Sodom and Gomorrah and the partial rescue of Lot and his family interrupts the main flow of the narrative, yet it still serves to reinforce the structural and thematic configuration of the surrounding stories. It functions in particular as a kind of parodied replay of such themes as unexpected divine visitors, equivocal human response marked more by incredulity than faith, and births of national ancestors. Moreover, as E. M. Good has noted, the story is not without its comical moments: for example, "Lot's ludicrous delay is comically ironic" (94). More germane to the birth story of Isaac is the etiological tale of Moabite and Ammonite origins: the kinship between Israel and its closest neighbors is recognized—they are cousins; yet the quality of the kinship is undercut because Moab and Ammon are the products of an incestuous union. Such a use of an invented story about the questionable origins of one's hated relatives is a stock-in-trade strategy of ethnic humor. In fact, ⟦12⟧ according to N. Frye, "the possibilities of incestuous combinations form one of the minor themes of comedy" (1966: 181).

The second complication comes in the guise of a repeated story—Abraham's decision once again that his wife's "loyalty" (חסד) to him would be best demonstrated by a denial of her wifely status, a stratagem designed ostensibly as a self-protective measure when Abraham feels threatened on foreign soil (Genesis 20; cf. Genesis 12). Ironically, of course, Abraham's timorous action threatens the future of the clan since he loses his wife to another man's harem. Here the episode re-enacts an earlier cycle of human failing and propitious divine interventions (see Genesis 12); even more significantly, it retards and even jeopardizes the long awaited fulfillment of the promised birth of Isaac. Moreover, it embodies the U-shaped plot line so endemic to comic tales: the innocuous beginning that locates Abraham and describes his status as resident alien, the precipitous decision to have his wife lie about her status, the induction of Sarah into the royal harem, the timely divine intervention which averts permanent harm to Abimelech's household, the return of Sarah to her husband along with lavish gifts, the rather incongruous prophetic intercession in which the "guilty" Abraham prays in behalf of the "innocent" Abimelech in order to heal the divinely inflicted barrenness of the royal household—all these elements, whatever their inner complexity, move ineluctably along the comic trajectory, averting potential disaster and ultimately reintegrating all protagonists in their rightful society.

At last the oft-delayed birth of the promised child takes place. Isaac comes as a gift out of season, and his birth is a happy surprise to the aged couple, resolving the long-standing problem of Sarah's barrenness. Hence Yhwh fulfills the promise—even if not necessarily according to human timetables. The festive occasion now evokes a laughter from Sarah different from what we heard before: "'God has made laughter for me; everyone who hears will laugh over me.' And she said, 'Who would have said to Abraham that Sarah would suckle children? Yet I have borne him a son in his old age'" (Gen 21:6–7). Once again is heard a play on the name Isaac, sounding the notes of laughter in response to such an amazing turnabout in the fortunes of

the erstwhile barren couple. As we recall, the divine announcement of
the promised birth had initially been greeted by skeptical laughter in
the face of absurdity; but now promise finally joins hands with fulfillment to create joyous laughter. Sarah's laughter is full-throated, vibrant, and infectious because it is born in one of life's most beautiful
moments—the birth of a child. In contrast to Abraham's earlier
laughter that was marked by disbelief, or Sarah's initial laughter that
was choked back in denial, Sarah's new laughter is wonderfully contagious: she extends it beyond the charmed [[13]] circle of Yhwh, Abraham, Sarah, and Isaac, announcing that "everyone who hears will
laugh over me." But ultimately it is Isaac who becomes the chief
bearer of this richly ambiguous tradition of laughter—for his very
name ("he laughs") tells the tale. In the end Isaac emerges from this
complex of comical stories as a being who is a sexual joke of sorts—
but a joke as profound as it is whimsical, as serious as it is playful, for
it contains all the mysterious rhythms of laughter and life both human
and divine.

We would normally expect such a story to end here and finish with
a fairy tale flourish, "and they lived happily ever after." But this is not
the way of the Genesis narrators, who are telling a series of connected
family stories which are open-ended by the necessity of the case. Thus
the story continues, and the narrator strikes a note of discord: Sarah
remains hostile about the disturbing presence of Hagar and Ishmael in
Abraham's clan (Gen 21:8ff.). During the festive event of Isaac's wean-
ing, Sarah spies Ishmael while he is "playing" (מצחק, Gen 21:9).
Though we have here still another word play on Isaac's name, the exact meaning is opaque. Is Ishmael playing with Isaac (מצחק עם יצחק—so
the Greek)? Or is Ishmael simply playing (so the Hebrew which lacks
the name of Isaac)? Or is Ishmael playing Isaac—that is, pretending to
be Isaac and thus usurping his role as legitimate heir (so the interpretation of G. Coats: 97)? We simply do not know the precise intent—
only the presence of the root צחק echoes Isaac's name, suggesting
some type of pun. In any event, Sarah is angry over Ishmael's activity
and demands the permanent expulsion of a rival wife and a potential
rival to her own son: "Cast out this slave woman with her son; for the
son of this slave woman shall not be heir with my son Isaac" (Gen
21:10). Though Abraham is displeased—after all Ishmael is his firstborn son—he complies with Sarah's demand, but not until he receives
further clarification from Yhwh about the exact status of his two sons:
" . . . through Isaac shall your descendants be named; yet I will make a
nation of the son of the slave woman also, because he is your
offspring" (Gen 21:12–13).

Again, as in Genesis 16, we have a bittersweet conclusion: Hagar and her son are banished to the desert where the forlorn mother laments the imminent death of her son; but Yhwh hears (שמע) Ishmael's voice (note the twofold play on Ishmael's name in Gen 21:17) and rescues boy and mother, reiterating one last time the promise of a great future for this other son of Abraham. This little narrative offers in miniature a U-shaped plot line. Beginning with an integrated society (the larger family unit of Abraham, Sarah, Hagar, and the two sons), the story has a downturn in the expulsion of Hagar and Ishmael; but in contrast to a tragic ending, the story has a wonderful upturn when Yhwh intervenes, ⟦14⟧ saving both mother and son and reaffirming the promise of a new society—"a great nation" to which Ishmael and his descendants will rightfully belong.

If Hagar's story has moments of pathos and near tragedy, the portrayal of Abraham's greatest trial represents the sharpest descent of Isaac's whole story into what is potentially a terrifying tragedy. The imperious divine voice startles us: "Take your son, your only son Isaac, whom you love, and go to the land of Moriah, and offer him there as a burnt offering upon one of the mountains of which I shall tell you" (Gen 22:2). If Yhwh's action has been puzzling before, now it becomes utterly incomprehensible, perhaps even contradictory: Abraham is to take the son of promise, whose name evokes and echoes "laughter," and sacrifice him to the God who originally gave him. Talk about the Joban God who gives and takes away! Here the story indeed comes dangerously close to tragedy, and E. M. Good uses the language of "tragic irony" to characterize the inexplicable command to kill Isaac (195).

Yet we must once again be alert to the U-shaped plot. Even this sudden jolt in the story need not catch us completely off guard. As Frye reminds us, "An extraordinary number of comic stories, both in drama and fiction, seem to approach a potentially tragic crisis near the end, a feature that I may call the 'point of ritual death'" (1966: 179). Frye's observation provides a legitimate and illuminating context for interpreting this famous story which has undoubtedly elicited more volumes of commentary than any other text in the Isaac sagas. We, the readers, know at the outset that the commanded sacrifice is a test for Abraham: like Job, Abraham must pass a trial by ordeal. We also know that despite Abraham's occasional moments of weakness, we can generally count on him to trust Yhwh (cf. especially Gen 12:1–4 and 15:1–6). Thus we are somewhat prepared for Abraham's instantaneous response in faith: as Kierkegaard's "prince of faith" he is ready to sacrifice Isaac to God. We know further that such heroes of faith, after enduring their trials, receive their due reward. Finally, in such a world, we know about dramatic interventions by a divine figure—the fabled *deus ex machina*. Therefore we are predisposed for Yhwh's last-minute intervention to save Isaac by staying Abraham's hand and substituting a ram. Like the preceding story about the divinely sanctioned expulsion of Hagar and Ishmael, the story of Abraham's most demanding trial ends happily: Isaac is spared, Abraham receives a reaffirmation of the promise of abundant blessing, and father and son return to their rightful society.

Too often interpreters have unduly isolated Genesis 22 from its literary context, thus failing to see how well it fits into the dominant [15] structure intrinsic to the surrounding narratives. Isaac's whole story, like the tales of Abraham and Jacob, not only fits into an overarching U-shaped plot line, but each individual episode similarly has a U-shape. We find, in short, "a series of little U's" (A. Bingham) all intertwined with the comprehensive U-shaped pattern. Thus Genesis 22 is not exceptional in its basic structure.

The emotional intensity of this tale of a father's willingness to offer up his son to a demanding deity gives Genesis 22 special force. In the present movement of Genesis, it serves as the *climax* of Abraham's story, while at the same time functioning as the *center* of Isaac's story. Commentators have traditionally stressed its climactic role for Abraham in his relationship to Yhwh, but we must not lose sight of how well it epitomizes Isaac's whole career both in its U-shaped structure and in its characterization of Isaac as a type.

We have already noted how Genesis 22 is *almost* a tragedy, a dimension evident in the Medieval mystery play *Abraham and Isaac*. What is crucial, however, in the biblical form is the absence of any heart-rending cries of either father or son—in sharpest contrast to David's lament over Absalom. Moreover, as we have emphasized, Genesis 22 breaks off from the tragic arc at the strategic moment—as opposed to the genuinely tragic tale of Jephthah's daughter where no fiat from heaven stays the executioner's hand. For Isaac there is a joyous upswing which puts his story back into a comic light, a comedy in the shadow of threatened death, but nonetheless a comedy with its celebration of life.

Here also in Genesis 22 we find a piquant representation of Isaac as a type: he is passive victim and survivor. A rapid review of his story from the vantage point of his role in Genesis 22 illustrates his passive, submissive nature: he is born to over-aged parents (Genesis 21); he is protected from the assumed threat of his older half-brother whose potential as a rival is taken care of by his mother Sarah (Genesis 21); he is preeminently the victim in his near sacrifice at the hands of his father, emerging as a survivor only because of divine intervention (Genesis

22); he is a compliant son in the idyllic, romantic tale of Abraham's match-making on his behalf (Genesis 24); he is the one to yield ground in order to avoid conflict with the Philistines in a series of well-disputes (Genesis 26); he is duped by his shrewd, strong-willed wife and his wily younger son and tricked into giving his deathbed blessing to the "wrong" son (Genesis 27); he somehow survives for apparently twenty more years after the "deathbed" debacle and after his death is buried by his two sons (Genesis 35).

The only time Isaac acts "independently" he imitates his father's pattern of perpetrating a lie about his wife's marital status in order to 〚16〛 protect himself while in foreign territory—a case of like father, like son (Genesis 26). R. C. Culley has perceptively contrasted this episode with the two earlier parallels in the Abraham cycle (Genesis 12 and 20), singling out for special comment Isaac's dull-witted, awkward handling of the situation. First, argues Culley, Isaac misperceives the danger of the situation, since no one apparently wants Rebekah—in contrast to Sarah. Second, misperception is coupled with an unnecessary act of deception to create an awkward, abnormal situation: Isaac continues to live with his wife who is purportedly his sister. Not surprisingly, Isaac cannot control his sexual urges and gets caught in a bit of sexual play with Rebekah. It is comically ironic that he is fondling or "playing around" (מצחק) with his alleged sister. Once again we hear a word-play on Isaac's name—echoing that intimate connection of eroticism, play, and earthy humor which are staple ingredients of the comic mix from time immemorial. Abimelech's discovery leads to a sharp rebuke of Isaac from a justifiably angry king because of the danger of guilt and divine punishment (Gen 26:10–11). Here again, however, the U-shaped pattern asserts itself: despite his reprehensible conduct Isaac gets off scot-free, and Yhwh blesses him beyond measure; so that once more Isaac receives divine protection and material prosperity simply because he is Abraham's heir (Gen 26:2–5, 12–13). "All ends well," as Culley laconically puts it. In fact, "the shape of the story suggests . . . the hero as a bumbler who in spite of his inept handling of the situation comes out on top" (Culley: 39). Thus on the one occasion when Isaac acts on his own he hardly appears as a strong, resourceful individual and only emerges successfully because of who he is—passive recipient of divine favor—not because of his ability to act wisely and independently.

In sum, apart from the *partial* exception of the episode in Genesis 26 involving his wife, Isaac through and through is a victim, characteristically acquiescent to personages stronger and more clever than he. Paradoxically, the brightest, happiest moment in Isaac's whole life perhaps occurred when he was most passive—the occasion of his birth. A child of his parents' old age, he bore a name that evoked laughter; yet, as we have seen, laughter can have many faces, often mirroring incredulity as well as joy, embarrassment as well as amusement, cruelty as well as relief. As passive victim Isaac is one more often laughed at or over rather than one who laughs himself or laughs with others (though he does enjoy sexual play with his wife! Gen 26:8). Although sometimes a victim is a candidate for tragedy (Jephthah's daughter is the chilling biblical example), such is not the case with Isaac: he is survivor as well as victim, emerging, from difficult and even dangerous circumstances as one who is successful and blessed. His story always has a comic ⟦17⟧ upturn, aborting the possibility of tragedy. He is typically an innocent, passive man and is set up again and again—a classic half-pathetic, half-humorous dupe whose story is filled with ludicrous moments. His role is widely attested in comedy through the ages—his type of comic figure is well depicted in Charlie Chaplin's pose as a rumpled tramp who is often laughed at, but who survives all his hard times.

To illustrate most vividly Isaac's role as dupe and victim who is manipulated but who nonetheless comes forth as a survivor, we turn lastly to Genesis 27. If Genesis 22 is the center of Isaac's story, then surely the climax comes in Genesis 27: the account of the famous deathbed scene when he is deprived of what should have been his last noble gesture, the passing on of his inheritance in the form of the paternal blessing to his firstborn son who is also his favorite. Though the story contains elements of pathos, it is dominantly cast in a comic mode, as Gunkel saw long ago and as Thomas Mann captured so pointedly in his title of this section, *Der große Jokus*, in *Joseph und seine Brüder*. This episode has the potential for a tragic development—note only the similar opening scene in *King Lear*, where the old father passes on his inheritance to his daughters; but the Genesis story takes a significantly different turn and ends happily.

Let us look more closely at the story in light of its comic dimensions. The opening lines of the deathbed scene, when we read how Isaac thinks first of his stomach, strike a humorous note: "prepare for me delectable food such as I love and bring it to me that I may eat; that I may bless you before I die" (Gen 27:4). (The earthiness of the Genesis narratives comes out often in the eating scenes: Isaac's favorite son, Esau, already has manifested a similar propensity of thinking of food first, the future second—another case of like father like son.) The clever rogue Jacob pulls off the hoax, though he expresses doubts and misgivings when his enterprising, resourceful mother first conceives the plan and urges him simply to follow her instructions. The story is marked by turns with both ludicrousness and pathos. Picture the scene: an old man, blind and senile, lying on his deathbed, hungrily awaits his beloved elder son's arrival with choice cuisine; but meanwhile the younger son, the favorite of his mother, enters and identifies himself as Esau. The dissembling Jacob has been preposterously outfitted with animal skins on his arms, aping the appearance of his hairy brother, lest his blind father feel his smooth, hairless skin and discover the ruse. To complete the disguise Jacob wears his brother's garb in order to emit the right body odor. Jacob then proceeds with a bold-faced lie when his blind, befuddled father becomes suspicious. The dialogue between deceiving son and confused father is immediately followed by the moving account ⟦18⟧ of Esau's later arrival and his anguished plea for a blessing (Gen 27:18–40). Pathos is indeed present, but more pervasive is comic incongruity and irony: Isaac blesses the "wrong" son who is paradoxically the "right" son according to the prenatal oracle (Gen 25:23). What a bizarre way of working out the divine will! Though somehow involved, God is curiously absent. Moral categories are not invoked; apparently they are just not appropriate (cf. Gunkel, 1964: 307). Isaac is deceived, Esau is cheated out of his blessing; yet nobody gets seriously hurt, at least not in any ultimate sense.

Gunkel seems to have been the first modern scholar to discern the comic, humorous aspects of Genesis 27: "The substance of the story is and remains that a deception finally has a happy ending: Jacob the rogue really wins for himself the blessing; Esau draws the shorter one, without being morally guilty, and the hearers are the happy heirs of the deceiver" (307). Like the near tragedy of Abraham's aborted sacrifice of Isaac, this story of deception has the happy outcome characteristic of comedy—though this ending must await the adventures of Jacob the rogue during his sojourn in a strange land, where he will show his marvelous ability as a trickster who ultimately manages to come out on top. Isaac's "wrong" blessing for his two sons therefore will finally be "right" for both of them: Jacob as deceiver will become Israel, a "prince of God" who prevails against both God and men, reflecting perhaps the image of his grandfather Abraham; whereas Esau as the deceived seems to display at crucial times the image of his father Isaac, a victim who is usually outwitted and manipulated by personages more resourceful than he, but who nonetheless emerges as a magnanimous, generous survivor (cf. his deportment in the reunion with Jacob in Genesis 33). Apropos of the plot line of comedy, the two brothers become reconciled in the end, even though becoming founder figures of two separate societies (Genesis 33).

The final encounter between Isaac and his twin sons, so decisive in determining the dynamic of the subsequent story of Israel, meshes with the recurrent pattern of comical moments in Isaac's story which begins with the dramatic announcements of his birth. His name, "he laughs," indeed begets his character and destiny, but in a different sense from what such a happy appellation might initially suggest. Apart from the one occasion of his birth, he is not usually the source of joyous laughter, nor is he a clever wit himself. Again and again he is laughed over, often manipulated, victimized, even duped—but his life at bottom is not tragic, for he survives and survives and survives. In fact, Isaac lives longer than either his father, Abraham, or his son, Jacob. According to biblical chronology, he lives twenty years after the deathbed scene. In the conventional style that describes a complete and successful life, the narrator tells us that "Isaac breathed his last; and he died and was gathered [[19]] to his people, old and full of days" (Gen 35:29). The burial scene epitomizes the typical ending of comedy, stressing that the different protagonists are reintegrated into the society to which they properly belong: the dead father "gathered to his people," and his two reconciled sons united at his burial.

In conclusion, the Isaac story contains all three ingredients of the comic vision as we have defined it. First, its plot line both in the parts and the whole follows the U-shaped pattern intrinsic to comedy. Though it indeed has its moments of near tragedy and pathos, each time we find the decisive upturn to a happy ending. Second, style and theme display typical comic traits: word plays are plentiful, especially the pivotal pun on Isaac's name; ludicrous and farcical moments abound; and comic irony and incongruity are pervasive. Finally, the characterization of Isaac as passive victim is best construed as comic. A hallmark of his role is his ordinariness; things typically happen to him, he is never the powerful protagonist actively shaping events. But in his very ordinariness, in his tendency to drift along on currents that sometimes threaten to submerge him, in his ability to survive and somehow to muddle through—in all these ways he is a comic hero familiar to us all, one who evokes from us a secret smile of recognition, a half-comic, half-pathetic figure who incarnates and mirrors the human, all too human, and is therefore all the more laughable and lovable.

III

Our interpretation of the Isaac story as a fundamental embodiment of the comic vision which characterizes biblical narrative, as well as our general remarks on the relationship between comedy and tragedy in the Bible, makes clear our agreement with the observation that the Judaeo-Christian vision is not a tragic one (see Frye, Steiner). We have argued that the account of Abraham's near sacrifice of Isaac, with all its implicit pathos and horror, must be read, finally, in its proper comic context. Even the Book of Job, which to many interpreters appears to have dressed its protagonist in tragic garb, we have defined as comic (see Whedbee). There remains one obvious choice for a biblical representation of the tragic vision, the story of King Saul. This story offers the clearest example of what might properly be called biblical tragedy—though we might use Steiner's phrase, "tempered tragedy" (xiii). For just as Denmark will be a better place under Fortinbras and Scotland under Malcolm, we know that Israel finds security and prosperity under Saul's successor, the king after God's own heart. Nevertheless, all the essential tragic ingredients meet us in the story of Saul, chief among them, and indispensable to the tragic vision, the Aeschylean paradox of human guilt and the wicked gods (see Ricoeur: 211–31).

[20] "Saul is the one great tragic hero of the Bible," says N. Frye (1982: 181), an observation most biblical exegetes would take as a commonplace. Few of us would quarrel with G. von Rad's classic statement that "Israel never again gave birth to a poetic production which in certain of its features has such close affinity with the spirit of Greek tragedy" (325). E. M. Good offers a compelling reading of this narrative in terms of its tragic dimension, and more recently, both W. L. Humphreys (1978, 1980, 1982) and D. M. Gunn (1980, 1981) have argued at length for its tragic character. In order to advance our thesis about the comic and tragic visions in the Bible, we propose to set the tragic story of Saul over against what we would classify as the comic story of Samson, a narrative which resembles Saul's at enough points to deserve Wellhausen's designation of Samson as a *Vorspiel* to Saul. Both are hailed as deliverers of Israel from the Philistines, both fail at the task, and both die seeming ignominious deaths at the hands of their oppressors in the process. How then is one a comic figure and the other tragic? The difference between the comic vision and the tragic vision becomes clear when we compare different handling of similar elements.

We have already alluded to the difficulty of differentiating sharply between comedy and tragedy, except in their extreme forms. Thus we shall find some crossovers in these stories, just as we found moments of pathos and near tragedy in the story of Isaac. Nevertheless, the difference between the two visions is evident in spite of a certain admixture of comic and tragic elements. As S. Langer remarks, "The matrix of the work is always either tragic or comic; but within its frame the two often interplay" (1981a: 72). This interplay, we have suggested, is essential to the vitality of these visions, for without the tempering of a comic perspective, tragedy moves into the realm of melodrama, while comedy without a recognition of tragic potential becomes farce (cf. Frye, 1965: 50).

Stock elements of comedy abound in the story of Samson in Judges 13–16: wit and humor, bawdy riddles and amorous escapades, a rapid pace, an episodic structure, and a hero of incredible vitality. The Philistines are the blocking characters who inhibit movement toward a harmonious society; they are caricatured, as is Samson himself, and clear distinctions are made between hero and villains. Unmistakably tragic elements appear as well—the hero's betrayal, blinding, and death providing the most obvious examples. When Milton sought to make a tragedy of the Samson story he produced a powerful drama, but even here the inherent comic plot line which he took over from the biblical tradition defeats the realization of the tragic vision. Neither in *Samson Agonistes* [[21]] nor in the biblical account does the death of the hero carry the final or the central message. It is entirely in keeping with the spirit of the biblical story, as we shall argue below, that Milton's Manoah offers us the crucial insight, "No time for lamentation now, / Nor much more cause; Samson hath quit himself / Like Samson . . . ," and the chorus assures us, "All is best, though we oft doubt. . . ."

Biblical scholars have been content to note either comic or tragic features of the Samson saga or both, without exploring adequately the nature of their relationship. Rarely do they give more than a superficial definition to the terms comedy and tragedy. J. L. Crenshaw is typical in concluding that the Samson saga is a tragicomedy because "neither tragedy nor comedy becomes sufficiently pronounced to drown out faint echos [sic] of its opposite" (129), yet he fails to move beyond generalities to make his case. While such assessments are cognizant of the interplay between comic and tragic elements, they fail to locate properly the matrix of the saga.[2] That matrix, in our opinion, is best described as comic, a designation which does not necessarily mean that we like the way the story ends. What Frye says about comic drama is applicable here.

> Does anything that exhibits the structure of a comedy have to be taken as a comedy, regardless of its content or of our attitude to that content? The answer is clearly yes. A comedy is not a play which ends happily: it is a play in which a certain structure is present and works

2. Similarly, the recent literary study of Vickery, who discusses tragic aspects of the story but fails to recognize that its form is comic.

through to its own logical [festive] end, whether we or the cast or the author feel happy about it or not (1965: 46).

In spite of Samson's suffering and death, the story, with its emphasis on restoration and resolution, exemplifies the comic vision, and only when viewed in its proper comic context can its tragic moments be rightly appreciated.

Similarly, the Saul story has its moments of comic incongruity, such as the unsuspecting lad who seeks lost asses and finds a kingdom (chs. 9–10), and the future king who hides among the baggage when he is chosen by lot (11:20–24). These incidents bring comic relief to the foreboding atmosphere of ch. 8, which predisposes us to expect the worst from the institution of a monarchy. But the real alternative to the tragic perspective in 1 Samuel 8–2 Samuel 1 is provided by the story of David, which gives the narrative another, sanguine, mood alongside the somber mood of Saul's tragic tale. Shortly after David is introduced comes what must count as one of the great comic scenes in the Bible, the slaying of the Philistine champion, "a man of war from his youth," by a ruddy, handsome shepherd boy with a sling. David's story follows the plot line of romance and his spectacular rise in these chapters epitomizes the romantic hero's successful quest (see Frye, 1966: 186–206). Like many of [[22]] Shakespeare's plays, the narrative of 1 Samuel 8–2 Samuel 1 is contrapuntal. Two plots, David's rise and Saul's demise, are developed at the same time, each preserving its own integrity, while interwoven and connected by intricate verbal, thematic, and structural patterns (cf. Frye, 1965: 27). For purposes of this analysis we shall consider only the tragic tale of Saul.

Let us begin with the plot line in the stories of Samson and Saul, Judges 13–16 and 1 Samuel 8–2 Samuel 1. Each of our heroes meets his death fighting Yhwh's battles against the Philistines. But preceding the death account in each story comes the point where the hero experiences his moment of greatest desolation. These two parts of each story, the low point in the fortunes of the hero and the account of his death, provide the points of greatest similarity between the tales and thus serve well to demonstrate the way in which the comic and tragic visions clearly diverge, one moving toward reconciliation and affirmation, the other toward isolation and lamentation.

The Samson saga has the characteristic comic U-shaped plot. Its low point is reached when Samson is shaved and Yhwh leaves him, a departure all the more devastating because Samson, at first, does not realize it. On three earlier occasions, when Delilah had tried to subdue him, Samson tricked her and remained invincible. But her fourth attempt brings about his undoing, just as she knew it would (16:18). In what we might consider a moment of hubris, Samson sets out "as at other times" to better the Philistines, only to discover the bitter reality that "Yhwh had left him." Betrayed by Delilah, bereft of his hair, his strength, and the presence of his god (and these three things are inseparably connected in the narrative), Samson is blinded and imprisoned. He is brought out for "sport" at a sacrifice to Dagon, where vast numbers of Philistines gather to celebrate victory over their enemy. In this, his moment of deepest humiliation, Samson calls on Yhwh with a petition for vindication and death (16:28–30).[3] His prayer, with its conventional invocation and plea to be remembered, expresses his sense of abandonment by Yhwh (see Greenberg: 12), as he makes urgent supplication for divine favor just this once: "O Lord Yhwh, remember me please and strengthen me please only this time, O God. . . . " Samson's prayer reestablishes his relationship to Yhwh and thus gives the plot its upward surge. This restoration of broken relationship is decisive for the comic vision in Judges 13–16. Yhwh's departure from Samson, which occurred when he was shaved, is not final; rather a responsive deity is swayed by prayer. Samson's request for strength "only this time" is granted as is his desire to die with the Philistines. Strictly speaking, his death is not a suicide, for death is in Yhwh's hand, not Samson's. The distinction is an important one: Yhwh's power—not Samson's own or some mysterious force [[23]] which resides in his hair—enables Samson to bring about the destruction of the Philistines and his own death. Samson's death is the logical conclusion of the narrative; it brings release from a world of darkness (an aspect heightened by Milton) and vindication for the ignominy he has suffered at the hands of the Philistines (the object emphasized in the biblical account).[4] At his death, Samson fulfills the destiny Yhwh had appointed for him, to "be the first to deliver Israel from the Philistines" (13:5). Moreover, his final triumph over the Philistines surpasses his earlier exploits, winning him even greater glory: "The dead that he killed at his death were more than those he had killed in his life" (16:30). Finally, his burial by his brothers in the tomb of Manoah his father serves as the final symbol of his integration into the society which he represents, but in which he has functioned so obstinately and independently.

3. Taking v. 30 as part of Samson's prayer; for fuller discussion, see Exum 1983: 34 and note.

4. Following G. Mendenhall (76–77) in taking נקם as vindication, not vengeance. Vindication is Yhwh's prerogative, with Samson acting as the legitimate agent.

In contrast to the U-shaped plot of Judges 13–16, the story of Saul in 1 Samuel 9–31 displays the inverted U plot structure typical of tragedy. The story develops against the negative backdrop of Yhwh's misgivings about kingship in ch. 8, and its movement to catastrophe is impelled by the rejection stories of chs. 13 and 15. Saul encounters various setbacks, from anxiety over his loss of prestige in the eyes of the people (18:7) to his inability to apprehend David; and his fortune, not to mention his sanity, deteriorates until the narrative reaches its lowest point with the vision of Samuel conjured up by the medium at En Dor. For sheer starkness and terror, and in its gripping evocation of isolation and hopelessness, this scene stands out amid biblical narrative. Notice, for example, the number of references to Saul's anguished state of mind: he is afraid (v. 5), his heart trembled greatly (v. 5), he is in great distress (v. 15), filled with fear (v. 20), there is no strength in him (v. 20), he is terrified (v. 21). After this journey into the abyss of divine abandonment, Saul's death can only be seen as anticlimactic.

The scene is set at night. Night not only covers the movements of the king, hiding him from Philistine observation, but symbolizes as well the realm of darkness and uncertainty he is about to enter. Night is traditionally the time of spirits and necromancer's rites, and it provides an archetypal symbol for the ultimate darkness, death. It is no accident that just as Saul left his first meeting with Samuel in ch. 9 at the break of day, i.e., the dawn of his career, he both arrives and departs from his last encounter with Samuel while it is still night.

The isolation Saul experiences manifests itself even before this final rejection by Samuel. Try as he may—and there have been no indications that Saul was not a faithful Yahwist—Saul cannot get Yhwh to answer him ("And when Saul inquired of Yhwh, Yhwh did not answer him either by dreams, or by Urim, or by prophets," 28:6; indeed, Yhwh [24] never addresses Saul directly in the narrative, but speaks to him only through Samuel, or, as in ch. 14, through the sacred lot). Why does Saul seek out the prophet Samuel, who has already rejected him? When Gunn (1980: 108) answers that Saul can stand no more ambiguity, he identifies the root of the dilemma of the tragic hero. Not content to let his tragic destiny unfold, the tragic hero stalks it. Like Oedipus, who relentlessly pushes for the full truth to be disclosed while the answers steadily close in upon him, Saul *must know*.

A feeling of uncertainty and apprehension permeates the chapter; what occurs is not only secretive but forbidden as well. Ironically it was Saul himself, apparently in the service of Yhwh, who put the mediums and wizards out of the land (v. 4). Now Yhwh's silence and the failure of ordinary means of inquiry drive Saul to consultation with the dead.

Though reluctant, the medium whose life stands threatened by Saul's edict against necromancy becomes the sole source of the knowledge he seeks. Neither Saul nor Samuel is identified at first; Saul goes in disguise and instructs the woman, "Bring up for me whomever I say to you" (v. 8). Both Saul's and Samuel's presence at the seance is revealed at the same time: when she sees Samuel, the woman recognizes *Saul.* Saul, for his part, recognizes Samuel on the basis of the woman's description, "an old man . . . wrapped in a robe." It has taken twelve verses to establish the mood and set the scene, during which time suspense has been mounting as we await the fateful confrontation.

With characteristic brusqueness, Samuel asks Saul's reason for disturbing him. Saul's reply that "the Philistines are waging war against me" recalls the situation of ch. 13, when Saul first erred by offering the sacrifice in Samuel's absence; and when he implores, "I have called you to *reveal to me what I should do,*" we remember that he did not wait for Samuel to tell him what to do then ("Seven days you shall wait until I come to you and I will *reveal to you what you shall do,*" 10:8). Samuel's reply, "Why do you ask me?" (ולמה תשאלני), puns ironically on Saul's name, and his answer reiterates in painful detail what Saul knows already: because Saul disobeyed in not carrying out the ban against the Amalekites (ch. 15), Yhwh has rejected him and given the kingdom to David. Moreover, Israel will be defeated and Saul and his sons will die in the forthcoming battle. Overcome by weakness and fear Saul collapses (v. 20), prefiguring as it were his fall on the field of battle.

Though the meal that follows provides one of several points of contact between Saul's last meeting with Samuel and his first (in this case the meal which takes place in ch. 9),[5] it seems at first glance somewhat incongruous in this terrible rejection scene. A remark by ⟦25⟧ George Steiner with reference to Racine's *Bérénice* not only provides, in our opinion, the clue to the meal's function, but also sheds helpful light on the nature of the tragic vision in 1 Samuel 28—a vision as terrifying and uncompromising as any in the tragic corpus, yet ever so slightly tempered.

> Can Bérénice remain standing under the hammering of sorrow on Racine's naked stage or will she have to call for a chair, thus bringing on to that stage the whole contingency and compromise of the mundane

---

5. Saul, from the outset, is not prepared to encounter Samuel (his servant in ch. 9 provides both the idea and the money). At the beginning and end of his career, Saul makes a journey of inquiry (דרש, 9:9; 28:7) which leads him to Samuel. He is urged on by a servant or servants who know where to seek the answers: "Behold there is a man of God in this city," 9:6; "Behold, there is a woman master of spirits at En Dor," 28:7. His servant's description of Samuel, "All that he says comes true" (9:6), is darkly ironic in its anticipation of all the troubles Samuel will prophesy for Saul.

order of the world? I admit that, today, this question and the executive conventions from which it springs, seem to me to crystallize the truth of absolute tragedy with an integrity, with an economy of means, with a transcendence of theatrical "business" and verbal orchestration beyond that which we find on Shakespeare's loud and prodigal scene. It needs no cosmic storms or peregrine woods to reach the heart of desolation. The absence of a chair will do (xiii–xiv).

Henri Bergson, in a classic essay on "Laughter," makes a similar point.

No sooner does anxiety about the body manifest itself than the intrusion of a comic element is to be feared. On this account, the hero in a tragedy does not eat or drink or warm himself. He does not even sit down anymore than can be helped (94).

In a scene built around dialogue, Saul's words are dramatic in their brevity, "I will not eat." The meal which Saul allows to be prepared and which he eats with his servants meliorates the despair and pathos of the scene. Saul would have it otherwise, but he gives in, as he has before, to human urging. Pure tragedy would have left him without any resource. Samson prays for and receives strength (כח, 16:30) from Yhwh; but as for Saul, we are told he has no strength in him (v. 20). Relief comes as he receives nourishment from the medium whose kindness offers a dramatic contrast to Samuel's severity (cf. Preston: 36). This delicate tempering of the tragic vein enables Saul to eat, rise, and go his way— though he goes now with the sure knowledge of the fate that awaits him: "Tomorrow you and your sons shall be with me. . . . " (28:19).

In the account of Saul's death in 1 Samuel 31, the narrative yields fully to the tragic vision. Wounded and fearing abuse by the Philistines, Saul tells his armor-bearer to thrust him through. But the young man is afraid. As in the ill-fated decision to make the offering himself in ch. 13, it appears that Saul has no option but to take matters into his own hand. Unlike Samson, whose prayer brings reconciliation to Yhwh, Saul *cannot* call on God to let him die, because already in ch. 28 God has effectively and decisively ended communication. Thus, whereas Samson's death was in the hands of Yhwh, Saul's comes by his own hand. In contrast to Samson's death which belongs to a larger, comic resolution, Saul's death stands in tragic isolation. Whether grounded in a "failure of nerve" (so Good: 78) or symbolic of a "final moment of grandeur [when] he seizes [[26]] control of events" (so Humphreys, 1980: 79–80), Saul's suicide functions as his last desperate attempt to wrench from his destiny its final meaning. As an act of his own will, it can be compared to Oedipus' self-blinding even though in both cases the circumstances are from God.

Apollo, friends, Apollo
Has laid this agony upon me;
Not by his hand; I did it.

Tragic events pile up in 1 Samuel 31. First, Israel is routed and many are slain (v. 1); then Saul's sons meet their deaths (v. 2); next comes Saul's suicide and that of his armor-bearer (vv. 3–6), after which the Israelites abandon their cities to the Philistines (v. 7). The next day brings further dishonor: the Philistines mutilate and desecrate Saul's body (vv. 8–10). They send messengers throughout their territory to carry the good news, and, as a token of their victory, they exhibit Saul's armor in the temple of Ashtaroth and his body on the wall of Beth-shan. The scene recalls the Philistines' celebration of Samson's defeat and their merrymaking in Dagon's temple over his disgrace ("Our god has given [Samson] our enemy into our hand," Judg 16:23, 24). But no *deus ex machina* steps in to aid Saul and bring about a comic resolution, as in the Samson story. The cruelest part of Saul's fate lies in his death in isolation from Yhwh. Typical of the tragic vision, there is no reconciliation, no restoration, no future for the house of Saul.

Catastrophe does not strike the tragic protagonist alone. Like the curses that work themselves out in the house of Atreus and the house of Oedipus, Saul's misfortune extends beyond himself to his whole family. Three sons, Jonathan, Abinadab, and Malchishua, are also killed in the battle on Mount Gilboa and their bodies exhibited with their father's at Beth-shan. Accounts which lie outside the boundaries of the Saul story in 1 Samuel 8–2 Samuel 1 describe the tragic circumstances which befall the remaining members of the house of Saul. Ishbosheth is slain in his bed (2 Samuel 4). In 2 Samuel 21, other sons of Saul meet tragic deaths as the result of blood guilt on Saul's house for apparent crimes against the Gibeonites. Only Mephibosheth is spared; but Mephibosheth has his own troubles as a cripple to whom David shows questionable loyalty (2 Samuel 9) and whose loyalty to David is questioned (2 Sam 16:1–4; 19:24–30). Finally there is Saul's daughter Michal, who is taken from David, whom she loves, and given to Palti, only later to be taken from Palti and returned to David (1 Sam 18:20; 25:44; 2 Sam 3:15–16—the fact that Palti followed after her weeping suggests the severing of a strong bond). Michal and David quarrel over his behavior before the ark of Yhwh (2 Sam 6:12–23) and the outcome for Michal has an air of tragic [[27]] finality about it. She dies childless, bringing to an end another branch of the house of Saul.

In our introductory remarks, we alluded to characteristic thematic and stylistic habits of comedy and tragedy. Here we would like to consider the different handling of that most common feature of biblical narrative, repetition.[6] Frye, in the *Anatomy*, observes that repetition overdone or not going anywhere is comic (168). Samson, as we are all aware, keeps doing the same thing, and in this, he is quite laughable. True, he encounters obstacles and suffers temporary setbacks, but we see over and over again that Samson bounces back, and we come to expect it. Samson exemplifies Ben Jonson's theory of the "humor" and Bergson's concept of mechanical behavior as a central element of comedy. He is obsessed by a fatal weakness for women, and this leads him into repeated scrapes with the Philistines (14:1–15:8; 16:1–3; 16:4–22). Twice he falls for the same ruse and reveals his secret to a woman, and the repetitive factor in these episodes accentuates his incorrigibility. The Philistines threaten one woman and bribe the other to "entice" (14:15; 16:5) Samson, first (ch. 14) in order to learn the answer to his riddle and then (ch. 16) to discover the secret of his strength (in both cases the key word is נגד). Both women manipulate him by appealing to his affection, "You only hate me, you do not love me," 14:16; "How can you say 'I love you' when your heart is not with me?" 16:15. After enduring the Timnite's urging for seven days (14:17) and Delilah's every day (16:16), Samson gives in. In both cases "he told her" (14:17; 16:17) "because she harassed him" (14:17; 16:16). The betrayal of his secret leads both times, once indirectly and once directly, to the handing over of Samson to the Philistines. In 15:13 they *bind* him with two new ropes and *bring him up* from the rock of Etam. In 16:21 they *bring him down* to Gaza and *bind* him with bronze fetters. The climax of both accounts occurs when Samson calls on Yhwh (ויקרא [שמשון] אל יהוה, 15:18; 16:28), in both cases bringing about a dramatic turn of events. The extensive repetition in the story both amuses and instructs, for each account leads to the same point: the strong man cannot save himself; Samson depends on Yhwh for life and death.[7]

---

6. Space does not allow consideration of a common repetitive technique in biblical narrative, the paralleling of scenes. Another, different version of Saul's death appears in 2 Samuel 1. Though investigation of the relationship of this account to 1 Samuel 31 would take us too far afield, suffice it to say that it helps to mitigate the starkness of the death of Saul, especially by accenting the continuity under David, the good, true king. At the same time, it offers us David's lament over Saul and Jonathan, which surely heightens the tragic grandeur of Saul, while emphasizing, through its focus on Jonathan, the tragic fate of Saul's house. In the Samson narrative, our sense of the comic movement is fostered by Judg 15:18–20, which presents a potential death account corresponding to 16:28–30. Here Samson's death is averted and his boastfulness undercut by Yhwh's rescue in a delightful comic resolution (see Exum, 1981: 21–25).

7. For detailed discussion of the parallels, see Exum, 1981: 3–9.

The repetitive phenomenon in Judges 13–16 differs noticeably from the twofold account of Saul's disobedience and rejection and other doublets in the narrative, such as Saul's casting his spear at David, and Saul's pursuit of David which both times results in David's sparing Saul's life—all of which have a cumulative effect. When, for example, Samuel rejects Saul for disobedience the first time (ch. 13), a number of details remain hazy. It is not altogether evident wherein Saul's disobedience lies: he did wait the seven days required by Samuel and only [[28]] then made the offering because "the people were scattering." Nor is the accusation, "You have not kept the commandment of God," quite clear, since the narrative records no instructions from Yhwh but only from Samuel (10:8). Even the outcome lacks an apparent resolution, for it leaves us in the dark about Saul's response. Having delivered his diatribe, Samuel simply goes off to Gibeah, leaving Saul to prepare for battle, and the narrative makes no further reference to Saul's error in offering the sacrifice. But by the second rejection scene, there is no mistaking that Yhwh has had second thoughts about the fledgling monarch. Ch. 15 reinforces and spells out what ch. 13 presented tentatively, and it confirms what we may have suspected about Saul there. Yhwh clearly gives the command to annihilate the Amalekites and Saul equally clearly does not carry it out, whatever the reason. Here we see more deeply into Saul's personality and the motivation behind his decisions, particularly his desire to win the favor of the people. Saul may well be acting in good faith; that is, he may truly believe that a sacrifice of the spoils to Yhwh in Gilgal is compatible with the demands of holy war.[8] But whereas his defense in ch. 13 seemed reasonable, it is somewhat feeble in ch. 15, as he shifts his pronouns as well as the blame: "*They* have brought them from the Amalekites; for the people spared the best of the sheep and of the oxen, to sacrifice to Yhwh *your* God; and the rest *we* have utterly destroyed" (15:15). No doubt attends the outcome; the conclusion strikes a tragic note: "And Samuel did not see Saul again until the day of his death but Samuel grieved over Saul. And Yhwh repented that he had made Saul king over Israel" (15:35).[9]

Samson repeats his folly and Saul repeats his errors. The repetition has different force and is evaluated differently in the comic and tragic worlds. Samson is not judged negatively by Yhwh. Though certainly not

8. See Gunn's analysis of ch. 15 (1980: 41–56), where he argues that Saul understands זבח [['sacrifice']] as compatible with חרם [['spoils']] whereas Samuel and Yhwh do not.

9. Saul does apparently see Samuel again, ch. 19. The statement in 15:35 that Saul did not see Samuel again signals forcefully the break with the old order represented by Samuel and prepares for the introduction of the new order symbolized by David in ch. 16.

the most perceptive of heroes, Yhwh never castigates him for it, and commentators who condemn Samson for betraying his Nazirite vow engage in a moral evaluation which the narrative itself does not make (see Exum, 1983). In contrast, Saul is judged negatively by both Yhwh and Samuel; and each repeated weakness, each instance of vacillation, each violent and unstable action adds to the case against him.

A comparison of the treatment of the two heroes shows how little Samson is held accountable by Yhwh (biblical exegetes are not so forgiving). Judges 13–16 does not make an issue of obedience. At best, it is implied in 13:5 and 16:17, but demands for obedience, warnings against disobedience, and homilies about the results of disobedience are strikingly absent in the story. Neither Yhwh, nor the narrator, nor any of the characters censures Samson for any of his actions, though his parents demur at his choice of a spouse (14:3). This lack of specific moral judgment finds [[29]] its home in comedy. The comic hero is neither good nor bad, as Langer points out, "but is genuinely amoral—now triumphant, now worsted and rueful, but in his ruefulness and dismay he is funny, because his energy is really unimpaired and each failure prepares the situation for a new fantastic move" (1981a: 78). Tragedy, on the other hand, plunges its protagonist into moral conflict. Obedience plays a central role in the tragedy of Saul. Samuel stresses its importance for both king and people: "If you fear Yhwh and serve him and obey his voice and do not rebel against the commandment of Yhwh, and if both you and the king who reigns over you will follow Yhwh your God, it will be well; but if you do not obey the voice of Yhwh, but rebel against the commandment of Yhwh, then the hand of Yhwh will be against you and your king" (12:14–15 following LXX). This admonition sets the stage for Saul's failure and consequent rejection when he obeys the people (15:24) rather than Yhwh (15:1, 19, 20, 22). And Samuel does not miss a last opportunity to remind Saul that his disobedience has cost him the kingdom (28:18).[10]

On various occasions people around him call attention to Saul's weaknesses and shortcomings. Samuel calls him a fool (13:13) and rebukes him for his feelings of inferiority (15:17), his own son admits that he has "troubled the land" (14:29), and David twice forces him to

---

10. Obedience (שמע בקול) is repeatedly connected with the notions of kingship (divine versus human) and rejection (of Yhwh or of Saul). In ch. 8 Samuel is told to listen to (שמע בקול) the people and make them a king like the nations even though their request means the rejection (מאס) of Yhwh as king (cf. also 12:1). Ch. 12 announces divine forbearance if the people and their king obey Yhwh (vv. 14–15; note the pun on Saul's name, vv. 13, 17, 19). Saul, however, obeys the people rather than Yhwh and is therefore rejected (מאס) as king (ch. 15). The themes come together a final time in 28:16–19.

admit his failings ("You are more righteous than I," 24:17; "I have played the fool and erred exceedingly," 26:21). Such negative estimations expose Saul's vulnerability while assuming his accountability.

Although space does not permit a full investigation of the subject, one of our observations about different styles and techniques at work in comedy and tragedy can be well illustrated by the death scenes in Judges 16 and 1 Samuel 31. We hasten to add, however, that it is difficult to generalize about these matters, since the same literary devices can serve both comic and tragic modes. Fine distinctions between what is particular to the stories and what is typical of comedy and tragedy remain to be tested and probably can never be fully drawn. Nevertheless, we believe these two accounts demonstrate our point about the playfulness and artifice of the comic expression and the high seriousness of the tragic style.

The techniques of irony and reversal as used in Judg 16:23–31 are not appropriate to the seriousness of tragedy. The entire scene depends for its surprise and delight on the technique of ironic reversal, and its unfolding is splendidly manipulated by the skillful employment of paronomasia. The Philistines assemble to praise their god for victory over their Israelite enemy, but in the end Yhwh (through Samson), not Dagon, is the victor. The Philistines rejoice at the captivity of one who has [[30]] greatly multiplied (הרבה, v. 24) their slain, and ironically, these very merrymakers at his death become the slain who outnumber (רבים, v. 30) those he killed in his life. When Samson is brought out for the amusement of the Philistines, he leans on the two pillars which support the house (v. 26); later he will lean on these supporting pillars again, but this time for destruction (v. 29). At first, the sightless Samson depends on a mere lad for support (הנער המחזיק בידו) but his petition to Yhwh to strengthen him (וחזקני) results in a dramatic change of circumstances. The crowning pun, and the one which carries the scene, revolves around Samson's prayer itself: the people call (קרא) Samson to make sport, but while they watch, Samson calls (קרא) on Yhwh! This superb ironic twist reverses the downward movement of the narrative and turns Dagon's festival into Yhwh's victory.

The situation is different in 1 Samuel 31. The tragic vision at this point, we suggest, could not tolerate a delight in word play such as we find in Judges 16.[11] The account is terse and straightforward, with an

---

11. This is not to say that tragedy cannot employ paronomasia—surely it can—but the handling of puns in tragedy would differ, we think, from the zestful twists in meaning exploited by Judges 16. The occurrence of paronomasia in other comic and tragic narratives in the Bible requires investigation. But the fact remains that word play is absent from the stark account of 1 Samuel 31.

almost uncharacteristic lack of repetition. Of the few repeated terms, the recurrent phrase, "Saul and his (three) sons," reminds us of the end of the Saulide dynasty prophesied by Samuel, and the reappearance of such words as "fall" (נפל), "dead" (מות), "slain" (חלל), and "fled" (נוס) casts a somber shadow over the whole.

Restoration in Judges 16 comes from God. In spite of the brute fact of Samson's death among the enemy, the story ends, as comedies typically do, on a note of triumph: through Samson, Yhwh achieves a glorious victory over Israel's oppressors. There is no restoration in 1 Samuel 31, but there is relief. Just as in ch. 28 relief had come in the form of human kindness on the part of the woman of En Dor, so now it comes from the men of Jabesh-Gilead. Again, it is a kindness of the *night*. In one of the many instances of inclusion in the Saul narrative, the men of Jabesh act on Saul's behalf as he had on theirs, at the beginning of his kingly career (ch. 11). Then he delivered them from the threatened shame of mutilation; now they retrieve his mutilated body, sparing it further humiliation. Saul's burial does not have the integrating symbolism of Samson's. The fact of divine rejection overshadows this act of acceptance into human society, though it does not negate it. Moreover, the treatment of Saul's body raises uneasy questions (cf. Humphreys, 1980: 83–85). Mutilation and desecration of the body occur; in a practice uncommon in Israel, the body is burned; and only then are the bones buried in Jabesh, a location remote from Saul's home in Benjamin.[12] The tragedy of King Saul ends with fasting (1 Sam 31:13) and lamentation (2 Sam 1:17; cf. also the tragic vignette of Jephthah's daughter). David's lament, "How are the mighty fallen," like the chorus' "Behold, this was Oedipus, ⟦31⟧ greatest of men," serves as a commentary not just on the fate of Saul, but on the tragedy of the human condition in general.

Comedy can embrace pain and death in the larger context of restoration. For Samson, this is possible because he is an instrument of the divine plan in which we implicitly trust. In contrast, tragedy shows the uncompromising terror of suffering and death which Saul must face alone. Here we find a crucial difference between the tales: divine intention and motivation are ambiguous in Saul's case but not in Samson's. Though we are introduced to Samson with high expectations which remain unrealized (ch. 13),[13] we are nevertheless repeatedly reminded that Yhwh controls Samson's folly and ludicrous escapades,

---

12. Restoration of the bones does occur in 2 Samuel 21, an illustration of the logical evolution toward comedy in the Bible.

13. Greenstein notes a number of anomalies in the story besides this one, all of which he sees as part of the riddle the text poses for us: "With Samson, the expected is

"for [Yhwh] was seeking an occasion against the Philistines" (14:4).
This fact allows perhaps for perplexity on the part of the reader, but
not ambiguity. We, like Samson's parents, may find it odd that Samson
desires a Philistine wife, but the text assures us that "it was from Yhwh,"
14:4. Not simply sexual desire but also the spirit of Yhwh drives Samson
to his confrontations with the Philistines (14:19; 15:14). Significantly,
Yhwh does not promise that Samson will ultimately deliver Israel from
the Philistines, only that he will be the first to do so, 13:5. The opposite holds true for Saul, of whom Yhwh says, "It is he who will deliver
my people from the hand of the Philistines" (9:16). Do we have here a
hint of divine unreliability? In the comedy, Samson fulfills Yhwh's plan
for him; part of Saul's tragedy derives from the fact that Yhwh's
prophecy of 9:16–17 does not come to pass.[14]

In the Saul narrative the portrayal of the deity is uncomfortably
ambiguous (see chs. 8 and 9). Any way you look at it, Yhwh has an ambivalent attitude toward kingship.[15] Gunn (1980) has argued, with
good evidence, that the deity's angry feelings of rejection as king by
the people (ch. 8) give rise to a predisposition to reject Saul. Rejection
(מאס) appears at strategic points in the narrative. "Because you have rejected the word of Yhwh, he has rejected you from being king," 15:23,
echoes Yhwh's bitter complaint of 8:7, "They have not rejected you,
but they have rejected me from being king over them." Yhwh selects
Saul but at the same time views him as an unwelcome usurper of divine
leadership. Thus the first king must pay dearly for the people's sin
("evil" according to 12:17 and 19) of requesting a human monarch. To
use Gunn's phrase, Saul becomes kingship's scapegoat. Whether one
accepts Gunn's thesis or sides with commentators who defend Yhwh as
justified in rejecting Saul, such widely differing interpretations bear
witness to a complex picture of deity in the narrative.

But it is not just Yhwh whose portrayal is ambiguous. Saul himself
appears as a particularly complicated personality. He emerges as ⟦32⟧
a strong leader (ch. 11), yet wavers in precarious situations (chs. 13 and
15). Appearing not to want the kingship at the beginning of his career,
at the end he struggles to hold on to it at all costs. Though capable of

---

the unexpected" (246). This unpredictability or toying with our expectations is another
feature of the comic. Tragedy tends to develop along clearer defined lines and is less likely
to surprise (cf. Sypher: 207).

14. Yhwh predicts two things for Saul in 1 Sam 9:16–17: "He shall save my people
from the hand of the Philistines," and "He it is who shall rule over my people." Both are
unrealized, for Saul does both only for a time. Fulfillment occurs with David.

15. Like Gunn, we are not concerned with the problem of sources here but only
with the final product.

magnanimity (11:13) and inspiring loyalty among his followers, he sometimes displays sinister, inflexible qualities one hardly anticipates—e.g., his willingness to carry out his rash oath and have his own son killed in ch. 14, his evil designs against David, and his slaughter of the priests of Nob. If Gunn is correct in arguing that Saul acted in good faith in chs. 13 and 15, then even Saul's best intentions bring about the worst of consequences. Is his problem that he is, as Good puts it, "a man not fitted for a job that should not have been opened" (58)?

The tragic vision until relatively modern times has typically cast as its hero a royal figure such as we find in Saul. The privileged position of kings, which enables them to break laws ordinary people must respect, renders them well-suited to tragic treatment. In Israelite as in Greek thought, the king in his role as mediator and representative stands in a special position between the sacred and the profane (C. Segal: 44–46) and, as the Deuteronomistic Historian so fondly points out, the people's welfare depends upon the king's proper performance of the royal functions symbolized by obedience. We observe Saul at the height and depth of this worldly fortunes. When we meet him, he stands "head and shoulders above the people"; yet all too soon we discover that he is little in his own eyes, and we follow his demise to his final rejection when his imposing stature lies "full length upon the ground, filled with fear." Saul is thrust into a position of leadership he did not seek only to have it torn away from him and promised to another who is better than he. Though he remains head and shoulders above the people who, like us, are less significant in the shaping of history, he is not so far above us that we fail to recognize in his *hamartia* our own potential to make similarly destructive, though certainly less far-reaching, errors of judgment.

And what of Samson? We are told he "judged Israel," but commentators have long observed that he does not behave like a judge. Samson, rather, is the typical rogue, a Hebrew Rob Roy, a Til Eulenspiegel in biblical dress. His wit and prowess provide the occasion to ridicule the Philistines and have a good laugh at their expense. He constantly gets the better of them, and the narrative shows a hearty, lusty approval of it all. Comedy may serve as a release for anti-social instincts and in this context wit in its various expressions often functions, as it does in Restoration Comedy, as a form of aggression (see E. Segal). Indeed, the frequently cruel laughter at the Philistines gives vent to Israelite hostility—so much so that J. A. Wharton has aptly described ⟦33⟧ these anecdotes about Samson as "resistance stories" (see especially 53–54). The narrative allows no place for remorse over the Philistine casualties of Samson's pranks and angry outbursts. The comic spirit which animates these escapades does not permit us to pause over any of them long enough to ponder the potential tragic dimension before plunging us into another laughable adventure. Like the story of Isaac, we have a plot composed of a series of little U's. Only in ch. 16, with Samson's betrayal, blinding, and death does a tragic perspective threaten seriously to intrude. But here also the comic vision prevails. Immediately after the betrayal and blinding, we catch a glint of hope and a hint of victory which is to come: Samson's hair begins to grow (v. 22). The clue to its direction planted, the comic movement proceeds, as we have observed, reversing the fortunes of our hero and his captors, and finally bringing about a victory for Yhwh and Israel.

A typical comic hero, Samson displays a remarkable absence of character development, a factor Milton was forced to alter considerably if his hero was to attain tragic proportions. We all know that the biblical Samson does not learn from past mistakes. This simple, if not simplistic, characterization is not a function of the short span of the story—only four chapters as opposed to the much longer narrative about Saul. One gets the impression that even if there were further Samson stories, they would be more of the same. Characteristics of the picaresque are evident not only in the episodic structure of the narrative but also in the hero who moves from one adventure to the next with little or no character development. In the end, of course, Samson is released from his "humor." Whether or not he learned anything about himself or his mission in the process the narrative does not say. We may take our clue from other comic heroes that the freedom from an obsessive trait does not necessarily bring with it a deeper self-understanding (see Frye, 1965: 79).

Whereas Samson's insouciant, comic character does not develop (as was also the case with Isaac), Saul's tragic one becomes a veritable battleground for opposing emotions and traits. Unquestionably Saul is a troubled man. His rigidity with regard to Jonathan (ch. 14), his suspicions of David and attempts on his life (chs. 18, 19, 22, 23, 24, and 26), his massacre of the priests of Nob (ch. 22), his random paranoia regarding the loyalty of family and servants (chs. 19, 20, 22) are all signs that something is amiss. The tragic hero is haunted by demonic forces from both within and without. We witness as Saul, driven by petty fears and jealousies, becomes a disintegrated personality, but most disturbing is the realization that the evil spirit which torments him and makes his plight even more desperate is the agent of none other than Yhwh. In this acknowledgement of the root of Saul's distress, we discover why Saul [[34]] alone of biblical heroes attains a truly tragic stature, and we reach the core of the tragic vision: the problem of evil.

In no other biblical story is the problem of evil so pressing and so uncompromising as in the story of Saul. Saul's downfall is of his own making, and in more than one instance he has incurred the divine wrath. But whereas Saul is guilty, he is not really evil. The tragic vision gives rise to the uneasy awareness that the hero's punishment exceeds any guilt. The question is not why is Saul rejected. That we know, regardless of whether or not we consider the rejection justified by Saul's actions. The question is why is there no forgiveness.

Saul encounters God's dark side in a way that Samson never experiences it, for Samson endures only a temporary abandonment. Saul knows the demonic side of God not only through divine absence, but also, paradoxically, through Yhwh's persecuting presence, in the form of an evil spirit. In Greek tragedy, the hero faces an indifferent, arbitrary world alone. Saul, in contrast, knows the agony of rejection by the God whose aid he repeatedly seeks—the biblical God whom we expect to be trustworthy—and more, he feels directly the terror of divine enmity. In a turn of phrase as telling as it is disquieting, Samuel exposes the problem "Yhwh has become your enemy" (28:16).[16]

Critics from Aristotle on have found various ways of formulating the problem of hostile transcendence, for it constitutes the essence of tragedy. Paul Ricoeur offers a particularly discerning discussion in *The Symbolism of Evil*, where he writes,

> The tragic properly so called does not appear until the theme of predestination to evil—to call it by its name—comes up against the theme of *heroic* greatness; fate must first feel the resistance of freedom, rebound (so to speak) from the hardness of the hero, and finally crush him, before the pre-eminently tragic emotion—φόβος—can be born (218; cf. Frye, 1982: 181).

It is hardly necessary to point out that when we speak of predestination to evil in the biblical story of Saul, we are not speaking of predestination in any simple sense, but rather as something undefinable and irreducible, and therefore all the more terrifying. Saul is caught between his own turbulent personality and the antagonism of God toward human kingship. He displays heroic greatness in his refusal to acquiesce to the fate prophesied by Samuel, taking extraordinary steps to hold on to his kingdom. A lesser man, a man without hubris, might merely

---

16. Reading ערך as "your enemy"; cf. Symmachus, Aquila, Theodotion, Vulg., Targ. Some commentators follow LXX (cf. Syr) in reading רעך, in which case Samuel's statement is not so radical and merely reiterates what he has said before (15:28).

accept his destiny. Saul, however, wrestles against it. Again, to borrow an insight from Ricoeur which fits the story of Saul admirably,

> Without the dialectics of fate and freedom there would be no tragedy. Tragedy requires, on the one hand, transcendence and, more precisely, hostile transcendence [[35]] . . . and, on the other hand, the upsurge of a freedom that *delays* the fulfillment of fate, causes it to hesitate and to appear contingent at the height of the crisis, in order finally to make it break out in a "denouement," where its fatal character is ultimately revealed (220–21).

Yhwh rejects Saul on two occasions early on in the narrative, and while tormenting Saul with an evil spirit, proceeds to further the fortunes of his rival. Since a large part of the narrative develops the plot of David's rise, we see Yhwh act simultaneously to subvert Saul and strengthen David. Saul manages to delay his downfall but not to avoid it. He rules some years after his rejection; there are signs that he still commands loyalty even though he himself doubts it (23:7, 19; 24:2; 26:1); he manages apparently to keep the Philistines at bay; and he even shows on occasion a conciliatory attitude toward David (19:6–7; 24:17–23; 26:21–25). Moreover, to the end, he seeks Yhwh's counsel (ch. 28). But, as we have seen, he meets ultimately with divine silence and a crushing reiteration of rejection from the ghost of Samuel.

IV

Tragedy confronts us with what R. Sewall has called "the terror of the irrational." The tragic hero is the victim of forces she or he cannot control and cannot comprehend. Faced with an inhospitable world, the tragic hero encounters on all sides unresolved questions, doubts, and ambiguities (see Sewall, Steiner). In contrast to tragedy, the comic vision can tolerate the presence of evil, resolving the fact of evil into a larger, harmonious whole. Though comedy is no stranger to ambiguity and doubt, and on occasion catches glimpses of tragic despair, it mitigates their terror. Even death, as we have tried to show for the story of Samson, is not a serious threat, for out of death can come restitution and renewal.

The exceptional quality of Saul as a tragic hero heightens by way of contrast the more dominant comic movement of biblical narrative. The biblical world view of a harmonious universe with a benign deity results in a natural evolution toward comic resolution. As G. Steiner observes, tragedy is alien to a universe which operates according to principles of reason and unthinkable in relation to a deity who acts in accordance with the demands of justice (4–5). We suppose the ways of the biblical God to be rational and just and thus we expect biblical stories to turn out for the best. Here the stories of Isaac and Samson fit our expectations, and, as we have argued, are inherently comic, however much subsequent interpreters have attempted to transform them into tragedies. In the all-embracing comic vision of the Bible, it is the presence of tragedies, like that of Saul, and perhaps a Jephthah or a Jeremiah, not their absence which is striking. But their presence in the wider biblical [[36]] story, like the presence of tragic moments in the individual comic stories, contributes to the fullness and richness of biblical narrative.

These three stories of a patriarch, a judge, and a king epitomize, in our judgment, the characteristic patterns of comedy and tragedy in the Bible. One cannot remain on the level of narrative genres to deal fully with comedy and tragedy. As we have implied in the title, "Reflections on the Comic and Tragic Visions," and as we have sought to show in this study, comedy and tragedy express essentially different views of reality. It remains the task of biblical scholarship to delineate more precisely the interplay between the genres of comedy and tragedy and the differing visions of existence reflected in the concrete forms of biblical literature.

Works Consulted

Bergson, Henri
  1980   "Laughter," in *Comedy.* Ed. Wylie Sypher. Baltimore: Johns Hopkins University Press. Pp. 59–190.

Bingham, Anne
  1981   "Ruse, Romance, and Resolution: The Comedy of Jacob," Unpublished Essay, Pomona College, Claremont, Ca.

Brooks, Cleanth
  1955   *Tragic Themes in Western Literature.* New Haven: Yale University Press.

Coats, George W.
  1980   "Strife Without Reconciliation: A Narrative Theme in the Jacob Traditions," in *Werden und Wirken des Alten Testaments.* Ed. R. Albertz, *et al.* Göttingen: Vandenhoeck & Ruprecht. Pp. 82–106.

Corrigan, Robert W., ed.
  1981a   *Comedy: Meaning and Form.* 2d ed. New York: Harper and Row.
  1981b   *Tragedy: Vision and Form.* 2d ed. New York: Harper and Row.

Crenshaw, James L.
  1978   *Samson: A Secret Betrayed, a Vow Ignored.* Atlanta: John Knox.

Culley, Robert C.
  1976   *Studies in the Structure of Hebrew Narrative.* Semeia Supplements 3. Philadelphia: Fortress.

Exum, J. Cheryl
1981 "Aspects of Symmetry and Balance in the Samson Saga," *JSOT* 19:3–29. Errata in *JSOT* 20:90.
1983 "The Theological Dimension of the Samson Saga," *VT* 33:30–45.
Freeman, James A.
1982 "Samson's Dry Bones: A Structural Reading of Judges 13–16," in *Literary Interpretations of Biblical Narratives*, II. Ed. K. R. R. Gros Louis with J. S. Ackerman. Nashville: Abingdon. Pp. 145–60.
Frye, Northrop
1964 "The Argument of Comedy," in *Theories of Comedy*. Ed. Paul Lauter. Garden City, N.Y.: Doubleday. Repr. from *English Institute Essays*. New York: Columbia University Press, 1948.
1965 *A Natural Perspective: The Development of Shakespearean Comedy and Romance*. New York: Harcourt, Brace & World.
1966 *Anatomy of Criticism*. New York: Atheneum.
1982 *The Great Code: The Bible and Literature*. New York: Harcourt Brace Jovanovich.
Good, Edwin M.
1965 *Irony in the Old Testament*. Philadelphia: Westminster.
Greenberg, Moshe
1983 *Biblical Prose Prayer*. Berkeley: University of California Press.
Greenstein, Edward L.
1981 "The Riddle of Samson," *Prooftexts* 1:237–60.
Gunkel, Hermann
1913 "Simson," in *Reden und Aufsätze*. Göttingen: Vandenhoeck & Ruprecht. Pp. 38–64.
1964 *Genesis*, 6. Aufl. Göttingen: Vandenhoeck & Ruprecht.
Gunn, David M.
1980 *The Fate of King Saul: An Interpretation of a Biblical Story*. JSOT Supplements, 14. Sheffield: JSOT.
1981 "A Man Given Over to Trouble: The Story of King Saul," in *Images of Man and God: Old Testament Short Stories in Literary Focus*. Ed. Burke O. Long. Sheffield: The Almond Press. Pp. 89–112.
Humphreys, W. Lee
1978 "The Tragedy of King Saul: A Study of the Structure of 1 Samuel 9–31," *JSOT* 6:18–27.
1980 "The Rise and Fall of King Saul: A Study of an Ancient Narrative Stratum in 1 Samuel," *JSOT* 18:74–90.
1982 "From Tragic Hero to Villain: A Study of the Figure of Saul and the Development of 1 Samuel," *JSOT* 22:95–117.
Krieger, Murray
1960 *The Tragic Vision: The Confrontation of Extremity*, vol. I of *Visions of Extremity in Modern Literature*. Baltimore: Johns Hopkins University Press.
1971 *The Classic Vision: The Retreat from Extremity*, vol. II of *Visions of Extremity in Modern Literature*. Baltimore: Johns Hopkins University Press.

1981   "*The Tragic Vision* Twenty Years After," in Corrigan 1981b: 42–46.
Langer, Susanne
1981a   "The Comic Rhythm," in Corrigan 1981a: 67–83. Repr. from *Feeling and Form.* New York: Scribner's, 1953.
1981b   "The Tragic Rhythm," in Corrigan 1981b: 113–23. Repr. from *Feeling and Form.* New York: Scribner's, 1953.
McCarter, P. Kyle, Jr.
1980   *1 Samuel. Anchor Bible*, 8. Garden City, N.Y.: Doubleday.
Mendenhall, George
1973   *The Tenth Generation: The Origins of the Biblical Tradition.* Baltimore: Johns Hopkins University Press.
Preston, Thomas R.
1982   "The Heroism of Saul: Patterns of Meaning in the Narrative of the Early Kingship," *JSOT* 24:27–46.
von Rad, Gerhard
1962   *Old Testament Theology*, vol. I. Tr. D. M. G. Stalker. New York: Harper & Row.
Ricoeur, Paul
1967   *The Symbolism of Evil.* Tr. E. Buchanan. Boston: Beacon Press.
Robertson, David
1977   *The Old Testament and the Literary Critic.* Philadelphia: Fortress.
Segal, Charles
1981   *Tragedy and Civilization: An Interpretation of Sophocles.* Cambridge, MA: Harvard University Press.
Segal, Erich
1972   "Marlowe's *Schadenfreude*: Barabas as Comic Hero," in *Veins of Humor.* Ed. Harry Levin. Harvard English Studies 3. Cambridge, MA: Harvard University Press. Pp. 69–91.
Sewall, Richard B.
1980   *The Vision of Tragedy.* New Haven: Yale University Press.
Steiner, George
1980   *The Death of Tragedy.* New York: Oxford University Press.
Sypher, Wylie
1980   "The Meanings of Comedy," in *Comedy.* Ed. W. Sypher. Baltimore: Johns Hopkins University Press. Pp. 191–260.
Vickery, John
1981   "In Strange Ways: The Story of Samson," in *Images of Man and God: Old Testament Short Stories in Literary Focus.* Ed. Burke O. Long. Sheffield: The Almond Press. Pp. 58–73.
Westermann, Claus
1981   *Genesis.* BKAT. II. Teilband, Genesis 12–36. Neukirchen.
Wharton, James A.
1973   "The Secret of Yahweh: Story and Affirmation in Judges 13–16," *Interpretation* 27:48–65.
Whedbee, J. William
1977   "The Comedy of Job," *Semeia* 7:1–39.

Wiesel, Elie
    1976   *Messengers of God: Biblical Portraits and Legends.* New York: Random
                House.
Williams, James G.
    1978   "The Comedy of Jacob: A Literary Study," *JAAR* 46/2, Supplement B.

Analysis of Hebrew Poetry

Introduction

Hebrew poetry has not received as much recent critical attention as Old Testament narrative, but the studies of the subject that have appeared have been by significant scholars who have submitted groundbreaking opinions. Of course, analysis of Hebrew poetry predates Old Testament literary criticism. Some might therefore ask why articles on the topic appear in this volume. The answer is principally that important literary critics, such as Adele Berlin and Robert Alter, contributed vital works on poetry. In addition, the general emphasis on literary detail that prevailed during the 1970s and 1980s created a good climate for new debates on this vital older issue.

Berlin's study of biblical parallelism (originally published in *Hebrew Union College Annual* in 1979) refines some traditional notions about Hebrew poetry. Since Robert Lowth's seminal work on Old Testament poetry in 1753, most scholars have accepted the idea that Hebrew verse consists of parallel thought sequences in consecutive lines. Lowth's categories of parallelism—synonymous, antithetical, and synthetical—were not thought absolutely comprehensive, yet the notion of parallelism was almost universally acknowledged. Berlin shows that parallelism exists not only in thought patterns, but in grammar and sound structures as well. She thereby clarifies the nature of poetry's overall fabric of composition.

J. Cheryl Exum (1981) demonstrates her own accurate understanding of parallelism, then also discusses other literary facets of poetry such as simile, metaphor, imagery, and tone. In so doing she illuminates biblical poetry much like other critics illuminate secular poetry. Her analysis illustrates Isaiah's theological brilliance, yet reveals its literary artistry at the same time. Creativity and exegesis mesh.

As the introduction to this volume indicated, Old Testament poetry is still being debated. Kugel, Alter, Berlin, Exum, and others will continue to discuss the nature of this literature. What has already been written, however, has been stimulating. More analysis will most likely only improve our grasp of poetry and poetic technique.

The Grammatical Aspect of Biblical Parallelism

ADELE BERLIN

[[31]] The grammatical aspect of parallelism—grammatical equivalence and/or contrast—is one of the fundamental aspects of biblical parallelism. There is almost always some degree of grammatical correspondence between parallel lines, and in many cases it is the basic structuring device of the parallelism—the feature that creates the perception of parallelism. In this chapter I will examine this grammatical aspect more extensively in order to see exactly which grammatical equivalences are present and how they manifest themselves.[1] Since the study of grammar is usually subdivided into morphology and syntax, I will subdivide grammatical parallelism into these two categories. Syntactic parallelism is the syntactic equivalence of one line with another line. (Most studies of grammatical parallelism have dealt only with a comparison of the syntax of the lines as a whole.) Morphologic parallelism involves the morphologic equivalence or contrast of individual constituents of the lines. Many lines contain more than one type of grammatical parallelism; and sometimes the boundary between morphologic and syntactic parallelism is indistinct.

Those who have studied the grammar of parallel lines are well aware that the surface structure of the lines is identical in only a small percentage of cases. One such case is

---

Reprinted with permission from *The Dynamics of Biblical Parallelism* (Bloomington: Indiana University Press, 1985) 31–63, 144–46.

1. Many of these grammatical equivalences were first presented in Berlin, *HUCA* 50. Kugel (*Idea*), Geller (*Parallelism in Early Biblical Poetry*), and Sappan independently put forth a few of the same and others. I will here combine and enlarge upon all of these studies.

Ps 103:10   לא כחטאינו עשה לנו
                          ולא כעונתינו גמל עלינו

    Not according to our sins did he deal with us;
    And not according to our transgressions did he requite us.

The surface structure of the two lines is the same, both in respect to syntax and morphology. Every component of the first line is mirrored in the second. ⟦32⟧ The syntax of both lines is Negative—Prepositional Phrase—Verb—Indirect Object. The corresponding terms are morphologically identical ⟦note: "The symbol // indicates 'parallel to' in the traditional sense of occurring in parallel lines"—from the preface to Berlin's book⟧:

לא // לא
"not // not"
negative particle

כחטאינו // כעונתינו
"according to our sins // according to our transgressions"
preposition + noun (masc. pl.) + possessive suffix (1st person pl.)

עשה // גמל
"he dealt // he requited"
verb (*qal*, 3rd person, masc., sing., perfect)

לנו // עלינו
"to us // on us"
preposition + 1st person pl. suffix

This is actually an example of grammatical identity or repetition. While there is not lexical repetition (the same words are not used in both lines), there is the repetition of the same grammatical structure. This verse is the exception, for more often we find grammatical equivalence: the second line substitutes something grammatically different, but equivalent, for a grammatical feature in the first line. The substitution may involve only one element, e.g., a pronoun in place of a noun, in which case we have morphologic parallelism; or it may involve a transformation in the syntax of the entire line, e.g., from indicative to interrogative, and then we would speak of syntactic parallelism. The important thing to remember is that although there is a difference in the two grammatical structures, they are in some way equivalent to one

another. In nonparallelistic discourse only one would occur, and
either one could substitute for the other (semantics permitting); but in
parallelistic discourse they are *both* present. Thus grammar has been
projected from the axis of selection to the axis of combination.

Morphologic Parallelism

In this section I will present examples of morphologic pairings from
different word classes, and pairings from the same word class with
different morphologic elements. [[33]]

Morphologic Pairs from Different Word Classes

This type of parallelism involves words from different parts of speech.
The following kinds of pairing may occur.

Noun // Pronoun

Ps 33:2   הודו לה׳ בכנור
                          בנבל עשור זמרו לו

>   Praise YHWH with the lyre;
>   With the ten-stringed harp sing to *him.*

Ps 33:8   יראו מה׳ כל הארץ
                          ממנו יגורו כל ישבי תבל

>   Let all the earth fear YHWH;
>   Let all the world's inhabitants dread *him.*

Noun/Pronoun // Relative Clause[2]

Ps 105:26[3]   שלח משה עבדו
                          אהרן אשר בחר בו

>   He sent *Moses his servant;*
>   Aaron *whom he had chosen.*

---

2. A relative clause is not a morphological element; a relative pronoun is. But since
the relative pronoun is often omitted in poetry, I will speak of relative clauses. This is actually more correct, for it is the whole clause, not just the pronoun, which is equivalent
to the noun in the parallel line.

3. The lexical pair עבד // בחר has been conventionalized, occurring in different parts
of speech in Isa 41:8, 9; 42:1; 43:10; 44:1, 2; 65:9, 15 (noted in Watters, 174) and also in
Ps 89:4; 105:6 and perhaps Hag 2:23.

Lam 5:1 זכר ה' מה היה לנו
הביט וראה את חרפתנו

Attend, YHWH, *what has happened to us*;
Look and see *our disgrace*.

Song 3:1 על משכבי בלילות בקשתי את שאהבה נפשי
בקשתיו ולא מצאתיו

On my couch at night I sought *the one I love*;
I sought *him* but did not find him.

Prepositional Phrase // Adverb

Ps 34:2 אברכה את ה' בכל עת
תמיד תהלתו בפי

I bless YHWH *at all times*;
Always praise of him is in my mouth.

Ps 42:9 [cf. also Ps 121:6] יומם יצוה ה' חסדו
ובלילה שירה עמי ⟦34⟧

By day may YHWH commission his faithful care;
And *in the night* may a son to him be with me.[4]

Job 5:14 יומם יפגשו חשך
וכלילה ימששו בצהרים

By day they encounter darkness;
And they grope as in the night *at noon*.

Isa 52:3 חנם נמכרתם
ולא בכסף תגאלו

You have been sold *without a price*;
And not *for money* will you be redeemed.

Substantive (noun, adjective, participle) // Verb. This category will be
treated in greater detail in the section on syntactic parallelism, since it
often involves a nominal clause parallel to a verbal clause. I cite several
examples here, first those which employ the same root in both word
classes, then those which utilize different roots.

---

4. יומם is more often paired with לילה, which serves as the adverbial form—compare,
for example, Exod 13:21, 22; Isa 4:5. But an adverb can be introduced by a preposition—
cf. Blau, *Grammar*, 103.

Ps 145:18   קרוב ה׳ לכל קראיו
                                לכל אשר יקראהו באמת

YHWH is near to all *his callers*;
To all *those who call him* in truth.

Ps 97:9   כי אתה ה׳ עליון על כל הארץ
                           מאד נעלית על כל אלהים

For you, YHWH, *are highest* over all the world;
You *have been heightened* greatly over all gods.

Ps 34:19   קרוב ה׳ לנשברי לב
                           ואת דכאי רוח יושיע

YHWH is *near* to the heartbroken;
And the dispirited he *will save*.

Mic 6:2   כי ריב לה׳ עם עמו
                          ועם ישראל יתוכח

For YHWH *has a quarrel* with his people;
And with Israel *will he dispute*.

There is really nothing unusual about such pairings, for the members of each category are normally used as substitutes for each other in biblical [[35]] Hebrew: pronouns take the place of nouns, prepositional phrases and adverbs often serve the same syntactic function and are not always distinguishable, and a relative clause may serve as a subject or object—the same syntactic slot also filled by nouns and pronouns. The evidence seems to indicate that any word classes that serve the same syntactic function can be paired in morphologic parallelism.

Morphologic Pairs from the Same Word Class

It is perhaps more usual to find that word pairs are from the same word class—i.e., nouns // nouns, verbs // verbs—but even here the words need not be morphologically identical. Singulars can parallel plurals, perfects can parallel imperfects, as in the following examples.

Contrast in Tense. The paralleling of *qtl* and *yqtl* verbs is a well-known and amply documented phenomenon.[5] It occurs with verbs from the same root, as in

---

5. Cf. Cassuto, *Biblical and Oriental Studies* II, 58–59; Held, "The YQTL–QTL (QTL–YQTL) Sequence of Identical Verbs in Biblical Hebrew and in Ugaritic"; Dahood, *Psalms* III, 420–23.

Ps 29:10   ה׳ למבול יָשָׁב
                                  וַיֵּשֶׁב ה׳ מלך לעולם

> YHWH sat enthroned at the Flood;
> YHWH sits enthroned, king forever.

Isa 14:25   וְסָר מעליהם עלו
                                  וסבלו מעל שכמו יָסוּר

> And his yoke shall drop from on them;
> And his burden shall drop from his shoulder.[6]

Isa 60:16   וְיָנַקְתְּ חלב גוים
                                  ושד מלכים תִּינָקִי

> You shall suck the milk of nations;
> And the breasts of royalty you shall suck.

The same phenomenon is found in prose:

Gen 1:5   וַיִּקְרָא אלהים לאור יום
                                  ולחשך קָרָא לילה

> And God called the light Day;
> and the darkness he called Night.

Exod 4:11   מי שָׂם פה לאדם
                            או מי יָשׂוּם אלם . . . [[36]]

> Who makes speech for man;
> or who makes a mute . . .

Lev 25:10   וְשַׁבְתֶּם איש אל אחזתו
                                  ואיש אל משפחתו תָּשֻׁבוּ

> You will return each man to his land holding;
> and each man to his family you will return.

Verbs from different roots appear in *qtl–yqtl* parallelism in

Ps 26:4   לא יָשַׁבְתִּי עם מתי שוא
                                  ועם נעלמים לא אָבוֹא

> I do not consort with scoundrels;
> And with hypocrites I do not associate.

---

6. Cf. Yoder, *Fixed Word Pairs*, p. 9, n. 21.

Job 6:15   אַחַי בָּגְדוּ כְמוֹ נַחַל
כַּאֲפִיק נְחָלִים יַעֲבֹרוּ

My brothers are as treacherous as a wadi;
Like a wadi-stream they run dry.

It is important to emphasize that the *qtl–yqtl* shift, of which we have given only a few examples, occurs not for semantic reasons (it does not indicate a real temporal sequence) but for what have been considered stylistic reasons.[7] But it is not just something vaguely "stylistic"; we can now recognize it for what it is—a kind of grammatical parallelism.

Contrast in Conjugation. Verbs from the same root but in different conjugations may be paired,[8] such as

<table>
<tr><td>Ps 24:7</td><td align="right">שְׂאוּ שְׁעָרִים רָאשֵׁיכֶם</td><td>qal</td></tr>
<tr><td></td><td align="right">וְהִנָּשְׂאוּ פִּתְחֵי עוֹלָם</td><td>niph^cal</td></tr>
</table>

Lift up, O gates, your head;
And be lifted up, O eternal doors.

<table>
<tr><td>Ps 38:3</td><td align="right">כִּי חִצֶּיךָ נִחֲתוּ בִי</td><td>niph^cal(!)</td></tr>
<tr><td></td><td align="right">וַתִּנְחַת עָלַי יָדֶךָ</td><td>qal</td></tr>
</table>

For your arrows have struck me;
Your hand has come down upon me.

This phenomenon was called the active-passive sequence by U. Cassuto,[9] and the factitive-passive sequence by M. Held (*JBL* 84, 272–82). However, [[37]] the shift is not limited to specific conjugations or grammatical voice, as can be seen from the following verses listed by M. Dahood: Ps 64:5 (*qal–hiph^cil*); Ps 77:12 (*Ketiv*) (*hiph^cil–qal*); Ps 139:21 (*pi^cel–qal*).[10] In addition to the verses cited by the aforementioned

---

7. Cf. Cross and Freedman, *Studies in Ancient Yahwistic Poetry*, 127–28; D. N. Freedman, *Pottery, Poetry, and Prophecy*, 210; Clines, *I, He, We*, 47–48.

8. I have limited this section to verbs from the same root because different verbal roots occur in different conjugations. Therefore, the pairing of, say, *bqš* in the *pi^cel* with *mṣ^ʾ* in the *qal* is not a strong morphological contrast because these are simply the conjugations in which these verbs are used. The contrast is most perceptible when different conjugations of the same root are paired. (This pairing also adds a lexical and phonetic dimension to the parallelism.)

9. *The Goddess Anath*, 47–48 = *Biblical and Oriental Studies*, II, 58–59 (original: *Tarbiz* 14, 1–10).

10. *Psalms* III, 414. Dahood also lists Ps 29:5; 38:3; 69:15.

scholars,[11] the following verses contain the pairing of the same verbal root in different conjugations.

Gen 6:12   וירא אלהים את הארץ והנה נִשְׁחָתָה   *niph*ᶜ*al*
                       כי הִשְׁחִית כל בשר את דרכו על הארץ   *hiph*ᶜ*il*

God saw the earth: it looked corrupt—
for all flesh had corrupted its way on earth.

Gen 17:17   הלבן מאה שנה יִוָּלֵד   *niph*ᶜ*al*
                   ואם שרה הבת תשעים שנה תֵּלֵד   *qal*

Can a son be born to a hundred-year-old man;
Can Sarah, a ninety-year-old woman, give birth.[12]

1 Sam 1:28   וגם אנכי הִשְׁאִלְתִּהוּ לה'   *hiph*ᶜ*il*
                כל הימים אשר היה הוא שָׁאוּל לה'   *qal*

And I, in turn, lend him to YHWH;
for as long as he lives he is lent to YHWH.

Isa 1:19–20   טוב הארץ תֹּאכֵלוּ . . .   *qal*
                        חרב תְּאֻכְּלוּ . . .   *pu*ᶜ*al*

. . . the good of the earth you will eat;
. . . you will be devoured by the sword.

This is a play on words made possible because the root ᵓ*kl* occurs in different conjugations with different meanings: the *qal* means "to eat" and the *pu*ᶜ*al* is used in the sense of "to be consumed."

---

11. The verses listed by Cassuto and Held are: Isa 6:11 (?); Jer 15:19; 17:14; 20:7; 31:3, 17; Ps 19:13–14; 24:7; 69:15; Lam 5:21. Held hesitates to include Isa 6:11 because many modern commentators, following the reading of the LXX, emend תשאה to תשאר. This emendation, notes Held, seems to be supported by Isa 24:12 (*JBL* 84, 275, n. 2). However, while it is true that Isa 24:12 contains the same idea and many of the same terms found in 6:11, this does not mean that all of the terms need be identical. The word נשאר may have been used in 24:12 because it makes a good phonologic complement to the word שער at the end of the verse. The phonetic pattern in 6:11 is entirely different. Here one might see an ABBA pattern composed of שאו—אדם—אדמה—תשאה. In my opinion emending תשאה is unnecessary; the verbs תשאה and שאו exemplify a contrast in tense, conjugation, and number.

12. Cf. Kselman, *JBL* 97, 168. There is no need to change יולד to אולד or to explain the *lamed* as emphatic, as Kselman does. The syntax of the two parallel lines need not be identical—see below, Syntactic Parallelism.

Isa 33:1

הוֹי שׁוֹדֵד וְאַתָּה לֹא שָׁדוּד
וּבוֹגֵד וְלֹא בָגְדוּ בָךְ
כַּהֲתִמְךָ שׁוֹדֵד תּוּשַּׁד
כַּנְלֹתְךָ לִבְגֹּד יִבְגְּדוּ בָךְ

Ho, Plunderer and you are not plundered;
And Betrayer and they did not betray you.
When you have done being a plunderer, you will be
    plundered;
When you have finished betraying, they will betray you.

The root *šdd* occurs here in the *qal* and *hophᶜal* forms; the root *bgd*
only in different forms of the *qal*. Not only does *šdd* show variation in
conjugation, but repetition of the same pattern for both verbs is
avoided by using *šdd* in passive constructions and *bgd* in active (imper-
sonal) constructions. [[38]]

Isa 66:13	כְּאִישׁ אֲשֶׁר אִמּוֹ תְּנַחֲמֶנּוּ *piᶜel*
	כֵּן אָנֹכִי אֲנַחֶמְכֶם *piᶜel*
	וּבִירוּשָׁלַ͏ִם תְּנֻחָמוּ *puᶜal*

Like a man whose mother comforts him;
So will I comfort you;
And in Jerusalem you will be comforted.

Jer 20:14	אָרוּר הַיּוֹם אֲשֶׁר יֻלַּדְתִּי בּוֹ *puᶜal*
	יוֹם אֲשֶׁר יְלָדַתְנִי אִמִּי אַל יְהִי בָרוּךְ *qal*

Cursed be the day on which I was born;
The day on which my mother bore me, let it not be blessed.

Jer 23:19 [cf. Jer 30:23]	הִנֵּה סַעֲרַת ה' חֵמָה יָצְאָה
	וְסַעַר מִתְחוֹלֵל *hitpaᶜel*
	עַל רֹאשׁ רְשָׁעִים יָחוּל *qal*

Look, the storm of YHWH goes forth in fury;
And [it is] a whirling storm;
Upon the heads of the wicked it will whirl.

Hos 12:13–14	וּבְאִשָּׁה שָׁמָר . . . *qal*
	וּבְנָבִיא נִשְׁמָר . . . *niphᶜal*

. . . And for a wife he guarded [the sheep];
. . . And by a prophet it [Israel] was guarded.

Mic 6:14b   ותסג ולא תַפְלִיט   *hiph^cil*

                          ואשר תְּפַלֵּט לחרב אתן   *pi^cel*

You will conceive/labor but will not bring forth;
And what you bring forth I will deliver to the sword.

Job 22:30   יְמַלֵּט אי נקי   *pi^cel*

                        וְנִמְלַט בבר כפיך   *niph^cal*

He will deliver the unclean;
And he will be delivered through the purity of your hands.

Furthermore, just as word pairs may be found in juxtaposition and collocation, in addition to parallel lines, so, too, the pairing of verbs of different conjugations occurs in these arrangements.

Gen 7:23   וַיִּמַח את כל היקום . . . וַיִּמָּחוּ מן הארץ   *qal . . . niph^cal*

And he blotted out all existence . . . they were blotted out from the earth.

Gen 25:21   [[39]] וַיֵּעָתֶר לו ה' . . . וַיֶּעְתַּר יצחק לה'   *qal . . . niph^cal*

Isaac entreated yhwh . . . and yhwh was entreated by him [i.e., responded to his plea].

Lev 13:19–20   . . . וְנִרְאָה אל הכהן: וְרָאָה הכהן . . .   *niph^cal . . . qal*

. . . and it shall be seen by the priest. And the priest saw. . . .

Josh 6:1   . . . ויריחו סֹגֶרֶת וּמְסֻגֶּרֶת   *qal pi^cel*

Jericho was closed and shut tight. . . .

Isa 45:1   לרד לפניו גוים

                       ומתני מלכים אֲפַתֵּחַ   *pi^cel*

                       לִפְתֹּחַ לפניו דלתים   *qal*

                       ושערים לא יסגרו

Treading down nations before him;
And the loins of kings I will loosen.
Loosening [opening] doors before him;
And not letting gates be closed.

Isa 57:20   והרשעים כים נגרש כי השקט לא יוכל   *niphᶜal*
            וַיִּגְרְשׁוּ מֵימָיו רֶפֶשׁ וָטִיט   *qal*

And the wicked are like a tossing sea that cannot be calm;
And its waters toss up mire and mud.

Ezek 14:6   שׁוּבוּ וְהָשִׁיבוּ   *qal hiphᶜil*

return and let return

Zeph 2:1   הִתְקוֹשְׁשׁוּ וָקוֹשּׁוּ   *hitpaᶜel qal*

gather yourselves and gather

Mal 2:10–11   . . . בָּגְדָה יְהוּדָה . . . מַדּוּעַ נִבְגַּד אִישׁ   *niphᶜal . . . qal*

why is a man betrayed . . . Judah betrayed. . . .

Ps 92:13–14   . . . צדיק כתמר יִפְרָח   *qal*
            . . . בחצרות אלהינו יַפְרִיחוּ   *hiphᶜil*

The righteous will bloom like a palm. . . .
. . . in the courts of our God they will be allowed to bloom.

Both a shift in tense and a shift in conjugation are found in

Hos 5:5   וישראל ואפרים יִכָּשְׁלוּ בעונם   *niphᶜal, yqtl*
          כָּשַׁל גם יהודה עמם   *qal, qtl*

And Israel and Ephraim will be tripped by their sin;
Judah also tripped with them.

⟦40⟧ M. Held's explanation for the shift in conjugation is that "the device is stylistic and would seem to aim at stressing and emphasizing the effect or result of the action referred to in the first stichos" (*JBL* 84, 274). He also suggests (*JBL* 84, 275) that there were fewer available parallel pairs for verbs than for nouns, and so rather than repeat the same verb in the same form, it was modified slightly. This is doubtful, for, as we will see in chapter 4 ⟦not reprinted here⟧, every word has a potential pair, so there are as many possibilities for pairing verbs as for pairing nouns. Lists of word pairs contain more nouns than verbs because it is often the verb that is gapped, or omitted, in biblical poetry (cf. O'Connor, *HVS*, 122–27). However, Held's observation on the effect of this type of parallelism appears to be correct. Using the same root in a different conjugation (and also in a different tense) is, at times, more effective than using totally different roots because it produces the assonance and the play on words which is so much a part of biblical rhetoric. In this respect, verses containing the same verbal root in different conjugations are part of the same phenomenon as verses containing the same root in any part of speech (e.g., Job 11:18; Ruth 2:12—and see below, pp. 45 ⟦327⟧, 55 ⟦338⟧, 71).

Contrast in Person. Shifts in person in parallel lines have been noted by many commentators. My contribution to their discussion is that these shifts should be viewed not as isolated "poetic" devices, but as examples of morphologic parallelism similar to those already presented (cf. also Kugel, *Idea*, 22).

Ps 104:13   משקה הרים מעליותיו
מפרי מעשיך תשבע הארץ

> [*He*] waters the mountains from *his* upper chambers;
> From the fruits of *your* work the earth is sated.

Song 1:2   ישקני מנשיקות פיהו
כי טובים דדיך מיין

> Let *him* kiss me with the kisses of *his* mouth;
> For *your* love is sweeter than wine.

Lev 23:42   בסכת תשבו שבעת ימים
כל האזרח בישראל ישבו בסכת

> You shall live in booths for seven days;
> every citizen in Israel [*they*] will live in booths.

⟦41⟧ Ps 20:8 contains third and first person contrast. Eccl 5:1 has second and third person contrast, along with other grammatical contrasts to be discussed below.

Contrast in Gender. There may be incidental morphologic parallelism when a masculine noun is paired with a feminine noun, as in the common pair הרים // גבעות, "mountains (masc.) // hills (fem.)." The real contrast, however, comes when the same noun (or same root) appears in two different genders. Cassuto pointed out that there are Ugaritic and biblical examples which show that often a masculine word is used in reference to a male or masculine term, and a feminine synonym is applied to a female or feminine term.[13] He cited

---

13. *The Goddess Anath*, 44–46 = *Biblical and Oriental Studies*, II, 66–68 (original: *Lešonenu* 15, 97–102). Cf. also Watson, *JBL* 99 and Watson, *UF* 13.

Jer 48:46 [cf. also Deut 21:10–11] אוי לך מואב
אבד עם כמוש
כי לקחו בניך בשבי
ובנתיך בשביה

Woe to you, Moab;
Lost is the people of Chemosh,
For your sons are taken into captivity;
And your daughters into captivity.

Nah 2:13b וימלא טרף חריו
ומענתיו טרפה

And he filled his lairs with prey;
And his dens with prey.

Isa 3:1 כי הנה האדון ה׳ צבאות מסיר
מירושלם ומיהודה משען ומשענה

For lo, the Lord YHWH of Hosts removes from Jerusalem and
Judah support and support.

In Isa 3:1, Cassuto explains, the word משען, "support (masc.)" harks
back to Judah (here grammatically masculine, cf. Isa 3:8), and משענה,
"support (fem.)" to the feminine Jerusalem. This pattern is chiastic.

These three verses contain three sets of nearly identical word pairs:
שבי // שביה, טרף // טרפה, and משענה // משען. Cassuto suggested that
these sets, or at least the second term in each, were chosen in order to
match the gender of another word in their respective lines. That is, the
choice of these words was based on morphologic considerations.

[[42]] But there is a slightly different way to view the phenomenon
in these three verses. Surely there were other word pairs which were of
the required gender (for example, compare Jer 48:46 with Num
21:29). One must ask why such similar terms were chosen in these
verses. The use of such closely related parallel terms is so striking as to
indicate an intent to emphasize their morphology. These pairs suggest
to me not so much that they were selected to match the gender of
other words in their lines, but that they were intended to parallel each
other morphologically, much like the pairs composed of the same root
in different conjugations. There are other sets of nearly identical
terms—one masculine and one feminine—although they do not cor-
relate with the gender of the surrounding words.

Jer 23:19 [cf. Jer 30:23]   הנה סערת ה׳ חמה יצאה
                                   וסער מתחולל

    Lo, the storm [s^crt] of YHWH goes forth furiously, and [it is] a
    whirling storm. [s^cr]

Isa 52:2 [cf. Jer 48:46]

התנערי מעפר קומי שבי ירושלם
התפתחי [התפתחו *Ketiv*,] מוסרי צוארך שביה בת ציון

    Arise, get up from the dust, captive [$šby$] Jerusalem;
    Loosen the bonds from your neck, captive [$šbyh$] Maiden
    Zion. [cf. RSV]

Other verses employ both masculine and feminine forms of the same
root, although they may not be exactly synonymous or parallel:

Ezek 25:13   . . . ונתתיה חרבה
                                   מתימן ודדנה בחרב יפלו

    . . . I will lay it in ruins [$ḥrbh$];
    From Tema to Dedan they shall fall by the sword [$ḥrb$].

Ezek 25:15   . . . יען עשות פלשתים בנקמה
                            . . . וינקמו נקם

    . . . because the Philistines acted in their vengeance [$nqmh$]
    and they avenged with vengeance [nqm] . . .
    [This verse is part of a larger play on the root nqm.]

    The use of the same adjective in different genders, although this is
determined by the modified nouns, may also be considered morphologic parallelism since it often serves to stress or contrast the adjectives. [[43]]

Gen 11:6   הן עם אחד ושפה אחת לכלם

    They are *one* [masc.] people and they all have *one* [fem.]
    language.

Isa 66:8   היוחל ארץ ביום אחד
                            אם יולד גוי פעם אחת

    Can a land travail in *one* [masc.] day;
    Can a nation be born at *one* [fem.] stroke.

Ps 51:19   זבחי אלהים רוח נשברה
לב נשבר ונדכה אלהים לא תבזה

[True] sacrifices to God are a *contrite* [fem.] spirit;
A *contrite* [masc.] and crushed heart, God, you will not disdain.

This last verse is especially interesting, because the word רוח may be
either gender, and, indeed, the pair לב and רוח appears in Ps 51:12
where both are masculine. Perhaps רוח has been used in verse 19 as a
feminine form in order to produce the feminine-masculine pairing
which stands out in נשבר // נשברה.

Is there any evidence for this type of morphologic parallelism involving different roots? There are verses in which there is agreement in gender within a line and contrast of gender from one line to the next.

Ps 144:12   אשר בנינו כנטעים . . .
בנתינו כזוית

For our sons are like saplings . . .
And our daughters are like cornerstones. . . .

Ps 126:2   אז ימלא שחוק פינו
ולשוננו רנה

Our mouths will be filled with laughter;
Our tongues with joy.

Prov 1:8   שמע בני מוסר אביך
ואל תטש תורת אמך

My son, heed the discipline of your father;
And do not forsake the teaching of your mother.

The arrangement of the genders in these verses may be accidental, but
the result is a morphologic parallelism. The question remains: is this
juxtaposition of genders effective (in the sense discussed in chapter 1;
cf. p. 24 [not reprinted here])—in [44] other words, is it meaningful
in focusing the message on itself? To put it more plainly, does the
morphologic parallelism in these verses belong to the poetic function,
or is it a random happening of no poetic significance. The case for poetic significance cannot be proved, for the following reason: most parallel terms are not chosen for grammatical reasons, but because they
are lexically associated (this will be discussed at length in chapter 4
[not reprinted here]). Since all nouns in Hebrew are either masculine

or feminine, there are inevitably many combinations containing one term in each gender, e.g., גבעות // הרים, שמחה // ששון. Even pairs which appear to be morphologically based, such as אם // אב, בנות // בנים, are better explained through the process of word association. Therefore, I would hesitate to consider the last three cited verses, and others like them, as examples of morphological contrast.

However, there is a verse which does seem to contain an effective morphological contrast.

Isa 3:8a   כי כשלה ירושלם
                                  ויהודה נפל

> For Jerusalem has stumbled [fem.];
> And Judah has fallen [masc.].

The word יהודה may be grammatically feminine, as in Ps 114:2 and Lam 1:3, or masculine, as in Hos 5:5. By choosing to construe it as masculine here (and also in Isa 3:1), Isaiah has created a morphologic parallelism. In Isa 3:8 the two genders appear to balance each other, and may even create a merismus.[14] The presence of this alternation in gender heightens the effect of the parallelism.

Contrast in Number. Here, too, one must take into account that some word pairs will contain one singular and one plural for lexical reasons. Most of these fall into one of the following categories:

a. Some words, such as שמים, מים, חיים, are grammatically plural although they have a singular meaning. They will most likely be paired with a singular term.

b. Some words usually occur in the dual or plural, e.g., עיניים, שפתיים, but often have a singular parallel mate.

c. Some words, although grammatically singular, have a collective meaning, e.g., גוי, and will often parallel a plural. [[45]]

d. One of the principles by which words are paired is subordinate // superordinate (a part and its whole). Some of these pairs contain one singular and one plural, e.g., מלכים // דוד (Ps 144:10), ערי יהודה // ירושלם (Jer

---

14. The pair *Jerusalem // Judah* also creates a merismus by employing a part and its whole. The effect of totality is emphasized by the chiastic word order. The verbs also constitute a totality since both verbs can apply to both subjects: Jerusalem and Judah have stumbled and fallen. This is a distributional reading, something warned against by Kugel (*Idea* 40–41). Heeding the warning, and influenced by Kugel's discussion of "sharpness" (*Idea*, 7–11), I would go on to see an even more dramatic picture of totality in Isaiah's words: Jerusalem's stumbling will lead to Judah's fall. Thus the grammatical and the lexical parallelisms work toward the same end.

7:17), ‏ציון // בנות יהודה‎ (Ps 48:12).

   e. There are what we can call for now traditional, logical, or natural pairs, such as ‏כוכבים // ירח‎, "moon // stars" (Job 25:5); ‏בניה // בעלה‎ "her husband // her sons" (Prov 31:28); ‏זקנים // אב‎, "father // elders" (Deut 32:7);[15] ‏שנים // אחד‎, "one // two" (Deut 32:30).[16]

   Thus, there are many verses in which, for lexical-semantic reasons, a singular term will parallel a plural one. But, in addition to these, there are numerous verses which contain this type of parallelism for nonlexical reasons. These verses contain a singular term paralleled by a plural (or a compound, which generates a plural predicate) for no apparent reason other than to create a morphologic parallelism.[17] This is most striking when the same root appears in both lines in different numbers.

Song 1:3   ‏לריח שמניך טובים‎
                               ‏שמן תורק שמך‎

    Your *oils* give sweet fragrance;
    . . . *oil* is your name.

Ps 80:6   ‏האכלתם לחם דמעה‎
                         ‏ותשקמו בדמעות שליש‎

    You have fed them *tear*-bread;
    You have made them drink *tears* in measure.

Prov 14:12 = 16:25   ‏יש דרך ישר לפני איש‎
                       ‏ואחריתה דרכי מות‎

    There is a [seemingly] right *path* before man;
    But its end is *paths* of death.

Judg 5:28   ‏מדוע בשש רכבו לבוא‎
                    ‏מדוע אחרו פעמי מרכבותיו‎

    Why does his *chariot* tarry in coming;
    Why have the poundings of his *chariots* delayed.

---

   15. A person has only one father but more than one elder (or perhaps even "grand-father"—cf. Prov 17:6).

   16. This follows the rule for paralleling numbers: x // x + 1.

   17. Watters has also observed the paralleling of a singular with a plural, but explains the phenomenon as being necessary for metric reasons: "By so varying the singular-plural aspect of the words in pair, the lines are balanced in more uniform lengths" (105). Cf. Kugel, *Idea*, 20–21.

Job 6:15   אחי בגדו כמו נחל
                                          כאפיק נחלים יעברו

My brothers are as treacherous as a *wadi*;
Like a wadi-stream [lit.: a stream of *wadis*] they run dry.

⟦46⟧ Equally effective is the pairing of demonstrative pronouns of
different number.

Isa 66:8   מי שמע כזאת
                                          מי ראה כאלה

Who has heard *such a thing*;
Who has seen *such things*.

Jer 5:9   העל אלה לוא אפקד נאם ה'
                                          ואם בגוי אשר כזה לא תתנקם נפשי

Shall I not call *such* (*deeds*) to account, says ʏʜᴡʜ;
Shall I not avenge myself on *such a nation*.

Job 10:13   ואלה צפנת בלבבך
                                          ידעתי כי זאת עמך

These things you hid in your heart;
I know that *this* is in your mind.

Job 12:9   מי לא ידע בכל אלה
                                          כי יד ה' עשתה זאת

Who among all *these* does not know;
That the hand of ʏʜᴡʜ has done *this*.

Job 18:21   אך אלה משכנות עול
                                          וזה מקום לא ידע אל

These are the abodes of the perverse;
And *this* is the place of him who ignored God.

Lam 5:17   על זה היה דוה לבנו
                                          על אלה חשכו עינינו

Because of *this* was our heart faint;
Because of *these* our eyes dimmed.

It is also striking to find two parallel verbs in different numbers.

Hos 5:5b
וישראל ואפרים יכשלו בעונם
כשל גם יהודה עמם

And Israel and Ephraim *stumble* in their sin;
Judah also *stumbles* with them.

Isa 2:4 [but cf. Mic 4:3]
לא ישא גוי אל גוי חרב
ולא ילמדו עוד מלחמה [[47]]

Nation will not *raise* [sing.] a sword to nation;
They will no longer *learn* [pl.] war.

Deut 32:7
זכר ימות עולם
בינו שנות דור ודור

Remember [sing.] the days of old;
Consider [pl.] the years of ages past.

Although many scholars prefer to read בין or בינה instead of בינו, there
is no evidence to support such a reading. The parallelism is clearly singular // plural. This pattern is continued in the following lines of the
verse

שאל אביך ויגדך
זקניך ויאמרו לך

Ask your *father* and *he* will tell you;
Your *elders* and *they* will say to you.

so that even though the pair זקנים // אב may not be primarily a morphologic pair, it reinforces the morphologic parallelism which precedes it.
   The four-part parallelism in Deut 32:7 is only one of several that
have a morphological pattern based on number. Other examples are

Isa 40:4
כל גיא ינשא
וכל הר וגבעה ישפלו
והיה העקב למישור
והרכסים לבקעה

Every valley will be raised;
And every mountain and hill will be lowered;
And the depression will become level;
And the ridges a plain.
[singular // plural; singular // plural]

Ps 92:13–14   צדיק כתמר יפרח
                                              כארז בלבנון ישגה
                                              שתולים בבית ה'
                                              בחצרות אלהינו יפריחו

The righteous will bloom like the palm;
Like the cedar in Lebanon he will flourish;
Planted in the house of YHWH;
In the courts of our God they will be allowed to bloom.
[singular // singular; plural // plural] ⟦48⟧

Ps 126:5–6   הזרעים בדמעה
                                              ברנה יקצרו
                                              הלוך ילך ובכה נשא משך הזרע
                                              בא יבוא ברנה נשא אלמתיו

Those who sow in tears;
In joy will they reap;
He who indeed goes crying, carrying the seed-bag;
Will indeed come joyfully, carrying his sheaves.
[plural // plural; singular // singular]

As in the case of gender, the use of the same or similar adjectives
in different number emphasizes the adjective and yields a morphologic
parallelism.

Gen 11:1   ויהי כל הארץ שפה אחת ודברים אחדים

The whole earth was the same language and the same
words.[18]

Isa 54:7   ברגע קטן עזבתיך
                                          וברחמים גדלים אקבצך

For a small [sing.] moment I abandoned you;
But with great [pl.] mercy I will gather you up.[19]

As we can see from Ps 126:5–6, either a singular or a plural can be
used generically in Hebrew. Moreover, we often find that a verse or
passage uses both—thereby producing a morphologic parallelism.

18. On אחדים cf. Ezek 37:17.
19. ברגע and ברחמים are not normally considered word pairs, but can be construed
here as such because they each occupy the same position in their respective lines. The
fact that they are phonologically similar, and that both are modified by similar adjectives,
adds to the impression that they are parallel terms.

Prov 14:33　　　　　　　　בלב נבון תנוח חכמה
　　　　　　　　　　　　ובקרב כסילים תודע

In the heart of *a wise man* Wisdom rests;
But in the midst of *fools* it makes itself known.

Prov 18:15　　　　　　　　לב נבון יקנה דעת
　　　　　　　　　　　　ואזן חכמים תבקש דעת

The heart of *an intelligent man* acquires knowledge;
And the ear of *wise men* seeks knowledge.

Prov 29:27　　　　　　　　תועבת צדיקים איש עול
　　　　　　　　　　　　ותועבת רשע ישר דרך

The abomination of *righteous men* is a perverse man;
And the abomination of a *wicked man* is one whose way is
straight.

Job 4:7　　　　　　　　　זכר נא מי הוא נקי אבד
　　　　　　　　　　　　ואיפה ישרים נכחדו 〚49〛

Think now, what *innocent man* ever perished;
Where *have the upright* been destroyed.

Compare also Ps 1:1–3, which speaks of the righteous in the singular,
and the parallel section in verses 4 and 5, which describes the wicked
in the plural.

Singular-plural alternation apparently varies freely. I have chosen at
random one term, ישרי לב, "upright ones," which always occurs in the
plural, and have noted that it is paralleled by צדיק, "righteous one," in
Ps 64:11; 97:11; and probably 94:15, and paralleled by צדיקים, "righteous
ones," in Ps 32:11 and by יודעיך, "those devoted to you," in Ps 36:11.

Finally, there is the striking juxtaposition in Lam 3:38 of הרעות
והטוב, literally "the evils and the good," and the use of what is generally interpreted as a dual // plural (along with a plural // singular) in

Ps 75:11　　　　　　　　　וכל קרני רשעים אגדע
　　　　　　　　　　　　תרוממנה קרנות צדיק

All *the [pairs of] horns* of the wicked [pl.] I will cut;
But *the horns* of the righteous [sing.] shall be held high.

Before leaving this section a few comments are in order about the
importance of the recognition of singular-plural parallelism on the
evaluation of the correctness of the Massoretic Text. The MT contains

several cases of singular-plural parallelism which are not reflected in the Versions.

Gen 12:3a

ואברכה מברכיך
ומקללך אאר

I will bless *those* who bless you;
and *he* who curses you I will curse.[20]
[Versions: those who curse you]

Isa 44:26

מקים דבר עבדו
ועצת מלאכיו ישלים

He confirms the word of his *servant*;
And the counsel of his *messengers* he fulfills.
[Versions: his servants]

Ps 114:2

היתה יהודה לקדשו
ישראל ממשלותיו

Judah became his *holy one*;
Israel his *dominions*.
[Versions: his dominion] [[50]]

Deut 26:13

. . . ככל מצותך אשר צויתני
לא עברתי ממצותיך

. . . according to *your entire commandment* which you commanded me; I have not transgressed *your commandments*.
[Versions: all your commandments]

We should not conclude from these examples that the MT is corrupt, or that the Versions had a different text, but rather that the Versions were simply not sensitive to this type of parallelism or could not render it idiomatically (as we often cannot in English) into the languages of their translations.[21]

Contrast in Definiteness A noun is considered definite in Hebrew if (1) the definite article precedes it, (2) it has a possessive suffix, (3) it is

20. Cassuto comments on this verse: "The difference between the plural *those who bless you* and the singular *him who curses you* was introduced, it seems, for the sake of diversification and variation in the parallelism, for which reason a change was also made in the order of the words of the two clauses" (*From Noah to Abraham*, 315).

21. For a similar approach to textual traditions see S. Talmon, "The Textual Study of the Bible—A New Outlook."

in the construct state. We find cases in which one type of definite noun parallels another, thereby producing equivalence.

Ps 33:17

שקר הסוס לתשועה
וברב חילו לא ימלט

> *The horse* is a false savior;
> And with *his many troops* he will not escape.

Ps 126:6

נשא משך הזרע . . .
נשא אלמתיו . . .

> . . . carrying *the seed-bag*,
> . . . carrying *his sheaves*.

Ps 25:9

ידרך ענוים במשפט
וילמד ענוים דרכו

> He guides the lowly in *the judgment*;
> He teaches the lowly *his way*.

Eccl 7:1

טוב שם משמן טוב
ויום המות מיום הולדו

> A name is better than good oil;
> And the death-day than his birth-day.

The second part of this verse contains two different (but equivalent) types of definite terms; they contrast morphologically with the two indefinite terms of the first part. There are a number of verses in which a definite noun is paired with an indefinite one, yielding a contrast. (This is all the [[51]] more striking in light of the observation that the definite article tends to be omitted in poetry.)[22]

Ps 50:17

ואתה שנאת מוסר
ותשלך דברי אחריך

> You hated *discipline*;
> And you threw *my words* behind you.

Ps 108:3

עורה הנבל וכנור

> Awake, *the harp* and *a lyre*.

---

22. Cf. D. N. Freedman, *Pottery, Poetry, and Prophecy,* 2 and now F. I. Andersen and A. D. Forbes, "'Prose Particle' Counts of the Hebrew Bible."

Ps 114:6

ההרים תרקדו כאילים
גבעות כבני צאן

The mountains danced like rams;
Hills like sheep.

Prov 10:1

בן חכם ישמח אב
ובן כסיל תוגת אמו

A wise son makes *a father* glad;
But a foolish son is the despair of *his mother.*

Job 3:3

יאבד יום אולד בו
והלילה אמר הרה גבר

Perish *a day* on which I was to be born;
And *the night* which intended that a male be conceived.[23]

Lam 3:47

פחד ופחת היה לנו
השאת והשבר

Panic and *pitfall* were ours;
The desolation and *the destruction.*

Contrast in Case. There are no longer case endings in biblical Hebrew, but a noun in the nominative (i.e., the subject) in one line may
be paralleled by a noun in the accusative (direct object) in the second
line. For example,

Hos 5:3

אני ידעתי אפרים
וישראל לא נכחד ממני

I have known Ephraim;
And Israel has not escaped my attention.

[[52]] Since this type of parallelism involves the syntax of the lines, it will
be discussed below as a form of syntactic parallelism (subject // object).

Miscellaneous Contrast. I have illustrated what I find to be the major morphological features that can be used as equivalences in parallelism. There remains, of course, the possibility that others, too, are so
used. In fact, any morphologic category that has two or more mem-

---

23. Cf. Andersen, *Job*, 101, where the correspondence between the indefinite and
definite is recognized in this verse.

bers, and any form that has two or more realizations, is a potential candidate for morphologic parallelism. One such example is

Prov 16:16   קנה חכמה מה טוב מחרוץ
                     וקנות בינה נבחר מכסף

Acquiring wisdom—how much better than gold;
And *to acquire* understanding is preferable to silver.

To conclude this section on morphologic parallelism I offer a verse in which *every* parallel term shows some kind of morphologic parallelism.

Jer 9:10   ונתתי את ירושלם לגלים מעון תנים
                   ואת ערי יהודה אתן שממה מבלי יושב

I will turn Jerusalem into rubble, a jackals' den;
And I will make the cities of Judah a desolation, without an inhabitant.

The same verbal root is used in the *qtl* and *yqtl* forms. None of the paired nouns match in respect to number: *Jerusalem* (sing.) // *cities of Judah* (pl.); *rubble* (masc. pl.) // *desolation* (fem. sing.); and even *jackals* and *inhabitant*, although they are not strictly speaking parallel,[24] contrast in respect to number.

I have isolated and systematized a number of morphologic parallelisms. Many of them involve words that are semantically parallel, although some do not. Those that do not, like Job 12:9, may at first elicit the reaction "but those are not parallel." But this is just the point. Parallelism is more than semantic parallelism. A morphologic parallelism is just as parallel as a semantic one, although it is of a different nature. As for morphologic pairs that are also semantic or lexical pairs—while I have stressed the grammatical nature of these pairings, I want to make clear that this does not preclude other aspects of pairing that they may manifest. In fact, morphologic pairing can be viewed as just one subprinciple of the process of [[53]] linguistic association whereby all pairings of individual terms can be explained. This is the subject of all chapter 4 [[not reprinted here]].

In summary, I have shown, first of all, that members of different word classes can be paired, and, furthermore, within a word class, all

---

24. The pair מעון תנים and מבלי יושב are neither lexically nor grammatically parallel, but they are phonologically similar (both begin with *mem* and have the same number of syllables and accent pattern), and they occupy the same position in otherwise parallel lines.

of the major morphological features can be contrasted: one tense with
another, one gender with another, and so on. So far, Jacobson's dictum that "pervasive parallelism inevitably activates all the levels of language . . . the morphologic and syntactic categories and forms . . . in
both their convergences and divergences" has been exemplified in respect to morphology. I will now exemplify it in respect to syntax.

Syntactic Parallelism

Once again, my assumption is that parallel lines are equivalent in some
way. In syntactic parallelism, the syntax of the lines is equivalent. In
linguistic terms, this would mean that their deep structures are the
same (cf. Greenstein).[25] I am not interested in discovering, through
tree diagrams or other technical notation, what the deep structure is,
but rather in showing, as simply as possible, what kinds of transformations occur in parallel lines.

Let me illustrate first by a series of English sentences.

1. John eats the bread.
2. John does not eat the bread.
3. Does John eat the bread?
4. The bread is eaten by John.

Sentence 1 is the basic indicative sentence. Sentence 2 transforms it
into the negative, sentence 3 into the interrogative, and sentence 4 into
the passive. Every language has its own rules for how these transformations are made, but most have the same or similar transformations.

In syntactic parallelism, in addition to lines with the same syntactic
surface structure—i.e., no transformation—one also finds the pairing
of lines in which a transformation has occurred. One should be aware,
however, that it is not the original sentence that has been transformed,
but rather another, unrealized sentence that is parallel to it. This will
become clearer from the examples and will be explained further after
all the types of transformations have been presented. The transformations that I have found to ⟦54⟧ be involved in biblical parallelism are:
(a) nominal-verbal, (b) positive-negative, (c) subject-object, (d) contrast
in grammatical mood. (The verses cited may contain ellipsis and/or the

---

25. Greenstein ("How Does Parallelism Mean?") defines parallelism in terms of this
syntactic equivalence (see above, chapter 2 ⟦not reprinted here⟧). I would allow for the
possibility of other kinds of parallelism in which the syntax is not equivalent. (Cf. chapter
4, note 42 ⟦not reprinted here⟧.)

addition of terms, and also rearrangements of their components, but this does not affect their syntax.)

Nominal-Verbal

There are two basic sentence types in Hebrew: those without a finite verb (nominal) and those with a finite verb (verbal). The two are paired in the following verses.

Mic 6:2b
כי ריב לה' עם עמו
ועם ישראל יתוכח

For YHWH has a quarrel with his people;
And with Israel will he dispute.

Ps 34:2
אברכה את ה' בכל עת
תמיד תהלתו בפי

I bless YHWH at all times;
Always praise of him is in my mouth

Ps 49:4
פי ידבר חכמות
והגות לבי תבונות

My mouth speaks [words of] wisdom;
And my heart's murmurings are [thoughts of] understanding.

Lam 5:19
אתה ה' לעולם תשב
כסאך לדור ודור

You, YHWH, will sit forever;
Your throne is for eternity.

Although they do not involve entire clauses, nominal and verbal forms are paired in

Deut 32:1
האזינו השמים ואדברה
ותשמע הארץ אמרי פי

Give ear, O Heavens, so *I may speak*;
And let the earth hear *the words of my mouth*.

More striking are those in which the same root appears in both a nominal and verbal form. [[55]]

Ps 73:11   ואמרו איכה ידע אל
                                      ויש דעה בעליון

> They say, "How could God know?
> Is there knowledge with the Most High?"

Ps 97:9   כי אתה ה׳ עליון על כל הארץ
                                      מאד נעלית על כל אלהים

> For you, YHWH, are the highest over all the world;
> You have been heightened greatly over all gods.

Ruth 2:12   ישלם ה׳ פעלך
                                      ותהי משכרתך שלמה מעם ה׳

> May YHWH repay your deeds;
> May your recompense be paid in full from YHWH.[26]

Nominal and verbal forms of the same root also occur in passages not generally considered parallelistic.

Exod 12:10   ולא תותירו ממנו עד בקר
                                      והנתר ממנו עד בקר באש תשרפו

> You shall not leave any of it over until morning,
> and whatever is left over of it until the morning you shall
> burn with fire.

Lev 13:12–13   . . . מראה עיני הכהן. וראה הכהן . . .

> . . . the sight of the priest. If the priest sees . . .

Lev 13:17 [cf. Lev 13:34]   . . . וטהר הכהן את הנגע
                                      טהור הוא

> . . . the priest shall declare clean the affected person; he is
> clean.

Lev 13:46   . . . בדד ישב מחוץ למחנה מושבו

> . . . he shall dwell apart; his dwelling is outside the camp.

These are only a few of the many verses in which a nominal and verbal clause are paired. This is sometimes accomplished through the

---

26. Both clauses are verbal but there is still the contrast between *yšlm* (a verb) and *šlmh* (an adjective).

use of the verb "to be" which, like other verbs, is a finite verb in the perfect and imperfect, but which, unlike other verbs, ordinarily has no participle form and is therefore totally absent or unrealized in what we would translate as the present tense. Below are verses which contain a finite form of "to be" in one line and a nominal clause of being in the other. [[56]]

Gen 42:31   כנים אנחנו לא היינו מרגלים

> We are honest; we are [Heb.: were] not spies.

1 Sam 3:1   ודבר ה' היה יקר בימים ההם
>   אין חזון נפרץ

> The word of YHWH was rare in those days;
> a vision was not [Heb.: is not] common.

Job 29:15   עינים הייתי לעור
>   ורגלים לפסח אני

> Eyes I was to the blind;
> And feet to the lame was [Heb.: am] I.

Here, as in the *qtl–yqtl* parallelism, there is no intent to convey a real difference in time, and so even though there appears to be a "present tense" and a "past tense," the tense of both parallel lines should be translated the same way. (Nominal clauses are extratemporal—cf. Blau, *Grammar*, 84.)

Positive-Negative

In this type of parallelism a statement phrased in the positive is paired with one phrased in the negative. (This is not to be confused with Lowth's "antithetic parallelism," which need not involve a negative transformation.) It is not simply a matter of transforming "John eats the bread" into "John does not eat the bread," for the pairing of two such sentences would make no sense. Rather, the negative transformation is performed on a parallel (i.e., equivalent) sentence, yielding possibilities like:

1. John eats the bread; John does not leave the bread uneaten.
2. John eats the bread; John does not drink the milk.
3. John eats the bread; Mary does not eat the bread.

These and others like them can be considered positive-negative parallelism.

Prov 6:20   נצר בני מצות אביך
                                   ואל תטש תורת אמך

Guard, my son, the commandment of your father;
And do not forsake the teaching of your mother.

Prov 3:1   בני תורתי אל תשכח
                                   ומצותי יצר לבך [[57]]

My son, do not forget my teaching;
And let your heart guard my commandments.

Hab 3:17   כחש מעשה זית
                                   ושדמות לא עשה אכל
                                   גזר ממכלה צאן
                                   ואין בקר ברפתים

The olive crop has failed;
And the fields do not produce food.
The sheep have vanished from the fold;
And there is no cattle in the pens.

Compare also 1 Sam 3:1 and Gen 42:31 quoted in the previous section.
The same device is often found in prosaic passages:

Gen 37:24b   והבור רק אין בו מים

The pit was empty; there was no water in it.

Deut 9:7   זכר אל תשכח

Remember, do not forget.

1 Sam 3:2b   ועינו החלו כהות לא יוכל לראות

His eyes began to dim; he was not able to see.

1 Kgs 3:18b   ואנחנו יחדו אין זר אתנו בבית

We were alone; no stranger was with us in the house.

Subject-Object

Many parallel lines are structured so that the terms which are semantically parallel serve different syntactic functions in their respective
lines. It is common for one of the terms to serve as the subject and its
mate to serve as the object (direct or indirect). This structure is related

to the transformation of passivization: "John eats the bread; the bread is eaten by John," but, since here, as in the case of positive-negative parallelism, more is going on than the transformation of the original sentence, I prefer to call this subject-object parallelism.

Gen 27:29   הוה גביר לאחיך
                             וישתחוו לך בני אמך

    Be a lord over your brothers;
    Let the sons of your mother bow before you. ⟦58⟧

Gen 37:33   חיה רעה אכלתהו
                             טרף טרף יוסף

    A wild animal has eaten him;
    Joseph is surely devoured.

Jer 1:5   בטרם אצורך בבטן ...
                             ובטרם תצא מרחם ...

    Before I formed you in the belly . . .
    Before you came out of the womb . . .

Jer 20:14   ארור היום אשר ילדתי בו
                             יום אשר ילדתני אמי אל יהי ברוך

    Cursed by the day on which I was born;
    The day on which my mother bore me, let it not be blessed.

Hos 5:3   אני ידעתי אפרים
                             וישראל לא נכחד ממני

    I have known Ephraim;
    And Israel has not escaped my attention.

Ps 2:7   בני אתה
                             אני היום ילדתיך

    You are my son;
    I, today, have fathered you.

Ruth 1:21   אני מלאה הלכתי
                             וריקם השיבני ה׳

    I went forth full;
    and YHWH brought me back empty.

Lam 5:4

מימינו בכסף שתינו
עצינו במחיר יבאו

 Our water for money we drink;
 Our wood comes for a price.

Some of the verses manifesting a contrast in conjugation also involve subject-object parallelism. For example, Jer 20:14 contains a contrast in conjugation, subject-object, and positive-negative parallelism.
It is not unusual for a verse to contain several different types of grammatical parallelism. [[59]]

Contrast in Grammatical Mood

Another set of transformations involves changing a sentence from one
grammatical mood into another. If we take the indicative mood as the
base, then "John eats the bread" becomes in the interrogative "Does
John eat the bread?"; in the jussive, "Let/may John eat the bread," and
so on. It should not surprise the reader at this point to find that in parallelism a line in one grammatical mood may be paired with a line in
another mood.

Ps 6:6

כי אין במות זכרך
בשאול מי יודה לך

 For in Death there is no mention of you;
 In Sheol who can acclaim you?
 [indicative // interrogative]

Ps 73:25

מי לי בשמים
ועמך לא חפצתי בארץ

 Who [else] is there for me in heaven?
 And having you I lack no one/nothing on earth.
 [interrogative // indicative]

Isa 44:8

היש אלוה מבלעדי
ואין צור בל ידעתי

 Is there any god besides Me?
 There is no other rock, I know none.
 [interrogative // indicative]

Ps 19:13

שגיאות מי יבין
מנסתרות נקני

Who can discern errors?
Cleanse me from hidden [guilt].
[interrogative // imperative]

It is interesting to note that in Ps 6:6, Ps 73:25, and Isa 44:8 the interrogative implies a negative answer, and the parallel indicative supplies
the negative.[27] In Ps 19:13 the answer to the question is "You, God"
and this is presented indirectly (as the implied subject) in the parallel
line. Thus we have here rhetorical questions which provide their own
answers (cf. also Isa 41:26 and Ps 24:8, 10).

There are many cases of imperative // jussive or jussive // imperative
parallelism. Some involve second person jussive and imperative (by
definition, [60] second person). Verses of this type in Psalms have
been listed by M. Dahood (*Psalms* III, 423–24). There are also verses
containing an imperative and a third person jussive.[28]

Deut 32:1

האזינו השמים . . .
ותשמע הארץ . . .

Give ear, O heavens . . .
And let the earth hear. . . .

Mic 6:1

קום ריב את ההרים
ותשמענה הגבעות קולך

Rise, dispute before the mountains.
And let the hills hear your voice.

Prov 3:1

בני תורתי אל תשכח
ומצותי יצר לבך

My son, do not forget my teaching;
And let your heart guard my commandments.

Eccl 5:1

אל תבהל על פיך
ולבך אל ימהר

---

27. Most positive rhetorical questions imply a negative answer, and vice versa. For
exceptions see R. Gordis, "A Rhetorical Use of Interrogative Sentences in Biblical Hebrew," *The Word and the Book*, 152–57.

28. The jussive and the imperfect indicative are indistinguishable in form in most
cases, so the identification is based on the context. The sequence of imperative followed
by jussive (or other similar combinations) often has a causal nuance: "Do X so that he
may do Y." For various combinations see Andersen, *The Sentence*, 112–13. The combinations in parallel lines are the same as those found in prose sentences.

> Do not be rash with your mouth;
> And let not your heart be hasty.

All categories of syntactic parallelism that I have listed involve transformations, but, as I have already mentioned, it is not the original sentence that is transformed, but rather another sentence that is syntactically parallel to it. One can analyze the operations involved as a multistage process.[29] I will do this for three verses.

1. The original sentence: "A wild animal ate him." [Gen 37:33]
2. The construction of a syntactically identical parallel: *"A wild animal surely devoured Joseph."
3. A transformation performed on the parallel line, in this case a passivization: "Joseph was/is surely devoured [by a wild animal]."

Some parallelisms involve more stages.

1. The original sentence: "I went forth full." [Ruth 1:21]
2. A syntactically identical parallel: *"I came back empty." [61]
3. A transformation of the parallel, in this case passivization (because the verb is intransitive there is an element of causation introduced): *"I was made to come [= I was brought] back empty."
4. A further transformation—here a reactivization of the passivization, specifying the causative agent: "ʏʜᴡʜ brought me back empty."

A slightly different set of transformations obtains in Hos 5:3.

1. The original sentence: "I have known Ephraim."
2. A syntactically identical parallel: *"I have known Israel."
3. A passivization: *"Israel was known to me."
4. A negativization of the passivization: "Israel was not hidden from me."

---

29. This transformational grammar model is for the purpose of analysis only. I am not suggesting that the biblical author consciously performed these transformations when composing parallelisms any more than we do when we form interrogative or passive sentences. The legitimacy of such an analysis, however, is reinforced by Jakobson when he says that "the analysis of grammatical transformations and of their import should include the poetic function of language, because the core of this function is to push transformations into the foreground. It is the purposeful poetic use of lexical and grammatical tropes and figures that brings the creative power of language to its summit" ("Verbal Communication," 80).

A parallelism may consist of lines at any stage in this process. Thus some parallel lines will be exactly the same syntactically (on the surface structure) and others will undergo one or more transformations. The same is true by analogy for morphologic parallelism. The same morphologic element may be repeated, or any equivalent on any level may be substituted. Let us take interrogative particles as a final example.

On the morphological aspect, we have the same element in both lines in

Isa 66:8   מי שמע כזאת
                                      מי ראה כאלה

> *Who* has heard such a thing?
> *Who* has seen such things?

and different but equivalent elements (all interrogative particles) in

Isa 40:18   ואל מי תדמיון אל
                                     ומה דמות תערכו לו

> To *whom* can you liken God?
> And *what* likeness can you compare to him?

Job 5:1   הֲיֵשׁ עוֹנֶךָ ...
                                     ואל מי מקדשים תפנה

> ... *is there* one who answers you?
> And *to whom* of the Holy Ones will you turn?

Isa 10:3   ... ומה תעשו
                                      ... על מי תנוסו
                                     [[62]] ... ואנה תעזבו

> What will you do ...
> And to *whom* will you flee ...
> And *where* will you leave. ...

And we have already seen that an interrogative sentence may be paired with one that lacks an interrogative particle or, indeed, the interrogative mood altogether (e.g., Ps 6:6; Ps 73:25).

The purpose of this chapter was to examine the role of grammar in parallelism. At the risk of getting lost in taxonomy, I have taken pains to cite examples of many different grammatical pairings. The weight of this evidence indicates that grammar as a whole—morphology and

syntax—is used not only to construct grammatically acceptable sentences, but is also used to construct parallelisms. In other words, parallelism uses grammar for a supergrammatical purpose; it makes
grammar serve in the poetic function—as part of the parallelism. Perhaps this is clearest when lines are not truly grammatically parallel but
are made to look as if they were. There are a few lines whose surface
structure is the same but whose deep structure is not (Greenstein also
considers these to be grammatically parallel). The illusion of syntactic
repetition adds to the perception of parallelism.

Ps 105:6
זרע אברהם עבדו
בני יעקב בחיריו

The seed of Abraham his servant;
The sons of Jacob his chosen.

Both lines contain noun in construct—personal name—appositional
noun with 3rd singular possessive suffix: the syntax looks the same.
This sameness is reinforced by the fact that every word has its semantic
mate and they occur in the same order: *seed // sons, Abraham // Jacob, servant // chosen* (cf. [[p. 313]] note 3 for this pair). But in reality the syntax
of the two lines is not quite identical, for *his servant* is in apposition to
Abraham while *his chosen* is in apposition to *sons*. A "syntactic" translation would be

The seed of his servant Abraham;
The chosen sons of Jacob.

Another example, this one with a tension between the syntax and
the word pairs, is

Ps 49:5 [cf. Ps 78:2]
אטה למשל אזני
אפתח בכנור חידתי [[63]]

I will incline to a proverb my ear;
I will open with a lyre my riddle.

Again the syntax is identical: verb—preposition + noun—noun +
suffix. The syntax is even identical at a higher level: verb—indirect object—direct object. But if one then equates the words with their grammatical functions, one emerges with preposterous equations: *to a
proverb // with a lyre; my ear // my riddle*. The syntax pulls the verse in one
direction, toward one set of equivalences, while the word pair *proverb //
riddle* pulls in another.

P. Kiparsky has said that "the linguistic sames which are potentially relevant in poetry are just those which are potentially relevant in grammar" (*Daedalus*, 1973, 235). I think that this chapter has given ample proof of the correctness of this statement, perhaps in ways that linguists did not anticipate. But my purpose is not to prove linguistic theories; it is to show how they may help biblicists toward better readings of the text. Biblicists must understand that grammar is important not only because it permits the parsing of lines, but because it helps to make poetry poetic. Parallelism activates grammatical equivalences just as it activates semantic and lexical equivalences. Therefore, before a scholar corrects a grammatical inconsistency, or dismisses it as poetic license, he must first consider its relevance to the poetic function. Above all, he must realize that, no matter whether grammatical parallelism was intentional or accidental, it is potentially important in the structure of a poem and ultimately to its meaning.

Bibliography

Andersen, F. I., *Job* (Tyndale O.T. Commentaries, London: Inter-Varsity Press), 1976.

_____, *The Sentence in Biblical Hebrew* (The Hague: Mouton), 1974.

Andersen, F. I., and Forbes, A. D., "'Prose Particle' Counts of the Hebrew Bible," *The Word of the Lord Shall Go Forth. Essays in Honor of David Noel Freedman in Celebration of His Sixtieth Birthday*, ed. C. Meyers and M. O'Connor (Winona Lake, Ind.: Eisenbrauns), 1983, 165–83.

Berlin, A., "Grammatical Aspects of Biblical Parallelism," *HUCA* 50 (1979), 17–43.

Blau, J., *A Grammar of Biblical Hebrew* (Wiesbaden: Harrassowitz), 1976.

Cassuto, U., *Biblical and Oriental Studies*, Vol. I (Jerusalem: Magnes), 1973, Vol. II, 1975.

_____, *From Noah to Abraham—A Commentary on the Book of Genesis, Part II* (Jerusalem: Magnes), 1964.

_____, *The Goddess Anath* (Jerusalem: Magnes), 1971.

Clines, D., *I, He, We and They: A Literary Approach to Isaiah 53*, JSOT Supplement Series, I (Sheffield: JSOT Press), 1976.

Cross, F. M., and Freedman, D. N., *Studies in Ancient Yahwistic Poetry* (Missoula, Mont.: Scholars Press), 1975.

Dahood, M., *Psalms I* (Anchor Bible, Garden City: Doubleday), 1966; *Psalms II*, 1968; *Psalms III*, 1970.

Freedman, D. N., *Pottery, Poetry, and Prophecy. Collected Essays on Hebrew Poetry* (Winona Lake, Ind.: Eisenbrauns), 1980.

Geller, S., *Parallelism in Early Biblical Poetry* (Missoula, Mont.: Scholars Press), 1979.

Gordis, R., *The Word and the Book. Studies in Biblical Language and Literature* (New York: Ktav), 1976.

Greenstein, E., "How Does Parallelism Mean?" *A Sense of Text, JQR Supplement* (Winona Lake, Ind.: Eisenbrauns), 1982, 41–70.

Held, M., "The Action-Result (Factitive-Passive) Sequence of Identical Verbs in Biblical Hebrew and Ugaritic," *JBL* 84 (1965), 272–82.

———, "The YQTL–QTL (QTL–YQTL) Sequence of Identical Verbs in Biblical Hebrew and in Ugaritic," *Studies and Essays in Honor of Abraham A. Neuman*, ed. M. Ben-Horin et al. (Leiden: Brill), 1962, 281–90.

Jakobson, R., "Verbal Communication," *Scientific American* 227/3 (1972), 73–80.

Kiparsky, P., "The Role of Linguistics in a Theory of Poetry," *Daedalus* 102/3 (1973), 231–44.

Kselman, J. S., "The Recovery of Poetic Fragments from the Pentateuchal Priestly Source," *JBL* 97 (1978), 161–73.

Kugel, J., *The Idea of Biblical Poetry. Parallelism and Its History* (New Haven: Yale University Press), 1981.

O'Connor, M., *Hebrew Verse Structure* (Winona Lake, Ind.: Eisenbrauns), 1980.

Sappan, R., *The Typical Features of the Syntax of Biblical Poetry in Its Classical Period* (Ph.D. Dissertation, Hebrew University), 1974.

Talmon, S., "The Textual Study of the Bible—A New Outlook," *Qumran and the History of the Biblical Text*, ed. F. M. Cross and S. Talmon (Cambridge, Mass.: Harvard University Press), 1975, 321–400.

Watson, W. G. E., "Gender-Matched Synonymous Parallelism in the OT," *JBL* 99 (1980), 321–41.

———, "Gender-Matched Synonymous Parallelism in Ugaritic Poetry," *UF* 13 (1981), 181–87.

Watters, W. R., *Formula Criticism and the Poetry of the Old Testament* (Berlin: Walter de Gruyter), 1976.

Yoder, P., *Fixed Word Pairs and the Composition of Hebrew Poetry* (Ph.D. Dissertation, University of Pennsylvania), 1970.

Of Broken Pots, Fluttering Birds, and Visions in the Night:

Extended Simile and Poetic Technique in Isaiah

J. CHERYL EXUM

[[331]] The prophet Isaiah of Jerusalem and his redactors were masters of poetic style and technique. They employ imagery and figures with great facility and versatility and succeed remarkably (whether or not they so intended) in merging sound and sense into an artistic whole.[1] As a rule, the literary tropes and rhetorical figures we find in the first 39 chapters of Isaiah are not just embellishments but rather mediums of persuasion. They are forceful ways of making a point; they center attention and involve the listener in making essential connections necessary for interpretation. Too often in biblical studies, however, in our intense pursuit of the theological message we tend to neglect its medium, as if form were some kind of container from which the message can be extracted. True, we may acknowledge a striking image or point to a chiasmus here

Reprinted with permission from *Catholic Biblical Quarterly* 43 (1981) 331–52.

1. Whether or not certain literary features were intended by the prophet or his editors is a question I doubt we can answer. Moreover, it is, in my opinion, the wrong question, as pursuit of it leads into the intentional fallacy. See W. K. Wimsatt, Jr. and Monroe C. Beardsley, "The Intentional Fallacy," in *The Verbal Icon: Studies in the Meaning of Poetry* (Kentucky: University Press, 1954) 2–18. On figurative language in Isaiah, see I. Engnell, *A Rigid Scrutiny* (Nashville: Vanderbilt University, 1969) 262–67; K. Nielsen, "Das Bild des Gerichts (Rib-Pattern) in Jes. I–XII," *VT* 29 (1979) 309–24.

and there, but seldom do we follow up such observations with genuine literary questions. The idea that a literary work has a meaning apart from its form has been criticized by L. Alonso-Schökel, who considers it "the most widely extended hermeneutical presupposition among exegetes. If the meaning precedes the form, then we must undo what has been [[332]] done, prescinding from the form, in order to arrive at the meaning. . . . "[2] Inasmuch as it does not treat biblical poems seriously as poems (which is not to say it does not treat them seriously as theological documents), the approach Alonso-Schökel describes does not give the poets of Isaiah—and other biblical books as well—their due.

In this study, I shall concentrate on a fundamental quality of poetic discourse, its metaphorical character. In particular, I want to look at an easily isolatable figure of speech, the simile—grammatically identified by its comparison of one thing to another through the use of "like" or "as." I do not intend thereby to suggest a narrow understanding of metaphoric language; indeed, metaphoric language can and should be defined so broadly as to include all modes of open and fluid discourse.[3] Thus while I have selected the texts below because they contain extended similes (similes that move beyond a single comparison), I propose to explore their larger poetic and metamorphic context as well. My concern is not so much *what* these examples mean— their historical situation, the theological perspective of the prophet, and certainly not his *ipsissima verba*—as *how* the poems mean; in other words, what effect do they produce? How do tropes and figures work and what results do they yield? In asking such questions, literary analysis participates in the goal of all exegesis: the poem is taken apart so that its readers may put it together again with greater appreciation and understanding.[4]

We may turn once more to Alonso-Schökel for our point of departure:

> Die Propheten haben fast durchweg in Bildern gesprochen. Die Exegese hat sich bemüht, die Bilder in Begriffe zu übersetzen. Manchmal ging man noch weiter und behauptete, oder glaubte doch wenigstens, eine derartige Übersetzung sei eine Rückübersetzung.

---

2. "Hermeneutical Problems of a Literary Study of the Bible," *Congress Volume Edinburgh* (VTSup 28; Leiden: Brill, 1975) 4.

3. See P. Wheelwright, *Metaphor and Reality* (Bloomington: Indiana University, 1962) 45–69.

4. Cf. J. Ciardi, *How Does a Poem Mean?* (Cambridge: Riverside, 1959) 663–64, 996–98. Ciardi stresses that analysis is no substitute for a poem, but only a means of preparing for more perceptive reading. The question "What does a poem mean?" invites paraphrase; the question "How does it mean?" calls for "pointing out the emotional sequences of the poem in time and the accompanying shifts in technical management" (p. 998).

So als habe der Prophet erst in reinen Begriffen gedacht und dann diese Begriffe "der Schwachen wegen" in Bildern eingekleidet. Derartiges trifft zu bei den didaktischen Gattungen—und bei schlechten Dichtern. Was die Propheten nicht sind. Der Dichter erlebt unmittelbar im Bild, oder aber er trifft intuitiv als erste Gestalt des gestaltlosen Erlebnisses ein sprachliches Bild. *Wir dürfen das Begriffsmässige* ⟦333⟧ *aus der Ganzheit herausschälen und in Begriffsworten formulieren—wir dürfen aber nicht unseren Extrakt mit der Ganzheit gleichsetzen.*[5]

⟦The prophets spoke consistently in pictures. Exegesis attempted to translate the pictures into concepts. At times it went even further and asserted—or at least believed—such a translation was a retranslation.

Thus the prophet first supposedly thought in pure concepts and then clothed these concepts in pictures "for the sake of the weak." Such an approach fits didactic genres—and poor poets, which is something the prophets were not. The poet lives immediately in pictures, or intuitively he chances upon a word picture as the first form of a formless experience. He may peel the conceptual out of the totality and formulate it in conceptual words, but we may not equate an extract with the totality.⟧

For analytic purposes, content and form are separable, but in the working of a poem they are not. The meaning of an image cannot be reduced to what it signifies. One reason for this irreducibility lies in the nature of words and images to be connotative rather than simply denotative. Figurative language embraces ambiguity. In fact, much of its power derives from its plurisignificance, from its ability to be suggestive of multiple meanings. But to observe that figurative language is not precise is not to claim that it cannot capture and convey meaning with deftness.[6] Three examples from Isaiah, 30:12–14; 31:4–5; and 29:1–14, will serve to illustrate this premise.

Isaiah 30:12–14:
Broken Pot and Enclosed Simile

[12]Therefore thus says the Holy One of Israel,
"Because you reject this word,
and trust in oppression and perverseness and rely on them,

---

5. "Die stilistische Analyse bei den Propheten," *Congress Volume Oxford* (VTSup 7; Leiden: Brill, 1960) 159, italics mine.

6. See esp. P. Wheelwright, *Metaphor and Reality*, 40–43. In *The Burning Fountain: A Study in the Language of Symbolism* (Bloomington: Indiana University, 1968) 73–101, Wheelwright discusses the following characteristics of poeto-language: referential congruity, contextual variation, plurisignification, soft focus, paralogical dimensionality, assertorial lightness, and paradox. Cf. J. Ciardi, *How Does a Poem Mean?*, 711.

¹³therefore this iniquity will be to you
   like a crack running down,⁷ bulging in a high wall,
when suddenly, in an instant comes its breaking;
   ¹⁴and its breaking is like the breaking of a potter's vessel,
smashed so ruthlessly
   that there is not found among its fragments a sherd
to take up fire from the hearth
   or to dip up water out of a pool."⁸

A simile is made up of two elements, a tenor and a vehicle, which interact with each other in various ways. The tenor is the subject to which the metaphor is applied, the vehicle is the metaphoric description itself.[9] Precisely because a [[334]] simile depends on interactions between tenor and vehicle for its force, it cannot be reduced simply to a paraphrase of its tenor. As I. A. Richards has observed,

> The co-presence of the vehicle and tenor results in a meaning (to be clearly distinguished from the tenor) which is not attainable without their interaction.... The vehicle is not normally a mere embellishment of a tenor which is otherwise unchanged by it but ... vehicle and tenor in co-operation give a meaning of more varied powers than can be ascribed to either.[10]

Richards goes on to point out that the contributions of vehicle and tenor to the meaning of the metaphor may vary considerably; in some cases, for example, the tenor may be prominent with the vehicle almost incidental, while in others, the vehicle may be primary with the tenor playing a minor role.[11] In Isa 30:12–14 the tenor is iniquity, and the poem seeks to portray metaphorically the effects of iniquity. In this

---

7. Following W. H. Irwin, *Isaiah 28–33: Translation with Philological Notes* (BibOr 30; Rome: Biblical Institute, 1977) 83. Cf. G. Fohrer, *Das Buch Jesaja* (3 vols.; 2d ed.; Zürich: Zwingli, 1967), 2. 95: "wie ein Riss, der einstürzen will"; O. Kaiser, *Isaiah 13–39* (Philadelphia: Westminster, 1974) 291: "like a break, sinking and bulging."

8. See P. Reymond, "Un tesson pour 'ramasser' de l'eau à la mare (Esaie xxx,14)," *VT* 7 (1957) 203–7.

9. The terminology was introduced by I. A. Richards and is widely accepted. See *The Philosophy of Rhetoric* (Oxford: Oxford University, paperback reprint, 1971) 96.

10. *Philosophy of Rhetoric*, 100. For a different point of view, see D. Davidson, "What Metaphors Mean," in *On Metaphor* (ed. S. Sacks; Chicago: University of Chicago, 1979) 29–45.

11. *Philosophy of Rhetoric*, 100–101. For an exploration of various types of relations between tenor and vehicle in biblical material, see E. M. Good, "Ezekiel's Ship: Some Extended Metaphors in the Old Testament," *Semitics* 1 (1970) 79–103.

particular instance, the vehicle dominates. Moreover, these verses offer an excellent example of enclosed simile,[12] or a simile within a simile, in which a vehicle of the first has become the tenor of a second (the breaking of a wall is described in terms of the breaking of a pot). The poet seems to have got so wrapped up in the vehicle that the original tenor (iniquity) all but fades into the background. Rather than discussing iniquity, the poem sharply exposes the nature of its results through description of, first, one vehicle (the complex of cracking, falling, bulging, and breaking images) and, then, another (imagery of breaking, smashing, fragments, and sherds).

The clarity of the picture enables O. Kaiser to find the two similes "comprehensible without explanation"; they "show how complete the judgment will be."[13] But notice that each simile contributes an essential idea to the total picture. In the first, the words *pereṣ* [['crack']], *nōpēl* [['running down']], *nibʿeh* [['bulging']], and *šibrāh* [['breaking']] all fall within the semantic range of *collapse*.[14] The complex of images in the [[335]] second simile, *šēber* [['breaking']], *kātût* [['smashed']], *bimkittātô* [['among its fragments']], and *ḥereś* [['a sherd']], conveys the *thoroughness* of shattering. The two similes are joined at the climax of the poem, the collapse of the wall. The climax is delayed ever so slightly by the placement of the key term *šibrāh* [['breaking']] at the end of the stichos: "suddenly, in an instant comes—its breaking." Given the introduction in vv. 12–13a, this result is not unexpected; yet there is a certain aesthetic pleasure that comes from having our anticipation delayed and then confirmed. Withholding the term *šibrāh* until the end of the stichos also results in the appearance of the root *šbr* three times in succession, a repetition which, at this crucial juncture in the poem, lends emphasis to the debacle.[15]

---

12. I base this term on Wheelwright's "enclosed epiphor"; *Metaphor and Reality*, 75–76. On epiphor and diaphor, see below.

13. *Isaiah 13–39*, 296.

14. I am not convinced by H. Wildberger's attempt to pin down the imagery, *Jesaja* (BKAT X/13–15; Neukirchen: Neukirchener-V., 1978) 1174–75, 1178. A crack, he points out, does not itself bulge or fall; rather it is the cause of collapse. Thus he takes *pereṣ* to refer to a section of a wall threatened by a crack and reads *khwmh* with T[[argum]] and S[[yriac]], so that the resultant comparison is both to a wall bulging and ready to collapse and to a wall so high that it is likely to tumble. Although we cannot gain absolute certainty on the exact reading of the text, we can nevertheless explore the suggestiveness of its images.

15. For this reason, *ûšēbārāh* [['and its breaking']] (v. 14) should not be deleted as dittography with *BHS* and most commentators. Cf. W. H. Irwin, *Isaiah 28–33*, 84.

Had the poem simply stopped with the comparison to a wall and ended with something like "and suddenly in an instant comes its breaking, and it will be broken into many little pieces," it would not be nearly so successful. The enclosed simile allows the poet to pursue the breaking vehicle to the very end, to the last sherd so to speak. The second simile dramatizes the utter completeness of the shattering in a way the first could not have. In contrast to a high wall—with all the connotations of security that image might carry—a pot shatters easily into tiny fragments. V. 14b illustrates just how small these fragments are; a sherd large enough to be useful cannot be found. The total effect of the poem depends upon the juxtaposition and interaction of images of destruction on a large scale (the high wall) with those on a small scale (the potter's vessel).

Moving from the dominant vehicles to consider the tenor of the primary simile, we may observe that iniquity in the poem has a referent beyond itself. The text tells us this iniquity consists of trusting (*bṭḥ*) in oppression and perverseness and leaning (*šʿn*) upon them (v. 12). The context allows us to be somewhat more specific. Since negotiations with Egypt are dealt with earlier in this chapter (vv. 1–7), and since the terms *šʿn* and *bṭḥ* are used together of Egyptian negotiations in 31:1 in a way similar to v. 12, it is likely that iniquity in this case also refers to Judah's attempts to gain military support from Egypt.[16] Theoretically, such aid should provide protection against Assyria; thus the simile of a high wall, which can provide a formidable defense, is an apt one.

Coupled with trust (*bṭḥ*) in oppression and perverseness is rejection (*mʾs*) of "this word" (v. 12). No direct antecedent of "this word" occurs in the verses immediately preceding.[17] Most likely the phrase has a broader referent in [[336]] Isaiah's message in general. A major theme of the collection in chaps. 28–32 is Judah's reliance on political intrigue rather than on *Yhwh*. The word rejected here appears to be the same message of quiet trust in *Yhwh* rejected elsewhere (28:12, 16b; 30:15). This inference is further supported within chap. 30 itself by vv. 15–17,

16. Cf. Irwin's translation of *ʿōšeq wĕnālôz* as "perverse tyrant," i.e., Egypt, taking the phrase as abstract for concrete (*Isaiah 28–33*, 84).

17. A. Schoors (*Jesaja* [Roermond: Romen & Zonen, 1972] 181) connects "this word" with the lesson of v. 9. Similarly, O. Kaiser (*Isaiah 13–39*, 295), though in substance he relates it to "the whole message of the pre-exilic prophets." J. Vermeylen (*Du prophète Isaïe à l'apocalyptique* [EBib; 2 vols.; Paris: Gabalda, 1977–78], 1.414) takes the original referent to the inscription *raḥab hēm šābet* in v. 7. A number of commentators see it as a reference to Isaiah's message of quiet trust in *Yhwh*; see, e.g., R. B. Y. Scott, "Introduction and Exegesis to Isaiah, Chs. 1–39," *IB*, 5.332; G. Fohrer, *Jesaja*, 98; W. Dietrich, *Jesaja und die Politik* (BEvT 74; Munich: Kaiser, 1976) 157; H. Wildberger, *Jesaja*, 1177.

which appear to offer a strong thematic parallel to vv. 8–14. Both pericopes speak of the people's unwillingness to accept *Yhwh*'s guidance (*lō᾿ ᾿ābû* [['unwilling']], v. 9; *wĕlō᾿ ᾿ăbîtem* [['you refused']], v. 15); both have words of rejection ironically placed in the mouth of the people ("speak to us smooth things; prophesy illusions," vv. 10–11; "upon horses we shall flee," v. 16); and both portray judgment through simile (the broken wall and pot of vv. 13–14; the standard on a hill of v. 17). Whereas vv. 8–14 do not refer directly to the rejected word, vv. 15–17 do: "in turning and rest you shall be saved, in quietness and in trust will be your strength." The trust recommended in v. 15 contrasts markedly with the false trust chosen in v. 12. But an inaccessibly high wall with a crack (lack of trust in *Yhwh*) is as vulnerable to devastation as a potter's vessel, especially if the potter is *Yhwh* (cf. 29:15–16).[18]

Isaiah 31:4–5:
Fluttering Birds and the Effect of Diaphor

[4]For thus said *Yhwh* to me,
   "As a lion growls,
      or a young lion, over its prey,
   when there is called out against it
      a band of shepherds,
   at their noise it is not terrified,
      and at their multitude[19] it is not cowered,
   so *Yhwh* of hosts will come down [[337]]
      to fight over[20] Mount Zion and over its hill.
[5]Like birds fluttering,
      so *Yhwh* of hosts will defend Jerusalem;
   he will defend and deliver,
      he will spare and rescue."

18. Notice that in v. 14 the subject of the ruthless shattering of the potter's vessel and of the fruitless search for a sherd is not mentioned. Unlike the wall's collapse which is caused by a crack, an agent is needed here, and the audience is left to consider the identity of that agent. I have not in this analysis explored the broader associations of the broken pot imagery, e.g., H. Wildberger (*Jesaja*, 1178) mentions magical and symbolic uses, citing Jeremiah 19 and the Egyptian execration texts as examples.

19. The word carries the double meaning, "clamor" and "multitude"; I have chosen the latter to draw out the similarity with 29:1–8, discussed below.

20. The multiple meaning of *ᶜal* ("against," "over," "upon") is important for the poem, but I know of no suitable way of rendering it into English. I have chosen the translation "over" in an attempt to preserve something of the ambiguity as well as the comparison between *Yhwh*'s fighting *ᶜal* and the lion growling over (*ᶜal*) its prey.

Unlike Isa 30:12–14, which is unified through enclosed simile (the vehicle of one simile serving as tenor of the other), this example of extended simile is composite. I use the term "composite" in a literary sense: the poem consists of two similes, unrelated except through diaphor. Diaphor is defined by P. Wheelwright as one of the two main elements of metaphoric activity. Wheelwright uses diaphor to refer to the creation of new meaning by juxtaposition and synthesis and reserves the term epiphor for the outreach and extension of meaning through comparison.[21] The epiphoric elements in these two verses are the comparisons of *Yhwh*'s conduct to that of a lion (v. 4) or birds (v. 5). The diaphoric aspect consists of the synthesis or new meaning which results by placing the two similes together. The different epiphors in vv. 4 and 5 serve as vehicles for a single tenor, the action of *Yhwh*. Both epiphors use animal imagery to bring out selected aspects of the tenor. In the present form of the poem, there can be no doubt that it is the protective aspect of *Yhwh*'s action which the vehicles highlight. But serious questions have been raised by some critics about the meaning of v. 4 and about the unity of these verses. It appears that the verses are composite from a form-critical, as well as a literary, perspective. B. S. Childs and others have maintained persuasively that v. 5 represents a later stage in the development of the tradition, which reinterprets and transforms v. 4 into a word of promise.[22] As Childs points out, *ṣbʾ ʿal* normally means to fight against (cf. Isa 29:7–8; Num 31:7; Zech 14:12).[23] More important, the natural sense of the image of a lion guarding its prey against shepherds' attempts to rescue it would appear to be hostile, since shepherds are not normally thought of as harmful to sheep, nor lions as solicitous of their well-being.

Some commentators argue for a positive reading of the image in v. 4, maintaining that a lion does not necessarily have to be seen as an aggressor. H. Wildberger, [[338]] for example, connects *ʿal* with *yrd* [['come down']] rather than *ṣbʾ* [['fight']] and holds that the picture here is not of a lion that pounces upon its prey, but rather of a lion that protects its prey from those who seek to take it away.[24] Kaiser

21. *Metaphor and Reality*, 72–86.

22. B. S. Childs, *Isaiah and the Assyrian Crisis* (SBT 2/3; London: SCM, 1967) 58–59; W. Dietrich, *Jesaja und die Politik*, 183–85; H. Donner, *Israel unter den Völkern* (VTSup 11; Leiden: Brill, 1964) 136, 138–39; J. Vermeylen, *Du prophète Isaïe*, 422–23; F. Huber, *Jahwe, Juda und die anderen Völker beim Propheten Jesaja* (BZAW 137; Berlin: de Gruyter, 1975) 56–57.

23. *Isaiah and the Assyrian Crisis*, 58.

24. *Jesaja*, 1240–42; similarly, G. Fohrer, *Jesaja*, 120–21; A. Schoors, *Jesaja*, 188–89; R. Fey, *Amos und Jesaja* (WMANT 12; Neukirchen: Neukirchener-V., 1963) 134–36.

makes a similar point, claiming, "The lion will not allow anyone to steal from him what belongs to him," and compares this behavior to *Yhwh*'s determination to defend the city which belongs to him.[25] This interpretation strains the sense of the simile. Sheep belong to shepherds; there is no suggestion in this simile that the lion has a right to the sheep. Already at the beginning of the poem, the word "prey" (*ṭrp*) implies a destructive agent: a lion may defend its prey, but with the intention of devouring it, not of protecting it. Were it not for v. 5, there would be, in my opinion, little reason to take v. 4 as a promise.

Regardless of their merits from the standpoint of transmission history, the arguments of commentators who hold to a defensive image of *Yhwh* in v. 4 are nevertheless instructive. They bear witness to the power of diaphor, for it is through diaphor that we must read the total poem as a promise, and, moreover, diaphor compels us to seek the very kinds of positive connotations these scholars have drawn out. Taken by itself, the meaning of the first simile is not entirely transparent. The multiple meanings of *ʿal* ("over," as in the lion growling over its prey; "against"; "upon") in v. 4 contribute to its plurisignificance. It is only juxtaposition with the second which secures its meaning. Since the tenor is the same in both cases, we are led to seek similarity in the vehicles. Though the precise meaning of the fluttering-birds vehicle may be questioned,[26] the series of protective images which accompanies it (*gānôn* [['defend']], *hiṣṣîl* [['deliver']], *pāsōaḥ* [['spare']], *himlîṭ* [['rescue']]) makes its defensive symbolism indisputable and emphatic. Through diaphor, a simile whose meaning is explicit in v. 5 limits and controls the way we read a simile whose meaning is ambiguous in v. 4.

Isaiah 29:1–14:
Dreams and Visions in Literary Context

So far we have looked at two examples of extended simile in relative isolation. Obviously simile has more significance or force in relation to the poem in which it appears.[27] To give the biblical poetry qua poetry the attention it deserves, we need to broaden our perspective to consider both the effect of extended simile and the handling of other poetic elements within a larger poetic context. Isa 29:1–14 offers a good example for investigation for two [[339]] reasons. First, as one of the

25. *Isaiah 13–39*, 316.

26. See the commentators. I prefer to take the comparison to the way birds hover over a young bird which has fallen out of the nest to defend it.

27. See P. Wheelwright, *Metaphor and Reality*, 77.

five/six woe-complexes within the collection of Isaiah 28–32(33), it is a distinguishable literary unit. Second, it contains two examples of extended simile (vv. 7–8, 11–12). We may note, too, that vv. 1–8 are made up largely of simile.

Scholars generally agree that the woe-complexes which comprise the collection in Isaiah 28–32 are composite.[28] They exhibit no clear structure and display no regular strophic division such as we find, for example, in the Second Isaiah.[29] Rather, the complexes consist of independent oracles from different situations, put together on the basis of thematic or catchword connections.[30] It is not the intention of this study to pursue the exegesis of individual oracles or the process according to which they were joined to produce the complex in 29:1–14. I am interested more properly in the effect of the material as a literary whole. For this reason, I shall discuss 29:1–14 in terms of poems and, for want of a better term, stanzas[31] rather than in terms of oracles. A poem or stanza may, but does not have to be, identical to an independent oracle. It is important to observe that the meaning of an oracle in its literary context may be different from its original meaning. More than the sum of its parts, a poem is the parts in interaction. New associations produce new meanings. As Alonso-Schökel points out, "Neben dem Sitz im Leben steht der Sitz in der Literatur [next to the life situation stands the literary situation]."[32] Only the *Sitz in der Literatur* concerns me here.

I divide Isa 29:1–14 into two poems, vv. 1–8 and vv. 9–14. One reason for this division is the abrupt transition in v. 9, where an impera-

---

28. E.g., C. H. Cornill, "Die Composition des Buches Jesaja," *ZAW* 4 (1884) 84–85, 100; T. K. Cheyne, *Introduction to the Book of Isaiah* (London: Black, 1895) 162–63, 180–204; K. Marti, *Das Buch Jesaja* (KHAT X; Tübingen: Mohr, 1900) xvii–xix; B. Duhm, *Das Buch Jesaia* (4th ed.; Göttingen: Vandenhoeck & Ruprecht, 1922) 13–14, 194 et passim; O. Kaiser, *Isaiah 13–39*, 234–36; S. Mowinckel, "Die Komposition des Jesajabuches Kap. 1–39," *AcOr* 11 (1933) 271, 279–92; and the references cited below, n. 30.

29. On poetic structure in Isaiah 40–66, see J. Muilenburg, "Introduction and Exegesis to Isaiah, chaps. 40–66," *IB* 5.

30. For principles of linkage, see esp. J. Ziegler, "Zum literarischen Aufbau verschiedener Stücke im Buche des Propheten Isaias," *BZ* 21 (1933) 131–35, 142–49, 237–41; G. Fohrer, "The Origin, Composition and Tradition of Isaiah I–XXXIX," *ALUOS* 3 (1961–62) 19–21, 26–29; L. J. Liebreich, "The Compilation of the Book of Isaiah," *JQR* 46 (1956) 268–69; 47 (1956) 121–22; J. Vermeylen, *Du prophète Isaïe*, 383–438.

31. I use this term for a unity of thought and structure within a poem and do not mean by it to suggest a consistent metrical scheme. Stanzas of a poem do not have to display the same number of lines, though in 29:1–8 this turns out to be the case.

32. "Stilistische Analyse," 162. With L. Alonso-Schökel, I want to emphasize that literary study of the final form of the text is simply a different enterprise from form-critical investigation, not a rejection of the form-critical and tradition-critical method. See also J. Muilenburg, "Form Criticism and Beyond," *JBL* 88 (1969) 1–18.

tive enjoining obduracy on the part of unspecified agents follows
directly upon a message of ⟦340⟧ deliverance for Jerusalem. Another
is the fact that the poems treat different themes: the first, the attack
and subsequent deliverance of Ariel; the second, the withholding of
understanding. The first poem is unified by means of catchword connections; the second, by theme. The two poems function together to
create a new literary meaning, in a sense, a new poem.[33] The new poetic complex, 29:1–14, works through juxtaposition, and, of course,
the fact that vv. 9–14 come last decidedly colors one's total impression
and interpretation. What the two poems have in common and what
forges the literary unity of the complex is the concern with visions. Interestingly, "vision" is the only key term the poems share (*ḥāzôn*, v. 7;
ḥāzût, v. 11; cf. *haḥōzîm*, v. 10). Each poem describes and concentrates
attention on the vision by means of extended simile, vv. 7–8 and
vv. 11–12. In vv. 1–8, simile functions as resolution of the poem's
meaning; in vv. 9–14, as illustration of the poem's message.

The entire poetic complex reveals particular sensitivity to considerations of euphony. While space does not permit a thorough examination of the poems along these lines, it is nonetheless important to
acknowledge the intimate connection between thought rhythm and
sound rhythm and to keep these connections in mind as we read the
poems.[34] Let us, therefore, note briefly some of the various kinds of assonance we find in the complex before proceeding. Some of the examples below, as well as others, will be discussed as we analyze each of
the poems individually.

1. *Repetition of the Same or Similar Word in a Stichos*

    1a *ᵓărîᵓēl ᵓărîᵓēl*

    1c *šānâ ᶜal šānâ*

    2b *taᵓăniyyâ waᵓăniyyâ*

    5c *lĕpetaᶜ pitᵓōm*

    9a *hitmahmĕhû ûtĕmāhû*

    9b *hištaᶜašᶜû wāšōᶜû*

    14b *haplēᵓ wāpeleᵓ*

    14c *ḥokmat ḥăkāmâw*

    14d *ûbînat nĕbōnâw*

---

33. My comments about stanza (n. 31 above) apply *mutatis mutandis* to my use of
"poem" as a convenient designation for a poetic unity of thought and structure. Because
29:1–8 and 29:9–14 are united through juxtaposition, the new unity qualifies as a new
poem; but because both vv. 1–8 and vv. 9–14 exhibit a striking inner unity, I limit my use
of the term "poem" to these two units.

34. Cf. J. Muilenburg, "The Literary Character of Isaiah 34," *JBL* 59 (1940) 357.

2. *Repetition of Similar Sounding Words in a Stichos*
   5a   *kĕ⁾ābāq daq* ⟦341⟧
   6b   *bĕra⁽am ûbĕra⁽aš*
         wĕqôl gādôl
   6c   *sûpâ ûsĕ⁽ārâ*
   7a   *kaḥălôm ḥăzôn*

3. *Similar Word or Sound at the Beginning and End of a Distich*
   1cd   *sĕpû . . . yinqōpû*
   3bc   *wĕṣartî . . . mĕṣurōt*
   9cd   *šākĕrû . . . šēkār*

4. *Repetition of the Same Word or Root in Successive Stichoi*
   3abc *⁽ālāyik . . . ⁽ālayik . . . ⁽ālayik*
   5ab   *hămôn . . . hămôn*
   14ab *lĕhaplî⁾ . . . haplē⁾ wāpele⁾*

5. *Alliteration or Assonance in a Distich*
   3bc   *wĕṣartî ⁽ālayik muṣṣāb wahăqîmōtî ⁽ālayik mĕṣurōt*
   5c6a *wĕhāyâ lĕpeta⁽ pit⁾ōm mē⁽im yhwh ṣĕbā⁾ôt tippāqēd*
   6bc   *bĕra⁽am ûbĕra⁽aš wĕqôl gādôl sûpâ ûsĕ⁽ārâ wĕlahab ⁾ēš ⁾ôkēlâ*
   7cd   *wĕkol ṣōbĕhā ûmĕṣōdātāh wĕhammĕṣîqîm lāh*

6. *Repetition between Successive Distichs or Tristichs*
   4, 8abcd, 11c–12

We are now ready to begin a close reading of the two poems which comprise the woe-complex 29:1–14. The discussion which follows will treat first 29:1–8, then 29:9–14. Next we shall consider the effect of the juxtaposition of these poems and inquire how they work together in the complex. Finally, we shall make some concluding remarks about the place of the complex in the collection of chaps. 28–32(33).

Poem I

¹Ah, Ariel, Ariel,
   city where David encamped!
 Add year to year;
   let the feasts go round.
²Then I will distress Ariel
   and there will be moaning and lamentation.
 And it will be to me like an Ariel, ⟦342⟧

³and I shall encamp like David³⁵ against you,
and I will besiege you with towers,
and I will raise siegeworks against you.

⁴Then deep from the earth you shall speak,
and from the dust your speech will be low.
And your voice will be like a spirit from the earth.
and from the dust your speech will whisper.
⁵And the multitude of foreigners will be to you³⁶ like fine dust,
and like driven chaff the multitude of adversaries.
And suddenly, in an instant,
⁶by *Yhwh* of hosts it will be visited,
with thunder and with earthquake and great noise,
whirlwind and tempest and flame of devouring fire.

⁷And it will be like a dream, a vision of the night,
the multitude of all the nations fighting against Ariel,
all those fighting it and besieging it³⁷
and those distressing it.
⁸It will be as when one hungry dreams of eating,
and wakes up, his throat empty;
or as when one thirsty dreams of drinking,
and wakes up and is faint, his throat parched.
Thus will be the multitude of all the nations
fighting against Mount Zion.

Like the extended simile in 31:4–5, we have in these verses the intervention of *Yhwh* and sudden deliverance of Jerusalem. There are other points of contact as well: *hā²aryēh* [['lion']] in 31:4 recalls *²ărî²ēl* [['Ariel']] of chap. 29, regardless of the actual meaning of that term. Both poems connect fighting (*ṣb²*) with Mount Zion (*har ṣiyyôn*, 31:4; 29:8), and through paronomasia, with *Yhwh* of hosts (*ṣēbā²ôt*, 31:4–5; 29:6–8). Both present a multitude (*ûmēhămônām*, 31:4; *hāmôn*, 29:5, 7, 8) at cross purposes with *Yhwh*. As was the case with 31:4–5, scholars have been troubled by the sudden transition to deliverance in this oracle and have questioned its unity on form- and tradition-critical grounds.³⁸

35. Following the LXX.
36. Following the MT and reading the suffix as dative, with W. H. Irwin, *Isaiah 28–33*, 52.
37. Reading with GKC §75qq as a pl. ptc. with suffix; cf. W. H. Irwin, *Isaiah 28–33*, 54; O. Kaiser, *Isaiah 13–39*, 264.
38. See esp. B. S. Childs, *Isaiah and the Assyrian Crisis*, 54–57. G. Fohrer (*Jesaja*, 72–76 and n. 75) disagrees, arguing that a proper understanding of v. 4 makes the assumption that vv. 5–8 are a later addition unnecessary (but he holds v. 8 a later addition, p. 76 n. 79).

[[343]] Our concern is how the poem manages this transition, for the situation at the beginning is clearly transformed by the end.

I divide the poem into three stanzas, vv. 1–3, 4–6, and 7–8.[39] The first deals with the attack of Ariel by *Yhwh* (*wahăṣîqôtî laʾărîʾēl*, v. 2); the third, with the deliverance of Ariel from its attackers (*wĕhammĕṣîqîm lāh*, v. 7). Stanza 2 effects the transition by introducing a multitude (*hămôn*, v. 5) and a sudden visitation by *Yhwh*. In stanza 3, it is this multitude (*hămôn*, vv. 7, 8) which takes over the role of fighting (*haṣṣōbēʾîm*, vv. 7, 8; *ṣōbĕhā*, v. 7) intimated by the name of *Yhwh* of hosts (*ṣĕbāʾôt*) in stanza 2 and the role of distressing (*wĕhammĕṣîqîm*, v. 7) Ariel ascribed to *Yhwh* in the first stanza. The transition is best appreciated through analyzing the way the poem performs itself.

The poem begins with a woe cry raised over Ariel. Whatever else Ariel may denote or connote, that it refers to Jerusalem/Mount Zion is clear both from the following stichos, "city where David encamped," and from the identification of Ariel with Mount Zion in vv. 7–8. The description "city where David encamped" is at this point ambiguous, since *ḥnh* may mean both "besiege" and "dwell." The command *ḥaggîm yinqōpû* [['let the feasts go round']] appears ironic; presumably the ground for the woe cry and the impending attack has to do with cultic observance,[40] a point to which we shall return below. The moaning and lamentation which result when *Yhwh* distresses Ariel, v. 2, are the opposite of what one expects at a religious festival, but, at the same time, fit readily the mourning called for by *hôy* [['ah']] in v. 1.

Two similes in vv. 2c and 3a play upon the double meaning of v. 1ab. Ariel will become "like an ariel." I doubt that it is possible for us to uncover the full significance of this pun.[41] If, as has been proposed, it means "altar hearth," we have a case of metonymy, in which the altar hearth as the holiest part of the temple stands for the holy city of Jerusalem. The association with the altar also fits the cultic setting indicated in v. 1d. In explaining the pun, scholars who accept this meaning usually understand the altar hearth (holy city) as symbolic either of its own sacrifice or that of its enemies. The issue is not etymology, since similar sounding terms may have suggested multiple meanings to the audience. If, as is also possible, Ariel calls to mind "underworld" (cf. Akkadian *arallū*), we have an image which accords well with the woe cry and lamentation in this stanza as well as with the picture of Ariel's muted cries from the *ʾereṣ* [['earth']] in the next.

---

39. Cf. O. Kaiser, *Isaiah 13–39*, 264, who divides the poem into three stanzas of ten lines each.

40. B. S. Childs, *Isaiah and the Assyrian Crisis*, 55.

41. See the discussion in H. Wildberger, *Jesaja*, 1104–5.

Although it means abandoning the principle of *lectio difficilior*, I follow the LXX in rendering v. 3a, "I will encamp like David against you." The pun in this case would be not only on Ariel but also on David's encampment: [[344]] Ariel will be like an ariel and *Yhwh* will encamp like David. V. 3bc secures a hostile meaning for *ḥnh* [['encamp']], and, though it does not help in delimiting the signification of Ariel, it does portray the situation of an ariel. The city is under siege. Assonance (*wĕṣartî, muṣṣāb, mĕṣurōt*) characterizes the means of attack in v. 3bc, while the siege receives emphasis at the beginning and end of the distich, where forms of the root *ṣwr* [['besiege']] appear. Whereas v. 2 addresses the city in the third person as "Ariel," v. 3 makes the address more personal by switching to the second person, underscoring at the same time the hostile nature of this encounter through the threefold repetition of *ʿālayik* [['against you']].

With v. 4 the poem changes its perspective on its subject from *Yhwh*'s action to Ariel's response. A shift in imagery occurs from the high to the low and from strength to weakness. This double imagery may already be present in Ariel: as Mount Zion, it is high; as suggestive of the underworld, low. That *Yhwh* must raise up siegeworks in stanza 1 suggests both the height of a wall and the strength of a fortified city. That Ariel speaks from the earth and dust in stanza 2 conveys notions of lowliness and weakness. Since *ʾereṣ* can mean not only "earth" but also "underworld," the imagery of v. 4 supports one connotation of Ariel as "underworld." This connotation is strengthened by the comparison in v. 4cd of Ariel's voice to a spirit which whispers from the netherworld.

V. 5 introduces something new into the poem, the *hămôn zārāyik* [['multitude of foreigners']] or *hămôn ʿārîṣîm* [['multitude of adversaries']]. Because of its anticipation of deliverance, v. 5ab has been considered either out of place or a secondary level of the tradition by many commentators.[42] Wildberger offers an interesting alternative by reading *zdyk* [['your insolent ones']] with the LXX and 1QIsa[a] and taking v. 5ab to refer to the arrogant rulers of Jerusalem.[43] If his interpretation is correct, Wildberger's division of the poem between vv. 5ab and 5c is to be preferred. Accordingly, the first two stanzas of the poem (vv. 1–3, 4–5b) present a threat, while the third (vv. 5c–7) reverses the situation by promising deliverance.[44] I prefer, however, to

---

42. O. Procksch, *Jesaia I* (KAT 9; Leipzig: Deichert, 1930) 373; R. B. Y. Scott, "Isaiah," 323; T. K. Cheyne, *Isaiah*, 188–90; K. Marti, *Jesaja*, 213; B. S. Childs, *Isaiah and the Assyrian Crisis*, 54–57; H. Donner, *Israel unter den Völkern*, 154–55.

43. *Jesaja*, 1099, 1101.

44. Ibid., 1101; he takes v. 8 as an addition.

take *hămôn* [['multitude']] in v. 5 as a reference to those besieging Ariel, primarily on the basis of the intratextual witness of the poem, where *hămôn* in vv. 7–8 clearly refers to those attacking Ariel. In my view, both *hămôn* and *tippāqēd* [['it will be visited']] in stanza 2 are ambiguous, and the ambiguity creates suspense and effects the transition to stanza 3, where their meaning is resolved.

The poem moves from image to image through association. The fortified city (image of strength) is threatened with siege (vv. 1–3) which will [[345]] humble it (image of weakness), v. 4. V. 4 portrays Ariel as speaking from the dust (*ᶜāpār*); in v. 5 a simile compares the multitude of foreigners to fine dust (*ʾăbāq daq*). One might view the foreign aggressor as the instrument of *Yhwh*'s siege. But the dust simile raises questions. It might mean that foreigners will cover the land as fine dust covers, that the foe will be innumerable. On the other hand, it carries connotations of insubstantiality and lowliness—at least this seemed to be the meaning of the dusty imagery in v. 4. The comparison of the *hămôn* to driven chaff in v. 5b appears to support the insubstantial aspect of the image. The third stanza will reveal that both ideas are, in fact, present: the multitude of *all the nations* (*kol haggôyīm*) presents a formidable adversary, yet one which turns out to be as insubstantial as a dream.

Vv. 5c and 6 present the unexpected intervention of *Yhwh*. Assonance draws attention to both the action and its suddenness: *lĕpetaᶜ pitʾōm mēᶜim yhwh ṣĕbāʾōt tippāqēd* [['and suddenly, in an instant, / by *Yhwh* of hosts it will be visited']]. If the multitude which attacks Ariel in v. 5 is *Yhwh*'s instrument, v. 6 may represent the decisive blow, and the meaning of the second stanza for Ariel is destruction. But since the nature of the multitude and the meaning of *pqd* [['visit']] are ambiguous, one cannot be sure. *Yhwh*'s appearance is described in storm imagery, where alliteration captures splendidly its force: *bĕraᶜam ûbĕraᶜaš wĕqôl gādôl sûpâ ûsĕᶜārâ wĕlahab ʾēš ʾōkēlâ* [['with thunder and with earthquake and great noise, / whirlwind and tempest and flame of devouring fire']]. V. 5 compared the multitude to dust and chaff. Since a storm settles dust and chaff blows away before a storm, it may be that *Yhwh*'s visitation will signify relief, and the meaning of the second stanza for Ariel is deliverance. Stanza 2 thus leaves us in suspense with two possible outcomes. It must be remembered, however, that both Ariel and the multitude attacking it are associated with dust and thus, for the moment, share the same position before *Yhwh*. Indeed, whereas Ariel's voice (*qôl*) was low, v. 4, *Yhwh*'s voice (*qôl*) is great, v. 6. If stanzas 1 and 2 contrast Ariel's present lowliness to its former height, within stanza 2 the contrast is between the lowliness of Ariel and awesomeness of *Yhwh*.

Stanza 3 clarifies the role of the *hămôn*; they are the nations (*hag-gôyīm*) fighting (*ṣb⁾*) against Ariel and distressing (*ṣwq*) it. *Yhwh* had the role of distressing (*ṣwq*) Ariel in stanza 1 and perhaps of fighting (*ṣb⁾*) it in stanza 2 (hinted at through the pun on *ṣb⁾*). If the multitude were *Yhwh*'s instrument of destruction in stanza 2, they cease to be here in stanza 3, where they meet their own disappointment. Such double-edged treatment of Israel's enemies is characteristic of Isaiah's thought. Assyria is *Yhwh*'s tool, but will be punished for its arrogance when *Yhwh*'s purpose is fulfilled (e.g., 10:8–19).[45] [[346]] The final stanza makes no direct mention of *Yhwh* as deliverer but rather points us back to *Yhwh*'s intervention in stanza 2, and requires that we take *pqd* [['visit']] in a positive sense.

In the first two stanzas of the poem, similes have been piling up. The first presented two comparisons (Ariel to an ariel, *Yhwh*'s encampment to David's); the second, three (Ariel's voice to a spirit and its enemies to dust and to chaff). The third stanza represents the crowning metaphoric touch, for it works entirely through simile. To be more precise, it works through two similes which operate in two directions at once. Stanza 2 used simile to associate both attackers and attacked with dust. Stanza 3 makes complex use of simile to associate both with dreams; each appears to be the subject of a dream of the other. V. 7 informs us through paronomasia that the attacking multitude (*hămôn*) will be like a dream (*ḥălôm*), a vision (*ḥăzôn*) of the night, in this case, a nightmare. As the menace vanishes when one awakes, so Ariel will experience the nightmare of siege.

In v. 8 the hunger and thirst imagery is apposite for the situation of a beleaguered people,[46] but the extended simile which elaborates the dream does not quite fit the picture. The dream of satisfying hunger and thirst is gratifying, and reality turns out to be a bitter disappointment. This can hardly be Ariel's dream and must be the dream of the attackers: they think they have Jerusalem in their grasp, but discover their anticipated victory to be an illusion. The enemy, compared first to a dream, is now the dreamer. The two different dream vehicles in vv. 7–8 point to a single tenor, the situation of attack.[47] By juxtaposing the two similes, the poem portrays the illusory experience of both attacker

45. On this distinctive element in Isaiah's preaching, see esp. N. K. Gottwald, *All the Kingdoms of the Earth* (New York: Harper, 1964) 175–96.

46. Cf. W. H. Irwin, *Isaiah 23–33*, 52, who points out (n. 16) that *Yhwh*'s intervention to break the siege (v. 6) is compared to a storm which breaks the drought.

47. The tenor in v. 7 is explicit, the multitude of nations fighting Ariel; that of v. 8 is implicit.

and attacked.[48] The conclusion of v. 8, "thus will be the multitude of all the nations fighting against Mount Zion," repeats the thought of the introduction in v. 7, with the result that the entire stanza is an *inclusio* in which phantom nations frame their phantom conquest.

Poem II

[9]Stupify yourselves and be in a stupor,[49]
  blind yourselves and be blind! [[347]]
 Be drunk, but not with wine,
  stagger, but not with beer![50]
[10]For *Yhwh* has poured out upon you
  a spirit of deep sleep;
 he has shut your eyes, the prophets,
  and your heads, the seers, he has covered.

[11]And the vision of all has become to you
  like the words of a sealed book.
 When they give it to one who knows how to read,
  saying, "Read this,"
   he says, "I cannot for it is sealed."
[12]And when they give the book to one who does not know how to read,
  saying, "Read this,"
   he says, "I do not know how to read."

[13]The Lord has said,
 "Because this people draw near with their mouth,
  and with their lips they honor me,
 but their heart is far from me,
  and their fear of me is a human command which is learned,
[14]Therefore I am again doing wondrous things with this people,
  wondrous and wonderful,
 and the wisdom of their wise shall perish,
  and the prudence of their prudent shall be hidden."

48. Thus Childs's observation (*Isaiah and the Assyrian Crisis*, 54) that v. 8 is an addition because it duplicates v. 7 is misleading. Likewise, Wildberger's assessment of v. 8 as an unnecessary variant of v. 7 lacking poetic quality (*Jesaja*, 1102) fails to recognize how much the poem accomplishes by this combination of images.

49. Following *BHS* and most commentators in taking *htmhmh* as hithpael of *tmh* (cf. Hab 1:5).

50. Reading impv.; cf. the LXX, Vg. Ehrlich, *Randglossen*, IV, 104, followed by W. H. Irwin (*Isaiah 28–33*, 56), considers both perfects substantival, to be taken as vocatives.

From the dream of the preceding poem, we move to the deep sleep of this one.[51] Vv. 11–12 are often taken as later commentary on vv. 9–10, with vv. 13–14 as a separate unit.[52] Since in their present position they exhibit a sustained relation to one thematic structure, the present literary analysis treats them as three stanzas of one poem.[53] Each stanza is a variation on the theme of incomprehensibility and inability to perceive (*Verstockung*). The poem has an A B A′ pattern in which the middle stanza illustrates the theme [[348]] through extended simile. In v. 11 the sealed book prevents discovery of its content, and in v. 12 the fact that it could not be read in any case removes even further the possibility of understanding. The first and last stanzas describe in chiastic order the confounding of the leaders from whom one would expect the greatest understanding, prophets and seers (v. 10) and the wise and prudent (v. 14).[54]

a	b
he has shut	your eyes the prophets
b′	a
and your heads the seers	he has covered (v. 10)
a	b
it shall perish	the wisdom of their wise
b′	a′
and the prudence of their prudent	shall be hidden (v. 14)

Parts of the body connected with perception and expression are brought into the picture in the framing stanzas. The first associates eyes and heads with religious leaders, the prophets and seers. The last deals with mouth, lips, and heart, which because they are in wrong relationship to *Yhwh*, result in the confounding of leaders, the wise and the prudent.

The poem is tinged with irony. Although those addressed by v. 9 are not specified, we may assume on the basis of the reference to "your

51. G. Fohrer points out the thematic connection; see "Origin, Composition and Tradition," 19; *Jesaja,* 77 n. 82.

52. E.g., H. Wildberger, *Jesaja,* 1113; G. Fohrer, *Jesaja,* 77–80; O. Kaiser, *Isaiah 13–39,* 269–74; R. B. Y. Scott, "Isaiah," 324–26; J. Vermeylen, *Du prophete Isaïe,* 404–6.

53. On semantic unity, see M. Riffaterre, *Semiotics of Poetry* (Bloomington: Indiana University, 1978), chap. 1, "The Poem's Significance," 1–22. Riffaterre's observation that mimesis may occupy considerable space while the matrix structure can be summed up in a single word (p. 13) describes aptly 29:9–14.

54. Interestingly, priests are not mentioned, cf. 28:7–8. Most commentators take the prophets and seers in v. 10 as glosses. Their presence is what creates the literary balance with the wise and prudent (v. 14).

eyes the prophets" and "your heads the seers," that the poem is directed to the Judahites in general. Or, on the basis of vv. 1–8, we may take the imperative more specifically as intended for the inhabitants of Jerusalem. Ironically, the people are being told in v. 9 to act precisely as they have been acting. Their self-delusion and wavering action are now attributed to the action of *Yhwh*, who, by pouring out a spirit of deep sleep upon them, makes it impossible for them to act otherwise.[55] The image of *Yhwh* pouring out a spirit picks up the liquid imagery suggested by *yayin* [['wine']] and *šēkār* [['beer']] in v. 9. Similarly, closed eyes (and perhaps covered head) resumes the imagery of sleep. With closed eyes and a covered head one would surely stagger as if drunk.

The introduction of a vision in v. 11 produces an ironic contrast, since a vision (*ḥāzût*) is something normally associated with eyes and with seers [[349]] (*ḥōzîm*), both of which are removed as a means of perception in v. 10. But the vision merely confirms the inaccessibility of revelation. The book is sealed just as the means of perception (eyes and heads symbolizing prophets and seers) were sealed in v. 10. V. 11 provides another example of understanding withheld from someone who, like prophets, seers, and wise, possesses knowledge which might bring understanding. In this case, it is knowledge (*ydᶜ*) of how to read, but it proves to be of no avail since it cannot be applied. The predicament is carried to the extreme in v. 12, where the irony of offering a sealed book to one who cannot read is inescapable.

The dominant vehicle in vv. 11–12 develops an indeterminate tenor, the vision of *hakkōl* [['all']]. Possible referents for *hakkōl* range from narrow to broad and include: (1) the eyes and heads of v. 10;[56] (2) the prophets and seers of v. 10, or the prophets, seers, wise, and prudent of vv. 10 and 14; (3) the situation of vv. 9–10, or the situation of the whole poem; (4) Isaiah's message of trust in *Yhwh*, or everything God has revealed to the people.[57] Since the unit of meaning peculiar to poetry is the finite, closed entity of the text,[58] I prefer to take *hakkōl* on the literary level as referring to the whole of vv. 9–14. Thus, the poem

---

55. See the discussion of H. Wildberger (*Jesaja*, 1115), who rightly stresses that "die Spannung zwischen der Selbstverstockung der Verblendeten und der Verstockung durch Jahwe darf auf keinen Fall aufgelöst werden . . . [[the tension between the self-hardening of the blinded and the hardening of Yahweh may under no circumstances be dissolved]]."

56. W. H. Irwin, *Isaiah 28–33*, 57; in this interpretation the comparison is not so much with the sealed book as with the reaction of readers and non-readers when confronted by the book.

57. H. Wildberger, *Jesaja*, 1115–16.

58. M. Riffaterre, *Semiotics*, ix et passim.

presents itself as illustration of its point; its message, like the words of a sealed book, will be lost on a people who cannot understand.

The third stanza returns to some of the images of the first, but whereas the first two stanzas address the people as "you," this one indicates their rejection by calling them "this people" (v. 13). The parts of the body here (mouth, lips, heart) are not confounded by *Yhwh* as in v. 10, but rather betray a relation to *Yhwh* which is learned rather than authentic. Verse 13 serves as reason for the judgment in v. 14. As in 29:1–2, the issue is cultic observance. The people go through all the motions of worship (*ngš, kbd*),[59] but their heart is not in it. Their commitment to *Yhwh* (*yir³ātām ³ōtî* [['their fear of me']]) amounts to no more than adherence to cultic regulations (*miṣwat ³ănāšîm mĕlummādâ* [['a human command which is learned']]).[60] W. Dietrich locates the *Sitz im Leben* of these verses in a petitionary service, perhaps in the year 701, in which the people ask *Yhwh* for deliverance from Assyria, and, as a corollary, for the success of their political endeavors. Since *Yhwh* has disapproved from the outset of their Egyptian intrigues (30:1–5; 31:1–3; cf. 29:15–16), such a petition can be viewed as no more than lip service.[61] While the text offers no clear support [[350]] for a definite situation as Dietrich advances, that vv. 13–14 have political undertones, and are not simply references to cultic practice in general, is likely.

The judgment in v. 14 is ironic. *Yhwh* will again work wonders so wonderful that only repetition can express it: *lĕhaplî³... haplē³ wāpele³* [['I am doing wondrous things . . . wonderous and wonderful']]. The wonders, however, are hardly what the people have in mind. The wisdom of the wise will perish, and the prudence of the prudent will be hidden. The mention of additional (*ysp*) wonders (*pl³*) is perplexing. What previous *pl³* of *Yhwh* does the poem have in mind? If we search within the poem itself, the likely referent would be *Yhwh*'s only other action in the poem, the confounding of the prophets and seers in v. 10. Just as the people were denied the guidance of their religious leaders in v. 10, so here the counsel of their wise is taken from them. According to this interpretation, *pl³* is doubly ironic, as both actions point to adversity for the people. If, on the other hand, we seek a reference within the complex 29:1–14, the wonderful (in a positive sense) deliverance of Ariel in vv. 1–8 suggests itself; and if we look even further, creation and the exodus come to mind.[62] An important clue for

---

59. On *ngš* and *kbd* as cultic terms, see O. Kaiser, *Isaiah 13–39*, 273 and n. d; G. Fohrer, *Jesaja*, 80; W. Dietrich, *Jesaja und die Politik*, 174; H. Wildberger, *Jesaja*, 1120.

60. On *miṣwat* as regulations for cultic life, see H. Wildberger, *Jesaja*, 1121–22.

61. *Jesaja und die Politik*, 173–75.

62. O. Kaiser, *Isaiah 13–39*, 274.

understanding the ironic nature of *pl'* here may be found in the context of the collection in chaps. 28–32(33). At the end of the first woe-
complex of the collection, 28:1–29, there appears the affirmation that
Yhwh makes wonderful (*hiplî'*) counsel, an assertion made in the light
of earlier statements about *Yhwh*'s incomprehensible speech (28:13)
and strange and alien work (28:21). The point seems to be that while
Yhwh's action may seem incomprehensible to the people, it is nevertheless guided by divine wisdom.[63] Similarly, the second woe-complex,
29:1–14, ends with a reference to *Yhwh*'s wondrous work, and again it
brings strange and incomprehensible results for those affected.

The above discussion has examined in some detail the interrela-
tions of form and meaning in the poems 29:1–8 and 29:9–14. It remains to consider briefly the way the poems function together as a
literary complex and the place of the complex 29:1–14 in the collection of chaps. 28–32. As we noted above, the major unifying principle
of the complex is the focus of each poem on vision and the use each
makes of extended simile in relation to the vision. The vision in 29:1–
8 resolves the ambiguities surrounding the poem's meaning (the nature of the *hămôn* [['multitude']] and of *Yhwh*'s visitation), whereas that
of 29:9–14 illustrates its theme of the withholding of understanding.
Whereas [[351]] the poems are similar in their use of extended simile
to elaborate the visions, there are some notable differences in the construction of the similes. In 29:1–8, the vision is the vehicle; in 29:9–14,
it is the tenor. The more complex first poem combines similes in vv. 7
and 8 to describe the situation of attack from the perspective both of
the victim and of the aggressor. In v. 7 the tenor is the multitude of attacking nations and the vehicle is the dream or night vision. In v. 8 the
implicit tenor is the situation of attack, while dream again serves as the
vehicle. The vehicle in v. 8 is dominant and illuminates the tenor with
the double illustration of the hungry person and the thirsty person. In
the second poem, the dominant vehicle (sealed book) is developed to
illustrate the tenor (the vision of all), and it does this with the double
illustration of a reader and a non-reader.

A second unifying principle of the complex 29:1–14 is *inclusio*. The
first stanza of the poem 29:1–8 and the last stanza of the poem 29:9–14
concern the cult. In 29:1, "Let the feasts go round, and I will distress
Ariel," hints at a disparity between Ariel's faith and Ariel's fate, but the

---

63. See J. C. Exum, "Isaiah 28–32: A Literary Approach," *SBL 1979 Seminar Papers*
(ed. P. Achtemeier; Missoula, MT: Scholars Press, 1979), 2. 143–46; D. L. Petersen, "Isaiah 28, A Redaction Critical Study," ibid., 115–17; J. W. Whedbee, *Isaiah and Wisdom*
(Nashville: Abingdon, 1971) 61–67.

reference remains vague. A more precise picture may be gained from 29:9–14, where performance of religious obligations without genuine commitment to *Yhwh* is denounced. The literary result of the balance between the two stanzas is that the latter now influences one's reading of the former and leads to the supposition that also behind vv. 1–2 lies a tacit objection to inauthentic cultic service. In neither poem, taken as a whole, is worship central. The theme of the first poem is attack and deliverance for Ariel; that of the second, withholding of understanding. In the final form of the complex, however, accusations against cultic observance receive an emphasis which neither of the poems alone gives. The Judahite's religious attitudes are brought into structural prominence through comments pertaining to the cult at the beginning and end of the complex.

The two poems are related not only in terms of their concentration on vision and their objections to certain cultic conduct, but also simply by virtue of juxtaposition. The deep sleep of obduracy which is imposed in vv. 9–14 counterbalances the welcomed dream of deliverance in vv. 1–8. Indeed, if the entire poetic complex be viewed as a semantic unity, *hakkōl* [['all']] in v. 11 raises the question whether the vision of deliverance of vv. 1–8 is also part of an inaccessible message, i.e., a lesson whose import will be lost on a people without understanding. In any event, vv. 9–14 offset the hopeful impression given by vv. 1–8, and the complex comes to an end on a note of confusion.

In the larger context of the collection in chaps. 28–32, the situation of confusion which prevails at the end of the second woe-complex is reversed in the third, 29:15–24. Again, juxtaposition produces new effect and now creates a new atmosphere of encouragement. The woe-complex of 29:1–14 [[352]] progressed from deliverance to delusion. The woe-complex of 29:15–24 contains a transformation from delusion to restoration. The transition between the complexes works smoothly, moving from understanding (*bînat nĕbōnāw*) which is hidden (*tistattār*) from the people (vv. 13–14) to counsel they try to hide (*lastir*) from *Yhwh*, implying thereby that *Yhwh* has no understanding (*lōʾ hēbîn*, vv. 15–16). In 29:17 transformation begins. Verse 18 mentions the words of a book (*dibrê sēper*) which, unlike the book of 29:11–12, is not sealed (*kĕdibrê hassēper hehātûm*, v. 11). As opposed to being inaccessible, the word is now available to those who could not normally perceive it, the deaf will hear the words of a book and the blind will see (v. 18). Sight given to the blind reverses the situation of 29:9–10, where the people are told to make themselves blind and *Yhwh* closes their eyes. The reversal reaches completion in v. 24. Whereas at the end of the complex 29:1–14, *Yhwh* hid understanding (*bînat nĕbōnāw*) from the wise; at the end of the complex 29:15–24 even those erring in spirit and those who murmur will know understanding (*bînāh*, v. 24).

The kind of effect created by juxtaposition of a promise of weal and a threat of woe we have observed within 29:1–14 and between 29:1–14 and 29:15–24 occurs throughout the collection in chaps. 28–32. The shifts from one to the other maintain a tension in the prophetic message. From a literary perspective, the tension builds suspense and creates interest. From a theological perspective, it underscores both the contingency of weal and woe on the people's response and the freedom of *Yhwh*. It is not enough to observe that judgment and promise alternate in the collection, nor even that the general movement within the whole is from judgment to promise and from confusion to clarity.[64] The literary task remains to show how the tension works, to explore how the component poems perform themselves and how they participate in the final literary product. Additional literary studies of the material in Isaiah 28–32(33) are needed to further this task. Perceiving the significance of literary patterns should lead us, in the final analysis, to deeper insight into theological patterns.

64. See *inter alia*, J. C. Exum, "Isaiah 28–32," 145–46; R. Lack, *La symbolique de livre d'Isaïe* (AnBib 59; Rome: Biblical Institute, 1973) 69–75; S. Mowinckel, "Komposition," 280–81.

Reader-Response Analysis

Introduction

Few scholars are neutral about reader-response criticism. Some critics find its emphasis on the reader's reception of the text exciting, even liberating. They believe the approach correctly explores the implications of the fact that biblical texts were written for an ancient audience, and they believe it is also helpful for describing the way the Old Testament affects contemporary audiences. Other analysts, however, are skeptical of the method. They claim reader-response criticism has few, if any, objective standards. They reason that if individual readers can interpret texts any way they wish, then exegesis will no longer take place. Readers will simply discuss the way the Scripture affects them personally.

Which opinion is correct? Perhaps reader-response criticism has not yet had enough time to develop a consistent pattern of Old Testament interpretation. Until it does, overly radical statements for or against the approach are premature.

Robert M. Fowler attempts to identify an ideal reader in his 1985 essay. Obviously, this reader must be defined for the methodology to have definite standards. By describing the ideal reader, Fowler reveals the way texts should be read, thereby indicating basic steps for completing a reader-oriented analysis of a biblical passage. Fowler believes that the Old Testament's original audience was serious, informed, and imaginative. Thus, only similarly minded modern readers can fully appreciate the Old Testament's message.

Willem S. Vorster analyzes biblical texts in his 1986 article, but in a very different way than the other exegetical studies in this volume. Instead of examining details such as character and plot, he notes how various interpretative traditions have read the succession narratives. He reveals that strict exegetical considerations have not always determined how texts have been read and explained. Other factors have always affected scholarship. What matters, then, is that these factors be

374

recognized and assessed. A reader's response will emerge, so this natural occurrence ought to be taken into account in a positive way.

In some ways, reader-response analysis represents the left wing of current literary studies because it allows critics to move interpretation beyond the text itself. Rhetorical criticism, with its emphasis on the text in its historical form, represents the discipline's right wing. The other approaches highlighted in this collection dialogue with rhetorical and reader-response analysis, yet remain independent of them. Which direction literary criticism of the Old Testament goes in the future depends on which variation of these two methodologies seems most attractive to thoughtful analysts.

Who is "The Reader" in Reader Response Criticism?

ROBERT M. FOWLER

The Reader and the Critic

[[5]] To begin, we need first to make a major distinction between the reader and the critic. Often a literary critic (or a biblical critic) will talk about being a reader of a text as if he or she were a reader only. But he or she is clearly more than that, for being a critic means being part of a guild, or an "interpretive community," as Stanley Fish (1980) likes to say. Such a guild has a history, it has a language, and it has rules and rituals for entrance into its ranks, and for subsequent advancement, demotion, or excommunication. In speaking as a critic one speaks to be heard chiefly by fellow critics, and thus the entire critical tradition of that particular interpretive community is evoked implicitly. To be sure, reader response criticism generally tends, more than other brands of [[6]] literary criticism, to grant value to *all* reading, whether expert or naive. But it is still reader response *criticism*, and that is where equivocation begins to creep in. Reader response critics do tend to value all reading, but insofar as they are critics working within the guild, the implicit critical presuppositions of the guild guide their work. They are not just readers; they are expert, critical readers. But the difference between being a critical reader and being simply a reader needs to be spelled out carefully.

One attempt to do just this is an article by George Steiner, entitled "'Critic'/'Reader.'" This is a rich and subtle essay, the intention of

Reprinted with permission from *Semeia* 31 (1985) 5–23.

which is to pose a fictional, heuristic antithesis of "critic" versus "reader." He is careful to note at the beginning and end of his essay that this polarity is indeed fictional; "in the ordinary run of things, 'criticism' and 'reading' interpenetrate and overlap" (451). Yet, to understand the overlap we need to understand the nature of the opposing poles, even if they never exist in a pure state.

Because Steiner repeats and develops his critic/reader antithesis in almost the fashion of a fugue, it is difficult to summarize adequately the variety of insights found in his essay. Nevertheless, the foundational motif of his fugue seems to be that "the critic is judge and master of the text," while "the reader is servant to the text" (449). More specifically, we can observe two ways in which the "judge and master" of the text contrasts with the "servant" of the text. The first of these is the observation that the critic steps back from the text to strike a magisterial pose of critical, objectifying distance, while the reader tries to eliminate the distance between himself and the text. Since the critic stands over against the text, criticism is by nature "adversarial," "competitive," even "parasitic," in its relationship with the text (433, 436, 437, 441). The reader, on the other hand, does not reify the text as an object, but finds in it a "real presence" and often a locus of "inspiration" or "revelation." In "dynamic passivity," a reader is read *by* the text (438–39); distance collapses as the reader seeks "to enter into the text and to be entered into by the text" (443).

A second way of formulating the antithesis is to say that a critic makes judgments about the text and declares them, while a reader does neither. Since it does not objectify the text, reading does not lend itself to discourse about itself. As Steiner says: "It is easy to say something about criticism worth looking at and/or disagreeing with. It is difficult to say anything useful about 'reading' in the sense in which this paper seeks to articulate the term. Criticism is discursive and breeds discourse. 'Reading' yields no primary impulse towards self-communication. The 'reader' who discourses is, in a certain manner, in breach of privilege. . . . Reading is done rather than spoken about . . . " (439). Criticism is the product of rational choice, and "the critic must declare; this is his public and [[7]] legislative ordination." On the other hand, "the reader will often hold his illumination mute" (448). After all, to the reader the text is "'a real presence' irreducible to analytic summation and resistant to judgment in the sense in which the critic can and must judge" (440).

The legislative duty of criticism has as a central task the evaluation and ranking of texts; part of the critic's job is to tell us what we should and should not be reading. Steiner calls the set of texts prescribed by

the critic the critic's "syllabus." The reader, too, has his selection of favored texts, which Steiner chooses to call the reader's "canon." The
crucial difference is that the critic chooses his "syllabus" by an act of
will, but the "canon" chooses the reader; a canon is unsought and un-
willed. "Canon," in Steiner's usage, refers to those texts and text fragments that capture our imaginations without our seeking it and often
without our being fully aware of it. "The canonic text enters into the
reader, it takes its place within him by a process of penetration, of lu-
minous insinuation whose occasion may have been entirely mundane
and accidental—decisive encounters so often are—but not, or not primarily, willed" (446). "The occurrence is banal to anyone whose mind
and body—both are involved—have been seized upon by a melody, by
a tune, by a verbal cadence which he did not choose by act of will,
which has entered into him unawares" (446). "The critic prescribes a
syllabus; the reader is answerable to and internalizes a canon" (445). "A
syllabus is taught; a canon is lived" (447).

A large part of the equivocation in reader response criticism regarding "the reader" can be explained by reference to Steiner's critic/
reader antithesis. It is helpful to recognize that reader response critics
can be positioned somewhere along a continuum running from the
pure (but probably non-existent) "critic" to the pure (but probably
non-existent) "reader" (cf. Mailloux, 1982: 22).

Toward one end of the spectrum we have some reader response
critics very much upholding the literary critical tradition, although in a
roundabout way, since they are trying to shift the critical focus to
something largely ignored by recent generations of critics: the reader
and the reading experience. Their affirmation of the critical tradition
is particularly noticeable when one common strategy is adopted. Often
a reader response critic will attempt to elucidate the history of the
criticism of a particular text by trying to find what has happened in the
reading experience that has given rise to convergent or (more often)
divergent critical assessments of the text. In other words, he or she will
presume to use the text to explain the history of its reading. The goal
here is to explicate, as much as possible, not the text per se, but all
previous readings of the text, thereby comprehending, encompassing,
and rising above a host of critical colleagues. As a critical strategy this
is a powerful move, because it puts the reader response critic in a position of not only standing over ⟦8⟧ against the text, but also standing
over against one's critical peers, in a most decisive manner.

We could call the critic pole of the critic/reader continuum the "objectifying" pole. What is objectified by the reader-oriented critic, however, is not the traditional text object, but the experience of reading

within a tradition of criticism. This could also be called the "sociological" or "ideological" pole, for we objectify our reading experience according to the critical presuppositions (or ideology) we share with our fellows in the guild.

The reader pole, or the other hand, is the pole of "subjectifying": this is the pole of the "individual" and the "psychological." A reader response critic positioned here will be less concerned to contribute to a critical tradition, and more concerned to contribute to a person (*not* a "critic") finding him/herself to be the subject of his or her reading experience. We frequently find here an unashamed acceptance of the nonexpert reader, and a challenge to the implicit authoritarianism of the critical community. Such "subjective" or "psychological" critics as David Bleich (1975; 1978) and Norman Holland (1975; 1982), for example, eagerly welcome their students as fellow readers with full reading privileges, a democratization of the classroom that their colleagues in the guild may look upon as foolish or even heretical. Most empirical study of reading (the psychology of perception, developmental psychology, etc.) also tends to slide to this end of the continuum (see Mailloux, 1982: 206).

Thus does Steiner give us one valuable measuring stick for sizing up "the reader." Applying this measuring stick, when reader response critics talk about "the reader," some are thinking primarily of Steiner's "critic," others are thinking primarily of Steiner's "reader," while most are probably somewhere in between. For me, and for most biblical scholars, I imagine, Steiner's antithesis is all too familiar. For us, Steiner's essay may even represent a pointed statement of knowledge we would just as soon repress, for most of us were readers of the Bible before we were critics of it, and we now struggle, in most cases, to reconcile the rational insights of criticism with the ecstasy of reading. Moreover, it would not be difficult to re-write Steiner's essay using the Bible as the paradigm in Western culture of a text that receives both the devotion of readers and the scrutiny of critics. And our experience with the Bible confirms Steiner's claim that reading is logically prior to criticism. Whether seen historically or ontogenetically, reading the Bible (or being read by it) precedes biblical criticism; the Bible was and is canon, in Steiner's sense of the word, long before critics placed it on their syllabus.

With a passion that I would suppose is missing in most other kinds of literature courses, a battle between critic and reader is fought in almost every college classroom where the Bible is read critically. In the first class meeting of an introductory course, the English professor is unlikely [[9]] to be presented with a hard-core element of Shakespeare

devotees, in the manner in which his biblical scholar colleague is likely
to be faced with at least a few students who can cite chapter and verse
of holy scripture. It is at once exhilarating and painful to have to fight
such battles, but it confirms for me that at least the literature I study as
a critic continues to matter to readers. If it should not matter to readers, why should it matter at all to critics?

I shall quickly abandon my battle imagery above, if it leads us to think
that one side is destined to victory and the other to defeat. The struggle
is indeed passionate and painful, but in those circumstances where one
side seems for the moment actually to vanquish the other, the results are
tragic. It sounds trite, but I find that a balance of readerly passion and
critical distance is desirable. An imbalance on either side is unhealthy,
and can be pathological. Steiner ably rebukes a current "hypertrophy"
(437) of criticism, and biblical critics would do well to take his remarks to
heart. But biblical critics also have a story to tell, and our story includes
many incidents of biblical criticism opposed and hounded mercilessly by
zealous readers. I would not tar all readers of the Bible with the same
brush, but the fact remains that just as there can be a pathology, a hypertrophy, of criticism, there can be a pathology, a blind zeal, of reading.
But inasmuch as most of us escape pathology, most of us live in the middle somewhere. Indeed, most biblical scholars of my acquaintance have
experienced an oscillation between Steiner's two poles; most of us have
moved from being readers to being critics, and then, for the lucky ones,
back to a post-critical readership (Ricoeur: 351).

The personal pilgrimages of numerous biblical scholars would, I
think, largely confirm Steiner's observations about critics and readers,
but we would have some insights to add to his. Many of us found *in
criticism* our "revelation" or our "ecstasy," because for the first time,
with the obtaining of critical distance, we could *see* the features of the
text that had hitherto read us, and we were enchanted and liberated by
what we saw. Without criticism, we saw in retrospect, it had been impossible to see and to know the text that had read us, not even to know
if it was the text we thought it was. He or she who "serves the text" with
utter devotion cannot objectify and thereby know what text is in fact
being served. In the case of the Bible, many are read by and serve 'versions' of the Bible that a critic in good conscience can only label perversions. But only with critical distance can one see perversions;
perversion is a concept of criticism. To add to Steiner's antithetical
comparison, the reader says of the text "It thou shalt not judge"; the
critic says of the text "If it is so worthy of respect, it will emerge from
judgment triumphant and with added glory." To the critic, the reader
appears to serve texts he does not know and cannot understand. To the

[[10]] reader, the critic appears to master and judge even those texts to which he is inferior. Must there not be a middle ground?

I see myself striving to be both a reader and a critic of the Bible: a *critical reader*, if you will. And unless I specify otherwise, the "reader" who will be mentioned frequently hereafter will be just such a critical reader. To be a critical reader means for me: (1) to affirm the enduring power of the Bible in my culture and in my own life; (2) and yet to remain open enough to ask any question and to risk any judgment, even if it should mean repudiating (1). Nothing less than both of these points, together, will do for me. Even more specifically, however, I am pleased to confess that: I was a "reader" of the Bible before I was a "critic" of it; I found becoming a critic to be liberating and satisfying, and therefore I judge criticism to be of inestimable value and a high calling; but I also recognize the prior claim of the text and the preeminence of reading over criticism, and so, accordingly, I seek and occasionally am apprehended by moments in which the text wields its indubitable power. The critic's ego says this just could be the cherished "post-critical naivete"; the reader's proper humility before the text says it is not for a reader to judge such things.

The Real Reader, the Implied Reader, and the Narratee

Keeping in mind that our initial question was "Who is 'the reader' . . . ?," at this point we split our question into the following questions: (1) Who is "the reader?" (2) How does "the reader" relate to "the author" by means of the text? And, (3) Just who is "the author?" The terminology I have adopted in addressing these questions is borrowed from Seymour Chatman's *Story and Discourse* (146–151; cf. Wayne Booth, 1983; Prince, 1973; 1982; Rabinowitz). Chatman distinguishes between real author, implied author, narrator, narratee, implied reader, and real reader. One needs such distinctions in order to explore with care "the interrelation of the several parties to the narrative transaction" (Chatman: 147).

The *real author* and *real reader* are easy enough to grasp. They are the living, flesh-and-blood persons who actually produce the text and read it.[1] But in the act of reading we encounter, not a flesh-and-blood

---

1. Booth speaks of "the flesh-and-blood author, who tells many stories, before and after a given tale," and "the flesh-and-blood re-creator of many stories" (1983: 428). Rabinowitz, who only deals with the audience side of the narrative act in his article, uses the term "actual audience" (126). Once beyond the narrator/narratee pair, Prince, like Rabinowitz, concentrates more on the audience side of the narrative than the authorial side; and Prince, like Chatman, uses the expression "real reader" (Tompkins: 9).

author, but the author's second self adopted for purposes of telling this tale, and similarly we as readers are not wholly ourselves as we read, but the reader the text invites us to be. The terms *implied author* and *implied reader*, therefore, have gained wide currency in recognition of the fact that a text implies a role or a persona for both the author and reader.[2] As Wayne Booth says, "the author creates, in short, an image of himself and another image of his reader; he makes his reader, as he makes his second self, and the most successful reading is one in which [[11]] the created selves, author and reader, can find complete agreement" (1983: 138). Finally, *narrator* and *narratee* are terms referring to the persons who are supposedly telling and listening to the story.[3] Every story may be supposed to have a storyteller and a listener, but as it happens some stories have only oblique, covert evidence of either a narrator or a narratee, while others may go so far as to have a narrator or a narratee overtly portrayed as a character in the narrative (as in *Thousand and One Nights*, where Scheherazade is the narrator and the sultan the narratee). Narrator and narratee are especially useful terms when it is clear that the implied author has distanced himself from his unreliable narrator or that the implied reader is expected to distance himself from a gullible narratee.

A number of critics, as I have noted, have proposed their own versions of these basic concepts. Their refinements often complicate matters, however, by drawing in some of the considerations about "the reader" that are better considered separately.[4] The terminology offered above is minimal and serviceable, without unnecessarily mixing in important but tangential reading concerns. It makes possible the careful consideration of a number of interesting phenomena in the narrative transaction, in spite of bearing within it the inevitable ambiguities and gaps of any critical vocabulary. I would like to address myself now both to the usefulness of this terminology and to its problems.

The critic/reader distinction introduced earlier, although not explicitly represented in this terminology, is implicitly present. It may be present, for example, in the way Chatman diagrams the functions of his

2. Booth is currently using the terms "the implied author of this tale" and "the postulated reader" (1983: 429). Rabinowitz speaks (only on the audience side again) of the "authorial audience" (126). In a similar vein Prince uses the term "virtual reader" (Tompkins: 9).

3. Chatman credits Prince for the coinage of "narratee," the counterpart of the "narrator." Booth speaks of "the teller of this tale" and "the credulous listener" (1983: 430). Rabinowitz uses the expression "narrative audience" (127).

4. For example, both Rabinowitz and Prince also want to talk about "ideal readers": for Rabinowitz, the "ideal narrative audience" (134), and for Prince, the "ideal reader" (Tompkins: 9). I want to reserve discussion of such ideal readers until later.

various critical entities (151, 267). On a horizontal line, he positions from left to right: real author, implied author, narrator, narratee, implied reader, and real reader (151). Arrows pointing toward the right tie together such successive pair of entities. The middle four terms are within a box labelled "narrative text," and within the box the arrows linking successive pairs are solid. In the heart of the box, narrator and narratee are in parentheses, to signify that they are optional features of a narrative (but the arrow connecting them is still solid). Lying outside the box of the narrative, however, are the real author and the real reader, and the arrows going from the real author to the box and from the box to the real reader are made of broken lines. Exile from the box, plus the broken arrows, together suggest that real authors and real readers have a tenuous relationship to the reading of a text. This is implied also in Chatman's explanation of his diagram: "The box indicates that only the implied author and implied reader are immanent to a narrative, the narrator and narratee are optional (parentheses). The real author and real reader are outside the narrative as such, though, of course, indispensable to it in an ultimate practical sense" (151).

This is the language of a critic of literature—or better, a theorist of [[12]] criticism—and not that of a reader. Indeed, real authors and real readers are outside the box of the critical concern, which is the realm of the critical apprehension of the literary text. Real authors, I suppose, are left to literary historians, while real readers are left to psychologists.

Bringing Steiner's language together with Chatman's, we would have to say that the "critic" will tend to focus on the text and on the critical entities immanent to it, while the "reader" will tend to take the reading experience to be an encounter with the discourse of a real author directed to him/herself as a real reader. That is, a critic will tend to live within Chatman's box, while a reader will not even recognize the existence of the box, thereby collapsing all of these careful critical distinctions into simply the author and the reader. Thus, Chatman's box does not divide neatly the realm of Steiner's "critic" from the realm of Steiner's "reader"; Steiner's language is not congruent with Chatman's language. However, if we may suppose for the moment that Chatman's "real reader" is in fact very close to being Steiner's "reader," then we may find in Chatman's language an insight that supplements the insights offered to us by Steiner. This is the recognition of just how much real authors and real readers have in common. Real authors often profess to write for real readers, and specifically disavow writing for critics. Similarly, the real reader believes in real authors; he *knows* he is encountering the real presence of a real author (and not just an implied one) when reading a narrative, while the critic knows no such thing. Thus Chatman's terminology helps to reveal an ally for Steiner's reader in the person of the real author (they are both willing exiles from the realm of criticism), while the terms inside his box specify helpfully some prominent concerns of the critical realm.

Working within Chatman's box for the moment, we can look at some of the concrete ways this terminology facilitates the critical discussion of reading. By distinguishing between the narratee and implied reader, for one thing, we indicate that there are often two major role models provided in the text for anyone reading it. The implied reader is the reader we must be willing to become, at least momentarily, in order to experience the narrative in the fullest measure (see Booth, 1983: 79–81, 138–39, and passim; 1979: 242 and passim; and Suleiman). The implied reader may relate to the narratee, in turn, in any number of ways, ranging from a close and intimate association to an ironic distancing, if the narratee appears to the implied reader to be gullible or otherwise deficient. In other words, a second benefit of Chatman's terminology is that it provides the vocabulary necessary to explore the myriad variations of distance that can exist between implied reader and narratee, between implied author and narrator, and moreover, between any of these four entities and the characters in the story. Actually, the possibilities are reduced considerably by the fact that the implied author and ⟦13⟧ implied reader, and, too, the narrator and narratee, are so closely linked. One might say that these pairs even represent mirror images. For example, the cluster of values and judgments that is the implied author is manifested in the implicit rendering of the text's reader—and vice versa. Similarly, the diction of the narrator is reflected like a sonar wave off of the outline of the posited narratee and returns to the sender to be emited again—each reflects the presence of the other (see Prince, 1987: 7–25). This, then, is a third benefit of our adopted vocabulary: it recognizes and provides a rudimentary way to talk about the dialogical process that is built into the text and demanded by the reading experience.

Granted the usefulness of Chatman's terminology, he glosses over one problem spot that requires attention: the nature of the implied reader (and *mutatis mutandis* the implied author). He places both of these entities within the box labelled "narrative text," claiming them to be "immanent" to the text. A clean break is therefore made between the reader in the text and the reader outside of the text, a division that is problematic, to say the least. In fact, one of the recurring debates among reader-oriented critics concerns the relationship between the text and the reader. Stated in its most extreme form, the question here is: *does the text control the reader or does the reader control the text?* For example, Wayne Booth and Wolfgang Iser both talk about someone very much like Chatman's implied reader, but it is clear they mean something rather differ-ent when they talk about this entity. Booth's version of the implied reader, although it invites and requires the cohesion of a real reader, is ultimately *in* the text, and is the creation of an author (see Booth, 1983: 138, 422–23). Iser's (1974) implied reader, however, is constructed by a real reader out of the material provided by the text, particularly its spots of "indeterminacy": "blanks," "gaps," etc. (Iser, 1978). Iser is careful to say that his implied reader is neither in the text, nor outside it, but is the unique product of the "interaction" of a text and a reader.

There are other points of view on the text vs. reader debate. Curi-ously outdoing even Wayne Booth in respect for the rhetorical power of the text, and outdoing even Wolfgang Iser in respect for the indepen-dence and creative activity of the reader, are the 'early' and 'later' po-sitions of Stanley Fish. In his early reader-oriented criticism, typified by *Self-Consuming Artifacts* (see also Fish, 1970 = Fish, 1972: 383–427 = Fish, 1980: 21–67), Fish engages in brilliant word by word analyses of the way texts manipulate the developing response of the reader; no one could make a stronger case for thoroughgoing textual control over the read-ing experience. Fish even goes so far as to argue that all readers are tex-tually directed in just the way he is describing. They just have not realized it because they have not paid attention to the ways texts have controlled them. In more recent work (1980), Fish still affirms the im-mense value of this kind of analysis in practical criticism; however, he [[14]] admits now that it is not the only way to conceptualize reading. In fact, he has now swung over to the position that the text cannot really control reading in any objective sense, for the text is invented in the process of being read—the text and all its features are only defined and therefore brought into existence by the reader's interpretive strategies. So, having said earlier, essentially, that the text controls the reader, Fish now says that it is the reader who objectifies the text and its character-istics in the first place, and thus controls it. From this latter position, Fish's earlier position may be explained as a convenient and powerful critical fiction, adopted by the critic because of its potential for persuad-ing a critical audience that already grants to texts an 'objectivity' and an 'authority' to control the reader. But now he wants to make clear that objectivity and authority are always, first, the reader's to grant.

Does this new position of Fish's now grant too much authority to the reader? In response to this question, Fish slides into the next sta-tion of his critical pilgrimage. The reader is not 'too powerful,' he says, and the critical enterprise is not doomed to subjectivism or solipsism, because the reader and his reading experience are defined and con-trolled by the critical community of which he is a part. The critical presuppositions employed by the reader to objectify and analyze the text are derived from the "interpretive community" in which the reading takes place. Readers may control texts, but that does not lead to anarchy, because interpretive communities control readers.

Fish has therefore bracketed Booth and Iser in his critical career, attributing at one point more control to the text than Booth, and then more control to the reader than Iser, and then locating the source of *all* control in the preexistent presuppositions of one's interpretive community. If Fish did not do what he does so brilliantly, one could dismiss him for a damnable protean slipperiness. But in sliding from one critical extreme to the next, he has helpfully highlighted, if idiosyncratically, what must be simultaneous foci for reader-oriented criticism. The issue is not about a two-sided relationship between text and reader, nor about the overarching preeminence of interpretive communities, but a matter of *text* and *reader* meeting *in the context of the critical community.* Granted that: (1) the community defines what the text is and tells the reader how to go about reading; at the same time, (2) the text (as defined by the community) molds its reader and constrains the critical gaze of the community; and at the same time, (3) the reader (as instructed by the community) construes the text and contributes to the evolution of the critical community. That is, granted the undeniable importance of the interpretive community, within that social setting the text will always have an objectivity and the reader a subjectivity that are also undeniable. Moreover, it is always possible that the objectified text will wield such power, or the subjectified reader exert such genius, that ⟦15⟧ the interpretive community will be re-made after their images.

All of this is to say that the implied reader is the locus of a great deal of equivocation in current criticism, but only because reading itself is a mysterious merger of text, reader, and context. Yet for all its ambiguity, the term implied reader is still useful. When I use it, I shall use it to refer primarily to the reader implied *in the text,* but I shall take care to observe that different *critical readers* will grasp that reader in the text differently, due largely to differences in *the contexts of reading,* which are constrained by the critical presuppositions prevailing at the time and place of reading. With judicious use, the rest of Chatman's terminology is also helpful.

The Ideal Reader

Besides the terminology discussed in the previous section, there is another common family of terms clustering about the notion of the "ideal reader." One hears, not only of the ideal reader, but also of the informed reader, the optimal reader, the superreader, the competent reader, the educated reader, and so on. What critics are grasping for amidst this assortment is an idealized reader intimately related to the implied reader, as I shall indicate below. But "ideal reader" adds greater intensity to "implied reader"; it reveals the critical impulse, not just to apprehend the reader implied in the text, but to apprehend the readers implied in many texts, so as to encompass and supersede them all.

A succinct description of the ideal reader is offered by Jonathan Culler: "The question is not what actual readers happen to do but what an ideal reader must know implicitly in order to read and interpret works in ways which we consider acceptable" (123–24). The ideal reader possesses not only "linguistic competence" but also "literary competence": an intimate acquaintance with Steiner's "syllabus" and a full grasp of the accepted critical means of working on it. The ideal reader is Steiner's "critic," par excellence. This is very close to Stanley Fish's version of the ideal reader, whom he prefers to label the "informed reader":

> Who is *the* reader? Obviously, my reader is a construct, an ideal or idealized reader, somewhat like Wardhaugh's "mature reader" or Milton's "fit" reader, or to use a term of my own, *the* reader is the *informed* reader. The informed reader is someone who (1) is a competent speaker of the language out of which the text is built up; (2) is in full possession of "the semantic knowledge that a mature . . . listener brings to his task of comprehension," including the knowledge (that is, the experience, both as a producer and comprehender) of lexical sets, collocation probabilities, idioms, professional and other dialects, and so on; and (3) has *literary* competence. That is, he is sufficiently experienced as a ⟦16⟧ reader to have internalized the properties of literary discourses, including everything from the most local of devices (figures of speech, and so on) to whole genres. . . .
>
> The reader of whose responses I speak, then, is this informed reader, neither an abstraction nor an actual living reader, but a hybrid—a real reader (me) who does everything within his power to make himself informed. (1980: 48–49)

Wolfgang Iser discusses several versions of the "ideal reader," and expresses dissatisfaction with all of them, finding them all too nebulous and lacking in theoretical rigor (1978: 27–38). In their place he offers his version of the implied reader, "a textual structure anticipating the presence of a recipient without necessarily defining him" (1978: 34). Iser has perhaps sensed correctly that the implied reader is at the core of all the talk about idealized readers, but he loses the use of a significant heuristic device by limiting himself to the reader implied by any one text, which is what his implied reader is.

Steven Mailloux, for example, has seen that the ideal reader is in a sense the implied reader writ large:

> The "ideal reader" is merely an abstracted version of the "implied
> reader." He is not a reader of a specific text but one implied by all lit-
> erary texts; or put another way, he is a hypothetical reader with the
> general ability to comprehend literature. . . . We have, then, a specific
> text's *implied reader*, which is really only a textual interpretation (or
> part of one) using a reader vocabulary. And we have an *ideal reader*
> who is also an interpretive construct, one that is abstracted from many
> specific instances of textual interpretation, one that defines the condi-
> tions of literary response. (1982: 203)

Mailloux's point is well taken, but it needs to be pushed further.
The ideal reader is not simply a hypothetical enhancement of the implied reader. The "ideal reader" is a fictive role created and assumed
by a critic as he or she presumes to address the critical community. It
is, in other words, a pose adopted *by the critic* for rhetorical purposes.
The fiction being acted out in the work of criticism is precisely the critical pretension to supersedure: to supersede the text, one's critical
community and its history of reading, and even one's own self. One
may not actually be the critic par excellence, but when playing the
game of criticism you cannot pretend to be anything less and still hope
to win over your critical audience.

This is hardly a revelation; numerous critics have admitted all of
this candidly. But we can push still further to observe that the role of
the ideal reader can be played in two major ways. First, there is the role
of the individual ideal reader per se. This is where I adopt the
stance—implicitly, perhaps, or explicitly, if I have nerve—of the su-
premely informed and [[17]] skilled individual reader-critic, possessing
impeccable linguistic and literary competence. We might call this the
Ideal Reader I. It is also possible, and very common, to construct a
kind of composite ideal reader out of the accumulated critical experience of one's critical community. In practice, this second, composite
form of the ideal reader—Ideal Reader II, let us say—often goes hand
in hand with the first. Rhetorically, they can uphold each other—I establish my credentials as a critic by demonstrating my personal knowledge of the syllabus and mastery of the critical tools, which is at the
same time a celebration of the history and current vitality of the entire
guild. The Ideal Reader I and the Ideal Reader II represent the opposing poles of another of those continua ranging from the individual to
the social, but in this case the continuum is narrow in its range, since
we are dealing with a dialectical relationship between subjective and
objective poles within a very specialized social group: critics in particular literary critical tradition.

Stephen Booth, in the preface to one of the most highly regarded
pieces of practical criticism done by reader-oriented critics, lays bare,

in just a few lines, his use of both versions of the ideal reader: " . . . the responses I attribute to my hypothetical reader of the sonnets cannot ultimately be more universal or other than my own. I have attempted to demonstrate that the responses I describe are probable in a reader accustomed to Elizabethan idiom. I have also quoted at length from the responses of the critics and editors who have preceded me in the study of the sonnets; their comments, glosses, and emendations provide the best available evidence that the responses I describe are not idiosyncratic" (Stephen Booth: x).

The most pyrotechnic use of the Ideal Reader, I and II, however, surely must be found in the practical criticism of Stanley Fish. We have already seen Fish's definition of the informed reader. Tucked into that definition is an admission that the informed reader is really Stanley Fish: it is "a real reader (me) who does everything within his power to make himself informed." After putting himself in the picture modestly, at first only within parentheses, Fish proceeds to say that of course he can claim to be an informed reader, and, moreover, so can anyone else in the guild: "Each of us, if we are sufficiently responsible and self-conscious, can, in the course of employing [Fish's critical] method, become the informed reader and therefore be a more reliable reporter of his [reading] experience" (1980: 49). It is, in other words, a rhetorical stance generally available to members in good standing of the critical guild. And in Fish's criticism (*Self-Consuming Artifacts*, for example), he makes use of this rhetorical stance masterfully.

Perhaps even more impressive is Fish's powerful use of the Ideal Reader II, the composite ideal reader. A frequent strategy in Fish's criticism is to examine an interpretive crux that has produced a diversity of ⟦18⟧ critical assessments, and then to seek a supposed common reading experience that lies at the base of the disagreement. Fish asks, What reading experience have critics shared unconsciously that allows them to agree enough to disagree about this passage? He surveys "the critical history of a work in order to find disputes that rested upon a base of agreement of which the disputants were unaware" (1980: 147). Fish elaborates thus:

> Typically, I will pay less attention to the interpretations critics propose than to the problems or controversies that provoke them, on the reasoning that while the interpretations vary, the problems and controversies do not and therefore point to something that all readers share. If, for example, there is a continuing debate over whether Marlow should or should not have lied at the end of *Heart of Darkness*, I will interpret the debate as evidence of the difficulty readers experience when the novel asks them to render judgment. And similarly, if there is an argument over who is the hero of *Paradise Lost*, I will take the

argument as an indication that, in the course of reading the poem, the identity of its hero is continually put into question. There will always be two levels, a surface level on which there seem to be nothing but disagreements, and a deeper level on which those same disagreements are seen as constituting the shared content whose existence they had seemed to deny. In short, critical controversies become disguised reports of what readers uniformly do, and I perform the service of revealing to the participants what it is they were really telling us. (1980: 177–78)

Rather than trying to reconcile differences and thus form his composite ideal reader at the "surface level," he forms his composite ideal reader from a base of unconscious agreement at a "deeper level." Wherever possible, Fish grounds the critical community on a hitherto unacknowledged but commonly shared foundation, thereby encompassing and surpassing the history of criticism. By descending to the "deeper level," he is able to transcend the critical disagreement altogether—"I perform the service of revealing to the participants what it is they were really telling us." This is skillful, rhetorical use of the metaphor of "levels." By supposedly descending to the "deeper level," he is actually putting himself in a position elevated above the debate. His skillful construction of an abstracted, composite, ideal reader is an indirect way of establishing his own credentials as, in his words, an informed reader. The thing that distinguishes Fish is that he uses the rhetorical strategy of the "ideal reader" so openly and so boldly.

Reading as a Temporal Experience

Were we to stop at this point, we would be left with still rather static abstractions of who "the reader" is. What we are missing is a model of ⟦19⟧ the reading experience itself. At this point reader response critics are making a significant contribution to criticism by recalling to the critical consciousness the richness and dynamism of the temporal experience of reading.

One distinguishing characteristic of reader response criticism is the emphasis placed on the fact that a reading experience takes place through time; it is fundamentally a temporal experience. This is a radical shift in perspective, because we have not been taught to monitor our reading experience as it occurs. Rather, we have been taught to read to the end of a text and then step back and comment on the final outcome of the reading. We view the whole of the text from the perspective of the end of the reading experience. The path we have had to follow to get to the end of reading is regarded merely as prelude to the end product. Only at the conclusion of reading do we dare ask our-selves: "What is *the* meaning of the story? What is *the* point of the story? What content did I get out of it?"

Most reader response critics resolutely resist the inclination to con-centrate on the end product of reading, what we have tended to call the point, the meaning, or the content of the story. The entire reading experience is to be valued—not just the end product of reading. Read-ing a text is a rich and dynamic experience; but focusing on the end product of reading lends itself to perceiving a text as a static, spatial form, like a painting or sculpture or piece of architecture. Also, the sheer physicality of writing has tricked us into thinking of texts as ob-jects existing in space rather than as experiences existing in time. As Stanley Fish puts it: "Literature is a kinetic art, but the physical form it assumes prevents us from seeing its essential nature, even though we so experience it. The availability of a book to the hand, its presence on a shelf, its listing in a library catalogue—all of these encourage us to think of it as a stationary object. Somehow when we put a book down, we forget that while we were reading, *it* was moving (pages turning, lines receding into the past) and forget too that *we* were moving with it" (1980: 43).

Fish also provides one of the clearest statements of the critical atti-tude needed in order to attend to the entire reading experience:

> The concept is simply the rigorous and disinterested asking of the question, what does this word, phrase, sentence, paragraph, chapter, novel, play, poem, *do*? And the execution involves an analysis of the developing responses of the reader in relation to the words as they succeed one another in time. . . .
>
> The basis of the method is a consideration of the *temporal* flow of the reading experience, and it is assumed that the reader responds in terms of that flow and not to the whole utterance. That is, in an utter-ance of any length, there is a point at which the reader has taken in only the first word, and then the second, [20] and then the third, and so on, and the report of what happens to the reader is always a re-port of what has happened *to that point*. . . . (1980: 26, 27)

Wolfgang Iser has described helpfully not just the linear, temporal encounter with the words one is reading, but the psychological phe-nomena of anticipation and restrospection that are also involved. While we read, we are actively involved in reviewing what has preceded and speculating about what lies ahead. Iser goes so far as to liken the reading experience to a recreation of the author's original act of creat-ing the text. Iser says: "We look forward, we look back, we decide, we change our decisions, we form expectations, we are shocked by their nonfulfillment, we question, we muse, we accept, we reject; this is the dynamic process of recreation" (1972: 293).

This represents a dramatic shift in literary criticism away from the formalism of the New Critics, which objectifies the text and devalues the reading experience. Walter Ong helps us to put this recent development into the broadest historical perspective. Ong, in numerous discussions of the shift from orality to the technology of writing, has described with great insight how the physicality of writing, and especially print, lends itself to be taken as static spatial form (1982: 135–38). Indeed, once the strict uniformity of printed language becomes deeply interiorized in the consciousness of the reader, it is well-nigh impossible to avoid the metaphor of language as a container or conduit, existing in space, which holds meaning within. According to this metaphor, the job of the reader or critic is to tap and drain off the contents—the meaning—of the container. Moreover, the metaphor promotes the idea that the container or text is a single entity, and that the contents or meaning is a single entity, and that therefore, in theory, we should all agree on what the meaning of the text is. This metaphor has a hard time accommodating the experience we have all had of disagreeing sharply over what a text says. Of course, a severe shortcoming of the metaphor is that it minimizes the active role of the reader in determining what the text is and what its meaning is. In short, it obscures the dialogical nature of true communication, which is inescapable even when the communication is taking place by means of a written text and therefore seems to be completely one-sided.

Reader response critics are rejecting the container metaphor altogether. The implications of this move are quite profound, yet we have scarcely begun to explore them. In arguing for a temporal model of reading, rather than a spatial one, we are actually returning to an understanding of language that has affinities with the language of oral culture. The written word is spatial; it constitutes a literate/visual mode of consciousness. The spoken word, however, is temporal; it constitutes an [[21]] oral/aural mode of consciousness. Since the world of orality lingers and is still so prominent in the biblical texts (see Kelber), the temporal model of reading employed by reader response critics is well-suited to the study of biblical narrative.

Therefore, who is "the reader" of reader response criticism? It is I, as critical reader. And it is I, as a supposed ideal reader, although I shall strike that pose by formulating and putting forth a composite ideal reader created out of the best that has been thought and said by my critical community. But that ideal reader, individual or composite, can only be an abstraction from the countless readers implied by countless texts. And each manifestation of "the reader"—critical, ideal, implied—is to be conceptualized as reading through time, in a dynamic, temporal experience. Or to put it as simply as possible, the reader has an individual persona (mine), a communal persona (the abstracted total experience of my critical community), and a textual persona (the reader implied in the text). And all of these personas are seen at their best through time.

Works Consulted

Bleich, David
    1975   *Reading and Feelings: An Introduction to Subjective Criticism.* Urbana, IL: National Council of Teachers of English.
    1978   *Subjective Criticism.* Baltimore and London: Johns Hopkins University.

Booth, Stephen
    1969   *An Essay on Shakespeare's Sonnets.* New Haven and London: Yale University.

Booth, Wayne
    1979   *Critical Understanding: The Powers and Limits of Pluralism.* Chicago and London: University of Chicago.
    1983   *The Rhetoric of Fiction.* 2d ed. Chicago and London: University of Chicago.

Chatman, Seymour
    1978   *Story and Discourse: Narrative Structure in Fiction and Film.* Ithaca and London: Cornell University.

Culler, Jonathan
    1975   *Structuralist Poetics: Structuralism, Linguistics, and the Study of Literature.* Ithaca: Cornell University.

Fish, Stanley
    1970   "Literature in the Reader: Affective Stylistics." *New Literary History* 2:123–62.
    1972   *Self-Consuming Artifacts: The Experience of Seventeenth-Century Literature.* Berkeley, Los Angeles, and London: University of California.
    1980   *Is There a Text in This Class? The Authority of Interpretive Communities.* Cambridge, MA and London: Harvard University.

Holland, Norman N.
    1975   *5 Readers Reading.* New Haven: Yale University.
    1982   *Laughing: A Psychology of Humor.* Ithaca and London: Cornell University.

Iser, Wolfgang
    1972   "The Reading Process: A Phenomenological Approach." *New Literary History* 3:279–99.
    1974   *The Implied Reader: Patterns of Communication in Prose Fiction from Bunyan to Beckett.* Baltimore and London: Johns Hopkins University.
    1978   *The Act of Reading: A Theory of Aesthetic Response.* Baltimore and London: Johns Hopkins University.

Kelber, Werner H.
1983   *The Oral and the Written Gospel: The Hermeneutics of Speaking and Writing in the Synoptic Tradition, Mark, Paul, and Q.* Philadelphia: Fortress.

Mailloux, Steven
1982   *Interpretive Conventions: The Reader in the Study of American Fiction.* Ithaca and London: Cornell University.

Ong, Walter J.
1982   *Orality and Literacy: The Technologizing of the Word.* London and New York: Methuen.

Prince, Gerald
1973   "Introduction à l'étude du narrataire." *Poétique* 14:178–96. [Now translated and abbreviated as "Introduction to the Study of the Narratee," in Tompkins: 7–25].
1982   *Narratology: The Form and Function of Narrative.* Berlin, New York, Amsterdam: Mouton.

Rabinowitz, Peter
1977   "Truth in Fiction: A Reexamination of Audience." *Critical Inquiry* 4:121–41.

Ricoeur, Paul
1967   *The Symbolism of Evil.* Translated by Emerson Buchanan. Boston: Beacon.

Steiner, George
1979   "'Critic'/'Reader.'" *New Literary History* 10:423–52.

Suleiman, Susan
1976   "Ideological Dissent from Works of Fiction: Toward a Rhetoric of the *roman à thèse*." *Neophilologus* 60:162–77.

Tompkins, Jane P., ed.
1980   *Reader-Response Criticism: From Formalism to Post-Structuralism.* Baltimore and London: Johns Hopkins University.

Readings, Readers, and the Succession Narrative: An Essay on Reception

WILLEM S. VORSTER

[[351]] Interesting shifts of focus in interpretation are presently taking place in biblical scholarship. While some scholars increasingly pay more attention to socio-historical aspects of these ancient documents, others concentrate their attention on matters relating to the reading of texts. In this essay I will deal with the latter, that is the reception of texts with special reference to the so-called Succession Narrative. The thesis of the paper is the following: Reading (including critical interpretation of [[352]] ancient texts) is an act of text production (cf. Riffaterre 1983: 3ff.) and not a neutral process of interpretation of the "meaning" of *the* or *a* given text. I hope to illustrate the value of recent attempts in science of literature to come to grips with the process of interpretation with reference to the act of reading by relating some of the insights to the study of the so-called Succession Narrative.

There seems to be nothing strange or extraordinary in the fact that certain hypotheses, presuppositions, and vantage points are taken for granted by scholars. Hypotheses often become axioms and even get the status of theories. Such has been the case for many years with views held by biblical scholars on what interpretation is about. Similar to other text interpreters, biblical scholars were of mind (and many are

Reprinted with permission from *Zeitschrift für die Alttestamentliche Wissenschaft* 98 (1986) 351–62. [The English translation of the original Afikaans article is reprinted exactly as originally published.]

still of mind) that interpretation (of ancient texts) consists of the reconstruction of the meaning of a particular text by studying its origin,
growth, making and transmission, and that meaning is something
which is inherent in a text. The focus was on the origin (author, redactor, Sitz) and on the text (growth, composition and structure) while the
reader and the act of reading as factors contributing to the meaning of
a text received little if any attention. In literary circles a shift in terms
of a paradigm shift (cf. Holub 1984: 1ff.) has taken place through the
years from interest in the author as the producer of the meaning of a
text, to the text as something which has meaning quite apart from what
the author intended, to the reader as the constructor of meaning.
Quite obviously this should not be seen in absolute terms since it is
clear that in any communication, also in the case of written texts, there
is an interaction between sender, message and receiver. There are,
however, far-reaching implications for biblical scholarship in the fact
that readers and interpreters attribute meaning to texts. I am convinced that we can learn quite a lot from "Reception theory," the um-
brella term for the shift " . . . in concern from the author and the work
to the text and the reader" (Holub 1984: xii). How do these insights
affect our understanding of the so-called Succession Narrative? and
should we as readers of Old Testament documents take the reader
(critic) and his contribution to the meaning of the text more seriously?

Reading and Readers

Broadly speaking, reception criticism deals with two matters (cf. Segers
1980: 29). On the one hand the actualization of readings of a particular text is studied. Here the focus is on the actual reception(s)
prompted by a text. On the other hand special attention is paid to the
text and how the reader is prompted by textual constraints and indicators to read the text in a particular way. Both aspects are of direct concern for biblical scholarship. The different actualizations of readings
of the [[353]] "Succession Narrative" and the rationalizations for these
readings are very fruitful fields of research (cf. Vorster 1985) and studies on the *Wirkungsgeschichte* of parts of Scripture certainly add to our
own understanding of that text. It is therefore necessary to come to
grips with both the reading process and the reader in and outside the
text (cf. Van Luxemburg, Bal, and Weststeijn 1982: 88–97) as we shall
see below.

　　Critical scholarship tends to concentrate on the text as a sign that
has to be interpreted and in this process little attention is paid to the
role of the reader in establishing the meaning of the text. In other

words, it is the sign and not the reader that receives attention. But what is the role of the reader in the process of communicating a message and how does reading contribute to the meaning of a text?

In a long forgotten article by Josef Balogh (1927) entitled "Voces paginarum" the author draws attention to the fact that the ancients, unlike us, used to read books (manuscripts) aloud and convincingly shows that the practice of reading silently was foreign to ancient readers. He refers to Nietzsche who made the following important observation: "Der antike Mensch las... mit lauter Stimme.... Mit lauter Stimme: das will sagen, mit all den Schwellungen, Biegungen, Umschlägungen des Tons und Wechseln des Tempos, an denen die antike öffentliche Welt ihre Freude hatte [Classical man read ... with a loud voice.... With a loud voice: that means with all the crescendos, inflections, alternations of tone and change of tempo, which the classical public world enjoyed]" (cf. Balogh 1927: 85). Nietzsche correctly observes that reading (aloud) is more than the mere repetition of what stands written. The implications and possibilities of reading aloud are manifold. One should only think of what the reader can make of a text by way of the use of gestures and facial expression, and who would deny the fact that tone of voice, accent and so on are means of attributing meaning to a text? What else is the reader doing when he accentuates certain words or phrases than interpreting the particular text in view of his understanding of that text? Although there is a difference between reading aloud and "reading" the Hebrew text in Aramaic, as a *methurgeman* used to do, the targums might point to what happens when a text is read (constructively). What happens when a person reads a text aloud is undoubtedly something different from repeating the written text in oral form. Something is added to the text, that is the reader's reading of the text, his presentation which is at the same time his reception of the text. Assuming that there was a "Succession Narrative" in ancient times one could imagine what a contemporary reader with the necessary competence to read Hebrew, to understand stylistic nuances and to use his imagination would have done with the story by reading it aloud! Bearing in mind the fact that ancient texts used to be read aloud and the fact that reading aloud is more than a mere repetition or representation of a text, the question arises whether silent reading or critical study is also a constructive operation in the sense of attributing meaning to the text. Is silent reading also a means of attributing meaning to a text?

[354] There are indeed various differences between reading silently and reading aloud but both are mental processes of construction. When a person reads a text he does not simply make a (verbatim) mental

imprint of the written text into his mind. In fact, a very complicated operation of selection both on the paradigmatic and syntagmatic level takes place in order to join the signs of the text into meaningful strings and conceptions. In addition a mental image is formed of the results of these processes of selection. The reader creates a mental picture of the world of the text, including the persons and their words and acts that are referred to in the text. This is also a means of attributing meaning to the text. Obviously it is the text that prompts the reader to attribute meaning to it and the reader decodes what has been coded but in the end it remains his decoding which might be different from both the sender's intended coding and another person's decoding. We exegetes know this too well. In short, there seems to be more to reading than a mere repetition of the written text in audible or mental signs. Reading is an act of production, of making a new text. This is of particular interest in the case of narration and we will return to it below.

Let us now turn to the reader. It has become customary to distinguish between readers inside and outside the text. Terms like "mock reader," "implicit reader," "implied reader," "model reader," "passive reader," "encoded reader," "narratee" referring to "readers" in the text, and terms like "original reader," "past readers," "composite reader," "naïve" or "ordinary reader," "the critic," "super reader," "informed reader," "ideal reader" referring to readers outside the text (cf. amongst others Fowler 1983), often add to our confusion about the reading process. The distinction between readers inside and outside the text is, however, a valid and useful one. A few remarks about the readers inside and outside the text are necessary. Let us first look at the readers outside the text.

There should be no doubt about the fact that there is a difference between an informed reading of the "Succession Narrative" and an ordinary or naïve reading by the man in the street. What is the difference then? Some would question whether a critic's reading should be called a reading. It nevertheless seems to be a kind of informed reading, not necessarily a valid, appropriate or even correct reading, but in any case a reading based on a particular reading competence. Appropriateness or validity is dependent on more than information as we shall see below. Be it as it may, any reader outside the text produces a reading on the basis of his understanding. He attributes meaning to the text on the ground of his reception of the signs in view of his reading abilities, experience, beliefs and conceptions about the text. "In reality every reader is, while he is reading, the reader of his own self" (Marcel Proust as quoted by Fowler 1983: 36 n 8). The difference between an informed and uninformed reader is not so much related to the reading process as [[355]] to the means by which meaning is attributed to the text. Readers outside the text are the persons of flesh and blood who are responding to the prompting of the inscripturated signs. What about the readers inside the text?

Readers inside the text are, unlike readers outside the text, not of flesh and blood. They are constructs of the author, readers of paper, so to speak (cf. Bal 1979: 2 for the metaphor in connection with characterization). The most important of these readers inside the text for the present purpose is the so-called implicit reader. This reader is an image of the reader which is prompted through a variety of indications in the text for the sake of the real reader. It is through these indications that the real reader knows how the text should be read (cf. Van Luxemburg, Bal, and Weststeijn 1982: 88f.). The implicit reader plays an important role in irony and other forms of covert communication which the real reader can grasp only through experience and an open mind for textual indicators. This is illustrated in the "Succession Narrative" by the abundant use of irony. David unwittingly pronounces judgment upon himself after hearing Nathan's parable; Absolom who was so proud of his hair meets his death because of his hair and Uriah, being faithful to his principles unwittingly brings disaster and even death upon himself (cf. Bar-Efrat 1978: 22). For the sake of the reader irony is used to express criticism of the characters. In this manner the reader is directed through the story by means of his image of the reader who knows how to read the story (in these cases as irony). The implicit reader is thus not in any way related to the real "original" readers and there is no reason to think that by constructing the image *implicit reader* one will be closer to the original reader. Like the narrator of a text the narratee or implicit reader of a text is a textual construction which only exists inside the text.

Now that we have distinguished between the two aspects of concern in "reception criticism," namely the study of the various receptions of a text by the actualizations of different readings and the study of textual indicators for the sake of the reader, for example in the implicit reader, it becomes apparent that reading is not merely a matter of receiving the meaning of the text. That is why Riffaterre (1983: 3) so aptly states:

> *The literary phenomenon is not only the text, but also its reader and all of the reader's possible reactions to the text*—both *énoncé* and *énonciation*. The explanation of an utterance should not, therefore, be a description of its forms, or grammar, but rather a description of those of its components that prompt rationalizations. . . . A relevant explanation of a rationalization will consist first in accepting the rationalization as a way of perceiving the text and, therefore, in recognizing that it is linguistic in

nature. We can confirm it by showing that the words impose it on us, and we can disprove it by showing that the words do not.

There is an interaction between the reader and the way in which a text works. Perception depends not only on the perceiver but also on ⟦356⟧ the indicators of the text which are perceived. In view of the fact that I regard the so-called Succession Narrative as a narrative irrespective of whether it ever existed outside the present context of 2 Samuel and 1 Kings, I shall next make a few remarks about the implications of text type and reading. These remarks are made in view of the fact that narrativity determines the character of the reading process in the same way as description would determine the reading process.

It is not always realized that there are only a few ways in which material can be organized in any given discourse. These include narration, exposition, argumentation, description and listing (cf. Brooks and Warren 1970: 56f.). In addition it is also clear that every communication does not necessarily have the function of informing the recipient. These functions vary. The function of some texts is indeed to inform. Others are, however, expressive (cf. confessions, prayers etc.), while others are persuasive, and yet others are social in their function (cf. Chatman 1978: 162ff.; Halliday 1978: 19f.). The way in which a text is organized and the function it has determine the way in which it should be read. These factors, in fact, make readings appropriate or inappropriate and impose on the reader certain constraints. They determine the parameters of the reading process. If this is true in general of the reader of texts, it is even more so in particular with the reading of narratives.

Narratives are the constructions of authors. They are not mere representations or imitations of "how things really happened." Once we have said this the way is open to come to grips with narratives like the "Succession Narrative." A narrative is the image of an author of a series of events and characters organized in terms of time and space. It is the result of an author's presentation of events and existents into a meaningful whole (cf. Chatman 1978). Both what is told and how it is told are the choice of the author. David of the "Succession Narrative" is a personage of paper and not a person of blood and flesh, and the point of view from which he is presented is the point of view of the narrator and his story. The world of the text and the story of the text is a made-up world and a made-up story even though it might be based on many historical events and persons. In reading a narrative like the "Succession Narrative" the reader creates his image of the world of the story, the characters and their deeds from the image which the narrator has created in his organization and selection of the material of his story. It would therefore be a mistake not to take seriously the indicators of the text of the story by reading into the text what it does not say, by reading the text for what it does not pretend to be and so on. This would be the case if one were to read the "Succession Narrative" as a description of episodes from the life of David without taking into account its narrative function.

In order to relate the brief introductory remarks about reception criticism and reading to the thesis of the paper and the "Succession [357] Narrative" the next section will deal with receptions of the "Succession Narrative" as actualized responses to the text. Both aspects of reception, that is actual receptions as well as text indicators, will receive attention.

Reading the "Succession Narrative"

As a result of the formcritical investigations of H. Gressmann and especially L. Rost the existence of a so-called Succession Narrative consisting of 2 Samuel 9–20 and 1 Kings 1–2 is taken for granted in Old Testament critical scholarship (cf. Koch 1961; Ackroyd 1981). The "Succession Narrative" is a hypothetical narrative which would have served as the Vorlage of a part of the books of Samuel and Kings. Whoever wishes to read the narrative, at least in its deuteronomistic edition, has to bracket out the mentioned sections in the Hebrew Bible. From the perspective of reception criticism this is not an unimportant observation. The demarcation of the text of the narrative is already part of the process of text production and the attribution of meaning to this text. The assumption that a "Succession Narrative" existed makes it possible for the Old Testament critic to reflect about its meaning and to construct possible backgrounds and origins for the text. In view of the perception of form critics like Rost and his many followers it is assumed that the "Succession Narrative" is a self-contained story (cf. however Coats 1981: 368ff.) about, let us say, the succession of David. It is argued that the theme is given in 1 Kgs 1:27 in the words " ... who should succeed you on the throne?" (cf. Schmidt 1982: 155). The story does not cover the reign of David since a substantial amount of relevant material precedes it, nor does it end with the reign of David since the death of David is already recounted in 1 Kgs 2:10. The remainder of 1 Kings 2 concerns Solomon and his succession (cf. 1 Kgs 2:11–46). The four chapters (2 Samuel 21–24) which stand between the two main sections of the "Succession Narrative" form a unit and it is argued that they may be excluded. The "Succession Narrative" is therefore a hypothetical narrative which could or could not have existed. At present it forms part of a cycle of narratives about the court history of David and is embedded into a larger written narrative. It is a construction of critical scholarship and as such a production of the mind. Both demarcation and composition are matters of construction which offer fascinating results when they are studied from the point of view of the reception of texts. It is the text of Samuel–Kings read in the light of the possible way in which Old Testament documents came about which prompted Rost and others to regard the mentioned text(s) as a narrative. Once the possibility of sources underlying the present narrative of Samuel–Kings was accepted the probability of the existence of a so-called "Succession Narrative" became an assumption which is not often questioned. This [[358]] leads to a number of very interesting detail studies about the exact nature and characteristics of the proposed narrative.

It is generally accepted that the "Succession Narrative" is a well-told story (cf. Ackroyd 1981: 383; Bar-Efrat 1978: 19ff.) despite the fact that little attention has been given to its narrative characteristics until recently (cf. however Bar-Efrat 1978; Gunn 1978; Fokkelman 1981). Tags of interpretation often reveal the interpreter's interest in a text as well as his assumptions and vantage points. The "Succession Narrative" has been characterized (cf. Gunn 1978: 20) as "history," "political propaganda," "wisdom" and/or "didactic literature," and also as ". . . story, told in traditional vein, as a work of art and entertainment" (Gunn 1978: 38). It is often regarded as the beginning of historiography in Israel and one of the best documented periods in the history of Israel (cf. Tucker 1971: 36).

Rost (1926) argued that the real concern of the story was dynastic politics and that it was written during the early years of the reign of Solomon in order to propagate his glory. In such a manner the succession of Solomon was facilitated since dating and purpose made this interpretation possible. This interpretation gave rise to anti- and propaganda interpretations of the story which, according to Veijola (1975) allegedly originate from the various stages in the growth of the story. Whybray (1968: 47) on the other hand, who also regards the "Succession Narrative" as a political document maintains that it is a novel " . . . albeit a historical one rather than a work of history properly speaking." In addition he regards the story as didactic literature, written from the same perspective as "Wisdom literature" (cf. Whybray 1968: 13). It was Gunn, however, who developed the idea of the "Succession Narrative" as a story written with the object of entertainment of the reader. He maintains that although the story is not fiction in the real sense of the word since it is based on historical persons and events, it is possible " . . . to detect demonstrably fictitious or highly conventional elements in the stories" (cf. Gunn 1978: 61). All these studies are in some respect concerned with the text type of the "Succession Narrative." Those who regard it as a descriptive text regard it as history in one form or another. Since perspective is sometimes taken as a characteristic of text type it is regarded as propaganda, didactic and/or Wisdom literature.

Tags like "history," "Wisdom literature" and others not only indicate the assumed text type of the "Succession Narrative"; they also describe a particular reader's frame of reference concerning the particular text. For those who regard the "Succession Narrative" as "history" the text seems to be descriptive in some way or another. It is assumed that the "Succession Narrative" presents the reader with information about the struggle in the Davidic dynasty about succession. It is perceived as a historical document which recounts the mentioned struggle. This is [[359]] different from the view that the "Succession Narrative" is a historical novel written from a wisdom perspective. Again historicity plays an important role while a theological perspective, namely "wisdom" is imposed on the text. Narrativity is thus combined with historicity and theological point of view. It would, however, be interesting to subject the "Succession Narrative" to a thorough scrutiny in connection with narrative point of view in order to determine how influential wisdom theology really was. I am of opinion that comments and references which can be related to parallel statements and views in so-called "Wisdom literature" are in fact very few and that "wisdom" is not the overall narrative perspective from which the story is told. These so-called trends of "Wisdom Literature" seem to be deduced from the way in which David is characterized in the narrative. As I have argued elsewhere (cf. Vorster 1985) David is characterized both with regard to the parable of Nathan and the story of the Tekoite woman as a man who was too clever by half. This to my mind has nothing to do with a wisdom perspective but with the narrator's way of manipulating the reader to identify with or reject the character's behaviour.

It is also clear that the pro- and anti-propaganda readings of the text are perceptions of the text rationalized by assumptions about the dating and the purpose of the narrative and furthermore prompted by the composition and the assumed theme of the text. These readings offer interesting results because the readers are constructively involved in attributing meaning to the text they are supposedly reading.

In most of the interpretations I have referred to focus on the perspective from which the "Succession Narrative" is told plays an important role and in fact leads the interpreters to believe that the story is what they think it is. Admittedly one should be aware of the fact that these interpretations are prompted by the text in view of the way in which the text is perceived. It is furthermore interesting to note that most of these perceptions are based in some way or another on the assumption that the "Succession Narrative" is a descriptive text giving information about the struggles for power in the court of David.

Recent studies of the "Succession Narrative" tend to focus much more on the narrative character of the text and interesting results have been reached with regard to narrative aspects like characterization, space, time and style (cf. Bar-Efrat 1978; Gunn 1978; Fokkelman 1981). Most of the old assumptions are questioned and new interpretations are given to the text as a whole and with regard to detail aspects (cf. Fokkelman 1981: 10ff.; also Vorster 1985). Perhaps the most important matter in this connection is the question of appropriateness of interpretation. If the "Succession Narrative" is a narrative, then the narrative character of its contents should be taken seriously. I have elsewhere illustrated how the perception of Nathan's parable and its application ⟦360⟧ in 2 Samuel 12 for example have led scholars to object against the authenticity of this David story in view of the so-called incompatibility between the parable of Nathan and its application. Since the days of Schwally and Gunkel it has been argued that it is hardly possible to reconcile the struggle of David for the life of the son of Bathsheba with his sentence on the man who stole the lamb from the poor man in the story of Nathan. In addition it has also been maintained that it is difficult to accept both the image of Nathan as the prophet who rebukes the king for his affairs with the wife of Uriah and the image in 1 Kings 1 where he is portrayed in his involvement to secure the succession of Bathsheba's second son to the throne of David as images of the same man (cf. Simon 1967: 208). In order to solve these so-called incongruencies various solutions have been suggested, ranging from interpolations to solutions inferred from the so-called juridical background of the parable. It is remarkable that in all these attempts it is not the narrative character of the parable and its application in a story which is focused upon, but "what actually happened" in the life of David (cf. Vorster 1985). In this way the point of the story is not only missed, but time and energy is spent to solve an alleged incompatibility in the text. Obviously the narrator of the Nathan and David story in 2 Samuel 12 had no interest in informing the reader about the "missing data" which modern scholars find of interest (cf. Garsiel 1976: 24; Simon 1967: 21). Moreover the incompatibility of the images of Nathan is a problem which arises in the mind of those who regard the "Succession Narrative" as something different from a narrative. If the "Succession Narrative" is a narrative then Nathan is a personage, a character and not a person. In the world of the story of David the character Nathan has a narrative function which has nothing to do with historical compatibility. The question therefore is whether the reader is willing to accept the "Succession Narrative" as a narrative and read it as a construction of an author or whether he prefers to impose judgments of historical compatibility on the characters and their actions. Prince (1982: 110) correctly observes: "If attempting to read a narrative maximally involves questions and answers about any and all of its meaningful aspects, reading it minimally involves questions and answers about what happens." Is the "Succession Narrative" then a narrative?

In addition to the obvious way in which the material is organized in a narrative discourse, Gunn (1978) and others (cf. Bar-Efrat 1978) have to my mind adequately indicated that the "Succession Narrative" is a story. The plot of the story is integrated into a meaningful whole in which previews and retrospection, characterization and point of view play an important role. The characters are shaped directly and indirectly with a view to the development of the plot and the omniscient narrator's finger is seen in his knowing everything and in his presence at every [[361]] scene. He even knows the "feelings" of God (cf. 2 Sam 11:27; 12:24; 17:14 etc.). The reason why critics have not paid more attention to the narrative characteristics of the text is mainly because of the lack of insight in narratology and the overemphasis on historical problems. Reading the "Succession Narrative" as narrative will obviously not solve all the problems of the text but it will undoubtedly lead to more adequate and appropriate readings of the story. I am specifically saying "readings" and not reading of the story since stories like other texts prompt the reader to attribute meaning to the signs in accordance with reader's expectation and many other factors. This can be illustrated by a simple example taken from 1 Kings 1.

1 Kings 1 portrays David as an old, helpless man, taken care of by a beautiful young Shunammite girl called Abishag. The narrator tells us that despite her beauty and care the king did not have intercourse with her. There he lay when Nathan sent Bathsheba to him to secure Solomon's succession. We are told that Bathsheba went to the king in his private chamber with Abishag serving him. She bowed before the king and prostrated herself while the King said: מה־לך (cf. 1 Kgs 1:16). What does this very simple question mean? And how did the narrated David say it? According to the New English Bible and the Good News Bible he said: "What do you want?" The Revised Standard Version translates: "What do you desire?" Is it a question of the king who has

lost all his power, weak and ready to die? Is it the voice of somebody who is portrayed in negative terms? Or can we imagine the spark in the eye of the old king who suddenly notices and remembers the intimate relationship with his beloved and says: What is it honey? To my mind the interpretation of the question depends on the interpreter's image of David and Bathsheba. The text is open to many interpretations, depending on one's image of the characters. This is one of the many examples of how the "Succession Narrative" prompts interpreters to interpret the text in different ways and attribute meaning to the text.

Reception criticism makes one aware of the fact that texts invite the reader to produce his own image of what is written. Various strategies are used by authors to convey messages and these strategies are there to be discovered. Some of the responses to texts are inadequate because they are prompted by factors outside the text. Others are appropriate since they are rationalizations of a reader's reception of the prompting of the text.

Works Cited

Ackroyd, P. R.
    1981   The Succession Narrative (so-called). *Interp.* 35:383–396.
Bal, M. (ed.)
    1979   Mensen van papier: Over personages in de literatuur.
Balogh, J.
    1927   "Voces Paginarum": Beiträge zur Geschichte des lauten Lesens und Screibens. *Philologus* 82:84–109, 202–240.
Bar-Efrat, S.
    1978   Literary modes and methods in the biblical narrative in view of 2 Samuel 10–20 and 1 Kings 1–2. *Immanuel* 8:19–31.
Brooks, C., & Warren, R. P.
    1970   Modern rhetoric. 3rd ed.
Chatman, S.
    1978   Story and discourse: Narrative structure in fiction and film.
Coats, G. W.
    1981   Parable, fable and anecdote: Storytelling in the Succession Narrative. *Interp.* 25:368–382.
Fokkelman, J. P.
    1981   Narrative art and poetry in the books of Samuel: A full interpretation based on stylistic and structural analyses. Vol. 1, King David (II Sam. 9–20 & I Kings 1–2).
Fowler, R. M.
    1983   Who is "the reader" of Mark's Gospel? in Richards, K. H. (ed.), Society of Biblical Literature 1983 seminar papers, 31–53.

Garsiel, M.
  1976   David and Bathsheba, I, II & III. *Dor le Dor* 5:24–28, 85–90, 134–137.
Gunn, D. M.
  1978   The story of king David. Genre and interpretation.
Halliday, M. A. K.
  1978   Language as social semiotic: The social interpretation of language and meaning.
Holub, R. C.
  1984   Reception theory: A critical introduction.
Koch, K.
  1961   "Samuelisbücher." *RGG*. 3. Aufl.
Prince, G.
  1982   Narratology. The form and function of narrative.
Riffaterre, M.
  1983   Text production.
Rost, L.
  1926   Die Überlieferung von der Thronnachfolge Davids. (BWANT III,6.)
Schmidt, W. H.
  1982   Einführung in das Alte Testament. 2. Aufl.
Segers, R. T.
  1980   Het lezen van literatuur: Een inleiding tot een nieuwe literatuurbenadering.
Simon, U.
  1967   The poor man's ewe-lamb: An example of a juridical parable. *Bib* 48:207–242.
Tucker, G. M.
  1971   Form criticism of the Old Testament.
Van Luxemburg, J.; Bal, M; and Weststeijn, W. G.
  1982   Inleiding in de Literatuurwetenschap. 2e uitg.
Veijola, T.
  1975   Die ewige Dynastie. David und die Entstehung der deuteronomistischen Darstellung.
Vorster, W. S.
  1985   Reader-response, redescription and reference: "You are that man" (2 Sam 12:7), in Lategan, B. C. & Vorster, W. S., Text and reality: Aspects of reference in Biblical texts.
Whybray, R. N.
  1968   The Succession Narrative.

The Future of Old Testament
Literary Criticism

Introduction

Predicting the future is risky. So is declaring what a discipline should emphasize over the next several years. One can easily look foolish or presumptuous or both. Thus, a disclaimer is in order. Neither Gunn nor West professes prophetic powers. They both simply discuss reasonable possibilities for the future.

David M. Gunn correctly assesses the growing division between scholars who analyze narrative from a strictly historical viewpoint and those who favor literary criticism. These two "opposing camps" inform one another at times, but do not share the same goals. Literary critics are concerned with plot, character, and narration. Historical critics continue to stress form, source, and redaction analysis. Gunn sees no immediate end to this division. On a more positive note, Gunn predicts that larger blocks of narrative will be treated as units in the future (see p. 419 below). Books like Judges and Kings will continue to be favorite texts for analysis, but they will be placed within their overall context of Genesis–2 Kings. He thinks ideological and reader-oriented approaches will enhance, not hinder, such analysis.

Mona West (in an essay written specifically for this volume) argues that future poetry studies ought to emphasize the way poetic style produces meaning. Several good works on rhetoric have appeared, yet poetry's message has not been highlighted. West fears that past studies have lost sight of the communicative powers of Hebrew poetry. Like Gunn, West believes that literary criticism will continue to benefit Old Testament research, but only if it avoids the temptation to focus on purely rhetorical topics.

In a way, both Gunn and West state that literary criticism has not gone far enough. Like its predecessors, this new methodology can become enmeshed in atomistic discussions of form, style, and ideology. It too can become overly concerned with background issues. Gunn and West remind us that the heart of Old Testament literary analysis is the text and its meaning. The validity of the approaches listed in this volume must be decided, then, on the basis of whether or not they illuminate text and meaning. When literary criticism adheres to this principle it *will* have gone "far enough." It will have eliminated the abuses it set out to correct.

New Directions in the Study of Biblical Hebrew Narrative*

DAVID M. GUNN

⟦65⟧ Plainly things have changed. The study of narrative in the Hebrew Bible has altered dramatically in the past ten years, at least as far as professional biblical studies is concerned. That is now a truism. Nor has there been any lack of commentators charting that change. This brief paper, therefore, risks offering more of the obvious by presenting some further thoughts about directions that have been taken and directions that might be taken in our field of study.

So striking is the change, it has led me on more than one occasion to suggest that "literary criticism" was becoming, has become perhaps, the new orthodoxy in biblical studies. But perhaps I enjoy overstating the position and, in any case, the varieties of "literary approach," present and foreseeable, look like having the potential to fracture any too neat party line that might emerge to choke the reading of the Hebrew Bible.

Nevertheless, I believe it is true to say that criticism of biblical texts using the reading methods of contemporary critics of other bodies of literature has, in a relatively short time, become entrenched among the disciplines of the professional guild of biblical critics and will not go away in a hurry. Inexorably the label "literary criticism" is being displaced as the label for "source criticism" or "source analysis," a symbolic displacement.

If the historical critics still dominate, the domination is fast eroding. Already the text books are beginning to appear that signal the shift— Norman Gottwald's *The Hebrew Bible* pays attention to ⟦66⟧ the new lit-

Reprinted with permission from *Journal for the Study of the Old Testament* 39 (1987) 65–75.
*A paper delivered to the Rhetorical Criticism Section: "Directions in Biblical Literature," SBL Annual Meeting, November 23, 1986

erary approaches, though in my view this material hovers still on the fringes of his work, while James Crenshaw's *Story and Faith* goes further, basing his book (like Brevard Childs's pioneering Introduction) on the shape of the Hebrew canon rather than an historical scheme and taking seriously questions of aesthetic criticism. There are many of us who look forward to the introductory textbook which radically reverses the present priority and consistently (and logically) places literary questions—which might include, in the case of narrative texts, attention to structure, plot, informational gaps, redundancy, allusion, metaphor, modes of speech, point of view, irony—ahead of questions of history and development.

The life-force of modern historical criticism was a determination to deal with the biblical text in the same way as secular texts were treated, even if that should lead to the shaking of some dearly held verities. And that assumption, ironically, is at the heart of the current challenge which historical criticism faces—a challenge to both its notion of history and its notion of a text.

For two hundred years western biblical criticism has been concerned with the question of historicity (the history of Israel) and with the history of biblical literature. The two ran hand in glove, for without the one the other could not be written. Despite some spectacular successes, the major failure of both programs is now becoming obvious.

What compositional units have been securely established and dated (beyond, that is, the mere convenience of consensus)? Even those cornerstones of historical critical endeavor, the Pentateuch and (to a lesser extent) the book of Isaiah are currently the subject of rethinking, some of it radical, in this regard (see, e.g., Rendtorff, Van Seters; Merendino, Schmitt, Vincent). It is no exaggeration to say that the truly assured results of historical critical scholarship concerning authorship, date and provenance would fill but a pamphlet.

As for the history of Israel, the problems confronting this enterprise are daunting. Of particular concern for our present subject are those that are intimately bound up with the historian's understanding of the nature of biblical texts, especially the major narrative texts. Miller and Hayes in their major new volume (*A History of Ancient Israel and Judah*) are unwilling to discuss the history of Israel before the "eve of the establishment of the monarchy" (in practice Solomon is their starting point), and thereafter are constantly admitting to the fact that what follows is largely ⟦67⟧ intelligent guesswork. Yet, as Burke Long has remarked in a review of their work, despite the

> reordering and evaluating, occasional discarding and rewriting of the Biblical tradition, the fact remains that, without much of either corroborative or disconfirming information from outside the Bible,

> Miller and Hayes have swallowed the biggest pill of all: they follow the
> large outline [of Kings], the as-found built-in selectivity, the perspec-
> tives and implicit evaluations implied by an ancient writer's choices,
> and the causal coherence (supposedly separated out from divine
> agency) at the heart of the version of history they chose to depend on.
> In short, because they cannot write from sources, they must write
> from historiography, and from a single one at that.

In other words, he suggests, this 'history' is still essentially a paraphrase of the books of Kings. If there is to emerge something *other*
than a paraphrase it will come, it seems to me, through the efforts of
the social-world critics, using models drawn from sociology and anthropology, recognizing patterns of material organization (the domain
of actions) in mute remains, and seeking in the texts the embedded
data which encodes some of the cultural or ideational concerns (the
domain of notions) of the society (see Flanagan). The result will be
nothing like a what-happened-next history, its periodization will be
broad, and it will depend upon literary criticism (including structuralist criticism) for its appropriation of texts.

The move away from historical critical study gained impetus from a
variety of sources, including the rise of canon criticism and its concern
for the final form of the text (Childs). Dissatisfaction has also stemmed
from a renewed appreciation of what critics in other disciplines are doing with, and saying about, texts and criticism. Earlier in the seventies
this showed up in two ways (amongst others), one, the importing of
structuralist modes of analysis into the study of biblical narrative (and
it was mostly on narrative), especially in France and through the pages
of *Semeia* in the United States, and the other, the growth of close reading loosely related to what has become known as the "New Criticism."
With this latter movement belonged essentially James Muilenburg's
"rhetorical criticism" which influenced the work of a number of key
pupils (I think, for example, of James Ackerman at Indiana University,
himself a figure of significant influence), and new critical concerns
were much in evidence in the work of others both within the United
States and elsewhere (as, for example, in Europe, Luis Alonso Schökel,
to whom David Clines and [[68]] I in England early looked for support). If structuralism was more theoretically sophisticated and had, as
I believe, a powerful effect in promoting the legitimacy of synchronic
study of the text, it could also be somewhat arcane and remote from
the non-afficionado. (The work of David Jobling has served a notable
mediating function.) It has been, above all, the "new critical" interest
in the surface composition of the text that has continued to generate
and reform critical practice among the readers of biblical narrative;

and although much of this work has appeared in the form of short essays, lengthier treatments of more extensive texts are beginning to appear (see recently, e.g., Eslinger and Miscall).

Robert Alter's timely book on the "art" of biblical narrative capped this movement of the seventies and gave it a huge fillip. Adele Berlin's book on the poetics of biblical narrative also stands in this tradition—concerned with the mechanics, the how, of narrative composition and the discipline involved in moving from mechanics to meaning. Meir Sternberg's recent book on poetics moves such a narratology into a whole new dimension of discrimination and sophistication and will be fundamental to the emerging generation of narrative critics (reading Sternberg will be the new graduate hurdle, equivalent to reading Martin Noth in German!). So let me dwell on this book for a moment.

Brilliant as Sternberg's poetics is, I would risk suggesting that his *hermeneutic* is less satisfying. At base he seems to be saying that the narrative offers a determinable meaning, determinable through the practice of sophisticated reading habits. Despite the ambiguities of the text, despite the gaps (about which he has excellent things to say), there is security to be found in the reliable narrator who is aligned with God, and offers the voice of divine authority. (God, it almost seems, is author, narrator and main character.) Ambiguities, tensions, gaps, multivalence—these should not deflect the reader from perceiving in the text its ideological truth. The ideological concerns the reader brings can and must be filtered out, allowing an essentially objective deployment of reading technique which will enable the sifting of right and wrong readings and the delineation of that authoritative voice. It is rather like the classical distinction between exegesis and interpretation—the distinction between discovering the root meaning and applying or relating it to oneself or one's social context. Exegesis is the discovery of the truth in the text. To listen to Sternberg (always an immensely stimulating thing to do) is to get the impression of having finally found the path to truth-in-the-text. ⟦69⟧ "Interpretation" is not his concern. In other words, such a poetics seems to be still moored, theoretically speaking, to something like the new critical position of the text-in-itself as the locus of meaning. Perhaps this is to misunderstand him or misstate his position. But I gnaw at the matter because it touches a fundamental question of direction.

It has become my conviction, if not always affecting my critical practice, that the major challenge to biblical criticism mounted by literary criticism cannot be expressed in terms simply of a shift from "diachronic" to "synchronic" analysis but rather involves the question of normative reading. This is especially so for those many among biblical scholars who are interested in theology and, in whatever tradition, the authority of the Bible. For it seems clear to me that those theorists who recognize the reader's inextricable role in the production of meaning in texts have the future on their side (see Culler, Detweiler, Eagleton, Suleiman and Crosman; cf. Barton, Keegan). That is not to say that Sternberg is not interested in the reader. On the contrary, he would claim, rightly, to be extremely concerned to chart the ways in which manipulations of text manipulate readers. But others would say, more radically, that meaning is also and always the manipulation of the text by the reader. "Readers make sense," as Edgar McKnight nicely puts it (1985: 12). There is no poetics, however discriminating, that will settle the question of meaning (for a provocatively indeterminate reading of Samuel, see Miscall). There is no objective, ideologically sterile reader to appropriate an ideological prescription embedded in the text.

Reader-oriented theory legitimizes the relativity of different readings and thus threatens to unnerve conventional understandings of biblical authority. This has already happened at the level of critical practice through the challenge of feminist criticism (cf. Fewell)—which, even when deployed in a seemingly new-critical mode, as for example by Phyllis Trible, operates out of convictions about reading that align closely with reader-oriented theory. The step from Trible's kind of reading (especially in *Texts of Terror*) to "deconstructionist" criticism is but a short and natural one: deconstruction appears to offer powerful opportunities to feminist and other critics, whose reading is overt in its ideological (or theological) commitment. Many religiously conservative/orthodox critics are finding in literary criticism (especially of "historical" narrative) a refuge from the hobgoblin of historicity. Yet my prediction is that [[70]] troubling times lie ahead as the reader theory of the secular critics begins to corrode the edges of normative exegesis and doctrines of biblical authority which insist on viewing the Bible as divine prescription. The problem of the gap between "original setting and intention" and "contemporary interpretation" will merely have given place to the gap between reader and reader.

In one sense, therefore, we might say that there has not really been a change at all: the more it changes the more it is the same—there will be no end of readings and reflections and papers and books and the endless round of exegetical and theological disputation. Yet in the midst of all that there are great possibilities for a resurgence of participation in the joy of critical reading—by scholarly, student and lay readers alike. Biblical narrative read critically through an orientation to the reader's experience and commitment has great power to enliven that experience, especially in the context of a particular community of readers and the sharing of readings. I see the beginnings of this both in writing and in changing methods of studying biblical narrative (and in this regard readers in the western "first world" countries have something important to learn from the reading practices of the "base communities" of Central America).

We have moved from the poetics of biblical narrative to more general talk of hermeneutics. Let me come back to poetics and raise an issue that relates closely, I think, to the question of (in)determinacy and the relativizing of readings. Sternberg is but giving clear voice to general practice when he emphasizes as he does the reliability of the biblical narrator. In the spirit of deconstruction, let me cast doubt on this conventional and convenient reading assumption.

One has only to take the story of David, a favorite among the newer critics, to make the point that the narrator seems to have gone to some lengths to subvert this notion of reliability. The story has hardly started before we are faced with what most of us here would recognize as two factually irreconcilable accounts of the young David's arrival at court. Sternberg (as Alter previously) may speak of the provision of depth and perspective to the portrait, yet that does not really address the issue of reliability. And, of course, the classic disrupter is yet to come (2 Sam 21:19)—who *did* kill Goliath? When the books of Samuel are read in their final form (which Sternberg does not do) this question cannot be dismissed lightly (unless the reader wishes to pull historical-critical rabbits out of the hat). I would suggest that the so-called supplement at the end of 2 Samuel can be read as having a complex role of subversion to play, [[71]] reinforcing rival views of David that have already come into focus and forcibly pulling our attention back to this very issue of the narrator's reliability that faced us at the onset. That is all part of an engineered collapse of reader confidence as the story of the great king fragments to an end.

When Samuel–Kings is read alongside Chronicles, where is the reliable narrator? Where for that matter is the reliable narrator of the four Gospels? Or, to put it another way: Who among the four narrators is reliable? What *did* Jesus say? We can only maintain an unsullied notion of a reliable narrator by maintaining the compositional segmentation of the Bible—and postulating whole hosts of narrators who have nothing to do with each other. So it is no small irony that Sternberg's poetics turns out to be still locked into historical criticism through the controls of source analysis, the old "literary criticism." I suppose my point is really a canonical one—reading biblical narrative in terms of its final form really is a more radical proposition than perhaps is realized by those who most enthusiastically have embraced the program (and mocked its historical-critical predecessor). Are the books of Samuel a book or not? Is this work a narrative? What about Deuteronomy to 2 Kings? Or the whole Hebrew canon? In each case, is the question whether we have "a" narrator, let alone a reliable one, real? In short, what counts as the poetics of biblical narrative depends on what the theorist means by biblical narrative. And it is time the theorists of poetics took seriously what Brevard Childs has been wrestling with for a decade and more.

Bearing also on the issue of the reliable narrator is a feature of literary works that has long fascinated me and is now gaining consistent attention from critics—namely, irony. When appealing to irony as an interpretive strategy I have been constantly rebuffed by those who counter that this is but a tactic of last resort. What I have come to realize is that such rebuttal is itself but a disguised declaration of the rebutter's critical ideology—very likely a by-product of a commitment to a particular understanding of revelation and the authority of scripture. But as we attune ourselves to listening more openly for irony in biblical texts, we need to be thoroughgoing about it. It is one thing for characters to be presented trading ironic speech or action with each other— where the narrator lays out the elements of the irony in such a way as both to share its savor and yet to stay detached. What, however, if the irony be embedded in the very language that is being used by the narrator? It is inviting to read [[72]] thus the evaluations of David and Solomon in Kings, where the little word 'except' or 'only' (*raq*) harbors tremendous subversive possibilities (see 1 Kgs 3:3 [cf. 3:11!], 15:4 [cf. 9:4, 14:8]; and compare 2 Kgs 14:1–4 and 15:1–4, of Amaziah and Azariah). Another well-known passage well served by an ironic reading is Josh 11:23 ("So Joshua took the whole land, according to all that Yahweh had spoken to Moses"). Or, more radically, what if it is the *narrator* (rather than an explicit character within the discourse) who is the object of the irony (e.g., through the espousal of naive judgments, as in an alternative reading of those evaluations of David and Solomon)? If irony is at all pervasive in biblical narrative, as is increasingly being recognized, what makes us shy away from locating irony also in the treatment of the narrator by the (implied) author? The kind of formalist reading that Robert Polzin has offered of Deuteronomy to Judges suggests just this very possibility—the narrator is but one voice of several, and none is immune from undermining (and irony is a classical mode of undermining). Richard Nelson's treatment of Uspensky and the Deuteronomistic History leads in the same direction.

The issue of reliability is bound up with discriminations concerning point of view. This is a matter of crucial importance which will increasingly shape the direction of radical criticism of biblical narrative.

I close with a few further prognostications. First, I expect to see soon appearing some major new readings of extensive segments of narrative, with the book of Judges a favorite subject, Kings following hard in its wake, and soon the whole Deuteronomistic History. Yet as fast as that happens we shall see the demise of the Deuteronomistic History and the adoption of Genesis to 2 Kings as a standard unit (so already, from very different standpoints, both Miller and Hayes, and Miscall 1986). (And readings of this unit which include the book of Ruth should gain some attention, at least from those concerned with the Christian canon.) We should also see growing interest in the poetics of the books of Chronicles, Ezra and Nehemiah, and, likewise, other monologue-oriented narrative such as we find in the Pentateuch and Joshua—it is here that we may see the growth of the kind of rhetorical analysis that has become a feature of New Testament studies, grounded in an understanding of the rhetorical manuals of the Greco–Roman world. And I come back to a subject briefly mentioned above: the impact of feminist criticism of biblical narrative is still only beginning to be felt—it will force some major [[73]] shifts in its own right. (A major new impetus may well come from Mieke Bal's work, soon to appear in English.)

One last thought, to end where I began (a good rhetorical principle)—with historical criticism. The cry is for a rapprochement between the old and the new. A few scholars have been able to accommodate this—I think of David Clines for one (both in *The Theme of the Pentateuch* and in his new book on Esther), of Lee Humphreys for another, and of that inimitable master of intersecting disciplines, Walter Brueggemann. But I think this will continue to be rare. I see separate roads for a long way ahead. My view is that, practically speaking in the doing of major varieties of literary criticism, historical critical inquiry does not make much contribution. It is not necessarily that it is wrong. It is just that it is going somewhere else.

Bibliography

Ackerman, James S.

1974   "The Literary Context of the Moses Birth Story," in Kenneth R. R. Gros Louis, ed., with James S. Ackerman and Thayer S. Warshaw, *Literary Interpretations of Biblical Narratives: Vol. I* (Nashville: Abingdon), pp. 74–119

1982   "Joseph, Judah, and Jacob," in Kenneth R. R. Gros Louis, ed., with James S. Ackerman, *Literary Interpretations of Biblical Narratives: Vol. II* (Nashville: Abingdon), pp. 85–113

Alter, Robert
1981   *The Art of Biblical Narrative* (New York: Basic Books)
Bal, Mieke
1985   *Femmes Imaginaires: L'Ancien Testament au risque d'une narratologie cri-
        tique* (Montreal: Editions Hurtubise HMH; Utrecht: HES Uitgevers)
Barton, John
1984   *Reading the Bible: Method in Biblical Study* (London: SPCK and Phila-
        delphia: Westminster)
Berlin, Adele
1983   *Poetics and Interpretation of Biblical Narrative* (Bible and Literature
        Series, 9; Sheffield: Almond)
Brueggemann, Walter
1985   *David's Truth in Israel's Imagination and Memory* (Philadelphia: For-
        tress)
Childs, Brevard S.
1979   *Introduction to the Old Testament as Scripture* (London: SCM and
        Philadelphia: Westminster)
Clines, David J. A.
1978   *The Theme of the Pentateuch* (JSOT Supplement Series, 10; Sheffield:
        JSOT)
1984   *The Esther Scroll: The Story of the Story* (JSOT Supplement Series, 30;
        Sheffield: JSOT)
Collins, Adela Yarbro, ed.
1985   *Feminist Perspectives on Biblical Scholarship* (Chico, CA: Scholars)
Crenshaw, James L.
1986   *Story and Faith: A Guide to the Old Testament* (New York: Macmillan)
Culler, Jonathan
1982   *On Deconstruction: Theory and Criticism after Structuralism* (Ithaca, NY:
        Cornell University)
Detweiler, Robert
1985   *Reader Response Approaches to Biblical and Secular Texts* (= *Semeia* 31;
        Decatur, GA: Scholars)
Eagleton, Terry
1983   *Literary Theory: An Introduction* (Minneapolis: University of Minne-
        sota)
Eslinger, Lyle
1985   *Kingship of God in Crisis: A Close Reading of 1 Samuel 1–12* (Bible and
        Literature Series, 10; Sheffield: Almond)
Fewell, Danna Nolan
1987   "Feminist Reading of the Hebrew Bible: Affirmation, Resistance
        and Transformation," *JSOT* 39:77–87
Gottwald, Norman K.
1985   *The Hebrew Bible: A Socio-Literary Introduction* (Philadelphia: Fortress)
Gunn, David M.
1980   *The Fate of King Saul: An Interpretation of a Biblical Story* (JSOT Sup-
        plement Series, 14; Sheffield: JSOT)

1987 "In Security: The David of Biblical Narrative," *Semeia* [forthcoming]

Humphreys, W. Lee
1985 *The Tragic Vision and the Hebrew Tradition* (Overtures to Biblical Theology; Philadelphia: Fortress)

Jobling, David
1986 *The Sense of Biblical Narrative: Structural Analyses in the Hebrew Bible.* Vols. I & II (JSOT Supplements 7 & 39; Sheffield; JSOT) [the first edn. of vol. I appeared in 1978]

Keegan, Terence J.
1985 *Interpreting the Bible: A Popular Introduction to Biblical Hermeneutics* (Mahwah: Paulist)

Long, Burke O.
1987 "On Finding the Hidden Premises," *JSOT* 39:10–14

McKnight, Edgar V.
1985 *The Bible and the Reader: An Introduction to Literary Criticism* (Philadelphia: Fortress)

Merendino, R. P.
1981 *Der Erste und der Letzte* (VT Supplements, 31; Leiden: Brill)

Miller, J. Maxwell, and John H. Hayes
1986 *A History of Ancient Israel and Judah* (Philadelphia: Westminster)

Miscall, Peter D.
1983 *The Workings of Old Testament Narrative* (Semeia Studies; Philadelphia: Fortress and Chico, CA: Scholars)
1986 *1 Samuel: A Literary Reading* (Indiana Studies in Biblical Literature; Bloomington, IN: Indiana University)

Nelson, Richard D.
1988 "The Anatomy of the Book of Kings," *JSOT* 40:39–48.

Polzin, Robert M.
1980 *Moses and the Deuteronomist. A Literary Study of the Deuteronomic History, Part One: Deuteronomy, Joshua, Judges* (New York: Seabury)

Rendtorff, Rolf
1977 "The 'Yahwist' as Theologian? The Dilemma of Pentateuchal Criticism," *JSOT* 3:2–10 (and see the further discussion, pp. 11–60)
1986 *The Old Testament: An Introduction* (translated from the German by John Bowden; Philadelphia: Fortress), pp. 157–64

Russell, Letty M., ed.
1985 *Feminist Interpretation of the Bible* (Philadelphia: Westminster)

Schmitt, H.-C.
1979 "Prophetie und Schultheologie im Deuterojesajabuch," *ZAW* 91:43–61

Sternberg, Meir
1985 *The Poetics of Biblical Narrative: Ideological Literature and the Drama of Reading* (Indiana Studies in Biblical Literature; Bloomington, IN: Indiana University)

Suleiman, Susan, and Inge Crosman, eds.
1980 *The Reader in the Text: Essays on Audience and Interpretation* (Princeton: Princeton University)

Trible, Phyllis
  1978   *God and the Rhetoric of Sexuality* (Overtures to Biblical Theology; Philadelphia: Fortress)
  1984   *Texts of Terror: Literary-Feminist Readings of Biblical Narratives* (Overtures to Biblical Theology; Philadelphia: Fortress)
Uspensky, Boris
  1973   *A Poetics of Composition: The Structure of the Artistic Text and Typology of a Compositional Form* (translated from the Russian by Valentina Zavarin and Susan Wittig; Berkeley, Los Angeles/London: University of California)
Van Seters, John
  1975   *Abraham in History and Tradition* (New Haven and London: Yale University)
Vincent, J. M.
  1977   *Studien zur literarischen Eigenart und zur geistigen Heimat von Jesaja, Kap. 40–55* (Beiträge zur biblischen Exegese und Theologie, 5; Frankfurt and Bern: Peter Lang)

Looking for the Poem:

Reflections on the Current and Future Status of the Study of Biblical Hebrew Poetry

MONA WEST

In the summer of 1990, I had the opportunity to be part of a writer's retreat on the island of Canna in the Inner Hebrides of Scotland. When it came time to share my writing with the group and receive their feedback, one person pointed out that she could not hear "my voice" in the paper. The idea that I wished to express had become lost in the clutter of the "many voices" of quotations from scholarly sources and my own qualifying statements (something that graduate study teaches us quite well). Instead of the clutter, my friend advised me to "look for the poem" in what I was trying to say. In other words, I was challenged to seek a mode of expression that is unburdened by technical jargon, that is true to the self and not just the concatenation of the voices of others. Feminist theorists have called this process "finding one's voice" (Belenky et al. 1986).

This phrase has been helpful to me over the months as I have "looked for the poem" in my lectures, sermons, and articles. It has been a haunting phrase as I have done research for this article on the current and future status of the study of Hebrew poetry. Turning to the eyes of my own discipline for help, I have looked for the poem in Hebrew poetry and have not been able to find it. This is a paradox. On the one hand, studies like Berlin 1985, O'Connor 1980, and even Kugel 1981 have illuminated the beauty and brilliance of the inner workings of Hebrew poetry. On the other hand, scholars' attempts to define the essence of

Hebrew poetry have made the power of that poetry inaccessible to the nonspecialist. In ironic contrast to Cheryl Exum's opening statements in "Of Broken Pots, Fluttering Birds and Visions in the Night: Extended Simile and Poetic Technique in Isaiah," which emphasizes the neglect of form in the "intense pursuit of the theological message," I think that in biblical studies recent "intense pursuit" *of the medium* of Hebrew poetry we have lost the poetry's theological message (Exum 1981: 331; reprinted on p. 349 above).

Literary critical studies have given biblical scholars methodologies that make biblical texts more accessible to readers. Indeed, certain critical methodologies emphasize the role of the reader in determining meaning. The impact of literary methods on biblical narrative has been to liberate interpreters from solely historical concerns, and from methods that dissect and define the text according to sources (see Gunn [reprinted on pp. 412–22 above]). Formalism and narrative analysis, as well as Brevard Childs's emphasis on canon, have yielded a holistic approach to reading the Bible. Literary criticism has also liberated biblical narrative from scholars and specialists and given it back to nonspecialized readers by emphasizing plot, characterization, and theme. Literary criticism has served the specialist as well—especially through structuralism and semiotics.

Structuralism, formalism, reader response, and deconstruction have been applied to biblical narrative with great success. But, as the table of contents of this present volume indicates, newer literary critical methodologies have been more successful in their application to biblical narrative than to biblical poetry. Literary criticism has not liberated Hebrew poetry in the same way that it has freed biblical narrative.

Most of the major analyses of Hebrew poetry since the rise of newer literary-critical methodologies utilize the theoretical frameworks of rhetorical criticism and linguistics. Both of these methodologies have been helpful in freeing the text from strictly historical concerns by focusing attention on the literary artistry of the text itself; however, the artistic form of the text has been liberated at the expense of content and the role of the reader in the making of meaning.

James Muilenburg's development of rhetorical criticism as a supplement to form criticism moved the study of poetic texts like the Psalms away from diachronic issues of *Gattungen* and *Sitz im Leben* to synchronic matters of the particularity of the text "as it presently stands before us" (Melugin 1979: 95). Rhetorical criticism has been applied widely not only to the Book of Psalms, but also to the prophetic literature and Hebrew narrative as well (see Clines, Gunn, and Hauser 1982).

Rhetorical criticism's emphasis on the literary artistry of the biblical text worked well with Hebrew poetry, since the poetic function of language is to draw attention to itself in a way that helps communicate the poem's message (Jakobson 1960: 356). In applications of rhetorical criticism to Hebrew poetry, an effort was made to show how the literary artistry of the text embodied the text's meaning. While the relationship between form and meaning was emphasized, the structure of the text seemed to become the dominant focus of the exegetical enterprise.

Two of the major criticisms of rhetorical analysis of biblical texts have been its lack of a well-developed methodology and its tendency to be nothing more than an exercise in stylistics (Wuellner 1987: 451). This last criticism illustrates my concerns about the sacrifice of content and the reader for emphasis on artistic form.

In his essay "Where Is Rhetorical Criticism Taking Us?" Wilhelm Wuellner claims the rhetorical critics of the Muilenburg school are "victims of the fateful reduction of rhetorics to stylistics, and of stylistics in turn to the rhetorical tropes or figures. Reduced to concerns of style, with the artistry of textual disposition and textual structure" (1987: 452–53). In place of this "old" rhetoric, Wuellner calls for a "new" rhetoric, which, ironically, takes us back to the classical definition of rhetoric: the art of persuasion. According to Terry Eagleton, this

> oldest form of literary criticism in the world . . . examined the way discourses are constructed in order to achieve certain effects.
>
> It saw speaking and writing not merely as textual objects, to be aesthetically contemplated or endlessly deconstructed, but as forms of *activity* inseparable from the wider social relations between writers and readers, orators and audiences, and as largely unintelligible outside the social purposes and conditions in which they were embedded (Eagleton 1983: 205–6).

What is at the heart of this "new" rhetoric is the notion of a text revealing its context. Context takes into account the social worlds shared by writers, texts, and readers, and the activity of making meaning in the reading process. Context recognizes reading and writing as persuasive acts that grow out of particular rhetorical situations and engage readers, writers, and texts at the point(s) where all share social worlds. Context also recognizes that a reader's or writer's interaction with or employment of the persuasive power of language provides a means by which new social realities are constructed (Wuellner 1987: 450). Context is similar to what structuralists call intertextuality, or the "various cultural discourses on which [the text] relies for its intelligibility" (Culler 1982: 32), and what deconstructionists have identified as the political process in reading and writing.

It seems to me that the future of rhetorical analysis of Hebrew poetry lies in the application of a "new" rhetoric, much like the one
Wuellner outlines, based on G. A. Kennedy's *New Testament Interpretation through Rhetorical Criticism.* This methodology would take into account the persuasive nature of the text, the rhetorical situation of the
text, the particular strategies of persuasion, the way those strategies are
achieved through rhetorical techniques or style, and the identification
of the rhetorical work as a synchronic whole (Wueller 1987: 455–58).
New rhetorical criticism's emphasis on rhetorical situation would build
on form criticism's *Sitz im Leben.* According to Wuellner, however,
there would be one crucial difference: "The rhetorical critic looks
foremost for the premises of a text as appeal or argument" (1987: 456).
"New" rhetorical criticism, on the other hand, would go beyond "old"
rhetorical criticism by focusing on the stylistic features of a text while
also taking into account the persuasive content (and context) of the
text, as well as the importance of multiplicity of meaning that comes
from the interaction of readers and texts in the activity of reading.
Like reader response criticism, "new" rhetorical criticism emphasizes
that readers are not passive, simply receiving meaning, but active in
the making of meaning. New rhetorical criticism changes readers from
"judges" and "critics" of the text, to "validators" of the text (Wuellner
1987: 461). New rhetorical criticism emphasizes that the persuasive
language of poetic texts acts as a catalyst for the dynamic process of
reading and rereading.

If (old) rhetorical criticism's focus on the literary artistry of the
biblical text called to mind Jakobson's description of the poetic function of language, linguistic analysis of Hebrew poetry explores the ways
in which this poetic function is achieved. According to Jakobson, "the
poetic function projects the principle of equivalence from the axis of
selection into the axis of combination" (1960: 358). For Jakobson and
biblical scholars who have been influenced by him, the poetic function
is achieved through parallelism, and indeed this is what has been at
the heart of the debate over the definition of Hebrew poetry.

In *The Dynamics of Biblical Parallelism,* Adele Berlin uses linguistics
and Jakobson's idea of the poetic function of language to explore the
multifaceted nature of parallelism in the Bible. She identifies four aspects of parallelism—grammatical, semantic, lexical, and phonologi-
cal—that operate at the textual levels of word, line, or clause. She
claims that her book is not a study in Hebrew poetry, but a discussion
of biblical parallelism. Still, she observes that through a study of parallelism one may come to a "better understanding of poetic texts" (1985:
17). She also asserts that parallelism is useful in identifying poetic

texts: "It is not parallelism per se, but the predominance of parallelism, combined with terseness, which marks the poetic expression of the Bible" (1985: 5).

Berlin's work is a good example of the way in which biblical scholars have used linguistics in clarifying the phenomenon of parallelism as a distinctive characteristic of Hebrew poetry. However, linguistics has been criticized in two areas. Jonathan Culler claims, "Linguistics is not hermeneutic. It does not discover what a sequence means or produce a new interpretation of it but tries to determine the nature of the system underlying the event" (1975: 31).

In response to this first criticism, Berlin argues that linguistic analysis explains the multidimensional existence of parallelism, and parallelism in turn provides the reader with a "entree" into the meaning of the poem (1985: 17). She claims that while parallelism "in itself does not have meaning" (1985: 135), parallelism is at the heart of the interplay between a text's form and meaning. But it is still up to the reader to perceive the parallelism and understand its effect in order for meaning to take place.

While Berlin's comments are helpful in understanding the function of parallelism in engaging the reader, Culler's critique of linguistics is valid. What is needed in linguistic analyses of Hebrew poetry is a move toward hermeneutics. Berlin attempts this process in the last chapter of her book under the heading "The Effect of Parallelism." Here she interprets how parallelism produces certain meaning within the text. Her efforts are, however, only a beginning. More full-length works are needed that explain the "effect of parallelism." Parallelism in Hebrew poetry needs to go beyond linguistic identification of a multitude of types of parallelism to the interpretive enterprise of meaning. This movement will engage text and reader alike and possibly provide an avenue of accessibility to the text by the nonspecialist.

To understand the effect of parallelism one must first recognize it. Ziony Zevit demonstrates that psycholinguistics can be helpful in understanding how one might perceive parallelism. Zevit also provides a corrective to the type of linguistic analysis done by Jakobson that over-identifies different types of parallelism in the written text. Out of all the different types of parallelism that linguistics has identified (what Berlin called the "variety of linguistic possibilities"), Zevit isolates only the basic levels at which parallelism would have been operative for the *original hearers* of Hebrew poetry. Psycholinguistics has shown that "form and meaning of an utterance are stored independently and that *meaning* is more persistent" (1990: 392, emphasis added). This leads Zevit to the notion of "apparency of parallelism" in biblical poetry:

These psycholinguistic insights clarify the apparency of parallelism in biblical poetry. The types of data that can be consciously retrieved from short-term memory would have been what was apparent to the ancient audiences. This would have included the meanings of lines, their key words—both grammatically important words and *Leit-wörter*—and, since they were generally short and compact, their syntax (1990: 392–93).

Zevit reminds us that because we as modern readers encounter Hebrew poetry as a literary text, "we are able to offer sophisticated interpretations of this poetry on many levels" (1990: 401). This distinction between the hearers of Hebrew poetry and the readers of Hebrew poetry is important for the second critique of linguistics: overreading the text. Like the first, this critique also comes from Jonathan Culler, who cautions the ultimate manipulation of the text through linguistic analysis of its patterns (1975: 57).

Culler's two critiques of linguistics stand in a paradoxical relationship. Linguistics is not hermeneutics; it does not produce new interpretations. Linguistic analysis can make the text mean whatever it wants. This last critique of Culler does not have as much to do with meaning/interpretation as it does with the identification of patterns. Linguistics carried to the extreme can identify any number of patterns (types of parallelism) in a text, but it will have a difficult time indicating how those patterns make meaning. Again, I support a move from linguistics to hermeneutics as a corrective to linguistic overreading of the text. In attempts to explain the way patterns make meaning, more emphasis would be given to the content and meaning of Hebrew poetry.

No discussion of Hebrew poetry would be complete without mentioning James Kugel's *The Idea of Biblical Poetry* (1981) and Robert Alter's *The Art of Biblical Poetry* (1985). In a 1984 addendum to his book, Kugel outlines four areas of research that need more attention with regard to biblical style: (1) parallelism, or what he calls the seconding effect of B in the A,B pause sequence of a Hebrew sentence; (2) biblical syntax as it relates to the artificial division of the Hebrew Bible into either poetry or prose; (3) the contributions of ancient Near Eastern parallels to the prose vs. poetry debate; and (4) the role of meter in a definition of Hebrew poetry.

For all the debate over Kugel's conclusions about Hebrew poetry (or the absence of it), his critique of the history of parallelism and our preconceptions about poetry have caused us to look again at what we mean by poetry in the Hebrew Bible. Like Culler, but for different reasons, Kugel also cautions against overreading the text. However, I think the type of linguistic analysis of parallelism done by Adele Berlin has already moved the discussion of Hebrew poetry beyond issues of definition to the complexity of the Hebrew language and its effects.

Robert Alter's work has made Hebrew poetry more accessible to the nonspecialist, and at the same time illuminated the "art" of that poetry. For example, Alter's explanation of the horizontal movement of the poetic line focuses for the nonspecialist the workings of Hebrew poetry into semantic and syntactic parallelism, which, as Zevit and psycholinguistics have pointed out, were the two basic levels at which meaning would have been operative for the hearers of Hebrew poetry. Alter explains and exemplifies this horizontal movement of meaning as one in which the second part of the poetic line intensifies, heightens, or focuses the first part of the line (1985: 19).

Alter's understanding of the way a poem makes meaning by moving from line to story (vertical movement or the "narrative impulse") is a helpful way for the reader to focus on the content as well as the form of the poem. For Alter, this horizontal and vertical movement means that "the poetry of the Bible is concerned above all with dynamic process moving toward some culmination" (1987: 620). In chapters 4–8 of his book, Alter applies this theory of horizontal and vertical movement to the poetry of Job, Psalms, prophecy, and the wisdom literature. In his explanation of the form and meaning of these poetic texts he raises the most important question of all: Why poetry? What does poetry say or express that prose cannot?

Upon asking the same question, Murray Lichtenstein states more succinctly what we find in Alter. Lichtenstein claims that the "why" of biblical poetry lies in its "particular genius for effecting the direct, immediate involvement of its audience in a kind of emotional dialogue with both its form and content" (1984: 120). This dialogue operates on a number of levels within the poetry of the Hebrew Bible. The prophets' historical audiences were immediately involved with the word of Yahweh represented in the poetic utterance of the prophet, yet it is "the indeterminancy of the language of poetry" that has continued to involve readers and hearers of these texts over the centuries (Alter 1985: 141). Wisdom poetry "exploits this same potential for personal involvement as a mode of instruction" (Lichtenstein 1984: 121), while the poetry of the Psalms provides the kind of emotional dialogue that allows the individual (and the community) to express the entire gamut of human emotion.

In light of all that has been said here about rhetorical criticism and linguistics, I think Alter's and Lichtenstein's emphasis on the *why* of poetry as well as the *how* of poetry is important to the future study of Hebrew poetry. Old rhetorical criticism made us aware of the artistry of poetic texts and gave us an appreciation of the *how* of Hebrew poetry.

New rhetorical criticism moves us toward the *why* of Hebrew poetry in its emphasis on the persuasive nature of texts and the role of readers as validators. Linguistics has contributed to the *how* of Hebrew poetry by giving us a means by which we may define what we mean by poetry and by giving us a better understanding of the complexity of the Hebrew language. Asking the *why* of Hebrew poetry moves us toward hermeneutics and more thorough explanations of the effect of this poetry on its audience and readers.

I began this article with some comments on "looking for the poem" and "finding one's own voice." I have used the "many voices" of biblical scholarship in an attempt to assess where research on biblical poetry has been, and I have attempted to find "my own voice" as well as the "voice" of Hebrew poetry in my efforts to focus on content and the reader. The essence of my friend's phrase *looking for the poem* meant the absence of technical jargon that obscures the message to be conveyed. While the technical jargon of any discipline is necessary to know what we wish to convey, the primary goal of any critical method is to equip people (and poems) to find a voice with which to enter into dialogue with the subject. The method is never an end in itself.

Bibliography of Works Cited

Alter, Robert
   1985   *The Art of Biblical Poetry.* New York: Basic Books.
   1987   "The Characteristics of Ancient Hebrew Poetry." Pp. 611–24 in *The Literary Guide to the Bible.* Edited by Robert Alter and Frank Kermode. Cambridge: Belknap.
Belenky, Mary Field, et al.
   1986   *Women's Ways of Knowing: The Development of Self, Voice, and Mind.* New York: Basic Books.
Berlin, Adele
   1985   *The Dynamics of Biblical Parallelism.* Bloomington: Indiana University Press.
Clines, David J. A., David M. Gunn, and Alan J. Hauser (editors)
   1982   *Art and Meaning: Rhetoric in Biblical Literature.* JSOT Supplement 19. Sheffield: JSOT Press.
Culler, Jonathan
   1975   *Structuralist Poetics: Structuralism, Linguistics, and the Study of Literature.* Ithaca: Cornell University Press.
   1982   *On Deconstruction: Theory and Criticism after Structuralism.* Ithaca: Cornell University Press.
Eagleton, Terry
   1983   *Literary Theory: An Introduction.* (Minneapolis: University of Minnesota Press.

Exum, J. Cheryl
    1981   "Of Broken Pots, Fluttering Birds, and Visions in the Night: Extended Simile and Poetic Technique in Isaiah." *Catholic Biblical Quarterly* 43:331–52 [reprinted on pp. 349–72 above].

Gunn, David M.
    1987   "New Directions in the Study of Biblical Hebrew Narrative." *JSOT* 39:65–75 [reprinted on pp. 412–22 above].

Jakobson, Roman
    1960   "Linguistics and Poetry." Pp. 350–77 in *Style and Language*. Edited by T. A. Sebeok. Cambridge: MIT Press.

Kugel, James
    1981   *The Idea of Biblical Poetry: Parallelism and Its History*. New Haven: Yale University Press.
    1984   "Some Thoughts on Future Research into Biblical Style: Addenda to *The Idea of Biblical Poetry*." *Journal for the Study of the Old Testament* 28:108–17.

Lichtenstein, Murray H.
    1984   "Biblical Poetry." Pp. 105–27 in *Back to the Sources*. Barry W. Holtz. New York: Summit Books.

Melugin, Roy F.
    1979   "Muilenburg, Form Criticism, and Theological Exegesis." Pp. 91–99 in *Encounter with the Text*. Edited by Martin J. Buss. Missoula: Scholars Press.

O'Connor, Michael
    1980   *Hebrew Verse Structure*. Winona Lake: Eisenbrauns.

Wuellner, Wilhelm
    1987   "Where Is Rhetorical Criticism Taking Us?" *Catholic Biblical Quarterly* 49:448–63.

Zevit, Ziony
    1990   "Roman Jakobson, Psycholinguistics, and Biblical Poetry." *Journal of Biblical Literature* 109:385–401.

INDEX OF AUTHORITIES

Abbott, W. M., S.J. 28 n. 14
Achtemeier, P. 370 n. 63
Ackerman, J. S. 26 n. 7, 414
Ackroyd, P. R. 177 n. 4, 401, 402
Albright, W. F. 50, 56, 60 n. 25
Alonso-Schökel, L. 7, 33 n. 28, 34 n. 31, 56,
177, 186 n. 1, 350, 358, 358 n. 32, 414
Alt, A. 52 n. 4
Alter, R. 3, 5, 13, 14, 15, 16, 17, 18, 19,
93 n. 35, 164, 186 n. 1, 220 n. 4, 221,
222 n. 8, 224 n. 11, 310, 415, 417, 428,
429
Andersen, F. I. 333 n. 22, 334 n. 23,
343 n. 28
Anderson, A. A. 77 n. 7
Aristotle 41, 224 n. 12, 303
Arpali, B. 232 n. 27
Auerbach, E. 43, 180, 186 n. 1

Bal, M. 396, 399, 419
Balogh, J. 397
Baltzer, K. 52 n. 9
Bar-Efrat, S. 164, 179, 399, 402, 404, 405
Barr, J. 27 n. 10, 28 n. 11, 28 n. 13
Barthes, R. 4, 100, 103, 103 n. 6, 111, 112,
113, 114, 114 n. 23, 197 n. 11
Barton, J. 416
Baudelaire 272, 274
Baumgartner, W. 49 n. 1, 52 n. 8
Beardsley, M. C. 190 n. 6, 349 n. 1
Beattie, D. R. G. 206 n. 1, 207 n. 2,
209 n. 6, 215 n. 18, 215 n. 20, 215 n. 21
Begrich, J. 53
Belenky, M. F. 423
Bentzen, A. 51
Benveniste, É. 109 n. 14
Berg, S. B. 32 n. 22
Bergson, H. 293
Berlin, A. 17, 18, 164, 295, 311 n. 1, 415,
423, 426, 427
Bingham, A. 282

Blau, J. 314 n. 4, 339
Bleich, D. 379
Blenkinsopp, J. 28 n. 12, 201 n. 16
Boadt, L. 9
Boomershine, T. 143, 144
Booth, S. 388, 389
Booth, W. 381, 381 n. 1, 382, 382 n. 2,
382 n. 3, 384, 385, 386
Bovon, F. 111 n. 17
Breisach, E. 3
Brooks, C. 400
Brueggemann, W. 419
Buber, M. 186 n. 1, 198 n. 13
Büchner, G. 33
Budde, K. 56
Buss, M. J. 26 n. 6

Calloud, J. 100
Campbell, E. F., Jr. 208 n. 5, 209 n. 6,
212 n. 13, 213 n. 15, 217 n. 22,
217 n. 25, 220 n. 4
Carlson, R. A. 31 n. 19, 52 n. 6, 57
Cassuto, U. 56, 177, 199 n. 14, 315 n. 5,
317, 318 n. 11, 322, 323, 332 n. 20
Cervantes 41
Chabrol, C. 111, 113, 114, 115 n. 25
Chase, M. E. 178, 224 n. 12
Chatman, S. 229 n. 22, 381, 381 n. 1, 382,
382 n. 3, 383, 384, 386, 400
Cheyne, T. K. 358 n. 28, 363 n. 42
Childs, B. S. 27 n. 10, 29 n. 15, 32 n. 24,
46 n. 8, 356, 356 n. 22, 361 n. 38,
362 n. 40, 363 n. 42, 366 n. 48, 413, 414,
418, 424
Ciardi, J. 350 n. 4, 351 n. 6
Clements, R. E. 29 n. 15
Clines, D. J. A. 3, 5, 14, 15, 24, 33 n. 25,
35 n. 35, 317 n. 7, 414, 419, 424
Coats, G. 280, 401
Cooke, G. A. 213 n. 14
Cornill, C. H. 358 n. 28

Courtés, J.   144
Crenshaw, J. L.   186 n. 1, 288, 413
Crosman, I.   416
Cross, F. M., Jr.   57, 70, 70 n. 1, 73 n. f, 79,
    79 n. 11, 80, 81 n. 16, 84 n. 20, 84 n. 21,
    85, 85 n. 22, 86 n. 24, 87, 87 n. 27,
    317 n. 7
Crossan, J. D.   26, 33 n. 26, 39 n. 1, 186 n. 1
Crüsemann, F.   87 n. 27
Culler, J.   187 n. 3, 387, 416, 425, 427, 428
Culley, R. C.   144, 196 n. 9, 197 n. 12, 283
Cunnison, I.   104 n. 8

Dahood, M.   58, 81 n. 14, 58, 85 n. 22, 94,
    94 n. 37, 96 n. 39, 315 n. 5, 317,
    317 n. 10, 343
Dante   13, 41, 175, 182, 273
Darwin, C.   41
Davidson, D.   352 n. 10
Davies, P.   14
Detweiler, R.   416
Dietrich, W.   354 n. 17, 356 n. 22, 369,
    369 n. 59
Donner, H.   356 n. 22, 363 n. 42
Duhm, B.   56, 358 n. 28

Eagleton, T.   416, 425
Eaton, J. H.   81, 81 n. 15
Ehrlich, A. B.   232, 366 n. 50
Ehrmann, J.   103 n. 5
Eissfeldt, O.   51, 56 n. 18, 177
Eliot, G.   184
Eliot, T. S.   69
Engnell, I.   349 n. 1
Erman, A.   49
Eslinger, L.   415
Euripides   275
Ewald, H.   56
Exum, J. C.   8, 9, 165, 272 n. 1, 290 n. 3,
    295 n. 6, 295 n. 7, 297, 310, 370 n. 63,
    372 n. 64, 424

Falkenstein, A.   60 n. 26, 61 n. 27
Fewell, D. N.   416
Fey, R.   356 n. 24
Fichtner, J.   52 n. 8
Fielding, H.   15
Fish, S.   385, 387, 389, 390, 391
Fishbane, M.   178, 186 n. 1
Flanagan, J.   414
Flaubert   176

Fohrer, G.   29 n. 16, 51, 352 n. 7,
    354 n. 17, 356 n. 24, 358 n. 30,
    361 n. 38, 367 n. 51, 367 n. 52,
    367 n. 59
Fokkelman, J. P.   179, 186 n. 1, 402, 404
Forbes, A. D.   333 n. 22
Fortunatov, F. F.   103
Fowler, R. M.   374, 398
Franken, H. J.   52 n. 11
Frazer, H.   102 n. 4
Freedman, D. N.   57, 57 n. 19, 70, 70 n. 1,
    73 n. f, 79, 79 n. 11, 80, 81 n. 16,
    84 n. 20, 84 n. 21, 85, 85 n. 22, 86 n. 24,
    87, 87 n. 27, 90 n. 30, 177, 317 n. 7,
    333 n. 22
Freud, S.   102 n. 4
Froehlich, K.   39 n. 1
Frye, N.   3, 5, 16, 17, 30 n. 17, 39 n. 1, 43,
    44, 273, 274, 275, 276, 279, 281, 287,
    288, 289, 295, 302, 303

Galbiati, E.   186 n. 1
Galland, C.   12
Gardiner, J. H.   26 n. 2
Gardner, H.   35 n. 34
Garsiel, M.   220 n. 2, 404
Geller, S.   311 n. 1
Gerleman, G.   57, 209 n. 6
Gilfillan, G.   25 n. 2
Ginsberg, H. L.   60 n. 25
Good, E. M.   57, 178, 223 n. 9, 273, 277,
    278, 281, 287, 293, 301, 352 n. 11
Gordis, R.   32 n. 24, 343 n. 27
Gottwald, N. K.   91, 91 n. 32, 365 n. 45, 412
Green, B.   164
Greenberg, M.   290
Greenstein, E.   299 n. 13, 336, 336 n. 25,
    346
Greenwood, D.   26 n. 6
Greimas, A. J.   113, 116, 144, 146, 148, 149
Gressmann, H.   50, 401
Gross, B.   3
Gunkel, H.   49, 50, 51, 53, 70, 70 n. 3,
    81 n. 14, 187 n. 2, 220 n. 3, 220 n. 4,
    273, 284, 285, 404
Gunn, D. M.   5, 10, 14, 15, 19, 31 n. 20,
    220 n. 3, 220 n. 4, 226 n. 14, 228 n. 17,
    228 n. 18, 229 n. 20, 231 n. 24,
    231 n. 26, 287, 291, 296 n. 8, 300,
    300 n. 15, 301, 402, 403, 404, 405, 410,
    424

Hahn, H. F. 176
Halliday, M. A. K. 400
Halperin, J. 188 n. 5
Halpern, B. 219 n. 1
Hardison, O. B. 5
Harvey, J., S.J. 52 n. 10
Hauser, A. 424
Hayes, J. H. 413, 414, 419
Hayes, E. N. 105 n. 10
Hayes, T. 105 n. 10
Held, M. 317, 318 n. 11, 321
Hempel, J. 52 n. 8
Herder, J. G. 25 n. 2, 49, 56
Hertzberg, H. W. 233 n. 31
Hillers, D. R. 52 n. 11
Hinneberg, P. 51
Holladay, W. L. 57, 59 n. 24
Holland, N. 379
Holub, R. C. 396
Homer 44 n. 6, 176
Howard, R. 185 n. 15
Hrushovski, B. 177, 180
Huber, F. 356 n. 22
Huffmon, H. B. 52 n. 10
Humbert, P. 65 n. 29
Hummel, H. D. 177 n. 3
Humphreys, W. L. 287, 293, 299, 419

Irwin, W. H. 352 n. 7, 353 n. 15, 354 n. 16,
    361 n. 36, 361 n. 37, 365 n. 46,
    366 n. 50, 368 n. 56
Iser, W. 384, 385, 386, 387, 391

Jackson, J. J. 26 n. 6
Jacobs, C. M. 25 n. 1
Jacobson, R. 11, 12, 13, 100
Jahnow, H. 52 n. 5
Jakobson, R. 103 n. 7, 104, 336, 344 n. 29,
    425, 426, 427
James, H. 181
Janzen, J. G. 37 n. 37
Jeremias, J. 78, 78 n. 9
Jobling, D. 143, 414
Johnson, A. R. 81 n. 16
Jonson, B. 295
Josephus 245 n. 10
Joüon, P., S.J. 209 n. 6

Kaiser, O. 352 n. 7, 353, 354 n. 17, 356,
    358 n. 28, 361 n. 37, 362 n. 39,
    367 n. 52, 369 n. 59, 369 n. 62

Kant, I. 41
Keegan, T. J. 416
Keel, O. 86 n. 25
Kelber, W. H. 392
Kelsey, D. F. 28 n. 13
Kennedy, A. R. S. 209 n. 6
Kennedy, G. A. 426
Kermode, F. 19, 224
Kerrane, K. 5
Kessler, M. 26 n. 6, 30 n. 17
Kiefert, P. A. 39 n. 1
Kierkegaard, S. 41, 281
Kikawada, I. M. 26 n. 6
Kimhi, D. 232 n. 27
Kiparsky, P. 347
Kirby, J. C. 118 n.
Kissane, E. J. 76 n. 5
Koch, K. 53, 401
Köhler, L. 53 n. 14
König, E. 26 n. 3, 56, 58
Kraft, C. F. 83, 83 n. 17
Kramer, S. N. 60 n. 26
Kraus, H.-J. 77 n. 6, 81 n. 14, 84 n. 21,
    90 n. 31
Krieger, M. 276
Krinetski, L. 57
Krinetzki, L. 186 n. 1
Kselman, J. S. 318 n. 12
Kugel, J. 18, 310, 311 n. 1, 322, 326 n. 14,
    327 n. 17, 423, 428
Kuntz, J. K. 48, 83 n. 18
Kurošec, V. 52 n. 9

Labuschagne, C. J. 212 n. 13
Lack, R. 372 n. 64
Langer, S. 287, 297
Leach, E. 105, 106, 107, 109, 197 n. 11
Levenson, J. D. 219 n. 1, 228 n. 17,
    229 n. 20, 229 n. 21
Lévi-Strauss, C. 4, 104, 105, 105 n. 10, 107,
    108, 109, 110, 111, 146, 148
Licht, J. 186 n. 1
Lichtenstein, M. 429
Liebreich, L. J. 358 n. 30
Lindblom, J. 52 n. 7
Livingstone, E. A. 35 n. 35
Long, B. 10, 413
Louis, K. G. 26 n. 7, 231 n. 24
Lowes, J. L. 42 n. 4
Lowth, R. 18, 56, 310, 339
Luther, M. 5, 6, 24

MacLeish, A.   38 n. 38
Magonet, J.   186 n. 1
Mailloux, S.   378, 379, 387, 388
Malamud, B.   232 n. 28
Manchester, P.   39 n. 1
Mann, T.   284
Marin, L.   111, 115, 115 n. 25, 116
Marsh, J.   25 n. 2
Marti, K.   358 n. 28, 363 n. 42
Martinet, A.   103
Marvell   176
Mauss, M.   104
Mays, J. L.   11
McCarter, P. K., Jr.   228 n. 19, 270 n. 16
McCarthy, D. J.   52 n. 9
McKane, W.   210 n. 8
McKnight, E.   416
McRae, G.   37 n. 37
Meek, M. E.   109 n. 14
Melugin, R. F.   26 n. 6, 424
Mendenhall, G. E.   52 n. 9, 290 n. 4
Merendino, R. P.   413
Meyer, E.   49
Miller, J. M.   413, 414, 419
Miller, A.   276
Miller, P. D., Jr.   93 n. 34
Milton, J.   41, 277, 288, 290, 302, 387
Miscall, P.   19, 228 n. 16, 415, 416, 419
Moulton, R. G.   6, 26 n. 2
Mowinckel, S.   55, 358 n. 28, 372 n. 64
Muilenburg, J.   4, 5, 6, 7, 8, 9, 10, 26,
    26 n. 5, 48, 63 n. 28, 186 n. 1, 358 n. 29,
    358 n. 32, 359 n. 34, 414, 424
Murphy, R. E.   35 n. 32

Nelson, R.   418
Neusner, J.   40 n. 2
Nielsen, K.   349 n. 1
Nock, A. D.   42
Norden, E.   49, 50
Noth, M.   415

O'Connor, M.   321, 423
Oesterley, W. O. E.   106, 106 n. 12
Ong, W. J.   38 n. 39, 392

Palache, J. L.   187 n. 4
Parker, J. F.   100
Parker, S. B.   212 n. 12
Patte, A.   143, 145, 149

Patte, D.   100, 143, 145, 149
Patton, J. H.   60 n. 25
Perrin, N.   10
Perry, M.   180, 181, 182, 183, 232 n. 27,
    232 n. 30
Petersen, D. L.   370 n. 63
Petuchowski, J. J.   45 n. 7
Pfeiffer, R. H.   44 n. 6, 51
Piaget, J.   101 n. 1, 187 n. 3
Plato   41
Plaut, W. G.   45 n. 7
Polzin, R.   10, 11, 12, 19, 418
Preminger, A. S.   5
Preston, T. R.   293
Prince, G.   381, 381 n. 1, 382 n. 2, 382 n. 3,
    382 n. 4, 384, 405, 407
Pritchard, J. B.   50, 60 n. 26
Procksch, O.   363 n. 42
Propp, W.   146
Proust, M.   398
Rabast, K.   52 n. 4

Rabinowitz, P.   381, 381 n. 1, 382 n. 2,
    382 n. 3, 382 n. 4
Racine, J.   292
Rauber, D. F.   26 n. 7, 217 n. 23
Rendtorff, R.   7, 413
Reventlow, H. G.   52, 52 n. 12, 54 n. 15,
    54 n. 16
Reymond, P.   352 n. 8
Richards, I. A.   352, 352 n. 9
Ricoeur, M.   108, 109
Ricoeur, P.   4, 12, 42 n. 3, 44, 100, 108,
    274, 287, 303, 304, 380
Riffaterre, M.   367 n. 53, 368 n. 58, 395, 399
Robertson, D.   12, 27 n. 8, 275
Robertson, E.   214 n. 17, 215 n. 19
Robinson, J. M.   10
Robinson, T. H.   106, 106 n. 12
Rosenberg, J.   182, 183
Rosenzweig, F.   186 n. 1, 198 n. 13
Rost, L.   30 n. 18, 401
Rowley, H. H.   60 n. 25
Ryken, L.   35 n. 33

Sacks, S.   352 n. 10
Samuel, M.   178
Sappan, R.   311 n. 1
Sasson, J. M.   208, 208 n. 4, 210 n. 9,
    210 n. 10, 211, 211 n. 11, 215 n. 18,

215 n. 19
de Saussure, F.   101, 102, 102 n. 3
Schmidt, H.-C.   71 n. 4, 87
Schmitt, W. H.   401, 413
Scholes, R.   187 n. 3
Schoors, A.   354 n. 17, 356 n. 24
Scott, R. B. Y.   354 n. 17, 363 n. 42,
   367 n. 52
Segal, C.   301
Segal, E.   301
Segers, R. T.   396
Sewall, R.   304
Shakespeare, W.   13, 175, 289, 379
Shaw, G. B.   41
Sievers, E.   56
Simon, U.   232 n. 27, 404
Smith, P.   25 n. 1
Smith, H. P.   233 n. 31
Speiser, E. A.   68, 166
Steiner, G.   276, 287, 292, 304, 376, 377,
   378, 379, 380, 383, 384, 387
Stendahl, K.   15, 24
Stern, J. P.   33 n. 27
Sternberg, M.   17, 165, 180, 181, 182, 183,
   188 n. 5, 230 n. 23, 232 n. 27, 232 n. 30,
   415, 416, 417
Stuart, D. K.   70, 70 n. 2, 80 n. 12, 81 n. 16
Suleiman, S.   384, 416
Sypher, W.   300 n. 13

Talmon, S.   332 n. 21
Theocritus   176
Todorov, T.   101, 184, 185
Tolstoy, L.   13, 175
Tompkins, J. P.   381 n. 1, 382 n. 2, 382 n. 4
Tracy, D.   39 n. 1
Trask, W.   180 n. 9
Trible, P.   416
Tucker, G. M.   402

Uspensky, B.   418

Van Doren, M.   178
Van Luxemburg, J.   396, 399
Van Seters, J.   413
Veijola, T.   402
Vermeylen, J.   354 n. 17, 356 n. 22,
   358 n. 30, 367 n. 52
Via, D. O.   10
Vickery, J.   288 n. 2

Vincent, J. M.   413
Virgil   176
von Rad, G.   51, 52 n. 4, 108, 287
von Ranke, L.   49
von Soden, W.   60 n. 26, 61 n. 27
Vorster, W. S.   374, 396, 403, 404
Vriezen, T. C.   209 n. 7

Walsh, J. T.   186 n. 1
Wardhaugh, R.   387
Warren, A.   400
Warshaw, T. S.   26 n. 7
Watson, W. G. E.   322 n. 13
Watters, W. R.   313 n. 3, 327 n. 17
Watts, J.   19
Weightmann, D.   107 n. 13
Weightmann, J.   107 n. 13
Weiser, A.   29 n. 16, 51, 55
Weiss, M.   53 n. 13, 186 n. 1
Wellhausen, J.   49, 287
Wenham, G. J.   199 n. 14
West, M.   410
Westermann, C.   9, 52 n. 7
Weststeijn, W. G.   396, 399
Wharton, J. A.   301
Whedbee, J. W.   165, 274, 287, 370 n. 63
Wheelwright, P.   350 n. 3, 351 n. 6,
   353 n. 12, 356, 357 n. 27
White, H. C.   144
Whybray, R. N.   30 n. 18, 402
Wiesel, E.   277
Wildberger, H.   353 n. 14, 354 n. 17,
   355 n. 18, 356, 362 n. 41, 363, 366 n. 48,
   367 n. 52, 368 n. 55, 368 n. 57,
   369 n. 59, 369 n. 60
Wilder, A. N.   10, 39 n. 1
Williams, J. G.   277
Wimsatt, W. K., Jr.   349 n. 1
Wolff, H. W.   37 n. 36, 55
Woolf, V.   184
Wright, G. E.   52 n. 10
Wueller, W.   425, 426
Wundt, W.   50

Yoder, P.   316 n. 6

Zevit, Z.   427, 428, 429
Ziegler, J.   358 n. 30
Zimmern, H.   49

INDEX OF SCRIPTURE REFERENCES

Genesis

1   105
1   110
1:1–2:3   204
1:1–2:3   205
1:5   316
1:29   106
2–3   100
2   110
2   144
2   145
2   150
2:4   146
2:4   151
2:4   152
2:4   153
2:4–15   145
2:4–3:24   186
2:4ff.   205
2:5   146
2:5   149
2:5   151
2:5   152
2:5   153
2:5   154
2:6   146
2:6   147
2:6   149
2:6   151
2:6   152
2:6   154
2:6   155
2:6   156
2:6   157
2:7   146
2:7   151
2:7   152

Genesis (cont'd.)

2:7   153
2:9   146
2:9   149
2:9   151
2:9   152
2:9   153
2:9   155
2:9   159
2:10   146
2:10   147
2:10   149
2:10   151
2:10   152
2:10   153
2:10   154
2:10   155
2:10   156
2:10   157
2:10–14   153
2:11–14   151
2:16   155
2:16   156
2:16   157
2:16   158
2:16–3:21   145
2:16–3:21   147
2:17   147
2:17   149
2:17   155
2:17   156
2:17   158
2:19–23   159
2:20   147
2:20   149
2:20   155
2:20   156

Genesis (cont'd.)

2:20   157
2:20   158
2:22   147
2:22   149
2:22   155
2:22   156
2:22   157
2:22   158
2:23–24   155
2:23–24   158
2:25   147
2:25   148
2:25   149
2:25   155
2:25   156
2:25   158
2:25   159
3   16
3   144
3   145
3   150
3:1   147
3:1   148
3:1   149
3:1   155
3:1   156
3:1   158
3:1   159
3:3   147
3:3   149
3:3   155
3:3   156
3:3   157
3:3   158
3:4   147
3:4   148

Genesis (cont'd.)

3:4 149
3:4 155
3:4 156
3:4 160
3:4–5 155
3:5 147
3:5 149
3:5 155
3:5 156
3:5 159
3:6 147
3:6 148
3:6 149
3:6 155
3:6 156
3:6 158
3:6 159
3:7 147
3:7 148
3:7 149
3:7 155
3:7 156
3:7 159
3:7–8 160
3:13 147
3:13 148
3:13 149
3:13 155
3:13 156
3:13 160
3:14 147
3:14 148
3:14 149
3:14 155
3:14 159
3:15 147
3:15 148
3:15 149
3:15 155
3:15 156
3:15 160
3:16 106
3:16 147
3:16 148
3:16 149
3:16 155
3:16 156
3:16 159
3:16 160
3:17 147

Genesis (cont'd.)

3:17 148
3:17 149
3:17 155
3:17 156
3:17 160
3:17–18 155
3:18 147
3:18 148
3:18 149
3:18 156
3:18 159
3:19 147
3:19 148
3:19 149
3:19 155
3:19 156
3:19 159
3:19 160
3:21 147
3:21 148
3:21 149
3:21 155
3:21 156
3:21 160
3:22 146
3:22 151
3:22 152
3:22 153
3:22 154
3:22–24 145
3:23 146
3:23 151
3:23 152
3:23 154
3:23–32 111
3:24 146
3:24 151
3:24 152
3:24 154
3:33 146
4 110
4:7 106
4:7 107
6–8 199
6:12 318
7:10 200
7:11 199
7:11 200
7:12 200
7:17 200

Genesis (cont'd.)

7:23 320
7:24 200
8:3 200
8:4 200
8:5 200
8:6 200
8:10 200
8:12 200
8:13 200
8:14 199
11:1 330
11:6 324
12 279
12 283
12:1–3 68
12:1–4 281
12:3 332
12:10–20 196 n. 9
15:1–6 281
16 281
17 277
17:17 278
17:17 318
17:18 278
17:19 278
18 277
18:9–15 278
20 279
20 283
20:1–18 196 n. 9
21 282
21:6–7 279
21:8ff. 280
21:9 280
21:10 280
21:12–13 280
21:17 281
22 197
22 282
22 283
22 284
22:2 281
24 199
24 283
24:1–10 199
24:11–31 199
24:32–61 199
24:62–67 199
25:21 320
25:23 285

Genesis (cont'd.)
26   283
26:1–14   196 n. 9
26:2–5   283
26:8   284
26:10–11   283
26:12–13   283
27   196
27   198
27   283
27   284
27   285
27:4   284
27:14–17   171
27:18–40   285
27:29   341
32–33   198
33   285
35   283
35:29   286
37   167
37   173
37   175
37:24   340
37:26–27   173
37:29   168
37:32   167
37:33   167
37:33   341
37:33   344
37:34–35   167
37:36   168
38   168
38   169
38   172
38   173
38   175
38   183
38   207
38:11   170
38:11   171
38:13   170
38:14   170
38:15   170
38:16   171
38:16–18   171
38:17   171
38:18   171
38:18   172
38:19   171

Genesis (cont'd.)
38:20   171
38:21   171
38:22   171
38:23   171
38:24   172
38:25   172
38:26   172
39   173
42:31   339
42:31   340
45:5   32
45:7–8   32
50:20   32

Exodus
2:10   95
4:11   316
12:10   338
12:34   216
13:21   314 n. 4
13:22   314 n. 4
15:22–27   196 n. 8
16:10   85 n. 23
17:1–7   196 n. 8
17:8–16   239
19:9   85 n. 23
20:34–38   85 n. 23
21:22–25   45
24:16   85 n. 23

Leviticus
13:17   338
13:46   338
13:12–13   338
13:19–20   320
19:9   217
23:22   217
23:42   322
24:20   45
25:10   316

Numbers
14:45   239
17:7   85 n. 23
21:29   323
31:7   356

Deuteronomy
4:2   108

Deuteronomy (cont"d.)
7:13–31   253
7:24–26   253
9:7   340
12:9   213
12:10–11   240 n. 5
21:10–11   323
24:19   217
25   207
25:17–19   237
25:17–19   239
25:18   240 n. 6
26:13   332
27:15–26   60
28:3–6   60
32   7
32   52 n. 10
32   54
32   214
32:1   337
32:1   343
32:4   80
32:7   327
32:7   329
32:30   327

Joshua
2:15   222 n. 7
6:1   320
7   252
7:14–21   252
7:21   244 n. 8
7:25   252
9   196
11:23   418

Judges
3:11   200
3:30   200
3:31   200
5   28
5:28   327
5:19–21   60
5:19–21   67 n. 32
6:3–5   239
8:28   200
12:14–15   297
13–16   289
13–16   290
13–16   291

Judges (cont'd.)
13–16   296
13–16   297
13:5   290
13:5   297
13:13   297
14:3   297
14:29   297
15:1   297
15:17   297
15:18–20   295 n. 6
15:19   297
15:20   200 n. 15
15:20   297
15:22   297
15:24   297
16   298
16   298 n. 11
16   299
16:4–31   190
16:17   297
16:18   290
16:23   294
16:23–31   298
16:24   294
16:24   298
16:26   298
16:28–30   290
16:29   298
16:30   290
16:30   290 n. 3
16:30   298
16:31   200 n. 15
28:18   297

Ruth
1:1–5   218
1:6   216
1:6–23   217
1:9   213
1:21   341
1:21   344
2   188
2   209
2:1–23   216
2:8–9   217
2:9   217
2:11–12   217
2:12   214
2:12   322

Ruth (cont'd.)
2:12   338
2:14   217
2:15–16   217
2:17–18   217
3   188
3   209
3:1–18   208
3:1–18   213
3:2   214
3:3–4   213
3:5–9   214
3:9   215
3:10–13   215
3:11   215
3:12   215
4:1–12   208
4:5   209
4:5   209 n. 6
4:5   212
4:6   210
4:9   211
4:10   209
4:10   209 n. 6
4:10   212
4:10–11   211
4:11   212
4:11   212 n. 13
4:11–12   212
4:13   212
4:13–22   211
4:14   212

1 Samuel
1–7   201
1:28   318
1:1–2:11   191
1:1–2:11   194
3:1   339
3:1   340
3:2   340
4–5   305
4:18   200 n. 15
8–15   201
8–2Sam 1   289
8–2Sam 1   294
8   291
8   297 n. 10
8   300
8:7   300

1 Samuel (cont'd.)
9   292
9   292 n. 5
9   300
9–10   289
9–31   291
9:6   292 n. 5
9:9   292
9:16   300
9:14ff.   193 n. 7
9:16–17   300
9:16–17   300 n. 14
10:8   292
10:8   296
11   299
11   300
11:13   301
11:20–24   289
12   297 n. 10
12:1   297 n. 10
12:13   297 n. 10
12:14–15   297 n. 10
12:17   297 n. 10
12:17   300
12:19   297 n. 10
12:19   300
13   292
13   293
13   296
13   299
13   300
13   301
13:5   300
14   291
14   295
14   301
14:1–15:8   295
14:4   291
14:4   300
14:8   292
14:15   295
14:16   295
14:17   295
14:19   300
14:36–64   252
15   292
15   296
15   296 n. 8
15   297 n. 10
15   300

1 Samuel (cont'd.)
15   301
15:1–3   238
15:5–6   241
15:7–9   242
15:9   246
15:10f.   246
15:13   295
15:14   300
15:15   296
15:18   295
15:20   292
15:23   300
15:28   303 n. 16
15:35   296
15:35   296 n. 9
16   295
16   296 n. 9
16   302
16–31   201
16:1–3   295
16:2   302
16:4–22   295
16:5   295
16:15   295
16:16   295
16:17   295
16:20   293
16:21   295
16:28   295
16:28–30   295 n. 6
16:30   293
17:1–18:5   186
18   302
18–20   221
18:1   222
18:5   291
18:7   291
18:15   291
18:20   221
18:20   291
18:20   294
18:21   291
18:26   221
18:28   221
19   230
19   296 n. 9
19   302
19:1   222
19:4–5   222

1 Samuel (cont'd.)
19:6–7   304
19:12–17   222
20   302
20:6   222
20:17   222
20:41   222
20:20ff.   222
20:28–29   222
22   302
23   302
23:7   304
23:19   304
24   229
24   302
24:2   304
24:17   298
24:17–23   304
25   192
25   219 n. 1
25   227
25   228
25   228 n. 16
25   229
25:3   228
25:13   193
25:14   193
25:20   193
25:21   193
25:25   228
25:35   193
25:44   221
25:44   294
25:29–30   229
25:43–44   193
26   229
26   302
26:1   304
26:21   298
26:21–25   304
28   292
28   293
28   299
28   304
28:6   291
28:7   292 n. 5
28:16   303
28:16–19   297 n. 10
28:19   293
29   190

1 Samuel (cont'd.)
30   192
30:1–2   192
30:25   192
31   293
31   294
31   295 n. 6
31   298
31   298 n. 11
31   299
31:1   294
31:2   294
31:3–6   294
31:7   294
31:8–10   294
31:12   252
31:13   299

2 Samuel
1   295 n. 6
1:17   299
1:26   222
2–5   31
3:13–15   221
3:15–16   294
4   294
5   220 n. 3
6   220 n. 3
6:12–23   294
6:23   222
7:1–3   240 n. 5
9   294
9–20   30
9–20   220 n. 3
9–20   401
9–24   31
11   31
11   191
11   201
11   205
11   224
11   227
11   231 n. 25
11   232 n. 28
11–12   223
11–12   225
11–12   229
11–12   230
11:2–5   192
11:4   224 n. 13

2 Samuel (cont'd.)
11:4   231
11:5   224
11:6–15   192
11:16–17   192
11:18–25   192
11:26   224
11:26–27   192
11:26–27   223
11:27   405
12   404
12:7–10   205
12:9   224
12:10   224
12:15   224
12:20   213
12:24   223
12:24   224
12:24   405
13   194
13   201
13:3–5   194
13:6   194
13:7   194
13:8–16   194
13:17   194
13:18   194
13:19–20   194
14   196
15–18   31
15–19   201
16:1–4   294
17:8–13   202
17:14   405
19:24–30   294
21   294
21   299 n. 12
21–24   401
22   57 n. 19
22   70
22   70 n. 1
22   72 n. b
22:3   90
22:17   95
24:17   271

1 Kings
1   226 n. 15
1   405
1–2   30

1 Kings (cont'd.)
1–2   201
1–2   220 n. 3
1–2   225
1–2   229
1–2   230
1–2   401
1:4   225
1:15   225
1:16   405
1:20   227
1:27   401
2:10   401
2:11   200 n. 15
2:11–46   401
3:3   418
3:11   418
3:18   340
9:4   418
14:8   418
15:4   418
15:5   205
17:17–24   196 n. 8
21   257

2 Kings
2:19–22   196 n. 8
4:1–7   196 n. 8
4:18–37   196 n. 8
4:38–41   196 n. 8
6:1–7   196 n. 8
14:1–4   418
15:1–4   418

1 Chronicles
10:10–11   252 n. 11
10:13   237 n. 2

Esther
4:13–14   32

Job
1–2   198
1:13–19   188
3:3   334
4:7   331
5:1   345
5:14   314
6:15   317
6:15   328

Job (cont'd.)
7:12   176
10:13   328
11:18   322
12:9   328
12:9   335
18:21   328
22:30   320
25:5   327
29:15   339
31   60
42   198

Psalms
1:1–3   331
1:4   331
1:5   331
1:6   63
2:1   66 n. 31
2:7   341
3   60
3:1   66 n. 30
6:1   66 n. 30
6:6   343
6:6   345
7   66
7–10   67 n. 32
7:1   66
7:3   66
7:6   66
8   52
8   52 n. 12
8   66
8:1   66
8:9   66
9–10   61
10:1   66 n. 31
15:1   66
15:1   66 n. 31
18   57 n. 19
18   70
18   70 n. 1
18   71
18   73 n. g
18   76
18   79
18   83 n. 18
18   85
18   87
18   88

Psalms (cont'd.)

18   89
18   90
18   93
18   96
18:2   76
18:2   77
18:2   88
18:2   89
18:2   90
18:2–4   72
18:2–4   76
18:2–31   71
18:2–31   87
18:3   77
18:3   80
18:3   82
18:3   88
18:3   89
18:3   90
18:3   91
18:4   73 n. k
18:4   77
18:4   86
18:4   89
18:4   91
18:4   92
18:4   94
18:5   94
18:5   95
18:5–7   72
18:5–7   77
18:5–7   78
18:5–25   88
18:6   94
18:7   88
18:7   89
18:7   93
18:7   94
18:7   94 n. 36
18:7   96
18:8   78
18:8   83 n. 19
18:8   84
18:8   84 n. 21
18:8   86
18:8   94
18:8–11   72
18:8–11   77
18:8–11   78

Psalms (cont'd.)

18:8–16   71
18:8–16   78
18:8–16   78 n. 8
18:8–16   83
18:8–16   86
18:8–16   87
18:9   83 n. 19
18:9   84
18:9   85
18:9–15   78
18:10   83 n. 19
18:10   85
18:10–11   85
18:10–11   94
18:11   83 n. 19
18:12   78
18:12–13   73
18:12–13   76
18:12–13   77
18:12–13   78
18:12–13   85
18:13   83 n. 19
18:14   78
18:14   83 n. 19
18:14   89 n. 28
18:14   90
18:14   94
18:14–16   73
18:14–16   77
18:14–16   78
18:14–16   86
18:15   86 n. 25
18:15   87
18:15   92
18:16   78
18:16   83 n. 19
18:16   88
18:17   78
18:17   79
18:17   95
18:17–20   73
18:17–20   77
18:17–20   78
18:18   73 n. k
18:18   79
18:18   86
18:18   89
18:18   89 n. 29
18:18   92

Psalms (cont'd.)

18:19   79
18:19   92
18:20   79
18:20   95
18:20   96
18:20   96 n. 39
18:21   89 n. 28
18:21–25   74
18:21–25   79
18:22   89 n. 28
18:25   89 n. 28
18:26   80
18:26–27   80
18:26–27   84 n. 20
18:26–27   88
18:26–31   74
18:26–31   76
18:26–31   80
18:28   89
18:28–30   80
18:28–31   88
18:29   88
18:29   90
18:29   91
18:30   95
18:31   80
18:31   87
18:31   88
18:31   89
18:31   89 n. 28
18:31   90
18:32   81 n. 13
18:32   82
18:32   87
18:32   88
18:32   89
18:32   90
18:32–37   74
18:32–37   76
18:32–37   80
18:32–46   88
18:32–51   71
18:33   88
18:33   89 n. 28
18:33   89 n. 28
18:33   91
18:33–35   81
18:34   95
18:34   96

Psalms (cont'd.)

18:35 81 n. 13
18:35 89 n. 28
18:36 80
18:36 81 n. 13
18:36 89
18:36 89 n. 28
18:36 93
18:36–37 81
18:37 81 n. 13
18:37 95
18:38 89
18:38 92
18:38 92 n. 33
18:38–43 75
18:38–43 82
18:38–46 87
18:39 92
18:39 95
18:40 92
18:40–41 82
18:41 89
18:41 89 n. 28
18:41 92
18:42 89
18:42 92
18:42 92 n. 33
18:42 93
18:42 93 n. 34
18:43 80
18:43 92
18:44 89
18:44–46 75
18:44–46 82
18:45 92
18:46 80
18:46 92
18:47 88
18:47 89
18:47 90
18:47–49 75
18:47–49 82
18:47–49 83
18:48 88
18:48 89 n. 28
18:49 82
18:49 89
18:49 92
18:49 93 n. 35
18:50 88

Psalms (cont'd.)

18:50–51 76
18:50–51 82
18:50–51 83
18:51 91
19:13 342
19:13 343
19:13–14 318 n. 11
20:8 322
22 62
22:1 66 n. 30
24:7 317
24:7 318 n. 11
24:8 343
24:10 343
25 61
25:1 66 n. 30
25:1–3 67 n. 32
25:9 333
26:1 66 n. 30
26:4 316
28:1 66 n. 30
29 62
29:5 317 n. 10
29:10 316
30:2 76
31:1 66 n. 30
31:9 96
32:11 331
33:2 313
33:8 313
33:17 333
34:1–3 67 n. 32
34:2 314
34:2 337
34:19 315
35:17 66 n. 31
36:11 331
38:3 317
38:3 317 n. 10
42–43 33
42–43 33 n. 28
42–43 61
42:5 34
42:7 34
42:9 314
42:11 34
43:1 66 n. 30
43:5 34
46 61

Psalms (cont'd.)

48:12 327
49:4 337
49:5 66 n. 31
49:5 346
50:17 333
51:1 66 n. 30
51:12 325
51:19 325
52:1 66 n. 31
58:1 66 n. 31
60:9 66 n. 31
62:3 66 n. 31
64:5 317
64:11 331
68:6 342
69:15 317 n. 10
69:15 318 n. 11
73:11 338
73:25 342
73:25 343
73:25 345
75:11 331
77:12 317
78:2 346
80:6 327
89:4 313 n. 3
92:13–14 321
92:13–14 330
94:15 331
95 63
95:3 63
95:7 63
95:11 213
97:9 315
97:9 338
97:11 331
103:10 312
104:13 322
105:6 313 n. 3
105:6 346
105:26 313
107 61
108:3 333
114:2 326
114:2 332
114:6 334
118:5 96
119 61
121:6 314

Psalms (cont'd.)
121:7–8   67 n. 32
126:2   325
126:5–6   330
126:6   333
139:11–12   67 n. 32
139:21   317
144:6   73 n. i
144:10   326
144:12   325
145:1   76
145:1–3   67 n. 32
145:18   315
150   60

Proverbs
1:8   325
3:1   340
3:1   343
6:20   340
8:22–31   60
10:1   334
14:12   327
14:33   331
16:16   335
16:25   327
17:6   327 n. 15
18:15   331
29:27   331
31:28   327

Ecclesiastes
5:1   322
5:1   343
7:1   333

Song of Solomon
1:2   322
1:3   327
3:1   314

Isaiah
1–39   354 n. 17
1–39   358 n. 30
1:19–20   318
2:4   329
3:1   323
3:1   326
3:8   323
3:8   326

Isaiah (cont'd.)
3:22   216
4:5   314 n. 4
5:8–22   60
5:25–30   61
6:11   318 n. 11
9:7–20   61
10:3   345
10:11   66 n. 31
13–39   352 n. 7
13–39   353 n. 13
13–39   357 n. 25
13–39   362 n. 39
13–39   367 n. 52
13–39   369 n. 59
13–39   369 n. 62
14:25   316
14:32   66 n. 31
23–33   365 n. 46
24:12   318 n. 11
25:1   76
28–32   354
28–32   358
28–32   370
28–32   370 n. 63
28–32   371
28–32   372
28–32(33)   358
28–32(33)   360
28–32(33)   370
28–33   352 n. 7
28–33   353 n. 15
28–33   354 n. 16
28–33   361 n. 36
28–33   361 n. 37
28–33   366 n. 50
28–33   368 n. 56
28:1–29   370
28:7–8   367 n. 54
28:12   354
28:13   370
28:16   354
28:21   370
29   361
29:1–2   369
29:1–2   371
29:1–3   362
29:1–3   364
29:1–8   355 n. 19
29:1–8   358

Isaiah (cont'd.)
29:1–8   358 n. 31
29:1–8   359 n. 33
29:1–8   360
29:1–8   368
29:1–8   369
29:1–8   370
29:1–8   371
29:1–14   351
29:1–14   357
29:1–14   358
29:1–14   359
29:1–14   369
29:1–14   370
29:1–14   371
29:1–14   372
29:2   362
29:2   363
29:3   363
29:4   361 n. 38
29:4   363
29:4   364
29:4–6   362
29:5   361
29:5   362
29:5   363
29:5   364
29:5–7   363
29:5–8   361 n. 38
29:6   364
29:6–8   361
29:7   359
29:7   361
29:7   362
29:7   365
29:7   365 n. 47
29:7   366
29:7   366 n. 48
29:7–8   356
29:7–8   358
29:7–8   362
29:7–8   364
29:8   361
29:8   361 n. 38
29:8   363 n. 44
29:8   365
29:8   365 n. 47
29:8   366
29:8   366 n. 48
29:9   368

Isaiah (cont'd.)
29:9–10   367
29:9–10   371
29:9–14   358
29:9–14   359
29:9–14   359 n. 33
29:9–14   360
29:9–14   367 n. 53
29:9–14   370
29:9–14   371
29:10   367 n. 54
29:10   368
29:10   369
29:11   368
29:11   371
29:11–12   358
29:11–12   367
29:11–12   371
29:12   368
29:13   369
29:13–14   367
29:13–14   371
29:14   367 n. 54
29:14   368
29:14   369
29:15–16   355
29:15–16   369
29:15–16   371
29:15–24   371
29:15–24   372
29:17   371
29:18   371
29:24   371
30:1–5   369
30:1–7   354
30:4   356
30:4   357
30:5   356
30:8–14   355
30:9   355
30:10–11   355
30:12   354
30:12   355
30:12–13   353
30:12–14   351
30:12–14   352
30:12–14   356
30:13–14   355
30:14   354
30:15   354

Isaiah (cont'd.)
30:15   355
30:15–17   354
30:16   355
30:17   355
31:1   354
31:1–3   369
31:4–5   351
31:4–5   355
31:4–5   361
31:12   354
32:2   63
34   63
34   359 n. 34
34:5   63
34:6   63
34:8   63
40–66   358 n. 29
40:4   329
40:9–10   65
40:12–31   64
40:15   64
40:18   345
41:8   313 n. 3
41:9   313 n. 3
41:24   64
41:26   343
41:29   64
42:1   65
42:1   313 n. 3
42:1–4   66 n. 31
43:10   313 n. 3
44:1   313 n. 3
44:2   313 n. 3
44:8   342
44:8   343
44:26   332
45:1   320
52   361 n. 36
52:2   324
52:3   314
52:13   65
54   361 n. 37
54–57   361 n. 38
54:7   330
55   64
55:1   67
55:6–9   67 n. 32
56   366 n. 50
57   368 n. 56

Isaiah (cont'd.)
57:20   321
60:16   316
65:9   313 n. 3
65:13–14   65
65:15   313 n. 3
66:8   324
66:8   328
66:8   345
66:13   319
??:7   354 n. 17
??:9   354 n. 17

2 Isaiah
40:1–11   62
40:28   62

Jeremiah
1:5   341
2:1–4:4   53
2:5   66
2:29   66
3:1   59
3:1–4:4   58
4:1   59
4:6   64
4:8   64
4:21   66
4:23–26   60
5:6   64
5:7   66 n. 31
5:9   328
5:15–17   67 n. 32
5:21   66 n. 31
7:17   327
8:22   66
9:9   66 n. 31
9:10   335
15:19   318 n. 11
17:14   318 n. 11
19   355 n. 18
20:7   318 n. 11
20:14   319
20:14   341
20:14   342
23:19   319
23:19   324
29:14   355 n. 18
30:23   319
30:23   324

Jeremiah (cont'd.)
  31:3   318 n. 11
  31:17   318 n. 11
  48:46   323
  48:46   324
  50:35–38   60

Lamentations
  1:3   326
  3:38   331
  3:47   334
  5:1   314
  5:4   342
  5:17   328
  5:19   337
  5:21   318 n. 11

Ezekiel
  1:26   68
  14:6   321
  16   214
  16:8   214
  16:9   213
  25:3–17   62
  25:13   324
  25:15   324
  37:17   330 n. 18

Hosea
  2   35
  2   35 n. 35
  2:2   36
  2:2–5   36
  2:5   36
  2:6   36
  2:6–7   36
  2:7   36

Hosea (cont'd.)
  2:8   36
  2:9   37
  2:9–13   37
  2:13   37
  2:14   36
  2:14–15   36
  2:16   37
  2:16–17   37
  2:17   36
  2:19–20   68
  4:16   95
  5:3   334
  5:3   341
  5:3   344
  5:5   321
  5:5   326
  5:5   329
  6:14   37
  11   37 n. 37
  11:8   37
  12:13–14   319

Amos
  1:3–2:16   62
  4:6–11   61
  5:18–20   67

Micah
  4:3   329
  6:1   343
  6:1–8   7
  6:1–8   54
  6:2   315
  6:2   337
  6:14   320

Nahum
  2:13   323

Habakkuk
  1:6   95
  3:17   340

Zephaniah
  2:1   321

Haggai
  2:23   313 n. 3

Zechariah
  14:12   356

Malachi
  2:10–11   321

Romans
  15:4   31

Hebrews
  1:2   40
  2   66
  2   66 n. 30
  2   66 n. 31
  2–4   67 n. 32
  4   66
  4   66 n. 31
  6   66 n. 31
  7   66
  8–11   67 n. 32
  10   66
  11   66 n. 31
  12–13   67 n. 32
  21–22   68